D1385044

EUROPEAN ECONOMIC HISTORY

EUROPEAN ECONOMIC HISTORY

TENTH CENTURY TO THE PRESENT

THEORY AND HISTORY OF ECONOMIC CHANGE

Elias H. Tuma
University of California, Davis

Harper & Row, Publishers
New York, Evanston, San Francisco, and London

To Dory

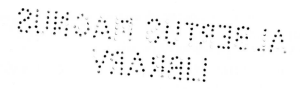

CONTENTS

PREFACE

The present state of economic history is turbulent. The scope, methods, and relevance of the discipline are all being questioned. I have had to address myself to some of these problems, express some of my own views even in a textbook, and let some of the outcomes be decided by the practical limitations of writing and publishing a book.

Most writings on the economic history of Europe either discuss the industrial revolution and what followed or they go all the way back to antiquity. I have chosen to begin with the tenth century, the time in which modern Europe began to emerge, and to close with a survey of the twentieth century. I have tried to keep the presentation in terms of topics rather than countries, but I have covered as many countries as possible, including those of Scandinavia, Eastern Europe, and Russia, which do not usually get much attention.

Part One is devoted to questions of method and theory of economic history. In Chapters 1 and 2 I consider the various approaches, including the new economic history, and I explain my own choice of an approach to the topic. In Chapter 3 I present various theories of economic change as illustrations of the contribution of history to the formulation of theory and of its relevance to current problems of economic development and growth. I have paid special attention to theories of decline, a subject that has often been totally neglected.

Parts Two to Four cover the standard material, but I have tried to combine fact and theory by introducing each topic with a theoretical framework in order to show the relationship between history and theory to guide the analysis that follows. Ample space is devoted to demography and technology as they relate to forces of demand and supply and as they influence economic change in theory and practice. The appendix to Chapter 17 presents the main technological innovations since the eighteenth century. The countries and periods in which these inventions first appeared might have some relevance as to when and where economic change took place or failed to do so.

I have tried to maintain a certain flexibility by making each topic as self-contained as possible. For example, Part One can be used independently of the rest, and so can the discussions of trade unions, agriculture, international trade, and finance. However, the two main parts for use in two quarters or semesters are Chapters 1–14 as one block and Chapters 1–3 and 15–24 as another. The book has been designed to make it usable for both economics and history students. Readers who wish more depth are provided with a fairly comprehensive bibliography at the end of each topic.

Tables, figures, and quoted extracts have been used with permission. Unless otherwise requested, full acknowledgment has been given in the bibliography at the end of each chapter.

Many people have helped in this effort. Colleagues in various institutions have been kind enough to read an extensive outline and comment on it; reviewers for the publisher have made highly constructive criticisms; I have also received helpful criticisms from Alan Olmstead on several chapters. My students in economic history, graduate and undergraduate, have read the manuscript and have made many helpful suggestions. I am grateful to all these people. Mrs. Evelyn Showalter did an excellent job of typing the manuscript, for which I am thankful. Last, but not least, I am highly indebted to the editors and staff of the publisher who were ready to help at every step to make this undertaking possible. No doubt there are errors of omission or commission which I have failed to catch. I alone am responsible for them.

E. H. T.

Davis, California

EUROPEAN
ECONOMIC
HISTORY

THE
STUDY
OF
ECONOMIC
HISTORY

THEORIES AND CONCEPTS

PART
ONE

INTRODUCTION

Positive economics tends to deal with the present. Economic theory is a ready-made tool having little evident connection with the past, and mathematics and statistics have become the only additional equipment the graduate in economics needs in order to sell his skill. Thus many students are upset to find that a course in economic history is a prerequisite for graduation. They may be curious about the past, but curiosity is not enough when their time and effort are being fiercely competed for.

While students are asking what economic history can do for them, economic historians are still asking what it is. They cannot agree on a definition, on the subject matter, or on the underlying methodological and philosophical bases for studying economic history. For example, John Clapham defines economic history as "a branch of institutional history, a study of the economic aspects of the social institutions of the past." Herbert Heaton regards economic history as the "story of man's efforts to satisfy his want," a story which cannot be confined to the economic sphere. A definition advanced by W. H. B. Court regards "economic choice as the centre of economic history." These definitions have much in common, but they vary in their scope, focus of attention, and approach to the study of history.

For practical purposes, however, it may be possible to adopt an operational defini-

tion that specifies the areas to be studied. For example, one might examine the behavior of consumers and producers, the distribution of income and welfare, the processes of production—including technology, decision-making, and organization—and the factors of production. Or one might specify as relevant topics the institutions that regulate economic behavior and their impact on economic development and change. Such an operational definition would permit communication and be flexible enough to allow disaggregation for purposes of measurement and precision. Our own approach will be worked out in the next chapter.

But regardless of how it it defined, why study the past at all? Because, in the first place, the present cannot be understood without a framework. As Gustavson put it,

> History gives perspective . . . history . . . is a mountaintop of human knowledge from whence the doings of our generation may be scanned and fitted into proper dimensions. History enables a person to see himself as part of that living process of human growth which has emerged out of the past and will inexorably project itself out beyond our lifetime. We are the product of the past but not the *completed* product.[1]

[1] C. G. Gustavson, *Preface to History*, pp. 2–3.

This means that by knowing the origin or the history of an institution or an organization, we would know, at least roughly, what to expect of it, and why certain behavior occurred the way it did.

Second, since there is a certain degree of regularity in social and economic behavior, knowledge of the past is indispensable to understanding the present and possibly the future. Students of economics are the first to admit such regularity. Economic behavior under similar conditions is presumed to be similar. Economic fluctuation has been observed to occur with a high degree of regularity. Certain measures and policies have been introduced in various periods to deal with similar problems. Some of these fail and others succeed. Knowledge of such experiences is invaluable in assessing these measures' chances of success or failure. A knowledge of history may in fact be the most important source of a theory of economic behavior.

Third, the growth of knowledge is a cumulative and long-term process. By learning what has been accomplished in the past, we avoid duplication and erect a foundation on which to build new knowledge. This is obvious in technological and physical matters, but it is equally true in the social sciences. Today's economic theorists have been building on what was started more than two centuries ago. Knowledge of what was formulated earlier is an efficient shortcut in the development of science. Without it, progress could come to an end.

Finally, while curiosity may be an insufficient motive to study history, we *are* naturally curious about the past. This curiosity is a force which makes the study of history desirable.

THE DEVELOPMENT OF ECONOMIC HISTORY

For one or another of the above reasons, writing in economic history has been going on for a long time, although it was usually lost in more general publications on history and society.

The Greeks and Romans, the Chinese and Arabs, and the medieval Europeans all wrote economic history. Though they did not classify the material as such, their history books were replete with discussions of trade, agriculture, government finances, and reforms and regulations. These books did not distinguish among economic, political, and social matters. Such distinctions became apparent only when, early in the seventeenth century, separate treatises began to appear dealing with trade, commerce, tariffs, or agriculture. From that time on, writing in economic history continued almost uninterrupted, becoming gradually more diverse in both method and substance. An examination of the major writings roughly from 1600 to 1900 shows that trade, commerce, and related fields were the main topics treated during the seventeenth and eighteenth centuries. But national debt, coinage, and production began to attract attention, particularly when manufacturing and industry started to gain ground.

During the first half of the nineteenth century a new trend appeared. Studies of specific industries such as cotton, wool, iron, and later railways were undertaken. However, no general economic history was written until about the middle of the nineteenth century. In fact, on the assumption that an economic history has to be an "historical work of a general character," some recent writers have denied that such history was written even then. The discipline's progress into the institutions of learning was also slow and painful. The first academic lecture on the subject was not delivered until around the middle of the century.

However, during the next half-century extensive literature developed. Textbook writers began to include a section on economic history as such. A rich crop of monographs and specialized researches, such as those of the German historical school, was written. Indeed, the German historical economists regarded historical analysis as the main approach to economic inquiry. Their studies were diversified and in many cases quite comprehensive in terms of national economies. However, with a few exceptions, general economic histories were not produced until later in the twentieth century, partly because of the lack of data, but also because of the previously shaky position of the subject. The debate over its meaning, methods, and objectives continued in Europe as well as in America. The tendency of the field to develop from the narrow and specialized to the general and comprehensive may also be explained by the changing trend of economic activity in western countries. Its diffusion from trade and agriculture into manufacturing and industry and from local and regional markets into national and international ones made it imperative that history writing become more comprehensive and general. The evolution of what may be called an international economy may also have been influential in modifying the methods and the substance of research into economic history. Partial explanations of data became inadequate for understanding economic change in a much larger and more integrated society.

To discuss the development of research in economic history as a progressive trend would obviously be misleading. The different phases of its development usually overlapped, both in chronology and content. Nevertheless, each phase had its own emphasis or objective and, therefore, a slightly different approach to the problem. These phases may be roughly classified as follows: descriptive–quantitative, descriptive–qualitative, institutional–analytical, and synthetic–comparative.

TRADITIONAL VERSUS
NEW ECONOMIC HISTORY

We are now on the threshold of a new phase which has been called "econometric

history" or "cliometrics," in contrast to what has become known as "traditional" economic history. The contrast between the traditional and new economic histories is complicated by the fact that neither presents a uniform picture of what it consists of or how it approaches the problem of study. However, a survey of selected traditional works suggests certain characteristics which differentiate them from the new approaches.[2]

Traditional economic historians have tended to touch on many topics in their research simultaneously, often without dealing with them thoroughly. For example, in almost every major study one finds an apparent interest in the methodology of historical research, but no systematic treatment of the subject. They have tended also to approach their problem from a given perspective, which they failed to define comprehensively or in detail. The writers often left a wide leeway for reinterpretation. Frequently even the topic itself has been so poorly defined that it is difficult to determine which data are relevant. As a result, misinterpretation and misunderstanding have been hard to avoid.

In part, the problem has been due to the broad interests of traditional economic historians. However, it is chiefly a logical consequence of their concept of economic history as a study of total society or one made within the framework of total society. They felt that they must treat not only the economic variables, but also the political, social, and cultural institutions. This interdisciplinary bent has often precluded a high degree of specialization and thoroughness.

Looking at traditional historians from another standpoint, it may be noted that their concern with qualitative analysis has resulted in broad but somewhat vague conclusions. They wanted to explain major events and formulate laws of behavior. Their broad generalizations could often be used

[2] See E. H. Tuma, *Economic History and the Social Sciences, Problems of Methodology*, Berkeley: University of California Press, 1971, especially chaps. 10 and 11.

to predict only directions of change, not magnitudes or timing. Their approaches were reinforced by their strict adherence to empirical or historical evidence. When such evidence was lacking, the treatment of the material could not be quantitative or systematic, thus leaving room for impressionistic interpretation.

At the same time, traditional interpretations tended to be inductive: Historians observed particular events, comparing and contrasting them, and then formulating possible explanations of all those events which belonged to the class as a whole. Such explanations were often the beginning of new theories of behavior, rather than confirmations of more general theories. This approach continued even after economic theory had become highly developed. Consequently, there was a tendency for historians and theorists to drift apart, not by choice, but by the logic of their approaches and interests.

The above characteristics may be observed in greater or less degree in most traditional studies of economic history. The new economic historians have, however, exaggerated the degree to which a rift has occurred between theorists and historians. They have also exaggerated the harm that might ensue from such a rift. As a remedy, the new economic historians seek to reunite history and theory and to bring research in economic history into the orbit of scientific method. Their proposed innovations include: (1) a more extensive use of economic theory in the analysis of historical data; (2) the use of econometric and statistical tools; (3) abidance by the rules of scientific method; (4) more precise specification of the model, hypothesis, and criteria relevant to the research; and (5) the explicit use of the counterfactual hypothesis approach to permit testing and confirmation of hypotheses.

These innovations imply that the economic historian should be guided by economic theory in interpreting his data. This of course is advisable whenever possible. However, economic theory may not exist, may not apply, or may be too restricted to cope with the interdisciplinary problems treated by the historian. Another implication is that quantitative data should be emphasized, and that when it is not available one should make estimates rather than depend on qualitative information. This approach is possible only if enough information is available about a given situation to permit estimation of the missing data, and if the problem under study is narrow enough to deal with by estimates. A more serious problem arises in the suggestion that explicit use be made of the counterfactual hypothesis approach. According to this approach, the impact of a phenomenon is evaluated in terms of what might be the situation in its absence. This requires that it be possible to determine what the counterfactual situation would be. In the absence of sufficient knowledge to do so, one could only resort to hypothetical conditions. This alternative approach could change the character of research in economic history by precluding exploratory research in areas in which the counterfactual conditions cannot be even approximately specified.

What is important is that the new economic historians are anxious to reduce vagueness and lack of specificity in historical research. Even when concepts are difficult to define, specification of their operational meanings should result in a great improvement in the quality of research. Such specification should increase the probability of obtaining relatively precise measurement and promoting clear communication. In fact, the impact of the new economic history has already been felt. More systematic and precise analyses have been on the increase. What remains to be done is to bring about a *rapprochement* between the traditional and the new historians to take advantage of the best of both approaches without seriously compromising either.

BIBLIOGRAPHY

Clapham, J. H., "Economic History," in *Encyclopedia of Social Sciences*, V, New York: Macmillan, 1931, pp. 315–320.

Court, W. H. B., "Economic History," in *Approaches to History*, H. P. R. Finberg (ed.), Toronto: University of Toronto Press, 1962.

Fogel, R. W., "The Specification Problem in Economic History," *Journal of Economic History*, XXVII (Sept. 1967), pp. 283–308.

Gras, N. S. B., "The Rise and Development of Economic History," *Economic History Review*, I (1927–1928), pp. 12–34.

Gustavson, C. G., *Preface to History*, New York: McGraw-Hill, 1957.

Redlich, F., " 'New' and Traditional Approaches to Economic History and Their Interdependence," *Journal of Economic History*, XXV (Dec. 1965), pp. 480–495.

Two main trains of thought can be derived from the debates concerning research methods and scientific treatment of historical data. First, there is no one best method of handling such data. The right method can be determined only in terms of the study's objective. Second, the most appropriate and feasible method is closely associated with the intellectual and technical environments in which the research takes place. Let us look at each of these observations separately.

OBJECTIVES
OF RESEARCH

The objectives of historical research may be divided into the general and the specific. The general objectives relate to the explanation of a type or class of events, rather than to any specific event or member of that class. For example, one's general objective might be to find out why prices rise or decline in a given time or environment, or why labor unions decide to strike or to compromise under given circumstances. A more specific objective might be to explain why prices declined in the 1930s, or why the AT&T workers struck in 1968. While the two types of objectives may be interconnected, each of them must be approached in a somewhat different way. Each demands certain methodological emphases, research

talents, and interests. Frequently a division of labor between the generalists and the monograph writers becomes inevitable. The student should be able to identify his objective before choosing his method of data collection and analysis.

The general objective aims at the formulation of an empirical law of behavior or an explanation of a general phenomenon far broader than the event under consideration. The specific objective tends to explain a single event which may or may not be consciously related to the formulation of theory. The general objective requires a certain degree of abstraction, reductionism, and comparison. The specific objective, unless pursued in the context of an already formulated theory, does not.

Abstraction in this context means conceptualizing the problem in a form general enough to make the concepts applicable beyond the specific event under consideration. The concept must be comprehensive enough to include features common to a whole class of events, leaving out the detail that may characterize any one member of that class. Therefore, in pursuing a general objective, the researcher must be able to reduce many individual features to a set of common characteristics which may be generalized to the class as a whole. This means that comparison, either cross-sectional or longitudinal, is necessary to permit abstraction and reductionism. It means too that a group large enough to indicate all the possible common features must be observed. Comparison in the study of history is a substitute for the laboratory experiment of the physical scientist.

The researcher who pursues a specific objective, such as the explanation of the performance of one firm or one individual, is more limited in his use of data. Every detail is relevant, regardless of whether or not it fits into a generalized conception. Reductionism is not possible, either in time or in space. Generalization is unique to the subject matter under study, and any extension of the conclusions beyond its confines can be only exploratory and heuristic.

It should be reiterated, however, that the general and specific objectives are not mutually exclusive. The generalized result may constitute a theoretical guide for the unique conclusion. On the other hand, the specific monograph performs the function of testing the more general conclusion, and it may also be a link in a chain of studies that eventually lead to a theory.

INFLUENCE OF THE ENVIRONMENT

The researcher's approach is also determined by the intellectual and technical environments in which his work is carried out. Each scholar is certainly to some extent the product of a school of thought or combination of philosophical inclinations. The men of the Enlightenment approached their topics differently from the Fabian socialists; the laissez-faire thinkers differed from the Marxists; and the evolutionary determinists differed from the upholders of individualism and free will. Any one of these approaches might be consistent with scientific method. Yet any one could also be based on assumptions which may not be realistic enough to permit empirical testing. The realism of the assumptions themselves determines the extent

to which the conclusions may be inferred from them, but does not effect the scientific nature of the method employed.

The intellectual environment is influential in two other ways: On one hand, the writer must take his audience into consideration and try to approach the problem in a way to which they may be receptive. On the other, since the author derives his information from his environment, his observations are influenced by the way in which people behave or express themselves in the case under study. Both these influences leave an impact regardless of whether the study objectives are general or specific. For example, students adopt many methodological and philosophical patterns from their teachers and in turn instill them in their own students. Thus a basic continuity of scholarship prevails between generations.

Similarly, the researcher approaches a given environment with a methodological scheme in mind. Often he needs to adjust it to cope with the specific case study. Methods applicable to the study of the industrial revolution may be totally inappropriate to a study of technology in the Middle Ages. Likewise, biographies, war records, philosophical treatises, or personal business records must be treated differently from official records or professional writings.

The environment in which the research is conducted is influential in another way. The extent to which scientific method has developed and the technical facilities available for handling masses of data largely determine the approach to be followed in historical analysis. Current interest in scientific method has made it fashionable for researchers to insist on model building, hypothesis formation, and empirical testing. Advances in computer science, mathematical tools, and statistical analysis have induced economic historians and other social scientists to take advantage of these facilities. This expansion of methodological interest is a logical step, given the potential advantages of the new technological facilities. The researcher needs to be sensitive to such influences, and to be able to select the appropriate method of observing, analyzing, and interpreting his data.

METHODS

Many methods of data handling can be utilized, although they can hardly be experienced in pure form. Some of the more important are discussed below.

Quantitative and qualitative analysis

The approach may be quantitative or qualitative. The quantitative approach attempts to measure all variables in precise terms. Numbers are important to this method, although they may not actually be used. For example, observations may be ranked in a descending or ascending order on an *ordinal scale* and thus be comparable with each other. This procedure is complicated by the fact that many observations are difficult to classify objectively as definitely more or less. Nevertheless, even if only subjective ranking is possible, it is helpful to use some system of clearly specified standards. Economists are accustomed to using this approach, especially when treating welfare questions and living standards. However, the historian frequently meets complicated situations in which the data are insufficient even for such impressionistic but systematic ranking.

A more sophisticated quantitative approach is what is called the *"interval scale measure,"* in which researcher tries to set up a scale with equal units upon which to measure his observations. The scale itself is arbitrary. However, to the extent that the units are carefully standardized, the results should be comparable and hence sufficient to indicate what has taken place relatively precisely. This approach is similar to the index number approach used in computing changes in living standards. Social scientists

have been prone to use index numbers as a means of bringing rigor into their analysis. Some researchers have even devised indices which are limited in application to specific subject matters. The absolute numbers established in such cases can of course only make sense when placed on the given scale. For example, it would mean little to say that the cost of living index has gone up five points, unless we can add information regarding the expected change, the average change over a similar period, or some information relating such a change to the breadbasket of the individual or family. Nevertheless, to the extent that interval scales allow precise comparison and some rigor, they are an improvement over the ordinal scale. They are also amenable to statistical analysis and the formation of generalizations.

The third and highest level of measurement is what is known as the *ratio scale* or *cardinal measure,* in which the absolute number has an inherent meaning relative to what is being described. This scale subsumes both the ordinal and the interval scales and also allows the application of statistical theory. The zero point in this scale is not arbitrary, since when we classify an observation as zero, it means that there is nothing in existence belonging to the class of events under observation. This measure is applicable to material things which can be added, divided, or multiplied. Most social scientists have given up hope of using it, although economists still struggle to achieve its precision and objectivity. Economic historians are apt to do the same. However, as students of society as well as economics, they find it difficult to do so.

Traditionally, economic historians have tended toward ordinal scales and qualitative analysis. They have frequently resorted to describing their observations impressionistically, rarely ranking them systematically. They have been satisfied with describing a situation as highly developed, or an economy as well developed, or the standard of living as comfortable, or technology as progressive.

Though they may have been measuring these conditions against other experiences, much has been left unsaid. Such observations need not be discarded as worthless. On the contrary, they are often so well detailed that they can form the basis for hypotheses and insights. This is true of most general studies that are reductionist in nature.

The economic historian often deals with concepts and variables that are not amenable to quantification even on an ordinal scale. Three alternatives present themselves in such cases: The historian may ignore the non-quantifiable, thus restricting the scope of his research. He may operationalize the concept by decomposing it into behavioral phenomena that are observable and measurable. Or he may retain the impressionistic, qualitative approach. The choice of method depends on the objective, the problems, the tools that are accessible, and the basic interests of the researcher. It would be misleading, however, to suggest that these alternatives are mutually exclusive. Actually each may be used as a check on the usefulness and applicability of the others. In fact, a certain division of labor may be not only advisable but indispensable to arriving at relatively rigorous and meaningful conclusions. However, research, regardless of whether it is quantitative or qualitative, should be as systematic as possible. Systematization and clarity are sure ways of reducing the problems inherent in economic history and the other social sciences.

The interdisciplinary approach

Economic history may be approached as a study of the economic conditions of the past, separated from their social and political environment. Or it may be approached more comprehensively as a study of total behavior, including economic, social, and political aspects of society. The question is whether economic behavior can be isolated and explained independently of its socio-political and cultural environments. If it

cannot, how can the researcher approach such complex behavior in a meaningful way?

If the period under study is short enough for the institutional framework to be assumed constant, economic behavior may be studied independently of other influences. If, on the other hand, the period is relatively long and the case study is so broad that the institutional framework is not uniform, isolation of the economic aspects of the situation becomes superficial. To take an example, would it be possible to study trends in international trade without investigating the political relations between the nations participating in trade? Or could one approach the economics of war without involving the social, cultural, and political institutions which are affected by it and thus impinge on the economic behavior of the societies under consideration?

Moreover, if the investigation relates to a micro problem, it may be legitimate to treat its economic aspects separately. It is difficult to do so if the study treats a behavior influenced by a total society in which various factors interact. We can approach the economics of agriculture only by specifying the significance of land in society, its relation to the power structure, its importance as a cultural component of the community, and the laws or tenure arrangements that regulate ownership, tenancy, and land transactions. Unless such specifications are made, the reader will be left with an incomplete picture and inadequate explanations of the changes in agriculture.

Whether or not an interdisciplinary approach should be pursued depends also on the nature of the problem and the questions asked. For example, if the investigation is mainly designed to show *what* happened in a given time or place, isolation of the economic behavior and variables may be justified. If the investigator is searching for an explanation of *how* economic events occurred, it may still be possible to hold the noneconomic factors constant, assuming that a mechanistic theory of economic behavior is adequate. For instance, it may be sufficient to say that the GNP rose because investment increased. However, if we are seeking to discover *why* such processes were effective or why certain economic behaviors took place, it may be impossible to ignore the noneconomic factors. A society's institutions, both economic and noneconomic, suggest potential or expected economic behavior because they relate to the fundamental objectives of such behavior. A theory of economic behavior shows, at least mechanistically, how certain processes lead to certain results. The actual results indicate whether the theory or the processes under investigation did in fact coincide with reality and whether the institutions were sufficiently understood to be able to predict or anticipate behavior. The economic historian who searches for nonmechanistic explanations therefore has no option but to apply an interdisciplinary approach to his research.

Description, analysis, and synthesis

There is a common misconception that history is simply a narration of what happened in the past. Certainly history depends on the descriptive narrative, because it provides the data for historical analysis. Essentially, descriptive history tells *what* happened and sometimes *how* it happened, but without explaining *why* it did. Obviously, these aspects tend to overlap, but the emphasis in descriptive history is on recording events. The narrative historian is not free of rules and standards. He needs criteria for determining the relevance of information; he needs standards of measurement to render the data meaningful; he needs rules of verification to establish the reliability of his data. He also needs a system of concepts in order to construct the data correctly and bring them to life. Nevertheless, few economic historians are satisfied with this achievement. Most of them search for explanations.

Analytical history utilizes the data gathered by the narrative historian. The analysis involves the dissection of events into smaller behavioral units in order to explain how and why each such unit took place. Such an approach depends on available theory, on the apparent logical relationships between events and the conditions immediately surrounding them, and possibly even on guesswork. For example, the analytical historian may try to explain why a certain recession took place or why a certain industry failed. If a theory concerning the class to which such behavior belongs is available, he tries to place that behavior in its theoretical perspective and formulate an explanation. If no such theory exists, he may try to explain it by whatever tools are available and meaningful to him. Although the analytical historian emphasizes partial considerations and isolated phenomena, he also depends on logical explanations and theoretical premises within which to integrate the individual case.

In contrast, synthetic history seeks generalizations which go beyond the specific instance and help to explain other events belonging to the same class. While the theorist formulates generalizations by intuition or logic, the historian approaches the problem empirically. In seeking a general explanation of a phenomenon, such as price changes, he observes as many instances as possible, tries to isolate the causes of each of them, and then synthesizes the explanations to derive a generalization that will apply to all. Synthetic history is thus inductive history based on empirical data and on investigation of more than one event in that class of events to be explained.

For purposes of synthesis, the researcher makes use of the findings of the analytical historian as shortcuts, rather than using the results of the narrative historian. Synthesis is thus possible only if the two other processes have been accomplished. At this stage of historical research, the historian and the theorist begin to join forces. The historian can offer generalizations to the theorist and help him by testing the validity of his formulations. On the other hand, the theorist is in a position to reinforce or to discourage the historian pursuing a certain line of thinking, depending on whether his generalizations are consistent with or contrary to what the theorist has concluded.

Synthetic history is highly dependent on comparative research. Comparison brings out the common characteristics of various cases. Contrast brings out differences which should be considered in arriving at conclusions. Therefore, synthesis is essentially a process of comparison in search of generalizations. Comparative economic history may be distinguished not only by its objectives but also by the method and the logical grounds on which it is carried out. It implies the expectation that similar conditions produce similar results and that any deviation from such an expectation has to be explained. It also implies controlling some of the independent variables by varying some conditions in order to observe and explain the differences in results. As mentioned earlier, comparison is a form of experimentation, although one that involves difficulties, especially when social and human behavior is under study. All the qualifications for good research associated with case studies must be applied uniformly to every case considered. Whether the comparison is cross-sectional—involving several cases within the same period of time—or longitudinal—involving one case over a long time or many cases from consecutive periods—it has to be justified in terms of uniform expectations under similar conditions. Whether the similarity of conditions or of results can in fact be established is debatable. The researcher must use his ingenuity to justify his selection of cases and establish enough similarities to render the comparison meaningful. Yet in spite of these difficulties, comparative method remains the most dependable and promising substitute for scientific experimentation.

Problems of the economic historian

While the approach to the study of economic history may vary, certain problems are common to all approaches. Knowing these problems may help to reduce their impact on the quality and reliability of results.

It has often been argued that scientific method implies objectivity and detachment on the part of the researcher. The same observations and conclusions should be reproducible by other observers regardless of personality differences. Interpretations may differ, but the data and the conclusions drawn from them must be independent of the researcher. Social scientists have been trying to promote such objectivity, but their success is debatable, for various reasons. The behavior the economic historian deals with as a social scientist is variable. Unlike material things, which have a high degree of homogeneity and constancy, man changes from one moment to the next and observations of him can hardly remain unaffected. Moreover, social behavior is so complex that it is hardly ever observed in totality. There is no assurance that observers will notice the same aspects of behavior every time an experiment is repeated. Third, to observe and understand human behavior requires that the values of the community under observation be internalized to some degree. Various observers may internalize different aspects of those values or internalize them differently from each other. Fourth, each observer begins with a unique background which affects his observations. Finally, observers may differ in their objectives and expectations and therefore may tend to emphasize different aspects of a situation.

These problems are not insurmountable, however. Two conditions are necessary to promote objectivity, though they may be insufficient. First, the observer and analyst should specify the conditions under which he approaches his research, including his own biases, his unit of study, his method, and his expectations. The second condition is that he should regard his observations and conclusions as tentative and subject to change.

A second major problem that faces the economic historian, regardless of his approach, relates to the quality of the data and the field of research. More often than not, the historian deals with a vast area for which records are neither sufficiently accessible nor reliable. The historian has to search for his data wherever he can find them: in biographies, church records, archaeological findings, war chronicles, and even cultural habits and legends which may not be recorded. The historian should be willing and able to search through all these records, compare them, and compare what they indicate with the findings of other disciplines. For example, archaeologists have devised methods of dating, such as carbon-14, which may be invaluable in establishing benchmarks in the recording of history. Again, an important source of information may be the technology of war and weapon manufacturing. The economic historian may have to depend completely on military historians and experts to decipher the relevance and significance to his problem of observations in these areas. His openmindedness and readiness to learn from others are sure ways of improving the quality of his work and of reducing errors and the chance of having to update his findings too soon.

These problems are all related to the fact that the study of economic history is complex. Its complexity derives in part from the vastness of the field, but it is mostly due to the dynamic nature of society. The difficulties are greatest when the subject of research is a total society or economy and when no theory of dynamic macro behavior has been formulated. In such cases the researcher must find ways of allowing for change and for seeking uniformities of behavior which endure over sufficiently long periods to be observable and for their effects to be measurable.

Another aspect of the field's complexity is the frequent inconsistency between real and apparent phenomena. Recent thought in the social sciences emphasizes behavioral observations and discourages introspection.

Yet often the real explanations can be discovered only by indirect inference. A good illustration of this problem is the impact of international diplomacy on the mobility of capital. The publicized explanations are rarely the actual causes for extending or withholding international aid or loans, or for facilitating or hindering trade movements. The historian cannot afford to take the official explanations at face value, yet rarely does he have adequate documentation to go beyond that level.

Given these complications, the economic historian can never be fully satisfied with his explanations. He must search for trends, for durable and comprehensive explanations, rather than for immediate, mechanistic causes. The latter serve as stepping-stones towards the discovery of trends, in which the power of historical analysis lies. The historian's biggest problem is to know where to stop in searching for causes, for he may end up asking questions that have long ago lost all relevance to his problem. This knowledge he acquires only by experience and by defining his questions carefully.

THE FRAMEWORK OF THE STUDY

As a textbook, this study is primarily a survey of economic history. It depends largely on monographic and secondary sources. It is reductionist because, regardless of our interest in exhaustive and comprehensive coverage, a certain degree of elimination will be necessary. However, it is not a descriptive survey. It will not narrate all the facts, nor remain confined to narration. Analysis and exploration are integral parts of the study. We seek to confront the student with major questions derived from the economic history of the modern world. We shall present certain explanatory theories and ideas from the literature. But we shall also try to leave him enough room to use his imagination, to challenge these explanations, to discard or accept as he sees fit, and to try his own abilities in sifting through the data to arrive at hypotheses that appeal to his senses of curiosity, logic, and scholarship.

Economic change

The theme of this volume is the study of economic change. In recent decades there has been a confusion between the concepts of development, growth, and change. In the language of the new economic historians, there is little differentiation among these concepts. However, other approaches have tended to associate development with basic structural changes in the economy, such as changes in organization, attitudes, and entrepreneurship, or in the structure of the market. In contrast, growth has been associated with the economics of relatively advanced economies in which the basic structure is fairly well established and research deals with temporary fluctuations within the structural framework. The concept of economic change subsumes both development and growth. It also extends to the economics of stagnation and decline. It covers market and nonmarket economies, including primitive, precapitalistic or presocialistic economies. Economic change, or lack of it, covers all economic phenomena observed during the period under consideration.

The study will be partly narrative, showing what changes took place in various periods. It will be analytical in exploring the processes of change and the obstacles preventing it. And it will investigate the institutional and philosophical bases which may help explain why change did or did not take place. It is a study of the direction and rate of change, as well as the influences impinging on it.

The study of economic change requires awareness of the major changes in history and the factors associated with them, regardless of whether or not these are economic. For example, the revival of trade may be associated with war, marine technology, population increase, the discovery of new territories, or merely with affluence. How much each of these factors contributed is relevant in explaining the change in trade. But a dynamic study of change is hardly possible, given the present state of economic and statistical theory. At best, change can be studied only in intervals or in a comparative–static framework. That is, we can study the differences between one situation and another, either cross-sectionally or longitudinally. To make such measurement meaningful, it is necessary to establish a standard unit and relate the degree of change to a given point of departure as a percentage or as a rate, such as the amount of change per unit of time. Finally, the amount of change realized must be compared with other changes or with a theoretically expected amount of change if it is to be meaningful.

The system approach

To cope with the interdependence among various aspects of the economy and society, we shall adopt what may be called a *system approach*, a macro approach which has been common in economics at least since the Keynesian revolution. We regard the economy as a composite of interdependent sectors. A change in any one of these is bound to leave an impact on other sectors as well as on the system as a whole.

We look at this interdependence primarily from a structural–functional standpoint, which assumes that each sector contributes to the continuation of the system and is supported by it. However, a factor may cease to be functional or in fact become dysfunctional in its relation to the system as a whole. It is therefore essential to explore the possibilities and meaning of obsolescence in society. This process may be quite significant in explaining why one economy or industry lags behind another or becomes retarded relative to its earlier rates of development and growth.

Because of the flexibility of the system's

boundaries, we shall regard it as an open one, allowing for the flow of both inputs and outputs.

Although the system concept implies an equilibrium situation, we shall use it in a flexible manner, implying only relative stability or minor change which cannot be observed or measured continuously. When disequilibrium is severe, however, change is serious enough to deserve study and explanation. Such severe disequilibria constitute the differences that can be studied by a comparative–static approach.

In a formal model, the role of each sector and the factors that hold the system together are specified in advance. However, since the nature of the system and the significance of the individual sectors tend to vary over a long period, such as the one covered in this study, we shall avoid a rigid specification of these roles. In general, we shall consider society as a total system, of which the economy is a subsystem. The components of the system are held together by the scarcity of resources and the common interest of the members in survival. Rationality is a unifying factor, since each group or individual will act in accordance with its objectives within the framework of the society as a whole. Conflict of interest is contained, although consensus may break down and conflict triumph. The system is unified by the processes of production, distribution, and exchange, although the patterns of each of these processes may vary with changing balances of power, changes in resources, disequilibria between inputs and outputs, and the state of technology.

In dealing with individual sectors of the economy, the economy becomes the system and each sector a subsystem. Therefore, we shall precede the discussion of each sector by a brief analysis of its place in the economy, using this as a point of departure in analyzing change in that sector. For example, when treating population changes, we shall begin by discussing the role of population as a factor of production, as a generator of

demand, as a competitor for other resources, and so on. It will be attempted, however, to maintain a close connection between the individual sector and the system as a whole. Even though the system may be more than the sum of its parts, it changes through change in its parts. Thus an economy changes only if industry, manufacture, agriculture, or the labor force change, individually or in combination. The general explanation aims simply at a summation of these various changes and how they interact in the system as a whole.

We shall try to unite the traditional and the new approaches to economic history. We shall try to take advantage of the achievements of economic theorists as much as possible. In approaching a given topic, we shall explore the relevant processes and functions as suggested by economic theory. The empirical findings may or may not be consistent with the theoretical expectations. Should empirical evidence be lacking, we shall depend on theory to suggest possible explanations, but we shall refrain from creating hypothetical data. In other words, we shall regard economic theory as a guide, rather than as a substitute for historical explanation. We shall try, whenever relevant, to illustrate theoretical generalizations by historical data, but we shall not attempt to test such hypotheses formally.

We shall also try to make use of statistics. Whenever possible, unanalyzed data will be subjected to scrutiny and analysis. However, statistics will not be a fetish. They will be used as a tool to render our findings more precise and more verifiable. The reader should be warned that the absence of statistical data for the earlier centuries covered in this volume should not be interpreted as undermining the significance of statistics or statistical theory. He is urged to recognize these gaps in the literature and expend efforts to fill them.

Our approach will lean heavily on comparative method. We shall try to present information topically for the various countries, simultaneously and when possible in tabular form. Qualitative data which cannot be tabulated will be presented in chart form or in the form of checklists which will indicate whether a given feature existed or did not exist in the areas under consideration. Every such table or chart will be discussed in a comparative framework. Thus a standard of comparison and a system of bringing out common features and differences will be established. However, as in the case of statistics, gaps in the literature may be expected and should be noted. Our emphasis on such gaps derives from our conviction that to know what is missing and search for it is as important for education as taking an inventory of what is already known and learning it.

Although this book deals with Europe, the actual unit of study will be determined by those political and regional boundaries which have a direct impact on economic behavior and relations. When economic relations are determined by the feudal structure, the manorial estate will be the unit of study. However, as the city-state replaces the feudal order, the unit of study will be modified; as communication and political unification give rise to the nation-state, a new unit will be the object of our analysis. Finally, when international and regional combinations and integrations begin to supersede the nation-state, our unit will again undergo change. As much as possible, the generality of the economic institutions, the extent of the market, and the ease of factor and product mobility will determine the unit.

It would, however, be unrealistic to suggest that economic change can be studied within the confines of a political or geographical boundary. Therefore, we shall search for continuities between Europe and other areas. The impact of the Orient on modern Europe and the impact of modern Europe on the New World are important illustrations of such continuities. Thus we shall try to relate the economics of medieval and modern Europe and those of the Americas, if only to suggest the degree to which the economic history of an area cannot be studied in isolation. To identify economic units we shall make use of maps, knowing full well that political boundaries often change radically and swiftly, but that economic boundaries are usually more lasting.

Frequently European economic histories center around England, France, and Germany, because these countries have gone forcefully through an industrial revolution. However, our theme of economic change tends to give attention to all countries, whether industrialized or not, if only for the sake of comparison and contrast.

The period we shall cover begins with the tenth century A.D., unlike most textbooks, which go back at least to the fall of the Roman Empire. Our rationale for this choice is that the tenth century marks the beginning of what has become modern Europe. At this time revival had reached a high point, and most of the institutions characterizing the Middle Ages had taken shape. Moreover, data are relatively available for this period. Although these reasons may be unconvincing, all attempts to cover earlier periods have been superficial enough to warrant discarding, in order to begin on more solid ground.

In this chapter we shall briefly sketch a few theories of economic change which have direct applicability to the understanding of the economic history of Europe, and which have an apparent claim to being emipirically or inductively derived. This brief survey is intended only to introduce some of the more commonly debated explanations of historical change. These theories relate to long-term changes; they deal with trends that often cover centuries; all of them are almost general enough to be called universalistic; and all of them touch on basic institutional and organizational structures that outlive short-term economic fluctuations. The selection is admittedly arbitrary and is mainly influenced by the writer's biases, although it implies neither endorsement nor rejection. It is intended to offer a few tools with which to approach the mass of data and the long stretch of history surveyed in this study. In the final analysis, the reader should be the sole judge of the relevance and adequacy of these theories.

Theories of change are rarely set out neatly and formally. Even more rarely are they presented in a pure or ideal form. Therefore, any classification of them must be arbitrary. The process of change may be initiated from within or from without the system; it may be inherent or built into the system, or it may come about only by conscious effort. Theories of change therefore may be internal or external; they may be evolutionary and deterministic, or revolutionary and individualistic; or they may belong to a combination of these categories. Deterministic theories have almost gone out of fashion, even though evolutionary change, which is deterministic, is still accepted as a meaningful process.

The theories summarized below are not unique to the history of Europe, nor are they derived from the history of Europe alone. Some have resulted from studies of the Orient or of the New World. They will be presented in two groups: (1) theories of evolutionary or developmental change; (2) theories of economic decline.

EVOLUTIONARY OR DEVELOPMENTAL THEORIES

These theories usually anticipate change in a progressive direction, from a relatively lower to a relatively higher level of economic development. The more general of these have been related to what have been called *stage theories*. Therefore, we shall divide this group into stage theories and nonstage theories.

Stage theories

German historical economists. Historical analysis often leads to generalizations which may be called theories even though they lack some of the basic characteristics of causal theories. Stage theories generally fall in this category. Their main function is classificatory; they describe an economy as moving from one stage to another, but without determining either the rate or the cause of change. Although it is still with us, the stage approach is commonly associated with the German historical school, which arose and declined during the nineteenth century. The rise of this school has been explained as a reaction to the classical deductive economic school which began with Adam Smith. The German historians emphasized empirical data, relativism, induction, and the need to accumulate monographic material before making generalizations. One common feature of their contributions was the specification of stages through which an economy or society passes. They also emphasized that economic policy should vary with the stage of development, rather than follow universal abstract laws of economic behavior. While many economists have questioned the validity of the stage approach, few would deny the impact this school has left on economic thinking.

Friedrich List (1798–1846) emphasized the relativism of economic laws and policies and the role of protective forces in the early stages of development. He conceived of the economy as proceeding from primitive conditions into what he called the agricultural stage. Since agriculture is insufficient to sustain an economy, it then evolves into the stage of agriculture and manufacturing. Once agriculture and manufacturing have been developed, the need for commerce arises, and all productive forces are put to use. Up to this stage, protective policies may be necessary, but once the economy has matured to this degree, free trade becomes possible and prevails.[1]

Another stage theory was advanced by Bruno Hildebrand (1812–1878), who used the means of exchange as the criterion for differentiating stages. He felt that every economy goes through three stages. Starting from a natural economy in which exchange, if it exists, is mainly in kind or barter, it develops into a money economy in which money becomes common as a medium of exchange. However, the economy eventually develops to a stage in which money is not only a medium of exchange but a unit of account. In this stage, credit becomes common and more significant in trade relations.

Karl Bucher (1847–1930) advanced a more sophisticated theory. His differentiating criterion was the proximity between the producer and the consumer. At first the economic household is self-sufficient; this is the domestic economy in which little or no exchange takes place. Next arises the town economy, at which stage goods pass from the producer to the consumer and from the countryside to the town. A certain division of labor is already evident at this stage. The final stage, however, is the national economy, in which the division of labor becomes more advanced and intermediaries appear.

Still another contribution which should be mentioned, at least for its novelty, is that made by Wilhelm Röscher (1817–1894). According to Röscher, the economy may be compared to the individual. The complexity of its organization and behavior may be classified into infancy, adolescence, maturity, and senescense. Here we have the elements of a theory of decline. Such theories will be discussed below.

The two most important theoretical contributions by the German historical school are those of Werner Sombart and Max Weber, although it is debatable whether Weber should be included in this school of thought.[2] Sombart (1863–1941) confined his analysis to the evolution of capitalism. He perceived its beginning to be around the year A.D. 1200. The first stage is early capitalism which extends up to 1750, the beginning

---

[1] One might easily associate this theory with the infant-industry argument popular in recent literature on economic development.

[2] We shall treat him outside our discussion of the stage approach.

of the industrial revolution. Early capitalism is characterized by small-scale production units, manual labor or nonmechanization, feudal attitudes and traditionalism, and minor factory production. The organizational structure is dominated by guild craftsmen, informal relations, and nonscientific, intuitive approaches to industry and trade. This stage, however, develops into what Sombart called *full capitalism,* which is conventionally regarded as the period of the industrial revolution. This stage is characterized by rational decision-making, acquisition and the competitive spirit, and innovation, contractual relations, and specialization. The feudal and traditional attitudes of the earlier stage are removed. The third stage is late capitalism, in which the features of full capitalism spread and the advantages of the early industrializers diminish. Here begins the period of cartels, combinations, monopolistic practices, and the need for control. This stage, according to Sombart, began with the end of the First World War. He emphasizes, however, that while public control expands, a large private sector will still prevail in late capitalism.

Walt W. Rostow. The most recent stage theory was advanced by Walt Rostow (b. 1916). Rostow revived the stage concept little more than a decade ago. He responded primarily to the Marxist approach, rather than imitating the German historical economists. He observed the pattern of economic change throughout the world to be uniform and classified the stages into which an economy goes as follows: (1) Traditional society is the first stage. The production function is limited because while a change in output and technology may occur, there is a "ceiling on the level of attainable output per head," due to limited technology and organization. This stage is mainly agricultural and is closely tied to the family and clan. (2) The second stage is that of the "preconditions for takeoff." This stage began in western Europe in the late seventeenth

and early eighteenth centuries, almost simultaneously with the beginnings of the application of modern science to agricultural and industrial production. These preconditions are externally generated by such forces as invasions, communication of ideas, and expansion of the market. This stage is also accompanied by the building up of a central political power to replace the earlier traditional structure. (3) The third stage is the "takeoff," which is the "interval when the old blocks and resistances to steady growth and economic progress are finally overcome." The initiative for takeoff is in some cases mainly technological, but more generally it

> . . . awaited not only the build-up of social overhead capital and a surge of technological development of industry and agriculture, but also the emergence to political power of a group prepared to regard the modernization of the economy as serious, high-order political business.[3]

During this stage industries expand rapidly, savings and investment of domestic income rise, new techniques spread in agriculture and industry, and incomes increase conspicuously. (4) The next stage is the "drive to maturity." This is the period in which growth is sustained at a high level of saving and investment, output increases more rapidly than population, and new habits and institutions develop.

> Formally, we can define maturity as the stage in which an economy demonstrates the capacity to move beyond the original industries which powered its take-off and to absorb and to apply efficiently over a very wide range of its resources—if not the whole range—the most advanced fruits of (then) modern technology.[4]

(5) Maturity is followed by the "age of high mass-consumption," in which production

[3] W. W. Rostow, *The Stages of Economic Growth,* p. 8.
[4] *Ibid.,* p. 10.

shifts towards durable consumer goods and services. Two things seem to have happened in those countres achieving this stage:

> . . . real income per head rose to a point where a large number of persons gained a command over consumption which transcended basic food, shelter, and clothing; and the structure of the working force changed in ways which increased not only the proportion of urban to total population, but also the proportion of the population working in offices or in skilled factory jobs—aware of and anxious to acquire the consumption fruits of a mature economy.[5]

At this stage the expansion of new technology is no longer of a high priority. Rostow also suggested a sixth stage which he called "beyond consumption," but which he left vague because "it is impossible to predict. . ."[6]

Rostow claims that his theory is not merely descriptive, but dynamic in that it takes into consideration the role and composition of investment, the impact of war, the role of government, social decisions, and the reaction of the population to economic conditions. He allows for variation in the length of each of the stages and for the possible stagnation of certain economies. To illustrate, he classifies various countries according to the stages they have achieved at certain periods, as shown in Figure 3.1.

The student may choose to question the validity and relevance of the stage approach in general as well as the above theories. For example, do economies usually evolve progressively? Are the conditions for change sufficient for change to take place, or are they only necessary? Given the generality of these theories, how useful are they in formulating policy or predicting and controlling economic conditions and behavior? The study of history may be a means to test these hypotheses and to search for more meaningful and reliable generalizations.[7]

Karl Marx. Karl Marx (1818–1882) viewed history as a dialectic process in which internal forces cause change and modification in the total economy, which was his unit of study. A change is a result of the contradictions between a *thesis* and its *antithesis*. The synthesis of these contradictions in the new form becomes the thesis, thus starting the process anew. This dialectic process is best reflected by what Marx called the "mode of production," the set of relationships between owners and users of the means of production. These are largely determined by the technology, which also determines the kinds and uses of the means of production. Without disregarding the social and political formations and values of society, Marx emphasized the economic and material values in his interpretation of social and economic change.

Marx's analysis concentrated on the capitalistic system, in which the power of capital predominates, the separation of labor from labor power is complete, the alienation of the worker from the means of production is under way, and the class struggle is evident. But he did not entirely ignore precapitalistic and postcapitalistic societies. Marx noted a number of stages in the evolution of economic history, each of which leads into the next after it has broken down because of its inherent internal contradictions. His analysis of the precapitalistic economic formations, as he calls them, starts with certain propositions:

[5] *Ibid.*, p. 10.
[6] *Ibid.*, p. 11.

[7] For further study of stage theories see W. S. Buckingham, *Theoretical Economic Systems,* chap. 3; *The Encyclopedia of the Social Sciences,* topics under economics, economic history, and the individual contributors in question; W. W. Rostow, *The Stages of Economic Growth;* Paul Baran and Ernest Hobshawn, "The Stages of Economic Growth: A Review," in *Issues in American Economic History,* Gerald D. Nash (ed.), pp. 540–549.

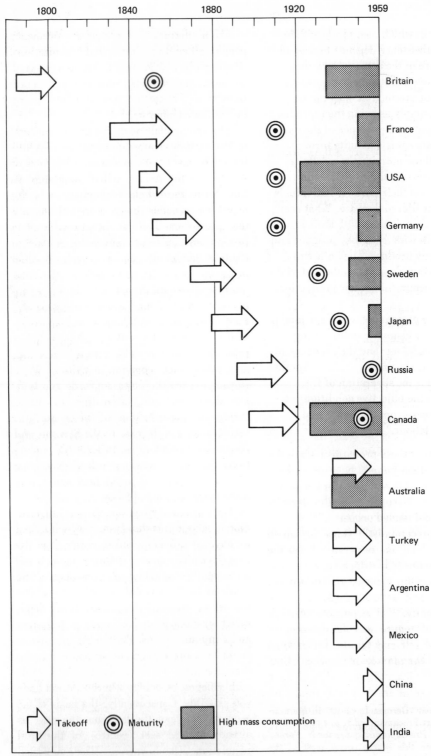

Figure 3.1 Pattern of stages of development.
SOURCE: W. W. Rostow, *Stages of Economic Growth*, opposite p. 1.

The way in which men produce their means of subsistence depends first of all on the nature of the actual means they find in existence and have to reproduce. This mode of production must not be considered simply as being the reproduction of the physical existence of the individuals. Rather it is a definite form of activity of these individuals, a definite form of expressing their life, a definite *mode of life* on their part. As individuals express their life, so they are. What they are, therefore, coincides with their production, both with *what* they produce and with *how* they produce. The nature of individuals thus depends on the material conditions determining their production.[8]

One of the prerequisites of wage labour and one of the historic conditions for capital is free labour and the exchange of free labour against money; . . . Another prerequisite is the separation of free labour from the objective conditions of its realization—from the means and material of labour.[9]

To the extent that these prerequisites are not fulfilled, capitalism cannot be said to have prevailed. Prior to this stage, Marx observes the existence of "free petty landownership, and of communal landed property."[10]

The first precapitalistic stage in which these forms of land tenure prevailed was the Oriental commune, in which private and communal ownerships coexisted. The worker was an owner and a "master of the conditions of his reality."[11] The purpose of work in this form of tenure was subsistence, or maintenance of self and family, rather than production for the market or creation of exchange value.

From migrant and nomadic movements, people settled down into tribal organizations, which evolved according to various external, climatic, geographical, and physical conditions as well as to the "special natural make-up" of the community.[12]

The communal relationship fundamental to the earliest economic formation took different forms in its evolution, the first of which was the Asiatic tribal ownership. In this form the whole community was the owner and smaller groups were only hereditary possessors. The individual was in effect propertyless unless he appeared as part of the total community, and his surplus product belonged to the highest unity in the community. Oriental despotism "therefore appears to lead to a legal absence of property." Part of the surplus or labor was appropriated to the common welfare, while the other part was used for wars, religious worship, and other such common activities. When surplus existed the power of lords and leaders developed and, according to Marx, therein lay the transition of the economy to serfdom, as was the case in the Slavonic and Rumanian communities. In terms of production, this stage was underdeveloped, with large areas of uncultivated land and a very elementary division of labor.

Marx's second form was the ancient, communal, state ownership system, which tended to have a stronger central power than the first. Its unity was also stronger, being based on kinship or on tribal relations between the heads of families as well as on conquest. The leaders or elites of the greater unity dominated strategic resources such as irrigation and communications. Politically, this system could be more democratic or more despotic than the first. Cities evolved side by side with villages, especially where external trade was possible. Consequently, the basis of the economy was not the land but the city "as already created seat (centre) of the rural population (landowners). The cultivated

---

[8] Selection from "German Ideology" in *Marx on Economics*, Robert Freedman (ed.), p. 4.

[9] Karl Marx, *Pre-Capitalistic Economic Formations*, p. 67. From this source comes most of the material on precapitalism.

[10] *Ibid.*, p. 67.

[11] *Ibid.*, p. 67.

[12] *Ibid.*, p. 68.

area appears as the territory of the city; not, as in the other case, the village as a mere appendage to the land."[13] Private property was separated from communal property and the individual was no longer a co-owner, but an occupier of the land.

> The precondition for the continued existence of the community is the maintenance of equality among its free self-sustaining peasants, and their individual labour as the condition of the continued existence of their property. . . . The tendency of this warlike community drives it beyond these limits,[14]

as was the case of the Romans, Greeks, and the Hebrews. However, the communal character of the organization was maintained by the need to retain power over the slaves, on whom production depended. The division of labor was more developed than in the Asiatic form of organization, and different types of internal conflicts existed: antagonism between town and country, between industry and commerce, and between citizens and slaves. Along with these antagonisms, Marx observed a gradual concentration of private property and transformation of the peasant owners into proletariat.

A third form of property was the Germanic or feudal estate ownership, which marked the beginning of the Middle Ages. Communal ownership and private property coexisted in this form. The conditions of the community varied according to local situations and whether labor service was provided individually or by groups. However, as Marx compared it with other formations,

> . . . the Germanic community is not concentrated in the city . . . which gives the community as such an external existence, distinct from that of its individual members. Ancient classical history is the history of cities, but cities based on land-

ownership and agriculture; Asian history is a kind of undifferentiated unity of town and country; . . . the Middle Ages (Germanic period) starts with the countryside as the locus of history, whose further development then proceeds through the opposition of town and country; modern (history) is the urbanization of the countryside, not, as among the ancients, the ruralization of the city.[15]

The Germanic form is distinguished from the ancient in that the communal land was only a supplement to private possession rather than a basis for state power. It was an association of individuals, not a union based on full agreement. "The community has no existence as a state, as a political entity as among the ancients, because it has no existence as a city. . . ."[16] Finally, this stage was marked by its dependence on enserfed small peasantry, against whom unity of the free community seemed essential. The antagonism between lord and serf in the country had its counterpart in the towns between the corporative or feudal trade organization and the apprentice, journeyman, and casual laborer.

Though differentiated from each other, these three forms had certain common features: (1) Landed property and agricultural production were the bases of the economy, and the economic objective of production was use value, or utilization for subsistence, in contrast to utilization for exchange. (2) The land was appropriated "not by means of labour, but as the preliminary condition of labour," which the individual simply regarded as his own. (3) The real existence of the community was determined by the form of ownership of the objective conditions of labor. The stronger the element of communal ownership, the more dependent the individual was on the community. Conversely, the less significant communal property was, the more dependent the community would be on

---

[13] *Ibid.*, p. 71.
[14] *Ibid.*, pp. 73–74.

[15] *Ibid.*, pp. 77–78.
[16] *Ibid.*, p. 78.

the voluntary association of its members. (4) Evolution in all these forms depended on the successful reproduction and maintenance of the relationship between the individual and the community. As long as the basic relationships were maintained, variation within the system was possible.

> Evolution of slavery, concentration of landed property, exchange, a monetary economy, conquest, etc., as among the Romans, . . . appeared . . . up to a point to be compatible with the base, and merely innocent extensions of it, or else mere abuses arising from it.[17]

However, the limits were quickly transcended and the economic and social order was destroyed and replaced by another.

> The object of all these communities is preservation, i.e., *the production of individuals which constitute them as proprietors, i.e., in the same objective mode of existence, which also forms the relationship of the members to each other, and therefore forms the community itself. But this reproduction is at the same time necessarily new production and the destruction of the old form.*[18]

For example, to offset the impact of an increase in population, war and colonization were pursued, but as a result slavery developed and modified the relations of man to the land or the objective conditions of labor. Certain forms, however, were apt to survive longer than others. Where private property has been established, "conditions already arise which allow the individual to *lose* his property. . . ." Such a dissolution implied "a dissolution of the relation to the earth— to land or soil—as a natural condition of production" and communal property; it also implied a "dissolution of the relations in which man appears as the proprietor of the instrument," as in handicraft labor. Before

the dissolution of these relationships, the worker had a right to or owned the means of consumption necessary for his existence prior to production, while after dissolution he appropriated them only in exchange for his labor power.

These changes were regarded as part of the historical process which resulted from the internal contradictions of these economic formations. Thus, dissolution involved what Marx called "historic situation No. 1," which negated the relation of men to the land. Historic process No. 2 negated the relation of man to the instruments of labor. However, a third form could exist in which man owned neither the land nor the instruments of labor, but only the means of subsistence. At its worst, this condition led to slavery and serfdom, both of which were based on domination. These dissolutions represented the alienation of man from the objective conditions of production and rendered the worker a free agent—free to sell his labor power in the marketplace. In the age of dissolution, Marx observed the growth of monetary wealth, which further accelerated the process. However, monetary accumulation was only a necessary, not a sufficient condition for dissolution. Its effectiveness depended on the existence of free labor alienated from the objective conditions of production. Thus the dissolution of the old forms led gradually to the capitalistic order, in which capital brought together labor and the instruments of labor that had been alienated from each other.

Marx observed that other factors were important in the dissolution, such as "the mass of commodities in circulation, [and] the mass of currency in circulation, creating new needs and consequently raising the exchange value of native products, raising prices, etc."[19] In the Middle Ages, for example, the division of labor between production and commerce led to the creation of a

---

[17] *Ibid.*, p. 83.
[18] *Ibid.*, p. 92.

[19] *Ibid.*, p. 113.

merchant class; commerce and interaction among towns not only improved communications but also helped to spread technology. The division of labor between towns led to the rise of manufacturing, which in turn changed the relationship between worker and employer into that between worker and capitalist. It also accelerated the accumulation of movable capital, especially through trade and adventure. Marx greatly emphasizes the development of exchange and exchange value, which "brings about the dissolution of labour's relations of property in its conditions of existence and also of labour as something which is itself part of the objective conditions of production."[20] This transformation of money into capital led into the new order in which new contradictions arose, leading to further transformation and economic change. The new order was the capitalistic system, which was Marx's major concern.

Marx's analysis of the capitalistic system and its process of change was more detailed and systematic than that of the precapitalistic periods, but it also was based on a system of relationships which he presupposed for that type of economy. This model was based on the labor theory of value, the competitive rationale of the market economy, the maximizing behavior of employers, and the absence of strong institutions to combat the power of the market. His analysis seems only a documentation of his preconceived theory, according to which economic change depends on the internal contradictions of the capitalist system itself, as represented ultimately in the class struggle.

Marx first establishes the breakdown of the feudal (Germanic) system and the process of primitive accumulation leading to capitalism. The agricultural revolution in England, foreign trade, colonization, and the movement of prices and credit, including public debt, permit accumulation of and domination by private capital. However,

20 *Ibid.*, pp. 113–114.

once the capitalistic order is initiated, change begins to modify it. Change within the system goes through a number of steps, as follows:[21] The alienation of the workers from the objective conditions of labor, which started in a previous period develops fully. Division of labor and capital domination are completed. Therein lies the conflict of interest between employer and employee, for although each desires the most for himself, the worker is dependent on the capital of the employer for the objective conditions of labor. Interaction in the marketplace between the buyer and seller of labor power results in the utilization of labor power in production so that a surplus value can be appropriated by the employer or buyer. The surplus value is the source of capital accumulation, which is a social function forced on the employer by the nature of the system. This is the first internal conflict: The capitalist is torn between his "passion for accumulation and the desire for enjoyment" through consumption. Accumulation of capital causes an alternation between relative declines and increases in the supply of labor, but ultimately it results in a redundant working population. Sooner or later the demand for labor tends to run short of the supply, even though absolute demand may rise. This redundant working population causes wages to fall and encourages accumulation through the employment of more labor. Wages are dependent on the market, which in turn reflects business fluctuations and the demand for labor supply.

The process of accumulation eventually results in a relative decline in the variable component of total capital, or in a declining demand for labor.[22] It also results in concen-

21 This section is based primarily on selections from Marx in Robert Freedman (ed.), *Marx on Economics*, pp. 166–212.
22 By *capital* Marx means the means of production, in the form of raw material and instruments of labor, which is *constant capital*, and labor power which undergoes an alteration of value in the process of production; this is *variable capital*. For details, see *Capital*, I, pp. 191–192.

tration and centralization of economic power and wealth in the hands of fewer individuals, who in turn intensify competition among themselves. Competition tends to lower the price of commodities on the market, thus driving the smaller capitalists out, while concentration and accumulation of capital tend to lower the demand for labor through economies of scale and higher labor productivity. The process of concentration is encouraged further by competition and the institutions of credit, which develop "in proportion as capitalist production and accumulations do." These fluctuations lead to a crisis which is reflected in a decline in the rate of profit, both because of the decline in the appropriation of surplus value owing to the relatively smaller labor force, and because of the lowering of prices. The crisis is intensified by the decline in consuming power caused by unemployment and depressed wages, or by a decline in effective demand. Society is no longer able to consume what it has produced. The fall in the rate of profit is checked momentarily by depreciation of existing capital, the creation of new capital and new technology, and the relative decrease of expenditure on wages. However, a further decline in the rate of profit tends to check the accumulation of capital; the internal contradiction of this process results in periodic crises. The increase of marriages during the period of prosperity and the increased unemployment in the following period lead to a reduction of wages which permits a revival of business; thus a new phase of the cycle sets in.

The periodic crises tend to become more and more intense as capitalist accumulation and concentration reach high levels. The misery of the workers also increases progressively. The breakdown of the system may be postponed by employers' efforts to discover new markets and new technologies, and even by compromise with the workers. However, the growing consciousness of the proletariat, their sociopolitical organization in trade unions and parties, and their determination to recover their share from the economy make recovery more and more difficult, until the system breaks down and socialism sets in. At this point collective ownership replaces private ownership, exploitation ends, and class conflict vanishes.

The final stages of economic organization are socialism and communism, which follow the breakdown of capitalism. Marx had little to say about these stages that would be relevant in this context. Nevertheless, for the sake of completeness, a brief summary may be presented.

In socialism and communism, which differ from each other primarily in the degree to which communism has been realized, all individuals are free, and the economy is planned by a social group on behalf of the whole community. Planning allocates labor "to perform the different kinds of work desired . . . and to serve as a measure of the value of each laborer's contribution to society, as well as to measure his share in that portion of output available for consumption."[23] The product is used partly for consumption and partly for accumulation of social services, since private property and accumulation have been abolished. The social and political institutions are no longer in the service of one group or class, and hence antagonism between classes is overcome. This harmony becomes a reality only gradually since communism, emerging from a capitalist society, retains some of its aspects. For example, while no market exchange prevails in a communist society, the individual still receives a reward equivalent to his contribution, as in a market exchange system. What happens after this phase and what sustains this harmony is not clear.

Max Weber (1864–1920). The significance of Weber's work to economic historians derives from the fact that while Weber was a disciple of the German historical school, he was a rebel against it; though he

---

[23] Robert Freedman, *Marx on Economics*, p. 267.

was influenced by Marx and paid tribute to him he went in the opposite direction from him. Weber was concerned with change and historical interpretation; he utilized economic concepts and tried to combine theory and empiricism; he was one of the few social scientists who managed to take a fairly broad view of socioeconomic history, both temporally and geographically.

Weber's controversial thesis focuses on the factors leading to what he calls western capitalism. He sees evolution of the socioeconomic system as a pattern of stages divided into traditional or precapitalistic, and rational or capitalistic, as in the West. Traditional society, he felt, lacks the presuppositions of western capitalism regardless of the stage it has attained.

Weber has been only remotely associated with the German historical school and with stage theory, partly because of his relative recency, and partly because of his emphasis on the development of capitalism. However, he was also concerned with precapitalistic society and looked at it in terms of stages. Interestingly enough, Weber's stages of development in agriculture, trade, and industry follow fairly similar patterns. He saw agriculture as beginning as a family or communal affair, in which division of labor was according to sex, women being the early agriculturists. During this stage the hoe was replaced by the plow. The second stage was clan agriculture in which the individual family became identified with the group and work was fairly cooperative. Clan agriculture was based on one or more ties: magical kinship, which was spiritual; military clanship, which was based on power and conquest; and blood kinship.

The third stage was the seigneurial proprietorship, which was based on chieftainship. Chieftainship sometimes evolved through internal differentiation within the community, either because of the development of a military class, through conquest and domination, or through voluntary submission to a chief for purposes of protection.

It also often developed directly through land settlement under feudal terms. The chief might derive his power from magic such as rain-making or from his ability to regulate trade with other communities. Finally, seigneurie could develop through the rise of a town nobility that regarded landownership as a symbol of its status. Seigneurial proprietorship varied from one place to another. However, in all cases, its substance depended on the ability to levy taxes and appropriate fiscal benefits in return for judicial and protective services. This system continued until the development of capitalism.

Stages in industry and mining followed a pattern similar to those of agriculture. First there was the house industry in which production was for personal use. Next Weber observes the development of tribal industry, which depended on a monopoly of either a certain raw material or a certain product. Tribal industry and mining were fairly differentiated either in terms of ethnic groups, skills, and prohibitions against certain subgroups, or for the sake of efficiency and division of labor. The third stage was the seigneurial form in which production for the market became common. The seigneur was ready to exploit the craftsmen under his jurisdiction, especially those who were slaves or serfs. This stage took various forms depending on the ease of securing and sustaining the slaves. The last precapitalistic form of industrial organization was the town industry, which was characterized by wage work and which eventually evolved into capitalistic production.[24]

The same pattern of stage development is observed in the case of trade. Exchange of goods in the first stage was among ethnic groups and was mostly in kind. Next came tribal trade, in which peddling and the beginnings of commercial specialization became characteristic. Commercial specialization was closely related to sects and other

[24] *Town industry* refers to the putting-out system discussed in detail in chaps. 8 and 12.

noneconomic forms of differentiation. The third stage, seigneurial trade, depended on the availability of a surplus for trading. Its rise was also due to the gift trade between seigneurs and to trade carried on for the benefit of the prince. Regardless of its form, it involved exploitation of their subjects by the seigneurs. Finally, we come to town or urban trade, which preceded capitalism. Town trade involved peddling, traveling, partnerships, a chain of trade posts and a central factory type of production, and trade from a central location mainly by correspondence.

Each of these forms and stages involved a higher degree of specialization, organizational sophistication, and scope of activity. The development of trade depended on three main factors. The first was the availability of transportation, whether by land or sea. Where facilities existed, trade was bound to develop. The second precondition was safety and protection. Whether trade was internal or external, safety was important; hence the need for caravans or convoys. Finally, the development of trade depended on the demand and availability of a fixed market to which the trader could direct his efforts; hence the development of the fairs which became characteristic of the precapitalistic economy.

The third and fourth stages in all these developments dominated the Middle Ages. These stages contained all the elements which capitalism had to overcome. The transition to capitalism was traumatic. It is his theory of this transition that makes Weber's contribution distinct from those of other stage theorists.

Weber proposes a conceptual scheme in which he defines economic action as the

> . . . peaceful use of the actor's control over resources, which is primarily economically oriented. Economically oriented action is action which is rationally oriented, by deliberate planning, to economic ends. An "economic system" is

an autocephalus system of economic action. An "economic organization" is a continuously organized system of economic action.[25]

Weber distinguishes what he calls "economically oriented action" as "(a) every action which, though primarily oriented to other ends, takes account, in the pursuit of them of economic considerations, . . . or (b) that which, though primarily oriented to economic ends, makes use of physical force as a means."[26] In that sense every action is economically oriented and must be taken into consideration in understanding economic phenomena and change. For Weber, action is an individual effort. He pays little attention to group or system action in his search for causal relationships.

Having defined his concepts, Weber presents a set of presuppositions which in combination lead to an ideal type of western capitalism. Such a system is characterized by rational capital accounting, which involves freedom of the market or "absence of irrational limitations on trading in the market" and presupposes rational technology or "one reduced to calculation to the largest possible degree, which implies mechanization."[27] Ideal western capitalism also presupposes "calculable law" or rational adjudication and administration, free labor, and commercialization of economic life. However, with commercialization, it becomes necessary to presuppose speculation, with the knowledge that "speculation reaches its full significance only from the moment when property takes on the form of negotiable paper."[28] Weber takes free labor to mean that "persons must be present who are not only legally in the position, but are also economically compelled, to sell their labor on

[25] Max Weber, *The Theory of Social and Economic Organization*, p. 158.

[26] *Ibid.*, p. 159.

[27] Max Weber, *General Economic History*, p. 208.

[28] *Ibid.*, pp. 208–209.

the market without restriction." Commercialization means "the general use of commercial instruments to represent share rights in enterprise," and also in property ownership.[29]

Given this conceptual construct, Weber asserts that

> . . . the impulse to acquisition, pursuit of gain, of money, of the greatest possible amount of money, has in itself nothing to do with capitalism. . . . But capitalism is identical with the pursuit of profit, and forever *renewed* profit, by means of continuous, rational, capitalistic enterprise. For it must be so: in a wholly capitalistic order of society, an individual capitalistic enterprise which did not take advantage of its opportunities for profit-making would be doomed to extinction.

Accordingly, Weber correlates rational economic action with capitalistic economic action "as one which rests on the expectation of profit by the utilization of opportunities for exchange, that is on (formally) peaceful chances of profit."[30]

The problem facing social scientists, as Weber sees it, is to explain why such capitalism evolved only in the West, in certain areas, and in a certain period in the history of civilization. Why did economic change, to put it within the context of our study, follow a certain pattern and take place in one environment and not in others? Even though Weber recognizes that it may exist in various degrees, he observes that capitalism as an economic way of life embodying all the above features was unique to the western world and to a given phase of its evolution. In explaining this phenomenon, Weber observes that two conditions were necessary: "separation of business from the household . . . and . . . rational bookkeeping." How-

ever, he notes, the peculiarities of western capitalism are closely related to "the capitalistic organization of labour."[31]

Weber looks into both external and internal factors to explain capitalistic development, though he suggests that external factors have only a partial and indirect relationship to it. For example, he finds accumulation of wealth through colonial trade of little significance, since it hardly helped in promoting rational organization of labor or income through market operations. The increase of population was not a crucial factor either, except in the sense that it made it easier to secure the necessary labor. Precious metal discoveries might have given rise to price revolutions, which would aid capitalism and development, but only if the labor organization were rational in the western form. Military requirements and consumer demand for luxury items were also merely supporting factors. The external elements that were significant, according to Weber, were geographical in character. International commerce in the West, for example, was greatly aided by the Mediterranean "as an inland sea, and abundant interconnections through rivers."

The features of capitalism and the external factors supporting its evolution were not unique to the western world. And yet capitalism as defined did not evolve except in the West. In the nonwestern societies traditionalism continued to prevail and obstruct the evolution of captialism, while in the West there developed what Weber calls the spirit of capitalism or the ethos of a rational economic system. This rationality, as defined by Weber, was not the same as the rational philosophy of the eighteenth century. It was not the practical or worldly rationality common to many countries and many groups. "The doctrines of Voltaire are even today the common property of broad upper, and what is practically more im-

---

[29] *Ibid.*, pp. 208–209.
[30] Max Weber, *The Protestant Ethic and the Spirit of Capitalism*, p. 17. The rest of this section is based primarily on this source.

[31] *Ibid.*, pp. 21–22.

portant, middle-class groups in the Romance Catholic countries"[32] in which the spirit of capitalism did not predominate. Rather, the spirit of capitalism was based on a "calling" which rendered capitalistic economic action rational. The calling itself might be irrational, but the economic behavior based on it was entirely rational.

The ethos of the capitalistic system seems to have originated in the Reformation and the later doctrine of Calvinism. The Reformation was the break from traditionalism, the source of new attitudes and a new outlook on man's destiny. In its first stages, however, it was still traditionalistic in some ways. Luther's idea of a calling was traditionalistic: Man had to accept the calling as a "divine ordinance" without associating it with work; he did not feel that "work in the calling was *a*, or rather *the*, task set by God."[33] In this sense, the Reformation cannot be said to have been responsible for capitalism. However, it was responsible for the evolution of certain religious sects and attitudes that have "taken part in the qualitative formation and the quantitative expansion of that spirit over the world,"[34] notably Calvinism, Methodism, Pietism, and the Baptist movement. Only Calvinism seems to have had a primary function in the evolution of capitalism. The other groups developed too late to make a difference, although they embodied the worldly asceticism associated with capitalism.

The impact of Calvinism may be seen through a brief study of its doctrines. Its most characteristic dogma is predestination. There are those who are elect and those who are not, and any person may be in one group or the other. However, to deserve to be in the elect group, it is an "absolute duty to consider oneself chosen, and to combat all doubts as temptations of the devil." It is also necessary to pursue "intense worldly activity" in order to gain the needed self-confidence. Therefore hard labor became the pattern, and St. Paul's ordinance "He who will not work shall not eat" became the motto. Another consequence of the dogma was reflected in the attitude towards social classes. Since one is known by the fruits of his labor, he is expected to strive for a higher status for the glory of God. Weber observes further that the Puritan approach gave a new meaning to the division of labor. Rather than being accepted as natural or divine, it was reinterpreted as a way of allowing each to do his best according to his calling. Thus while specialization increased the skills and quantitatively improved the well-being of the whole community, it also prevented the sin of idleness.

Looking at these effects in an economic perspective, Weber observes that "when the limitation of consumption is combined with the release of acquisitive activity, the inevitable practical result is obvious: accumulation of capital through ascetic compulsion to save."[35] Thus the Puritan outlook encouraged the evolution of "rational bourgeois economic life," including at least formal honesty and the methodical pursuit of economic activity. As long as the individual

> remained within the bounds of formal correctness, as long as his moral conduct was spotless and the use to which he put his wealth was not objectionable, [he] could follow his pecuniary interest as he would and feel that he was fulfilling a duty in doing so.[36]

Finally, according to Weber, Calvinism gave a rationale to the unequal distribution of income by regarding it necessary to be poor to remain obedient to God. Weber sees a connection between this rationale, economic theory, and the "productivity of low wages." The acceptance of low or unequal wages and the pursuit of hard labor, when

---

32 *Ibid.*, p. 77.
33 *Ibid.*, p. 85.
34 *Ibid.*, p. 91.

35 *Ibid.*, p. 172.
36 *Ibid.*, p. 177.

combined with the recognition of the activities of the businessman and profit-maker as a calling, were quite significant in the development of capitalism. Before asceticism and Puritanism declined, these behavior patterns had become part of the ethos of western society.

The result of this Calvinistic asceticism was intelligent and alert behavior based on order, merit, and rationality. The same ascetisism which was common in Catholic monasteries was brought out into the world. Furthermore, the rejection of penance, common to both Catholicism and Lutherism, meant that one had to order his moral life as a uniformly ascetic and vigorous whole, as proof of one's worth as one of the elect. Hard work, rational economic behavior, worldly asceticism, and individualism meant a total break from the traditionalism which had obstructed change, prevented a rational organization of labor, and hindered the separation of business from the household. This ethos permeated the socioeconomic life of the individual, affecting the state organization, the institutions of law, and the relationship of man to his total environment.

These observations led Weber to conclude that the development of capitalism was related to religion, that it evolved from within the social system, and that Calvinism was particularly significant in that development. "Where it [the spirit] appears and is able to work itself out, it produces its own capital and monetary supplies as the means to its end, but the reverse is not true."[37] In his conclusion, however, Weber emphatically denies that it is his aim

> . . . to substitute for a one-sided materialistic an equally one-sided spiritualistic causal interpretation of culture and of history. Each is equally possible, but each, if it does not serve as the preparation, but as the conclusion of an investigation accomplishes equally little in the interest of historical truth.[38]

[37] *Ibid.*, pp. 68–69.
[38] *Ibid.*, pp. 89–90.

Nonstage theories

Eli Heckscher. Eli Heckscher (1879–1952) dealt with economic change by analyzing the process of transition from the precapitalistic to the capitalistic form of production, or from the Middle Ages to the era of laissez-faire. Mercantilism appeared to him as a system of power, of protectionism, of monetary organization, and as a conception of society including views on religion and ethics. The most important characteristic of mercantilism to him was that it was a process of unification. As such it was important in advancing or preventing economic change, according to whether or not it was successful. While Heckscher did not credit the policy with such developments as the industrial revolution or modern capitalism, he felt that it certainly contributed to those objectives, as shown by the experiences of England, France, Germany, and to an extent Sweden.

On the eve of the mercantilist period, two forces were active: the universalism inherited from the Roman Empire and a particularism which aided the disintegration of the state. Though universalism was not perfect, it left enough harmony in society to prevent total disintegration. This harmony went beyond national or geographic boundaries and, therefore, was an obstacle to the creation of unified national states. The universalism of which Heckscher spoke was represented by different institutions such as the Church; the guild system; the structure of town administration, which was the same all over the West; international fairs; a common law of commerce and exchange; and the body of Roman law which was basic to modern European law. The effects of these universalistic features were adequate to sustain a somewhat similar social life in different areas and to determine the pattern of later development. Heckscher went one step further, relating these factors to certain philosophies of history. His observations, for example, refuted "the conception that economic factors are the only ones in history."

How they did so is not clear, especially as no evidence was presented to suggest that economic factors would have led to dissimilar social patterns.

Particularism, however, was more of an obstacle to unification. Parochialism guided the behavior of town and corporate administrations. The economic forces in society supported particularism and individualism, while universalism depended mostly on religious forces. Particularism was encouraged and sustained by two main economic conditions: poor communication facilities and the existence of a natural economy. However, exceptions can be found: In Sweden the state maintained a strong central authority on the basis of a natural economy.

State disintegration took the form of a transfer of power to spiritual and temporal vassals. However, in economic matters, power shifted mostly to the new towns, which gradually supplanted the central authority. The degree to which authority shifted varied from one city to another, and consequently disintegration of the state was not uniform. Venice was an absolute city. Most German towns, in contrast, had to submit to a territorial authority.

This disintegration was indirectly augmented by forces such as "transport difficulties [which] produced local differences, . . . the confusion in the system of weights and measures, . . . "[39] and conservatism in general. Obstacles were represented in economic policies such as toll payments, especially when no rational bases for such tolls existed. Heckscher dealt with the system of tolls and customs in detail, as an illustration of the need for and the efforts to overcome such disintegrative obstacles. That they had to be overcome before a more modern economic system could develop cannot be proven. However, evidence tends to suggest this.

Heckscher illustrated his theory by comparing England, France, and Germany, concentrating on their toll systems. He found that the efforts expended on unification of the toll system were paralleled by others in areas such as weights and measures, internal regulation of business behavior, and jurisdiction. The results were equally disappointing. As Heckscher explained,

> . . . every sphere of administration of economic importance had exactly the same characteristics as the toll system. The branches on which the ruling authority lavished greater care and affection showed greater results. Unification and serviceableness came about in those fields where the clear interests of the state demanded them or appeared to demand them. . . .[40]

In conclusion, while no concise theory of change is presented, Heckscher seems to associate the advance to capitalism with expansion of the market, easier mobility, uniformity of rules and regulations, and the security of property of the individual. To what extent these factors were sufficient is not clear, but the implication is that they were necessary.

Earl J. Hamilton. Earl J. Hamilton (b. 1899) has advanced what might be called a theory of change, even though he treats the relevant factors as contributing rather than directly causative. His thesis is mechanistic: He describes given conditions as leading to given results without explaining how the effects are produced. Hamilton is interested in the mobility of precious metals, especially their inflow from the New World to Europe. His theory may be summarized as follows: The inflow of precious metals, much of which was minted, increased the quantity of money and thus led to a rapid rise of prices relative to wages. The lag of wages behind prices resulted in what is called *profit inflation*. The inflation of profit was a significant factor in the revolutionary economic change experienced during the industrial revolution. However,

---

39 Eli F. Heckscher, *Mercantilism*, I. pp. 43–44.

40 *Ibid.*, p. 127.

. . . without a conjuncture of liberal institutions, public and private stimuli to mechanical research, expansion of commerce, epoch-making advances in pure science, progress in agriculture, rich natural resources, a favorable climate, insular protection against military invasion, and many other factors, the Industrial Revolution could not have occurred,[41]

in spite of the apparent profit inflation. This tendency was observed in England between 1751 and 1800, in Spain between 1729 and 1800, and in France during the eighteenth century. Hamilton notes that a price revolution in the fourteenth century failed to bring about similar results because of the Black Death. Yet, when the effects of the Black Death were removed, there were

. . . sweeping advances in English industry, commerce, and finance in the second half of the sixteenth century and the first half of the seventeenth synchronized with a lag of wages behind prices during the Price Revolution precipitated by the great influx of Mexican and Peruvian treasure.[42]

Where wages lagged only slightly behind prices during this period, as in Spain, the results were modest. Where the lag was noticeable, as in France, the upsurge was much more impressive in spite of the religious wars and the civil strifes of the period.

Hamilton's thesis has been subjected to many criticisms, in terms of both accuracy and applicability. Nevertheless, it raises major questions. One might think of it as a theory of both rise and decline. Doing so gives the role of capital extraordinary significance, especially where credit institutions are not highly developed. The usefulness of the quantity theory of money is itself brought into sharper focus. It is possible that such a theory may be directly applicable to the development policies being advanced in present-day societies; these policies might provide a rationale for the necessarily unequal distribution of income inherent in it. Finally, one may wonder whether the role played by profit inflation can be replaced by some other institutional arrangements to advance change upward or to prevent it from turning downward.

Alexander Gerschenkron.   Alexander Gerschenkron (b. 1904) has made observations which may be considered a theory of change, although his emphasis is on the rate or pattern of change, rather than on its causal explanations. Gerschenkron regards historical determinism as out of fashion. He considers history as relevant for guiding policy-makers, and regards variations in historical experiences as the rule rather than the exception. Nevertheless, certain broad trends can be observed and synthesized to form a theory. Observing the pattern of change in nineteenth-century Europe up to the First World War, Gerschenkron suggests that the rate and pattern of development are directly related to the degree of the economy's backwardness on the eve of economic change. The relevant factors include the structure and organization of industry, the institutional arrangements affecting development, the intellectual climate, and the "spirit" or "ideology" of the countries concerned.

Backwardness is a relative concept. In this context it implies certain characteristics which are reflected by the "tension between the actual state of economic activities in the country and the existing obstacles to industrial development, on one hand, and the great promise inherent in such a development, on the other."[43] The comparison of various experiences suggests that

---

[41] Earl J. Hamilton, "Profit Inflation and the Industrial Revolution," in *Enterprise and Secular Change,* Lane and Riemersma (eds.), p. 323.

[42] *Ibid.,* p. 334.

[43] Alexander Gerschenkron, *Economic Backwardness in Historical Perspective,* p. 8.

. . . assuming an adequate endowment of usable resources, and assuming that the great blocks to industrialization have been removed, the opportunities inherent in industrialization may be said to vary directly with the backwardness of the country. Industrialization always seemed the more promising the greater the backlog of technological innovations which the backward country could take over from the more advanced country.[44]

The idea that cheap labor may be an asset is misleading, since it often discourages higher productivity and innovation. In the late-comer countries to development such as Germany, France, and Russia, it seems that

. . . to the extent that industrialization took place, it was largely by application of the most modern and efficient techniques that backward countries could hope to achieve success, particularly if their industrialization proceeded in the face of competition from the advanced country.[45]

This theory questions current thinking that developing countries ought to make use of less advanced techniques in order to live within their means. Gerschenkron observes another tendency which runs contrary to some current thinking: that successful development has tended to proceed on a broad base rather than by concentrating on a leading sector.

In viewing the economic history of Europe in the nineteenth century, the impression is very strong that only when industrial development could commence on a large scale did the tension between the pre-industrialization conditions and the benefits expected from industrialization become sufficiently strong to overcome the existing obstacles and to liberate

the forces that made for industrial progress.[46]

The scale on which commencement takes place determines the degree of tension, and the tension must be great before an adequate response will materialize.

This theory is illustrated by the pattern of development and the role of banks in England, France, Germany, and Russia. Even though a large-scale, fast-moving banking institution, such as the Credit Mobilier, may not last long, its impact forces the old institutions to adopt new patterns and remove the tensions between backwardness and advancement. Where tension does not exist, as in England, slow development of banking on a small scale is adequate. German banks combined the characteristics of both the English and the French banks.

Another example of Gerschenkron's theory is provided by the role of the state. The tension and pressure for rapid development render active participation by the state indispensable, as is best illustrated by the behavior of the Russian governments. However, inconsistencies in state action can lead to prolonged stagnation, reversal, and even hindrance of development, especially if the basic institutional obstacles have not already been removed, or if the natural endowments are not sufficient. As development progresses and backwardness declines, the economy becomes able to sustain itself, and the role of the state becomes less significant.

The degree of backwardness has another important impact on the preconditions for change. The more backward an economy, the higher the degree of ideological commitment necessary to initiate and sustain change. This ideology or faith is a force that goes beyond the desire for the material benefits that accrue from development. Under conditions of severe backwardness, pros-

---

[44] *Ibid.*, p. 8.
[45] *Ibid.*, p. 9.

[46] *Ibid.*, p. 11.

pects of profit or promise of better allocation of resources are inadequate. It takes a
Saint-Simon or a Marx to break the stagnation which characterizes backwardness, as
can be seen from the European experience.

> In conditions of Russian "absolute"
> backwardness . . . a much more power-
> ful ideology was required to grease the
> intellectual and emotional wheels of in-
> dustrialization than either in France or in
> Germany. The institutional gradations of
> backwardness seem to find their counter-
> part in men's thinking about backward-
> ness and the way in which it can be
> abolished.[47]

The student may ask himself many questions based on this theory in looking at the
economic history of Europe. He may raise
the issue of its relevance to other theories of
change. Or he may seek in it a guide for
policy recommendations for present-day societies. He might even ask whether the theory
might not be applicable in explaining economic decline. Is it possible, for instance,
that stagnation may once again take hold of
an economy at a certain stage of its development, as in the case of the "arrested civilizations" described by Toynbee?

Frederick Jackson Turner. Frederick
Jackson Turner (1861–1932) has advanced
a thesis probably familiar to most American
students, at least in a simplified form. However, the extensions of the thesis, especially
those made by W. P. Webb, are less familiar.
Turner's frontier thesis is not an interpretation of history presented for one generation
or age, nor in fact for any one country or
region. It is meant as an hypothesis, derived
through observation, to be subjected to testing, and if validated to be applied to other
experiences of colonization and change. In
fact, some of the analytical details of Turner's thesis have been applied to the colonization of Russia. The frontier hypothesis has

also been applied to medieval Germany, to
Hispanic-American history, to the conflict between European powers, and to the international sphere.

Turner insisted that no study of culture
or history can afford to isolate history, soci-
ology, economics, and political science as
separate areas of study. They must all be
integrated with a detailed study of the phys-
iography of the country. The study of institutions is equally important, since they
reflect the pattern of social and economic
relations in the community.

In trying to explain the history of America, however, Turner paid special attention
to political institutions and their origin. His
point of departure is a given environment
with people of certain qualifications. In
studying the pattern of change, Turner observed

> . . . the familiar phenomenon of the
> evolution of institutions in a limited area,
> such as the rise of representative govern-
> ment; the differentiation of simple
> colonial governments into complex or-
> gans; the progress from primitive indus-
> trial society, without division of labor,
> up to manufacturing civilization.[48]

These changes are common to other civilizations. But, in addition, there is in America

> . . . a recurrence of the process of evo-
> lution in each western area reached in the
> process of expansion. Thus American
> development has exhibited not merely
> advance along a single line, but a return
> to primitive conditions on a continually
> advancing frontier line, and a new de-
> velopment for that area. American social
> development has been continually begin-
> ning over again on the frontier. This
> perennial rebirth, this fluidity of Amer-
> ican life, this expansion westward with
> its new opportunities, its continuous
> touch with the simplicity of primitive

[47] *Ibid.*, pp. 25–26.

[48] Frederick Jackson Turner, *The Frontier in
American History*, p. 2.

society, furnish the forces dominating American character.[49]

This rebirth and achievement and the peculiar pattern of development are due to the unique American frontier. While immigrants come into the country as Germans, Italian, or Irish,

> . . . the frontier is the line of most rapid and effective Americanization. The wilderness masters the colonist. It finds him a European in dress, industries, tools, modes of travel, and thought. . . . Before long he has gone to planting Indian corn and plowing with a sharp stick; he shouts the war cry and takes the scalp in orthodox Indian fashion.[50]

Thus the colonist succumbs to the harshness of frontier life and tries to adjust to it, rather than overcome its obstacles and reinstate his traditional pattern. In the process, his way of life becomes peculiarly American. The farther away from the shores of Europe, settlement assumes a more independent character.

The frontier in Turner's studies seems to be a functional concept related to population centers. It is not a political boundary, but "the edge of settlement." It is a moving frontier defined by the advance of population, which attracts pioneers and immigrants. "The very essence of the American frontier is that it is the graphic line which records the expansive energies of the people behind it, and which by the law of its own being continually draws that advance after it to new conquests."[51] Furthermore, being an area of insecurity, the frontier is also the area that needs defenses. Therefore, the settlement and the military frontiers coincide. Thus conceived, the frontier seems to play a passive role, the energies of the people being the moving force.[52]

Turner studied settlement in detail, tracing its movement on the map, in numbers, and in terms of institutions. He compared experiences in different regions until the frontier ceased to exist, around 1880. Settlement advanced in spurts. The new frontiers usually were marked by natural boundaries such as the Allegheny Mountains, the Mississippi, the Missouri, arid lands, and the Rocky Mountains. Each new settlement had to overcome similar natural obstacles. The internal development within a settlement region depended on its proximity to older settlements and on the ease of communication with them. Isolation and difficult transportation led to more rapid improvements within a region. Although the pattern differed with time and place, certain similarities are observed not only between different regions but also between American settlement and that in other countries.

Line by line as we read this continental page from West to East we find the record of social evolution. It begins with the Indian and the hunter; it goes on to tell of the disintegration of savagery by the entrance of the trader, the path-finder of civilization; we read the annals of the pastoral stage in ranch life; the exploitation of the soil by the raising of unrotated crops of corn and wheat in sparcely settled farming communities; the intensive culture of the denser farm settlement; and finally the manufacturing organization with city and factory system.[53]

Each region of settlement had its influence on the economic and political history of the nation as a whole. "The evolution of each into a higher stage has worked political transformations." The nation went through stages, as did each region, but the two interacted as separate units rather than as parts of the same greater unit. The impact of each

---

[49] *Ibid.,* p. 2.
[50] *Ibid.,* pp. 3–4.
[51] *Ibid.,* p. 41.
[52] This statement contradicts Turner's emphasis to some extent.

[53] Frederick Jackson Turner, *The Frontier in American History,* p. 11.

region varied according to its resources and industries—fishing, fur trading, mining, cattle raising, and farming. These occupations advanced unevenly, making it necessary to "distinguish the frontier into the trader's frontier, the rancher's frontier, or the miner's frontier, and the farmer's frontier."[54] The differential regional impact persisted long after the frontier had vanished, reflecting the diversity of values brought in from earlier settlement and the necessary amalgamation of these values within each region. This is the essence of what Turner called *sectionalism*.

Each of the new frontiers had obstacles as well as attractions. Balanced against each other, these factors determined the rate and pattern of settlement. Trading established trails which opened the way for the farmer who chased the game away and sent the hunter and trader into new frontiers. "The trails widened into roads, and the roads into turnpikes, and these in turn were transformed into railroads. The same origin can be shown for the railroads of the South, the Far West, and the Dominion of Canada."[55]

The frontier also determined the degree of cooperation within the community. Indian threats were unifying elements and "particularism was strongest in colonies with no Indian frontiers." Equally important were the resources of the frontier. In the case of farming, for example, the pattern was also determined by the location of passes and rivers, the fertility of the soil, and the availability of salt springs, mines, and army posts. Turner paid special attention to the availability of salt, particularly after the frontier had advanced beyond mountain ranges and communication with the seaboard was difficult.

In general, however, the advance of the frontier proceeded in stages. Turner approvingly quoted from Peck's "New Guide to the West," a description of the pattern of farmer settlement. "First comes the pioneer, who depends for the subsistence of his family chiefly upon the natural growth of vegetation, called the 'range,' and the proceeds of hunting."[56] The pioneer's implements are primitive, his house is a log cabin, and clearing land is one of his main functions. The preemption law enables him to dispose of his property to the next group. This second group of immigrants "purchase the land, add field to field, clear out the roads, throw rough bridges over streams, put up hewn log houses with glass windows. . . ."[57] Next come the capitalists who offer favorable terms which constitute enough incentive for the settler to seel and move on where cheaper land is available for new settlement.

In this respect the frontier offered an opportunity and an incentive for saving and accumulating capital in the form of investment in new settlement. Those who had the capital were able to employ it from the comfort of their established homes. Thus the frontier was also a source of absentee ownership and of class conflict between settler and landlord. The settler resented being dependent on the landlord and therefore was ready to move on when opportunity offered itself—that is, when a new frontier became available.

Accumulation of capital was facilitated by the creation of credit institutions to accommodate the demand arising in new settlement areas. As the area of settlement expanded transportation was extended, particularly by the railroads. However, the frontier raised technical obstacles. Often the crop of one area was unsuitable for another. The implements of the hills were not good for the prairies. The frontier thus provided the laboratory for technological innovation and adaptation. As life became more complex and the power of capital, speculation, and credit became formidable, the settler sought relief in government legislation. Thus the

---

54 *Ibid.*, p. 12.
55 *Ibid.*, p. 14.

56 *Ibid.*, p. 19.
57 *Ibid.*, pp. 20–21.

frontier encouraged certain institutions, which were forced to change as it declined. While the frontier existed, it acted as a safety valve which relieved both social and economic pressure. When the safety valve was demolished alternative outlets became necessary; these were found in legislation.

Having outlined the pattern of settlement, Turner went on to describe the effects of the frontier on American society. "The frontier promoted the formation of a composite nationality for the American people . . . and decreased our dependence on England."[58] It conditioned legislation and the role of government. In a sense it was the source of nationalism and Americanism. However, as long as the public domain existed, it was difficult to pursue a well-planned conservationist method of purchasing and disposing of public land. The frontier determined legislation regarding land, tariffs, and internal improvement at the same time as it worked against sectionalism.

> But the most important effect of the frontier has been in the promotion of democracy here and in Europe. . . . The frontier is productive of individualism. . . . So long as free land exists, the opportunity for a competency exists, and economic power secures political power. . . .[59]

This safety-valve approach is regarded as the source of individualism as well as of the laxity of legislation and government administration. For example, each period of "lax financial integrity coincides with periods when a new set of frontier communities had arisen. . . ."[60] Finally, the frontier was the soil in which certain intellectual traits developed, such as

> coarseness and strength combined with acuteness and inquisitiveness; that masterful grasp of material things, lack-

ing in the artistic but powerful to effect great ends; that restless, nervous energy; that dominant individualism, working for good and for evil. . . .[61]

Throughout his essay Turner kept the past in sight. The frontier developed new methods to replace traditional ways of doing things, and as a result a new constitution and a new society arose. In his long career, Turner wrote many essays, but he did not significantly improve on his original presentation. To the end of his life he held to his ideas that the frontier was the determinant of social and political institutions, and searched for examples to support his theory.

The relevance of the frontier thesis may be seen from its extension into what has been called the Great Frontier and the 400-Year Boom by W. P. Webb (1888–1963). Webb called the New World the "Great Frontier" and Europe the "Metropolis." Around A.D. 1500 the Metropolis was already crowded with people, relative to its land and resources. Discovery of the Great Frontier opened up new vistas which changed the whole institutional, cultural, and political structure of the Metropolis. The main gains were free land, open space, and precious metals. Wealth flowed in from the Great Frontier to the Metropolis, while the inflow of precious metals increased the quantity of money and created the price revolution. The two factors combined led to what has been called the "Boom," which ended around 1930. The 400-Year Boom was based on the relative abundance of land and goods, given the population dependent on these resources.

Webb recognized that the Age of Discovery required preconditions. At the same time, the Great Frontier idea was enhanced by the willingness of the *individual* to play his role in realizing benefits from his opportunities. The individual was instrumental in ruling himself, enriching himself, and saving his soul; his three institutional frame-

---

[58] *Ibid.*, pp. 22–38.
[59] *Ibid.*, pp. 30, 32.
[60] *Ibid.*, p. 32.

[61] *Ibid.*, p. 37.

works were Protestantism, capitalism, and Democracy.

The Great Frontier idea is a general thesis, but it raises many significant questions to which the student may address himself: What is the optimum ratio between land and people? What constitutes a resource? Could technology and science change the conditions and postpone the end of the boom? Why did not the same consequences characterize other areas of settlement, such as Australia and New Zealand?

THEORIES OF ECONOMIC DECLINE

Decline may be defined as relative stagnation where per capita output or productivity remains fairly constant over a given period of time. It may also be an absolute fall in the rate of increase in output or income per capita. Or it may be a decline in rank relative to the changes experienced by other economies. As far as can be ascertained, no general theory of decline has been formulated, although there have been theoretical models of stagnation.[62] These models generally have not been observed or illustrated in history, nor do they treat the question of decline in the precise manner implied by the measurement of rates of change. To illustrate their relevance to history, we shall approach the economics of decline by referring to specific economies that have risen to primacy but have eventually fallen into relative backwardness.

Frank W. Walbank (b. 1909)

Walbank advanced a theory of the decline of the Roman Empire in the West. Although it deals with an earlier period

[62] Schumpeter's and Hansen's models are notable examples. Historical experience in this area is not totally lacking. Observations have been made of the impact of population changes on economic conditions, as in Malthusian theory; and of changes in technology and entrepreneurship, as in Schumpeter.

than we are concerned with and is primarily a theory of political decline, it is a complete and general theory based on historical observations. Walbank's causes are mainly economic, and his description of decline touches all aspects of society.

The causes of the decline of the Empire, according to Walbank, were best reflected in the conflicts and contradictions inherent in its structure. The main causes of these conflicts were the institution of slavery and the low level of technology which reduced the living standard to subsistence. Because of these problems, all attempts to save the Empire were fruitless, and some led to further weakening of the economy and society. These internal causes were augmented by the advance of Christianity and the barbarian invasions, both of which reduced the impact of attempted reform.

The theory is interesting primarily because of its view of the process of decay as logically inevitable and hence determinate in nature. The empire had expanded its frontiers and flourished by conquest. Conquest brought booty into the treasury and wealth to individuals; it also secured slaves to do the work and sustain economic production at a low level of technology. Within this framework, a middle class began to grow. However, a time came when further expansion at the frontier was no longer possible or even desirable. The sources of slaves and booty were thus exhausted. Slavery itself was undermined by the advance of Christianity. The functions of government required means and resources which had been derived from these external sources, but now had to be secured from within.

One of the most destructive approaches to this goal, according to Walbank, was the creation of what he called the *corporative state*, a concept he borrowed from the literature on modern Fascism. The state began to interfere in economic affairs openly: The *collegia* (craft guilds) were legalized and recruited to serve the government; serfs were tied to the land; the middle class was pressured into contributing more than they thought possible; and the state took direct action by controlling the markets for both raw material and products. The response to these efforts which were compounded by the pressure of the invading barbarians, was the decline of towns and cities, disintegration of the central power, return to the land under a feudalistic structure, decentralization accompanied by regional autarchy, and the further decline of available resources. Defenses were weakened and the army became dependent on peasants and mercenaries who were poorly equipped and trained to defend the Empire. Often the state resorted to inflationary financing by debasing the currency. People lost confidence in the currency and often returned to a natural economy to avoid dealing with it.

On the eve of its fall, the Empire was characterized by declining urban and total populations, because the members of the middle class were against raising families. Technology remained stagnant and did not raise productivity to compensate for the loss of external resources. Economic incentives vanished, and interest in the safety of the Empire was greatly reduced. The decay was also reflected in the decline in creative and scientific literature and in an increasing dependence on religion and superstition. Furthermore, the society was progressively more polarized between the nobility and churchmen on one hand and the workers on the other; the middle class had declined conspicuously. When the invasions came, the Empire was already doomed.

Walbank finds that there were two possible solutions:

> The bourgeoisie might have been persuaded to abandon their privileged position, pay higher wages to the proletariat, develop techniques, and abolish slavery. Alternatively: the depressed classes might have seized power by a violent revolution and carried through the technical changes themselves.[63]

[63] Frank C. Walbank, *The Decline of the Roman Empire in the West*, p. 70.

The first alternative was impractical because in the presence of slavery there was no incentive to pay higher wages or improve techniques. The second alternative might have worked, had the lower classes been better organized or more tightly consolidated. However, there was a "wedge between the free artisan and the slave," and the slaves themselves were divided according to their degree of prosperity.

Walbank raises many questions. To what extent do internal factors determine the fate of nations and economies? Is it true that the corporative state cannot survive, that slavery precludes technological innovation, or that decentralization is detrimental to the development of the economy? He also explores, on the basis of his analysis, the implications for present-day societies. We shall leave these questions to the student.

Henri Pirenne (1862–1935)

Strictly speaking Pirenne's is a theory not of decline but of revival. However, the two kinds of change are so intertwined that it is quite relevant in this context. Pirenne was directly concerned with economic and social change, with universalities, and with philosophies of history. He was interested in the impact on society of economic factors, especially foreign trade and commerce, which might be considered external to the economic system. For him, internal change could hardly be isolated from the events occurring in the surrounding environment. Though Pirenne did not generalize his thesis as a philosophy of history or as a universal idea, its implications are easily generalizable. Can external factors determine the course of a society's history, regardless of the internal strengths or weaknesses? Or are theories like the challenge and response of Toynbee or the creative destruction of Schumpeter more relevant? One can safely suggest that the general implication of Pirenne's thesis is that external pressure on society may redirect change towards new outlets which permit survival and reconstruction.

Since Pirenne was more of an historian than an economist, his treatment was mainly empirical and factual, containing little or no economic theory or deductive analysis. However, he attached much significance to economic phenomena because of their simplicity, their susceptibility to statistical treatment, and their additive and anonymous character. Pirenne tried to explain the transition of Europe from the ancient to the medieval structure without considering national or geographic boundaries, which were diffuse at that time. He succeeds in guiding the reader carefully through time and place, using social, political, economic, and cultural benchmarks to maintain a tight framework. In summary form, Pirenne's thesis is as follows:

1. The Germanic invasions destroyed neither the Mediterranean unity of the ancient world, nor what may be regarded as the truly essential features of the Roman culture as it existed in the 5th century, at a time when there was no longer an Emperor in the West. . . . The Orient was the feudalizing factor: Constantinople, the centre of the world. In 600 (A.D.) the physiognomy of the world was not different in quality from that which it had revealed in 400 (A.D.).

2. The cause of the break with the tradition of antiquity was the rapid and unexpected advance of Islam. The result of this advance was the final separation of East from West, and the end of the Mediterranean unity. . . . The Western Mediterranean, having become a Musulman lake, was no longer the thoroughfare of commerece and of thought which it had always been.

The West was blockaded and forced to live upon its own resources. For the first time in history the axis of life was shifted northwards from the Mediterranean. The decadence into which the Merovingian monarchy lapsed as a result of this change gave birth to a new dynasty, the Carolingian, whose original home was in the Germanic North.

With this new dynasty the Pope allied himself, breaking with the Emperor, who, engrossed in his struggle against the Musulmans, could no longer protect him. And so the Church allied itself with the new order of things. In Rome, and in the Empire which it founded, it had no rival. And its power was all the greater inasmuch as the State, being incapable of maintaining its administration, allowed itself to be absorbed by the feudality, the inevitable sequel of the economic regression. All the consequences of this change became glaringly apparent after Charlemagne. . . . The transitional phase was protracted. One may say that it lasted a whole century—from 650 to 750. It was during this period of anarchy that the tradition of antiquity disappeared, while the new elements came to the surface. This developement was completed in 800 by the constitution of the new Empire which consecrated the break between the West and the East, inasmuch as it gave to the West a new Roman Empire—the manifest proof that it had broken with the old Empire, which continued to exist in Constantinople.[64]

Pirenne asserts that "the conquest of Spain and Africa by Islam had made the king of the Franks the master of the Christian Occident, and without Mohammed, Charlemagne would be inconceivable."[65]

Pirenne's summary of his thesis contains all the elements explicit or implicit in his work. In order to sustain his theory, he had to establish a number of results as facts. First, he had to upset the prevalent idea that the Germanic invasions disrupted life in the

[64] Henri Pirenne, *Mohammed and Charlemagne*, pp. 284–285.
[65] *Ibid.*, p. 234.

Southern parts of Europe. Next he had to established his claim that the Arabs interrupted the flow of trade in the Mediterranean and thus blockaded the West. Finally, he had to perceive and argue the possibility that once the routes of trade were interrupted, Europe had to rebuild its own social and economic life independent of the old influences. The first two of these matters can be verified by empirical evidence. The third must remain a possibility, since there is no way of knowing what would have occurred had the interruption not taken place. Therefore, Pirenne's last conclusion can be established only with a certain degree of probability.

Several questions follow immediately from this thesis: For example, can the interruption of trade lead to the decline of an economy or a political system, or must the system already embody the seeds of decline before such interruption can have serious effects? Can this theory be related to the debates regarding balance-of-payments difficulties in present-day economies? To what extent is a system capable of rehabilitating itself and redirecting its energies in order to survive? Does a center of political power like Rome attract economic activity, or does that activity follow more economically rational determinants of its direction and scope? What relevance, if any, has Pirenne's theory to current economic thinking and developmental policy-making?

An eclectic approach to economic decline

Decline has been observed in more recent times—in Italy, Spain, and the Netherlands, for example—but no "theory" has been advanced to explain it, although individual experiences have been analyzed. These countries succeeded each other in power from the sixteenth to the eighteenth century. Although the conditions surrounding each of them differed, certain similarities may be observed and generalized as an eclectic theory of economic decline. These similarities include the sources of primacy as well as the apparent causes of decline. In each case the rise seems to have been based on the development of services, rather than on productive industries or manufacturing. The external market was important as a source of both raw material and demand for the service or finished product. Apparently, the size of population was an important determinant; an adequate domestic market was necessary for economic supremacy. Furthermore, the hegemony was relative: As long as external competition was not acute, economic rise was possible. Since the rise was not based on the inherent strengths of these economies, sustained supremacy would have required that internal factors be brought into predominance. Where such factors were available, decline was less noticeable, as the contrast between Spain and Holland shows.

The decline resulted from various conditions: First, there seems to have been some institutional rigidity. Contradictions developed between the economic and the sociopolitical arrangements. The flexibility needed to sustain economic development was lacking. The demands on the economy increased, while the techniques and organization of production failed to change rapidly enough to maintain the comparative advantage that had been enjoyed. In the second place, increased competition from other economies failed to arouse enough response to keep the prices down or to maintain low comparative costs, and external markets were easily lost. In the third place, there seems to be a basic need to maintain a balance between domestic and foreign markets. Borrowed or even hired manpower is a weak foundation for an economic empire. Finally, the sources of decline may be inherent in a mature economy. Although no definite features of a mature economy have been agreed upon, the imbalance between the capacity for production and the available market has been noted; this may be termed overproduction or underconsumption. Another feature is the lack of flexibility or mobility. Since large amounts of capital have been sunk, it is difficult to scrap them to modernize the economy. A third feature is the failure to improve on the technology; all available resources have been used, and, given the technology, no cheapening of production is possible. This problem may be linked to the appearance of new competitors and to obsolescence, and may be compounded by the exhaustion of resources and closure of the foreign market to domestic enterprise. Since a mature economy is also institutionally rigid, new blood finds it hard to break in. These conditions imply a high rate of diminishing returns and a failure to compete for the international markets on which the economy originally depended; hence the relative decline. If compounded by a high rate of population increase, the decline may even be absolute.

These conditions of rise and decline are not comprehensive enough to provide a theory. However, they do raise several questions: For example, what characterizes a mature economy? How much can an economy depend on the international market without endangering its continued prosperity or leadership? What is the optimal ratio in a given economy between domestic and foreign dependence and how can one determine that ratio? What degree of institutional flexibility sustains leadership? Finally, can we determine the contemporary relevance of these observations?

GENERAL REMARKS

The above survey of theories of economic change does not exhaust thinking about development or decline. However, it serves to illustrate the relevance of history in formulating generalizations about change and the way such generalizations relate to the present and possibly the future. The survey shows that theories of change cannot be regarded as final judgments on how or why things happened, nor can they be used with great confidence in forecasting trends in the future. Nevertheless, it also shows clearly that essential questions about change can be posed on the basis of these theories, mistakes can be avoided, and doctrines can be scrutinized. Most of all, the survey shows the complexity of change and the futility of isolating economic from noneconomic factors in the dynamics of society. Which of the above theories fits a given situation is a question which can be answered only in context and with full knowledge of the prevailing conditions.

BIBLIOGRAPHY

Baran, Paul, and Ernest Hobshawn, "The Stages of Economic Growth: A Review," in *Issues in American Economic History*, Gerald D. Nash (ed.), Boston: D. C. Heath, 1964, pp. 540–549.

Buckingham, W. S., *Theoretical Economic Systems*, New York: Ronald Press, 1958, chap. 3.

Cipolla, C., "The Decline of Italy," *Economic History Review*, 2nd series, V (1952), pp. 178–187.

Freedman, R. (ed.), *Marx on Economics*, New York: Harcourt, Brace & World, 1961.

Gerschenkron, A., *Economic Backwardness in Historical Perpective*, New York: Frederick A. Praeger, 1962, chaps. 1–2.

Hamilton, Earl J., "Profit Inflation and the Industrial Revolution," *Quarterly Journal of Economics*, LVI (1942), pp. 256–273; reprinted in *Enterprise and Secular Change, Readings in Economic History*, F. C. Lane and J. C. Riemersma (eds.), Homewood, Ill.: Richard D. Irwin, 1953.

Hamilton, E. J., "The Decline of Spain," *Economic History Review*, VIII, No. 2 (1938); reprinted in *Essays in Economic History*, I, E. M. Carus-Wilson (ed.), New York: St. Martin's Press, 1962, pp. 215–226.

Havighurst, A. F. (ed.), *The Pirenne Thesis*, Boston: D. C. Heath, 1958.

Heckscher, Eli F., *Mercantilism*, I, London: George Allen and Unwin, 1934.

Kamen, Henry, "The Decline of Castile: The Last Crisis," *Economic History Review*, XVII, No. 1 (1964), pp. 63–76.

Marx, Karl, *Pre-Capitalistic Economic Formations*, E. J. Hobshawn (ed.), Jack Cohen (tr.), London: Lawrence and Wishart, 1964.

Marx, Karl, *Capital*, I, New York: International Publishers, 1947.

Pirenne, Henri, *Mohammed and Charlemagne*, Cleveland: World Publishing Co., 1957.

Rostow, W. W., *The Stages of Economic Growth*, New York: Cambridge University Press, 1960.

Taylor, George Roger (ed.), *The Turner Thesis*, Boston: D. C. Heath, 1956.

Turner, F. J., *The Frontier in American History*, New York: Henry Holt, 1921. [Copyright 1920 by Frederick Jackson Turner. Copyright 1948 by Caroline M. S. Turner. Reprinted by permission of Holt, Rinehart and Winston, Inc.]

Walbank, Frank W., *The Decline of the Roman Empire in the West*, New York: Henry Schuman, 1953.

Webb, W. P., *The Great Frontier*, Boston: Houghton Mifflin, 1952.

Weber, Max, *General Economic History*, New York: Collier Books, 1961.

Weber, Max, *The Protestant Ethic and the Spirit of Capitalism*, New York: Charles Scribner's Sons, 1958.

Weber, Max, *The Theory of Social and Economic Organization*, New York: Oxford University Press, 1947.

Wilson, C. H., "Economic Decline of the Netherlands," *Economic History Review*, IX, No. 2 (1933), reprinted in *Essays in Economic History*, I, E. M. Carus-Wilson (ed.), New York: St. Martin's Press, 1962, pp. 254–269.

THE
MIDDLE
AGES

EUROPE IN THE MAKING

PART
TWO

THE SETTING: THE TENTH AND ELEVENTH CENTURIES

Every society requires a set of institutions to define its political, economic, and social relationships. Usually these are broad enough to allow a certain degree of individual action and change to take place without completely disrupting the functioning of society. These broad institutions are the most important criteria by which a society can be defined. Identifying them should enable us to construct a model of the behavior of the members of that society, and to identify change when it occurs and assess its impact.

When we speak of medieval Europe, it would be misleading to imply a tightly knit society or a well-organized economy or polity, with a set of institutions which apply uniformly. The geography, the ethnic structure, the traditions, and the internal influences in the various regions were quite different from each other. In effect there were numerous societies or economies, each with its own set of institutions or identifying marks.

The Europe of the tenth and eleventh centuries was subject to at least four sources of influence which were differently distributed in various regions. First, there was the influence of the Roman heritage with its complex culture, laws, and traditions, which had survived the fall of Rome several centuries earlier. This influence was felt mostly in the southern and southeastern areas of the continent. The second influence came from the Germanic invaders who settled the land and assimilated with the native population, but who retained certain characteristics of their own cultures. A third major influence came from the Arabs who had penetrated various parts of Europe. Although their expansion had been stopped and some of their conquests retrieved, their economic and sociocultural interaction was still important. The Kingdom of Granada was to last three more centuries. The fourth influence came from the more universalistic institution of the Church. By this time Christianity had advanced abroad, and the Church as an organized institution, with its power centered in Rome, was becoming a dominant influence throughout Europe. Its influence was felt in religion, politics, and most effectively economics.

The impact of these influences was not uniform, however, varying conversely with the strength of the native people. For example, the impact of Germanic occupation on Roman population centers was much less than it was on the less civilized Slavic territories.

THE MEDIEVAL ECONOMY: AGRICULTURE

If we look at the map of Europe around the year A.D. 1000 we find it divided into kingdoms, some of which were relatively large, such as France, England, and the Holy Roman Empire, which combined most of what is now Germany and Italy. These political entities had some common features which held them together, but such unity was largely nominal. A closer look at the map would show the internal divisions of these entities into separate duchies, counties, archbishoprics, bishoprics, and towns. In most cases, these smaller units were almost completely autonomous or were tied to the realm by an agreement involving only paying homage or extending aid when needed. However, even these smaller units are not appropriate for economic analysis, because they are not total economies. To form an economy, the unit must share a market, a system of economic arrangements, and a common currency, and its individual parts must be interdependent with each other. Medieval political entities usually consisted of more than one autonomous economic unit. The duke usually was an overlord; under him were different lords on whom he had conferred a fief which functioned as the economic unit. The fief might itself be a unit or it might be composed of several units known as *manors*. The manor might be shared by more than one lord, and a lord might control more than one manor. This overlapping has probably been a source of confusion between the concepts of feudalism and manorialism. In this context feudalism implies political and military status; manorialism, on the other hand, relates to the economic structure. We shall discuss the manorial economy in some detail below. Before we do that, let us look at the density and distribution of population and suggest a general model of the medieval economy of this period.

Population

Population data for the period under consideration are scarce and not highly dependable. Various methods of estimation have been used, based on such data as the rise of new cities, the expansion of old ones, or the erection of new city walls. Total population

Table 4.1. Estimates of population in selected areas, A.D. 950–1348

AREA	PERIOD	POPULATION
Asia Minor and Balkan Territories	c. 950	5–8,000,000
Constantinople	1000–1050	200,000
Russia	Early 1000s	2,000,000
	Early 1200s	6,800,000
	c. 1348	8,000,000
Iberia	c. 950	7,000,000
	1280–1290	8,300,000
	c. 1348	9,500,000
England	1086	1,100,000
	1348	3,700,000
British Isles	1086	1,720,000
	1348	5,250,000
France	1000s	6,700,000
	1328	13,400,000
Paris	1348	90,000
Denmark	1348	192,500
Finland	1348	58,000
Norway	1348	123,000
Sweden	1318	162,240
	1348	212,160
Italy	Late 1200s	8–9,000,000
Germany	1100	4,000,000
	1200	7,000,000
Poland	1348	1,200,000

SOURCE: *Based mainly on J. C. Russell, "Late Ancient and Medieval Population,"* Transactions of the American Philosophical Society, *New Series, Vol. 48, Part 3 (1958), pp. 99–123. Other estimates vary greatly, but all sources seem to agree on the trends.*

has occasionally been estimated by regarding urban population as about 1.5 percent of total population. Estimates have been made on the basis of hearth-tax records. The density of settlement in certain areas has also been used to estimate the total population. Such estimates are very rough and should be interpreted very cautiously and only as trends. The estimates in Table 4.1 cover a longer period than we are discussing, to allow comparison and to suggest the apparent trend. The significance of the population changes suggested by these figures will be analyzed below. Here we shall concentrate only on the figures relevant to what has been classified as the rural era.

The relatively sparse population of Europe in this period included a few large concentrations—such as Venice, Rome, Paris, and London—which were important centers of government and seats of power. Few other cities exceeded 5–10,000 people before the end of the eleventh century.

A model of
medieval agriculture

Economic activity depends on the factors of production, on effective demand, and on the market or its substitute, in which the forces of supply and demand interact. The factors of production are conventionally land, labor, and capital. In more complex societies we also speak of entrepreneurship or risk-taking as a factor of production. In this discussion we shall speak of land and capital as one factor; we shall leave out entrepreneurship temporarily, but we shall say a few words about technology. The following are our assumptions:

1. Land tenure, the arrangements regulating disposal of the land, determines the distribution of income and power and the relationships between the social groups dependent on the land. The owner may be dependent on others to cultivate his land, but he disposes of the right to cultivate, to earn an income, or to fill an occupation.

2. The significance of land tenure increases with economic dependence on agriculture, and it decreases as alternative means of livelihood prevail. Therefore, as long as agriculture remains the primary source of livelihood, landownership carries with it not only economic power, but also political and social power and influence.

3. Land tenure is most significant where the methods of production are primitive and agricultural labor seems homogeneous. As long as the worker is replaceable, his bargaining power remains weak. The power of the landlord or employer increases in proportion.

4. Where economic alternatives and mobility are lacking, tradition tends to be a powerful stabilizer of society. Tradition, rather than contract, regulates the relation-

ships between the social and economic groups in such a society. And, since tradition changes slowly, the same system of relationships tends to prevail for long periods. In such cases change comes about only when a forceful catalyst impinges on and undermines these relationships.

5. Land is only one factor of production. Labor is at least as important. The supply of labor is closely related to the size of the population and to the availability of economic alternatives as well as to the level of technology. Let us look at these implications separately:

a. The larger the population, the larger the labor force, given the technology and other resources. However, the population also represents the consumers for whom the production is intended. In an economy with low technology, production usually is labor-intensive and population is an important source of productive capacity. For example, where land is available, an increase of population could lead to an expansion of settlement, cultivation, and production. The same is true of manufacturing and handicrafts, which require simple tools, most of which are custom-made. Given the available factors in either case, population changes determine the degree of expansion of production and the relative supply of products.

b. Whether in a subsistence or in a commercial economy, the supply of products depends to a large extent on the demand for them. In either case, an increase in population means an expansion of potential demand. The demand becomes effective to the degree that the population is creating purchasing power to exchange for the new products.

c. Population may have an impact on other areas of an economy. The density of population may be a determining factor in the creation and expansion of social investment. For example, population agglomerations in cities and townships make it economically feasible to build roads, public services, schools, and hospitals. They make it possible to realize economies of scale as well as external economies, both of which invite new investment.[1] They also create the institutional groundwork for improving the quality of product and for raising productivity, either beacuse of competition or because of the institutional and legal controls set up to protect the consumer.

6. An improvement in technology permits higher production and productivity and a rise in the standard of living. It also permits diversification of production and division of labor. The rise in productivity releases part of the population to produce additional commodities, thus creating additional effective demand. However, in the absence of higher technology, the increase in population may be a burden rather than an asset. Arable land is extended beyond the economic margin, per capita income falls, and in the extreme case starvation and disorder may be experienced. The economy may suffer stagnation or even a decline, unless offsetting forces are introduced.

The manor

The early medieval economy may be represented as an agrarian subsistence economy in which tradition played a major role. Control of the land and other means of production was conferred from above by enfeoffment. The common unit of settlement was the manor. The micro unit of cultivation and social unit within the manor was called the *manse* in France, the *hufe* in Germany, the *hide* in England, and in Denmark the *bool*. This unit contained the operational family, which might or might not be an extended family, whose members worked and lived together. It also represented the control unit for tax levy and collection, both for the state and for the manorial administration.

The manor, or agricultural village, varied in size and internal relationships, depending on its geography and terrain. It has been observed that hilly terrain was often char-

acterized by independent homestead farms; meadowland encouraged dispensation, servile labor services, and substitution of rents in money or kind; the same was true of newly settled areas. Flat grain land often seemed resistant to change, compared to other areas. Finally, it seems that crops needing less labor than others, as in the Mediterranean area, usually encouraged free relationships between the landlord and the peasants. Yet these differences were only matters of degree and do not indicate any substantial variations in the organizational structure.[2]

The manor usually included a landlord, a small minority of free tenants, a majority of serfs, and a small group of cottars or squatters who lived on the margin of the community. Slavery existed on certain manors, but it was no longer common. The size of the manor varied from a few hundred acres to many thousand. To an extent its size was determined by the social and political power of the landlord, and the landlord's relations with his tenants varied accordingly.

At least formally, the lord controlled all the land. He dispensed land and duties and controlled the distribution of income. In most cases, he also supervised the enforcement of law and order. He protected the individual peasant and the whole community against outsiders, and against famine. Though the lord might live on the manor, it was common to find him residing in town or on one of several other manors he might control. He therefore employed an agent, *the bailiff*, who represented him in all respects, including enforcing the law in the

---

[1] External economies imply indirect benefits; economics of scale mean that the cost of production decreases as the scale of production increases.

[2] A different classification arranges manors according to the combination of types of tenure represented, seven of which may be differentiated, as follows: (1) "typical" manor with *demesne*, villein or servile land, and free holdings; (2) demesne and villein, but no free holdings; (3) demesne and free holdings but no villein land; (4) no demesne; (5) only free holdings; (6) only villein land; (7) only demesne land. These various types are explained below. The significance of these combinations will become clear when sociopolitical and economic relations are faced with a crisis, as we shall see.

community. Often the bailiff had the help of a reeve who was one of the peasants or *villeins,* as they came to be known. If he owned more than one manor, the lord often employed a steward to represent him and supervise them on his behalf. The system of control was quite detailed. The steward knew how much seed was needed for sowing, how many people and plows would be available, who owed what dues and in what form. He watched over the purchase or sale of rights to make sure the transaction was authorized. He also supervised the bailiffs to make sure that they did not cheat the lord.

There were three main forms of land tenure. Though the landlord was the sole owner, he usually held only a part of the land personally. The lord's *demesne,* as it was called, could be as much as a third of the area of the manor. The demesne land was cultivated by serf labor, the obligatory services of other peasant groups, or by wage labor hired among the cottars. The second type of holding was the free tenant holding, which the tenant cultivated as he saw fit, although he had certain obligations towards the lord as rent, which he usually paid in kind. The third type was the villein or serf holding. The serfs paid rent in the form of labor services, *corvée.* They might owe the lord up to three days work every week. Moreover, they could leave the lord only at the pleasure of the lord. Both they and the free peasants were obligated to help on the demesne during periods of bad weather or disaster. The cottars owed little and were entitled to little. Some held one or two acres but had no oxen or plows for cultivation. They lived, formally at least, at the mercy of the landlord. Often they provided wage labor on the farm and elsewhere.

These relationships, both obligations and rights, were upheld by tradition and were reinforced by the fact that this was a subsistence agriculture. Any possible market was far away and the means of a landlord were required to take advantage of it. Under the circumstances, the power of the lord was almost unlimited. For example, the serf had to pay a fee, the *merchet,* upon marriage of his daughter; he paid another, the *chevage,* for any absence from the manor; upon a serf's death, the lord was entitled to take his horse and war equipment, *heriot* and *relief.* Finally, the serf was expected to pay homage by utilizing the lord's facilities, such as his mill and bakery, *banalities,* especially in England. The significance of these additional obligations is that they symbolized the lord's hold over the serf. The serf was also personally tied to his master. His movement was restricted. His plans for his children were subject to control; for example, he could not send them into a religious order without permission. He could not dispose of his land rights, nor of his movable property —especially the beasts and draft animals— without explicit permission of the manor lord. Thus tradition sustained the social relations by creating symbols and providing an economic foundation for them. Many of these symbols outlived the tenure arrangements which brought them into existence.

The manor land was distributed among the peasants according to convenience, equity, and security. The arable land was held in strips, each of about an acre. The strips of each holder included lands of different fertilities and locations. Everyone was entitled to good and poor land, as well as to distant and near locations. This intermingling of holdings was also regarded as a security measure, for it insured that a peasant had company in the distant fields. The number of strips held by a family depended on the land/labor ratio in the manor, and on the number of working members in the family or the number of plows the family could muster. However, since redistribution was avoided as much as possible, inequity was not uncommon. Differentiation also resulted from differences in laws of inheritance. In France and Italy division among the heirs was the rule, although primogeniture was not uncommon among the nobility. In contrast, Germany avoided division of the estate by applying primogeniture. England did the same, leaving the estate to either the eldest or the youngest son.

The manor also included meadows and forest land. These were held in common. Usually, however, the number of beasts that could be grazed was controlled by the landlord.

Cultivation and labor

The land was cultivated by primitive methods, although after the year A.D. 1000 the wheel plow, drawn by eight oxen, seems to have come into use, especially on the demesne land. Cultivation followed the two- or three-field system of rotation, according to which either a half or a third of the land was held fallow every year. The rotation systems were used to restore fertility to the soil, since manure was the only fertilizer known and its quantity was limited.

The manor was an independent unit. Most of the tools were handmade, often by the peasant himself. In manors large enough to support specialization, a craftsman might be found. The manor had a church and possibly a school, both of which were supported by the lord.

This type of agricultural settlement was common in most areas west of the Elbe, although there were variations according to the size of the demesne, the ratio of serfs to free peasants, and to whether the lords were lay or ecclesiastic, and whether or not the settlement was new. Despite their differences, such manors had two features in common: They combined relatively large-scale operations on the demesne with small-scale operations on the individual holdings, and most of the holdings were fragmented into strips widely spread across the land of the manor.

These features were not characteristic of the lands east of the Elbe, however. This territory was inhabited by the Slavs, whose organization was based on family and clan relations. The Slavs were less agricultural than in the West and depended more on hunting, gathering, and fighting. Some had settled on land that was already in cultivation, while those close to the Germanic settlements imitated the Germanic way of life, concentrating on agriculture. The fighters among them were organized around a lord, on whose estate they lived. They were supported by slaves or the *wend*, dirty folk. However, even those nominally free were subject to the lord, who in turn was subject to a prince, but under whom there might be lesser lords. Cultivation on these estates was communal and no field ways were open to individual holdings. Each field was cultivated by the whole community, and dues were either based on the number of plows mustered by the peasant, or levied on the group of neighbors rather than on the individual.

This pattern was relatively uniform among the Slavs and among the Baltic people, who were collectors and herders. Baltic leaders arose from the families and clans and formed a modest nobility related in blood to the rest of the community.

Finally, a word should be said about conditions in the area under the Arab conquest. In general, the Arabs were relatively few. They lived in towns and had their country estates, which they had received in return for military and government services, worked for them. The Berbers, who came a little later, were more interested in farming, and usually settled in the hilly northern parts of Spain. Farming was mainly dry, although the Arabs managed to improve greatly on the irrigation systems they found and to introduce fruits, vegetables, rice, and cotton. Slave labor was common, especially when slaves were brought in by professional traders from the Slavic countries and other areas of Europe. However, the majority were free farmers, including Christians who refused to be converted. Their only symbol of subjugation was the payment of a *Jizya* or a poll tax. Feudalism, as described above, did not develop in Moslem Spain, except in the areas closest to the Christian settlements. In fact, feudalism seems to have taken hold only as reconquest began.

In general, the manorial structure described above was fairly stable. The land/labor ratio was favorable enough in the early period to allow some flexibility. The relationship between the lord and the peasants was sustained by spiritual or political power. The lord, whether lay or ecclesiastic, was the peasants' protector, but he was also entitled to enforce his rule. Another stabilizing element was the absence of alternative opportunities, which was compounded by the difficulty of transportation and communication. Distance was an obstacle which would have remained even if opportunity had been available. Moreover, to initiate an enterprise outside the traditional framework would have required capital, which the average producer who lived at a subsistence level did not have. On the positive side, the producer had traditional rights, including security against starvation.

Together, these reasons precluded any major destabilizing action by the producer. On the other hand, the lord as yet had no reason to seek change in an economy in which he had a large vested interest. He enjoyed the luxury, the prestige, and the power of his position. As long as these two forces were balanced and external or new forces did not emerge, relative stability was assured. The test of stability would come when the system was faced with a crisis.

THE NONAGRICULTURAL ECONOMY

Although agriculture was the main occupation in this period, there were other ways of earning a living. The period was characterized by fighting, invasions, and defenses. The lords therefore usually lived in walled towns. Where no towns existed, new ones were built as places of fortification; these were known as *bourgs* or *burgs*. Initi-

ally these fortifications were inhabited mainly by a fighting garrison, by the lord and his attendants, and by the surrounding population during times of danger. However, these inhabitants generated demand for services and manufactured products. By the beginning of the eleventh century business life became noticeable. Merchants, artisans, and craftsmen moved to the towns in response to the demand. Soon the *bourgs* became too small to accommodate the newcomers. Therefore, either the area within the walls was extended or building around the walls was encouraged; this became known as the *faubourg* or outside bourg.

Until this time trading had been based on agricultural products and controlled by the lord or his agents. As Ashley has suggested, the villages in England were totally self-sufficient except for four items: salt, iron for plows, tar needed as a remedy for scab which infected the sheep, and millstones.[3] These usually were imported from their places of origin or from periodic markets and fairs. Slaves and luxury items were the main components of international trade. However, the end of the eleventh century witnessed the beginning of merchant guilds in English towns. The picture was little different on the continent except in the well-developed cities of the South.

The faubourgs saw the change to professional traders, but the lords still had control over commercial activity in the town. In addition to agricultural products, woolen items were made locally. Weaving became a specialty in Flanders. The Meuse valley concentrated on metallurgy. Copper-works flourished in Namur, Huy, and Dinant; these towns sent agents to Saxony to secure copper from the mines. Tournai specialized in stoneworks that were exported. The Italian towns were involved in silk weaving. Tools were manufactured in most localities that were large enough to support an artisan.

[3] W. J. Ashley, *An Introduction to English Economic History and Theory*, p. 36.

In spite of these activities, commercial exchange was still fairly limited and mostly in kind. Monetary exchange was not common practice, although it was known in virtually all areas. In fact, some wages and dues were paid in money. However, the limited international exchange encouraged the localization of currency.

At the end of the Carolingian period, circa 1000 A.D., the silver pound was the main denomination minted, although the gold *solidus* was still used in Byzantine and Arab territories. The Carolingian silver pound was about 491 grams of silver; it was divided into 240 *deniers* or pence (*denarii*), each containing about two grams of pure silver. Halfpennies (*oboli*) were also minted. Actually these last two denominations were the only real money. Larger denominations such as the *sou* or shilling, equaling 12 pence, and the pound, equaling 20 sous, were only units of account. At this time minting was still a state monopoly and the metal content of the currency was under control. However, the breakdown of the Empire and the solidification of feudalism led to extensive decentralization of minting rights, accompanied by confusion, corruption, and periodic debasement of the currency. Minting rights were taken over by princes and granted to churchmen by the various kings in their territories. Soon many currencies were in circulation. Often they were acceptable only within certain fiefs. Furthermore, the princes who had the minting rights periodically reissued the currency with the same nominal value but with less content and lower purity of the precious metal, thus increasing the supply of money to their own advantage. The consequences of such devaluation were limited, however, since the currency was restricted to their own territories and monetary exchange was still not very common.

In all societies some form of borrowing exists. However, this period saw the beginnings of formalized credit, both for commercial and for consumption purposes. While little detailed information is available, it is clear that commercial credit did exist. The Church was an indispensable source of credit, especially for consumption purposes. Credit for consumption, which was considered charity, was intended to relieve distress and prevent starvation, especially in periods of famine. Such credit was secured against a property in one of two forms, either as "live gage" (*vif gage*), in which case the revenue of the property was used to reduce the debt, or "dead gage" (*mort gage*) in which the revenue was not necessarily applied to reduction of the debt. Up to this time there is no evidence of usury or interest payment on debts to the Church. Commercial credit probably carried an interest, although no documentation is available. However, there is no evidence of any banking operations before the end of the eleventh century.

In general, this urban life was sufficient to complement the dominant rural society. Economic activity was on a small scale and catered to the needs of the manor lords and public authorities.

BIBLIOGRAPHY

Ashley, W. J., *An Introduction to English Economic History and Theory,* New York: G. P. Putnam's Sons, 1892, chap. 1.
Bloch, M., *French Rural History,* Berkeley: University of California Press, 1966, chaps, 3–4.
Hole, Edwyn, *Andalus: Spain Under the Muslims,* London: Robert Hale, 1958, pp. 46–56.

Pirenne, H., *Economic and Social History of Medieval Europe*, New York: Harcourt, Brace & World, 1937, chaps. 2–3.

Postan, M. (ed.), *The Cambridge Economic History of Europe*, Second edition, I, New York: Cambridge University Press, 1966.

Vinogradoff, P., *Growth of the Manor*, London: George Allen, 1911.

Watt, W. Montgomery, *A History of Islamic Spain*, Edinburgh: Edinburgh University Press, 1965, pp. 48–51.

Weber, Max, *General Economic History*, New York: Collier Books, 1966, chaps. 4–5.

If any one feature may be regarded as uniquely characteristic of the twelfth and thirteenth centuries, it is change in a uniform direction. This process was arrested only by the plagues which swept Europe during the fourteenth century. Most of the fifteenth century was required for recovery.

EXPANSION
AND COMMUTATION

Change in the twelfth and thirteenth centuries was predicated on a number of developments. Some of these were external to the economy, such as the increase of population, urbanization, and the Crusades.[1] Others were internal, such as the growth of monetary and credit institutions, better technology, and more aggressive entrepreneurship. Table 4.1, p. 50, shows that the population trend which began in the tenth century continued until the early fourteenth. The population increase was accompanied by a shift of economic emphasis from the countryside to the towns and cities. The increase of urbanization was accompanied by several other developments which became important determinants of socioeconomic life. For example, a larger demand for

[1] "External" and "internal" are relative terms relating to the direct impact a given factor has on the economy.

agricultural products and a larger supply of nonagricultural items developed. The expansion in the market and increase in exchange resulted in a higher demand for a medium of exchange. Once trade had developed, international exchange became a necessity. This complex economic life required certain controls which were provided by either the market or legislation or both. It also meant a larger demand for factors of production, including capital, and an expansion of credit and banking institutions. However, since the demand for factors is derived from the demand for products, we shall concentrate on the latter.

Two main tendencies can be observed in this period. The first was an expansion of cultivation through colonization and settlement, accompanied by a strengthening of the institutional (feudal and manorial) structure; the second was a tendency for these institutions to change in response to the same forces which tended toward expansion. These two tendencies were complementary. Without modification of its internal relationships, the manor might have broken down much earlier than it did, centuries later.

Colonization
and settlement

The expansion of agriculture in this period was mainly quantitative, although manorial and feudal arrangements were now exercised more efficiently. Expansion of production was mainly the result of new settlement and the clearing of previously uncultivated land. The frontiers were continually extended, and the wastelands and forests were reduced and converted into arable land. The settlers were led by those lay or ecclesiatic lords who could secure land grants and round up enough people to man the new settlements.

In Italy land reclamation and improvement continued throughout the twelfth and thirteenth centuries. Fruit trees were planted; dykes and river embankments were built, especially by the Benedictine order in the twelfth century. The Cistercians helped provide water for cultivation. An irrigation canal in Milan, *la Muzza*, was started in 1220 and finished in 1239. In southern and central Italy settlement was extended to the hilly areas, which were of marginal or submarginal fertility.

There seems to have been a concerted effort towards reclamation in France, the Low Countries, and West Germany. The efforts were started by the monastic orders, although some believe that the laity were the pioneers. The Cistercians and Benedictines were of great importance in clearing the wastes in the northern part of Flanders, the forests and wastes of Roussillon, Bavaria, the high valleys of the Vosges, and the Alps of Switzerland and the Dauphine. The Cistercians are held responsible for clearing the forests of Normandy and large parts of what today is Belguim. Monastic efforts seem to have been most important in Germany between the Rhine and the Elbe. Bishops and archbishops were equally interested; early in the twelfth century Archbishop Frederick of Bremen is said to have been the example followed by many others in attacking the wasteland in Holland. Lay princes were also involved. Even the king of France is said to have encouraged the reclamation of the interior of his kindom.

The pace of settlement was not uniform. In Normandy the peak was not reached until about 1260; in most places the expansion continued until 1300, except in the lands east of the Elbe, in which it lasted much longer. Labor was recruited from all walks of life, although the main source was the peasantry. It was common for peasants to settle in faraway places to avoid overcrowding and to enjoy the favorable conditions offered them by the new lords. In Germany and sometimes in France, a *locator* or middleman was employed to search for the land and the labor for new settlements. In France, although new *bourgs* or *villes neuves* arose, the manorial structure was retained and even strengthened by better organization. The peasants were related to the lord as their forefathers had been, even though their condition might be better.

The history of agriculture in Spain in this period was different from that of the rest of Europe. Moorish Spain was gradually reconquered, and a large part had been regained by the end of the thirteenth century. The clergy, the nobility, and especially the military, benefitted from grants by the king. As territories were recovered, western institutions, including feudalism, were introduced. Spain thus not only experienced a delayed introduction of manorial agriculture, but retained slavery much longer than the rest of Europe. Spanish agriculture was relatively advanced. The Arabs had encouraged irrigation and they left a complete system of canals. Fruits, vineyards, olives, cotton, rice, and grains were grown. The most important export item was wool, derived from the Merino sheep, also brought into the country by the Arabs from Africa in the twelfth century. The sheep has great significance for Spain, as indicated by the *Mesta*, or guild of the migratory sheepherders, which became a strong force sparing neither meadows nor forests. Even though conservation measures were taken in the thirteenth century, the Mesta left its imprint on Spanish agriculture for a long time.

The Norman conquest left many areas

of England completely devastated, and much property changed hands. However, the available evidence suggests that in the period of reconstruction the tenure arrangements of earlier times were retained. The manorial structure and the open-field system seem to have been strengthened.[2] In addition, the land subjected to clearing and assarting (the legal conversion of forest into arable land), which were common in this period, was held under the same arrangements as previously settled land. Although some individual holdings may have resulted from assarting, they were the exception. It may be noted that, as in other countries, the Cistercians played an important role in clearing and assarting.

The greatest expansionary movement was that of the Germans into the lands east of the Elbe. The movement had begun earlier, but a new and sustained momentum prevailed at the beginning of the twelfth century. German settlement was conducted by the Church and by laymen and was based on blood relations, faith, and conquest. Missions were established in the newly opened lands, which were pushed eastward for purposes of security and defense. An important element in this movement was the Teutonic Order, whose members, the Knights, had decided to invade the land upon their return from the Crusades. The expansion was continuous; at the beginning of the thirteenth century the settlers crossed Pomerania. Around the middle of the century they settled the lands of the Teutonic Knights in Prussia and on the Baltic. The settlement of Prussia was effective by 1280. However, the peak of settlement in this period was reached after 1300; by 1350 the settlers had entered Red Ruthenia (parts of Poland and the Ukraine) and spread over Hungary.

The migrants came from all walks of life. German social patterns were adopted, including the village and town layout and the institution of primogeniture. The settlements were usually ethnically homogeneous, although in some cases Slavs and Germans intermixed. When new lands were being cleared, the Germans usually predominated. The pattern was uniform: A locator searched for suitable land and sometimes recruited settlers; each settler owed the same obligation to the lord or prince; thus seigneurial relations became established. Often the locator settled down as an agent of the lord. He might even be given a judgeship or he might receive his dues and move on to another enterprise.

The settlement might take the form of a compact village with field land all around it; or it might be a street village in which the homesteads stood in rows, or a series of separate or irregular homesteads. The three-field system was the common form of cultivation. Though strip holdings existed the more common pattern was the consolidated holding, with field-ways reaching to the field. At the beginning of settlement, the tenants had favorable terms, although the lord remained the ultimate owner. A new form of dues, money rent, was charged, in contrast to rent in kind which was common in old settlements. While labor services were not demanded at first, reaction soon set in and services were often required, even by the Teutonic Knights, who were among the first to charge money rents. Although at the beginning of settlement the villagers had elected the headman, *schulze*, he later became an appointee of the lord and the office became hereditary and was used as a means of oppressing the peasants.

The advance of the Germans eastward had other significant effects. By introducing the three-field system, the Germans improved productivity and diversified agriculture. They introduced the heavy plow, brought in fruit trees, and encouraged cattle farming. They improved the breed of horses, especially on the *vorwerke* estates which were held by military leaders. Further-

---

[2] Whether the open-field system existed in this period has been questioned by some scholars, although with little evidence.

more, they established towns with markets and this laid the foundations for commercial agriculture east of the Elbe.

The German system of colonization was copied to some extent in Poland, where the manorial structure was apparent at the beginning of the eleventh century. During the twelfth and thirteenth centuries relatively large estates developed, which were often associated with knighthood. However, another group evolved in Poland at this time, namely the gentry, who were below the nobility but above the peasants. Many of them had no tenants and cultivated the land themselves, as the yeomen did three centuries later in England. Polish agriculture emphasized stock raising which was supplemented by fishing, hunting, and other specialization. Serious colonization began around the twelfth century and took German tenure patterns during the thirteenth and fourteenth centuries. It was directed by landowners, churchmen, and the monarchy. Here also the Cistercians were active, especially in importing settlers, notably from Flanders and Germany. When these were not available, they turned to local people. They used the system of locators, who usually became headmen of the colonies. An interesting aspect of this movement is the virtual absence of labor services, at least at the beginning. Dues were in money or kind.

A similar colonizing trend developed earlier in Hungary, and much later in Lithuania. In contrast, no evidence exists of such expanded settlement in Scandinavia at this time. Although villages were established, emphasis in the Scandinavian territory continued to be on hunting and stock raising, rather than on cultivation and clearing the land.

Commutation and the decline of serfdom

The expansion of agriculture was accompanied by changes in the internal relations on the manor. Labor dues were replaced by money rents; most dues became fixed, in contrast to the arbitrary and variable dues levied previously; and decision-making concerning cultivation shifted from the landlord or his agent to the individual holders. The agreement became contractural rather than traditional; henceforth in England it was recorded in court and the peasant held a copy of it—hence the name *copyholder*. The copyholder had a French counterpart, the *censier*, who paid a fixed *cens*. This change has been known as *commutation*, since labor services were commuted to fixed dues in money form, or the tenancy was transformed into share tenancy (*metayage*) to avoid servile labor on the demesne. Commutation has been generally accepted as a fact, although its rate and form varied from one place to another. It is apparent that both the lords and peasants played a major role in the process.

Causes. Different reasons for commutation have been advanced by different people, but none seems sufficient to cause the change by itself.

The increase in population put new pressures on the manorial economy, since more of the product was needed for subsistence. It would have caused a reduction in the standard of living of the peasant below subsistence or in the surplus appropriated by the landlord while his dependents were increasing in number. The peasant who lived at subsistence had no incentive to increase his production, but neither did he want to reduce his standard of living. On the other hand, the lord had no desire to reduce his standard. His only alternative was to increase pressure on the peasants for additional dues, which was impractical. Therefore, it seemed rational to renegotiate and commute the services to money rent, leaving the peasant free to make his own decisions, increase his production, or leave farming altogether. The landlord was thus relieved of supervision and could expect a guaranteed income.

Expanding colonization offered new opportunities to peasants and lords for maintaining or even improving their living standard. The peasant found it desirable to join new settlements in which the terms were more favorable than he had had before. Once relieved of labor dues, he was free to go. The landlord found it worthwhile to offer better terms in order to recruit people because it was good business. It therefore became necessary to change the old relations.

The rising urban economy offered other opportunities. The peasant who was still tied to the land could escape to town and find a hiding-place as well as earn a living, probably a better one than he had enjoyed previously. It became increasingly difficult to keep the peasantry under control in the face of these new outlets. The lord who had to sustain a larger family or more dependents also found it attractive to participate in the urban economy. To do so, however, required capital and free time. Commutation offered him both. Therefore, it was rational for him to modify the terms, reduce the usurpation of his land by his subordinates, and guarantee his income by shifting the responsibilities to the peasants themselves.

A third factor was the increase in the use of money and the resulting higher interest in receiving money rather than kind. By commuting the dues, the landlord shifted the burden of marketing and exchange onto the peasant. This reduced not only his responsibilities but also the risks of price fluctuation. The peasant, on the other hand, was interested in participating in the market as long as his dues were fixed and he could reap the results of his labor. Should there be price rise, he could increase the supply without fear of losing a larger share of the landlord.

Another factor is what has been called the "demonstration effect" of the Crusades. The Crusaders were introduced to a totally different way of life in the East. Once they had tasted the comforts of such living, they were anxious to continue it. Therefore, they were attracted to urban living and enterprise, leaving the rural economy in the hands of the peasants. The Crusades were also important as a source of demand for and supply of products. The demand for war material tended to stimulate certain industries, notably those producing food, clothing, and arms. Such demand, especially when backed by an inflow of purchasing power in the form of booty, was a stimulating influence on the economy. At the same time, the Crusaders brought back items which, when made available on the market, gave incentive to further exchange. They also returned with precious metal which added to the supply of money, thus stimulating further the forces of demand and supply.

Another cause has been advanced for commutation and renegotiation, as follows: Expansion brought submarginal land into cultivation and the lack of sufficient fertilization rendered soil fertility low. Therefore, it seemed more rational for the landlord to secure a fixed money income than to accept dues in kind or labor, the value of which was no longer guaranteed. This argument indicates that commutation was favorable for the landlord, but the evidence suggests that the peasants were more anxious to reduce their dues to fixed money rents. This is not consistent with the low fertility explanation. If we accept the low fertility assumption and the declining income of the farmer as a fact, it may be true that the landlord had to reduce rents by converting them to money in order to sustain the peasant. However, it is not evident that low fertility was common, nor that land had become scarce enough for settlement to have reached marginal or submarginal areas, nor that rents were reduced until their value was depreciated through price inflation. Therefore, the low fertility argument has little to support it in this period.

Internal conflict was growing on the manors. The peasant and the lord's other followers were no longer ready to accept their social and political lot. This unrest is best illustrated by the increasing encroachment on the lord's rights within the manor. Especially in France, there was a growing tendency by the bailiffs and their accomplices to usurp the rights of the lords, appropriate much of their dues, and often take over parts of the demesne. Another symptom of the conflict was the increasing need for individual and collective adjudication, especially in England where public courts were gaining at the expense of manorial courts. The authority of the lord to increase dues or to demand certain types of services was questioned. Under these circumstances, the lord found it expedient to anticipate trouble and circumvent it by modifying the terms and changing them into money payments.

Had all these reasons been inadequate to modify the terms of tenancy, the decline of population caused by the plagues and wars in the following centuries would have completed the change, as we shall see below.

The impact. Although there were variations in the rates, types, and results of commutation in different areas, certain common effects can be noted. First, commutation gave new strength to the manorial structure, since it removed some of the grounds for conflict between the lord and his followers. Serfs who might have objected to a continuation of the status quo were enfranchised, given a large measure of freedom, and freed from degrading servile labor. However, their tenure still assured them of land on an hereditary basis, and they were protected against outsiders as previously. They were required only to pay a fixed amount of money rent plus certain symbolic obligations associated with their status. If they had any grievances left, these were relatively minor.

Free tenants and cottars were not affected by commutation, except that their rent in kind was replaced by a money rent. There is no evidence that the lord's power was yet reduced. He continued to be the master, to levy dues and gather taxes, and to supervise the courts, except where, as in England, public courts had been established for certain types of cases. Use of his utilities continued to be required of the peasants. Moreover, the lord was relieved of certain obligations he had had, to the disadvantage of the peasant. The lord's status *vis-à-vis* other lords was not affected by the general loss of servile labor. Therefore, from a sociopolitical standpoint, the change had a strengthening impact on the manor.

The major impact of the change was economic. Commutation was a necessary step to release the productive forces that were tied within the manorial structure. The easier mobility of capital and labor was an important factor in the colonization movement which extended to all parts of the continent. Since the serf could replace his labor services with money payments, he could participate in colonization, improving his lot and possibly increasing his productivity. Colonization utilized the population increments which otherwise might have become a burden on the manorial economy. The free peasants may also have been affected, although not as strongly because they could have left even before commutation, at least in principle. The economic impact of commutation was probably as important for the landlords whose families and dependencies had grown. The new arrangements put capital and time at their disposal and thus made it possible to seek new avenues of income.

Although the economic effects of commutation were primarily relevant to individuals or groups, its impact was significant also on an aggregate level. Commutation and expansion were significant in increasing the product surplus by which a larger nonagricultural population could be sustained. Although the technological changes in agriculture were minor and productivity was not greatly increased, total production advanced significantly as a result of the expansion of cultivation over large areas of new arable land. Even if we preclude any shifts of the production function, the expansion was sufficient to increase the surplus by a proportionate ratio.[3] Since not all those in the nonagricultural group enjoyed the nobility's high standard of living, the additional surplus sustained an even larger nonagricultural population. The majority of those fed by this surplus were themselves productive and hence added to the economic welfare of the community. Thus, while the population increase and growth of the urban economy helped to bring about the change in agriculture, commutation and colonization were necessary for them to take place.

While no adequate data are available, it may be presumed that the standard of living improved as a result of these changes. To the extent that the fixed dues were less than the variable ones extracted previously, the commutations were a means of redistributing income from the lords to the servile population. Furthermore, since the dues were delivered in money terms, any upward price movement meant an increase in the real income of the peasant, at the expense of the landlord. Finally, to the extent that the new arrangements increased incentives and possibly productivity or production, the lot of the peasant was bound to improve. In contrast, although the lords lost by redistribution, to the extent that they were able to benefit from their new opportunities, they were more than compensated. It is true that their share in the additional total income was probably less than it would have been under previous arrangements, but this was the price they paid to avoid greater losses. However, the change was not always an improvement for the peasant, particularly in areas where the landlord was directly in charge of cultivation or where there was a labor shortage. The cultivator lord was anxious to retain his land and even enlarge his demesne. This was the case in England, in contrast to the disintegration of the demesnes in France and later in Hungary.[4] In such cases, the lord might be willing to commute services, but would not give up land. He might even insist on unfavorable terms. With little land, the peasant had no place in the manor except as a wage worker. This might be an economic improvement, but socially and politically it was not. Where labor was in relatively short supply, the lord tended not to resist commutation, but whenever possible he reverted to the use of servile labor. This was particularly true in the lands east of the Elbe. Although servile labor had been relatively rare in that area at the beginning of colonization, a wave of reaction took place around the end of the thirteenth century. The need for labor services, especially on the knightly estates, *allod* or *vorwerke*, caused the lords to reinstate servile labor and revive serfdom. The Teutonic Knights also resorted to this method of securing labor a little later, as we shall see below. An interesting countermovement was the introduction of the system of "gardeners' rights" in the eastern territories. According to this institution, introduced to secure labor, the lord would bring into the town a group of "gardeners" who would be given landholdings too small to provide a living. To supplement their income the gardeners would work on the lord's estate for wages, usually a given percentage of the produce paid in kind. These people had a heritable right to their holdings, but they remained dependent on the lord for supplemental work. In a sense, this group was similar to the cottars described above, except that the gardeners had rights and obligations toward

---

[3] Suppose 100 workers, with the appropriate amount of land and capital, are necessary to support 10 members of the nonagricultural or leisure class. Then 1000 would support 100. An upward shift of the production function would allow a larger surplus and thus would support an even larger leisure or nonagricultural population.

[4] However, in England there was a stronger tendency for commutation. Because of the diminishing need for military service resulting from the end of the Hundred Years' War, the king welcomed a substitution of shield money or *scutage* for the military service.

the lord, while the cottars had none. While the magnitude of this reversion to servile labor is unknown, it is apparent that the lot of the people affected was far from improved.

Finally, one belated experience of feudalism in agriculture should be noted. Russia, about which we have said very little, was during this period divided into various segments with little unity among or within them. Feudalism developed fully, but without commutation, during the thirteenth and fourteenth centuries. In some places commutation took place during the fifteenth century or later. However, in general the situation in the West was common also in Russia, except for the lag in time and in the development of the institutions that led to the breakdown of the feudal structure.

To summarize, the manorial institution was by the end of the thirteenth century well established. Though the internal relations had undergone change, the forces were balanced enough for the general structure to persist. However, the effects of commutation were felt far beyond the confines of the manor. The economic horizon had expanded. Income and decision-making power were redistributed in favor of the majority of the people. Man was gaining control over nature, as reflected in his invasion of the land and in his efforts to extract more and more output for his enjoyment. However, the forces of change remained active, and the apparent stability was again put to the test in the next two centuries.

DECLINE
AND REVIVAL

The trends towards expansion and freedom were to a large extent reversed by the events of the fourteenth and fifteenth centuries. The period has been described as one of crises, of transition, of decline, and even of preparation for the commercial revolution to come. Although society was rocked to its foundations, those foundations were strong enough to weather the crisis, reverse the decline, and make the transition possible. This crisis was caused by famine and plague and the ensuing population decline; internal and external wars, including the Hundred Years' War between France and England; the rapid development of the cities and the urban economy; and the expanding international horizon. The last two of these influences will be treated in detail in the next chapter. We should note here, however, that the growth of the urban economy involved a larger volume of exchange between the country and the city and made it necessary to consider the terms of trade between these two sectors.

Demographic instability:
famines, plagues, and war

Early in the fourteenth century, Europe experienced some of the most serious famines that had ever occurred. Before complete recovery was possible, France and England began a war which continued intermittently for 100 years. The severest blows came from the periodic plagues which hit hardest in 1348 but recurred until the last decade of the century. In fact, local plagues took place as late as 1485 (in Pavia).

The most direct effect of these shocks was on the population. Population data for the Middle Ages are still sparse, but there is enough evidence to suggest a trend. For example, the population of England is estimated to have been 3.7 million in 1348; in 2 years it declined to 3.1 million; after the 1360–1361 plagues it declined to 2.74 million, to 2.45 million after the 1369 plague, and to 2.25 million after the 1374 plague. In Florence 3 merchant families lost 7 out of 14 children, 5 out of 9, and 5 out of 12 respectively. In Bordeaux the canons of Saint-Seurin lost 12 out of 20 members; in Hamburg the 40 butchers in the city were reduced by 18. The town of Givry in Burgundy lost 615 people out of a population of 1800. The population of Brabant, on which detailed estimates are available,

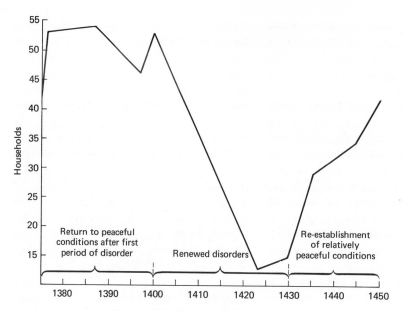

Figure 5.1 Military operations and numbers of households in Ouges, Burgundy.

During the first three-quarters of the fourteenth century epidemics and wars had reduced the population of Ouges by 30 percent.

SOURCE: *The Cambridge Economic History of Europe*, I, p. 676.

declined continuously between 1374 and 1496. A reverse of the declining trend came only in the sixteenth century. The population of the Scandinavian countries around A.D. 1400, or after the plagues, is estimated as follows: Denmark: 105,500 (preplague: 192,500); Finland: 35,100 (from 58,000); Norway: 90,750 (from 123,000); and Sweden: 106,560 (from 212,160). The city of Toulouse is estimated to have contained 30,000 people in 1335; 26,000 in 1385; 20,-700 in 1398; 19,000 in 1405; and 8,000 in 1430.[5] Thus the decline is evident, although not uniform. Nevertheless, it is estimated that "when the plague subsided, the population was reduced by 50 or 60, or even 70 percent in some places, by 15 to 20 percent in others, and on the average by 30 percent."[6]

The impact of war on population was due to loss of life and to displacement. Although

[5] *Cambridge Economic History of Europe*, I, p. 664.

[6] *Cambridge Economic History of Europe*, I, pp. 674–675.

the evidence is not fully reliable, an indication of the effects may be seen in Figure 5.1, which relates the number of households to war activities over a period of three-quarters of a century.

The recovery of the population trend was slow. The upturn in England and in France did not come until 1420–1430. By 1545, the population of England had reached 3.22 million. The French population picked up around 1460 and might have reached 15 million by 1500. The population of Italy around 1500 was about 5.5 million and about 8.5 million in 1550. It may be safely concluded that by 1500 all European countries had recovered their population losses and resumed growth.

The effects

The impact of a population decline depends on the age distribution of those lost, their social and occupational composition, and their skills and incomes. We may assume that famines and plagues would hit hardest at the poor, the undernourished, the very old and the very young, and possibly at the slum population. On the other hand, war would probably hit hardest at those of military age and those close to strategic locations such as cities. These assumptions are illustrated, although inadequately, by the available data. The cities suffered more than the rural population; children and old people suffered more than the healthier working population. Therefore, the economic impact must be differentially distributed among different locations and different social and economic groups. We may be able to trace the effects of population decline by observing its impact on the demand for and supply of agricultural products and on the terms of trade between country and city.

On prices. The decline of population precipitated a decrease in the need demand for agricultural products. If the population did decline about 30 percent during the plague period, we should expect the demand, at least for subsistence, to decline by the same proportion. The decline of population and the war also caused depopulation and destruction of producing units in the countryside, resulting in a decline of supply. However, to the extent that the decline of population was more drastic in town than in the country, and among the nonproducing than the producing population, we may expect the demand for food to have declined more than the supply. The obvious result in a market situation would be a relative decline in the average price of agricultural products.

In actuality this seems to have been the case in most localities. The available evidence shows that price changes were not uniform and that the price decline lagged behind the plagues by about a quarter of a century, during which the prices of wheat and other grains were probably rising. This rise may be explained by a shortage of supply caused by the plagues and the war. However, as the farmers adjusted to the new market situation, a surplus developed, causing the price

decline. It is also possible that the plagues hit the country before the urban areas, causing the shortage and the later surplus. However, there is little doubt that a general decline of agricultural prices was experienced, especially in the fifteenth century, when the effects of the plagues were felt throughout the continent.

The price decline of agicultural products was not matched by a decline in nonagricultural prices. Estimates from England of the fourteenth and fifteenth centuries suggest that prices of iron, horseshoes, lathes, tiles, hurdles, and cloth had in many cases doubled, while the price of corn remained relatively stable.[7] Estimates also show that in Krakow the price index of wheat declined from 100 in 1361–1400 to 84 in 1401–1450, and to 59 in 1451–1500. In contrast, industrial products rose from 100 to 180 in the second period, although they declined to 96 in the third. While there are only scattered data, there is little doubt that the terms of trade turned against the farmer for most of the period between 1350 and 1450.

On wages. The impact of war and population decline also resulted in a relative shortage of labor, which led to a general increase in the level of wages. In Krakow the wage index rose from 100 in 1361–1400 to 128 in 1401–1450, but returned to 100 in 1451–1500.[8] With the average wage in Navarre between 1421 and 1430 set at 100, the real wage seems to have risen from an index of 55.7 in 1351–1355 to a high of 116.9 in 1401–1405, after which it slowly declined to 93.8 in 1441–1445. On the estates of the bishop of Winchester, a rising trend seems evident. Setting the average for the period 1300–1319 = 100, wages in 1320–1329 averaged 124, 169 in 1360–1379, and 188 in 1380–1399, at which level it stayed until

[7] For more detail, see *Cambridge Economic History of Europe*, I, pp. 682–683 and 692.

[8] Compare these figures with the wheat price changes mentioned above.

1460–1479. During the same period the price of corn dropped from an index of 90 to 47.[9] It should be noted that the wage increase seems to have been common to various trades. Data from the Westminster estates show that the wages of carpenters rose from 4.53 pence per day to a high of 6.09 pence between 1330 and 1369; those of laborers and tilers almost doubled between 1300 and 1359; while thatchers' wages increased even more. In all cases, however, there was a small decline in the second half of the century.[10]

On agricultural incomes. These scattered estimates suggest a relative increase in the costs of production and a relative decline of revenue, assuming the production function to have remained constant. There is no evidence that it changed. Therefore, the farmer who traded in the market and who employed wage labor was at a disadvantage. The terms of trade and the relation between revenue and cost were both against him.

It is easy to conclude that the standard of living of the rural population was lowered as a result, but such a conclusion would be an oversimplification. The effects varied according to the status of the farmer, the size of his estate, and the measures he took in the face of the new difficulties. Let us begin with the wage workers and the cottars. These people had little agricultural product to sell. They sold their labor, a commodity which was relatively scarcer than before. Therefore, they were in a more favorable position than previously, in at least two ways. On one hand, they could earn a higher wage. On the other, they were in a position to acquire better land and on better terms. The same may be said of the small farmers, who could cultivate more land than they had had at their disposal before the decline and could enlarge their holdings on much more favorable terms. They also were in a position to

renegotiate their terms of tenancy. Therefore, at first glance we may conclude that these two groups improved their position and raised their standard of living. Before we accept this conclusion, however, we should examine the sociopolitical conditions to see whether they would have permitted realization of these potential benefits.

The middle-size farmers and peasants had enough land to live on and depended on the market to sell their products and procure what they did not produce themselves. These people suffered a loss of manpower and any attempt to replace the loss by wage labor would have entailed a rise in the average cost of production without a comparable rise in revenue. The available data suggest that such farmers had to settle for a lower net income. Furthermore, their real net income was lower still because of the unfavorable terms of trade at which they exchanged their products for nonagricultural items. They might have been able to increase their production by substituting good land for any marginal land they held, but given the inelasticity of demand for agricultural food products, the gain could not have been sufficient to offset these negative effects. Therefore, it seems likely that this group, which constituted a large segment of the rural population, was hurt badly in this period.

The lords were in an even worse position than the middle-size farmers for several reasons: They received fixed rents; they depended on wage labor; and they participated in the market in which the terms of trade were against them. But since the lords were more powerful economically, politically, and socially, they were more able to cope with the situation. In fact, some of them were able to maintain their position or even improve it.

The lords resorted to both positive and negative measures, depending on the locality, the obstacles, the period, and the political and social power they wielded. Some lords, particularly in England, in the lands east of the Elbe, and among the ecclesiastics, took direct charge of cultivation and often worked

[9] *Cambridge Economic History of Europe*, I, pp. 687–691.
[10] *Cambridge Economic History of Europe*, I, p. 689.

with their hands. Members of the various Church orders took to cultivation, thus avoiding the use of wage labor. Other lords managed to consolidate their holdings and increase the size of their estates, compensating for the low average net income by increasing the total product and hence the total income. Still others managed to keep their estates in cultivation by offering better terms of tenancy, including the security of long-term leases, thus accepting lower net returns as the price for continued income. Some even offered freedom where freedom had been slow to come in order to avoid having idle land. Others gave up farming, either leasing the land or selling it, and took up new occupations in trade and the urban economy.

Finally, some landlords created a shift in the production function by introducing crop rotation and by substituting more profitable industrial products for those they had traditionally produced. Industrial crops and legumes replaced grain. Idle or fallow land was thus reduced while fodder crops were used to increase stock raising. Crop rotation and substitution were evident in parts of England around the end of the fourteenth century. An improved field rotation system to increase pasture and encourage stock raising was evident in Flanders also in the fourteenth century. Enclosure for consolidation of the pastureland in response to the demand for wool was evident a little later, although on a very small scale.[11]

The lords' negative measures, however, were more conspicuous, if only because they drew equally negative reactions from the peasantry. These measures may be described as "second serfdom," at least figuratively. The lords were aided in applying these measures by the state and city governments. Some lords reactivated old manorial obligations which tied the peasant to the land. In many areas even wage workers were prohibited from leaving the land without the lord's permission and the cities cooperated by denying protection to the escapees. Fugitives were punished severely. Other lords, especially east of the Elbe, including many in Hungary, Poland, and Russia, converted money dues into labor services to guarantee the availability of labor. The lords east of the Elbe and in Spain seized sovereign rights and imposed their wishes on the towns, appropriating public *corvées* and making them private labor services to be applied to their own estates. The second serfdom became the rule rather than the exception east of the Elbe. Finally, the various states encouraged export and restricted import to aid the lords by sustaining higher prices, regardless of the impact on the general welfare of the consumers.

The success of these positive and negative measures is hard to estimate. On one hand, the conditions at the base of the difficulties were gradually subsiding. On the other, the peasants did not accept these measures passively. They reacted violently all over the continent. Their problems were compounded by heavy direct and indirect taxes levied to sustain the governments and to finance internal and external wars. Furthermore, debasement of the currency often depleted the value of any money incomes they might have been able to earn. The first peasant revolt took place in Flanders in the second half of the fourteenth century. The French peasants' revolt in 1358 has become famous as the *Jacquerie*. England experienced a serious uprising in 1381. In Spain a revolt took place around the end of the fourteenth century; one occurred in Bohemia around 1400; Italy experienced revolts in 1430 and again in 1460. The Kents revolted under Jack Cade in 1450, and the territories around the Alps revolted in the sixteenth century. In all cases, however, the governments managed to suppress these revolts.

The end of the medieval period was brighter than the middle. Population had begun to recover, and the national economies were beginning to regain their health. The manorial structure was intact and in various places it had even been strengthened.

---

[11] The enclosure movement will be discussed in detail later; in brief, it meant fencing in the land and consolidating the holdings.

BIBLIOGRAPHY

Bloch, M., *French Rural History*, Berkeley, University of California Press, 1966, chaps. 3–4.

Kosminsky, E. A., "Services and Money Rents in the Thirteenth Century," *Economic History Review*, 2nd series, V, 1935, p. 2. Reprinted in *Essays in Economic History*, II, E. M. Carus-Wilson (ed.), New York: St. Martin's Press, 1962, pp. 31–48. This source gives variations in rates of commutation.

Lucas, Henry S., "The Great European Famine of 1315, 1316, and 1317," *Speculum*, V (1930), reprinted in *Essays in Economic History*, II, E. M. Carus-Wilson (ed.), New York: St. Martin's Press, 1966, pp. 49–72.

Lyashchenko, Peter I., *History of the National Economy of Russia, to the 1917 Revolution*, L. M. Herman (tr.), New York: Macmillan, 1949, chaps. 6–7.

Malowist, M., "The Problem of Inequality of Economic Development in Europe in the Later Middle Ages," *Economic History Review*, 2nd series, XIX (April 1966), pp. 15–28.

Pach, Z. P., "The Development of Feudal Rent in Hungary in the 15th Century," *Economic History Review*, 2nd series, XIX (April 1966), pp. 1–14.

Pirenne, H., *Economic and Social History of Medieval Europe*, New York: Harcourt, Brace & World, 1937, chap. 3.

Postan, M., (ed.), *The Cambridge Economic History of Europe*, Second edition, I, New York: Cambridge University Press, 1966, chaps. 5–8.

Tuma, E. H., *Twenty-Six Centuries of Agrarian Reform*, Berkeley: University of California Press, 1965, pp. 37–43.

In dealing with the urban economy, we can no longer use the manor as our unit of study. Moreover, because of the interdependence between town and country, our unit is no longer a self-contained entity. The economy that was closed in the early period is no longer closed to the same extent. Therefore, before discussing the urban economy of the Middle Ages, we shall specify our unit of study and identify its features through a model of its institutional structure and behavioral superstructure.

THE MEANING AND
IMPLICATIONS OF URBANIZATION

Urbanization is a loose concept. In modern times it is often described in terms of the size of the population of the community. Thus, a city may be any concentration of people larger than a given number, say 100,-000. A population between 10,000 and 100,-000 may be classified as a town. Such a classification leaves too many unknowns, at least from an economic point of view. It may also be vague politically and socially, unless the institutions of the community are specified. The center of power may be outside the largest agglomeration of people, unless the community is based on democracy. For our purposes, an operational meaning of urbanism is more useful. An urban community is

primarily nonagricultural by occupation, and is administratively self-contained. Members of the community may still have direct contact with agriculture, but the majority derive their living from other occupations. Thus, urbanization is a matter of degree, and communities may be classified on a continuum from fully agricultural to fully nonagricultural. The administrative self-containment is more easily specified: Either the community has an administration of its own or it does not. This, obviously, does not preclude interdependence with other administrations such as the county or the state.

There has been a tendency to associate urbanization with industrial development, since urbanization grows as industrial activity grows. While this association may be valid, industrialization is not a necessary condition for urbanization. Urban centers have grown in many parts of the world with little or no industry. However, other nonagricultural occupations must be sufficient to sustain them. Conversely, industry may grow in an area without creating an urban community around it—without incorporation.

Urban centers were frequently associated with military and defense activities, as in the fortifications of the tenth and eleventh centuries, or with manorial and feudal administration. Indeed, many cities were reduced to residences of bishops, archbishops, princes, or manorial lords. Such towns, while they might be administrative units, hardly concerned themselves with any productive occupation. Such communities rarely grew in size until other requirements for growth were satisfied. Our concern is not with these, but with those communities which had economic significance, be they towns or villages.

The significance of urbanization. The economic significance of urbanization may be reflected in several ways:

1. Urbanization indicates that surplus food is being produced in sufficient quantities to sustain the nonproducers in society. In the absence of such surplus, food must be imported to feed the nonproducers. Therefore, we may positively associate urbanization with the accessibility of food surplus, and the growth of the community depends greatly on the accessibility of such a surplus.

2. Urbanization implies an exchange of one form or another. Unless the surplus is exacted as dues or extracted by looting and piracy, a payment of some sort must be rendered in return. The payment may be material or otherwise. For example, the tithe is delivered in return for religious gratification and payment of dues is exacted by the manor lord, at least nominally, in return for protection. Whatever the reasons, a payment must be rendered in money or kind. The exchange may be in barter form or in money. Barter, however, is possible only in small communities where the magnitude of exchange and the surplus are both relatively small, and where the items exchanged are so standard that their exchange value is easily recognized—e.g., a cow for so many bushels of wheat. As urbanization and the volume of exchange grow, barter becomes impractical. It becomes necessary to use a common medium of exchange, the best-known form of which is money of a specified range of denominations. This arrangement allows anonymous exchange. People with commodities do not need to know the person with whom they trade; nor do they need to wait for someone who happens to need their commodities and who has what they need. They can trade with anyone who has the money and who is willing to trade, either for his own use or for secondary exchange to earn a profit. Thus urbanization is associated with both monetary exchange and the rise of professional trading.

3. Urbanization also requires and provides a clearing-house in which various commodities are exchanged. It thereby stimulates the development of markets in which both agricultural and nonagricultural commodities are exchanged through a common medium. The development of a market expands the horizon of the rural community. It gives the producers as well as the products a new outlet, encouraging both product and factor mobility. This mobility is both geographical and occupational: The producer may move out of agriculture or from one urban occupation to another. However, mobility may be restricted by the tendency toward specialization. Since the larger market implies a larger total demand and a larger demand for specific commodities, it becomes economically rational to specialize. Division of labor is a necessary condition of market expansion and is closely interdependent with urbanization.

Another implication of the growth of markets which has many consequences is the fact that the market town functions as the connecting link between various agricultural districts and between these districts and the outside world. Such contact is important in terms of economic as well as social and political relations. Participation in the market stimulates the forces of supply and demand and has a demonstration effect on the levels of consumption and production, which includes the demonstration of new technologies and items of trade. Thus, the rise of towns as economic centers is closely related to an expansion of knowledge and techniques, both domestically and internationally. In modern society, this function of communicating knowledge has been partly responsible for the international exhibitions and fairs, as it was for the fairs of the Middle Ages.

Structural features of towns. Certain structural features characterize urban economic units. Anonymity and monetary exchange tend to undermine the traditional blood relations common in agrarian and manorial society. In place of cooperation and informal relations, urbanization encourages competition and formality. The economic agents participating in the urban market do not know each other and may never meet again once the transaction is over. Therefore, there is little check on their behavior outside the market itself. In the absence of perfect information and mobility, the market may be an inadequate check. Hence, urbanization creates the need for regulation of economic life, especially if humanism has not been completely superseded by economic rationality. Regulation becomes necessary also to protect those who are not familiar with the market mechanism or the ethos of the community.

Anonymity, formalism, and competition tend to isolate the individual who previously identified himself with a group and therefore to create a need for him to establish an identity based on common interest. Initially, this common bond is occupation, since political parties arise later in a town's development. The rise of urbanism is usually accompanied by an expansion in group organizations such as clubs, guilds, or church associations.

As centers of exchange and trading, towns must be accessible. Therefore, they are usually built in economically strategic areas. They may be on rivers and seacoasts where water transportation is available, or in locations to which roads can be built, or close to sources of raw material. However, a town's location must be strategic for its other purposes as well. A central location is ideal for administrative purposes. On the other hand, a town should be easy to defend militarily.

The problem becomes more complex when a town is expected to serve all three functions. In such cases there may be a division of labor between towns. The center of power and political administration may not be the economic center, in which case it remains relatively small. In contrast, the economic center tends to grow, especially if it is serving other functions.

The structural aspects described above should be considered relative to the conditions prevailing at the time. Although the functions may remain the same, the means by which they are fulfilled may vary. For example, a change in technology could easily change a town's defense requirements or render its means of transportation obsolete. It might also reduce the dependence on natural conditions. Under these circumstances, the growth of particular towns may be checked or advanced, depending on their new comparative advantage.

AN OVERVIEW OF URBANIZATION

If a general trend can be specified for the Middle Ages, it is this: Except for the Mediterranean areas where urban life was fairly sophisticated, the tenth and eleventh centuries witnessed mainly the creation of fortifications or *bourgs* and *faubourgs*. These new concentrations had a minor economic function, although they served as administrative and military centers. Accordingly, they were located close to the manorial estates which supported them, regardless of trade and transportation considerations. They had little need to maintain contact with the outside world; in fact restricted contact might have been considered safer from a military standpoint. The next two centuries witnessed a strengthening of feudalism, a decline of central power, an expansion of colonization and settlement, and some growth in towns and urbanization. During this period economic considerations were important and towns grew up where strategic considerations could be satisfied. These towns grew in size and economic importance and outlived most of the bourgs. Some of these towns reached their peak in the fourteenth and fifteenth centuries and extended their power to the political and military spheres. This was the case with the city-states of Italy and the Mediterranean area. In fact, the thirteenth and fourteenth centuries may be regarded as the era of city-states, even though nominally central power might be represented by a king. During the fifteenth century the power of the city-states began to decline, just as the manorial and feudal lords had been overshadowed. Power was shifting into the hands of centralized authorities, and nation-states were in the offing.

CULTURE AND TECHNOLOGY

At least in one sense the fourteenth and fifteenth centuries were definitely a period of expansion and development. The Renaissance is known for its artistic, literary, and philosophical achievements. It was rich in painting, sculpture, and architecture, as well as in philosophical discourse. And it saw technological and exploratory achievements which laid the foundation for the commercial revolution that was to come. All these innovations occurred in what has been called a period of decline. Looking at it from this point of view, one wonders whether the description is accurate.

Among the most important innovations of the Renaissance was the wider use of the water mill which was first used in the eleventh century as a source of power. It was put to use in grinding grain, in sawing lumber, and in weaving and dyeing. The water mill has in fact been credited with creating an industrial revolution in the thirteenth century. However, it was of limited utility because it depended on the availability of water. In the twelfth century, the windmill came into widespread use.

Another important innovation was double-entry bookkeeping, which was invented in Italy when the Italian cities were still flourishing business and trade centers. This development has been regarded as so essential to rationalizing economic and business relations that it contributed to the rise of capitalism. Probably more important was the invention of the printing press, which revolutionized book publishing, spread literacy, and facilitated communication. Paper-making was known to the Arabs in the twelfth century; France and Italy acquired the skill in the thirteenth century and Germany in the fourteenth. The combined impact of paper-making and printing can hardly be exaggerated, but its immediate result was to increase the supply of books available at a much reduced cost and relatively free of errors, compared to the tedious and imperfect system of copying by the scribes. Also in the thirteenth century the art (or science) of cartography advanced greatly. Probably equally important was the invention of gunpowder. Not only did it revolutionize military activities, but it was put to use in quarries, in opening tunnels, and in defenses.

Advances in the art of navigation are best reflected by the expansion of international trade and of fishing on the high seas, and by the long voyages which led to the discovery of the Cape of Good Hope on one side and America on the other. That both discoveries came within such a short period is not accidental. It reflects the spirit of the period, the readiness of Europe to expand, and the advance of shipping and technology. It also reflects the developments in business and economic organization which made the funding of such long voyages possible.

The pattern of change in this period and the growth of urbanization and economic activity may be seen from the distribution of these technological innovations among

Table 6.1   Technical innovations in Europe, twelfth–fifteenth centuries

PERIOD	ITALY, SPAIN, AND PORTUGAL	CENTRAL AND NORTHERN EUROPE	FRANCE AND LOW COUNTRIES	ENGLAND
A.D. 1100	Magnetic compass in use in 1100 Paper-making by Moors	Mold-board added to plow		
1150	Stamp-mill used in paper-making		University of Paris founded	Old London Bridge built
1200	Venetian glass-making Italian silk-throwing mills	Cogs[a] built for northern trade Rise of Hanse towns and League	Fulling mills in wide use	
1250	Gold florin coined Naviglio Grande (Grand Canal of Lombardy) Plate armor made in Milan		Great age of stained glass	
1300	Spectacle-making in Venice Catalan atlas Majolica ware	Use of open sea route around Skaw Salt-glazing of pottery	Flax-breaker Forge	
1350	Italian Renaissance begins	First summit-level Canal (Germany) Cast-iron canon (Germany) Cast-iron Stuckofen furnace Osmund furnace	Wind-driven scoop wheel Modern lock (Damme) Dutch drift nets	
1400	Portuguese voyages organized by Prince Henry the Navigator		Hollow-post mill (Holland)	King's College built (beginning of Cambridge University)
1450	Patents introduced at Venice Double-entry book-keeping (Italy, 1494)	Gutenberg's printing press (Mainz) Blast-furnace introduced Intensive silver mining Instrument-making at Nuremberg	Laying dry of drowned lands	

[a] *A broad-beamed boat for fishing and transport.*
SOURCES: *T. K. Derry and T. I. Williams,* A Short History of Technology, *pp. 726–730;* Cambridge Economic History of Europe, *II, pp. 459–469.*

the nations of Europe over the period as a whole. (See Table 6.1.) In general, they were concentrated in Italy, Spain, and Portugal, although a shift towards Germany and central Europe began in this period. England had little to show in terms of innovation or invention.

Finally, we should note the fact that in this period the Roman Empire in the East came to an end. Constantinople was overrun

Table 6.2. City walls extended, tenth–fourteenth centuries

	TENTH	ELEVENTH	TWELFTH	THIRTEENTH	FOURTEENTH
France		Geneva	Angoulême	Bordeaux (2)	Agen
		Rouen	Bourges	Cahors	Avignon
			Grenoble	Clermont	Cavaillon
			Marseilles	Limoges	Geneva
			Poitiers	Cahors (2)	Grenoble
				Geneva (2)	Limoges
				Marseilles (2)	Rodez
Germany and Low Countries	Cologne	Bruges	Utrecht, 1122	Bonn, 1243	
	Verdun	Antwerp	Metz, 1150	Middleburg, 1250	
	Liège	Tournai	Strasbourg	Nimegue, c. 1230	
		Ghent	Aachen	Maastricht, c. 1230	
		Douai	Brussels, 1122		
		Ypres	Louvain, 1149		
			Antwerp, 1183–1201		
			Malines, 1183–1201		
			Dijon, 1130		

SOURCE: *J. C. Russell, Late Ancient and Medieval Population, pp. 106–111.*

by the Ottoman Turks in 1453. Thus ended the last fortress of western civilization and the traditions of the Roman Empire outside Europe.

URBAN EXPANSION

The population increase in the three centuries preceding the plagues has been accepted as a fact. However, how much urban expansion occurred is less clear. Available data are neither adequate nor comprehensive enough to give a full comparative picture. Nevertheless, tentative estimates of the degree and distribution of the change may be attempted. The southern urban centers were fully established during the twelfth and thirteenth centuries. Their populations increased but not many new centers were established. In contrast, new towns were growing in the northern and eastern regions of Europe. The first developed in Flanders in the eleventh century, among which were St. Omer, Ghent, Douai, Bruges, and Arras. Ypres followed at the beginning of the twelfth century. Next came the towns of Brabant. New towns such as Laon, Soissons, Rheims, Senlis, and Noyon were built in France. Bayonne on the Atlantic became strong enough to com-

mand the traffic with Spain, while Bordeaux commanded that with England. La Rochelle advanced to the forefront in the thirteenth century. However, the most impressive expansion was made in Germany during the twelfth and thirteenth centuries. Some towns were built on the sites of old castles, such as Frieburg-im-Breisgau (1120); the "old town" of Brunswick (1100–1120); and Lübeck (1158). The Dutch towns developed a little later; Amsterdam was first mentioned in 1275 and had town status by 1306.[1] In today's Switzerland, we find 19 towns which were built in Roman times, only 8 of which were towns in the Middle Ages. These were the sites of bishoprics. However, 9 were built in the tenth and eleventh centuries; 16 were added in the twelfth century; 97 in the thirteenth; and 12 in the fourteenth. About 23 of these remained small villages. Town expansion was similar in England, where the king did not depend on natural development but took steps to "plant" towns in various districts of England and Wales. It is estimated that by the end of the Middle Ages there were 531 towns in England. Of these, 172 were planted, while 359 were "organic," growing in a natural evolution of the popu-

[1] *Cambridge Economic History of Europe*, III, p. 13–14.

Table 6.3.   Comparative estimates of town population in Germany

WESTERN CITIES	CENTRAL CITIES	EASTERN CITIES	NORTHERN CITIES
ELEVENTH CENTURY			
Cologne 20,000	Regensburg 25,000		
Strasbourg 15,000			
THIRTEENTH CENTURY			
Cologne 45,000	Nuremberg 15,000	Magdeburg 16,000	
Strasbourg 30,000			
PRE-PLAGUE			
Cologne 50,000	Nuremberg 25,000	Vienna 25,000	Hamburg 30,000
Strasbourg 30,000			
LATE MIDDLE AGES			
Cologne 30,000	Nuremberg 23,000	Prague 30,000	Hamburg 22,000
Strasbourg 20,000	Augsburg 18,000	Vienna 25,000	Lübeck 18,000
Frankfurt 10,000	Zürich 11,000	Breslau 14,000	Bremen 18,000
Trèves 9,000	Regensburg 10,000	Frankfurt-am-Oder 10,000	Brunswick 18,000
Wismar 7,000	Basel 10,000	Stettin 9,000	Magdeburg 12,000
Mühlhausen 7,000	Ulm 9,000	Brno 8,000	Rostock 8,000
Mainz 6,000	Salzburg 7,000	Görlitz 8,000	Osnabrück 5,000

SOURCE: *Russell*, Late Ancient and Medieval Population, *pp. 111–125.*

lation and the economy. The planting of towns was concentrated in the twelfth and thirteenth centuries, when 67 and 65 were established, respectively. Wales had 84 planted out of a total of 87 towns. Of these, 20 were planted in the twelfth and 46 in the thirteenth centuries.

The expansion of urban population centers may be noted in part by the extension of city walls. Although the degree of expansion remains uncertain, its tendency is shown in Table 6.2. As the distribution shows, the expansion in France occurred mostly in the thirteenth and fourteenth centuries, with several cities extending their walled area more than once. Germany and the Low Countries show more activity in the twelfth and thirteenth centuries.

The magnitude of expansion may also be seen from the rough estimates of city population at various times shown in Table 6.3. These figures show that only two cities had populations around 20,000 in the eleventh century. Before the plagues, the number had more than doubled and the largest city in each district of Germany had reached 25,000 or more. Cologne had reached about 50,000 people. The number of cities with several thousand people and with a town status had increased greatly by the late Middle Ages, although the size of the individual city populations might have declined due to the plagues and not been restored.

We may compare these figures with estimates for older cities. Paris, for example, is thought to have contained about 25,000 people in the twelfth century, 60,000 at the end of the thirteenth, and 80–90,000 in mid-fourteenth century. Rome had about 35,000 at the end of the twelfth century. Milan is estimated to have had 52–54,000 people between the twelfth and fourteenth centuries; however, its population in 1540 is estimated at 68,500 people. Bologna had 70–80,000 in 1250 and Venice was even larger. These scattered figures suggest a time lag between the development of the South and the North. They also show increasing urbanization both absolutely and relatively.

ECONOMIC BASES OF MEDIEVAL TOWNS

These urban centers had to be accessible and to have a comparative advantage in one or more products. A look at Figure 6.1 shows the first consideration to be of vital importance. The need for accessibility had to be satisfied by natural means until the advent of more modern means of transportation, such as the railway and air transport. Most of the new towns were therefore built near the seacoast or on or close to navigable rivers. This was true of the French, Dutch, German, English, and Scandinavian towns, as well as those of Italy and Spain. Bayonne, Bordeaux, Bruges, Ghent, Mainz, Lübeck, Hamburg, Danzig, Riga, Prague, and Krakow were all either on the seacoast or on major navigable waterways.

Comparative advantage is more difficult to establish and analyze in the absence of detailed monographs concerning individual town economies. Observers usually note a city's more distinctive features, and describe its domestic economy. Certain functions are common to all urban population centers and may be taken for granted. But none of these is sufficient to stimulate the growth of the city as an economic center unless other resources are available. The city of Paris is said to have had 282 trades listed at the end of the thirteenth century, but most of them

produced only for domestic consumption. The fame of Paris was rather as a center of government and learning.

A city grows economically when it controls a resource or produces commodities more efficiently than the surrounding areas. For example, it may control the grain produced in a district and act as the gateway for its disposal. Or it may have a certain specialization whose products may be used as payments for what the city needs and imports. Therefore, international or inter-economy trade is our best clue to the comparative advantage each city enjoys. Its exports would show what the city or the district it controls specializes in, and its imports would show what it lacks. A summary of the areas of specialization and the directions of trade may be seen in Figure 6.1. These will be discussed further below.

TRADE AND DEVELOPMENT

In the period under discussion trade gradually grew from local to intercity to international, depending on the prevailing obstacles and facilities. Economic historians have usually treated trade in northern Europe separately from that in the South, allowing for some trade between the two. However, there is little to be gained by this separation, especially since the distinction tended to disappear as shipping and communication improved. It is true that most of the trade was intraregional, but this was a natural result of the difficulty of transportation. Trade outside a region tended to be limited to essential nonperishable foodstuffs or to luxuries.

The southern towns were in contact with the Orient and acted as middlemen between that area and the rest of Europe. They imported spices from India; rice, oranges, apricots, figs, raisins, medicaments, dyestuffs, and alum from Africa, Persia, and Syria; damask from Damascus; muslin from Mosul; and gauzes from Gaza. In return

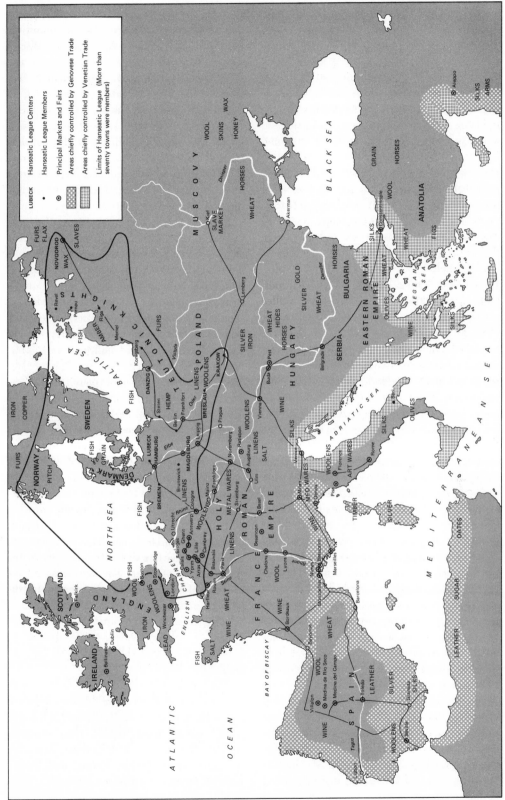

Figure 6.1　Industry and commerce in the middle ages.

they shipped European timber, arms, and sometimes slaves. The southern towns also expanded the manufacturing of textiles such as silk and flax mixed with cotton, which they exported largely to the North. Florence specialized in woolens. However, the woolen industry flourished also in the central and northern areas. The Flemish towns of Ghent, Ypres, and Bruges gradually became major exporters of woolens. Spain and England provided raw wool, which was an important item of trade; eventually England started to manufacture its own wool and export it. The Italians adopted the silk industry from the Arabs and soon it became a specialty of Lucca, Naples, Florence, Genoa, and Venice. In addition, Venice became the most important glass-making city, importing skilled artisans from Constantinople. Florence became famous for its swords. English towns produced canon and exported lead, tin, and copper; these three items were also exported by Bohemia and Poland. Liège produced a variety of armor and war material for export. The wine industry was probably one of the most important items of trade from Bordeaux to England, and from the Rhine country.

In time a certain degree of specialization evolved and certain trade items became staples. For example, the staples of the English trade were wool, hide, and cloth as exports; fine cloth, wax, wine, linen, and groceries as imports. However, other items were mentioned at various times, such as pearls, masts, coal, and steel. The Germans exported metal, wax, and feathers, in addition to the grains that came from east of the Elbe. The northern and north-eastern regions specialized in furs from the Baltic and from Russia. The Baltic and the Scandinavian countries exported fish, which was in high demand as a source of protein and as a meat substitute during Lent. Fish traveled as far as Spain, and northern fishermen are said to have reached Newfoundland. The fishing industry created a high demand for lumber for shipyards and for salt as a preservative.

Salt as a necessity, was also an important item of trade from the Bay of Biscay. Sweden exported copper and iron, which was usually of a relatively good quality. The Baltic trade is represented in Table 6.4. In addition to wool and wine, Spain exported sugar, iron, oil, rice, leatherwork, textiles, hardware, fruits, and onions. It also supplied a good breed of horses. Coral came from North Africa, while gold, fish, fur, and grain from the Black Sea region traveled throughout Europe.

Service itself is an important item of trade. Bordeaux, for example, was mainly a shipping center. Genoa and Venice were major carriers of trade and the most important links between the Orient and Europe. Bruges became the major trading center in central and northern Europe in the thirteenth century. Often the carrying industry was the basis of economic and political wars. Most of the trade was carried by foreigners, especially Hanseatic German merchants. However, the towns produced merchants who acted as middlemen, deriving profits and returns on their services. Towns that did not have the resources for trade often depended for growth on the services they could provide, as we shall see when we discuss the medieval fairs.

The volume of trade and the total product of the city economies are hard to estimate because of the lack of data, although examples can be found to give an idea of the change. For instance, the expansion of the Flemish cloth industry is illustrated by the fact that

the number of lead seals which Ypres had attached to the cloths manufactured by its weavers as checking marks rose from 10,500 in 1306 to 92,500 in 1313. . . . The number of pieces of Flemish cloth which in 1368 found the way from Hamburg via Oldeslae ran to at least 23,000. . . .[2]

[2] Fritz Rörig, *The Medieval Town*, p. 76.

Table 6.4.   Baltic trade

IMPORTS				EXPORTS			
Woolen cloths, linen, yarn, works in metal, needles, salt, Rhine wines, beer passing to the West				Wax, tallow, hides, corn, leather			
NORWAY		SWEDEN		DENMARK		BERGEN	
EXPORTS	IMPORTS	EXPORTS	IMPORTS	EXPORTS	IMPORTS	EXPORTS	IMPORTS
Timber	Corn	Pitch	Corn	Herring	Linen	Butter	Flax
Resin	Wine	Ashes	Meal	Salt fish	Wax	Salmon	Cloth
Pitch	Metal-work	Iron	Wine	Horses	Honey	Dried cod	Ale
Furs	Beer	Hemp	Linen	Cattle	Beer	Fish oil	Corn
Fish	Salt	Copper	Cloth	Corn	Wine	Fine furs	Malt
Blubber	Spices	Timber	Metal-work		Cloth	Timber	Biscuit
	Fruits	Salt fish					Flour
		Meat					Wine
							Spirits
							Copper
							Silver

SOURCE: *J. W. Thompson,* Economic and Social History of Europe in the Later Middle Ages, *1300–1530, p. 167.*

Trade through Bruges was an even more impressive indicator. It is estimated that in 1350 "no less than forty Spanish ships arrived . . . in early summer," with fruits, silk, and iron to be distributed to various places. Other indicators are the number of fairs held every year and the expanding distribution of their locations. Finally, the total involvement in trade of the Hanseatic towns, which at their peak numbered about 77, indicates the growth of trade, as will be seen later.

Probably the least development of the urban economy occurred in Russia and the eastern territories. It has been suggested that when trade in the West had reached a high level in the thirteenth century, the East was just beginning to trade. Even after it began to catch up in the fourteenth and fifteenth centuries and when the West was going through a crisis, the East remained about two centuries behind. Development was advanced in the Baltic region and in the southern region around the Czech and Carpathian Mountains. Prague had reached a population of over 30,000 in the fourteenth century. However, the central region—central Poland, Lithuania, and most of Russia—did not

catch up until the fifteenth century. The East was more agricultural than the West, less urban, and little involved in international trade. It was also experiencng a revision in its institutional foundations that precluded urbanization; namely, the revival of serfdom. Unlike the West, the East depended on agricultural and mineral resources and the services of foreign traders. Grain and silver were the most important items of trade, although gold, lead, iron, and copper were exported. The ships built in Russia were mostly for river transportation; they were uncovered and had weak masts. Moreover, while the Russians concluded reciprocal trade treaties with other countries, there is little evidence that they implemented them before the sixteenth century.

Nevertheless, even in this agrarian environment, urbanization and trade were able to develop. Towns were often built by the estate or feudal lord and carried his name. Moscow developed from the feudal *votchina* of a prince; Novosil was originally the *votchina* of the former Prince Novosilsky; Odoyev belonged to the Prince Odoyevsky; Skopin to the Romanov family. Towns, however, remained small and urban occupations were limited to the exchange and manufacture of essentials, except for the luxuries exported to the West. Unlike the other towns, Novgorod, which was the center for foreigners, was quite advanced in trade and urban economic activities. In the thirteenth and fourteenth centuries the merchants in Novgorod had already formed an association which monopolized trade and shared in public office. In general, however, the impact of the urban economy was quite limited until the sixteenth and seventeenth centuries, long after the western urban economy had reached a high level of sophistication.

BIBLIOGRAPHY

Beresford, Maurice, *New Towns of the Middle Ages*, New York: Frederick A. Praeger, 1967.

Derry, T. K., and T. I. Williams, *A Short History of Technology*, New York: Oxford University Press, 1960.

Dickenson, R. E., *The West European City*, London: Routledge and Kegan Paul, 1962.

Kirchner, W., *Commercial Relations Between Russia and Europe, 1400–1800*, Bloomington: Indiana University Press, 1966, introduction and chap. 1.

Lopez, R. S., and H. A. Miskimin, "The Economic Depression of the Renaissance," *Economic History Review*, 2nd series, XIV (April 1962), pp. 408–426.

Lyashchenko, Peter I., *History of the National Economy of Russia, to the Revolution*, L. M. Herman (tr.), New York: Macmillan, 1949, chap. 8.

Malowist, M., "The Problem of Inequality of Economic Development in Europe in the Later Middle Ages," *Economic History Review*, 2nd series, XIX (April 1966), pp. 15–28.

Pirenne, H., *Economic and Social History of Medieval Europe*, New York: Harcourt, Brace & World, 1937, chap. 6.

Pirenne, H., *Medieval Cities*, Garden City: Doubleday & Co., 1956.

Postan, M. M., and E. E. Rich (eds.), *The Cambridge Economic History of Europe*, II, New York: Cambridge University Press, 1952, chaps. 5–7.

Postan, M. M., E. E. Rich, and Edward Miller (eds.), *Cambridge Economic History of Europe*, III, New York: Cambridge University Press, 1963, chap. 1.

Rörig, Fritz, *The Medieval Town*, Berkeley: University of California Press, 1967.

Russell, J. C., *Late Ancient and Medieval Population*, Philadelphia: The American Philosophical Society, 1958.

Thompson, J. W., *Economic and Social History of Europe in the Later Middle Ages 1300–1530*, New York: Frederick Ungar Publishing Co., 1960.

Van Houtte, J. A., "The Rise and Decline of the Market of Bruges," *Economic History Review*, 2nd series, XIX (April 1966), pp. 29–47.

7

OBSTACLES
AND
FACILITIES
IN THE
MEDIEVAL
URBAN
ECONOMY

The modern economist is accustomed to dealing with an economy in which the "invisible hand" of the market rules supreme. Buyers and sellers meet in the marketplace and after an interlude of bargaining they conclude a transaction, with each party satisfied that he has obtained the best possible terms. In such a situation, the welfare of society is thought to be well served. Competition, perfect information, and the rational behavior of the economic agents provide the only necessary regulation. As long as effective demand prevails, supply responds, the relative price acting as the control signal.

This idealistic picture is unrealistic for an age in which the obstacles were too many and the facilities too few for this happy ending to be realized.

The Middle Ages were a period in which economic life was frequently subjected to noneconomic influences which rendered its smooth functioning impossible. Our discussion of the facilities for economic activity and the obstacles to it can be divided into two areas: the physical and structural framework, and the internal policies and organization.

THE PHYSICAL AND STRUCTURAL FRAMEWORK

Natural obstacles

The first problem that faced the medieval economy was that of transportation. In an age when energy was confined to manual and animal sources, and the limited use of water and wind, man depended heavily on nature. The climate and the terrain were important determinants of the ease or difficulty of transporting trade items from one place to another. Pack animals could travel only when the climate was moderate, where roads existed, and when the load was bearable. The Romans had left a system of roads in various parts of Europe, but in many cases these were either partially or totally destroyed. Transportation in such places was limited to the immediate district which tied the countryside to its urban center. Roads between cities often did not exist, to prevent access as a measure of security. Even when roads did exist, the load a pack animal would carry was far too small to permit extensive trade and commerce. However, more efficient transport was provided by animal-drawn carts. The *bronnette*, a two-wheeled cart, was more common, but the *car* or *carrette*, a four-wheeled cart, was capable of carrying twice or three times the load. Long-distance road transport also depended on *colliers* or professional carriers. Artificial road-leveling and drainage were common, especially near the entrance to cities; in some cases these entrances were even paved. England, France, and Italy had laws regarding the maintenance of roads and thoroughfares, but these laws were not always enforced, except in big towns where commerce was important. In some cases the roads were maintained under pressure and with the cooperation of the territorial princes and the religious orders who made contributions toward their maintenance.

Waterways were more important than roads, especially for long distances and big shipments. However, we should distinguish between river and ocean shipping. In the absence of steam, water navigation depended on natural elements. Rivers might not be navigable in the icy season, and traveling upstream might be hazardous or even impossible if heavy loads were to be carried. Therefore, river transportation was useful mostly for downstream shipments of large cargoes such as timber, which could be floated to their destination with little difficulty from northern Europe. Sea shipping was more advanced, and some improvements took place during this period which added to its speed and carrying capacity. In the eleventh century, the Italians adopted from the Orient two useful kinds of ships: the *lateen*, with triangular sails fore and aft, and the stern-port rudder ship. In the thirteenth century the *cog*, a broadbeamed sailing ship, with a carrying capacity of 100–500 tons, was built in northern Europe. In Eastern Europe the Slavonic *dubassy*, a kind of raft, was in wide use for transporting timber and other bulky cargoes.

By 1300 shipping between southern and northern Europe was under way, but carrying capacity was still limited. It would be misleading to suggest that this handicap was the limiting factor on trade, but when it was combined with other difficulties, it began to count. Unfortunately, there is little cost information available for this period. Estimates of transportation costs in the mid-fourteenth century indicate the cost of wool transport by road to be less than 1.5 percent of the value, while that of grain was about 15 percent. The cost of sea transport in the thirteenth century is estimated to be about 10 percent of f.o.b. value.[1] The distribution

[1] *Cambridge Economic History of Europe*, II, pp. 143–155.

of trade routes on land may be seen in Figure 6.1 (p. 79).

Another problem facing trade was the insecurity of travel on land and sea. Robbers and pirates were quite common in the sparsely populated or poorly guarded areas. Often piracy was a national service performed in the economic interest of warring cities or nations. There is much evidence that the Italian cities in the South and the Hanseatic towns in the North sanctioned actions against competitors on the high sea until their nationals were granted the trading privileges they desired. Consequently, it was customary to form convoys under armed escort. This practice added to the cost of transportation and the price of the product, and limited trade to those items which would give high profits.

Given the slow means of transportation and the difficulty of preserving commodities, long-distance trade was limited to nonperishable goods. However, since the greater part of production was agricultural, nonperishable items were relatively limited in number. Furthermore, since the volume of trade depended on the amount of surplus product, trade was also limited by the low level of technology and the relatively low productivity.

Political and social environment

The most significant obstacles to the development of economic activity in this period emanated from the political and social structure and from the dominant attitudes toward life, occupation, and money-making. These obstacles resulted in segmented and imperfect markets, restricted mobility of the factors of production, and a dampening of the profit incentive usually associated with economic development and commercial expansion. They have often been blamed for the slow development toward the industrial revolution.

Political structure. The political structure, which determined the extent of the market, was complicated by the feudal organization on one hand and the rise of city-states on the other. National boundaries were virtually meaningless in Italy, Germany, Scandinavia, and east of the Elbe, and only a little less so in France and England. The contest between the cities and the feudal lords was often decided by where the king or emperor stood. In Germany, after bitter struggles, the individual cities achieved the autonomy they wanted. They became allies rather than subjects of the king, required only to pay certain taxes and accept his authority only nominally. In countries where the princes and feudal lords became strong at the expense of the king, the relationship of the towns with these princes was also one of alliance. In fact, the cities had the right to form alliances among themselves, weakening the central authority still further. Where such alliances prevailed, the cities controlled their own economic affairs, but they were also segmented into separate markets.

The exception to this diffuse structure prevailed where the central power was stronger, as in Austria, where consolidation took place fairly early. Many towns lost power over their destiny. Vienna, for example, was subject to seigneurial rule and no alliance among Austrian towns was allowed. Even municipal matters gradually fell under the rule of the feudal lord, although the towns continued to seek autonomy.

In Italy, which was nominally a part of the Empire, the results were more clearly in favor of the towns. As early as the twelfth century, Italian cities were fighting for imperial recognition of their autonomy, at the expense of the feudal lords. Their success was economically more meaningful than that of the German cities. They became large units, both territorially and demographically, in contrast to the relatively smaller German "states," which had "the stamp of territorial feudalism," both the tendency toward decentralization into city-states was evident. The Italian cities grew from within, independently of the countryside, and therefore the rural nobility had to assimilate itself within the new urban structure. This often led to internal conflicts between the old and the new classes. But, it also made room for the emerging merchant and bourgeois classes.

In both France and England the central power maintained a certain degree of influence. The king of France often supported the cities against the feudal lords, sometimes even meddling directly in city affairs. For example, he appointed the mayor of Paris and turned the city corporation into a public authority to be used against the merchant guilds, which were striving for autonomy. It is true that sometimes the feudal lords had great influence in the court, which they used against the towns. The towns in France never achieved the autonomy which the German and Italian cities enjoyed, but not because France was united. The French cities generally handled their internal affairs, including the law courts, the police, and the markets.

England was probably the most unified country in this period. The cities had their own policies, but in many cases approval of them by the king was necessary. Early in this period, the cities won representation in Parliament and the king often found it expedient to support them in order to retain them as allies against the House of Lords. Even the peers found it to their advantage to remain friends with the mercantilist groups, primarily for economic reasons. Such alliances gradually shifted control of the economic interests of the towns from foreign to local hands. The shift began about 1350 but was not completed until the end of the sixteenth century.

In the Low Countries there were three principalities—Flanders, Brabant, and Holland—with no unified policy among them. Flanders had an active unifying policy up to the thirteenth century, after which the policy became a passive one and the cities were given more autonomy than before. The cities of the other principalities developed a little later. In the new towns autonomy was easier to come by. The same was true of the Scandinavian kingdoms, in which urban life was a late development. Although these kingdoms were united, the feudal structure still dominated throughout the thirteenth and fourteenth centuries. Poland reverted from a unified kingdom to tribal feudalism in the twelfth century. It recovered in the thirteenth and fourteenth centuries, at the expense of a weakened Teutonic order. Nevertheless, decentralization remained characteristic of eastern Europe.

An important qualification of the above outline may be noted. A city's autonomy seemed to depend in part on whether the princely or feudal authority was lay or ecclesiastic. This was true in the South as well as in central Europe. Lay lords were more flexible in forming alliances with their cities and in accepting the autonomy they had achieved. The ecclesiastics, in contrast, often insisted on swearing in the commune or city council to maintain loyalty. They were less willing to let go until they were forced to do so.

Effects of the structure. The impact of these political divisions on the economic and commercial life of Europe was mixed. On one hand, it permitted the evolution of new economic groups which often became powerful enough to gear town policies toward economic expansion and trade. On the other, it left room for conflicting interest groups whose policies were not easily reconcilable. Frequently the city had to cope simultaneously with its own ruling groups, with the wishes of the central power, with those of the prince or feudal lord, with the Church, and with its competitors in other cities and territories. Taxes and dues could be levied by more than one authority. Tools could be set up at too many points on the road which a merchant traveled. Security on the road was difficult to guarantee in the absence of unity and cooperation. Even the otherwise healthy competition between cities could lead to warfare and the closing down of markets. In fact, as a result of this decentralization, the trader found himself a stranger in every other city, losing his privileges and subjected to dues and obligations that hindered his activities.

However, these forces also enhanced economic and trade relations. The state and the Church were quite helpful in expanding trade and ensuring security.

The king of England, and to an extent the king of France, interfered whenever there was corruption in the city. In times of famine they applied measures to guarantee the availability of food. They tried to maintain law and order and offered protection and sometimes privileges to foreigners in order to expand trade and improve the prospects for their nationals in other countries. However, they also interfered by controlling wages and prices, especially in time of war. They tried to protect the quality of the nation's products by establishing the machinery for supervision and laws to guarantee observance. In 1275 the English king levied an export duty on wool to protect the textile industry, and early in the fourteenth century he introduced a customs system. He also controlled the imposition of tolls. The king of France was less successful in implementing national measures. However, he did make arrangements with individual towns regarding taxes, the quality of products, and maintenance of law and order. The town interests were given a high priority in the policies of the state. In the fifteenth century, the king pursued an active policy of encouraging manufacturing. For example, he tried to substitute local for Venetian silk, encouraging the city of Lyons to establish silk manufacturing. When Lyons resisted, Tours was chosen. In 1480 the silkworkers' guild in Tours included 22 Italians, 1 Greek, 2 Burgundians, and 17 Frenchmen trained for the purpose. The king's efforts were so successful that half a century later the industry had 800 masters and 3–4,000 apprentices. The king also concluded trade agreements with Holland and Flanders and ended the trade war with England.

Attempts to guarantee the safety of foreigners as well as nationals were made by the princes of the low countries. Reciprocal trade treaties were exchanged in the twelfth and thirteenth centuries, and when necessary the princes protected their towns against foreigners. They tried to create links among their territories to expand the market. They even tried, though not too successfully, to unify the currency within their territories. Though the Scandinavian countries developed a little later than the rest of Europe, their policies were initially more permanent in character. For example, regular taxation was introduced in the thirteenth century to commute the *ledung* or fleet service into regular money payments. Assessment of land was also introduced as a tax base, thus bringing land into the market. A unique feature of the Scandinavian policy was the concern for the welfare of the people which was evident from the start and resulted in the protective policies of the fifteenth century.

The role of the state in Italy and Spain, hard to define because of the many authorities, was similarly positive in many cases. The central authorities tried to guard against famine, encouraged production, and often supplemented the market in guiding economic behavior. One common approach was to control exports, stockpile goods, and encourage imports to maintain reserves. Cities were obligated to take care of thoroughfares, while food and trade were usually redirected towards metropolitan areas. The leaders tried also to protect living standards by maintaining a balance between prices and wages and by restraining the forming of monopolies and workers' associations. They also tried to regulate trade in precious metal in an attempt to conserve as much of the area's "wealth" as possible. To encourage production, cultivation of the soil was made obligatory, with loss of land being the punishment for failure to cultivate it. Tariffs on imports were avoided in order to let the market determine the movement of international trade. There is evidence of conservation policies to protect forest land and to maintain a reasonable ratio between pasture and arable; however, they did not apply in Spain where the Mesta was anything but conservationist.

The policies toward trade and manufacture in Italy and Spain varied. Some observers describe the twelfth and thirteenth centuries as a period of mercantile favoritism, with a shift in favor of manufacturing taking place in the fourteenth and fifteenth centuries. Attempts to encourage industrialization through the protection of textiles were common. In general the Spanish monarchy and the territorial princes in Italy encouraged economic activity, apparently convinced that such development would advance their own power. Their policies included fostering the immigration of skilled people. Nevertheless, it is safe to conclude that up to the fifteenth century economic policies were mainly in the hands of the cities rather than in territorial princes or kings.

The state was also influential on the economy in two other ways: by creating demand and by encouraging credit. The courts' demand for luxury goods was an important factor in trade, although it is difficult to estimate the degree to which trade depended on it. A royal wedding was a great opportunity for certain merchants; an act of war benefited others. Supply followed demand, and resulted in a certain degree of market lubrication and expansion.

In part such demand depended on the immediate availability of credit. Whether for consumption, for public services such as upkeep of the government, or for war, the king or prince needed money. Revenues from traditional sources were no longer adequate in this period. Taxes and dues were imposed but always met opposition. Therefore, the rulers resorted to borrowing. Sometimes forced loans were contracted, but more frequently the lenders were quite willing to cooperate, either in anticipation of return or to obtain concessions and privileges. This was especially true of those merchants who had widespread interests to protect.

Borrowing by rulers seems to have become common around the middle of the thirteenth century, at a time when economic and trade expansion was rapid. However, the extent of borrowing varied. In England, France, and the low countries the rulers used credit regularly. They borrowed on the security of future revenues and often assigned specific revenues to specific loans. They also gave tax-farming concessions to their lenders, who thus could gain a profit in addition to their interest. They even pledged personal possessions and valuables, including their crowns, as security.

The German emperors and princes were more in need of credit than the English and French, since their traditional sources of revenue were no longer enough. They borrowed from both lay and ecclesiastic lenders and often had to mortgage their land or give personal promises as security; sometimes they pledged personal relics and treasure. Royal borrowers, like common ones, hid the interests they paid by integrating it with the principal, thus reducing the effects of prohibitions against usury. In fact, royal borrowers often protected their lenders against prosecution on charges of usury. By their regular demand for funds, they encouraged banking institutions and credit.

Culture and the Church. Finally, we should take into consideration the cultural values predominant in this period. At this time Rome had finally become the center of Christianity, since the Byzantine Empire was on the decline. Religion had a strong hold on the individual. Despite the Church's activities, lust for material wealth and earthly accumulation were frowned upon. Without exaggerating this influence, it cannot be denied that the merchants and profit-makers were still looked down upon in terms of morality and honesty, although statements to the contrary may be found here and there. The extent to which this influence reduced incentives is hard to estimate, but its practical implications may be represented by the influence of the Church.[2]

The Church was an imposing force which

2 Recall Weber's theory discussed in Chapter 2.

influenced the economic and social life of the period with its universalistic message and its centralized power in Rome. While bishops and archbishops were frequently territorial princes and feudal lords, the impact of the Church was much broader. The Pope had emissaries throughout the Christian world; he received tithes and gifts from various areas; he received commodities from other countries to sustain his spiritual empire. Cathedrals were built to reflect the universality of the Church. Deriving its power from a wide spectrum of classes and localities, the Church was able to dispense protection to Christian merchants throughout its vast areas of influence. Facilities and protection were provided to merchants by its bishops. It also controlled large sums of capital which it could pump into the economy or hoard; it usually did the former in various ways. Although the Church's universalism may be looked upon as both a positive and a negative force from a political point of view, there is little doubt that it encouraged cooperation and facilitated the mobility and security of Christian merchants on soils other than their own.

The impact of the Church was felt also in regulating the relations between buyer and seller, debtor and creditor, and employee and employer. In principle the Church was opposed to exploitation, to unjust prices, and to usury. Wages were supposed to be fair so that the employee would be able to live; prices had to be just in the sense that profits were to be a reasonable percentage of total revenue. Interest on credit was not allowed, unless the capital was put to risky use in anticipation of profit, or if the repayment was made later than had been originally agreed upon. The extent to which these principles were upheld is difficult to determine, especially since members of the Church were themselves parties to usurious transactions. That the charging of interest was not as strictly prohibited as is often claimed may be suggested by the fact that a decree of 1240 in Barcelona limited the rates charged by the banks to 18 percent. However, by upholding these principles, the Church set itself up as a guardian of the welfare of the people of all classes.

This policy should not be interpreted as designed to hinder trade or economic and credit activities, as has often been suggested. In fact, the Pope had his own merchant groups who transacted business for the Church and advanced credit. Bishops were both lenders and borrowers, and many Italian merchants found their way to northern Europe as lenders to bishops who wanted to borrow in order to pay the Pope for promotions they had obtained. It has been suggested that the Pope often encouraged the bishops to borrow from the merchants in order to speed up his payments. When the bishops failed to repay on time, the Pope sided with the lenders and pressured the bishops to honor their agreements. Bankers also received direct help and protection from the Pope. It is said that Pope Gregory IX once declared that "any injury to them [the bankers] was to be regarded as an injury to the Holy See."[3] The Pope also employed merchant companies and bankers to collect his funds from different countries. It is estimated that only one Italian company was employed regularly by the English Crown late in the thirteenth century, in contrast to 14 such firms employed by the papacy to collect the £70,000 levied in England. Obviously, these various materialistic interests of the Church enhanced business and credit and international economic activity in general.

INTERNAL POLICIES AND ORGANIZATION

Within the general framework described above, the main determinants of policy in this period were the towns themselves and the organizations of craftsmen and merchants within them.

[3] *Cambridge Economic History of Europe*, III, p. 448.

The towns

The significance of town policy in this period derives from the fact that the central power in most states was weak and each town was responsible for its own destiny. The rise of towns was often at the expense of the feudal structure. Therefore, each town had to assert its autonomy from that structure to assure its prosperity and growth. For these reasons, it seems realistic to look at the town as an independent unit of study functioning within the larger but loose framework described above. The significance of the term *town* varied according to the size of the metropolitan area and the power of the feudal lord in its vicinity. For our purposes, we shall regard the town as the territory to which legislation by the city authority applies.

Town policy varied according to the economic basis of the town, which changed as time went on. The policy also depended on the balance between the power of the central authority and that of the internal oligarchy. When trade was the major source of income, town policy favored trade and traders; when manufacturing became important, it usually tended toward protection of the relevant industries. One might invoke Gerschenkron's theory of economic backwardness in this connection. The cities' protectionism varied directly with their degree of backwardness. As backward cities caught up, they tended to revert to either competition or cooperation, according to whether there was glut or shortage in the market.

The variations between liberalism and protectionism can be outlined as follows: In the early period, tenth–eleventh centuries, the few existing cities or towns and the feudal lords who were strengthening their own power were anxious for growth. They were not afraid of competition and there was a great demand for supplies to feed the urban populations. Therefore, the policy emphasized liberal measures to encourage trade and artisanship. However, as trade expanded and more urban centers were created, the tendency turned toward more active intervention, both to ensure the arrival of supplies and to control a larger share of the trade. The merchants and merchant guilds had their heyday in the twelfth and thirteenth centuries. The beginning and expansion of manufacturing followed, together with the crisis in procuring supplies caused by war and the plagues. In this period, the policy tended toward protectionism, regulation, and the beginning of economic nationalism.

Town policy was guided by three basic goals: to secure enough revenue for city affairs including defense; to protect the native traders and craftsmen; and to protect the consumer against famine and fraud. Revenues were derived from tolls taken at the gates of the city and on the crossings of trade routes, especially when trade was carried out by foreigners coming to the city. They came also from taxes or assessments on the business community within the city. Many cities collected dues by levying lump sums on the merchant and craft guilds, thus relieving themselves of the burden of collecting and guaranteeing a more equitable distribution of the tax burden, since guild members were not unjust to each other. Finally, the city often collected revenues by sponsoring markets or renting grounds for fairs, which also served to fulfill other aspects of their policies.

The protection of native businessmen against outsiders also meant securing a larger share of the trade for the city as a whole. Different approaches were used to reach this objective. The most extreme was to exclude outsiders altogether from certain territories. "Genoa forced Narbonne in 1166 to give up the transport of all pilgrims embarking at any port from Montpellier to Nice; Venice . . . insisted that Ravenna should withdraw from the pilgrim business in 1234 and enforced the same prohibition on Ancona in 1264."[4] Retail trade was kept largely in the hands of the native people. Many cities guar-

anteed their native traders a favored position, as Bologna did in 1116. The townsman was assured the function of a middleman between foreign traders and the local consumer. Direct trade between foreigners within the city limits could be prohibited, as it was in Bologna, Genoa, and the Baltic towns. Certain trades and products might be forbidden to foreigners. Genoa and Venice were foremost in this regard. Barcelona prohibited banking to foreigners in 1268. Cities were also anxious to divert trade to their own markets, as was true of Polish and German towns and Genoa. Some towns tried to control trade routes leading to old and new markets. This policy was quite important in the Mediterranean area in the twelfth and thirteenth centuries and grew in importance at the beginning of the fourteenth century, when trade between the South and North was quite active. Certain sea routes were dominated by specific cities such as Venice and Genoa. As Figure 6.1 (p. 79) shows, trade zones were also established, especially in the North where the Hanseatic towns were predominant, as will be discussed below. Naturally the creation of trade zones aroused enmity, and control of trade routes had to be enforced by armed escort. Conflict could be avoided also by alliances or by trade agreements. Alliances between towns were common in various parts of Europe. Milan headed the Lombard League against Genoa and Pisa in 1168. The Hanseatic towns went to war more than once for control of trade zones. The effectiveness of these various policies is difficult to estimate. There is evidence, however, that the prohibitions were sometimes circumvented by partnerships formed between foreigners and native merchants.

Protection of the consumer against a shortage of supplies was served partly by the above measures. However, certain positive measures were also introduced. Some cities concluded bilateral treaties with other towns to make certain that trade would continue to flow in. Such treaties gave mutual privileges, toll concessions, and protection to the

---

[4] *Cambridge Economic History of Europe*, III, p. 164.

traders from each town in the zone of the other. An arrangement between Milan and Novara in 1230 gave Milan the right to buy corn and to import food without paying duties, and allowed Novara to carry its trade without harassment from Milan.

An effective way to secure food and other strategic supplies was the "tied import" policy, which was common in the cities of Germany, Poland, and Florence in various periods of shortage. The policy stipulated that a certain percentage of the imports must consist of the desired goods. It was often accompanied by severe restrictions on the export of strategic items. Export restriction sometimes meant total prohibition, but more frequently it was carried out by levying high export duties. It was common in the fourteenth and fifteenth centuries in virtually all parts of Europe. The towns often used the merchant and craft guilds as means of implementing these restrictions.

The towns also concerned themselves with the distribution and quality of their products. Distribution control was implemented mostly by regulating prices, especially those of foodstuffs and other necessities, to maintain a balance between wages and prices. Price-fixing was one method of control. However, more indirect methods were equally important. *Engrossing*, or accumulating inventories for speculation, was not allowed. It was equally forbidden to *forestall* by buying the goods before they reached the market in order to resell at higher prices. *Regrating*, or raising prices arbitrarily, was also against city rules. The idea of the just price upheld by the Church served as a guide and as a moral weapon to enforce the law. The city authorities also kept an eye on the quality of the goods to prevent adulteration and fraud, employing supervisors for the purpose. The guilds were also used to enforce these regulations. A common approach was to establish a "standard loaf" and make sure that the ratio of the prices of different loaves of bread was equivalent to the ratio of their weights to the weight of the standard loaf. This was a common procedure in Germany and France as early as the twelfth century.

These policies were not uniform throughout Europe, however. Towns varied in their relation to the outside; their economic needs varied; and the political and social environments in which they existed were not uniform. The most important influence on town policy, however, was the internal structure of the town and the business community, particularly the role of the guild versus other groups in the city.

Craft guilds

Guilds are combinations of people with a common interest, like trade unions today. In their urban setting, the merchant and the artisan were often severed from their previous relations and required a substitute source of security, companionship, and identity. Furthermore, the economic environment was not always friendly. Business affairs were not well guarded, and often the merchant was opposed by the feudal lord, the prince, or the city oligarchy. Guild organization or combination with members of his profession was a natural outlet for these frustrations.

Craft guilds seem to have spread mostly after the beginning of the thirteenth century. They found a place in middle-sized towns of 20–30,000 people, in which some division of labor prevailed and various economic interests existed side by side. They were insignificant in small towns and rural districts, and they were widespread but weak in areas such as the coastal towns, in which foreign trade was important. In the small towns there was little need for them, and in major trading areas the merchants were too powerful for them to gain any strength. Italy had the earliest and strongest guilds until the city communes became dominated by mercantile interests or by powerful seigneurial oligarchies. In Spain, the guilds were so threatened by town authorities that they sought royal protection, which eventually led to their total domination by the Crown. In southern

France, as in Italy, the communes dominated the guilds but let them exist. In central and northern France, however, the communes were weak while feudal power was strong. There the guilds had to pay dues to the feudal powers in order to exist. French guilds eventually became public authorities used by the royal power for fiscal purposes. The German and central European guilds became widespread and politically active to maintain their position against the rising mercantile interests. Guilds were even more active politically and sometimes militarily in the Low Countries, where the textile interests were very strong. They were least common in Scandinavia, where in fact they were denied any privileges unless their members were German immigrants.

The situation in England was unusual. Outside of London, towns were relatively small. Moreover, the royal power offered sufficient protection to the individual to obviate the need for combination. Nevertheless, guilds frequently became strong enough to invite restrictive laws and even prohibitions against them, on the assumption that they were opposed to the royal interests. This happened in 1256.

Prohibition was not confined to England. The city of Nuremberg had requested the guilds to submit their correspondence with foreign agencies to city supervision at an earlier date. Even where they grew to be strong, as in western and southern Europe, guilds were often subject to prohibition: in Rouen in 1189, in Dinant in 1255, in most Flemish towns in 1280, and in Brussels in 1290. However, such opposition was not sufficient to discourage them.

The economic functions of the guilds influenced local trade. They tried to gain dignity by solidarity and internal discipline, by imposing certain standards especially with regard to quality, and by restraining internal competition to some degree. For example, they restricted the number of apprentices a master could have and the working hours of the shop. They fought the rising costs of labor in times of shortage, and encouraged competitive expansion by members or outsiders when labor costs were low. In both cases, they had to fight the central authority to maintain their position. Their protective efforts were much weaker in the export trades where mercantile interests often dominated or penetrated their ranks. Such interests eventually subjected the artisans to control by means of the putting-out system or the farming-out of piecework by the merchant entrepreneur.[5]

It has often been argued that guilds hindered innovation. While they protected their members and guaranteed them a certain degree of equality, Pirenne concludes that

> the counterpart of the privilege and monopoly enjoyed by the guild was the destruction of all initiative. No one was permitted to harm others by methods which enabled him to produce more quickly and more cheaply than they. Technical progress took on the appearance of disloyalty. The ideal was stable conditions in a stable industry.[6]

This argument, however, gives no evidence that internal competition was totally lacking, or that the competition with outsiders was reduced by guild organization. Nor is there sufficient evidence to say how much the guilds influenced, positively or negatively, the processes of innovation, saving, and investment. Furthermore, changes in the textile industry demonstrate that when economic and technological conditions were appropriate, change did come about. The guilds were not able to stand in the way, even if they wanted to do so.

The power of the guilds varied according to their specialization as well as to the prevailing economic conditions. The bakers, the butchers, the goldsmiths, and the armor-makers were among the most powerful, compared

---

[5] The putting-out system will be discussed in detail in chaps. 8 and 12.

[6] H. Pirenne, *Economic and Social History of Medieval Europe*, p. 186.

with industries such as construction and transport, which were dominated respectively by municipalities and merchants. All of the former group were involved in making necessities for either peace or war. However, they were also subject to more strict control in the name of the public interest. In all cases, however, the power of the guild varied with the conditions of demand and supply in the market. In periods of relative shortage they were asked to cooperate with the authorities. In periods of relative abundance of supply, it was difficult to secure protection. Thus, the guilds were able to survive and grow during the fourteenth and fifteenth centuries, in part because of the shortage of supply and the high demand for their services.

The social functions the guilds performed were equally important to their survival. The guilds offered their members, especially the weaker among them, a social group to belong to. In fact, many scholars look for the origin of guilds in the need for a free association of members such as fraternities or church and social groups. Guilds provided the family craftsman with a mechanism by which his skill could be retained within the family, by regulating entry into the guild and restricting the number of apprentices in a shop. The guilds also provided the mechanism for an apprentice to rise in the ranks to journeyman and then to master. Guilds offered a form of social security to their members in times of need or crisis. Often they aided their members by collectively owning equipment and markets. Some documents on English guilds show that they were philanthropic and tried to guarantee work for all. They offered mutual assistance, held social festivities and common worship, and attended the funerals of members. Some guilds had subscription boxes out of which they made allocations to the elderly poor, the unemployed, families who had lost the breadwinner, and those who could not bury their dead. When members failed to complete a job they had undertaken, they could count on help from other members. Furthermore, the guilds provided a certain degree of political protection and representation for the individual. Therefore, even though economic benefits might have been modest—and there is little evidence that they were—the members derived sufficient social and political benefits from the guilds to fight to retain them.

Merchant guilds and combinations

The merchant interest group might be referred to as a guild, although its structure varied greatly from that of the craft guild. Since the merchants were interested mainly in trade, they were directly involved in foreign relations and in politics to the extent that these affected trade. They attained their power position by combining in merchant leagues, by dominating urban administrations, and by combining the towns in leagues to defend and expand their interests.

The need for combination has been debated and sometimes criticized as a sign of weakness and decline in the sense that powerful individuals or big family businesses did not care for combinations in corporate bodies. The widespread corporate structure of businesses in the fifteenth century has been associated with the alleged decline of business in that period. While there might have been an economic decline in the early part of the fifteenth century, it does not seem valid to associate it with the corporate structure. To understand the significance of merchant organization, we must look at it in perspective. The environment in which the merchants found themselves was not friendly. Having no institutionalized place in society, they had to carve one for themselves despite the hostility of the older nobility and the inaction of the weak central government. The economic structure was equally antagonistic. Political intervention in the market was common. Town policy discriminated against foreign traders and limited the areas in which they could function freely. Therefore, when opportunities prevailed, the merchants found themselves unable to take advantage of them.

They sought political power in order to cope with the political opposition they faced.

That the merchant guilds were not a symptom of economic decline or weakness may also be seen from the chronology of their appearance. Merchant guilds and associations were known in England and in Italy in the twelfth century, long before the period of economic decline. Their main interest was trade and social interaction. The Genoese established an association of partnerships, the *maona*, to counteract the unfriendly forces in the Mediterranean around the end of the twelfth century. A merchant guild in Barcelona can be traced back to 1258. In 1279 it secured the right to elect judges to hear marine cases, was represented on the city council by as many as a third of the membership, and together with the industrial interests contributed a majority.

The merchant guild in London succeeded in 1200 in persuading the king to abolish the weavers' craft guild to give the merchants a monopoly. The merchants were known as freemen, in contrast to the craftsmen, and a craftsman could become a freeman only if he renounced his craft and removed all the craft equipment from his house. This monopoly lasted for more than a century, until 1335. However, a new organization had been growing in the meantime, the Company of the Staple, which was created with the help of the King around the middle of the thirteenth century. The Staple originally meant a place to which English merchants could bring their commodities for sale. At first it was located in England, making it necessary for foreigners to come to England to buy English goods. However, after many changes, the Company of the Staple was permanently placed in Calais in 1363. It served fiscal and supervisory functions for the Crown, and also protected English merchants and held a monopoly on English products.

The merchants of the Italian towns were more successful in achieving their goals by dominating the city communes and by iden-tifying the interests of the cities with their own. Venetian and Genoese trade routes generally served the interests of the merchants. Similarly, the alliances between towns mentioned above were made to guarantee the native merchants protection, privilege, and even the concession of certain trade zones and commodities.

The most significant merchant associations of the thirteenth–fifteenth centuries were those of the Hanseatic towns. These merchant leagues evolved into town confederations and into political forces that dominated most of northern and eastern Europe for a period of more than two centuries.[7] The Hanseatic League was first an association of foreign merchants, of which the best-known were the Hansa of London and the Teutonic Hansa which prevailed in northern and eastern Europe. As early as 1237 the merchants of Amiens, Corbie, and Nesle succeeded in securing privileges from the merchants of London to trade anywhere in England in return for certain regular payments. The only restriction was that they could not trade in wine or corn. The Hansa of London was headed by Bruges, and became known as the Steelyard, the area on the Thames in which the members lived. It followed set standards of efficiency and management, with rank differentiation clearly established. However, each member was free to pursue his interests and trade individually within the common framework. The Hansa of London finally succeeded in the first half of the fourteenth century in securing for its members royal protection and the privilege to trade wherever they pleased and to stay in England 40 days, as long as they agreed to pay the ordinary taxes. London, however, was only one of the four main "factories" established in the thirteenth century on which Hanseatic trade depended. Bergen in Norway was another, Novgorod in Russia the third, and Bruges the fourth. London was mainly for wool and

[7] Actually, the Hanseatic Confederation lasted through 1669, the year of the last Diet assembly.

cloth, Bergen supplied fish, Novgorod the produce of Russia, and Bruges served as a buying center for the Low Countries. These factories were the stations for collecting and exporting trading items, but their leadership and direction came from the German towns.

The chief Hanseatic towns were in the Teutonic Hansa, which was led by Lübeck and which established stations as far east as Novgorod. The power of the merchants grew strong enough to dominate their towns and bring them into a confederation in 1367. At the peak of its power, the League included 77 towns and was powerful enough to defeat the king of Denmark in battle, after which the treaty of Stralsund was signed in 1370 giving the League a free hand in most of northern Europe. The zone of influence and the towns and stations of the League are shown in Figure 6.1 (p. 79). Clearly, the interests of the League went beyond the political boundaries and national interests of the towns themselves. Once their commercial interests were recognized, however, they were willing to reach agreement with other towns and countries. The relative economic significance of the League towns has been studied in terms of their tax assessments. At the peak in 1364, Lübeck and Cologne shared the top rank, followed by Colberg, Hamburg, and Danzig.[8]

The golden age of the League could not last forever. On one hand, national governments were beginning to take shape in various parts of Europe. On the other, the League began to suffer the consequences of its own success. Merchants began to emulate the older nobility by acquiring titles, building castles, and retiring prematurely from trade. Other merchants fought among themselves for leadership. Towns began to look toward their own interests, regardless of the "common goal." The structure of the League itself was too loose to permit a lasting organization. Therefore, it gradually went

into decline, although it was not dissolved until the needs it filled could be satisfied by other means.

What impact did the merchant guilds and the Hanseatic League have on economic change? There is little doubt that the League was more aggressive than individuals could have been. Its members extended the zones of trade and commerce over areas that were previously isolated. They also helped to standardize methods and patterns of trade and thus set a standard for a certain degree of competition within the specified zone of influence. More significant was their competition with other alliances or trade zones, such as the Staple, the Milan League, and the Venetian traders. Such competition obviously stimulated better conditions for production and consumption. Another important effect of the League was the enlargement of the scale of operation, which resulted from the increase of trade and the limited membership. It also provided for some pooling of resources, which in the absence of capital-recruiting mechanisms might have been impossible to obtain. Finally, the rise of the merchant class itself might have been difficult without association, and the traditional forces might have retained their hold on society.

We can conclude then that these associations were vehicles for social and economic change. Whether the change might have been slower or more rapid without them is hard to determine. There is little evidence, however, that they hindered innovation, while they clearly improved management, organization, and shipping and encouraged manufacturing for export. Furthermore, there is little evidence that countries with no associations but with similar technological background progressed faster than the Hanseatic towns. While the question of hindrance or facilitation of economic development might be difficult to answer firmly, the changes that occurred suggest a positive rather than a negative role for these associations in advancing trade and the market.

[8] A full ranking of each of the towns may be found in J. W. Thompson, *op. cit.*, p. 164.

The fairs

Fairs have been common to most periods of economic history, although their functions have changed from one period to another. In general, fairs are markets with a higher tempo of activity than normal and a greater variety of commodities offered, and they have a seasonal character for which one can build expectations. A fair may be related to religious or social festivities: Since people will assemble for such occasions, buying and selling promise good profit, and therefore the mechanism for them is created. Or the fair may be related to an economic need: If the usual demand is too small to support a permanent and comprehensive market, a periodic fair may be held to satisfy it. Or the fair may be for political purposes, as is the case with most modern fairs or exhibitions. These three functions can be observed in varying degrees in most fairs. The medieval fair between the eleventh and fifteenth centuries may be classified as mostly of the economic variety.

In the early period, demand was insufficient to support large and active markets. Fairs were held in which cumulative demand and supply met periodically to satisfy the buyers and sellers who were unable to get satisfaction in the regular local market. In such cases, while demand creates supply, the anticipated supply tends to redirect demand to itself. Knowing that a fair will be held, the prospective buyer tends to postpone his purchase, hoping to find a bargain there in quality, variety, and price. Similarly, the prospective seller waits for the fair with the hope of making higher profits both by charging higher prices and by selling larger quantities. It should be expected, therefore, that if sufficient demand exists for a continuous, large, comprehensive market, the need for a fair declines and merchants find it at least as attractive to settle down and utilize that market. In other words, fairs generally serve an economic function where the demand is too large for the small village market but not large enough to support a large city market.

This pattern can be observed in the history of the fairs in Europe. Fairs grew in waves when demand was rising, but as the demand became large enough for permanent activity, they began to decline. The money-changer and the merchant preferred to settle down in Paris rather than keep moving from one fair to another. While the older and larger fairs were declining, new, smaller fairs grew up in areas of smaller population density or less intensive economic activity.

Usually fairs were sponsored by a count or the king as sources of revenue. Payments were received as taxes, as tolls on entry and exit, as transaction fees, as fees on weights and measures, and as dues for safe conduct. The sponsor usually gave protection and guaranteed justice under the supervision of public officials. When necessary, special privileges such as reduced tolls were offered to foreigners to attract them to the fairs.

Fair sites were spread throughout Europe, but they varied in commercial significance from one place and period to another. The Champagne fairs were the most famous, followed by those of Flanders. Each of these groups of fairs were held in a series of six every year, so that a fair was going on at all times. In the twelfth century, the Champagne fairs were held in the summer and winter at Troyes and in the spring and autumn at Provins; another was held at Lagny near Paris; the last was held at Bar-sur-Aube. Merchants came from all over Europe and the Hansa of the 17 towns of the Low Countries and northern France were not allowed to sell their cloth outside these fairs. The Italian towns which supplied silk and Oriental products were given special protection in order to secure these products.

The thirteenth century saw the rise of the Flemish fairs which were held twice at Ypres, and once each in Bruges, Torhout, Lille, and Messines. While these fairs were large and important, they were somewhat less international than the Champagne fairs. Nevertheless, they attracted merchants from a wide area and offered an equally varied supply of goods. Next in importance were the fairs of Chalon, which prospered around 1280, the four yearly fairs in Geneva of the fourteenth century, and the fairs of Lyon, which offered stiff competition to Geneva.

Germany also had its fairs, the most important of which was the fair of Frankfurt-am-Main, which served merchants of at least 32 towns. Fairs were also held in Switzerland and Austria. Scandinavia had weekly markets which sometimes increased their tempo to the level of fairs. Scania had a fair which was the most important center for the sale of herring, where Lübeck traded its tens of thousands of barrels of herring every season. In the interior and later in the Middle Ages fairs were smaller and more numerous as, for example, were those of Spain, Portugal, and Italy. The fairs of the British Isles were also small but less numerous relative to those of the continent.

The reasons for the rise and decline of the fairs, especially those of Champagne and Flanders, have been subjects of debate. The conditions for the fair had to be right. Good roads, a large suuply of local products, a complete yearly cycle, a safe-conduct policy,

and an increase in population were all contributing factors. The organization of merchants into corporate bodies made it feasible for them to gain representation and protection at the fairs. At least 15 Italian towns had consuls at the fairs of Champagne representing the interests of their merchants. Finally, the rise and success of the fairs may be associated with a prevalent need for a mechanism to advance international trade. Although most of these conditions continued, their significance declined as the basic foundations for fairs were shaken. The spread of manufacturing in Italy, the opening up of sea routes from the Mediterranean to the North Atlantic, and the increase in local demand to levels sufficient to support a permanent market were enough to cause a decline of the Champagne fairs. In broad terms the same explanation may be applied to the Flemish fairs. The fairs had served their function, which now was served by the cities and their permanent markets. In their time and place they were great facilities for expanding trade and manufacturing. As we shall see in the next chapter, they were also important as credit and money markets.

BIBLIOGRAPHY

Kalische, J., "Fairs," *Encyclopedia of Social Sciences.* E. R. A. Seligman and Alvin Johnson (eds.), New York: Macmillan, 1931.

Pirenne, H., *Economic and Social History of Medieval Europe,* New York: Harcourt, Brace & World, 1937, chap. 4.

Postan, M., E. E. Rich, and Edward Miller (eds.), *The Cambridge Economic History of Europe,* III, New York: Cambridge University Press, 1963, chap. 3.

Thompson, J. W., *Economic and Social History of Europe in the Later Middle Ages, 1300–1530,* New York: Frederick Ungar Publishing Co., 1960, chap. 5.

Weber, Max, *General Economic History,* New York: Collier Books, 1966, chap. 16.

8

THE FIRM
IN THE
MEDIEVAL
ECONOMY:
SCALE,
FINANCING,
AND
MANAGEMENT

So far we have been concerned with economic conditions in aggregate terms. However, it is important to know the features of the producing unit, the mercantile enterprise, and the ways by which inputs were secured and converted into outputs. Put in modern economic terms, we must ask these questions about the firm: Who makes the decisions? How is the scale of production determined? What labor relations prevail? How determinate is the behavior of the firm *vis-à-vis* the market? Had free competition prevailed, these questions would be answerable according to standard economic theory, prices being determined in the market and the level of production being a function of the demand for and the supply of the factors of production. However, the economic environment of the Middle Ages does not fit that theoretical framework. The influences which have been discussed in the previous chapters were also relevant to the individual firm.

THE CRAFT SHOP

This category of enterprise includes all those in which commodities are produced for the local or export market, regardless of whether they are finished, semifinished, or raw material. The crafts were classified into specific categories, either by action of the guild members or by public order. The individual craft was manned by a given number of artisan masters. This number was controlled in order to prevent a glut in the market which would lower prices and reduce profits. The master usually had one or two journeymen in his shop. These were fully qualified artisans who had not been admitted to the guild as masters and therefore worked in the shop for wages. In addition, the shop had a few apprentices in varying stages of advancement towards journeymanship. The period of apprenticeship was governed by the guild rules. The simple tools needed in the shop were owned by the master. Thus he was both an artisan and an entrepreneur, since he carried the risk of producing for an unspecified market or price. He was expected to make decisions regarding the quality and quantity of production, and he benefited from the profits and suffered the losses.

However, the degree of entrepreneurship inherent in this structure was quite limited under the conditions that prevailed throughout Europe in the twelfth to fifteenth centuries. The master–owner was both regulated and protected by the guild or corporation. His hours of work and the number of his apprentices were limited and the total supply he could produce was specified within a given range. Moreover, the craft shops were often concentrated in one quarter of the city and thus were subject to supervision as well as control by the guild or public authority. In the absence of a glut because of increased supply or a sharp decline of the demand because of some calamity, the firm was in a state close to equilibrium: The forces of supply and demand were given and the economic conditions in the shop adjusted accordingly. The master could not compete openly with his fellow masters, nor did he have any guarantees that he could sell at prices higher than those set by the guild. He could not sell products of inferior quality. In the absence of a major shift in the terms of trade between his craft and the other sectors in the economy, his standard of living tended to be stable.

When trade and population were expanding, fairs being opened and markets enlarged, it would be unrealistic to expect the craft shop to remain unaffected. However, the change that did occur was merely an extension of the existing framework. A trend toward increasing production for export was developing. The merchant who wanted goods for a distant market began to contract with certain artisans to produce for him at piece rates. He might even advance the material and some capital, in anticipation of the finished or semifinished product. To make his undertaking economically profitable, he enlarged his scale by contracting with different artisans to produce for him simultaneously. This was the beginning of the putting-out system, which reached its peak between the sixteenth and eighteenth centuries.

This extension of the production process had several significant implications. First, it relieved the master of the risk of producing for an unspecified market: Now he produced a given quality of goods for a given buyer on specified terms. Second, he became dependent on the merchant employers for orders and for supplies or credit. He could also expand his production by employing more journeymen and apprentices to cope with new orders, especially since craft guilds were relatively weak in towns in which international

trade was important. However, freeing himself of risks meant losing his independence and the security and satisfaction deriving from his position as master of the shop. Since the artisan producing for the export market depended on decisions which were not subject to local regulation, he became vulnerable to competition from artisans in other cities or countries whom he neither knew nor had any contact with. Furthermore, journeymen, apprentices, and independent artisans found themselves without work whenever a glut in the market was apparent. This vulnerability was reflected by the uncontrolled increase in the number of artisans who entered the market in favorable situations and who found themselves unemployed when crises arose. It is estimated that Ghent, a city of not more than 50,000 people in the mid-fourteenth century, had 4,000 weavers and 1,200 fullers. About the same date in Ypres 51.6 percent of the town's trade was in the cloth industry. A town producing for the local market had more diversification and hence less vulnerability. Only 16 percent of the workers in Frankfurt-am-Main depended on the cloth industry.[1]

Thus the decision-making in the production process was shifting gradually towards a less regulated free market. Risk was also shifting from the artisan to the merchant capitalist who farmed out the production. In place of the secure artisans, a new group of proletariat was coming into existence which had neither protection nor organization. However, it would be premature to describe that group as a class, since it lacked organization, consciousness, and intercommunication. Finally, a new factor of production, capital, was gaining in importance. Neither the artisan nor the master needed capital of his own, since the merchant capitalist would provide it in advance if necessary. There was a growing dependence on capital, in contrast to the conditions in earlier periods

---

[1] H. Pirenne, *Economic and Social History of Medieval Europe*, p. 189.

or in local industry, in which availability of capital was of little significance either for entering the market or for expanding production. Nevertheless, production was still in small, loosely organized, and poorly managed enterprises. Change and development in these areas were much more conspicuous in mercantile and banking enterprises.

MERCANTILE ENTERPRISES

This classification includes all trading firms, regardless of their form of organization. Such firms do not produce commodities, but sell them. They often have other interests such as banking, but trading is their primary concern. In fact, it is difficult to separate the mercantile from other interests in scale, financing, or management. Looking at twelfth- to fifteenth-century business activities, several features become apparent. First, it is clear that there was no one pattern common to all countries or to the period as a whole. The structure of the firm varied according to time and place. Second, in the various zones of influence certain features predominated. Third, as time went on business organization and the managerial process tended to become more complex. Finally, regardless of time, place, or scale of operation, there was some consciousness of risk and a tendency toward diversification to hedge against it.

To discover the important features of mercantile enterprise in this period, it is useful to compare the Italian pattern with that predominant in the northern and Hanseatic towns, as the two major zones of influence. The Italian firm tended to be larger, better organized and managed, and more innovative in business and accounting techniques than its counterpart in the North. Especially in the export business, the Italian firm tended to branch out in different directions, while the northern firm was generally owned by an individual and concentrated

its operations within a narrow sphere. While partnerships and companies were common in both North and South, the Italian firms were much larger, both in scale of operation and in area of trade. In 1336 the Peruzzi had at least 18 branches spread throughout Europe and North Africa; the Acciaiuoli had at least 17 branches in 1341; the Medici had at least 8 branches with a larger staff in each. An idea of the capital investment involved can only be inferred. The Medici had an investment of 88,269 florins in 1451; in 1403 Philip the Bold, head of the Burgundian state, had a total revenue of 96,000 li. tour. (about 60,000 fl.); Henry of Luxembourg's total receipts in 1312–1313 amounted to 191,500 florins. For comparison, it may be noted that £200 Genoese were sufficient for a merchant to undertake an overseas venture. This figure is a little less than the amount the Medici had invested per staff member.[2]

Such large companies hardly existed in northern Europe. Even among the relatively advanced Hanseatic towns, the firm was small, manned usually by the individual merchant and sometimes represented abroad by a mutual agent. Certain large companies were in existence in southern Germany, but these were exceptions. It is true that the Hanseatic merchants sometimes pooled their resources and enlarged their scale of operations, but such arrangements were made only on a temporary basis.

Merchants, like craftsmen, had to learn the art of trade. A period of apprenticeship in a counting-house was the most usual approach. A merchant might learn the trade within the family business, as was common among the Italians. He might also learn by experience, beginning as a peddler on a very small scale until he could undertake more substantial ventures. As business operations grew in scale and sophistication, manuals were made available to advise merchants of the most appropriate ways of conducting

[2] *Cambridge Economic History of Europe*, III, pp. 84–86.

business. These described the main characteristics of a trading or banking center, identified the crowded and the less crowded places, and sometimes even shed some light on dealing with certain groups or clients.

Merchants were also expected to have an education and to use the abacus. Gradually they became more and more acquainted with systems of bookkeeping, although double-entry bookkeeping was not common until late in the fifteenth century. In all these respects, the Italians were far ahead of the Hanseatic merchants. They adopted bookkeeping and the bill of exchange or some variant of it long before the northern merchants. They also began to settle down and establish permanent representatives in their areas of trade while the Hanseatic merchants were still traveling with their merchandise.

In both the South and the North, business relations were based on contract. Even where merchant guilds and associations served as regulating agencies, individual transactions were governed by specific contracts. However, business management practices differed according to the needs and scale of the business, rather than according to any ideology regarding business activity. It is interesting to note that business ethics were put down in writing as early as the thirteenth century. The author of the *King's Mirror* is unknown, but the message of the book is set out as a general doctrine:

The merchant should be brave and adventurous; he should be polite and gentle, but should also be careful to check the quality of his purchase; he should avoid vice, but should go to good inns and live well; he should know languages, especially French and Latin and must study law and local customs; he should know some arithmetic and astronomy in order to be able to navigate. The merchant should sell quickly at reasonable prices because a quick turnover stimulates trade; he should maintain his ship in good condition and should

buy shares only in good ships; he should choose his partners carefully, and should keep reinvesting his profits, especially by acquiring land which is the safest form of investment.[3]

The Italian companies probably went further by holding a reserve against unexpected difficulties.

Management of the business was at first usually directed by the traveling merchant himself. However, as the system of traveling began to decline, about the time that fairs were declining, merchants began to depend on partners, correspondents, factors or commission agents, or on innkeepers in the places they or their agents went to. The Italians usually depended more on partners or correspondents than did the Hanseatic merchants. The latter used commission agents and innkeepers. They also made extensive use of mutual agents, whom they represented in their own town and who represented them in return.

PARTNERSHIPS

Partnerships are a form of combination by which resources may be pooled and risks more broadly distributed. Probably the most primitive form of economic partnership is the family, in which members are recruited to do certain chores, funds are pooled, and benefits and losses shared. This traditional form of partnership reached a high degree of development and sophistication in the Middle Ages, especially among the mercantile and banking enterprises. However, there comes a time when outsiders must be brought into the business, or when capital and labor do not exist in the same family and therefore must be brought together by a partnership. Medieval businesses took advantage of this mechanism, in various forms,

[3] *Cambridge Economic History of Europe*, III, p. 48.

in the Italian as well as in the Hanseatic zones. In fact, there was a high degree of similarity in the forms of organization used in both areas.

Southern forms

Probably the most common form of non-permanent partnership among the Italians was the *commenda* partnership, according to which one party did all the work and traveled with the merchandise, while the other contributed all the capital.[4] The profits were distributed after each venture according to a standard formula: one-quarter for labor and three-quarters for capital. Decision-making varied according to the specific agreement. Sometimes the *contractor* or traveling partner made all the decisions; in other cases the *stan* or contributor of capital stipulated the merchandise and its destination; in still others, all decisions were joint. The risk in this kind of partnership was limited to the contribution of each party, and could be reduced by participating in more than one partnership simultaneously. A variant of the *commenda* which came into being near the end of the twelfth century in relation to the Syrian trade was the *accomendatio,* a partnership between several contributors of capital and one traveling partner. The arrangements were the same as under the *commenda,* the only difference being that the *accomendatio* allowed people with small means to participate in international trade.

Another temporary form of partnership was the *societas maris,* according to which the *contractor* contributed his labor and one-third of the capital, while the remaining two-thirds were contributed by the *stan.* In these

[4] According to some authorities the *commenda* is of Arab origin and goes back to the days of the prophet Mohammed. (See J. W. Thompson, *Economic and Social History of Europe in the Late Middle Ages, 1300–1530,* p. 441.) Mistakenly, however, this form of partnership is explained as a way of avoiding the Moslem prohibition on usury, although it predated the Moslem law. Indeed, Mohammed went on a venture organized as a *commenda* before he received the prophecy.

cases, the profits were divided equally between the two parties.

A form of partnership which qualified more as a credit mechanism than a business partnership was the *sea loan.* The amount of the loan might vary, but its characteristic feature was that repayment was contingent upon the safe arrival of the ship, the cargo, or both. In such cases, the lender assumed only the risk of sea travel, while the traveling merchant assumed the economic risks associated with the marketplace, such as failure to sell, price fluctuations, and even robbery and loss after arrival. A distinctive form of the sea loan was the *bottomry loan,* which included capital advances to build a ship, equip it, or repair it in foreign ports. Sea loans were also limited to single ventures, although like the other temporary contracts they might be renewed again and again.

Sea loans lost their popularity around 1250, to be replaced by the *combium maritimum.* In this new form interest on the loan could be hidden by making repayment in another currency at a given rate of exchange. This made it possible to avoid any conflict with prohibitions on usury, at a time when the interest rate, which apparently included a premium as insurance on risk, was between 40 and 50 percent. A variant of this contract was the *combium quasi nauticum,* according to which loans were advanced on the security of the goods being shipped. This form was used for travel over land and provided insurance against robbery, as well as a mechanism by which advances could be made for bogus ventures.

Finally, ordinary partnerships, *campagnia,* were not uncommon. These were more permanent and carried with them an unlimited liability of all the partners. In such enterprises all parties to the partnership might contribute labor as well as capital. Such partnerships often sold shares to outsiders and guaranteed them a certain rate of return, commonly 8 percent, which was paid before any dividends were allocated out of profits.

Northern forms

Partnerships in the Hanseatic zone had certain similarities with the Italian forms, although they were usually on a smaller scale. A common form was the *Sendeve*, which was limited to one venture, with one party contributing the labor and the other the capital. All the decisions were made by the party contributing the capital. Usually this was an agreement by which a servant, a fellow-merchant, or even an innkeeper undertook to sell the capitalist's goods against a commission. In such cases, all the risks of the venture were assumed by the party contributing the capital. A contrasting form of agreement was the *Wederlegginge*, in which the traveling partner was also the managing partner, making the decisions and assuming the risks. The most common form, to which we have already alluded, was the *Gegenseitige Ferngesellschaft*, or mutual agency partnership, under which partners in different towns represented each other, but without publicizing the partnership.

The English experience was similar to that of northern Europe. While partnerships were common, they were smaller, less developed, and less widespread than they were in the Italian zone. It was common to entrust goods to someone else who would sell them for a commission, or to finance a share partner who would serve as *contractor*. Occasionally partnerships were concluded among parties who were both active for a single venture. Decision-making in all these cases was agreed upon in advance and was somewhat regulated by trading companies such as the Merchant Adventurers and the Company of the Staple. As elsewhere, diversification was common to avoid risk.

The English seem also to have been slow in adopting new business techniques such as double-entry bookkeeping, which did not come into use before 1500, although it was used as early as 1340 in the Italian zone. Similarly, the English were less anxious to make use of marine insurance, apparently because their trading zone was limited to the Channel area and hence relatively free of risk. They made use of a form of the bill of exchange around 1450, almost two centuries later than the Italian, although in this case they were ahead of the Hanseatic towns. A unique feature of English trading companies was the separation of imports from exports; each was a specialized activity conducted by a different company or group.

Sources of capital

The sources of capital mentioned so far, the family and the various forms of partnership, were supplemented by more indirect sources. For example, the Church supplied funds to its cameral merchants, who for all practical purposes acted on their own in the market. Although they usually received a commission, in effect they made all the decisions while the Church assumed all the risks. A similar source of funding was the lay leadership, such as territorial princes or city authorities, who often borrowed large sums which eventually were channeled into the market. One might even conceive of financing the production and supply of war material as a form of public funding of economic activity. Moreover, inflationary financing through debasement often meant the expansion of economic activity at the instigation of public authorities.

A more important and lasting form of funding was the system of credit or deferred payment. Deferred payment in its simplest form means extending the opportunity to a merchant or producer to undertake an enterprise and repay his debt only after consummation of the activity, at which time he would ideally have begun to accumulate profits as a source of capital for future ventures. The landlords permitted mining on their land against deferred payment of rent, either as a fixed sum or as a share of the output. Several of the partnerships mentioned above were financed in this manner.

In such cases, the risk was assumed entirely by the active party, who also made all the decisions.

Deferred payments were important also in trade and merchandising. Credit exchange at the fairs was common. A trader would buy on credit, resell at another fair or market, and repay the debt at the next fair, having completed the business undertaking and made his profit. However, as the fairs declined and merchants ceased to travel, a new system evolved. The simplest form was to promise to repay on a given date (a promissory note in modern terms). Such a method functioned only where the two parties knew each other and a certain degree of trust prevailed between them. In international or intercity trade, a promise was not sufficient. Moreover, it might be difficult for the seller to wait for his money until the buyer had disposed of the goods in another town. Therefore, a new system of deferred payment was devised, which eventually became known as the *bill of exchange*.

Although the bill of exchange took different forms, its standard concept may be described as follows: Merchant A and Merchant B live in two different towns. Each of them has a correspondent in the town where the other resides. Thus A's correspondent X resides in B's town, and B's correspondent Y resides in A's town. Merchant A buys from B a certain quantity of goods but cannot pay immediately or cannot pay in the currency of B's town. Therefore, he signs a draft or a bill of exchange to B, either directly or through Y, for the amount specified to be paid at a given time, in a given currency, and at a specified rate. Either directly through A or indirectly through Y, the bill of exchange is now in the hands of B who approaches X to accept the responsibility of payment. X pays the specified sum to B and holds the bill of exchange until the agreed time when he can collect the sum from A. This system of credit, in its direct and indirect forms, is shown diagramatically in Figure 8.1.

This process is much simplified if X and Y are one and the same agency, acting as correspondent to both merchants, as many bankers do in modern times.

Eventually, the bill of exchange became negotiable so that it became possible for the person holding it to sell it to another party at a discount, relieving himself of the risk and allowing him to reinvest his money, at a cost which is the *discount rate*. The bill of exchange was a landmark in the history of banking, since it removed the need for payment in specie or for transfer of specie. Book transfers became increasingly significant across boundaries, as they had been in local banking for many years.

Profit was an obvious source of capital, encouraging saving and expansion and reducing dependence on outside sources. The rates of return were high in the Middle Ages, especially on international ventures. A 30 percent return on invested capital was not unusual, and 40 or 50 percent was quite common on trips to the Orient. Even on short trips, such as those from Genoa to Sicily, the merchant could easily receive a net return of 25 percent. Unfortunately there is no way of isolating these sources to estimate their relative significance.

It should be noted that where the demand for credit prevailed, ways and means were created to cope with it. Mechanisms were also created to avoid prohibitions on usury and profit; the partnership was itself such a mechanism. The rationale was often advanced that a company or partnership, unlike an individual, had no soul and therefore could not be charged with the sin of usury. Another mechanism was to agree on a given date of amortization in anticipation of failure to pay on that day; when the debtor failed to comply with the letter of the contract, it became legitimate to charge him a penalty for breach of contract. Annuities were regarded as sales for which the payment was spread over a long period and paid in fixed annual amounts, thus accommodating the required interest. These mechanisms were supple-

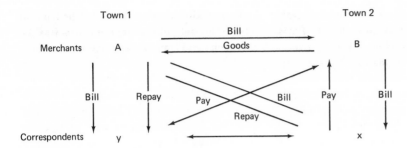

Figure 8.1 System of credit.

mented by the conscious diffusion of interest in the principal or in the rate of exchange for international transactions.

Merchant banking and other facilities

The combination of trade with banking was an important feature of the Italian companies. Most of them were in effect merchant bankers, accepting deposits, advancing credit, and participating in trading activities. This feature was also common outside Italy. The Fuggers of Augsburg, who were second only to the Medici in size, outdid the latter in the variety of their pursuits. The Fuggers were bankers for royalty and for the Pope in the second half of the fifteenth century. They consequently gained control of the German silver mines. The family business, which began early in the fifteenth century, developed so extensively that by the end of the century it

> . . . controlled the mines and metal resources of Germany, Austria, Bohemia and Spain—the California, Nevada, Colorado, and Montana of Europe. They owned the quicksilver and silver mines of Almaden and Guadalcaucal in Spain; copper and silver in Tyrol, and in Hungary. In 1505 they branched out into the East Indian trade.[5]

[5] J. W. Thompson, *Economic and Social History of Europe in the Later Middle Ages, 1300–1530*, p. 426.

In addition to banking and mining, they retained their interest in weaving and textiles, both cotton and wool. They also traded in silk, furs, spices, citrus, arms, and ammunition. Though most of the operations were in the hands of family members, they took on partners and combined with other companies in order to reduce risk and gain a tighter hold on business in general.

Two other methods of facilitating trade by pooling resources deserve mention. The first was the development of galley or shipping lines in the Italian and a few other cities in the fourteenth and fifteenth centuries. To own a ship is not an easy matter; even a partnership may be too small to do so. Therefore, state-owned ships were built and chartered to individuals and partners to run at their own risks for mercantilistic purposes. The galley ships usually traveled in groups or convoys at regular intervals from Genoa or Venice to the Orient and the West.

The second development was merchant interest in mail-carrying. Once the traveling merchant decided to conduct his business through correspondents, factors, or branches, a regular means of communication became necessary. As early as 1181 the merchants agreed among themselves to have mail carried from one place to another. Gradually, however, cities became interested and concluded treaties guaranteeing the safe passage of the mailbag, *scarsella*, handled by special couriers. Frequently this arrangement was made under the auspices of the merchant association. By about 1350 the *scarsella* was leaving at regular intervals, twice a month at first, from Bruges to Paris, Montpellier, and Barcelona. A little over a century later, by ordinance of June 19, 1464, the king of France established postal service throughout his kingdom; this was the first such service in medieval Europe.

BIBLIOGRAPHY

DeRoover, R. A., *Money, Banking and Credit in Medieval Bruges*, Cambridge, Mass.: The Medieval Academy of America, 1948.

Pirenne, H., *Economic and Social History of Medieval Europe*, New York: Harcourt, Brace & World, 1937, chap. 4.

Postan, M., "Credit in Medieval Trade," *Economic History Review*, I (Jan. 1928), pp. 234–261.

Postan, M., E. E. Rich, and Edward Miller (eds.), *The Cambridge Economic History of Europe*, III, New York: Cambridge University Press, 1963, chap. 2.

Thompson, J. W., *Economic and Social History of Europe in the Later Middle Ages, 1300–1530*, New York: Frederick Ungar Publishing Co., 1960, chaps. 18–19.

Usher, A. P., "The Origins of Banking: The Primitive Banks of Deposit, 1200–1600," *Economic History Review*, IV (April 1934), pp. 399–428; reprinted in *Enterprise and Secular Change: Readings in Economic History*, F. C. Lane and J. C. Riemersma (eds.), Homewood, Ill.: Richard D. Irwin, 1953, pp. 262–292.

9

MONEY, PRICES, AND THE LIVING STANDARD

What impact did the economic changes in the Middle Ages have on the daily living of the people? Who benefited from them, how much, and at what cost? To be able to answer such questions we need data on the monetary institutions, the levels of prices and wages, the level of employment, and the significance of public service in society. In one respect our job is simplified by the fact that we are dealing with change rather than with an absolute standard. Nevertheless, the lack of data prevents any absolute conclusions, although tentative observations and suggestions may be made.

To understand the impact of prices and price changes, we should recall that the period under study witnessed numerous new currency issues in most of the countries of Europe. The new issues were often debasements of the former currencies and therefore nominal additions to the money supply. They therefore often had a direct impact on the price levels and the standard of living in the area in which they circulated.

MONEY

In modern times we think of money as a unit of account, as a medium of exchange, and as a store of value. In the twelfth to fifteenth centuries, all these functions were served by the various currencies, although certain denominations served certain functions more than others. For example, small silver currency was used mainly as a medium of exchange, especially in local exchanges. This was the role in the twelfth century of the *denier* in Italy, France, and parts of Germany; the penny of England; and the *pfennige* or *bracteates* of the Baltic area, Saxony, Poland, Silesia, and Bohemia. However, large-scale international trade required larger denominations. These silver pieces were related to the silver *groat*. Venice was the first to issue a larger silver piece; the *grosso* or *metapan* appeared in 1202 and was fixed at 2.18 grams of .965 fine silver, equal to 24 deniers. Verona followed in 1203 with a grosso known as the *soldo veronese*, which was equal to 12 deniers. Florence issued a *soldo* in 1237, and Milan did the same around the middle of the century. The Duchy of Apulia in southern Italy soon after issued a *ducat*. Naples issued a grosso known as the *gigliato* or *carlino* in 1285–1309.

The pattern spread quickly to other countries. France issued the *gros tournois* in 1266, equal to 4.22 grams and to 12 deniers. However, in 1290 it was made equal to $13\frac{1}{8}$ deniers by reducing the value of the denier and raising that of the gros tournois. Aragon issued the *croat* about the same time. The Low Countries began to issue large silver in 1266: Holland was the first, followed by Brabant in 1268, Liège in 1295, and Flanders in 1302. All these issues were based on the gros tournois of France. In the Holy Roman Empire, princes and town imitated the gros tournois in the fourteenth century. Hungary, in contrast, issued *grosehen* like the gigliato of Naples. England issued a groat equal to only four pennies, since the penny had not deteriorated in value as did the denier.

These currencies were related to each other conceptually and sometimes nominally. However, the real value—in content and fineness—varied from one currency to another and even from one period to another. For example, the French raised the value of the gros tournois by reducing the value of the denier, as mentioned above. Around the middle of the fourteenth century they reduced its value by reducing the fineness of the metal, as represented by the new issue of the *blanc*. A similar debasement took place in the Empire in the minting of the *albus*. The silver *mark* of Cologne was equal to 55 groschen in 1226, to 91 in 1350, to 70 in 1378, and to 100 in 1459. In England debasement was carried out by reducing the weight of the coin rather than the fineness of the metal. However, debasement was at its worst in the case of the denier, which in the late Middle Ages was reduced to a token silver content and became known as black money, or *monnaie noire*.

The monetary exchange was further complicated by the fact that bimetallism was common in all the European countries. Gold was minted, first as a continuation of the Roman and Arab heritage, and later as a European tradition. The Byzantine *solidus* and the Arab *dinar* were in circulation in some parts of Europe most of the time. Native gold coins were minted between the mid-tenth and late twelfth centuries in Salerno and Amalfi (*Taris*). A serious attempt to mint gold coins was made in 1231 when Emperor Frederick II minted the *augustale*, but it was significant only as an innovation. A more successful and permanent attempt was made in 1252 when Genoa issued the gold *genovino*; Florence about the same time issued the *florin* which was equal to the geno-

vino and had 3.5 grams of fine gold. It is interesting that the genovino was circulated mostly in the South and gradually replaced the dinar in the Mediterranean area, while the florin found its way northward and became a model for most gold currencies. Venice copied the florin in 1284 by issuing the *zecchino* or gold ducat. About the same time the florin was imitated in Aragon, France, the Low Countries, the Holy Roman Empire, and Hungary. However, various other denominations were also minted periodically, including the *gulden* of the Empire and the Low Countries. France established a national gold coinage around 1290 with various issues; a standard was not established until the *écu* was issued in 1385 equal to 4.079 grams of fine gold and set equal to the *livre tournois*, which was the standard unit of account. In 1344 England minted the *noble*, equal to half a mark or a third of a pound. However, both the écu and the noble eventually were debased by reductions either in weight or in fineness.

Both gold and silver currencies underwent debasement. This was true in Venice, Genoa, and Florence. The Florentine gold florin in 1252 was established equal to 20 *soldi*, but was equal to 111 in 1480. The general policy of debasement was often considered consciously protective and a public service. Sometimes it was intended to check the outflow of specie. It was observed that whenever the price of the metal rose relative to the nominal value of the coin, the currency tended to disappear. Debasement was introduced to check the drain. Or debasement and revaluation were introduced to maintain a given ratio between gold and silver or between one national currency and another, to reduce the impact of speculation.

The confusion inherent in these various monetary policies and units was somewhat mitigated by two factors. On one hand, there was a tendency toward unification of currencies, as happened in the Low Countries and among the Hanseatic towns. The other factor was the existence of what has been termed "ghost money," which served as a standard or unit of account. For example, in 1340 the florin was set equal to 1.6 pounds = 32 shillings = 384 pennies; the pound was equal to 20 shillings = 240 pennies; the shilling was equal to 12 pennies. However, only the florin and the penny were real money; the pound and the shilling were ghost money used only to maintain the relationship between the florin and other currencies. Regardless of the currency in use, there was a tendency to express the value of the transaction in terms of these standard units even though they might not be real, and even though the rate of exchange between a given currency and the unit of account varied. However, there is evidence that the price level was affected directly by debasement of the currency, and that in turn these price movements had significant effects on the distribution of wages, income, and wealth.

PRICES AND WAGES

Price movements are meaningful only when related to a context. The impact of a price change depends on the causes of the change, the responses to it, and on how its effects are distributed. Most of the general influences on prices and wages—such as demographic changes, economic processes, and the policies of guilds, towns, and territorial rulers—have been discussed in previous contexts. The unique local situations are too numerous and insufficiently known to pinpoint. However, we can consider the findings of various researches and try to infer from these illustrations tentative observations regarding price and wage movements.

If relative shortage causes a price rise, which in turn generates an increase in the supply, the change may be a catalyst to the economy and the effects may be generally positive. On the other hand, if prices go up and the supply does not respond, the effects may lead to economic frustration; either the

demand finds a substitute and thus induces reallocation or the prices continue to rise and thus create an atmosphere of speculation and profiteering before demand is reduced to the level of supply at a relatively high price level, at which time reallocation takes place. The first situation increases the available commodities and employment and hence tends to raise living standards. The second may or may not lead to such an increase, depending on the pattern of reallocation and the response of the supply to the change in demand. In fact redirection of resources towards the commodity in question may reduce the quantity of goods on the market, even though the total expenditure and output may remain the same. Thus those who demand the given commodity are satisfied at the expense of those whose commodities are reduced through reallocation.

A more relevant evaluation of price changes can be made by comparing the rates of change in prices and wages. If a lag of wages behind prices results in a reduction in real income, the welfare effect of a price change is obvious, although it may not be measurable. However, a reduction of the real income of one group usually implies an increase in the real income of another, namely those who do not depend on fixed incomes or on lagging wages and salaries. Hence, a redistribution of income takes place in favor of profit-makers.

Debasement and price changes

One of the main reasons for debasement was to increase the nominal money available to the treasury by increasing the quantity of money and appropriating the difference between the original and the new quantities. The relation between debasement and price change has been studied by comparing French and English prices of wheat, found to be a good indicator and subject to common conditions in the two countries. The adjusted price series for the two countries from 1295 to 1395 is shown in Figure 9.1. The

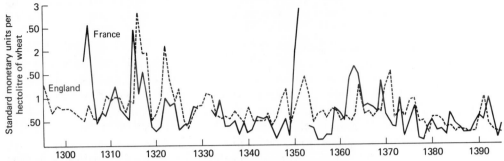

Figure 9.1 Adjusted maximum wheat prices in France and England, 1295–1395.

Prices are expressed in standard monetary units, of which six are drawn from the French mark. Frence prices failed to absorb debasement effects, 1346–1348 and 1355–1358. French prices rose enough to absorb debasement effects, 1310–1313, 1326–1329, 1341, 1343–1345, and 1359–1361. Where curve is broken, evidence is lacking to establish it.

SOURCE: H. A. Miskimin, *Money, Prices, and Foreign Exchange in Fourteenth Century France*, p. 74.

graph shows no secular price rise; actually one may observe a secular decline in the maximum price level of wheat in both countries. However, serious recurrent price fluctuations are observable with certain divergences between the levels in France and England.

Mr. Miskimin's study is based on the assumption that in the absence of price changes to absorb monetary debasement, the divergence between the two price levels would be greater than if the prices responded. In other words, when currency is debased in one country only, unless the price in that country goes up, the two price levels would diverge from each other, assuming all other influences are held constant. Surveying the various periods of serious fluctuation, it appears that in some instances prices did go up to absorb currency debasement, but when they did not the divergence was quite evident. The instances in which the price level responded or failed to respond have been marked on the figure. For example, the divergence of 1340 is explained tentatively by the failure of French prices to rise in response to the debasement of that year. The probability is greater that French prices rose in response to the debasements of 1346–1348 and 1355–1358, but the rise could not have been sufficient, although the evidence is in-

sufficient to warrant firmer conclusions. A more successful absorption of debasement is evident in the price rises of 1310–1313, 1326–1329, 1341, and 1343–1345. The evidence is even more conclusive for the years 1359–1361 in which French prices responded fully to debasement.

Studies of wages and prices

The relation between prices and wages has been studied for England, Valencia, Aragon, and Navarre. England has been studied by Thorold Rogers, Lord Beveridge, and others. A synthesis of the available material shows the patterns of change of prices of a consumer's basket and the wages of workers in the building industry in southern England from the thirteenth to the twentieth centuries.[1] The data are neither complete nor precise enough to warrant firm conclusions. Nevertheless, certain trends are observable. Using an index number series with 1451–1475 equal to 100, a secular rise in the price of the consumer basket is apparent between 1270 and 1380, followed by relative stability up to 1500, after which a sharp rise begins.

[1] A consumer's basket means a standard quantity of consumer goods, of given quality, that can be purchased periodically to measure the changes in the cost of living.

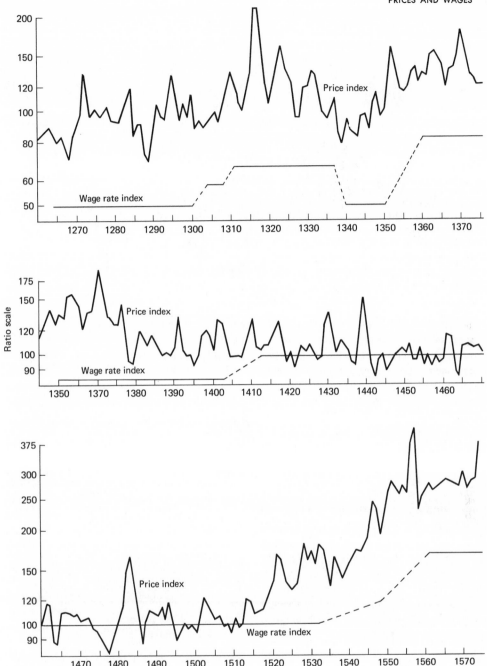

Figure 9.2 Indexes of wage rate of building craftsman and price of composite unit of consumables in southern England, 1264–1954. SOURCE: E. H. Phelps-Brown and Sheila V. Hopkins, "Seven Centuries of the Prices of Consumables Compared with Builders' Wage-Rates," *Economica*, rev. series 23 (Nov. 1956); reprinted in *Essays in Economic History*, II, E. M. Carus-Wilson (ed.), p. 184.

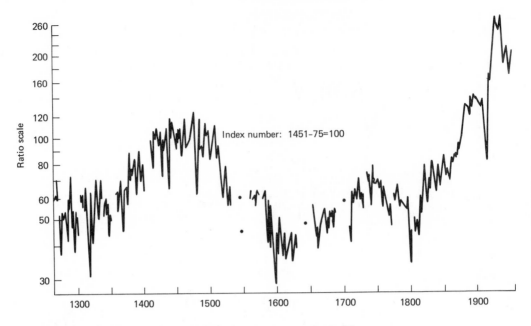

Figure 9.3 Changes in the equivalent of the wage rate of a building craftsman expressed in a composite physical unit of consumables in southern England, 1264–1954.

Source: Brown and Hopkins, "Seven Centuries of the Prices of Consumables Compared with Builders' Wage-Rates," p. 186.

However, there are serious recurrent fluctuations throughout the period, as shown in

In contrast, the wage rate in terms of consumable equivalents tends to rise slowly at the beginning of the fourteenth century and takes a sharp rise near the end. It then maintains a stable pattern for more than a century, after which it begins to decline. Here also we observe serious recurrent fluctuations, as Figure 9.3 shows. The extent to which the wages of builders and craftsmen are representative is not evident, although a certain pattern may be assumed.

The studies of Valencia, Aragon, and Navarre cover a shorter period but they are equally informative. In these studies the price index was computed for several consumer goods while wages were a composite of various trades and of various levels of skill in each trade. Inspection of the data for Valencia shows a high degree of secular stability of both money prices and wages between 1380 and 1500, even though short-

run fluctuations were quite frequent, as Figure 9.4 shows. The result seems to be a stable real income over most of the period with only a few exceptions. With 1421–1430 as a base period, the index ranges between 87.5 in 1413–1415 and 111.4 in 1461–1465, ending at 89.9 in 1500. This means that the standard of living of the wage groups represented in this index held its own over a period of more than a century, in spite of the economic changes that were taking place.

A sharp contrast may be observed in the movement of both money prices and wages in Navarre, where both rose sharply between 1350 and 1400 and then became stable for most of the century, as shown in Figure 9.5. While a lag existed between prices and wages, the real wage tended to rise until about 1400, after which a slow decline set in until the mid-fifteenth century. The data are unclear after that date. With 1421–1430 as a base period, the real wage rises from 55.7 in

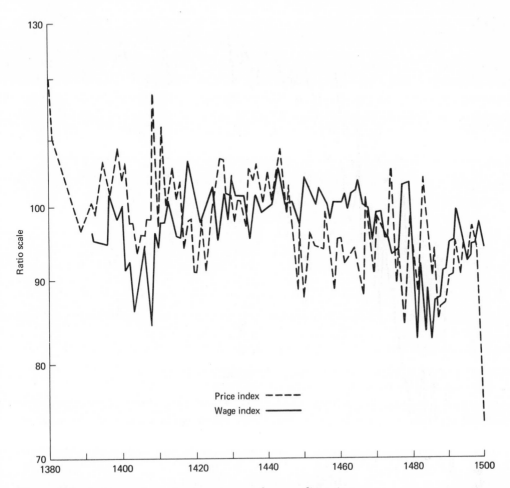

Figure 9.4   Index numbers of money wages and commodity prices
in Valencia.
SOURCE: E. J. Hamilton, *Money, Prices, and Wages in Valencia,
Aragon, & Navarre*, p. 73.

1351–1355 to a high of 116.9 in 1401–1405, but goes down to 93.8 in 1441–1445. These observations are similar to those made for Valencia in the first half of the fifteenth century, the period common to both studies.

The case of Agaron is similar to that of Valencia in terms of the secular stability of money prices and wages, although the periodic fluctuation tended to be more severe in Aragon, as shown in Figure 9.6. The real wage also shows severe short-run fluctuations, although at a higher level of prosperity than was the case in either Valencia or Navarre. With 1421–1430 as a base period,

the real wage index fluctuates from a low of 74.6 in 1411–1415 to a high of 147.7 in 1446–1450, ending at 124.7 in 1496–1500. Throughout most of the fifteenth century the index is higher than the base period, thus suggesting a trend towards improvement of the living standard of those wage workers it represents.

Herman Van Der Wee's study of the Low Countries relates the value of the currency to real wage levels. Figure 9.7 summarizes the changes in the silver content of the Brabant and Flanders groat from 1365 to 1500. In contrast to other currencies, there seems

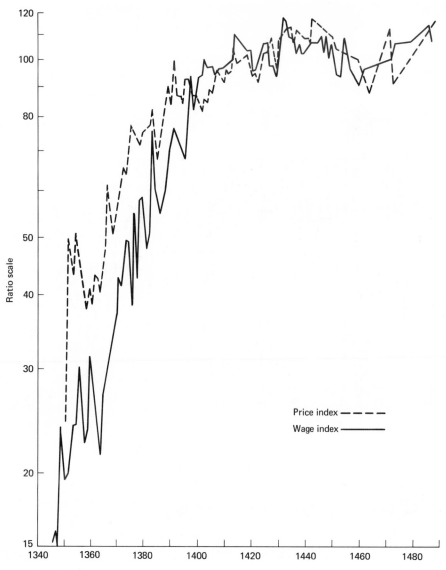

Figure 9.5   Index numbers of money wages and commodity prices in Navarre.
SOURCE: E. J. Hamilton, *Money, Prices, and Wages in Valencia, Aragon, & Navarre*, p. 181.

to have been relative stability in the silver content, although the nominal value was not as stable. Nevertheless, several major fluctuations took place during that period, especially in the value of the Brabant groat, as between 1370–1380, 1420–1430, and 1465–1490. The last two of these periods were ones of expansion and rising prices, although wages were relatively stable in nominal terms. Thus in these periods the real income of the wage earners was lowered, as can be seen in Figure 9.8. It should be noted that the pattern of real wages of masons were similar to those of other urban and agricultural wages. Though the real wage is given as purchasing power in terms of rye,

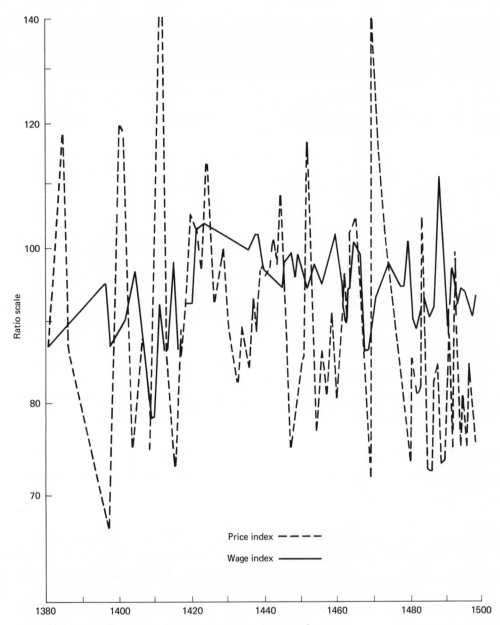

Figure 9.6   Index numbers of money wages and commodity prices in Aragon.
SOURCE: E. J. Hamilton, *Money, Prices, and Wages in Valencia, Aragon, & Navarre*, p. 113.

there was a high degree of similarity in the movement of rye prices and those of other commodities.

Real wages were influenced by currency movements, by the market conditions in- cluding famines, and by the apparent lag of wages behind prices. Wages seem to have been rigid relative to price movements both upward and downward. When prices went up, the impact was felt by the wage earners;

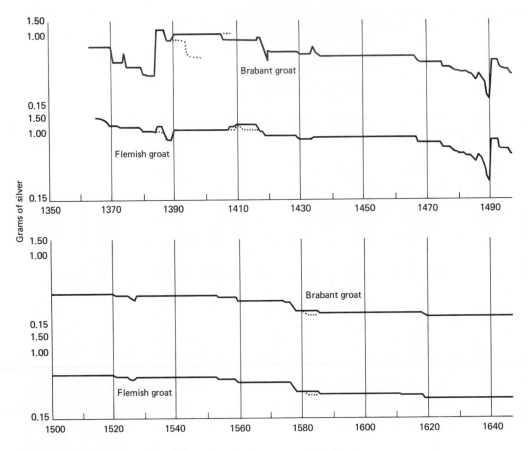

Figure 9.7 Official weight of fine silver in the groat of Brabant
and Flanders, 1363–1650.
SOURCE: Herman Van Der Wee, *The Growth of Antwerp and the
European Economy*, II, pp. 26–27.

when they dropped the employers suffered.
However, a downward movement tended also
to result in unemployment which eventually
affected the wage earners.

The overall standard of living was also
influenced downward by the decline of the
textile industry which, in addition to the
agricultural famine that began in 1437,
caused great hardships for the whole population. The fifteenth century was generally a
period of hardship. The only temporary re-
coveries occurred after monetary reforms in
1389–1390 and 1465, and these affected
chiefly the wage workers, the agricultural
groups, and the small farms. As Table 9.1
shows, the percentage of the population

classified as poor rose radically in the fifteenth century in all areas except the city of
Antwerp, which was on the verge of becoming a major trade and financial center. However, it should be noted that these figures
cover only one census year in which the
standard of living was exceptionally low.
The end of the fifteenth century witnessed a
recovery, at least for the building workers,
as shown in Figure 9.8.

These findings, which are neither complete or necessarily representative, suggest
that the real wage went up between the mid-
fourteenth and mid-fifteenth centuries and
declined slowly after that, with serious
slumps prevailing in the meantime. The rise

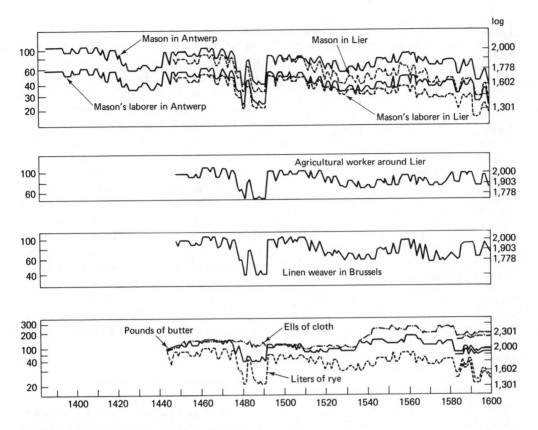

Figure 9.8   Comparison of trends of real income of wage earners
in Antwerp, Lier, and Brussels, 1382–1600.
Calculated on logarithmic figures: interquartile moving medians
over 13 years with application of the option method. *Top*, comparison of purchasing power in liters of rye, of the annual income
of masons and mason's laborers in Antwerp and Lier (adjusted by
the summer–winter ratio of daily wages and by the employment
index of the urban building sector). *Middle two*, comparison of
purchasing power in liters of rye, of the income of linen weavers in
Brussels and agricultural workers around Lier (adjusted by the
employment index of the urban building sector). *Bottom*, comparison of purchasing power of the annual income of an Antwerp
mason in liters of rye, in ells of cloth from Weert and in pounds
of butter.
Source: Herman Van Der Wee, *The Growth of Antwerp and the
European Economy*, II, pp. 90–91. For the figures, see vol. II, part
II, appendix 48.

and decline may be associated with demographic changes, since population tended to
recover after the middle of the fifteenth century from the consequences of the plagues.
One might expect the conditions of the wage
earners to have been better in the advanced
economies of the Italian cities, in Flanders,
and in the other export-producing centers.
However, the evidence available for Brabant
and Flanders does not support this hypothesis. Therefore, the trend may be assumed to
be somewhat uniform, given the generality of
demographic effects and the high dependence
of the export market on wage workers.

Table 9.1. Poverty hearths in Brabant in the fifteenth century as percentage of total hearths

	1437	1480	SECOND HALF OF FIFTEENTH CENTURY
Antwerp	13.5%	10.5%	
Small towns around Antwerp	9.3%	17.3%	
Antwerp countryside			26.0%
Louvain	7.6%	18.3%	
Small towns around Louvain	8.75%	35.7%	
Louvain countryside			16.2%
Brussels countryside			46.6%

SOURCE: *Herman Van Der Wee, The Growth of Antwerp and the European Economy, II, pp. 70, 294. "By poor hearths the census meant people who did not possess any fortune and who had no sufficient income to pay ducal or governmental taxes"* (p. 35).

Effects of economic changes on other groups

Wage workers were only one group in a population which was still mainly agricultural. We have noted in Chapter 5 and in Table 9.1 the possible effects of the economic changes of the fourteenth and fifteenth centuries on the rural groups. The effects were differentially distributed, but most of the middle-size peasant farmers were negatively effected. The impact on the landlords was mixed; many of them were not only able to cope with the problems but succeeded in improving their lot. The cottars and workers benefited from the expanding opportunities.[2]

The merchants and manufacturers, as well as the bankers and service producers, depended primarily on profits. Since profits are the difference between costs and revenues, it should be possible to evaluate them. Unfortunately, data for this period are not available, although illustrations can suggest tentative observations. Since technology was not highly developed, the highest cost item in

manufacturing was probably labor. Fixed capital was a relatively small percentage of the total cost, while raw material was probably a little more. As we have seen, labor costs did go up gradually until the early years of the fifteenth century when they began to decline in four of the five areas studied. Thus, in the absence of technological change and higher labor productivity, the unit labor cost rose for a period, and then declined throughout most of the fifteenth century. The cost of capital in the form of interest charges generally declined from the thirteenth through the fifteenth centuries. Commercial loans, which are of particular interest in this context, carried a rate of interest between 20 and 25 percent in Italy during the thirteenth century. In the fourteenth century they were between 7 and 15 percent, and around 10 percent in the early fifteenth century; the range, however, continued to be between 7 and 15 percent. The rate in thirteenth-century northern Europe ranged between 15 and 20 percent in Champagne, and between 10 and 16 percent in the Low Countries. It remained the same in the Low Countries in the fourteenth century and dropped slightly in the fifteenth century. Personal loans were always higher, while public loans, many of which were forced loans, were always lower. Thus, while labor costs were rising, capital costs were declining. Since the production function is not known, it is difficult to estimate the degree to which these trends offset each other. Nevertheless, we know that prices of manufactured goods were rising. Assuming no reduction of total demand, as indicated by the price structure, it seems that profits were rising throughout the period. Even where they remained stable, the profit rates were relatively high, particularly in the service industries such as banking and trade.

Another indication that the profits of merchants and bankers were relatively high may be the relatively high rates of interest on capital. Merchant bankers were willing to pay guaranteed returns of 8 percent or

[2] For a fuller discussion of these groups, see Chapter 5.

more on deposits only because they could advance loans at higher rates, or because they could earn higher profit rates if they used the capital in their own businesses. Furthermore, commercial loans could be advanced at 20 to 25 percent rates only because the profit prospects were high. It is even more interesting to note that when the rates went down, the prices were still high and rising and thus the profit prospects were getting brighter. The lack of sufficient data precludes more precise conclusions, but the trend is unmistakable. Those who depended on profit were enjoying an improvement in their levels of income as a result of the lag of costs behind revenues, the redistribution of incomes in their favor, and the advances made in manufacturing and the service industries.

It would be helpful to construct a general index of the standard of living during the thirteenth to fifteenth centuries for various parts of Europe. However, in the absence of detailed income and price data, and of information regarding the distribution and level of employment, no such index seems possible. Nor is it possible to compare the changes in the different parts of Europe at this time. It is apparent that a certain degree of improvement in living standard was taking place, but that improvement was differentially distributed in favor of the rising bourgeoisie and skilled workers, while landowners and middle peasants were suffering a decline. The position of the workers who lived at subsistence could move only upward, except in periods of famine when starvation might have been their fate. The nobility and royalty managed to hold their own, when they did, by sharing the benefits of the commercial economy, by manipulating taxes and imposing forced loans, by raising the dues on their tenants, by inflating the currency through debasement and reminting, or, as in eastern Europe, by reviving serfdom. Within this class a certain degree of redistribution of wealth and income was taking place in favor of the more enterprising and those closer to the central government, which was gaining in importance in large parts of the continent.

BIBLIOGRAPHY

Cipolla, Carlo, *Money, Prices and Civilization in the Mediterranean World,* Princeton: Princeton University Press, 1956.

Einzig, Paul, *The History of Foreign Exchange,* New York: St. Martin's Press, 1962, chaps. 7–10.

Hamilton, E. J., *Money, Prices, and Wages in Valencia, Aragon, & Navarre,* Cambridge, Mass.: Harvard University Press, 1936.

Homer, Sidney, *A History of Interest Rates,* New Brunswick, N. J.: Rutgers University Press, 1963, chaps. 8–9.

Miskimin, H. A., *Money, Prices and Foreign Exchange in Fourteenth-Century France,* New Haven: Yale University Press, 1963, chap. 5.

Phelps-Brown, E. H., and Sheila V. Hopkins, "Seven Centuries of Building Wages," *Economica,* Rev. series 22 (Aug. 1955), pp. 195–206; reprinted in *Essays in Economic History,* II, E. M. Carus-Wilson (ed.), New York: St. Martin's Press, 1966, pp. 168–178.

Phelps-Brown, E. H., and Sheila V. Hopkins, "Seven Centuries of the Prices of Consumables, Compared with Builders'

Wage-Rates," *Economica*, Rev. series 23 (Nov. 1956). pp. 296–314; reprinted in *Essays in Economic History*, II, E. M. Carus-Wilson (ed.), New York: St. Martin's Press, 1966, pp. 179–196.

Postan, M., E. E. Rich, and Edward Miller (eds.), *The Cambridge Economic History of Europe*, III, New York: Cambridge University Press, 1963, especially the appendix on money.

Van Der Wee, Herman, *The Growth of Antwerp and the European Economy*, II, The Hague: Martins Nijhoff, 1963, pp. 289–308, 381–388, and 429–436.

10
THE MIDDLE AGES COME TO AN END

Although it may be an oversimplification to speak of the end of the Middle Ages, a comparison of the years 1450–1500 with the tenth-eleventh centuries may bring into focus the magnitude and quality of change that took place in this period. The comparison can be made in terms of the framework set up in Chapters 2 and 4. It will provide a general picture of the European economy to serve as a background for our study of mercantilism.

Table 10.1 summarizes the changes that took place in the Middle Ages. It should be pointed out, however, that these changes are both quantitative and qualitative, although the differences cannot be measured accurately because of insufficient data. It is also important to emphasize that some countries were ahead of others in one or more areas. Our discussion of these changes will emphasize the terminal period to avoid repetition.

SOCIOPOLITICAL STRUCTURE

The beginning of the period under study was characterized by a decline of the central power, the rise of feudal lordships, and the increasing autonomy of the local lord. Any relation with the territorial prince or monarch was one of vassalage and token homage based mostly on mutual aid in military and security matters. The lord was at the same time the political master and the economic patron. He owned the land, dispensed justice, and represented the community in political affairs. The community was highly polarized between the nobility and the serfs and tenants, although there was a small group of free peasants who owned their land and had some say in the affairs of the community. The lord controlled the spiritual and social life of the community since he supported the local church and sponsored festivities. That structure was relatively stable and unchallenged especially because of the diffusion of economic, political, and social power among the feudal lords and their representatives.

By the end of the era an almost total change in these relations had taken place in most of Europe. The major exception was in eastern Europe, where the political structure was still segmented and the class structure relatively rigid. Even where town power had grown, the lords were still powerful economically as well as politically. The Holy Roman Empire was widely segmented with many centers of power, many sets of regulations, and many autonomous bodies who often resorted to internal conflict and even war. This segmentation is best illustrated by the diversity of law codes. The Teutonic order had its own personal and local codes, the knights had the *Lehrenrecht,* the countryside had the *Landrecht,* the manors had the

Table 10.1. Comparative summary of the changes in Medieval Europe

TENTH–ELEVENTH CENTURIES	1450–1500
SOCIOPOLITICAL STRUCTURE	
Decentralized, feudalistic, and polarized society	Tendency toward central authority; decline of feudal power; city-states in decline; more diffusion and less polarization
No middle class	Bourgeoisie on the rise
Diffusion of political, spiritual, and economic power	Separation of political from the economic and spiritual power structures
Relatively stable class structure	Apparent rapid change in social relations
ECONOMIC STRUCTURE	
Subsistence economy based on agriculture	Commercial economy evident; agriculture still predominant, but trade and manufacturing important
Concentration of control of means of production	Control of means of production diffuse and less concentrated
Stability through inheritance and tradition; decision-making tradition-bound or mechanistic	Decision-making more rational; tradition on the decline; contractual agreements on the rise
Rigid interdependence between landlord and peasant or employer and employee	Anonymous relationship between employer and employee; room for mobility
Corporate organization—manorial, traditionally managed	Individualistic and cooperative organization—partnerships and pooling of resources with improved management techniques
Demand and supply relatively in balance at a low level of production; small surplus	Imbalance between supply and demand at a higher level; more surplus
Exchange mainly local; barter, segmented market	Exchange national and international; money terms; expanded market
Low level of technology	Improved technology: gunpowder, printing, water and windmills, ship-building
Land/labor ratio highly favorable	Land/labor ratio relatively unfavorable: need for alternatives
Limited horizon: poor transportation, distance —sparse rural population, lack of capital, local security and lack of incentives, no urge to change	Expanded horizon: land and water transport, reduced distance, credit facilities, demonstration effect, international mobility, increased urge to change
Internal security	Hazards of unemployment and destitution

Hofrecht, the cities had the *Stadtrecht,* the guilds had the *Zünfrecht,* and the peasants had the *Bauernrecht.* These laws were not codified and were often contradictory, while the central power was too weak to maintain uniformity or enforce the law. The closest to a central authority were the Hanseatic alliances, which were on the decline by the end of the fifteenth century.

A pattern of segmentation similar to that of Germany existed in Italy during the later period. While the Italian cities had vast territorial jurisdictions, each formed its own state authority. No central power existed to join them together, unify their laws, or form a political union among them. The cities did overshadow the feudal lords who had prevailed in the earlier period, and they enlarged the unit of political power, but they fell short of creating a unifying central power. This failure might have been due to the fact that the Italian cities were already showing signs of decline by the end of the Middle Ages. This apparent decline was in part due to overextension of each of the city-states and the failure to pool political and economic resources to maintain their international influence. However, the Italian cities were ahead of most other regions in redistributing power, reducing polarization, and permitting the emergence of a middle class of capitalists and manufacturers. The bourgeoisie were in fact responsible for the new structure of political power and the city policies.

In contrast, central power evolved in England, Scandinavia, the Low Countries, France, Spain, Poland, Hungary and Russia, although with varying degrees of success. England, for example, had already recognized the role of the people in managing their affairs. The Magna Carta had established a certain partnership between the king and the lords, by which the power of the monarchy was nationally acknowledged. The king of France was less well established and therefore was still groping for more power, often at the expense of a wider distribution of power among the towns and guilds. In both cases the central power became distinct from and superior to the locally dominant economic forces. The king was only one of many landlords, but he was the king of all. In this atmosphere the cities offered the opportunity for an economically powerful middle class to emerge and reduce the polarization in society. The king had the rights and duties of taxation, control over markets, protection against enemies, and maintenance of law and order. He also upheld standards of industry and production. Even when these powers were misused, their economic and political impact was radically different from that of the segmented and decentralized power structure of the earlier period. The power of the Church was also made subordinate to the lay authorities. Anti-ecclesiatic legislation was passed in various parts of Germany and Italy. The king of France took control of the Church property, thus further reducing possible segmentation of authority.

ECONOMIC STRUCTURE, ORGANIZATION, AND OUTLOOK

Economic activity in the early period was directed mainly towards subsistence or local use. Agriculture was the mainstay of the economy. Artisans and craftsmen were mostly part-time farmers. They catered to their own needs and to those in the local community, and produced little for trade outside the manorial economy. In contrast, the medieval economy of the later period was based largely on trade and commerce, for which crafts were developed and manufacturing expanded. There are no data on the percentage of the population occupied outside agriculture, or on the national income deriving from nonagricultural activities. We do know, however, that urban centers grew large and that they depended on nonagricultural production. The development of craft and merchant guilds is another indication of the growing dependence on nonagricultural employment. The expansion of trade into international markets suggests the development of ship-building, which flourished in various coastal cities, especially in Italy and the Low Countries. Trade and commerce indicate further that the economy had moved a long way since the beginning of the period. Urban centers and services, including middlemen, can be supported only if there is surplus production above the subsistence requirements of the producers.

Rise of the commercial economy

The change from subsistence agriculture to a commercial mixed economy was accompanied by a shift of control of the means of production from a monolithic to a multilithic structure. The landlord owners who had controlled the means of production were replaced. Land became less important and capital more important. Now there were many owners, including people whose economic power was independent of land. This diffusion of economic control over the means of production increased the mobility of factors and products. Indeed, commercial ventures were undertaken by people who would have been penniless outcasts in the earlier structure. This diffusion of control had significant effects on the stability of the economy, the distribution of income and wealth, and the decision-making process. It also led to more competition and efficiency in economic activity. We can easily observe this shift in at least three respects: The conflict between the urban and the rural economies, or between the bourgeoisie and the feudal lords; the growing power of the merchants and bankers; and the increasing dependence on contractual agreements.

The rise of the urban economy with its anonymous actors reduced the dependence on tradition and enhanced the relevance of the contract. Each contract was concluded by the parties on its own merits. Thus, these parties made their own decisions which were valid only for the duration of the contract. They were not bound forever by traditional patterns to which they had made no contribution. The shift to a contractual basis was a major blow to the stability of the traditional economy. The individual was enabled to pursue his self-interests, make his own decisions, and seek opportunity as he saw fit. He no longer was subject to a mechanistic process of decision-making. Relatively advanced managerial techniques, with sophisticated accounting and supervision methods, were a logical consequence of this change.

The early economic unit was run as a corporate structure: decision-making in the manor was controlled from above, and all members of the economy were subjected to these decisions. The manor has sometimes been described as a collective economy, but in fact the members had no share in the decision-making process, and their rewards were traditionally established or were determined from above. This corporate structure had by the end of the fifteenth century broken down even in agriculture and certainly outside it. Except for East Germany and eastern Europe, agriculture was now decentralized in the hands of tenants who made their own decisions. Whether *censiers*, copyholders, or *metayers*, the peasants were free agents as far as economic activities were concerned. They could leave the land, rotate the crops, diversify production, and sell products on the markets. They also reaped the fruits of their initiative and hard work. Individual enterprise had become a characteristic feature of agriculture throughout most of Europe.

Individualism and free enterprise were even more characteristic of the nonagricultural economy in the later period. While the craftsmen and merchants formed associations, their behavior was relatively unrestricted, and by the end of the period they could pursue their endeavors according to their own initiative. However, the change did not preclude certain collective efforts, represented by the various partnerships in trade and banking. Whether these were temporary or permanent, partnerships permitted cooperation, pooling of resources, distribution of risk, and enlargement of the scale of production, all of which had hardly existed in the manorial economy. These partnerships were based on individual initiative rather than on tradition or regulation. The capitalistic free-enterprise system was replacing the traditional corporate organization.

The change was in part related to the interaction between supply and demand. In the early subsistence economy, the forces of supply and demand were relatively in balance at a low level of output, leaving little room for expansion. The little surplus that was produced was not sufficient to stimulate trading and exchange. In the later period, production of surplus permitted exchange and acquisition of imported goods. The increase of demand was accompanied by high hopes of being satisfied by the larger market. The producer who managed to produce a surplus was no longer worried about disposing of it. Thus, the economy of the later period was not only one of surplus and exchange, but also one of higher production and consumption, or a potentially higher standard of living. The rise of the living standard was both quantitative and qualitative. Surplus and exchange meant diversification of the consumer basket, at least for those who participated in the market. Instead of depending on local products, the consumer could acquire products from other areas, thus satisfying both his needs and desires. The quality of the demand market was changed from one catering mainly to needs to one catering to both needs and wants in which economic forces played a more significant role. Once this change had taken place, the earlier stability deriving from the relative balance between demand and supply was bound to be disturbed. Although the balance might be restored, usually the fluctuations were more severe, although of shorter duration. For example, demand in the earlier period could be satisfied only at harvest or after. In the later period, such demand could be satisfied by imports at any time. Therefore, there was less reason to suppress it.

Basic changes

These various changes were obviously related to fundamental differences in the economic foundations of the two periods. The economies of the early period were based on three main interconnected conditions: low technology, a relatively favorable land/labor ratio, and a limited horizon. Production in agriculture was based on primitive methods and almost completely depended on nature. Men and beasts were the sources of power and, therefore, productivity was relatively low. Manufacturing was limited to the home or to a small shop in the larger manors. Its power too was manual and techniques were little developed. Knowledge and skill were transmitted mainly through observation and apprenticeship. While no major technological revolution took place before the end of the fifteenth century, certain improvements had occurred. Agriculture was using heavier plows; field rotation and some crop rotation were practiced; new crops had been introduced in some regions; even irrigation was used. There was some new awareness of the impact of legumes on the fertility of the soil. Finally, there was growing attention to in-

dustrial crops such as cotton, flax, and wool. Added to the expanding market, these new attitudes tended to encourage commercialization of agriculture for export purposes as well as for local exchange.

Technology had improved even more outside agriculture, and additional sources of power had been introduced. Water and wind were now utilized in mills for fulling and dyeing textiles and sawing lumber. Shipbuilding had advanced, and carrying capacity and speed had been increased by more than 100 percent. Gunpowder had come into use, thus modifying the art of war and reducing dependence on the knights and lords who had provided military service. Probably the most important invention was the printing press which revolutionized the expansion of knowledge and skill.

In manufacturing and trade, double-entry bookkeeping had become common practice. A significant organizational change had taken place in manufacturing. The increasing demand for export goods had rendered the old form of production inadequate, and in its place the putting-out system was coming into existence. Not only was production for the merchant capitalist under way, but a certain degree of specialization was also evident. This pattern of production was little developed as yet, but the trend was quite apparent.

Another fundamental difference between the two periods was the change in the land/labor ratio. The vast European continent was sparsely populated in the early period. Even though technology was at a low level, it was possible to absorb population increases by horizontal expansion on the land. Therefore there was little pressure to seek alternative sources of income outside agriculture. In the later period this situation had changed. Not only had technology in agriculture remained relatively stagnant, but much of the land had been settled. Although further expansion and clearing of the land were still to come, most of the easily accessible areas had been put to cultivation. The land/labor ratio had diminished through population increase and public policy. In Germany, for example, the state laid claim to the forests and wooded areas, thus reducing further the amount of available land, while individual princes controlled the water. The magnitude of the change can only be estimated. A reduction of the land/labor ratio by more than one-half seems plausible since less than half of the total population was outside agriculture. This estimate takes into account the effects of the Black Death, without which the land/labor ratio would have been reduced even further. The pressure on the land was an important influence towards seeking alternatives outside agriculture in trade and manufacturing.

This push factor was augmented by a pull factor which did not exist in the early period, namely a broader economic horizon. In the early period the means of transportation were poor, the markets were small and far apart, and capital was lacking both because of the low surplus and because of the lack of credit institutions. The hazards of leaving one's birthplace were many. Furthermore, there was enough economic security within the community to reduce the incentive to move out. All these conditions had changed by the later period. Transportation had improved both on the land and on water. Cities had taken the responsibility for maintaining roads, especially those leading to the fair or market under their jurisdiction. Central governments had begun to pay attention to roads. Wheel carts were being used. Water transportation had improved enough so that by the end of the period ocean-going vessels were being built and operated. The ship capacity had reached 600 tons, several times what it was in the early period. Finally, communication had been improved by the institution of a mail service.

A more important factor in expanding the horizon was the expansion of credit and the establishment of credit institutions. Though credit had always existed, in the later period banking institutions had become fully developed for deposit as well as loans. The importance of these facilities was that they allowed those with insufficient capital to undertake ventures which otherwise would have been out of their reach. The enterprising individual was no longer tied down by his inherited fortune or misfortune, and could pursue opportunities even on borrowed capital. Capital was also made more available through partnerships and joint ventures. An important indicator of the change was the openness with which interest charges were accepted in the later period. While the authorities still frowned upon usury, they allowed the charging of interest within the limits of the law. The governments of France, Spain, and the Low Countries, among others, fixed the maximum rates that could be charged. They themselves borrowed and paid the interest charges that were due. Thus, the credit market had become a legitimate place of business.

Another factor in the expansion of the horizon was the growth of international trade and the concomitant international mobility of labor. Italian artisans could move to Flanders, England, and Russia. Hanseatic merchants could roam all over the northern part of the continent. Merchant bankers opened branch offices or set up representations in other towns and countries. State governments established rules regarding foreigners. In 1471 France imported skilled people to operate the mines; Italians came for ship-building; Germans came for metal work and printing; miners came from the Rhine country and Swabia. Other countries were no longer mysteries to the medieval European, and the relatively static life he had led previously was no longer acceptable. The urge to move and change was growing more acute as the horizon was becoming more extensive. By the end of the fifteenth century Europeans had reached distant continents. The Cape of Good Hope had been discovered. The way to the Orient had been explored. North America had been reached. The stability which had characterized the early period had been shattered. Europe was on the verge of a leap into the wider horizon of the New World.

The cost
of change

These changes were not without costs. Nor were their benefits uniformly distributed. On one hand, the economic security which the individual had enjoyed in the corporate structure of the early period was removed. His fear of hunger had become genuine. His independence from his employer relieved the latter of his obligations to provide land for cultivation and food and seed in times of famine. Now the individual depended on employment, which was a function of a market over which he had no control. In other words, one of the costs of the change was alienation and the beginning of a proletariat whose fortune was in flux. The same problem existed on the national level in the greater sensitivity of the economy to price fluctuations. When barter was pre-dominant and exchange was limited, this problem was nonexistent. However, as monetary exchange became the rule, the local economy became subject to external influences on prices and employment such as inflation and dislocation. When the authorities tried to protect against these hazards, the results were often regulations which hindered economic activity. International competition and monetary fluctuations left their impact on the economies of the later period. Newcomers into the market began to replace older leaders. The Italian cities which had mastered trade in large parts of Europe had to contend with strong competitors. Florence, for example, was already losing ground in cloth manufacturing and trade to South Germany, Flanders, and the French Midi. Protection of the market by the central government was introduced to reduce the impact of competition, especially by protecting infant industries and securing carrying services for natives. These tendencies, however, were just beginning.

MERCANTILISM
A PERIOD OF TRANSITION
PART
THREE

11

THE
GENERAL
FRAMEWORK

The period extending roughly between A.D. 1500 and 1700 has been recognized as a critical one in the economic history of the western world. Some observers in fact suggest that the foundations of the economic upsurge of Europe and the West which occurred in the next two centuries were laid during this period. Why then do we separate the period 1500–1700 from those before and after? A simple answer is that it has been the custom to deal with these years separately as the mercantilist period. More important, these two centuries, while sharing certain features with the surrounding periods, have some unique characteristics.

The theories which deal with this era usually treat it as the stepping-stone towards the next period, thus depriving it of any significance of its own. For example, Max Weber discovered the rise of rationality necessary for modern economic behavior in the Reformation of this period. Marx discovered in this era the beginning of capitalism, primitive accumulation, and alienation, which became characteristic of capitalist society. Rostow saw it as the pre-takeoff stage of development, relating its significance closely to the takeoff. Hamilton discovered that the profit inflation which was enjoyed in this period contributed to the development of capitalism. Webb emphasized the significance of the Great Frontier which

was discovered and exploited as a step towards the developments of the next period. The era has also been described as one of commercial revolution since commerce expanded greatly, and as the period of the first industrial revolution because coal replaced wood as fuel. Probably the only comprehensive theory or framework which treats these years as a distinct state of being with its own policies and objectives is that of Eli Heckscher. However, Heckscher's theory does not deal with transition in general, but only with a specific series of historical experiences which constitute a transition from one state to another, namely from disunity to unity, as prerequisite for national economic development. All these theories, however, contribute to the attempt to formulate a general framework within which to place the events of the period as expressions of the transition.

THE ECONOMICS
OF TRANSITION

The economics of transition can provide an appropriate framework for our study. Transition may be characterized as follows:

1. Transition is a process with an objective which may or may not be known or consciously aimed at. A continuation of the process is sure to lead away from the pre-

existing conditions, but the consequences may or may not be identifiable because of the multiplicity and variability of objectives.

2. The process of transition is based on a feeling of disenchantment with the status quo and an anticipation of different and possibly better things to come. Discontent implies disharmony between what members of society have and what they wish to have. However, unless there is reason to expect realization of these wishes, the process of transition may never get off the ground.

3. The rate at which transition proceeds will vary according to the degree of disharmony, the certainty of accomplishment, and the external competition for the same results. The greater the disharmony the more anxious the members of society become to realize the transition. However, the process requires reinforcement which comes from evidence that realization is possible. The safe passage of one ship through the straits may be sufficient to induce people to undertake similar voyages. The first gold finds may create a rush to mine the gold. This process becomes even more rapid if there is fear that outsiders may lay claim to and exclude others from these finds. This is especially true if the objectives involve a scarce resource.

4. The process of transition encourages experimentation and the search for shortcuts. In the absence of known procedures for realizing objectives, experimentation becomes necessary. This process may even lead to unintended, high, nonrational costs such as war, enmity, and destruction. It may also compromise moral values by the assumption that the ends justify the means, although the policy-makers would not admit to such nonrational behavior.

5. The process also results in dislocations, hardships, and the redistribution of costs and benefits among the social groups in transition. To the extent that new methods are introduced, the field will be open to new actors, be they individuals, groups, or nations. Each ethos tends to create its own disciples who, as first-comers, have an advantage over the agents of the former ethos, many of whom may be displaced in the process of transition. One might consider these processes of dislocation and redistribution as concomitant with the processes of innovation and obsolescence, the benefits being concentrated in favor of the innovator and the costs to the disadvantage of the outdated. Before the process of transition is completed several dislocations may take place. These costs may also be a result of a misallocation or overextension of resources which makes a decline inevitable.

6. The process of transition will end only when the benefits have been perpetuated in favor of one or more actors, at which time a new ethos will have evolved to guarantee a certain degree of continuity and stability. By this time spheres of influence will have been established, competition or lack of it will have been institutionalized, and the new outlets will have been opened up for full exploitation. The end of the transition may also be brought about by the discovery of a new objective or resource superseding that to which the transition was originally directed. In such a case the expected benefits will have diminished in relative value so much that the costs of acquiring them will have become prohibitive.

AN OVERVIEW

This general framework is tentatively derived from the economic history of the period under consideration. Whether or not it fits other experiences remains to be seen. Europe underwent a transition between A.D. 1500 and 1700 in several directions, some of which are mentioned below.

Political change

Two important developments in the political sphere mark this period. The first is the continuation of the tendency toward the formation of the national state begun at the end of the medieval period. The mercantilist period saw an almost complete fulfillment of this tendency in most of the

European countries. The exceptions were Germany and Italy, which remained segmented until the nineteenth century. The second development was the political expansion into new lands, the setting up of colonies, and eventually the creation of empires. This expansion had important economic consequences because it expanded Europe's market for both raw material and finished products. It also meant an increase in the facilities for labor mobility from the Old to the New World.

The unification of the Russian state also occurred in this period. Until the fifteenth century Russia had suffered from fragmentation and foreign occupation. However, in this period a central authority was established and Russia became an active participant in the economic affairs of Europe.

The political structure of both the European countries and the colonies underwent fundamental changes in this period before stability could be established. For example, domination in the colonies was originally predicated on the acquisition of economic advantages by trading companies, in cooperation with local chiefs. Before the period was over, this domination had become political and the responsibility for maintaining it had shifted from trading companies to the national governments. However, this responsibility was to shift again to the governments of the colonies themselves in most cases.

The fact that in expanding the Europeans encountered societies that were less developed politically and technologically made the colonial relationship one of dependence rather than interdependence. The underdeveloped societies frequently lost their civilizations and sometimes their existence. This relationship was transitional also: The Europeans were transplanting their own cultures into the colonies and as soon as the number of migrants became relatively large, they rebelled and established their own independence. However, in this period the migrants were small in number and the natives were unable or unwilling to free themselves

of the foreign yoke. Consequently, during this period European hegemony was fully established.

Changes in economic philosophy

Another transition in this period was the shift from an economic doctrine based on ethics and morality to one based on rational calculation and accounting. This period witnessed the beginning of economic science. The mercantilists wrote books on economics and policy-makers tried to justify their actions in economic terms. Probably the most important development in this respect was the beginning of macro analysis, as represented by considerations of the impact of foreign trade on the economy as a whole. There was talk of the wealth of the nation, the prosperity of the country, and the welfare of the consumer. All these concepts were used in the aggregate for the first time. Considerations of the quantity of money were raised, also in aggregate terms. These concepts, however, were clearly connected with national policy. Thus restrictions were placed on exports or imports or on the flow of specie, and privileges were granted to traders and companies, in behalf of the welfare or wealth of the nation. These policies reached their peak in what came to be known as the Navigation Laws, which were not abandoned until the middle of the nineteenth century, even though most of them had lost their relevance long before then.

The transitory nature of these policies may best be illustrated by the attitude toward slavery and labor mobility. Slavery was rationalized as necessary for the cultivation of the new lands which supplied the raw material on which the national economies depended. To make the policy even more acceptable, the Pope sanctioned it as a means of converting the heathens, while the Protestants justified it as a way of saving the slaves from Catholicism. The national state let these rationalizations stand, since the end result was supposed to be beneficial for the economy as a whole. The attitude toward labor can also be illustrated by the survival of serfdom in many countries, especially in central and eastern Europe. Old customs were revived and new obligations introduced which resulted in the subjugation of most of the peasantry to new forms of servitude.

Intellectual change

The period was transitional intellectually and scientifically. This was the time of the Reformation which established new relations between man and God, between man and nature, and between man and the Church. The new relationships were more consistent with the economic events of the centuries to follow, as Weber has suggested. This rationality was accompanied by new approaches to the physical world. Interest in positive phenomena and in scientific explanation was growing. Scientific knowledge had been adopted from the Romans or the Arabs, now it was an indigenous product. Europe produced Galileo and Bacon, Descartes, and Newton in this period. While their theories were not put to use until later, they put Europe on its way to supremacy in scientific and technological achievement.

The economy

In the area of economic activity, this period had little innovation to offer. However, two developments deserve attention: the extensive commercial expansion in the form of chartered and regulated companies, and the putting-out system of production. Both developments were transitory and by the end of the period both were proving inconsistent with the economic requirements of industrialization and development. Monopolies were to be superseded by competition, free enterprise, and individualism. This change was made possible by the division between the economic and political roles played by these companies. As the companies' political roles were assumed by the national governments, it ceased to be expedient to give them monopolies. Their economic roles were opened to individuals and groups who were willing to take risks and compete for the benefits.

The putting-out system of production was the second important development. This was a mechanism by which capital and labor could be combined in production to satisfy the increasing demand for products. The weaknesses of this system were known in this period, but because its benefits outweighed its costs, it was tolerated. However, it was no longer adequate when demand increased appreciably and when mechanization made the gathering-in of producers necessary.

Another aspect of the economic transition was the predominance of trade and commerce and the dependence on external treasures as sources of wealth. The transition was completed when manufacturing became the basis for national wealth in the next period. This change was reflected in the socioeconomic relations in society. The producers and manufacturers were to gain in status, in part at the expense of the merchants. The countries that depended largely on services for their income were surpassed by those that developed manufacturing. Spain, for example, which depended more on services, was surpassed by England, which relied on manufacturing.

Government in transition

Finally, the system of government was transitional. Though unification and centralization had taken place, the relations between the head of state and the legislative agencies were not formalized. Nor were the relations between the Church and state fully stabilized. The regular sources of revenue were neither adequate nor well organized. Bankruptcies among the monarchs were common. New taxes and devious ways of extracting revenue were the order of the period. Sale of offices and nepotism were almost institutionalized and the personal and informal touch still characterized government. These conditions often proved incapable of sustaining government or of creating mutual trust between it and the governed. By the end of the period, however, a change toward more formal and rational methods of government and public finance had become apparent.

These developments have been described as transitions indicating that mercantilism was a passing phase, preparing for the next period.[1] Yet, without at least some of these developments, later developments might not

---

[1] Some authors take the opposite view, considering mercantilism as the normal state of affairs, and the short period of *laissez-faire* of the nineteenth century as the transitory phase: C. W. Cole, *Colbert and a Century of French Mercantilism*, II, New York: Columbia University Press, 1939, p. 557; contrast this with E. Lipson, *The Economic History of England*, 6th ed., II, London: Adam and Charles Black, 1956, 1964, pp. ii–iii.

have come about at all. For example, without the development of rationality, the primitive accumulation of capital, or the expansion of the market into the Great Frontier, Europe might have gone in a totally different direction. A pessimist might suggest a decline as the alternative result, since the resources of Europe had already been fully utilized, given the contemporary level of technology. However, we shall study historical, not hypothetical, developments. The next chapter will cover the internal changes in the various countries during 1500–1700. Chapter 13 will deal with overseas expansion and the organization of trade. And Chapter 14 will treat the achievements of mercantilism and its impact on later developments in Europe.

12

INTERNAL DEVELOPMENTS IN THE MERCANTILIST PERIOD

Europe was expanding outward in this period, either to new territories adjoining the mainland, as in Russia, or overseas to the Orient and America. Internally no revolutionary changes took place. Where expansion of industrial production and manufacturing occurred, it was usually horizontal with little change in technology or productivity.

The major innovations in industry were the more extensive use of the putting-out system and the substitution of coal for wood as a fuel. The putting-out system was widely used, especially in the textile industry in England, the Netherlands, and in other parts of western Europe. As an organizational innovation, it was indispensable in bringing together the managerial and entrepreneurial abilities of the merchant capitalist and the skill of the producer. It also permitted the use of labor on a part-time basis which not only supplemented incomes from agriculture, but also increased the supply of products in response to the expanding demand. The substitution of coal for wood as fuel was even more significant, especially in the metal industries. Since deforestation was advancing and the shortage of firewood was apparent, further industrial development might have been impossible without coal.

The sources of power continued to be man and beast, wind and water. Transportation was improved mainly by digging canals and improving the ship-building industry. The

techniques of banking and credit had already advanced considerably by the end of the fifteenth century, and few further improvements occurred. There was an expansion in the money and commodity markets, in credit, and in partnerships. These were closely related to foreign trade and will be discussed in that context. This chapter will concentrate on change in three main areas: population, agriculture, and industry and manufacturing.

POPULATION

Two significant trends are observable in this period: an increase of population during the sixteenth century and a decline in the seventeenth. The pattern was not uniform throughout the period or for the various countries. There was also some variation in the distribution between urban and rural population in the different nations. There seems to have been a tendency toward the growth of large urban centers in the West, in contrast to an apparent decline of urbanism in eastern Europe.

The recovery of the population, which had started around 1450, reached its peak sometime after 1500. The data are still incomplete and not totally reliable, but certain trends may be observed from the available information, represented in Table 12.1.

Table 12.1. Population changes in selected years and countries, fifteenth–eighteenth centuries

	YEAR	COUNT IN	NUMBER
Italy			
Sardinia	1485	Hearths	26,263
	1603	Hearths	66,669
Sicily[a]	1501	Inhabitants	502,761
	1607	Inhabitants	831,944
Kingdom of Naples (without the City of Naples)	1501	Taxed hearths	254,380
	1595	Taxed hearths	540,090
Spain			
Navarre	1553	Heads of families	30,833
	1587	Heads of families	41,901
	1678	Heads of families	43,184
Aragon	1495	Heads of families	50,391
	1603	Heads of families	70,984
	1650	Heads of families	22,688
Catalonia	1553	Heads of families	65,394
	1717	Heads of families	124,032
Valencia	1609	Houses	97,372
	1714	Houses	76,524
Castile	1591	Heads of families	1,340,320
	1646	Heads of families	807,903
	1723	Heads of families	965,610
Portugal	(1448–1481)	Hearths	252,261
	1527–1532	Hearths	278,468
Brabant	1496	Hearths	75,343
	1526	Hearths	97,013 = 363,000 inhabitants
	1693–1709	Inhabitants	373,000
Hainault (rural)	1468–1469	Hearths	29,212
	1540–1541	Hearths	34,286
Territory of Zurich (without city)	1467	People	26,700–28,900
	1529	People	48,100–58,700
	1585	People	69,975–85,000
	1649–1650	People	90,000
Switzerland	c. 1450	People	600,000–650,000
	c. 1575	People	800,000
Poland	1578	People	3,200,000
	1662	People	2,250,000
England and Wales	1570	People	4,123,708
	1600	People	4,811,718
	1630	People	5,600,517
	1670	People	5,773,646
	1700	People	6,045,008

[a] *Without Palermo and Messina and clergy and indigent people.*
SOURCE: Cambridge Economic History of Europe, *IV*, chap. 1 (*various tables synchronized selectively*).

These figures are not comprehensive enough to show the rise and decline clearly. Moreover, the decline was not absolute but rather a drop in the rate of increase, except in certain localities. Absolute declines can be attributed to population mobility rather than to loss of people. For example, Venice had 170,000 in 1568 and only 140,000 in 1700.

Naples with its suburbs had about 300,000 early in the seventeenth century and only 188,000 in 1688. The population in both cases may have moved to the countryside. However, the recurrent famines and plagues could easily have caused absolute population declines. For example, the French population increased until the French Wars of Religion in 1562, after which heavy losses were suffered because of the plagues of 1563–1564, 1567, and 1584, the famines and plagues of 1628–1638, the poor crops and diseases of 1646–1652, and the famines of 1660–1662 and 1693–1694. In addition the French population suffered because of religious persecution, just as Spain lost people by evicting the Moors and other religious and ethnic minorities. Reverses of the rising population trend were also experienced in the seventeenth century in the Balkan countries, in Scandinavia, and in the Holy Roman Empire. The declines in the Empire during the seventeenth century ranged from zero in Burgundy, Switzerland, and Austria, to over 50 percent in Mecklenberg, Pomerania, and Thuringia.

Had Europe remained closed, these population trends might have had significant effects on demand and supply. However, since the market had ceased to be local, the impact was not as grave as it might have been. Nevertheless, certain effects on wages, prices, and economic relations may be observed in agriculture and in the attitude towards industry and manufacturing.

The effect of this decline also might have been somewhat mitigated by the demographic changes reflected in urbanization. While certain urban centers declined among the Italian cities, the Hanseatic towns, and in eastern Europe, the trend was the opposite in England, Sweden, France, and the Low Countries. Paris had 300–400,000 inhabitants in the seventeenth century; Greater London passed the 100,000 mark in the mid-sixteenth century and exceeded 200,000 early in the seventeenth century. Geneva still had 70,000 in the 1640s, and Hamburg and Danzig had 60,000 in the same period. In general, such concentration has a stimulating effect on both manufacturing and agricultural production. On the other hand, it has been suggested that concentration might have had some negative effects, spreading disease and aggravating the impact of famines and plagues, thus contributing to the general population decline of the seventeenth century. The evidence, however, is not sufficient to provide any conclusions on this point.

AGRICULTURE

The developments in agriculture were of two types. Institutional changes were concerned with land tenure and labor relations. Economic and organizational changes were made in response to economic factors. Few if any involved technology or methods of cultivation. Expansion was accomplished either by extending the same techniques to new areas or by reorganizing the existing farms in order to increase the yield, as by changing the crops in response to the market demand.

These changes should be interpreted in the light of the changing and expanding market for food and other agricultural products. On one hand, there was an increase in the demand for wool and other industrial crops and fibers. The expansion of pasture in response to this demand reduced the supply of grain and other food products. Therefore, there was a relative increase in the demand for grain and more pressure on the remaining arable land. The responses to these two demand trends differed from each other and from one country to another.

England

While little change can be observed in the agrarian history of France in this period, England experienced the beginning of a fundamental change in agriculture. The sixteenth century witnessed the first movement for enclosure of the open fields and the common land. As the demand for wool increased, both for local industry and for export, English landlords were anxious to increase pastureland at the expense of arable areas. The movement for enclosure was reinforced by the relatively high cost of labor and by the declining fertility of the soil.

Enclosure for the purpose of creating pastures and sheep walks could be undertaken only at the expense of farmers and copyholders. Landlords accomplished their ends either by buying these landholders out or by evicting them, in the absence of title to the land. Thus enclosure led to unemployment and in some cases to depopulation of the countryside. Restlessness among the peasants became widespread, and the government was forced to interfere in opposition to enclosure. It is not surprising, therefore, that the enclosure movement proceeded slowly and remained relatively limited. Nevertheless, the sixteenth-century enclosures marked the beginning of larger-scale operations in English agriculture, consolidation of holdings, and proletarization of the rural population. The enclosure movement, which became more significant in the eighteenth century, did not disappear in the seventeenth. On the contrary, there is evidence of enclosure throughout that period, although on a smaller scale than during the sixteenth century.[1]

The tendency towards consolidation has been explained as a result of another process, namely land transaction on the market. Indeed, the period from the mid-sixteenth to the mid-seventeenth centuries has been described as the period of the rise of the gentry in England. The gentry, who rank below the peers and above the yeomen, were large landowners and farmers interested in farming as a business as well as in ownership of land.

The increase in their number in this period has been attributed to various factors. Expropriation of the monasteries put much land on the market, as did the sale of Crown land. The economic problems of the nobility led them to sell some of their land. Enclosure was also an important factor in freeing some of the land from the hold of the peasants. The gentry were in the best position to take advantage of the land market, since they could afford transactions on a relatively large scale. Hence, their significance as landowners increased during this century. While the data are incomplete, figures on manor ownership show that owners of ten manors or more declined by almost 40 percent between 1561 and 1680. The loss was a gain for those owning five to nine manors, but more for those owning four manors or less. Similar figures support the observation that large-scale farming was on the rise, at least among the gentry.

Spain

The increasing demand for wool was more strongly reflected in the policy of the Spanish government toward the migratory sheepherders of Spain. The National Association of the Honorable Assembly of the Mesta of the Shepherds had been chartered in 1273, but it reached the peak of its power and prosperity in the sixteenth century, although it remained in existence until 1836. The importance of wool as an export item and the increasing demand for it in Flanders and other countries led the Spanish monarchy to give strong support to the Mesta, often at the expense of farmers and arable land. Indeed, when the farmers wanted to enclose their farms for protection against the migratory sheep, the government made sure that the sheep highways, *cañadas*, were not affected. The sheepherders were awarded various rights of pasture, especially on common land, the land of the military leaders which was appropriated by the Crown, and land that might have been left fallow. Even though the "old 'five forbidden things' (*cosas veda-*

---

[1] On continued enclosure in the seventeenth century, see E. M. Leonard, "The Inclosure of Common Fields in the Seventeenth Century," *Transactions of the Royal Historical Society*, New series XIX (1905); reprinted in *Essays in Economic History*, II, E. M. Carus-Wilson (ed.), New York: St. Martin's Press, 1962, pp. 227–256.

dos)—the orchards, grain fields, vineyards, ox pastures, and mown meadows—were still to be respected by the Mesta,"[2] the farmers were obligated to prove that their land was being put to these uses before they could keep the sheep off their fields.

The government's policy of supporting the Mesta emanated from various objectives. First, wool was a source of foreign currency or specie, which was badly needed by the government. Second, the Mesta members were an important source of revenue since they were subject to taxes. Third, the Mesta was used as a political tool against the town authorities, the military leaders and nobility, and even the Church. Although at times policy turned against the Mesta, the Order was in such high esteem that the king was once elected Master of the Order, and the Master always held a very high position at the court. Fourth, the Mesta was a prototype in the organization of large-scale trade. The factories or trading posts established to handle wool provided the model for the *Casa de Contratacion* (House of Trade) established at Seville to handle international trade. Finally, the sheepherders were often an important means of trade and communication throughout the realm. This last function was served primarily by another sheepherder association known as the *Cabaña Reale de Carretero* (the Royal Association of Teamsters), which was chartered in 1497, and whose charter was renewed several times thereafter. The Teamsters' oxcarts carried domestic commerce in Castile "over a regular system or schedule of routes." According to a statement introduced on behalf of the teamsters,

> they usually spent the winters south of Toledo, where their oxen rested and regained their strength until April. On the first stage of their annual journey they carried loads of charcoal from the woodlands of Toledo to Talavera, the home of

the famous potteries, where they arrived about June. Thence they journed as far south as Seville [presumably with tile, terra cotta ware, etc., for shipment to America]. They then started north across the Guadiana Valley, bringing salt as far as Coria and Plasencia. Thence their route lay southeast to the highlands of Alcudia with wood for the mines of Almadén, whence they carried quicksilver to Seville for transportation overseas to the Mexican mines. Another circuit, after the wintering near Toledo led northward to Madrid, to which point grain was brought and exchanged for wool at Segovia. This wool was taken up to Vitoria; and the carts were there loaded with iron for the north coast, where they took on salt and carried it to Vierzo and Ponferrada [in the upland sheep country west of León]. Then they returned eastward to Poza, near Burgos, where salt was loaded for Valladolid, Salamanca, and other parts of Castile.[3]

Furthermore, wherever sheepherders appeared local trade was activated. The herders clipped their sheep on the way, sold what they could sell and stored the rest, and bought supplies for the next link in the journey.

The economic significance of sheep in Spain may be suggested by the size of the flocks, although estimates of these have varied within a range of 100 percent. A conservative estimate is that in the period of prosperity the flock was about 3.5 million sheep, excluding the Teamsters' flock and the sedentary flocks. Another indication of the significance of the Mesta may be inferred from the fact that the Fuggers were engaged by the king to handle the taxes due from them. The seventeenth century, however, was a period of decline for the Mesta. In part, this was a reflection of the growing strength of their opponents and the inability of the central government to protect them.

[2] Julius Klein, *The Mesta*, Cambridge, Mass.: Harvard University Press, 1920, p. 319.

[3] *Ibid.*, pp. 22–23.

But it was also due to the creation of new sources of wool and the growing importance of other textile material. It has also been explained as a reflection of the destructive role of migratory sheep in the Spanish economy, especially agriculture. Migratory sheep tended to restrict cultivation and cause deforestation and possibly erosion, both of which were harmful to production and conservation. The attempts to remove the privileges of the herders were finally successful; apparently the Mesta had served its functions and was no longer profitable.

East Germany

In Spain the trend towards consolidation of farms seen in England did not exist at all, even though both countries faced the same market conditions and both had an interest in sheep-raising. However, the agrarian difficulties of the fifteenth century and the rising demand for agricultural products in the sixteenth led in East Germany to an increase in the scale of operation, a strengthening of the landlords and the estates, the revival of serfdom, and the weakening of the towns to the advantage of the estate lords, the *Junkers*. In the sixteenth and seventeenth centuries the peasants were put under great pressure, often to the extent of attaching them to the land, demanding from them labor services, and even appropriating their holdings and integrating them into the demesne. The estates were also enlarged by appropriation of the lands of the monasteries and religious orders. The dukes, who were usually among the largest landowners, were willing to introduce laws to augment the estates and the new serfdom. The trend that began in the later Middle Ages was continued and strengthened until the power of the estates was reduced by the political centralization under Frederick Willliam of Prussia in the middle of the seventeenth century.

These developments in East Germany were economically important. Cultivation was intensified, the scale of operation was enlarged, and the grain export market was more effectively exploited. This was especially true when the estates were still powerful and the lords could export their products despite the restrictions on export in times of shortage imposed by the towns. The landlords improved their situation at the expense of the peasants and the towns. However, the effects were disastrous to the peasants, both economically and socially. Not only were they forced to pay higher dues, but they were reduced to serfdom.

Russia

A significant development of this period was the unification of large parts of Russia, the expansion of cultivation in that area, and its advent into the European economic community. Until the middle of the fifteenth century Russia was fragmented into several independent territories, each of which was dominated by one or another of the foreign forces surrounding the country. Ivan III of Moscow (1462–1505) freed Moscow from Tartar rule in 1480 and declared himself "Sovereign of all Rus." However, unification was not completed until the end of the sixteenth century.

Although slavery was declining, the feudal principalities disintegrating, and a system of landownership developing, the need for labor services in agriculture led to the legalization of serfdom by the end of the fifteenth century. In the sixteenth century slave labor was still in evidence, particularly in areas away from Moscow. On some farms indentured labor, secured against a loan, provided the labor services. Gradually the debtors lost the right to repay their debts and hence lost their freedom. Rent in the form of labor services was preferred by the landlords since, in the absence of wage labor, it allowed more intensive cultivation than money rent.

At the same time a tendency existed in the sixteenth century to commute labor services into money rent. This tendency was encouraged by the state in two ways: by exerting pressure to weaken the feudal lords, and by distributing land to the slaves, especially lands expropriated from princes and feudal lords. The impact of this policy is said to have caused a decline in cultivation and even depopulation in some villages, especially after the middle of the sixteenth century. Instead of sedentary farming, there was an increase in the cultivation of "visited land"; that is, the land was cultivated until fertility had declined, at which time the farmer moved to another area. Another effect of the policy was a decline in the scale of operation which caused a further decline in agricultural production. In part, the decline of agriculture was also caused by a shortage of labor around the end of the sixteenth century. New restrictions on labor movements were imposed in 1597 and all peasants who had run away during the previous five years were to be returned to their former landlords.

The beginning of the seventeenth century was marked by severe hardships for the peasantry and a victory for the landlords. The famine of 1607–1612 led to violent uprisings by the peasants, in response to which the restrictions on them were tightened. The Code of 1649 abolished the limitation on the period a landlord could search for runaway serfs and gave him unlimited rights to retrieve his lost peasants. While this measure helped revive cultivation, it led to a peasant war in 1667–1668.

Serfdom continued throughout the seventeenth century and was even extended to manufacturing. Throughout this period Russia was colonizing new land, increasing the arable area, and thus expanding production. Farming techniques were still backward, however, relative to the West. Russian farmers were familiar with manure fertilization, but crop rotation was almost unknown and the three-field system of rotation was little used. A wooden *sokha* with many teeth drawn by a horse was the common plow, although it was good only for shallow plowing. Plows of wood and iron were known but rarely used.

Sweden

This period was significant also in the history of Sweden, which emerged as the most powerful country in the Baltic area. In agriculture, however, there was no dramatic change either in organization or in technique. The main developments were the expropriation of Church property, colonization and the beginning of conservation, and some containment of the nobility in order to protect the peasantry. At the end of the Middle Ages the Church was an important landowner, while the Crown was relatively insignificant. Expropriation of the Church land increased the Crown lands more than fivefold. At the end of the Middle Ages the peasantry held about two and one-half times the amount of land held by the nobility. This ratio was changed slightly in favor of the nobility by the middle of the sixteenth century. However, after Gustavus Vasa (1521–1560) the nobility found ways of enlarging both their holdings and the scale of operation on the manorial estates. One important method was to acquire estates as gifts from the Crown, which entitled the owners to the land rent. This alienation of rent really meant transference of ownership to the nobility. Thus by 1652 the nobility had increased their holdings by two and one-half times, while the peasants had lost about 40 percent of what they had held a century earlier, despite the rise in population and the colonization of new land. It was in the second half of the seventeenth century that alienation was reversed: All land that had been acquired by the nobility without equivalent compensation had to revert to the Crown. Although the nobility had to surrender a large amount of land, they succeeded in retaining the better land in consolidated tracts. Thus the scale of operation continued to be relatively large.

Nevertheless, the impact of redistribution was significant. As Table 12.2 shows, the peasantry lost quite significantly. The nobility lost land during the second half of the

Table 12.2.   Distribution of land in Sweden
in selected years (percent of total)

	END OF MIDDLE AGES	AT DEATH OF GUSTAVUS VASA (1521–1560)	REIGN OF CHARLES VI (1700)
Crown	5.5%	28.2%	35.6%
Church	21.0	—	—
Nobility	21.8	22.4	32.9
Peasants	51.7	49.4	31.5

SOURCE: *E. F. Heckscher, An Economic History
of Sweden, Cambridge, Mass.: Harvard University Press, 1954, pp. 67, 126.*

seventeenth century, but they were still
ahead relative to their holdings in the sixteenth century. The Crown was the winner at
the expense of both the Church and the
peasantry. The Crown land, however, was
farmed by the peasants against a fixed
money rent until the reversion. Reverting
land was farmed against rent in kind (produce), apparently to avoid the monetary
problems of inflation and debasement which
were recurrent in this period. The rent in
kind was used to pay the army and service
people. The method of cultivation was relatively primitive. The strip system was followed except on the large consolidated
estates.

Government policy encouraged colonization, especially by Finns. However, the Finns
were in the habit of cultivating the land for a
few years and then moving on to virgin and
more fertile land. This practice was costly to
the forest areas, causing erosion and often
deforestation. For protection and conservation, restrictions were imposed on the Finns,
sometimes to the extent of persecuting them.
Nevertheless, the colonization movement was
important in increasing agricultural production.

The population ran ahead of production,
however, as suggested by the decline in
calorie intake of certain groups. It has been
estimated that on one manor the average
calorie intake declined by one-third between
the sixteenth and seventeenth centuries. This
decline is significant in two ways. First, it

suggests the low level of consumption in the
seventeenth century. Second, it indicates that
the level achieved in the sixteenth century
was relatively high, comparing favorably
with the level of the early twentieth century.
On another manor the consumption in 1555
was 4166 calories per day per person;
throughout the seventeenth century it ranged
between 2480 and 3000 calories. On the
royal manors, the average consumption of
the agricultural servant in 1573 was 4315
calories. The average calorie intake for the
whole population in 1912–1913 was 4402
calories, indicating the high level achieved in
the sixteenth century.[4]

The Low Countries

In contrast with the above experiences,
the Low Countries concentrated on technical
improvements in agriculture. The declining
land/labor ratio, increasing urbanization,
and economic expansion in other sectors
provided incentives to increase both production and productivity. Expansion on the land
was not possible. Therefore, the Dutch decided to attack the sea by draining swamps,
raising the level of the land, and rendering
new areas fit for cultivation—a process still
evident in Holland today. Drainage provided
large areas of arable land. Estimates run as
high as 80,000 acres drained by 1640. The
Dutch were interested also in increasing
productivity. They began a movement of
intensive agriculture by crop rotation and
continuous care; hoeing, deep plowing, and
fertilization became common procedures.
Crop rotation and the introduction of turnips and clover helped to revive the fertility
of the soil and to provide feed for cattle, as
they did about a century later in the agricultural revolution in England. The Dutch were
the first to substitute crop rotation for field
rotation, removing the need to rest the land
by letting it lie fallow every two or three

[4] Eli Heckscher, *An Economic History of Sweden*, Cambridge, Mass.: Harvard University Press,
1954, pp. 69, 116.

years. At the same time, they made it possible to increase dairy production without depending on natural pastures.

Overall changes
in agriculture

During the two centuries under consideration it appears that European agriculture was only slightly changed. Attempts at enclosure in England proved abortive. Techniques and yields were little improved, except for the more intensive farming and drainage methods of the Dutch. There was some interest in conservation. Large consolidated, and fragmented strip systems of holding and operation existed side by side. The peasantry was still a dependent group, consisting either of copyholders who paid quitrent or serfs tied to the land. The East and the West had developed two systems which contrasted with each other and by the end of the seventeenth century they had strengthened these differences.

In one respect European agriculture benefited from contact with the New World, namely the introduction of new crops. These spread quickly from one country to another. The Portuguese brought grain of paradise from West Africa, which was used as a pepper substitute and in spiced wines. Maize came from America as early as 1494 with Columbus; a certain variety also came from the Euphrates area in 1574. It found wide acceptance, especially in northern and eastern Europe in wet climates. The Spanish brought in sweet potato at the same time as maize. Tobacco came from the New World in 1561 through the French, who also introduced French beans which they found in Canada. The Jerusalem artichoke also came from Canada early in the seventeenth century. Probably the most important new crop was the potato, which was already being grown in Spain by 1573 and soon after was to become a staple food in Ireland. Pineapples came from America in the sixteenth century but were slowly accepted in Europe. Tomatoes were introduced in the sixteenth century. Red peppers and chilis were adopted and grown in Germany as early as 1542 and soon after were common in Spain. The turkey also came from America through the Spanish in the sixteenth century. These crops were important mainly because they added variety in the diet, except for the potato and maize which became staples. The techniques of cultivation and productivity were not affected by their introduction.

POLICY AND EXPANSION IN
INDUSTRY AND MANUFACTURING

The sixteenth and seventeenth centuries in general were distinguished more for external trade relations and expansion than for internal economic developments. The main internal changes were related more to policy matters than to implementation. The changes which took place in policy and production were unequally distributed among the various countries. Holland, England, and to an extent France were already on the threshold of modern capitalism, while eastern Europe and the Baltic countries were still in the grip of medieval institutions. Despite these variations, however, certain general observations may be made regarding the period as a whole.

Gradual change

The breakaway from medievalism was gradual, nonuniform, and often costly. The towns were still influential in regulating economic behavior in this period. Segmentation was still common. Guilds were still entrenched, probably even more than they had been a century or so earlier. The attitude toward trade and finance was based on the nonrational foundations that were to remain dominant in this period and most of the next century and a half. Yet on all these fronts change was underway in varying degrees.

Involvement
of government

Probably the most significant internal change was the direct involvement of the central government in economic affairs on all levels. The government set itself up to supervise and regulate production. It managed to encourage economic activity by subsidy, protection, and even direct participation. Withdrawal of these advantages often signaled a change of policy and the beginning of restriction, and with it a decline of those areas to which the advantages had formerly accrued. The central government, in addition to managing trade relations, supervised and regulated the guilds, wages and prices, and poor relief. Government action often centered on facilitating economic activity indirectly by encouraging mobility and internal exchange. This was done by sponsoring road and water transportation, importing skills, and setting up insurance institutions.

Principles of
mercantilism

Government policy was often arbitrary in its detail but it was consistent with certain general principles which have come to be identified with mercantilism. The most important of these principles were the following:

1. Nationalism and power are closely related to economic self-sufficiency. A country must produce what it needs so that in times of war or disturbed international relations it can stand on its own.

2. Economic self-sufficiency depends on regulated trade and production, which are the main sources of wealth. Production increases wealth and trade with others causes circulation of commodities to rise, thus increasing profits and making the country more important in its relations with others.

3. Trade can be a source of wealth only if the country produces goods that are either demanded at home as substitutes for imports, or demanded abroad and therefore increase the volume of exports. Trade increases wealth only if exports exceed imports in value. In other words, wealth through trade is represented by a positive balance of trade. A positive balance of trade is represented by an excess of the precious metals—

the international medium of exchange—brought into the country over those sent out. This principle has often been misinterpreted as the concept of bullionism, which is taken to mean the accumulation of precious metals. However, the mercantilists were not so naive as to want precious metals for their own sake. They recognized the relationship between these metals as an international medium of exchange and the flow of trade. In the absence of the international credit facilities current today, the mercantilist attitude seems consistent with remaining solvent in international trade and maintaining a reserve balance of international currency.

4. The government has a responsibility to advance economic wealth and prosperity as the guardian of society.

5. Poverty, disease, and idleness are social ills which reduce wealth and cause a drain on national resources. Therefore, public authorities have a responsibility in curing these ills.

6. Finally, national wealth and power are relative values which can be measured only by comparison with other nations. Therefore, the whole society must be involved in the international competition, even though some groups may have to bear the cost. Furthermore, there should be no hesitation in a beggar-my-neighbor policy, since the decline of a competitor means one's own victory and expansion.

The putting-out
system

The changes in production were much more limited. In general there was a tendency to expand existing lines of production with few innovations or new products. Technological change was probably least affected, although some products and techniques were adopted by one country from another. The most extensive change was in the area of industrial organization. Although certain large enterprises existed in the textile, mining, iron, and coal industries, the majority of the producers worked within the framework of the putting-out system.

The putting-out system involved two main parties: the master artisans or producers and the merchant capitalist, as the clothier. The clothier initiated production by placing orders with the artisans, who usually worked in their homes. The individual artisan often performed only one activity, such as spinning, weaving, dyeing, or fulling. The clothier contracted with a different artisan for each of these processes. Once a process had been completed, the clothier collected the product and transferred it to another artisan for the next process, until production had been completed. The clothier paid each of these artisans for the individual process he performed at an agreed-upon piece rate. When the product was finished it belonged to the merchant capitalist who marketed it, carried the risk, and paid the charges on the capital represented by the product. Frequently the clothier advanced the raw material and some capital to sustain the artisan until the work had been completed. The artisan owned most of his tools and used a part of his house as a workshop. He often employed wage workers and apprentices to do the work on his behalf.

The putting-out system was the beginning of the division of labor and of interaction between economic forces on a relatively large scale. It alienated the worker from the means of production by making him dependent on the merchant clothier. It made it possible to cope with an expanding market for commodities. It also created a larger market for raw material than had previously existed. On the other hand, it allowed flexibility, since it permitted the artisan to do other work on the side. It also sustained a widespread distribution of industry. It encouraged the employment of apprentices and children at very young ages, since payment was on a piece-rate basis. Finally, it allowed the master artisan a certain degree of freedom from supervision, which often encouraged abuse and embezzlement of the commodities.

Side by side with the small-scale putting-out system of production arose large-scale, vertically integrated capitalistic enterprises and state-sponsored, monopolistic operations. Some countries or governments, as in Spain, France, Sweden, Russia, and sometimes England, preferred to convert directly to a factory system of production. In other cases, as in mining and metallurgy, the nature of the product made it easier to produce on a relatively large scale. The textile enterprises supported by the government of Spain were vertically integrated so that all the processes were carried out in the same workshop. Colbert in France created and sustained many similarly concentrated operations, both in textiles and in other lines of production. Some of these included hundreds of workers. Dutch and German masters who set up works in Sweden produced metals on a relatively large scale rather than by small differentiated processes. Nevertheless, throughout the period putting-out was the most characteristic feature of internal economic life.

Manufacturing and industry in the sixteenth and seventeenth centuries

Probably the oldest industry in Europe was the textile industry. The utilitarian nature of textile in part explains this fact. However, equally important are the facts that textile manufacturing requires relatively little capital, is highly divisible, and can be practiced at any scale, and that its products are easily movable and marketable. It is not surprising that all the countries of Europe, in varying degrees, were anxious to encourage the production of textiles by subsidy, protection, or patronage.

France and England. The Low Countries already had a comparative advantage in the manufacture of woolens, lace, and hosiery. The French had an advantage in the production of silk. These countries, however, were in the race not only to be self-sufficient but also to dominate the textile trade. Colbert in France made it a primary objective to produce woolens as fine as those produced in England and lace as good as was produced in Holland. The French government conferred titles on manufacturers who introduced new lines of production or who expanded old lines. It exempted them from taxes and gave them pensions and subsidies as long as the quality and the scale of production were maintained as originally stipulated.

The woolen industry was the oldest and most important textile industry in England. English wool producers had previously sold their raw material in Flanders; now England was an importer of wool and an exporter of finished products of both high and low quality. An important advance was made in the manufacturing and use of cotton, which had been introduced about three centuries earlier. Expansion was carried out on a putting-out basis, largely because the raw material had to be imported by the merchant clothier. Attempts also were made to expand the silk industry, but England gained in that field only slowly. It is noteworthy that the silk industry was the first to shift from a putting-out to a gathered-in factory system of production during the eighteenth century. A more significant change took place in the production of hosiery. A knitting frame was invented in the second half of the sixteenth century by William Lee. The frame, completed in 1589, allowed higher-speed knitting, especially of worsted and silk stockings. Finally, the production of linen was expanded by insisting that hemp and flax be grown in England. Every farmer who had more than 60 acres of land had to grow hemp and flax on part of it. Nevertheless, the major expansion of the linen industry took place in the eighteenth century.

Both England and France paid special attention to the saltpeter and gunpowder industries. In fact, in virtually all European countries the state assumed a monopoly over these industries as well as over the manufacturing of shot, cannonballs, muskets, and artillery pieces. The Grand Master of the Artillery in France was in charge of the manufacturing of all armaments. Ordinances declaring this monopoly in France were issued in 1572, 1582, and 1601, and again in 1663. Although producers worked in their homes in towns and villages, they were under contract to deliver the product to the royal warehouse. Unlike the French system, the English armaments industry was highly concentrated. The state monopoly was less effective, however, mainly because of public opposition to monopoly. The industry did not become important in England until the middle of the seventeenth century.

In England and France metallurgy and mining were also important. As a rule, the monarch reserved to himself the right to control the mines as sources of revenue. The French kings granted large concessions to mining to stimulate the search for ore, requiring a tenth of the find to be paid into the treasury. The main ore in France was iron. It is estimated that the tax on iron in 1640 amounted to 72,000 livres, at a rate of approximately 5 livres per thousandweight of bar iron. The more valuable ores, which were quite rare, were under strict control. The English monarchy also had trouble controlling the mines, where precious metals were virtually nonexistent. In both countries the salt industry was important as a source of revenue. In France patents or concessions were given out to stimulate production and increase the receipts from the salt tax or *gabelle*. The industry was expanded significantly in both countries, but again the English government was less successful in maintaining control.

In both countries attempts were made to foster the introduction of new products and industries. In France particular attention was paid to artistic and luxury items designed to serve as import substitutes. The king was usually the most important patron of these products. Patents were granted for inventions, and even money grants were made to foster new industries, such as silk products, glass, earthenware, and mirrors. Italian craftsmen were lured into France by exceptional advantages. Some of these craftsmen were employed directly by the court, a system which provided both protection and control. The new industries in England were more functional and less luxury-oriented. Labor-saving machinery, furnaces with stronger blasts, and powerful pumps for raising water from the mines were among the most important new items encouraged. The use of coal was fostered because of shortages of charcoal and the extra heat coal provided. Finally, of great interest in both countries was the expansion of ship-building, especially in the second half of the seventeenth century. Colbert in particular was anxious to have ships built in France in order to ruin the Dutch.

Germany and Italy. The industries mentioned above were also common in the Italian and German cities and towns. Indeed, in many cases the artisans of these areas were far ahead of those in other countries. However, this period was one of relative decline for these territories. The lack of unity in Italy and the rise of competition from unified external powers helped to reduce the economic significance of the Italian cities. While they maintained their expertise, they were unable to retain either their control of the market or their monopoly over the production of such items as silk, glassware, and ships. The German cities also declined, because of both the weakening of the Hanseatic League and the rising autonomy of the feudal estates. Nevertheless, the Germans retained their expertise in metallurgy and mining, as can be seen from the efforts made to import German metallurgists into other countries.

The Netherlands. Probably the most important economic power of the period was the Netherlands. The Dutch dominated trade and finance as well as the manufacturing of specialized items. The textile industry flourished, particularly in luxury items. Wool and linen were specialties of Leiden and Harlem. Fish and cheese were staple export products. The shipping industry was important both for supplying the carry-

ing industry and for sale to other countries. The rise of Amsterdam to replace Antwerp as the financial center of Europe is an indication of the economic power of Holland. Unfortunately, we have no data on the expansion of the various Dutch industries. It is apparent, however, that the Dutch economy was more dependent on commercial and financial activities than on local industry.

Spain and Portugal. There was much less activity in industry and manufacturing in Spain and Portugal, since both countries had extended themselves in the international sphere. Portugal concentrated on wool, wine, salt, oil, and cork. Except for wool, these formed a weak basis for industrial expansion. Moreover, because wool had a ready export market in raw form, there was little incentive to expand local manufacturing. Spain also lacked natural resources other than agricultural products, some iron ore, and the wool of the Mesta flocks, which was a staple export item. There were attempts in Spain to expand the textile industry and some protective measures were introduced for that purpose. However, Spain had too many other external avenues to expend serious efforts on local manufacturing.

Sweden. Although until this period Sweden was less developed than France, the Low Countries, or England, signs of organized and systematic expansion were already evident. The iron industry received a great push forward from the government. The blast furnace had been introduced earlier, but attempts were now made to promote a process "in which pig iron was 'freshened' or 'fined' into a malleable product."[5] The resulting bar iron became Sweden's staple. Large hammer-works were promoted to cater to the production of bar iron. The copper industry received equal attention at a time when the silver industry was declining due to external competition. The expansive trend of

[5] *Ibid.*, p. 70.

the sixteenth century continued during the seventeenth, so that by the end of the century Sweden was contributing half of Europe's total copper output. As if to encourage the industry and stabilize prices, copper was adopted as a second metal for currency. Thus, in periods of declining demand, more copper was absorbed by the mints. The production of brass, a combination of copper and zinc, was another growing Swedish industry. However, iron remained the most important product, constituting about 50 percent of Sweden's exports. Iron output increased about fivefold between 1600 and 1720. Swedish iron found a ready market in England, which imported about 82.5 percent of its requirements from Sweden. This trend seems to have been largely due to the excellent quality of Swedish iron and the entrepreneurial skills of Swedish manufacturers. The Swedes adopted German and French furnaces, notably a stone blast furnace which could stand the heat needed to produce high-quality iron. Sweden also took advantage of other natural resources found in its forests. Tar and potash were important items of trade. Sweden had a monopoly on tar, which was badly needed in the ship-building industry.

Russia and eastern Europe. As we go east into Russia and eastern Europe, we notice similar expansive activities but on a lower level of development. In Russia urban centers had begun to emerge with crafts and manufacturing as their economic basis. However, producers of foodstuffs still constituted more than 30 percent of those economically employed in towns. Textiles absorbed about a third of the city dwellers. It is estimated that in 1638 Moscow had 2367 artisans, Kolomna had 159, Mozhaisk had 224, and Novgorod had about 2000. The artisans, however, were less organized than in the West. While they continued to produce independently, large enterprises, often based on "free" labor, were emerging to produce iron ore, salt, mining products, potash, and

other metallurgical items. These operations were family-owned and operated under public protection. The owners controlled large amounts of capital and were close to the court. State "factories" were also emerging dealing in mining, military equipment, construction, and minting. Artisans were imported from other countries to man these state enterprises. During the first half of the seventeenth century iron works were built and equipped to use water-driven machinery. Nevertheless, Russia still depended heavily on foreign manufacturers and trade was more important than manufacturing.

Regulation and control

The age of mercantilism is notable for government intervention in economic and social affairs. England and France offer good examples of the variations in government policies and their successful implementation.

France. Intervention in France was designed on one hand to encourage production and innovation, and on the other to guarantee quality. Serving the first objective were such policies as subsidy, tax exemption, and direct participation. These forms of intervention have been noted briefly above and require little further comment in this context. However, government regulation was much more extensive and far-reaching. Regulations were usually detailed and their implementation was a public responsibility. They were of two types: local or regional and general. Both evolved over a long period stretching back to the Middle Ages and reaching its peak in the days of Colbert (1661–1683). We shall discuss some of the regulations codified in Colbert's time as expressive of the trend.

Among the local regulations, those of the city of Beauvais concerning the manufacturers of cloth and serge are typical. The 56 articles of the regulation passed in 1667 touch on all aspects of the industry: the place of the master and his offspring in the industry, relations between masters and workers, the hours of work, holidays, relations to foreign craftsmen, the guild council and administration, and supervision. They specify the standards to be met in production, including the length of the cloth, its width, and the kind of raw material that may be used. Details on the colors, number of threads, quality of weaving, and the conditions for marketing woolen cloth in the city are also specified. A few examples of the regulations of Beauvais follow.

4. Sons of masters to need no certificate of apprenticeship if they have worked with their fathers for two years, but to be received in the guild they must be at least fifteen years old.

7. The wardens to visit the houses of the cloth and serge-makers at least once a week, so that each such house is visited at least every month.

11. Masters must open their shops, workrooms, and storerooms to wardens. If any defective goods are found, the wardens are to seize them and take them before *echevins*. If adjudged truly defective, the cloth is to be confiscated, and the master fined for a second or further offenses.

12. No unmarked cloth to be sold, bought, or kept.

13. Any fuller who spoils a piece of cloth, or causes it to shrink below the required specifications, is to be fined by the administrative judge. . . .

18. No master to take more than two apprentices.

19. Number of threads in the warp of serges *à deux envers* (with two wrong sides) fixed. Such serges to be 36 ells long before fulling, 26 to 33 ells long after fulling, according to quality. Ells to be those of Paris. Looms to be adjusted to make serges of the required specifications. Serges to be woven. Width to be at least one ell after fulling, when the serge

is ready for sale, and not to shrink further. The purchasers to be allowed to test this by putting the fabric in water.

21. Wide *ratines* to have a fixed number of threads in the warp. To be 30 to 34 ells long and 1¼ to 1⅓ ells wide when finished.

22. Spanish-style serges to have a fixed number of threads in the warp. White ones to be 28 to 31 ells long and one ell wide when finished. Gray ones to be 24 to 27 ells long and 1¼ ells wide when finished.

33. Weavers to pay one *sou* fine for each shuttle hole.

34. If a weaver makes the distance between the threads of the warp unequal, 6 *deniers* fine; or, in bad cases, 2 *sous*.

35. If the warp is not tight, 2 *sous* 6 *deniers* fine.

36. If a piece unevenly woven, 5 *sous* fine.

37. No weaver to leave his master until he has finished the piece on his loom, and until he has paid his master all he owes him.

55. One-half of all fines to go to the poor of Beauvais; one-fourth to the wardens; and one-fourth to the guild for expenses. . . .[6]

The Beauvais code was often exceeded in detail and restrictiveness. The code of Amiens contained 248 articles, although others were less detailed. By 1669 codes had been introduced in Paris, Lyon, Tours, Carcassone, Sedan, Chalons, Reims, and many other cities.

General regulations applied to the country as a whole and related more to relations with foreigners, but they were also detailed and comprehensive. Colbert's "Ordinances and regulations on the length, width, and quality of cloth, serges, and other stuffs of wool and linen" are considered

6 C. W. Cole, *Colbert and a Century of French Mercantilism*, II, New York: Columbia University Press, 1939, pp. 377–382.

among his most important achievements. These include 59 articles which go into minute detail concerning the specifications to be observed, including procedures of supervision and implementation. The main objective of these regulations was to introduce uniformity throughout the country. However, they were modified again and again, even during Colbert's lifetime. A few of the articles on dyeing are reproduced below:

1. In dyeing, five kinds of simple, un-mixed, or primary colors are made, from which all the others are derived or made up.

2. These colors are blue, red, yellow, fallow (*fauve*), and black.

3. Fabrics that are to be dyed in red or yellow should preferably be boiled with alum or tartar and other ingredients which do not give a color, in the manner which will be related hereafter.

4. Those that are to be dyed black should be boiled with gall and sumach, and, lacking sumach, with myrtle-leaved sumach [*rhus myrtifolia*] or *fovic* [a native French plant]; being well galled, they have a color between fallow and gray; and it will be observed that fallow and root color are really the same thing.

5. But the fabrics that are dyed blue and fallow are dyed from the white to blue or fallow, without other preparation than that which they receive from the fuller.

6. The fabrics of the best wool and those which are whitest and clearest are those which take the most beautiful and best color.

7. Fabrics which have been bleached with sulphur or with white lead should be well scoured and purged of the poor quality of these two ingredients, which prevent the penetration of the dye, spoil its beauty, and hinder the proper union of the colors. . . .[7]

Enforcement was regulated by a separate code which specified the role of the inspec-

[7] *Ibid.*, pp. 408–409.

tor, his relationship with the guild, and his connections with the local wardens. Implementation, however, was not an easy matter. Uniformity was hard to achieve. Furthermore, these regulations were not accepted wholeheartedly by those affected by them. In many cases, therefore, they proved to be more a menace than an effective instrument.

An equally significant aspect of Colbert's mercantilism was his restriction on capital export in the form of money or bullion. Although money could move freely within the country, its export was regarded as detrimental to the nation. However, in times of famines imports were undertaken at the expense of the treasury. The ban on the export of bullion was renewed by edicts in 1663 and 1670; while the import of precious metals was exempted from duty in 1678. However, the ban was ineffective in restricting silver export, especially to the Levant. Restrictions on the use of luxuries also caused problems, since they were in direct conflict with the encouragement given to the luxury industry. The fact that such restrictions were enacted in 1664, 1667, 1668, 1669, 1670, 1671, 1672, 1673, 1675, 1677, and 1679 shows how ineffective they were.

England. The internal policies of England had much in common with those of France. They were based on the premise that wealth comes from production and trade and therefore efforts should be expended to promote these objectives. At the same time, wealth and prosperity were considered relative values measurable only by comparison with other nations. England compared itself with Spain in the sixteenth century, with Holland in the seventeenth, with France in the eighteenth, and with Germany in the nineteenth. England utilized protection, prohibition, control, and encouragement by exemption from taxes and monopoly patenting to achieve its objectives. Intervention extended to manufacturing, labor, trade, wages, and finance.

The policies introduced were often re-activations of earlier policies and often caused conflict between interest groups. For example, an act of 1559 prohibited the import of girdles, rapiers, daggers, knives, saddles, stirrups, gloves, leather, laces, or pins made in other countries. The export of wool was always controlled, and by 1621 more than 30 statutes had been enacted to prohibit it, to the dismay of farmers. The conflict was similar to that surrounding the import and export of corn, which was controlled by the Corn Laws. These laws made trade in corn dependent on the local price, thus protecting the farmers at the expense of the consumers. A similar conflict arose from the restrictions on the export of leather and hides. An equally protective policy was applied to woolen cloth. This was accompanied by another forcing the use of native wool, under which judges and university professors were required to use robes made of native material. Finally, strict controls were imposed on the emigration of artisans and the transfer of tools out of the country.

Controls also extended to wages. The Statute of Apprentices of 1563 established a maximum wage rate. In 1601 a minimum wage rate was added. The government took steps to regulate apprenticeship by requiring seven years of it before admission to a guild was possible. Measures to standardize quality were imposed through the guilds. These measures were less comprehensive and detailed than those introduced in France, but they were equally detested by the artisans and the producers. Although they were mainly concerned with wool, they extended to all other branches of industry and manufacturing. The methods of control included "the direct intervention of the government; the creation of an administrative staff; the employment of the craft guilds as agents of national supervision; and the delegation of authority to private individuals."[8] Searchers

[8] E. Lipson, *The Economic History of England*, 6th ed., III, London: Adam and Charles Black, 1964, p. 327.

were authorized to enter and inspect all houses and workshops. However, these measures were ineffective, largely because of the general opposition to such intervention and the lack of mutual harmony among the various interest groups affected by them.

The guilds were established as companies, each with its ordinance which defined the status of its members and the standards of the industry to which it belonged. This incorporation was designed to aid the members and to control them. It also gave the guilds the responsibility of appointing searchers and supervising adherence to the regulations. During the seventeenth century grants of incorporation were made to the Feltmakers, the Musicians, the Turners, the Fruiters, the Gardeners, the Pinmakers, the Curriers, the Plumbers, the Founders, the Apothecaries, the Scriveners, the Bowyers, the Starchmakers, the Upholsterers, the Tillers, and the Bricklayers, among others.

An important method of control was to delegate a monopoly power to an individual or a group in a specific line of production or endeavor. This practice was especially common in those areas considered to be of strategic national interest, such as glass-making, alum, saltpeter, and gunpowder. Monopoly patents usually established conditions for the industry, and often involved the granting of licenses, supervision of the industry, or a monopoly over trade in a given product. However, these measures were relatively ineffective in the face of strong opposition to monopoly patents. The Navigation Laws, which related to international trade, were also important protective measures. These will be treated in the next chapter.

GENERAL REMARKS

The policies discussed above have been used only to illustrate what was common in varying degrees in most countries of Europe. But although we have discussed mercantilism as characteristic of the sixteenth and seventeenth centuries, neither the timing nor the duration of these policies was uniform in all countries. Mercantilism began before the sixteenth century in some countries and lasted much later than the seventeenth in others. The high point of Russian mercantilism came in the eighteenth century during the days of Peter the Great and Catherine II, both of whom made extensive efforts to create factories and encourage economic self-sufficiency. In some countries mercantilism continued to be the rule rather than the exception until the end of the Napoleonic Wars, although by the middle of the eighteenth century signs of its decline in western Europe were apparent, as in England and Sweden. On the other hand, mercantilism was on the decline, at least figuratively, in Germany and Russia. However, before any real decline could take place, a revival of mercantilist policies occurred in the 19th century, as will be seen in that context.

Trade and exchange, whether through barter or money, are inherent in economic society. Sufficiency on a domestic, national, or international scale is achieved through exchange carried on by merchants for profit. However, the mercantilist period went beyond mere trading, exploring and expanding into previously unknown territories. To reduce the risk and increase the spoils of such ventures requires extra effort and enthusiasm. Therefore, some additional explanations of the mercantilist expansion may be necessary. Several possible explanations follow, all of which were acting simultaneously.

CAUSES OF
THE EXPANSION

1. The earlier ventures, such as those of da Gama and Columbus, had been undertaken for the sake of exploration and adventure. Little trade or profit in the economic sense, outside of whatever spoils could be found, was expected from them. Their objective was mainly to search for new routes to already known lands. Thus, while trade might have been looming large in the background, these were not trading ventures. The same may be said of the voyages undertaken or sponsored by Henry the Navigator, who loved adventure and risk. Therefore, it seems appropriate to consider exploration and ad-

venture in themselves as one reason for the international activity of the period.

2. Once the Cape of Good Hope and America had been discovered, new horizons were opened and new expectations aroused. On one side, a new road to the sources of spices and Oriental luxuries was discovered. On the other, vast areas of unexploited natural resources were found. These discoveries activated two major forces: a pull factor and a push factor.

3. Whether the goal was to trade with or to settle in the new lands, the pull factor was important. The lure of profitable venture was strong enough to induce individuals and groups to organize voyages and transplant colonies to exploit the new areas. Profit from trade was high, and the new territories proved to be temptingly rich. Their riches included precious metals which could be mined at ridiculously low costs, if the passage across the ocean could be made safely. Therefore, it became attractive to participate in these ventures as soon as it was apparent that a few successes could bring great wealth.

The new lands, whether in the East or the West, whether on the mainland or across the oceans, proved to be politically and militarily weak relative to the European countries. All of them seemed to have a power vacuum. As soon as this became known, the European governments, one after the other, entered the race to establish their own spheres of influence. This domination resulted in what has become known as colonialism. Whether the flag followed the trade or trade followed the flag, a question often debated, is actually irrelevant. Once a power vacuum had been discovered or could be created, a European power was ready to step in, either directly or through intermediaries, to establish itself as a colonial power. Hence, a significant explanation of the expansion of both trade and settlement is the pull factor inherent in the tendency to dominate and spread influence.

But colonialism is a dynamic force. Once influence has been established, there is always the temptation to expand it into new territories. Self-containment prevails only when an opposing force renders further expansion too risky. When this happens the already dominant forces settle the conflict by dividing the area among themselves, establishing spheres of influence which prevail as long as the balance between these forces remains unchanged.

4. A pull factor is usually augmented by a push factor which gives a movement sustenance, continuity, and force. Europe in this period provided at least two bases for a push factor. The first was the religious–political–social situation. The Reformation created a religious turmoil which assumed a political character, often leading to persecution. People who were unhappy with these events had a reason to move to countries where they might be free and independent. Those who were not wanted were encouraged to emigrate or even transported to these new areas. Emigration and settlement were regarded as colonization by the individuals and groups looking for a new home, but they were also part of the colonial policies of the governments of the home countries.

The push factor had another, probably equally forceful, basis for expansion, namely the economic situation. By the end of the fifteenth century Europe had become fully settled, except for the Russian and eastern

European territories. The land was becoming relatively crowded while technology remained stagnant. Since productivity was not increasing, there was an apparent threat of economic decline. Although data are lacking to support this hypothesis, the recurrent famines and food shortages indicate that there were serious economic threats looming. Europeans found in the newly discovered lands a safety valve to relieve the pressure on the native resources and a way to supplement them. The Great Frontier which the Metropolis needed was discovered, and the Europeans were anxious to exploit it, both for their own welfare and for the good of the mother country, with which they maintained relations for many years.[1] Thus the economic pressure at home stimulated population movement and trade activity on both organized and unorganized levels. The attitude of the governments concerned was reflected in the various measures used to protect, finance, and man the trade and colonization movements.

It should be noted that the economic factor functioned as a pull factor only when the objective was temporary exploitation of the resources in the areas visited, rather than settlement. Settlement and colonization became significant objectives where the push factor was important, and more so where both the pull and the push factors functioned together.

THE PATTERN OF EXPANSION AND ORGANIZATION OF TRADE

Voyages from Europe to other continents had been common for a long time when the new wave of exploration, discovery, and trade began. The Italian cities had established trading colonies on the Mediterranean coast as far back as the eleventh century. Their merchants had gone to the Far East in

[1] On the Great Frontier see Webb's theory in Chapter 3 above.

Figure 13.1 Expansion of Russia in Europe, 1462–1796.

search of spices and other luxury items. The Italians—notably De Carpini, Marco Polo, and Odoric—also explored Asia during the thirteenth and fourteenth centuries. On the Atlantic, expeditions had reached Newfoundland, at least for fishing purposes. Thus, the contact between Europe and the outside world had already been established. This contact and the spirit of exploration, how-ever, were limited in comparison with the expeditions which characterized the period from the late fifteenth through the middle of the seventeenth centuries. These later expedi-tions extended to all corners of the earth. They were sponsored by various countries, although the early efforts were expended mainly by Portugal and Spain. The Dutch, the English, and the French came next in full force. Discovery and trade were the primary objectives in the early period, as reflected in the pattern and organization of these expedi-tions. Settlement and colonization became important almost 100 years after the Portu-guese had begun their explorations.

Russia

The exception to this pattern was the expansion of Russia, where the newly unified Muscovite state was expanding settlement, cultivation, and unification to new territories in its immediate neighborhood. The Russian territorial expansion is shown in Figure 13.1. The periods 1462–1505 and 1505–1682 were periods of major territorial change. New settlement in the Southeast reached the Terek River, and extended in the East be-yond the Volga as far as Yaik; in Siberia it reached the Tobol and the Irtysh. Although Russian expansion was mostly political, eco-nomic activity was an integral part of the movement. Settlers were chosen in family groups and dispatched under a leader, with the incentive of receiving land grants. Where they settled they established towns and forti-fications. Voronzeh was established in 1580; Kromy and Belgorod in 1593; Oskel in 1593; Valuyki in 1600. In the Southeast, Saratov was established in 1584–1589 and Samara in 1586. New towns founded in Siberia included Tynmen in 1586, Tobolsk in 1587, Berezov in 1593, Narym in 1596, Tomsk in 1604, Ilimsk in 1630, Barguzin in 1648, Verkho-Irkutsk in 1653, and many others. Security of the borders was directly connected with the establishment of markets and trade relations as well as the exploita-tion of new resources. By the end of the seventeenth century, the Muscovite state had reached the Pacific Ocean and the Caspian and Black Seas. Only in the West had there been difficulties because of the power of Poland and Lithuania.

The Russian expansion differed from the western European expansion in at least two ways: From the beginning it aimed at terri-torial domination and settlement, both to secure more power and resources and to guarantee the safety of the state. Second, Russian settlement followed the same pattern of institutions, including serfdom and class differentiation, as had prevailed in the Muscovite state itself. Nevertheless, Russian policy was similar to that of the West in some respects. It espoused expansion and trade and adopted measures of exemption, subsidy, and even direct participation. While no companies were created on the scale ex-perienced in the West, enterprises were established to handle local and, to a limited extent, foreign trade. The Russian govern-ment played an important role, as would be expected of a mercantilist state.

A good example of Russian policy toward trade and expansion was the sponsorship of the "Guest Hundred," a group of large mer-chants who had titles and riches, and were closely associated with royalty. The member-ship of the "Guest Hundred" was relatively small; in the sixteenth–seventeenth centuries it was around 158. The tsar himself also participated in trade indirectly by acquiring monopolies on the trade in grain, hemp, rhubarb, raw silk, potash, tar, and caviar. Nevertheless, international trade in this period was still largely in the hands of for-eigners, as it had been for many years.

Western expansion

In contrast, western expansion was into unknown areas. It involved risk and rela-tively large capital investments as well as high prospective returns. Royalty was there-fore always involved both economically and politically in sponsoring expeditions and

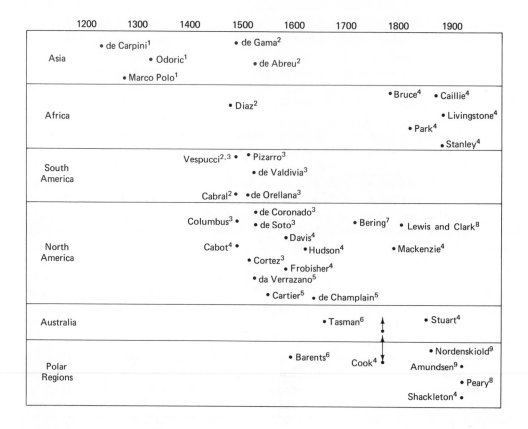

Figure 13.2 The time-place pattern of western explorers.
Superscript number 1 indicates Italy was the sponsor country; 2,
Portugal; 3, Spain; 4, England; 5, France; 6, The Netherlands;
7, Russia; 8, the United States; 9, Scandinavia.

settlement. Jean III of Portugal declared himself the "true spice merchant of the Indies." Isabella of Castile contributed seven-eighths of the capital for Columbus' first two voyages. Queen Elizabeth of England used her personal funds to finance Drake's piratical expeditions and to form in 1588 the Royal African Company, which dealt mostly in slaves, against a third of the profits. Colbert in France sponsored the creation of at least ten large companies to handle international trade and expansion.

European expansion into both the East and the West occurred about the same time. The extent and direction of exploration and settlement are shown in Figure 13.2 and

Figure 13.3. The map shows the routes followed and the coastal areas settled, together with the spheres of influence established by the European countries by the year 1771. As Figure 13.2 shows, exploration was concentrated in the period between 1475 and 1650. The figure also shows the distribution of the expeditions according to the nationality of the sponsor and the destination.

The pioneer country in the exploration of trade routes was Portugal, which extended itself simultaneously into both the East and West Indies. Early in the sixteenth century the Portuguese established ports or trading posts in Goa, Hormuz, Socotra, and Malacca, and on the coast of Brazil. In both

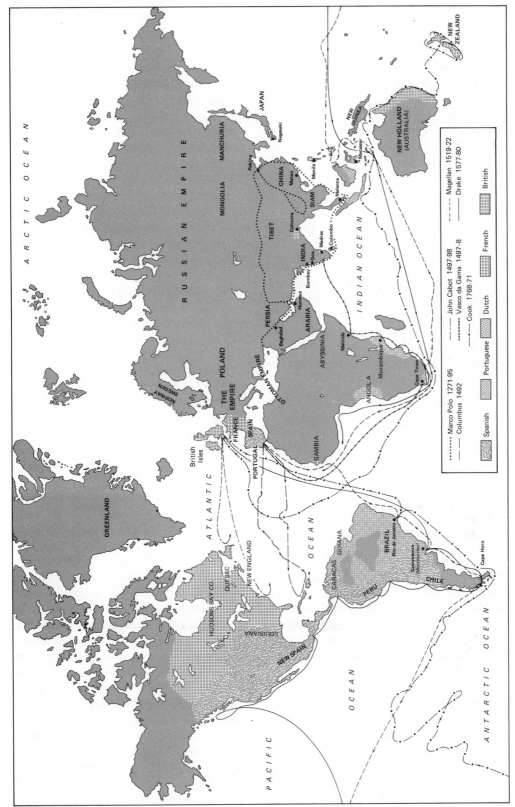

Figure 13.3   Exploration and settlement, with spheres of influence by 1771.

areas they acted as intermediaries in local as well as international trade. In the East they were particularly important as intermediaries in the trade between China and Japan. The pattern of their trading activities may be seen from the routes they followed and the commodities they carried:

> Ships sailing from Goa, by way of Malacca . . . carried assorted European goods to the Portuguese settlement at Macao, where they loaded silk goods, raw silk, and porcelain purchased in Canton. These were sold in Nagasaki, the returns being made, as a rule, in silver. Since the value of silver was higher in China than in Japan, a further profit could be made by exchanging silver for gold on return to Macao. . . . Silks were carried also from Macao to Macassar—a source of spice—and to Manila where they were sold for Mexican silver. There were many other local trades: the sandalwood trade . . . between the China Coast and the Lesser Sunda Islands; the slave trade, whether in African Negroes or in Chinese and Japanese *muitsai*; the import to India of horses from Mesopotamia and copper from Arabia; the export from India to China and Japan of hawks, peacocks, and even an occasional caged tiger.[2]

The Portuguese, however, soon met with competition in their Oriental trade activities. The Dutch and later the English did their best to replace them in the Orient. The Dutch came with more capital and more experience, which they acquired from the mistakes of the Portuguese. They were able to benefit from relations with the local chiefs. These same benefits were available to the English, who in effect were the successors of the Portuguese in the East. The Dutch and English, unlike the Portuguese, were more concerned with trade between the Orient and Europe than with local trade within the re-

2 E. E. Rich and C. H. Wilson (eds.), *Cambridge Economic History of Europe*, IV, New York: Cambridge University Press, 1967, chap. 3, pp. 192–193.

gion. The Dutch were at first mainly interested in spices and later in slaves. The English were interested in these, but they also shipped back to England cotton, muslins, and saltpeter, for which they usually paid in cash.

With the shift in influence from the Portuguese to the Dutch and English there came a change in the methods of organizing trade. The Portuguese conducted their trade largely as a government-sponsored activity with centralized authority under the supervision and direction of public officials. In contrast, the Dutch and English worked through largely autonomous companies chartered by the government. This contrast existed also in the Americas. The Portuguese and Spanish operations were the responsibility of public authority while the English, Dutch, and French interests were, at least up to the end of the seventeenth century, largely in private hands.

Portuguese–Spanish centralized approach

The tradition of direct royal participation in Portugal goes back to the days of Henry the Navigator. After discovery of the Cape of Good Hope and of trade sources on the coast of Africa, the Portuguese government became highly interested in the spice and slave trade. Though slavery began as a private monopoly, centralization soon followed. The government established Houses of Trade with territorial specializations as well as differentiation of responsibilities. For example, they established a *Casa de Ceuta*, a *Casa de Guinea*, and a *Casa da Mina* in Lisbon with authority to control the trade and economic life of the country—the *Vedores da Fazenda*. The first two of these *casas* dealt with the African trade. A *Casa da India* was established in 1517 with a treasurer seated in India. The *Casa da India* had a complete system of controls with "factories" and warehouses of its own. A state authority was responsible for the monopoly in spices and precious metals, and it made certain that private merchants handling other items paid a duty of about 20 percent. Control by public officials extended to organizing fleets, appointing captains, specifying trade items to be carried, and protecting the convoys. Although the Portuguese influence was reduced by the Spanish occupation of Portugal, 1591–1640, these institutions remained virtually intact. However, learning from the successful experiences of the Dutch and the English, Portugal permitted the creation of private companies in the seventeenth century. However, these remained under the control of the *casa*. Their success was limited, but their creation marked a decline of state control. By the eighteenth century trade between Portugal and the colonies was virtually free.

The Spanish experience was similar to that of Portugal. After some hesitation, the Spanish government began to regulate trade —as early as 1501. To implement a policy of control, a state agency was created, the *Real Ardiencia y Casa de Contratacion,* under a treasurer, a controller, a secretary, and a "factor" who regulated shipments. The *casa* acted also as a court of justice, a trade administration, and an academy of hydrography. After 1526 all ships were required to join a convoy for protection and supervision. The *casa* established consulates in various countries to facilitate trade and the administration of justice on its behalf. The state monopoly was somewhat flexible but remained in effect with minor revisions for many years. Gradually, however, the *casa* became an administrative bureaucracy manned by nobility and courtiers who acquired their positions as payoffs. Its influence declined thereafter because of bureaucratic abuse of power, severe attacks by pirates, and foreign competition and aggression.

The companies approach

England, Holland, and France were equally interested in trade and colonization, although they were latecomers compared with Portugal and Spain. The approach they followed was to encourage the creation of companies and give them privileges and protection to conduct trade and increase the wealth of the nation. Some of these companies were associations of merchants, such as the Merchant Adventurers of England, who traded individually but united under a common set of rules and moral principles. The members rendered mutual help to each other, but each made his own decisions and earned his own profits. The organizations which were more characteristic of the period were the chartered companies, such as the East India and the West India Companies. These were created by all three countries, although at different times during the century. The English East India Company was established in 1600; the Dutch Company in 1602, and the French Company sometime later under the influence of Henry IV. The West India Companies were created still later. These were joint-stock companies with permanent capital, and acted as legal persons. Each company was usually created by a charter or its equivalent, which gave it a monopoly of trade in a given region, in a given commodity, for a certain period of time, or any combination of these. The English Royal African Company was chartered for 1000 years.

A chartered company usually had political influence and responsibility in the colonies, in addition to its economic objectives. This political significance increased with the interest in colonization and settlement. Some companies even became interested in territorial expansion in the colonies, arousing the jealousy of the states which created them and on which they depended for protection. However, by the end of the eighteenth century, these companies had served their purpose and political responsibility for the colonies had shifted to the national governments, largely because of the increasing burden of administering the colonies. In a sense, the companies acted as feudal lords until their services were no longer needed.

In general, the companies were expected to fulfill certain obligations in return for the monopoly privileges they enjoyed. They were expected to deliver a certain number of slaves each year to the colonies, or send out a certain number of ships, or secure specific cargoes from one place or another. The most interesting obligation, but one which was not too common, was to carry out scientific exploration. Fernao Gomez, for example, obtained a monopoly of the trade of Guinea on condition that he would explore 100 leagues of the coast each year. In 1550 Fernao de Loronha acquired a trade permit in Brazil for 3 years on condition of exploring 300 leagues of the coast. The merchants of the Dutch East India Company were actually in direct contact with the geographer Plancius. Companies sometimes employed such scientific explorers as Berentz, Lemaire, and Hudson. It is even claimed that Captain Cook was as interested in purely scientific discoveries as he was in the commercial benefits of his adventures.

DIRECTION AND COMPOSITION OF TRADE

Production and trade, particularly international trade and expansion, were regarded as the main sources of national wealth. The composition of trade was determined by the demand for products, which varied according to the changing tastes and changing conditions in the colonies. The sixteenth century was a century of trade. The seventeenth and eighteenth centuries were periods of agricultural production, colonization, and mining, as well. Throughout these three centuries, there was a high degree of interdependence among the Orient, Europe, and the Americas in the sense that trade in any one direction was influenced by trade in other directions. Trade was triangular: Commodities from the Orient came to Europe either as a terminal point or in transit to the colonies in America. In return, the Americas sent their products to Europe. Europe provided the manufactured goods such as firearms, cloth, and liquor in return for what they received, although sometimes silver

from the Americas, rather than European finished products, found its way to the Orient. Spices continued to be a major and profitable item of trade from the Orient. The East India Companies were for a long time concerned primarily with spices and with silk and silk products from the Orient. This pattern changed slightly when gold was discovered in the Gold Coast and when the demand for slave labor in the Americas increased. Slavery became the most important trade item from Africa and many companies were chartered primarily for the slave trade. Slavery became increasingly more important as the sugar plantations and silver mines of America found themselves short of labor.

A certain degree of national specialization developed in both production and trade. The Portuguese, for example, in addition to their early monopoly of spices and the slave sources in Africa, led in creating sugar plantations. They also traded in dyes, cotton, and gold. Spain concentrated on the production and transport of precious metals, which constituted 95 percent of the Spanish imports from the colonies. However, in the process of providing labor for the mines, the Spaniards had to establish settlements. As a result they became involved in the production of hides, sugar, dyes, cacao, and tobacco, although on a relatively limited scale. The English were interested in tobacco and sugar as were the French and the Dutch. All countries took an active part in piracy and the slave trade, not only as a source of manpower for the sugar plantations each nation operated, but also as a trade item from which high returns could be expected. Thus the demand for sugar produced a high demand for slaves which sustained the triangular trade.

FINANCING, REGULATION, AND VOLUME OF TRADE

In Portugal and Spain most of the financing for trade and settlement came from the treasury, and the revenues from such ventures were directed to it. The government charged duties on all items traded and used these, as well as other taxes, to finance the *casas*. Therefore, financing was determined more by political considerations than by economics or profit. The national interest rather than the economic justification of the *casa* determined the amount of support it received. In contrast, the English, French, and Dutch companies were usually financed by the private funds of merchants, even though governments were often shareholders and subsidizers. Other groups were frequently contributors also, among them military officers, nobility, and royal households. The role of government was primarily to protect and regulate trade to maintain the monopoly abroad and to sustain a positive balance of trade at home. Three illustrations of government regulations will be discussed: the *asiento* system relating to the slave trade, the English Navigation Laws, and the "five big farms" tariff policy of France.

The *asiento* system

The significance of slavery is shown by the interest national governments took in it. Four sources of labor were available to man the mines and settlements of the New World. The first was family labor. This source was inadequate and became important only in such northern colonies as New England, where small family farms were common. The second source was the indigenous Indian population. This source was quickly depleted by disease and frustration when the Indians were forced to replace their mobile tribal way of life with regulated settlement. The third source was the system of indentured labor by which emigrants were financed against a commitment to work for a given period of time. Land grants were given out to anyone who could recruit a labor force of a specified size. This source, however, was inadequate for the sugar plantations and in tropical and subtropical climates where white settlement was limited. In these areas, the main source of labor was Negro slavery. The Portuguese and the

Spanish recognized that fact and took measures to hold onto their initial advantages in the slave trade. The Portuguese jealously guarded their trading posts on the coast of Africa, which were the main sources of slaves. The Spanish regulated the slave trade by a licensing system, the *asiento*, which required that all deliveries of slaves to the Spanish possessions remain in Spanish hands. The *asiento* system became the focus of national rivalry and was a factor in the sea battles which led to the destruction of Spanish shipping and the Armada.

Although for many years the *asiento* remained exclusively Spanish, the shortage of labor and the need for revenue led the Spanish government to issue licenses to non-Spaniards as early as 1521. The first such license was issued to Germans. However, the English and Dutch were already sharing in the trade through partnerships with Spaniards and Portuguese. The monopoly was not easy to enforce because of smuggling, piracy, and the high demand for labor in the colonies. However, Spain held onto its monopoly, at least formally, until the Treaty of Utrecht in 1713, when the *asiento* was given to the English South Sea Company allowing them to deliver one shipload of slaves a year to Spanish possessions in America. In British hands, the *asiento* became a source of conflict between planters and traders. The planters wanted the slaves to be delivered to them, while the traders wanted to sell where the market was more favorable. As a result of this conflict and Spain's declining ability to maintain a monopoly, the companies that held concessions became progressively weaker and individuals began to gain access to the slave trade. Nevertheless, as late as 1750, Spain was still interested enough in the *asiento* to retrieve the concession from the South Sea Company for £100,000 compensation.

The Navigation Laws

In the seventeenth century the rising interests of England in international trade and colonization were challenged by the

Dutch, whose trade activities were already highly developed. The Dutch were not concerned with colonial production, but with trade and carrying. However, their strength in these areas affected the balance of trade of the nations buying Dutch services and therefore could not be ignored. The Navigation Acts were an answer to this challenge, designed both to undermine Dutch and other competitors and to protect England's wealth and its balance of trade. Navigation ordinances and Acts were passed from 1650 on, but the Act of 1660 contained most of the important clauses and was to remain in effect, with periodic elaborations, until 1849. The main provisions of the Act have been summarized as follows:

a. No goods were to be imported from or exported to the king's possessions outside Europe, or imported from other places outside Europe, except in ships belonging to people of England, Wales or Ireland, or in ships built by and belonging to people in the overseas possessions themselves; ships, moreover, with English masters and crews three-quarters English.

b. No tobacco, sugar, corn, indigo, ginger, fustick or other dyewood produced in English possessions outside Europe was to be exported to any place other than England or Ireland or an English possession. [These are the so-called "enumerated commodities," the list of which was extended from time to time.]

c. A wide range of goods, including nearly all the principal products of the Mediterranean and the Baltic, and all the produce of the Russian and Turkish empires, was to be imported into England, Ireland or Wales only in English ships, with masters and three-quarters of the crews English, or in ships of the producing country or of the place of first shipment.

d. Foreign goods imported by English-built and English-manned ships were to be brought only from their places of origin or usual first shipment.

e. The coasting trade was completely reserved for English-owned ships, with masters and three-quarters of the crew English.[3]

In 1663 another Act was passed making it mandatory that all European goods destined for English colonies be laden in England or Wales and be carried directly to the colonies. The only exceptions to this rule were salt destined for the Newfoundland fisheries, Madeira and Azores wines, and horses and provisions from Scotland and Ireland.

The Navigation Laws which were passed between 1660 and 1696 had several implications. First, they tied the economies of the colonies to that of England and thus guaranteed the manufacturers in England a supply of raw material at favorable prices.[4] Second, the Navigation Laws secured employment for the masters and crews in English shipping, as well as for the ship-building industry and its craftsmen. The effects of guaranteed employment are hard to estimate in the absence of adequate information regarding the alternative opportunities in the labor market at the time, but no doubt such employment favored the interests of England and the Empire. Third, the Laws secured a market for finished products in the colonies at prices favorable to the English producers. Whether the colonists might have been able to secure goods at lower prices has been a subject of debate. However, the fact that English producers held onto these restrictions indicates that they derived benefits from them. Fourth, the Laws formally involved the government in international trade in spite of its tendency to keep the companies autonomous. There was no longer any question that trade must be geared to the national interest as perceived by the government or by the interest groups involved in trade. Fifth, the Navigation Laws made English ports points of transit and made reex-

---

[3] Ralph Davis, *The Rise of the English Shipping Industry*, London: Macmillan, 1962, p. 307.

[4] The impact of these Acts on the economies of the colonies has been debated, with no clear evidence on either side. See the bibliography at end of Chapter 14.

Table 13.1.   Export tax on coal, per
Newcastle chaldron

YEAR	IN ENGLISH VESSELS	IN FOREIGN VESSELS
1620	6s. 8d.	8s. 4d.
1660	8s.	16s.
1694	3s.	10s.
1710	3s.	12s.
1714	6s.	17s.
1757	10s.	21s.
1765	14s.	25s.

SOURCE: *Ralph Davis*, The Rise of the English
Shipping Industry, *London: Macmillan, 1962,
p. 311.*

port from England an important source of
revenue for the Exchequer. At the same time,
they prevented other nations from reexport-
ing goods to England. Finally, the Laws
legitimated piracy and attacks on foreign
ships in defense of the territorial and
shipping rights they guaranteed. Although
piracy was a common practice, official involvement had occurred only during wartime. The Navigation Laws made such
involvement legitimate also in peacetime, although at the risk of a full-scale war. The
success of the enforcement of the Laws is not
easy to measure, but the reactions to them
and the fact that they remained in effect for
189 years suggest that their results were felt
both at home and abroad.

In order to aid English shipping further,
a heavier duty was levied on coal exports
shipped in foreign vessels than on those
shipped in English ships. The differential
duty amounted to almost one-third of the
value of the coal exported, as Table 13.1
illustrates. Similarly, a bounty of five shillings per quarter was paid to corn exporters
whose produce was carried by English ships,
making foreign competition in corn shipping
virtually impossible.

The "five big farms"

The French policy of restriction was
similar in intent to those of Spain and England: protection of French interests and increase of the national wealth. It was also
similar in that it tried to maintain certain

monopolies. However, a unique French
policy was the division of France into two
main tariff areas: the "five big farms" (*cinq
grosses fermes*), and the rest, the "provinces
reputed foreign" (*provinces reputées étran-
gères*). The five big farms included Ile de
France, Normandy, Picardy, Champagne,
Burgundy, Bresse, Poitu, Aunis, Berry,
Bourbonnais, Anjou, Main, Orléanais,
Perche, Nivernais, Touraine, Thouars and
its dependencies, and the Châtellenie of
Chantoceaux. These provinces formed a customs union within which trade was free of
duties. However, goods going in or out of
this area were subject to duty, regardless of
whether or not their destination or point of
origin was another French territory. The five
big farms were subject to the *aides*—an
indirect sales tax levied on beverages, fish,
livestock, and wood—while the other provinces were exempt. This tax was usually
farmed out to collectors; hence the appella-
tion "big farms." This tariff system divided
France into two regions and thus reduced
the size of the market. It also allowed variations in the duties levied at the borders of
different farms, which tended to reduce uniformity and to cause dislocations in the
distribution and flow of trade.

The volume of trade

The available data are not adequate to
give a clear picture of the total volume of
trade, but certain tendencies may be illustrated for selected commodities.

Probably the most important commodity
in the early period of colonization and expansion was the bullion imported by Spain.
Obviously the importation of bullion and the
exchange of goods required services and
shipping industries to cope with the flow of
traffic. The relationship between the flows of
bullion and traffic is shown in Figure 13.4.
These graphs show the trend of international
trade activity between Seville, headquarters
of the *Casa de Contratacion*, and America.
Both the volume of traffic in tonnage and the
value of bullion rose until around 1600, with

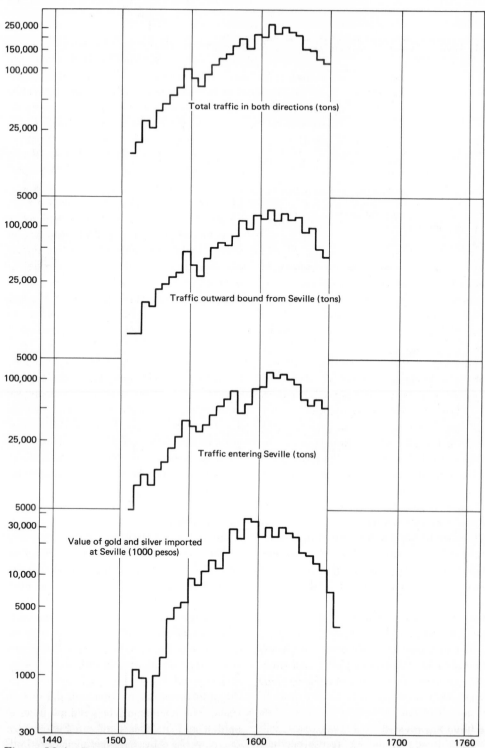

Figure 13.4   Trade between Seville and America.
SOURCE: *Cambridge Economic History of Europe*, IV, p. 485.
Trade with America after H. and P. Chaunu; gold and silver imports after E. J. Hamilton.

Table 13.2. England's tonnage of entrances and clearances and value of trade

	1686 (Thousands of Tons)		AVERAGE VALUE 1699–1701 (£1000)	
	ENTRIES	CLEARANCES	IMPORTS	EXPORTS
Germany	12.7 (3.5)[a]	7.8 (2.7)	732	779
Holland	36.8 (2.6)	76.9 (4.1)	518	1787
France			100	204
	82.5 (3.9)	41.9 (3.3)		
Flanders			68	252
Ireland and Channel Islands	48.6 (13.5)	61.4 (17.3)	332	290
Scotland	6.2 (3.2)	2.7 (1.9)	97	77
Norway	80.8 (34.1)	33.2 (14.1)	71[b]	42[b]
Russia	1.3	1.9	213	78
Baltic, except Russia	48.4 (22.1)	20.1 (5.5)	—	—
Sweden	—	—	123	62
Spain	19.9 (0.6)	12.5 (0.3)	516	517
Portugal	10.0	8	219	334
Italy	—	—	355	114
Turkey	6.8	3.9	50	35
East India	5.8	8.4	756	136
West Indies	43.7	30.7	743	344
Africa	0.7	3.3	22	129
North America	71.2	66.3	342	378

[a] *Parentheses indicate tonnage carried by foreign ships.*
[b] *Norway and Denmark.*
SOURCE: *Ralph Davis,* The Rise of the English Shipping Industry, *London: Macmillan, 1962, various tables.*

the value of bullion reaching the peak about two decades before the volume of traffic. This suggests that items other than bullion were important in the trade. However, Spanish trade began to decline under the pressure of Dutch and English competition. The height of British and Dutch trade was not achieved until later in the eighteenth century. Since comparative data are not available, we shall resort to selective data to suggest the magnitude of international trade activity in this period.

The Dutch East India Company organized fleets throughout the seventeenth and eighteenth centuries. The annual average of ships in these fleets varied from 10 to 38 sailing in any one direction between 1611 and 1781. The highest annual average was reached in the third decade of the eighteenth century. The tonnage of these ships and their significance to Dutch shipping are not clear. It is estimated that the Dutch merchant marine

employed between 30,000 and 40,000 sailors in the second half of the eighteenth century, after the decline had already started.

More detailed information is available regarding English merchant shipping. Table 13.2 shows the distribution of trade between England and other countries for the year 1686 and the average value of trade for the years 1699–1701, including the colonies. These figures give some idea of the volume of English trade and the countries with which England traded. In spite of rivalry, Holland was important both as a buyer and as a seller. Spain's exports to England were almost equally important, although its purchases were less than half those of Holland. The East Indian and West Indian colonies were much more important as suppliers than as buyers from England. Germany was both a big buyer and a big seller. Russia was one of the smaller customers, especially in terms of the entry and clearance of ships between

Russia and England. Apparently intermediaries carried the goods that were traded between the two.

The colonial trade

In the absence of detailed data on other European countries, it may be suggested that the pattern of trade between them and their colonies was similar to that of English–colonial trade. The same items of trade were common to all countries. Sugar refining was basic to the development of Bristol and Glasgow, but it was also important to Paris and Amsterdam. It is estimated that France had 30 domestic sugar refineries in 1683 and 5 more in the colonies. These refineries used more than 18 million pounds of raw sugar a year. This was brought by the French from the West Indies, although 20 years earlier it had been supplied by Dutch ships and crewmen. Amsterdam had 16 sugar refineries around the end of the century. The Portuguese had 30 sugar plantations in 1576, 76 in 1584, and 180 early in the seventeenth century. As we have seen, the sugar industry had significant repercussions on the slave trade and ship-building.

Slavery was important in the English, Dutch, and later the French trade. The significance of each nation's participation is not clear, however. It has been noted that by the end of the eighteenth century there were 40 "factories" on the African coast supplying slaves. Of these, 10 were English, 3 French, 15 Dutch, 4 Portuguese, and 4 Danish; apparently the remaining 4 were Spanish. It has also been estimated that from 1600 on more than 100 Spanish and Portuguese ships a year came to Africa to carry away slaves. In 1771, 192 British ships carried 47,146 Negroes to the West Indies. In 1788, 98 French ships carried 29,000 slaves to Santo Domingo.[5]

These figures are too few to permit a full evaluation. However, various guesses regarding the total number of slaves carried are available: One source estimates that from the Congo to America, an annual average of 7,000 slaves were shipped during the sixteenth century; an annual average of 15,000 during the seventeenth; and an annual average of 30,000 during the eighteenth century. During the first half of the nineteenth century an annual average of 150,000 were transported; 50,000 were shipped annually between 1850 and 1860, and 2,000 annually between 1860 and 1885. Another general estimate puts the total figure at 20 million transported during the whole period. A third estimate is that between 1576 and 1591 about 52,000 Negroes were shipped to Brazil alone. The West Indies imported 2,130,000 slaves between 1680 and 1786; France shipped about 30,000 annually to the French West Indies between 1780 and 1789.[6]

Even though these figures may be exaggerated, the magnitude can hardly be overestimated if we recall that around 1580 Spain and Portugal together had a total population of only 10 million; England and Wales had a population of about 4.5 million in 1600; and France claimed about 16 million in that year. In other words, a group as large as the total French population was transported as slaves from Africa to the Americas. To this should be added the white settlers and indentured workers who emigrated freely or by force. The shipping industry had to develop to cope with this activity; and with it developed all the related industries and services.

Slavery and colonization left an impact on the future development of both Europe and the colonies. Their qualitative effects were more important than can be ascertained from the fragmentary data at our disposal. Clearly they stimulated industry, organization, and political rivalry. But they also created a deep schism between social groups within the colonies and between countries on different continents.

[5] Scattered figures and estimates from Frank Tannenbaum, *Slave and Citizen, The Negro in America*, New York: Random House (Vintage Book), 1946, pp. 32–33.

[6] Frank Tannenbaum, *op. cit.*, pp. 29–36.

14

THE
IMPACT:
TRIUMPH
OF
MATERIALISM

The effects of mercantilism must be viewed as consequences of the whole process of mercantilist activity, political, economic, and social. Internal and external developments, which we have discussed separately, were in fact highly interdependent. The government policy toward both was guided by the same doctrine, objectives, and information. The regulation of wages or prices had an impact on economic conditions within and outside a given economy, and was in turn determined by these conditions. What happened at home was closely connected with what happened in the colonies.

Nor were mercantilist policies unique to the sixteenth and seventeenth centuries. Many of the policies pursued in this period had forerunners, and most continued throughout the eighteenth century and even longer. Many of the results of mercantilist policies were not apparent until the late eighteenth and early nineteenth centuries. Some observers have even questioned whether the mercantilist policy was ever abandoned or its consequences fully realized. They argue that mercantilism is an ongoing process and that new effects keep appearing in modified forms appropriate for the changing environment and frame of reference. However, since this approach renders evaluation impossible, we shall approach the subject as if mercantilism reached its peak in the sixteenth and seventeenth centuries and

as if the prevalent conditions at the time can be directly attributed to its policies.

TRIUMPH OF
MATERIALISM

Mercantilism has been described in various ways, but one apparently common feature noted by most observers has been the subjection of economic interests to the political and the emphasis on national unification and state power. Such a characterization seems appropriate, but it is insufficient. The most apparent phenomenon uniting the policies and activities of the various countries was the virtually complete triumph of materialism. Even though the goal of increasing state power and national wealth loomed large, these objectives had to be consistent with material incentives, profit motives, and the accumulation of private wealth. Where the national objectives were inconsistent with private objectives or where the latter were suppressed, the national objectives were not fully realized. The contrast between Portugal and Spain on one hand and Holland and England on the other provides a good illustration. In all these countries there was government intervention and interest in national aggrandizement. In all of them attempts were made to expand, colonize, trade, and accumulate wealth. However, in Portugal and Spain state objectives took precedence over private ones and material wealth was dissipated in the service of the state or national power. In contrast, the Dutch and English governments pursued the same objectives within a framework in which the material interests of individuals could be satisfied. The vested interests of the economic and business groups were always prominent in state policy formation in these countries. In France the conflict between state and individual interests was less conspicuous than it was in Spain and Portugal, but more than in England and Holland. The results were intermediate between those attained in the other two groups.[1]

The triumph of materialism was apparent in the conflict between economic objectives on one side and social and moral values on the other. Undoubtedly the material objectives triumphed. With the help of the Church and the state, individuals and groups were able to reinterpret their moral and social values to remove obstacles that might prevent realization of their economic objectives. Whether we call the process economic rationality, objectivity, or determinism, the end result was always the same. Enslavement of the Negro, annihilation of the Indian, indenture of the white immigrant, and piracy and pillage were given legitimacy. Whether material interests could have been reconciled with social and moral principles without compromising either is difficult to determine. But it is revealing that more effort was expended on rationalizing the situation than on trying to reconcile these goals. There were few if any attempts to secure wage labor in place of the slave. The Negro and the Indian were not offered any attractions to the job; either they were forced into the work or the master decided what terms *ought* to be attractive. The re-

[1] The argument presented here is different from that of J. U. Nef, who compared England and France between 1540 and 1640. Nef observed that government regulation and control was the determining factor.

sults were costly to all parties concerned, except possibly the individual colonizer, trader, and profit-maker.

Finally, the triumph of materialism is illustrated by the new criteria for supremacy among nations. It became clear in this period that the nation's power depended on the skill and ability of its members to subdue nature and produce material objects. It was not the richness of culture, as in the Far East, nor the homogeneity of the community, as among the Indians, nor the religious values which determined the status of the nation. It was the ability to produce, to mobilize, to put ships on the high seas, to produce firearms, and to put all the resources of the country at the disposal of its economic and business interests which determined supremacy. The schism that developed between producer and nonproducer, between materialist and nonmaterialist, and between the concrete and the introspective is most fully illustrated by the dualism that arose between European and non-European, and between white and nonwhite. This dualism has persisted and material criteria remain its basic determinants.

To understand the processes by which the triumph of materialism was realized, let us explore the effects of mercantilism on the various communities concerned. These include the colonies and spheres of influence outside Europe and the various social groups within the European countries.

THE COLONIES AND SPHERES OF INFLUENCE

The difference between colonies and spheres of influence corresponds to the distinction suggested above between colonization and colonialism, or between colonies of settlement and colonies of exploitation. Spheres of influence were established mainly for exploitation, economic and political, and concerned primarily non-European natives. The objectives and policies of the two types of colonies obviously overlapped, but in both types a clear distinction was made in the treatment of Europeans and non-Europeans, and of whites and nonwhites. The non-Europeans and nonwhites were regarded only as tools of production or as means to material wealth, whether their products were spices, slaves, sugar, or bullion.

The Europeans faced different environments in the three continents they reached. The Asian countries were fairly well populated, with old cultures and organized governments in addition to the spices and silks the Europeans wanted. Africa was a dark continent where the population was sparser, less organized, and more submissive. The Americas, rich in resources, were even more sparsely populated with a population that had a totally different conception of wealth and economy. The Europeans recognized these differences and adjusted their policies. They did not, however, modify their objectives, and paid little attention to their effects on the natives.

The Orient

The Portuguese, the Dutch, and later the English tried to befriend the chiefs in the Orient in order to secure spices and other commodities. These friendships lasted only as long as the chiefs were useful, however. If other sources were discovered, the previous sources were abandoned and even subdued. When it seemed feasible the Europeans took over the political administration of the areas from which they secured valuable supplies.

European involvement remained restricted to the ports and coastal areas, and the responsibility of carrying supplies from the interior was left to the natives. White settlement in these territories was out of the question. When settlement did occur, its purpose was only to secure supplies to ship to Europe. Any impact on the development or economy of the area was restricted either to the supply sources or to an indirect influence by demonstration, and thus had limited effects in the long run. This was true even of the English East India Company. Even after it had expanded its influence to encompass the political administration of India, the changes introduced were only in areas that could be exploited economically or that would make political administration and hence economic exploitation easier.

Gradually the relations between Europe and the Orient changed from trade relations to those of an empire, or of governor and governed, master and servant, superior and inferior. The economies of these colonies were geared to complement the home economies both as sources of supply and as markets for finished products.

Africa and slavery

In Africa there was less aspiration for imperial domination and more interest in short-run gains. Political domination was restricted to the ports, trading posts, and factories. The African chiefs insisted on serving as intermediaries in the slave trade, bringing the slaves to the coast for shipment to the Americas. The Europeans in return supplied firearms, chains, cloth, or cash. Otherwise they showed little interest in economic exchange in Africa. Sometimes they expressed deep concern for converting the Negroes to Christianity or for saving them from a harsh life. However, this policy was consistent with their trade objectives. Those chiefs who accepted baptism and conversion were left free and befriended, so that they could continue to supply the slaves from the interior. But although the slaves were baptized *en masse* they were still kept as slaves, sold in auction, or delivered to the sugar plantations.

No efforts were spared to get these slaves to their destination. They were chained, whipped, or amused with loud music to keep their spirits high. Whatever good treatment was rendered was designed to keep as many of them as possible alive and fit for marketing at high prices. The issues of humaneness and morality were dismissed lightly in the face of the demand for labor on the plantations and in the mines of America and the high returns that could be expected from the slave trade. Even though a third of the Africans who left their homes died before reaching the coast and many more never reached their destination alive, the survivors paid off well enough to sustain the trade for more than three centuries.

The buyers, whether intermediaries or plantation owners and managers, did not improve on the traders' treatment. The slave was given subsistence and kept on the job as long as he could work. His offspring were also slaves and could be sold separately. If he was taught anything, it had to be consistent with the institution of slavery. Questions of morality, freedom, brotherhood, and political rights were subordinated to economic and business objectives. Gradually the new generations of whites and Negroes came to believe that the institution was right and that racial differences justified it. The significance of the slave as an asset was expressed by the prestige attached to the owner of many slaves. The question of how much he produced or how many acres of land he owned might be raised, but the number of his slaves was a sufficient indicator of his wealth and influence. It indicated the size of his plantation, the level of production, and the stock of wealth he controlled.

The American Indian

The Negro slave was treated in a way designed to keep him alive and strong to serve as a tool and as a market asset. The American Indian was in a different category. He occupied the land which the new settler invaded. Therefore, he was not expected to be friendly. The white settler tried at first to secure by trade with the Indian those commodities which promised high returns, such as precious metals and furs. In return the settler offered firearms, some finished textile products, and liquor. As mines and plantations were established, he tried to use the Indian for labor. The Indian was resistant to the work regulations of sedentary settlement,

especially on lands that had been open to him alone. Thus, the settler faced a conflict: On one hand, he needed the Indian for work; on the other, he wanted to get rid of him in order to secure his land for exploitation and settlement. To reconcile the two objectives, reservations were assigned to the Indians, labor quotas were imposed on their chiefs, and they were spared slavery. However, their resistance was too strong to overcome. The labor quotas which caused the breakdown of the Indian family and required adjustment to a sedentary life depressed the Indians enough to reduce their numbers effectively. This oppression was reinforced by white diseases to which the Indian had no immunity, by the wars organized to subdue hostile tribes, and by the liquor provided by the whites which rendered the Indian helpless and unproductive. The Indian was on his way to annihilation, thus making room for the European settler and his Negro slave. One exception to this policy of annihilation was the mixed-blood policy practiced in the Spanish and Portuguese colonies. There, in order to increase the population and provide an adequate labor force in the colonies, mixed marriages were encouraged between whites and Indians. The result was the *mestizo* who is characteristic of the formerly Spanish territories. This intermarriage policy may have saved the Indian from annihilation, but it did not save his culture. The result was modification into a hybrid culture.

Indenture

Indentured labor had been used in the colonization of rural Europe as early as the eleventh century. It also had some connection with the system of apprenticeship. Two differences from apprenticeship should be noted, however. Indentured labor in America was not aimed at teaching a skill. In most cases unskilled work on the farm was expected. The primary objective of the arrangement, from the standpoint of the employer, was to secure labor for the new settlements. The worker's objective also differed from earlier experiences of indenture. Because the transportation cost to America was too high for the worker, he was willing to commit his services and often those of his family for a given period in exchange for the fare and a certain compensation at the end of his service. In order to gain access to the benefits of the New World, he agreed to sell his services for years in advance, thus helping also to solve the labor problem of his employer.

Once in America, the indentured laborer was treated differently from both the Indian and the Negro. His relationship with his employer was regulated by contract. His status was known to be temporary. He came from the same stock as his employer and his rights were protected by the imperial laws of the mother country. Neither the Indian nor the Negro had such rights or recourse to protection. The treatment of both the Indian and the Negro was founded on exploitation. The treatment of the indentured worker was based on a policy of colonization and permanence. The indentured worker was expected to become a "neighbor" and co-citizen. The effect of the policy toward the Indian and the Negro was to release the land and to produce wealth for the European powers. The policy of indenture was designed to produce wealth for the colonies, commodities for Europe, and power over the weak but rich continent. Indenture also provided an outlet for the unhappy, the unemployed, and the unwanted of Europe. Whether or not Europe was relatively overcrowded at the time makes little difference. Those who had no place in the Old World could find a place in the Great Frontier and thus relieve the Old Country of a burden as well as increase the outflow of products from the Great Frontier to the Metropolis. It was to the advantage of all concerned to encourage indenture, emigration, and settlement. As settlement and indenture increased, the pressure on the Indians increased. And as more land became available for cultivation, the attractiveness of slavery was sustained or even increased. The impact of these developments was to be felt much later in the colonies. The impact on Europe was immediate.

THE HOME COUNTRIES

The five countries that were most active in overseas expansion were affected in different ways by it. The effects were political, economic, and social.

Political effects

In the mercantilist period the pattern of power distribution that was to remain in effect for more than two centuries was established. Until the unification of Germany in 1871, Britain and France virtually dominated politics in Europe and in the world at large. It is true that Portugal, Spain, and Holland retained their empires or spheres of influence, but they had declined as European and world powers by the end of the period. Spanish weakness was best illustrated by the recurrent bankruptcies of the government which occurred roughly every 20 years. The Spanish Crown mortgaged its colonial revenues years in advance. As the currency was depreciated and as the monarchy defaulted on its debts, the lenders were also ruined. The Italian bankers and the Fuggers of Germany bore the main burden of these defaults. Despite this decline, however, Spain and Portugal left indelible cultural and institutional impressions on their colonies abroad. Holland retained its position as a serious competitor of France and England a little longer than the Portuguese and the Spanish.

Portugal and Spain declined in part because they failed to create viable economic foundations. They had extended themselves beyond their means, restricted private initiative, and concentrated on accumulating bullion and financial gain. The slight emphasis they placed on production and their limited natural resources were important handicaps in the way of future development. Further-more, both had been for many years targets of rivalry, first from the Dutch and later from the English and the French. The recur-rent wars in which Spain participated fur-ther weakened its polity and economy.

Britain and France came onto the scene a little later than Portugal and Spain and learned from the experiences of their fore-runners. They had more resources, especially manpower, to commit to the new economies they were striving to create. Both were favored by virtual unification and centraliza-tion of power. However, probably the most important reason for their continued influ-ence and political development was the fact that they built their political power on the basis of viable economic structures. They paid attention to production and the accumu-lation of real capital. While this was true also of Holland, the latter was a relatively small country with limited labor resources. Holland became the envy of England and France, who indirectly combined their forces to undermine its influence, until they eventu-ally succeeded in containing its power and in creating a vacuum which they could fill.

As a result, the mercantilist period came to a close with Britain fully established as a leader and France as a close competitor. Interestingly enough, this new power struc-ture did not seriously disturb the distribu-tion of influence in the colonies. Except for the English–French skirmishes in North America, it seems that the powers accepted the established distribution, regardless of their relative abilities to protect their im-perial territories. Possibly this acceptance was due to the fact that the powers gradually relaxed their earlier restrictions in regard to their colonies. This trend was especially true in the area of trade, which was a basic source of conflict. Once that problem had been contained, acceptance of the power structure became possible and meaningful.

Another political development resulting from mercantilist policies in the colonies was the change in the attitude of the European national governments toward sharing their power. At the beginning, the European coun-tries were primarily interested in trade and profit and were willing to delegate power and share it with their nationals abroad, as long as the material benefits were forthcom-ing. The chartered companies were full-fledged political authorities in the colonies. The flag of the mother country followed them and national resources were put at their disposal, but they made all the deci-sions within the colonies. Similarly, the grantee who received title to a given terri-tory was for all practical purposes the sole authority in that territory. However, gradu-ally the European countries became less will-ing to delegate authority and were even anxious to retrieve what had been delegated. It is at this juncture that the idea of empire became important. The overseas areas of influence were no longer only economic assets; they became political assets to be guarded and retained. This was true even of Portugal and Spain, which had never dele-gated full power to their economic agents. This is probably one reason why the Euro-pean governments held onto their colonies even though these colonies became economic liabilities. The idea of empire became an integral part of the political doctrine and was enhanced by the benefits accruing to smaller vested interests.

Economic effects

Capital accumulation. The theories of Marx, Weber, Hamilton, and Webb suggest in different ways one of the most important effects of mercantilism, namely the accumu-lation of capital which preceded the develop-ment of capitalism. Weber was indirect in suggesting this result since he emphasized the change of attitude to favor rationality, asceticism, and hard work. Given these favorable conditions, capital accumulation follows, however. Marx, Hamilton, and Webb emphasized the economic conditions favorable to accumulation: commerce and the exploitation of the colonies on one hand, and the inflow of bullion and profit inflation on the other. Whether they were realized through trading with the overseas areas or by acquiring resources at relatively low costs, the returns to Europe were high.

These returns were important not only as profits but as raw materials which rendered processing and industrialization possible. The supply of sugar led to the building of refineries which in turn created employment and income. Raw tobacco was equally significant in the creation of manufacturing, as was cotton. The discovery of these resources shifted the supply curve downward and to the right, making manufacturing and processing feasible as well as profitable. The slave trade created high demand for iron and coal and for woolen and cotton products; it also stimulated the ship-building industry. All these production processes were financed from the returns of the triangular trade. While the spice trade did not increase the physical or real capital in Europe, it helped to channel profits and capital into the hands of the entrepreneurial class which was inclined towards reinvestment and capital accumulation.

Thus the accumulation of capital was the end result of the total activity of the economy. It occurred in two ways: by the addition of real capital to the resources of Europe, and by the relative concentration of capital in the hands of the merchant and entrepreneurial class. The inflow of bullion served both kinds of accumulation by creating new purchasing power in Europe, by concentrating this purchasing power in the hands of the profit-makers, and by increasing the mobility and circulation of capital within the economies of Europe.

Profits. These two main aspects of capital accumulation have been described as effects of the commercial revolution and of the price revolution respectively. The commercial revolution related to the increase in trade and the acquisition of physical capital,

while the price revolution was a result of the inflow of bullion and the increase of the supply of money and precious metals. The precise magnitude of the increase in trade and commerce is difficult to establish; it is even more difficult to estimate the profits from mercantilist policies and international trade. Illustrations may be suggestive. In 1528 an *asiento* was given out to Germans to supply 4,000 slaves against a payment of 20,000 ducats into the Portuguese treasury. Assuming this payment to be 20 percent of the value, the total expected value of 4,000 slaves would have been 100,000 ducats, or 25 ducats per slave. The rough value of 13–20 million slaves traded would have been between 325 and 500 million ducats[2] The rate of profit could have been from 50 to 200 percent.

The profits of the companies varied. The English East India Company took a loss on one out of five voyages; on one voyage the rate of profit was 195 percent. On eight other voyages undertaken between 1609 and 1613 the rates of profit realized were respectively 334, 221⅔, 318, 311, 260, 248, 320, and 233 11/12 percent. Between 1651 and 1690 the paid dividends varied from 12½ to 60 percent.[3] There is no reason that other companies facing similar risks should have made less profit. These figures might seem high, but it must be remembered that they included profits from trade and the returns of shipping. Estimates of shipping returns alone are illustrated in Table 14.1. These rates were still above 50 percent after a serious decline had taken place. It is possible, therefore, that the returns to those companies which handled both shipping and commerce were much higher than the figures shown. It is interesting to note the decline in the costs of maintaining ships as well as in freight rates. A close look at the estimates suggests that the major cost items, wages

[2] A ducat was about 3.559 gr. gold.
[3] *Cambridge Economic History of Europe,* **IV,** p. 259.

Table 14.1.   Comparative costs and returns on shipping

| SIZE OF SHIP | IN VIRGINIA TRADE | | | | IN MALAGA TRADE (for two voyages in one year) | | | |
	250 TONS				120 TONS			
Year	1635	1680	1725	1770	1635	1680	1725	1770
Costs of voyage, £	803	749	549	531	512	500	404	348
Freight returns	1437	1312	1000	875	960	780	600	540
Returns—costs	634	563	406	344	428	280	196	192
Ratio of return to cost, 3:1	.78	.75	.73	.64	.83	.56	.48	.55

SOURCE: *Extracted with modification from Ralph Davis,* The Rise of the English Shipping Industry in the Seventeenth and Eighteenth Centuries, *London: Macmillan, 1962, pp. 370–371.*

and food, went down, as did the freight charges per ton. Apparently the decline was due to a slackening of activity rather than to an increase in productivity. This may also explain the decline in the rate of profit on shipping in the later years.

Inflow of bullion.   In Chapter 13 estimates of the amount of bullion coming into Spain were presented. Bullion as such has little significance in the economy. However, it becomes significant when it is minted or accepted in lieu of money. As an addition to the store of value or to purchasing power, the flow of bullion into Europe had at least three important effects. It enabled Europe to acquire commodities which required cash payments, including slaves from Africa and spices and silks from the Orient. Second, it increased the exchange of goods and money between Spain and the rest of Europe, encouraging trade and lubricating economic activity. Third, by increasing the supply of money relative to the increase in production, it caused prices to rise. To the extent that wages or costs of production lagged behind prices, there was a profit inflation which provided incentives and redistributed incomes in favor of capital accumulation and reinvestment. The impact on prices was a rise in nominal prices and a decline in the value of the currency. These two tendencies went hand in hand in various countries, although at various rates. The price rise was much higher in the sixteenth century than in the seventeenth century.

The graphs in Figure 14.1 show the trend in depreciation and debasement of currencies in various countries from the fifteenth through the eighteenth centuries. Without exception all currencies suffered a loss of fine silver content between 1500 and 1700. The magnitude of debasement and the time at which it took place varied from one place to another. Relative stability was characteristic of only the pound sterling after 1560. Dutch currency, first the florin and then the guilder, had some stability but much less than the English pound, at least after 1590. All other currencies seem to have suffered a continuous decline, especially after 1600. The impact of debasement was in part to raise prices and in part to redistribute wealth from the creditors to the debtors, among whom were many governments and royalty.

The trend of commodity price movements is not easily determined for this period. Detailed information for all commodities is not available and what is available has been debated about constantly. Among the available information, the price of wheat is probably the most representative. Figure 14.2 shows the trends of wheat price movements in five-yearly averages in different markets. The general trend seems to have been a steep rise until around 1600, after which a certain degree of stability may be observed. A certain decline occurred, especially after 1650 in Exeter, Arnhem, Ondenarde, Udine, Siena, and Naples. However, severe fluctuations seem to have been characteristic of all

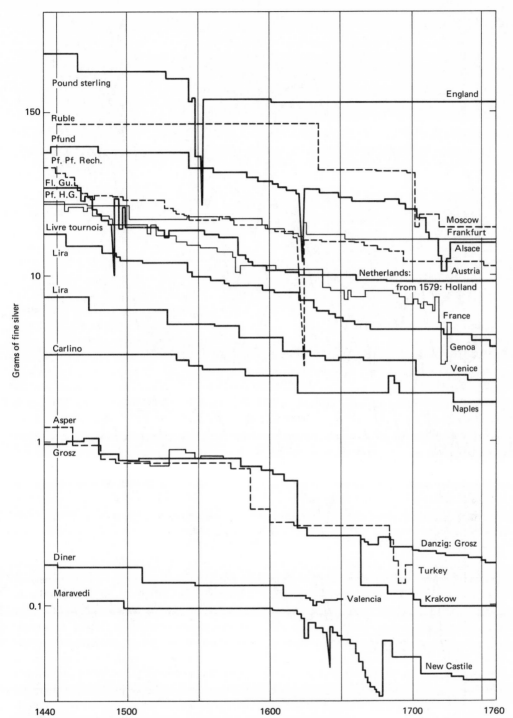

Figure 14.1 European moneys and their weights in fine silver, 1440–1760.

Values shown for the ruble and the asper are approximate. Abbreviations: Pf. Pf. Rech., Pfund Pfennig Rechengulden; Fl. Gu., Florin, which became Guilder after 1579; Pf. H. G., Pfund Heller Gulden.

SOURCE: *Cambridge Economic History of Europe*, IV, p. 458.

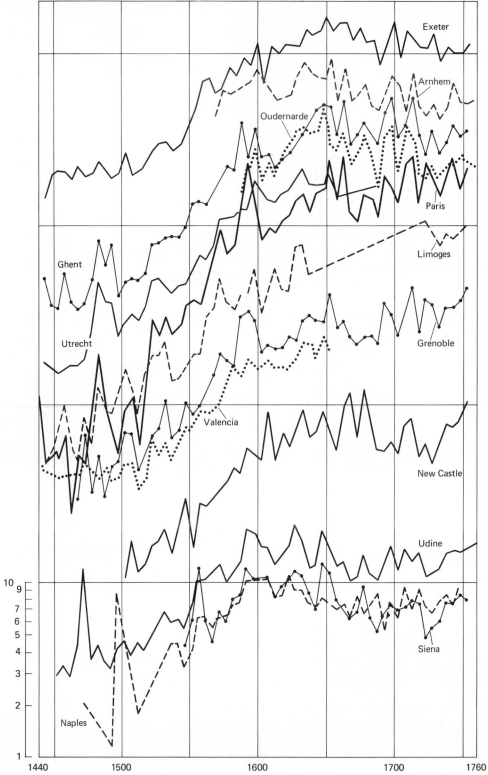

Figure 14.2 A and B Wheat in prices of moneys of account: five-year averages.
The boundary limits of the shaded area have been obtained by

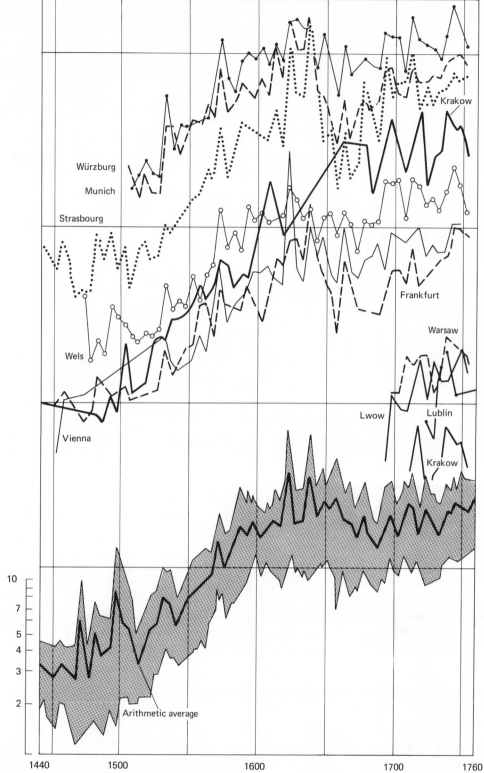

Würzburg

Munich

Strasbourg

Wels

Vienna

Krakow

Frankfurt

Warsaw

Lwow   Lublin

Krakow

10
7
5
4
3

2

Arithmetic average

1440   1500   1600   1700   1760

fitting graphically 59 series of wheat prices in Europe, of which 20
are given separately in the figure.
SOURCE: *Cambridge Economic History of Europe*, IV, pp. 474–475.

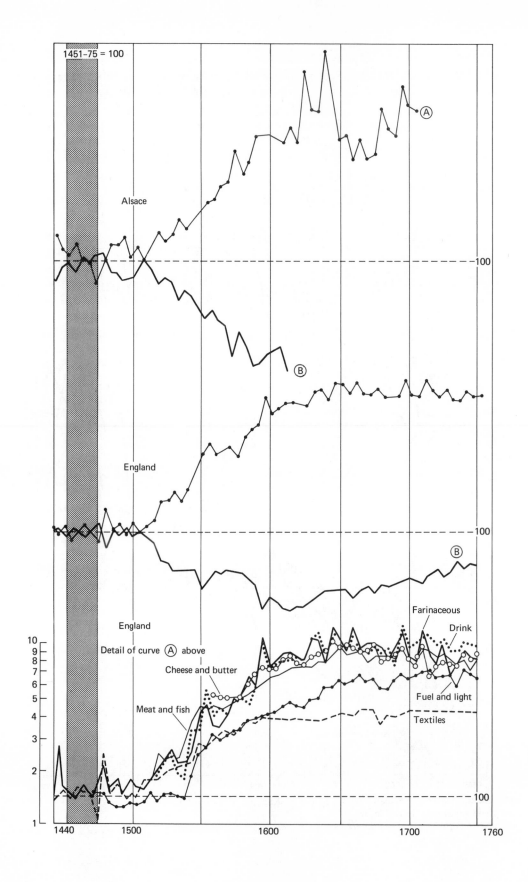

1451–75 = 100

Alsace

Ⓐ

Ⓑ

England

100

England

Ⓑ

100

Detail of curve Ⓐ above

Farinaceous

Drink

Cheese and butter

Meat and fish

Fuel and light

Textiles

100

10
9
8
7
6
5
4
3
2
1

1440   1500   1600   1700   1760

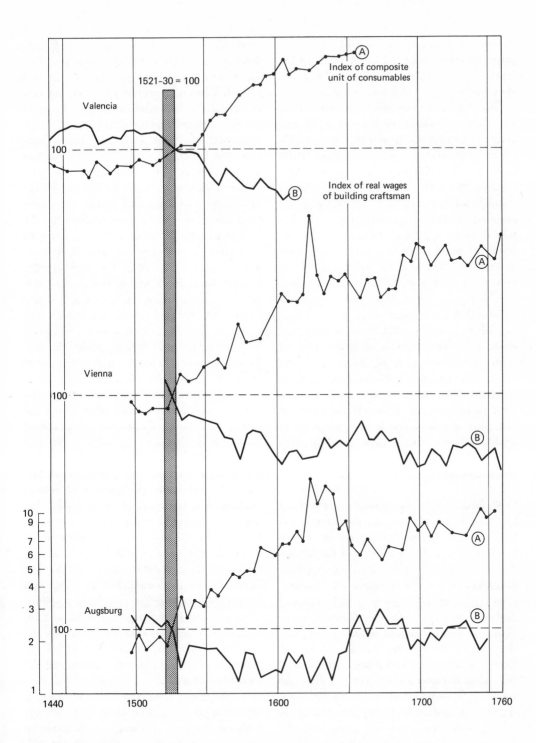

Figure 14.3 A and B   Builders' wages and the cost of living: five-year averages.
SOURCE: Cambridge Economic History of Europe, IV, pp. 482–483 (after E. H. Brown and Sheila Hopkins).

the markets. As can be seen in Figure 14.3A, prices of other consumables in England followed a similar trend; only textile prices show more stability and a lesser rise.

The impact of these price rises on welfare and living standards may be roughly suggested by comparing them with Figure 14.3B, which gives cost of living estimates in selected areas. Although there was much fluctuation, the cost of living index rose in virtually all cases. The precise measures represented need not be regarded as final, but they do suggest a trend. In contrast the real wages of builders in the same places went down after 1530 and did not begin to rise perceptibly until after 1700. Although this is only one wage series, there is no reason to believe that the tendencies of others would be different, at least not those representing the wages of other craftsmen. If the apparent contrast between cost of living and real wages can be accepted, the conclusion is inevitable that the wage earners were in an unfavorable position relative to the sellers of consumer goods. This is the meaning of profit inflation which was an important source of capital accumulation in the mercantilist period.[4]

Finance. Another economic effect of mercantilist activity was the development of financial centers and institutions in various parts of Europe. Until the end of the Middle Ages the Italian cities and some German financiers were the bankers of Europe. Antwerp which had risen to prominence had declined, especially after the Spanish occupation. However, the mercantilist period saw the rise of Amsterdam as the banker of Europe, a position which it held at least until the end of the seventeenth century. This rise was due to several factors. To begin with, Amsterdam had an alert city administration which noted the needs of trade and the weaknesses of other cities, and took advantage of their opportunities. In 1609 they

[4] See the description of Hamilton's theory in Chapter 3 above.

established the Bank of Exchange (*Wisselbank* to aid international exchange. This innovation came at a time when the decline of earlier financial centers had left a vacuum in Europe. To take advantage of the facilities the city offered and to strengthen its position, both the East and West India Companies of the Dutch made their headquarters in Amsterdam. The city authorities also showed religious tolerance by offering refuge to the Jews of Italy and Spain who, soon after their arrival, revived trade with the Mediterranean. Interests with large amounts of capital channeled money into land reclamation, which benefited the city greatly. Finally, Amsterdam was helped by the prosperous manufacturing towns of Haarlem and Leiden. In all three towns, one feature was common: Trading interests took precedence over all others and helped render Amsterdam a major financial and commercial center.

The intervention of governments in economic activities rendered their financial affairs complex. Organized institutional management became necessary. On one hand, there was increasing sophistication in the issue of annuities and public borrowing. On the other hand, the concept of central banking was born out of these needs. The Bank of Rialto of Venice was created in 1507 to handle deposits and transfers of funds. In 1609 the Amsterdam *Wisselbank* was created to handle similar tasks. The Bank of Sweden, established in 1656, was the first to take over the additional responsibility of issuing currency. The Bank of England, created in 1694 primarily to handle the finances of the government, combined the functions of deposit, transfer, loans, and the issue of currency.

At the same time, the need for government capital to finance local and overseas ventures made it necessary to tie taxes to government expenditure. Although the balance of trade was emphasized, little attention was paid to the idea of a balanced budget. Governments borrowed extensively to support projects they favored. Deficit spending was in vogue in all the countries of Europe. Public finance thus acquired significance, although the tendency was to regulate revenue according to expenditure rather than vice versa.

An equally important development was the expansion of the idea of joint-stock financing. Shares began to be floated and traded on the stock exchanges anonymously, as they are today. The floating of shares gained acceptance, thus making large ventures possible and allowing small investors to partake of their potential benefits. Some illustrations of the distribution of investors may suggest this effect. The English East India Company, which was among the first to be established, was financed primarily by large investors. Those with investments of £2000 or more held 72.4 percent of the company stock in 1691; investors of £301–1999 held 23.8 percent; investors of £300 or less held only 3.8 percent. These groups of investors respectively held 14.0 percent, 71.4 percent, and 14.6 percent in the Royal African Company, which came later. The initial stock of the Bank of England, which was established in 1694, was distributed as follows: small investors held 7.7 percent, medium investors held 44.2 percent, and 48.1 percent was held by large investors.[5]

The formation of companies and the sale of shares became so common and uncontrolled that many companies were established for speculative purposes without any economic base for their existence. Peculiar items of trade were used for speculation. The Dutch are said to have speculated in tulip bulbs. In 1636 a single bulb exchanged hands for 4600 florins. In 1672 government bonds were brought into trade on the exchange.

The trend reached its peak around 1720 when the French Company of the Indies went bankrupt. John Law, a Scotsman, had succeeded in attracting investors to buy

shares of the French Company of the Indies which he established and which managed to absorb most of the other French companies at highly speculative rates. He also established a bank which through government sponsorship managed to control all French finances. The floating of shares and the sale of shares on credit without sufficient security caused a speculative fever which raised share prices by 1000 percent within three years. In 1719 the company went bankrupt and so did John Law's bank. The French bubble was paralleled by that of the English South Sea Company, which followed similar speculative policies and met a similar fate about the same time, although it survived on a modest scale until the middle of the eighteenth century. These bubbles led to the Bubble Act of 1720, which made the formation of companies subject to Parliamentary approval.

Although some companies failed completely and many others were only moderately successful, one clear result of the expansion of the joint-stock company was greater mobility of capital and a changed attitude toward investment and the pooling of resources. The restriction of participation to kinship or membership in an exclusive association was no longer valid. Furthermore, investment in the joint-stock companies enhanced their status. They acquired a more permanent character and evolved better-organized administrations. The company became a legal person with a life of its own that did not disintegrate after each venture or when certain members withdrew their financial support. This newly acquired continuity was conducive to the reinvestment, accumulation, and development which were important in the following period.

Interest rates. Probably the best illustrations of the changes in financing and credit institutions are the rates of interest in the various markets. Commercial rates of interest on "best short-term credits" in Antwerp ranged between 7 and 12 percent from 1530 to 1562, except for the year 1536

<hr/>

[5] K. G. Davies, "Joint-Stock Investment in the Later Seventeenth Century," p. 285.

when the rate declined to 4–6 percent. The rates in Holland on private loans ranged between 1.75 and 4.5 percent between 1650 and 1700, with the low rate appearing near the end of the period. In Lyon, commercial bills carried rates ranging from 7 to 12 percent between 1530 and 1558, with an exceptionally low rate of 5 percent in 1542. However, in 1674 the French State Savings Bank paid 5 percent interest on savings; commercial rates must have been higher. Commercial rates for other countries are not available, but rates on long-term mortgages ranged between a 4 percent low in Germany, Italy, and the Netherlands, to a high of 10–14 percent in England during the sixteenth century. These rates were lower during the seventeenth century. In England the rate on mortgages was 10 percent, while commercial loan rates declined from 10 percent in 1571–1624 to 6 percent in 1651–1714 as averages.[6]

While the decline in the rate of interest may be due to a decline of economic activity, a more relevant explanation may be that money markets had become more efficient, the money supply had increased, and government regulations of prices and interest rates had become more effective. Probably an important factor was the improvement in public credit institutions and the declining competition by the governments for private funds. Finally, the decline in the rates during the seventeenth century, at least in England and Holland, and the change in the rate structure in general, may be due to the localization of the money markets in that century within national boundaries. Until the end of the sixteenth century Europe was virtually a single market. The rivalries of the seventeenth century and the successful unification of individual countries tended to localize the influences disturbing interest rates. This, in effect, was the beginning of the modern rate structure in the economies of Europe.

[6] Extracted from S. Homer, *A History of Interest Rates*, pp. 111–132.

Social effects

Redistribution of wealth. The accumulation of national wealth and the increase in economic activity affected the well-being of individuals. Those who participated in trade or who controlled manufacturing could become wealthy. The price revolution of the sixteenth century and the expanding overseas trade of the seventeenth created boom periods for the merchants and profit-makers. The landowners and the nobility, in contrast, were in a less favorable position to the extent that their interests were made subservient to those of the traders. The conflict between the merchant class and the nobility was well illustrated in Amsterdam. The regents of that city were of humble origin. Although the nobility looked down on them, they controlled the policies of the town and managed to establish a coalition with the merchants. The merchants of England fared equally well materially, although their political influence was less pronounced than that of the Dutch merchants. The French merchant class had less direct political influence. They, like most other economic groups in France, were controlled by and dependent on the government. Nevertheless, there was some redistribution of wealth and influence in their favor. Least affected of all were the merchant groups in Spain and Portugal where economic activity was carried on either by a monopoly or under strict control of the government.

The redistribution of wealth and influence had significant effects on income. Income followed wealth to a certain extent, and saving and investment followed income. The redistribution of income and wealth had repercussions on the accumulation of capital which was to be quite important in the years to come.

The artisans were kept busy and therefore their incomes continued to flow in. However, their earnings were regulated downward in order to support exports and discourage imports by keeping production costs low. They were kept under supervision and their interests were subordinated to those of the nation and the commercial groups. The protection the artisans expected from the guilds was severely circumscribed because the guilds themselves had become tools of government control.

The wage workers had no protection from the authorities or from their own organization. The proletariat, as a new phenomenon, was not organized and had no means of acquiring influence. The workers' problems were usually aggravated during times of famine or shortage, when the prices of consumables were high and their wages remained low or they were unemployed. They also suffered when inflationary prices were not matched by increasing wages, which was the common state of affairs. For these reasons, the mercantilist period witnessed an increase in pauperism, poverty, and destitution, especially in the towns. It also witnessed the beginning of organized efforts and formal policies to cope with poverty and unemployment problems.

Welfare policies. Public awareness of unemployment was rising in this period in the Netherlands, England, and France. While little information on the other countries is available, it is probable that some of them retained their former social structures which offered security through family ties, serfdom, guilds, or charitable organizations.

The problem seems to have come to light earlier in England than in France. In both countries the official policy was based on two grounds: charity towards the infirm, aged, and orphan; and harshness towards idleness and vagrancy. Charity was a matter of humaneness. Idleness was condemned as a way of reducing national wealth by consuming without producing. Work must be provided for the able-bodied, and those who refused to work must be punished and forced to do so. The measures taken in England and France were generally similar. In both countries, the disabled were herded into general hospitals

or institutions where they could be fed and taken care of.

London was the first city to establish a general hospital in 1533 which provided indoor relief and some productive activity for those who were able to work. In 1536 an Act was passed introducing a national system of relief. The Act was based on the following principles:

> . . . prohibition of begging; the organized collection and distribution of alms amongst the aged and impotent; the division of the able-bodied into two classes, those willing to work for whom work was to be provided, and those unwilling to work on whom punishment was to be inflicted; and the apprenticing of pauper children.[7]

This Act, however, left financing on a voluntary basis. The Act of 1572 levied a tax assessment to support the relief system, thus making a compulsory rate the basis of financing. It is interesting how comprehensive the class of able-bodied who were unwilling to work defined by the Act was:

> . . . scholars wandering about begging, seafaring men pretending losses of their ships or goods, persons feigning knowledge in physiognomy and palmistry or telling fortunes, proctors, patent gatherers, collectors for prisons and hospitals, fencers, bearwards, unlicensed minstrels and players in interludes, jugglers, tinkers, peddlers and petty chapmen, labourers loitering and refusing to work for reasonable wages, persons pretending losses by fire or otherwise, or posing as Egyptians.[8]

At first these people were treated very harshly. However, the Act of 1576 provided for the establishment of houses of correction in which people were put to work under

---

[7] E. Lipson, *The Economic History of England,* sixth edition, III, p. 416.
[8] *Ibid.,* p. 421.

severe discipline for 21 days, unless accepted for employment in the meantime. Although they received wages for their work, they paid for their own maintenance. However, to avoid the cost of maintaining houses of correction, parishes often shipped inmates to other places. The Act of 1702 required justices to fix the charges before conveyance to other areas.

Those willing to work were treated differently. At first, pressure was put on the employers to keep their workers on the job even in severe economic conditions. This method was inadequate. Therefore, the Act of 1576 provided that the unemployed be given raw material and put to work under supervision against regular payment for their product. Children who were too young to work were put under the care of a parish nurse. If they were able to work, they were apprenticed: boys from age 7 to 24, and girls to age 21. However, the Act of 1767 fixed the period of apprenticeship at 7 years.

Abuse of the system was common. Parishes were unwilling to take care of the poor when their numbers increased relative to their expectations. Inmates went to parishes that offered better conditions. Therefore, the Act of 1662 or the Law of Settlement allowed justices of the peace to order the conveyance of newcomers to the place they came from within 40 days of their arrival, thus establishing residence as a condition for aid. This Act, however, also restricted mobility. Those who wanted to move were required to obtain a license to do so and to promise to return to their former residence when the reasons for their movement had been eliminated. In 1697 the return provision was repealed. This system of poor relief remained in effect with little modification until the Speenhamland system was introduced in 1795.

Poverty, however, was also due to imbalance between wages and prices. Especially in periods of food and fuel shortage, prices soared and many people could not subsist on their incomes. Therefore, the government

introduced the system of the Book of Order in 1587. According to this system supplies were surveyed by public officials and ordered on the market, after allowing for personal needs, to be sold at regulated prices. This system, which required a highly organized administrative machinery, was adopted in 1631 as the framework for relief administration in general.

The French approach to the problem of poverty, which came about three-quarters of a century later, was similar. Lyon started a program for employing the poor around the middle of the seventeenth century. Until then their only resources had been voluntary charity and begging. Paris soon followed with a plan to remove idleness, create piety, and relieve the city from pauperism. An edict was passed in 1657 establishing a *Hôpital général,* which by 1661 was caring for 5000 poor people. Edicts to control begging and vagrancy were passed every few years until the end of the century. In 1660 a stringent edict was applied to France as a whole according to which, "all Bohemians, vagabonds, and vagrants . . . were to leave the Kingdom. If they failed to do so, royal judges and officials were authorized to send them to the galleys, attaching them to the first chain of galley slaves that came by, without trial or formality."[9]

General hospitals were established in the towns and provinces, combining work and upkeep under severe discipline. The capacity of these institutions, however, was limited because they were based on voluntary contributions. A compulsory assessment was introduced in 1662, but it was applied only to certain localities. Nevertheless, at their peak the total number accommodated in these institutions was about 20,000. To avoid undue burdens, a residence requirement was introduced according to which each parish cared for those born in it and for those who had resided there for one year. Finally,

[9] C. W. Cole, *Colbert and a Century of French Mercantilism,* II, p. 473.

around the end of the century, especially after the economic crisis of 1693–1694, public work projects were established to provide work for the unemployed.

These policies and measures suggest a major change from the medieval period. A wage-earner group had evolved and grown in numbers. The market conditions had become a determining factor in the level of employment. The security of tradition had vanished. Public awareness of the unemployment problem had become evident. However, as usual, the policy created to solve it seems to have aimed at larger outputs and the creation of national wealth.

DECLINE OF MERCANTILISM AND ITS LASTING EFFECTS

We have treated the economics of mercantilism by illustration rather than by a detailed history of its development in all countries of Europe. However, the development of mercantilism was far from uniform. In Russia it hardly began before the eighteenth century. In Scandinavia it scarcely developed at all, least as discussed above. In the Netherlands it was less rigid and less efficiently applied than in England or France. In the German territories it did not acquire a unified character until the middle of the nineteenth century. Even in England a distinction was made between internal and external policies. While mercantilist measures were relaxed internally, the Navigation Laws were forcefully implemented for many years.

While mercantilism declined in certain countries, it rose in others, and while the form it took and the efficiency of its application underwent change, certain aspects are still with us. If mercantilism means government intervention in economic affairs, then it has never declined. If it means emphasis on bullionism, it may be proposed that it was never strong in any country. If mercantilism means emphasis on commerce and a positive balance of trade, the observation

may be made that commerce remained important, although it was supplemented by industrial production as a focus of emphasis, while interest in a positive balance of trade has never declined. The change was in the methods and processes by which these material objectives were realized rather than in the objectives themselves.

Effects of mercantilism

Despite the difficulties of definition, certain lasting effects of mercantilism may be observed. First, after this period Europe was no longer a self-contained economic area, as it had been until the end of the Middle Ages. Economic activity and the capacity for both production and consumption expanded in such a way that the European countries became highly interdependent with the Americas, with Africa, and with the Orient. The manufacturing enterprises of Europe waited for the raw material of the colonies and planned production to supply the colonial market. The shipping industry became dependent on contact between the home countries and the colonies. Without external economic relations, the European countries would have found it hard to maintain their levels of production and consumption, given the prevalent technology.

Another lasting effect was the development of economic nationalism, which has never been eliminated. Even when free trade became a motto in European policy declarations, economic nationalism loomed large in the background.

Third, the experiences of mercantilism illustrated that no single approach to economic problems could be regarded as the best. They showed that experimentation was necessary and that when economic objectives were at least partially achieved, economic behavior required modification. This point is best illustrated by the changing attitudes towards mercantilist actions in England and France around the end of the seventeenth century.

Fourth, mercantilism influenced the distribution of wealth and income among economic groups. The redistribution was reflected in the accumulation of capital and the increasing emphasis on saving and investment, all of which were important in the economic developments of the next two centuries.

Finally, the mercantilist period fully represented the triumph of materialism in the western world. As time passed, it became more and more evident that this materialist system of ethics was a necessary condition for development and economic change. Regardless of whether one's doctrine was mercantilist or laissez-faire, it was clear that the road to economic power lay in the achievement of material benefits. One has only to look at developing countries today to see how nonmaterial values are subordinated to material goals in the interest of catching up with the western countries.

Decline of mercantilism

A question which has been debated extensively but unsuccessfully is that of the cause of mercantilism's decline. Cole proposes various explanations which he admits to be a mixture of speculation and factual observations. These, however, deal with government intervention and regulation in general, rather than with mercantilism in the conventional sense as represented by the sixteenth–seventeenth-century experiences.

The first explanation is a monetary one, according to which bullionism was adopted because business was still carried out through metallic currency. Credit and paper instruments of payment had not yet become fashionable. As nonmetallic instruments of payment became available, however, bullionism lost its function. This explanation assumes that bullionism declined, but one might argue that it has not, as illustrated by the continued emphasis on gold reserves.

Another explanation is that as the idea of economic growth became common, economic nationalism ceased to be rigid. During the mercantilist period, economic resources and opportunities were considered constant. Therefore, the only way of increasing national wealth was at the expense of others. As it became evident that opportunities and wealth could be increased through growth, mercantilism lost its rationale. Another aspect of the growth explanation is that the increased emphasis on investment enlarged the national wealth regardless of the stock of bullion.

A third explanation takes the stage approach as a point of departure. As an economy becomes well established, it has no reason to protect its enterprises and can depend on free trade and competition. This theory is used to explain the more rapid decline of mercantilism in England than in the less developed countries of Europe.

A fourth explanation takes nationalism and nation-building as the objective of mercantilism. As the nation is united and nationalism becomes a way of life, a mercantilist policy becomes unnecessary. A variant of this is the war explanation. War makes it necessary to protect national interests, and since the sixteenth–eighteenth centuries were plagued with recurrent wars, there was justification for mercantilism. However, when wars were no longer recurrent, the need for mercantilism declined.

A fifth explanation is based on technology. As long as technology was backward, nations found it necessary to adopt a policy of self-sufficiency. However, as technology developed and the means of transportation were revolutionized, the idea became meaningless; hence, the decline of mercantilism and the emphasis on the division of labor and comparative advantage.

A sixth explanation is a "Marxist" approach which emphasizes class structure as a point of departure. According to this theory the bourgeoisie was willing to use government influence to promote its own interests. However, as the bourgeoisie became strong enough to stand on its own feet, it had no reason to depend on government help and hence dissolved the coalition.

Cole adds another "theoretical or intellectual" explanation, namely that mercantilism was based on incorrect assumptions. As the errors of these assumptions were discovered and economic theory evolved, policy changed in the direction of freer trade, more individualism, and private enterprise. This explanation, however, assumes that policy usually is guided by theory and intellectual analysis, rather than by pragmatic considerations.[10]

Cole ends his survey of explanations by asking "What is Truth?" since all the explanations seem to have some evidence to support them. We are not in a better position than he was in to answer the question. One thing is clear: Materialism had triumphed. When guilds stood in the way, they were suppressed; when religious or Church regulations interfered, some form of rationalization was devised; and when moral values were in conflict with material interests, they were subordinated. Wealth, whether in the form of bullion or commodity production, became the main objective of the individual and the nation. Thus, when development and growth became technologically feasible, the western world was ready to take the challenge and bring about what became known as the industrial revolution.

[10] C. W. Cole, *French Mercantilism 1683–1700*, chap. 6.

BIBLIOGRAPHY

The following selected bibliography, which covers Chapters 11–14, includes mainly basic references. Journal articles and specialized studies are too numerous to include here. However, the interested reader will find comprehensive references in the bibliographies of the titles listed below.

Boxer, C. R., *The Dutch Seaborne Empire: 1600–1800,* New York: Alfred A. Knopf, 1965, especially chap. 10.

Carsten, F. L., *The Origins of Prussia,* Oxford: Clarendon Press, 1954, especially chaps. 8, 9, 11.

Cole, C. W., *Colbert and a Century of French Mercantilism,* 2 vols., New York: Columbia University Press, 1939.

Cole, C. W., *French Mercantilism 1683–1700,* New York: Octagon Books, 1965, especially chaps. 5 and 6.

Davies, K. G., "Joint-Stock Investment in the Later Seventeenth Century," *Economic History Review,* 2nd series, 1952, reprinted in *Essays in Economic History,* II, E. M. Carus-Wilson (ed.), New York: St. Martin's Press, 1962, p. 285.

Davis, Ralph, *The Rise of the English Shipping Industry in the Seventeenth and Eighteenth Centuries,* London: Macmillan, 1962.

Ehrenberg, Richard, *Capital and Finance in the Age of the Renaissance,* New York: Augustus M. Kelly, 1928, 1963. A study of the Fuggers and their connections.

Geyl, Pieter, *The Netherlands in the Seventeenth Century,* I

(1609–1648) and II (1648–1715), 2nd ed., London: Barnes and Noble, 1961, 1964.

Harper, Lawrence A., *The English Navigation Laws*, New York: Columbia University Press, 1939.

Heckscher, Eli, *An Economic History of Sweden*, Cambridge, Mass.: Harvard University Press, 1954, chaps. 3–4.

Heckscher, Eli, "Mercantilism," in *Encyclopedia of Social Sciences*, Edwin R. A. Seligman and Alvin Johnson (eds.), New York: Macillan, 1933.

Homer, S., *A History of Interest Rates*, New Brunswick, N.J.: Rutgers University Press, 1963, pp. 111–132.

Klein, Julius, *The Mesta*, Cambridge, Mass.: Harvard University Press, 1920.

Lipson, E., *The Economic History of England*, 6th ed., II and III, London: Adam and Charles Black, 1956.

Lipson, E., *The Growth of English Society*, Second edition, London: Adam and Charles Black, 1951, Part II.

Lyaschenko, P. I., *History of the National Economy of Russia to the 1917 Revolution* (translated by L. M. Herman), New York: Macmillan, 1949, chaps. 9–14.

Malowist, M., "The Economic and Social Development of the Baltic Countries from the Fifteenth to the Seventeenth Centuries," *Economic History Review*, 2nd series, XII, No. 2 (1959), pp. 177–189.

Nef, J. U., *Industry and Government in France and England, 1540–1640*, Ithaca, N.Y.: Great Seals Books, 1957.

Ramsay, G. D., *English Overseas Trade During the Centuries of Emergence*, London: Macmillan, 1957.

Rich, E. E., and C. H. Wilson (eds.), *The Cambridge Economic History of Europe*, IV, New York: Cambridge University Press, 1967.

Tannenbaum, Frank, *Slave and Citizen. The Negro in America*, New York: Random House (Vintage Book), 1946.

Thomas, R., "A Quantitative Approach to the Study of the Effects of British Imperial Policy upon Colonial Welfare," *Journal of Economic History*, XXV (Dec. 1965).

Unwin, George, *Industrial Organization in the Sixteenth and Seventeenth Centuries*, London: Cass and Co., 1957.

THE
MODERN
PERIOD
TECHNOLOGY AND DEVELOPMENT
PART
FOUR

15

INTRODUCTION
AND
FRAMEWORK

The modern period is usually defined as the period of the industrial revolution in Europe, which began around the middle of the eighteenth century. It has also been classified as the era of capitalism, of the takeoff and mature economy, of credit as well as money exchange, of free enterprise, of economic rationality, and of advanced technology. All these qualifications have one implication in common: They suggest that the modern period can be clearly distinguished from the age of mercantilism, both quantitatively and qualitatively.

AN OVERVIEW OF THE INDUSTRIAL REVOLUTION

The economic development of Europe brought many benefits. The quality of life and the standard of living of people in the industrialized nations have changed radically since the beginning of the modern period. The distribution of incomes has been altered and the dignity of work has been enhanced. These benefits, however, have been obtained at a cost. We shall attempt to discover the benefits and the costs which characterized the European experience, and to see how the costs were contained or reduced, how the benefits were increased, and how they were distributed among various income groups. We shall also study the impact of industrialization on the various economies involved and on the international relations among them, especially in the last quarter of the nineteenth century, when the number of industrialized countries had increased. Such a study should prove highly relevant to the emerging economies of today.

Industrialization came at various times and at different rates in different countries, although it has been common to use the term *industrial revolution* to describe the experience of Britain between 1760 and 1830, to indicate the high rate and comprehensiveness of economic change in that period. Therefore, we will consider specific changes without restricting our discussion to any given chronological period or country.

In all the countries there were certain features which were regarded as constituting industrialization: All aimed at higher incomes; all tried to switch from agricultural to industrial production; all faced problems of financing, labor movements, and balance of payments. Furthermore, all industrializing countries found it necessary to cope with increased problems of welfare and unemployment and more recently with problems of ecology. Some were able to depend on the market mechanism, while others depended on planning by the state or some other public authority. Still others used a mixture of planning and the market mechanism.

CHANGES FROM THE MERCANTILIST PERIOD

The differences between the mercantilist and modern periods may be reduced to three types: changes in the structure of the European economies, increases in the productivity of the factors of production, and changes in the forms of organization of the production units. The structural changes included a higher degree of urbanization, a higher volume and percentage of industrial output in the total production, and increased utilization of mechanical tools and nonmanual sources of power in the production process. The productivity changes were mainly due to increased productivity of labor, capital, and land as represented by higher per capita output.

The changes in organization included greater dependence on or utilization of the market mechanism, increased division of labor and standardization of production, crystallization of the wage working class, more anonymity in economic relations, and larger-scale production operations, which tended to encourage the development of a managerial class.

Since these various changes were closely interdependent, it would be difficult to determine a cause-and-effect relationship among them. However, two major causes of the change may be singled out: an increase in the demand for products and an advance in technology. The sources of demand may vary, but unless demand rises, there is little incentive for increased production. However, even if the demand increases, unless technology has also advanced remarkably, there is little reason to expect higher productivity. It is true that productivity may be increased by better organization, supervision, and training, but such improvements are bound to be limited unless accompanied by technological advances.

However, the processes and organization of production are also important to an understanding of the economic changes of the modern period. An increase in demand only indicates that it would be profitable to produce for the market. An improvement in technology indicates the feasibility of producing on a larger scale and at a lower average cost. Neither factor, however, shows how the production activity should be carried out, where the investment capital will come from, how to recruit or train labor and management, or how to market the product or build transportation facilities. These important aspects of economic activity are often explained as effects of the "invisible hand of the market." However, the economic historian cannot be satisfied with this explanation and must find out how and why things happened the way they did in their historical environment.

As we have mentioned, not all the countries of Europe developed at the same time or at the same rate, even though demand and technology might have been favorable. The failure to develop suggests that certain other facilities and obstacles must be taken into consideration. Such obstacles seem also to be operating in present-day societies, where development has lagged behind expectations even though technological knowledge has been accessible and the demand for higher production has been apparent. Although the change occurred mostly in the nineteenth and twentieth centuries, the eighteenth century saw significant noneconomic developments which were highly conducive to industrialization where they took place. It may be that the failure to experience those noneconomic events was in part responsible for the failure to industrialize.

NONECONOMIC DEVELOPMENTS IN THE EIGHTEENTH CENTURY

The eighteenth century witnessed the crystallization of mercantilism in some countries and its decline in others. In Germany, Russia and to some extent Sweden, it was the high point of the mercantilist period. In

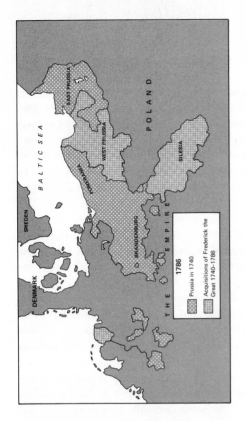

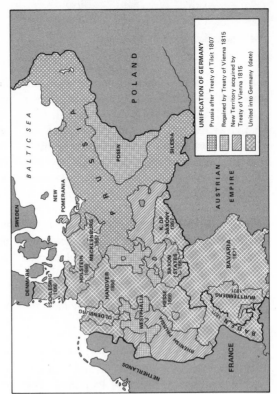

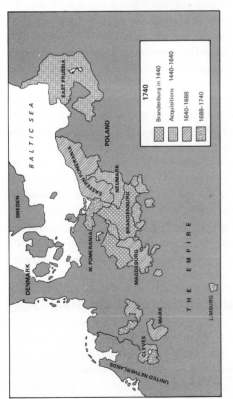

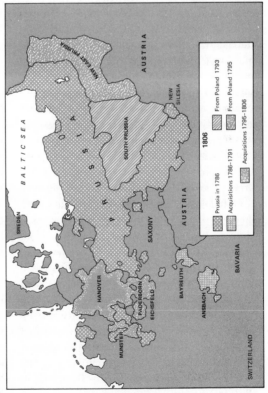

Figure 15.1   The expansion of Prussia and the unification of Germany.

Britain, France, and Holland mercantilism was on the decline. Frederick the Great (1740–1786) dominated this period in Germany, as did Peter I and Catherine II in Russia all of whom managed to strengthen the hold of government on the society and the economy. In contrast, Sweden went through a period regarded by historians as the era of freedom (1720–1815), during which the government turned away from imperialistic ambitions and concentrated on domestic development. The economic changes which took place in these countries will be treated in detail below; here only noneconomic developments will be noted.

Political developments

This was a period of political or territorial expansion in both Russia and Prussia, as Figures 13.1 (p. 156) and 15.1 show. The Russian expansion, which had started in earlier years, continued. During the eighteenth century the Russian state acquired parts of Kirghiz in the east, and Kuban, Taurida, the Crimea, parts of Poland, Lithuania, and Courland in the southwest and west. These additions and others which preceded and followed rendered Russia a giant economy, with extensive sources of demand and supply brought together in a unified political system. Similarly between 1740 and 1786 Frederick the Great was able to acquire Silesia and a large part of West Prussia; large parts of Poland were added between 1793 and 1795. Thus the Russian state multiplied its size several times in two centuries, while in half a century, Prussia more than doubled its size. These acquisitions were consistent with the contemporary European trend towards national unification and strengthening the national state. Although certain boundary changes took place during the Napoleonic period, Prussia's expansion and the trend toward unification continued until they were finally consummated in the German Empire, established by Bismarck in 1871 (see Figure 15.1).

In contrast, Britain and France had to adjust to the loss of colonies and boundary changes in the Americas. In 1713 France relinquished to Britain its claims to the Hudson Bay area, Newfoundland, and Nova Scotia. France also lost its empire in the St. Lawrence and Mississippi Valleys, which was ceded to Britain in the Peace of Paris of 1763. However, the American Revolution cost Britain the 13 colonies. The Revolution was an important blow to British mercantilism, although economic and trade relations with the new republic were maintained for many years.

An even more significant event for Europe was the French Revolution of 1789, which hit at the core of the *ancien régime*, shook the politics and economics of the continent, and introduced new codes which have become integral parts of modern national constitutions. The impact of the Revolution was felt in the domestic structures of the European countries. The Napoleonic Wars also had profound effects on international relations and on the national crises faced by each of the parties to them. The economic impact of the wars will be explored in due course.

Intellectual developments

The eighteenth century was the high point of the Enlightenment, the era in which reason replaced metaphysics, and exploration of nature replaced revelation. Interest was focused more on the real world than on abstraction: "Dare to use your own understanding" became the motto of this era. Man was no longer willing to depend on belief. The motto was applied to political thought, religion, society, and the place of the individual.

The place of the individual was now viewed as a function of social contract rather than of heredity or state authority. The power of the state was seen as the "product of the individual will," surviving only through a mandate from the members of society. By investing power in the state, the members forfeit their sovereignty. However, they retain the right to regain that sovereignty by withdrawing their support from the state. This philosophy was clearly expounded in Rousseau's *Social Contract*, and was embodied in the American Declaration of Independence, and later in the Declaration of the Rights of Man and of the Citizens of the French Constituent Assembly of 1789, which guaranteed the individual's freedom to act for his survival and mental health.

Economic behavior, which deals with more tangible matters and is more subject to observation and understanding, was directly affected by the Enlightenment. The triumph of materialism experienced during the preceding two centuries gained intellectual and philosophical backing from the worldly tendencies of the Enlightenment. A new economic doctrine evolved, that of laissez-faire or free enterprise, in which each individual serves his own interests, while the market expresses the general will or the wishes and desires of the constituents.

In the area of economic thought, the School of the Physiocrats preached a return to nature and to the land, to replace parasitic nonproductive activities. The Physiocrats emphasized the role of private property and the freedom of the individual to pursue his economic interests. Capital and labor should be freely mobile. Large-scale organization of production should be encouraged to increase productive efficiency. Free competition would lead to "human perfectibility." Although these views had only limited circulation at the time, in the long run they hit directly at mercantilism and at the manorial institutions which still dominated agriculture in most European countries. They also greatly influenced the classical economic doctrine initiated by Adam Smith and carried

further by his successors in the nineteenth century.

Adam Smith's *The Wealth of Nations*, published in 1776, was an expression of a trend that had begun a few decades earlier. The new doctrine emphasized freedom of the individual, the effectiveness of the market mechanism, the significance of division of labor in production, and the inadvisability of state intervention in individual activities. Smith felt that economic agents will express their desires and act according to their self-interests which, when they interact, will result in the national interest.

The Wealth of Nations was only the beginning. The laissez-faire doctrine was to undergo a more sophisticated development in the nineteenth century by various attempts to discover other economic laws regulating economic behavior on the assumption that such behavior followed reason and had a logic of its own. These intellectual and economic doctrines were strong foundations for the individualistic, competitive actions which had already challenged the mercantilist state.

The new forces acted simultaneously in various European countries. Where flexibility prevailed, change came peacefully. Where the structure was rigid, change was delayed and when it finally came, it was a violent process. The French Revolution was the most significant expression of the conflict; the Revolutions of 1848 in Germany, Italy, and in other countries of Europe were others. The industrial revolution and the economic development of Europe during the modern period can be understood only if viewed against this wider background.

BIBLIOGRAPHY

Beales, H. J., "The Industrial Revolution," *History*, New series, XIV (1929–1930), reprinted in Warren C. Scoville and J. Clayburn La Force (eds.), *The Economic Development of Europe, The Eighteenth and Early Nineteenth Centuries*, Boston: D. C. Heath, 1969, pp. 17–23.

Henderson, W. O., *Studies in the Economic Policies of Frederick the Great,* London: Frank Cass and Co., 1963.

Seligman, E. R. A., and A. Johnson (eds.), *Encyclopedia of the Social Sciences,* sections on the Enlightenment, economics, the industrial revolution, New York: Macmillan, 1931.

Toynbee, Arnold, *Industrial Revolution,* Boston: Beacon Press, 1956, pp. 1–6, 58–66 [first published in 1884].

16
POPULATION
AND
DEVELOPMENT

THE CONCEPTUAL FRAMEWORK

In earlier chapters, we discussed population as a source of both demand for products and supply of labor. These functions were reflected mainly by the number of people in an area. Although both are still important in the modern period, changes in the economic structure and the composition of production have added new dimensions. Thus a new conceptual framework is necesary. It is no longer sufficient to count heads. It is more important to observe the age structure of the population; the distribution of wealth and income, or purchasing power; the significance of want in addition to need as a form of demand; and the structure of the family, the inheritance laws, and their relationship to labor mobility and entrepreneurship.

The market industrial economy requires labor mobility. Labor must be able to respond to the demand and provide the input when and where it is needed, in contrast to the rigid structure of the agricultural subsistence economy. Moreover, labor mobility is a way of disseminating knowledge, new technology, and skills. Therefore, free mobility is an asset to the population factor in economic change. Where rigidity prevails, as in a tightly knit family structure or in a serf economy, population growth tends to become a burden on the available resources, income, and saving and investment.

Population movements, to be an asset, must be coordinated with wage movements in the market. The wage level will then act as an indicator of the demand for labor. Any obstacles to communication of the wage rates or to the response of labor to them will hinder development and render population growth a burden on the economy rather than an asset.

Wage and labor mobility, as they relate to population growth, may be approached also from the time perspective. Labor input is usually the largest cost component in industrial production. Therefore, it is important to observe the timing of population growth and internal migration, relative to economic development and change. Production costs can be reduced either by a local population increase or by labor movement to those areas where the demand for it is high. It has been claimed that proletarianization of the English peasantry as a result of enclosure was one of the most important factors in industrialization, partly because it kept labor costs relatively low. However, the natural increase of population, both in the country and in the cities, has also been considered important in this regard. Probably both factors were acting simultaneously, causing a significant downward trend in the costs of labor.

The opposite of such coordination between population growth and economic development could result in a Malthusian trap[1] which would dissipate the positive effects of the population increase and keep the economy stagnant.

Qualitative aspects of population growth

An industrial market economy, in contrast to an agricultural subsistence economy, requires skill and entrepreneurship more than manual labor power. Assuming sources of power are available and a contractual business form of organization exists, the sheer number of people becomes relatively unimportant. Therefore, population growth is an asset as a factor of production only to the extent to which skills and entrepreneurial and managerial abilities are increased. Failure to develop these qualities could render population growth a burden on the economy and an obstacle to development and change.

In discussing demography and economic change, it is essential to consider the qualitative features of population, such as educational receptivity, risk-taking, and the attitude toward saving and investment. Thus the social and economic class composition of the population and the impact of growth on them may be highly significant.

It has been common to associate urbanization with development on the assumption that development leads to urbanization, even though the reverse may not be equally true. Since both urbanization and development are dynamic processes, and since their impact tends to be cumulative, it is important to consider the trend in urbanization. To what extent are population increases absorbed in nonrural areas and how capable are the urban centers of employing these additional labor forces? The ability to absorb

[1] A Malthusian trap refers to a situation in which population growth surpasses economic growth so that all product increments are eaten up, investment goes down, and the economy stagnates until population pressure is relieved by war, famine, or disease.

additional people outside agriculture renders population growth an asset to the economy; failure to do so changes it into a burden, unless agriculture is still capable of absorbing additional people by extending or intensifying cultivation. Thus population growth can be studied meaningfully only in conjunction with other resources.

An important feature of population change relates to the population's age structure and life expectancy. A short life expectancy implies a higher percentage of children in the total population. Although a long life expectancy increases the number of dependents by the number of the elderly, such additional dependence is quite limited compared to that of the young created by the short life expectancy. The dependence of old people may be reduced by extending the productive period before retirement, but short life expectancy adds to the burdens on the economy by raising the costs of procreation through infant and child mortality. If 10 children were born for every 6 surviving into productive adulthood, the cost of producing these 6 would be raised 40 percent. A lengthening of life expectancy indicates not only improvements in the health and diet of the people, but also the potential productive resources represented by the population.

Does development lengthen life expectancy, or does life expectancy lead to development? The former relationship seems more logical, although the latter cannot be dismissed as irrelevant. Since both development and life expectancy change at varying rates, they tend to reinforce each other over a relatively long period of time, just as failure to change in either case tends to reinforce stagnation in the other.

Trends in European population

In the modern period two almost unique features are related to population and its role in development. On one hand, most of the countries of Europe had by 1750 become fairly unified nation-states. The exceptions, Germany and Italy, consisted of unified smaller units which enjoyed full sovereignty. Unification carried with it restrictions, some of which interfered with emigration from one national territory to another. This meant that the market for labor and products was less free than previously, and labor mobility became restricted by national boundaries.

Restrictions on labor mobility were a carry-over from the mercantilist period, when the productive population had to be retained within the economy in order to increase the national wealth, and population movements across borders were controlled to prevent the leakage of skill and technology into the hands of competitors.

On the other hand, the population of Europe had a gateway to the outside. Emigration to the Americas and to Oceania became an important outlet for population surplus in Europe. When population grew faster than the complementary resources and became a threat to development and the standard of living, emigration acted as a safety valve. One of the most important characteristics of population change in modern Europe was the people's readiness to seek opportunities elsewhere. By emigrating they helped reduce pressure on the local resources, and sometimes contributed to the effective demand for European products as well as to the supply of strategic commodities and raw material. It should be noted, however, that emigration provides a safety valve only when it is associated with certain local economic conditions. If emigration takes place when there is population pressure on resources, or when there is unemployment, it will contribute to the health of the local economy. If it takes place when local demand for labor is high or regardless of the labor market conditions, the effect may be detrimental.[2] The experiences of the various

countries of Europe provide good examples of these situations.

The neat relationship between emigration and pressure at home is complicated by another factor, however. Emigration from one country is also immigration into another. The former process usually results from a push factor which may be economic, social, or political. Immigration is usually due to a pull factor which is primarily economic. The potential migrant may make his decision by comparing the relative benefits of staying with those of migrating. His decision may be in favor of migrating even though local pressure on resources may be relatively small, because the attractions of the pull country may be relatively high. Unfortunately, it is difficult to break down migration figures by cause. However, it may be safe to assume that the majority of migrants give more weight to local conditions than to the uncertain prospects abroad and that therefore a closer relationship exists between emigration and population pressure than between the pull factor and immigration.

Summary

In a given area, population growth will be favorable to economic development if additional resources are available, if labor market conditions are predictable, if labor and resource mobility is feasible, if other outlets for surplus population exist, and if the population increase is gradual enough to permit periodic adjustments in the economy. Conversely, a population increase will be detrimental to development if the above conditions are not satisfied, although some favorable conditions may be sufficient to offset the unfavorable ones. Finally, population stagnation or decline will be unfavorable to development in the long run unless technology advances so that capital may be substituted for labor and per capita output raised.

The determining factor in all these cases may be the degree of harmony among the rates of change in population, resource utili-

[2] Some specialized studies consider construction and investment to be directly associated with migration. In this context it seems appropriate to generalize the factors as economic opportunities and complementary resources.

Table 16.1. European population, 1700–1960 (millions)

	1700[a]	1750[b]	1800	1850	1880	1890	1900	1910	1920	1930	1940	1950	1955
Austria	—	—	—	3.9	5.0	5.4	6.0	6.6	6.5	6.7	6.7	6.9	7.0
Belgium	—	—	3.0	4.3	5.5	6.1	6.7	7.4	7.6[c]	8.1	8.3	8.6	8.9
Bulgaria	—	—	—	—	2.8	3.3[c]	3.7	4.3	4.8[c]	5.7	6.7	7.3[c]	7.5
Czechoslovakia	—	—	—	—	—	—	—	—	13.0	14.0	14.7	12.4[c]	13.1
Denmark	0.8	—	0.9	1.6	2.1	2.3	2.6	2.9	3.2	3.5	3.8	4.3	4.4
France	20.0	22	26.9	36.5[c]	39.2	40.0	40.7	41.5	39.0	41.2	39.8	41.7	43.3
Finland	—	—	1.0	1.6	2.0	2.4	2.7	3.1	3.4	3.4[c]	3.7	4.0	4.2
Germany	16.0	—	24.5	31.7[c]	40.2	44.2	50.6	58.5	61.8	65.1	69.8	68.0[c]	70.1
Holland	—	—	2.2	3.1	4.0	4.5	5.1	5.9	6.8	7.9	8.9	10.1	10.8
Hungary	1.6	—	—	5.0	5.3	6.0	6.9	7.6	8.0	8.6	9.3	9.3	9.8
Italy	13.4	—	18.1	23.9[c]	29.6	31.7	33.9	36.2	37.0[c]	40.3	43.8	46.6	48.0
Norway	0.7	—	0.9	1.5	1.8	2.0	2.2	2.4	2.6	2.8	3.0	3.3	3.4
Poland[b]	—	—	—	—	8	—	9	10	27	31	33	25	27
Portugal	2.4	—	3.1	4.2	4.6	5.1	5.4	6	6	6.8	7.7	8.4	8.8
Russia[b]	—	20	37	60	88	—	111	140	150	176	192	181	197
Spain	8.0	8	11.5	15.5	16.6	17.6	18.6	19.9	21.2	23.4	25.8	27.9	29.0
Sweden	—	1.5	2.3	3.5	4.6	4.8	5.1	5.5	5.9	6.1	6.4	7.0	7.3
Switzerland	—	—	1.8	2.4	2.8	2.9	3.3	3.8	3.9	4.1	4.2	4.7	5.0
United Kingdom	9.5	10	16[b]	22.3	31.1	34.3	38.2	42.1	43.7	45.9	48.2	50.3	51.0
Yugoslavia	—	—	—	—	—	—	—	—	11.9	13.8	15.8	16.2[c]	17.6
Europe[b] (including Russia)	—	144	192	274	335	—	423	456	486	531	572	574	606

[a] SOURCES: *J. Beloch*, Zeitschrift für socialwisenschaft, *III* (*1900*), p. 5. *All other figures are from* Cambridge Economic History of Europe, *VI, Part I, p. 61.*
[b] SOURCE: *Extracted from Table III/2, William Woodruff,* The Impact of Western Man, *p. 104.*
[c] *Indicates boundary change.*

zation, and technology. As long as the discrepancies among them are relatively small, development may proceed smoothly. However, violent fluctuation in one or more of these conditions may hinder development and render population increases a burden rather than an asset. In the rest of this chapter, we shall survey the population trends in modern Europe and explore the influences and the effects of these trends on the demand and the supply factors. We shall also explore the extent to which population trends were in harmony with economic development and the changes in per capita incomes in the various countries.

POPULATION TRENDS

Population figures are incomplete and unreliable before the nineteenth century, and must be carefully interpreted. The estimates presented in Table 16.1 are probably the best

available. But, except for those covering the last 100 years, they are only rough approximations useful for the observation of trends rather than for detailed analysis.

The population estimates in the table suggest the following observations: (1) The population of Europe increased from 144 million to 574 million in 2 centuries, net of the effects of famines, plagues, war, and emigration. The increase in the last 2 centuries was almost fourfold, or 3.98 times. (2) A sharp increase was characteristic of only a few countries, notably Holland, Belgium, and the United Kingdom. The rest increased at lower rates, especially those that suffered greatly from war. Russia's population increased almost 10 times in this period, although a part of the change must have been due to annexation of new territories, as indicated. (3) The rate of change in these countries was variable. Some of them, such as France, experienced periods of stagnation and decline.

Table 16.2.   Annual rates of population growth in European countries during the nineteenth century[a] (Annual rate of growth per 1000)

	1801–20	1821–30	1831–40	1841–50	1851–60	1861–70	1871–80	1881–90	1891–1900
Sweden	4.8	11.2	8.4	10.8	10.3	7.7	9.1	4.7	7.1
Norway	5.1	14.7	9.7	11.7	14.0	7.9	10.0	4.1	11.3
Denmark	8.3	9.3	7.2	9.8	12.3	10.4	9.6	9.4	11.5
Finland	7.4	13.2	5.3	12.5	6.5	1.2	15.4	13.2	11.1
Great Britain and Ireland	13.0	13.7	10.4	2.5	5.5	8.3	10.2	7.8	9.6
Holland	5.5	9.6	9.3	6.7	7.2	8.4	11.7	11.8	12.7
Belgium	7.7	7.2	8.0	7.4	6.2	7.4	9.5	9.5	9.9
Germany	5.2	11.2	7.5	7.7	6.4	7.8	10.3	8.9	13.2
Austria-Hungary	5.3	9.8	5.3	3.6	6.8	7.5	4.4	9.1	9.6
Switzerland	4.6	9.0	6.0	7.4	4.4	6.3	6.5	3.9	11.4
France	5.5	6.2	4.6	4.4	2.4	2.8	2.0	2.2	1.6
Italy	2.4	9.3	6.8	7.0	4.9	6.0	6.0	7.6	6.2
Spain	4.2	6.2	5.1	3.5	7.8	5.1	3.7	3.8	4.9
Portugal	1.6	7.6	7.7	2.0	5.6	8.3	7.4	7.2	7.2
Russia	9.6	10.8	8.3	7.7	8.0	11.7	13.6	13.9	13.5
Balkans	4.2	3.3	6.3	6.3	5.2	6.2	4.6	11.0	10.5
Europe	6.5	9.4	7.1	5.8	6.2	7.7	8.3	9.0	9.9

[a] *After Sundbärg*, Aperçus statistiques internationaux, *p. 31.*
SOURCE: Cambridge Economic History of Europe, *VI, Part I, p. 62.*

The rates of growth in this period are shown in Table 16.2. These figures suggest that the northern countries, probably with the exception of Russia, experienced higher rates of growth than the rest of Europe. However, other countries tended to catch up in the latter part of the nineteenth century. The growth rates of the populations of France, Spain, Italy, and the Baltic countries were relatively low until the last two decades of the nineteenth century. More important are the relatively high rates of growth of the countries that developed more rapidly during the nineteenth century, such as the United Kingdom, Germany, Holland, and the Scandinavian countries. However, a decline in the growth rate seems to have characterized the period from 1840 to 1860 in many countries of Europe, and in Europe as a whole between 1841 and 1850. This was probably due to the potato famine of 1846, the 1848 revolutions, and emigration.

Sources of population growth

Before looking into the factors leading to these dramatic population changes, one should recall that they were net of migration.

Migration had an impact on both the actual population figures and the changes which might have occurred in its absence. The extent of migration from Europe during the last century and a half indicates its importance as an outlet for surplus population. Between 1815 and 1820 60,000 people left Europe; 133,000 left between 1821 and 1830; 542,000 in 1831–1840; 1,639,000 in 1841–1850, and 2,477,000 between 1851 and 1860.[3] More detailed information on emigration for the last decade is shown in Table 16.3. The figures in this table were accompanied by many qualifications which have been omitted because approximations are sufficient in this context. The figures show that emigration was quite high from the countries which developed rapidly, such as the British Isles, Germany, and Scandinavia, and from the countries which failed to develop, such as Spain, Portugal, and to an extent Italy. This suggests that emigration alone cannot explain economic development or its absence. The limited emigration from

[3] Brinley Thomas, *Migration and Economic Growth*, extracted from Table 121, p. 312.

Table 16.3. Emigration from Europe, 1851–1960 (Thousands)

ORIGIN	1851–1960	%	1851–60	1861–70	1871–80	1881–90	1891–1900	1901–10	1911–20	1921–30	1931–40	1941–50	1951–60
British Isles	20,501	33.6	1,313	1,572	1,849	3,259	2,149	3,150	2,587	2,151	262	755	1,454
Sweden	1,265	2.1	17	122	103	327	205	224	86	107	8	23	43
Norway	882	1.4	36	98	85	187	95	191	62	87	6	10	25
Finland	426	.7	n.a.	n.a.	n.a.	26	59	159	67	73	3	7	32
Denmark	575	.9	n.a.	8	39	82	51	73	52	64	100	38	68
France	548	.9	27	36	66	119	51	53	32	4	5	n.a.	155
Belgium	284	.5	1	2	2	21	16	30	21	33	20	29	109
Netherlands	631	1.0	16	20	17	52	24	28	22	32	4	75	341
Germany	6,485	10.6	671	779	626	1,342	527	274	91	564	121	618	872
Austria	4,241	6.9	31	40	46	248	440	1,111	418	61	11	n.a.	53
Switzerland	383	.6	6	15	36	85	35	37	31	50	47	18	23
Spain	5,184	8.5	3	7	13	572	791	1,091	1,306	560	132	166	543
Portugal	2,950	4.8	45	79	131	185	266	324	402	995	108	69	346
Italy	11,511	18.8	5	27	168	992	1,580	3,615	2,194	1,370	235	467	858
Russia	2,238	3.7			58	288	481	911	420	80			
Poland	3,048	4.9								634	164		
TOTAL	61,152		2,171	2,805	3,239	7,785	6,770	11,271	7,791	6,865	1,226	2,275	4,922

SOURCE: *William Woodruff*, The Impact of Western Man, *p. 106.*
n.a. = not available.

France, whose pattern of economic development differed from the countries mentioned above, supports this suggestion. The trend of emigration from Europe will become more meaningful when estimates of per capita income change are presented below.

Population growth can be a result of changes in birth rates or death rates, movement across national boundaries, or any combination of these. Since in the last two centuries Europe lost people because of migration, its growth cannot be explained by population movements across national boundaries. It therefore must be explained by changes in the birth and death rates.

Birth and death rates can give only rough mechanical explanations of the changes in population. But although more sophisticated measures such as fertility rates and replacement rates may be more useful for predicting trends, in the present context birth and death rates are quite adequate. Even these rates, however, are not easily assembled, especially for the years preceding the middle of the nineteenth century. Relatively dependable estimates are available only after 1841.[4] Inspection of these rates shows that: (1)

[4] See *Cambridge Economic History of Europe*, VI, Part I, p. 68, Table 9.

Birth rates almost invariably declined. The decline became conspicuous after 1875 in a few countries, but in most it did not appear until 1900. Since birth rates during the first four decades of the period were relatively stable, it may be safe to assume that no decline was experienced before that time. (2) The decline in birth rates varied from one country to another, but in most cases it was about 40 percent. The exception was the birth rate in France, which was the lowest of those observed in 1841–1850. The decline in France was from 27.3 births per 1000 of total population in 1841–1850 to 19.5 per 1000 in 1951–1955, with 2 low rates of 13.2 in 1916–1920 and 14.7 in 1941–1945, which were war years. In contrast, the birth rate in Germany declined from 36.1 per 1000 in 1841–1850 to 15.8 in 1951–1955. The closest to this decline was that experienced in England and Wales from 32.6 to 15.2 per 1000. All other experiences fall between these extremes. (3) In most countries the decline fluctuated, with an apparent rise after war periods as if to recover the lost population. Nevertheless, a relatively steady decline seems to have characterized the latter part of the nineteenth century, during which time industrialization and development occurred.

The changes in the birth rate should have

caused a decline, had not the death rates declined faster. It seems clear from Table 16.4 that except for the war years, the death rate declined continuously after the middle of the nineteenth century. The rate of decline, however, was not steady, and some countries reached a very low death rate long before others had shown a real improvement. For example, in Denmark and Norway the death rate was already down to 13.7 per 1000 in 1906–1910; in Sweden it was 14.3 and in England and Wales it was 14.7 in the same interval; in Austria it was still 22.5, in Italy 21.1, and in Rumania 26.0 per 1000 in the same period. Only the Scandinavian countries had a death rate lower than 20 per 1000 by 1876–1880; the Netherlands, Belgium, Switzerland, and the United Kingdom achieved that level by 1900.

Causes of changes in birth and death rates

Birth rates are much more difficult to explain than death rates. One generally accepted explanation relates the size of the family to the expected living standard. The higher the family's expectations, the greater the tendency to restrict the number of children in order to enjoy a higher per capita income. As development and industrialization progress, more commodities become available on the market. Higher per capita income becomes necessary to enjoy them; hence the limitation of the size of the family.

Another explanation connects the size of the family with its structure. As the family becomes less tightly structured and as mobility increases, members find it necessary to delay marriage until they have succeeded in establishing themselves economically. Delayed marriages reduce the fertile years and therefore the size of prospective families.

A third explanation, related to the above two, emphasizes the higher expectations for the offspring. In order to provide a brighter economic future for the children, parents must give them more care and education. Education lengthens the period of dependency, delays marriage, and increases the demands on the parents. The fewer the children, the more attention can be devoted to each of them; and the longer the period of schooling, the later the marriage will be. Both of these factors result in lower birth rates.

Finally, an explanation which has received wide circulation is based on the development of rationality, objectivity, and a new attitude toward religion and the Church. Given the advances in science and medicine, these new attitudes made it acceptable to reduce birth rates by using contraceptives. However, the available figures give no conclusive evidence on this explanation. Catholic Belgium has consistently had lower birth rates than Protestant Holland; Catholic Spain and Italy, in contrast, have consistently had two of the highest birth rates in Europe. It may be safe to suggest that, when combined with one or more of the previous explanations, attitude becomes an important determinant of the birth rate. When expectations for a higher standard of living rise, for example, it may be easier for Protestants to limit the size of the family than it is for Catholics.

Nutrition. Declines in the death rate have been explained by a number of factors, some of which are closely related to development. Natural death may be caused by old age, starvation and malnutrition, or disease. All these causes are interconnected. Therefore, improvements in diet and nutrition and advances against disease tend to reduce infant mortality, extend life expectancy, and delay death from old age. Especially after the middle of the nineteenth century, improvements were achieved on both fronts. Increases in agricultural output, the expansion of transportation, and the introduction of new crops were extremely important in improving the diet of the average person. Not only was more and better food produced, but it could be transported to all parts of the continent with sufficient rapidity to render famines less frequent and less destructive. As will be seen later, the expansion of canals and railroads had an immediate impact on food distribution and on the average diet.

Higher production and better transportation were capable of improving the diet and reducing the danger of famines, but they could not assure the achievement of such results. Their effectiveness depended on the distribution of incomes and on national welfare policies which would guarantee that the minimum requirements for nutrition and growth would be available to everyone. Variations in income distribution patterns, in national welfare policies, and in the national output or per capita income explain the differential changes in the death rates of the various European countries. The Scandinavian countries, though not the wealthiest or most developed, had at an early date formulated welfare policies which helped to guarantee minimum dietary requirements. British policies were less advanced, but the greater economic development in Britain tended to at least partly compensate for that deficiency and thus allow a larger number of people to enjoy the minimum requirements. Where there was neither development nor advanced welfare policies, the death rates declined more slowly. As will be seen below, in many countries, such as Italy, Spain, Portugal, and Yugoslavia, the per capita incomes remained low until far into the twentieth century, the distribution of income remained highly unequal, and no welfare policies prevailed to guarantee a nutritional minimum.

Sanitation and medicine. The battle against high mortality rates was won more decisively by improvements in sanitation and medicine. Mortality was especially high in the early nineteenth century among the younger people, as shown by the short life expectancy. It was caused primarily by infectious diseases such as typhus, cholera, smallpox, and scarlet fever. The discovery of a relationship between certain bacteria and these diseases made it possible to produce immunity by inoculation to destroy them. Immunization and improvements in sanitation reduced the danger of these diseases to almost nil by the end of the century. Similar successes were achieved with respect to other diseases so that the main dangers in the twentieth century have been respiratory and heart diseases, which generally strike older people. However, as in the case of diet improvements, those countries which could afford national programs to control these diseases were more successful in reducing the mortality rate. Improvements in the diet also increased resistance to disease. Hence, economic development, as represented by the per capita income, was an important factor in reducing mortality rates.

Summary

Population growth in Europe was due primarily to a reduction in the death rate which offset the decline in the birth rate and the loss of people through emigration. The declines in the birth and death rates were closely related to economic development and the rise in per capita incomes. However, they were more marked where national welfare policies guaranteed a minimum nutritional diet, where means of transportation were expanded, and where advances in medicine were implemented. These supplementary measures seem to have come at a time when economic development and industrialization were under way. The reduced infant mortality and increased life expectancy changed the structure of the population in favor of a higher percentage of adults. Thus, a larger labor force was created to advance economic development.

ECONOMIC DEVELOPMENT INDICATORS

The main hypothesis in this section is that economic development was virtually impossible until technology was developed sufficiently to increase total output at a faster rate than the population growth rate. Until such time, per capita income remained almost stagnant, and most people derived their living from agriculture. To explore the relevance of this hypothesis, we will use two indicators of development, per capita income and the rate of urbanization. Both should be used jointly, since while per capita income may be a clear indicator of development, the degree of urbanization is not. It is assumed that the larger the number of people in agriculture, the larger the number who live near subsistence and command relatively low purchasing power and demand for commodities.

Quantitative data are not sufficient to allow a systematic comparative survey of the various European countries, especially for the early years of their development. However, there is adequate information to show trends. Although data are not available, it is fairly certain that per capita income changed very little before the beginning of the nineteenth century, with the probable exception of minor changes in Britain and Belgium. In most western European countries, the change began around the middle of the nineteenth century. In eastern Europe, Russia, and the Mediterranean provinces of Italy and the Iberian peninsula the change came much later, although in northern and central Italy it came before the middle of the century. The income trend was parallel to the demographic trend. The dependence on agriculture began to decline in Belgium and the United Kingdom before the middle of the nineteenth century, in other western European countries a little later, and in Russia and eastern and southern Europe after the turn of the century. These trends may be more precisely indicated by some of the available statistics.

Agricultural population

The average real output in Britain increased by 60 percent between 1700 and 1800, if the year 1700 is taken as a base, and by 47 percent if the year 1800 is taken as the base year.[5] Thus the average annual rate was much less than 0.5 percent, since the total increment included compounded rates.

By 1800 only about 36 percent of the British labor force was still occupied in agriculture. However, this percentage represented a larger absolute number of people than were previously employed in agriculture. In the nineteenth and twentieth centuries the ratio of people employed in agriculture continued to decline, reaching 21.7 percent in 1851, 10.5 percent in 1891, and 5.0 percent in 1951. The absolute number of people occupied in agriculture, 1.7 million in 1801, was still the same in 1891 and was 1.6 million in 1911, after which it decreased radically.

The nineteenth century also saw a significant increase in per capita output. Throughout the century the annual rate, averaged from 30-year intervals, never went below 1.0 percent, and in 6 out of 7 estimates it was above 1.0 percent, reaching 1.9 percent near the end of the century. Thus it appears that as dependence on agriculture was declining, per capita output was increasing.[6]

At the opposite end of the spectrum were Russia and other eastern European countries such as Rumania, Bulgaria, Albania, and Hungary. In all these countries about 90 percent of the people were still occupied in agriculture as late as the end of the nineteenth century. It is estimated that the urban population of Russia in 1863 was less than 10 percent and that it was only about 13 percent in 1897. About 80 percent of the population of Albania were employed in agriculture as late as 1930.

These are extreme examples. In the majority of the European countries, about 50 percent of the population was in agriculture around the middle of the century, but no

[5] For a brief explanation of index numbers, see R. G. D. Allen, *Statistics for Economists*, London: Hutchinson and Co. Ltd., 2nd ed. 1951; pp. 100–116.

[6] Estimates extracted from Phyllis Deane and W. A. Cole, *British Economic Growth 1688–1959*, pp. 78, 80, 142–143, and 283.

absolute decline of agricultural population had taken place. Such declines had to wait for the twentieth century, even in France, Germany, and the Scandinavian countries.[7]

Per capita income

Since the second half of the nineteenth century, increases of income have been common, although their rates have varied. The per capita real income in Italy increased by less than 10 percent between 1861–1865 and 1896–1900. Between 1900 and 1950 it rose about 10 percent, and between 1950 and 1960 about 80 percent. Thus the development of the Italian economy belongs more to the twentieth than to the nineteenth century. This is consistent with the radical decline of dependence on agriculture from 41.1 percent in 1861 to 30.5 percent in 1900 and to 16.0 percent in 1960.[8] However, these figures are somewhat distorted by aggregating data on northern, central, and southern Italy. Northern and central Italy were similar to other western European countries, experiencing a declining agricultural population and a rising per capita output, while southern Italy showed stagnation throughout most of the nineteenth century.

Table 16.4 shows the trend in per capita output from 1870 for a few selected countries. A major advance in per capita output came as late as 1950, but since 1870 there has been a positive, and in many cases, impressive change in per capita output, especially in Belgium and the Scandinavian countries. A significant relative decline of dependence on agriculture is also apparent in these countries in this period. About 75 percent of the Swedish labor force was engaged in agriculture in 1861, 61 percent in

Table 16.4. Rates of growth of output per head of population

	1870–1913	1913–1950	1950–1960
Belgium	1.7	0.7	2.3
Denmark	2.1	1.1	2.6
France	1.4	0.7	3.5
Germany	1.8	0.4	6.5
Netherlands	0.8	0.7	3.6
Norway	1.4	1.9	2.6
Sweden	2.3	1.6	2.6
Switzerland	1.3	1.5	3.7

SOURCE: *From Table 1–3, Angus Maddison, Economic Growth in the West, p. 30.*

1891, and 48 percent in 1911, at which time an absolute decline began. Denmark had 52 percent in agriculture in 1871, 40 percent in 1911, and 28 percent in 1939. Holland, whose per capita output increased less than 0.9 percent annually after the mid-eighteenth century, had 40 percent of its labor force in agriculture in 1849; by 1900 the percentage had gone down to 30 and to 20 percent in 1947. However, an absolute decline began around 1956 when the percentage had declined to 11 percent. Prussia had 73.5 percent of its labor force in agriculture in 1816 and 69.3 in 1861; however, for Germany as a whole the figure was much less. Nevertheless, annual income per head in Prussia had already started to rise and in 1851–1855 it was rising 0.8 percent annually.

Conclusions

These scattered figures are too few and incomplete to permit firm conclusions. However, some general observations can be made which tend to be consistent with the impressions experienced earlier. (1) It does seem that development is usually related to a decline in the dependence on subsistence agriculture or on agriculture in general, although examples may be found to contradict this observation. (2) The decline in agricultural population itself is not sufficient. It contributes to development only if there are alternative nonagricultural economic opportunities. Thus a significant rise in per capita output tends to be associated with a decline

[7] William Blackwell, *The Beginnings of Russian Industrialization 1800–1860*; pp. 96–7; P. I. Lyaschenko, *History of the National Economy of Russia*, p. 504; *Cambridge Economic History of Europe*, VI, Part II, pp. 60 ff.

[8] S. B. Clough, *The Economic History of Modern Italy*, pp. 369 ff.

in the absolute number of people dependent on agriculture. (3) This generalization does not apply if a continuing dependence on agriculture is accompanied by an expansion of the cultivatable area, a rise in the land/labor ratio, and an increase in capital investment in agriculture, causing a rise in per capita agricultural output. (4) It should be noted that even though the rural population was declining relatively for many years in various European countries, per capita output did not rise appreciably until the second half of the nineteenth century. This suggests that until then productivity was not increasing.

Although not indicated by the above data, it may be suggested that the rise in productivity and per capita income depended on the introduction and utilization of new technologies and a rise in the capital/output ratio in the economy. This may explain the fact that urbanization need not be closely associated with development. Development depends more on technology and capital investment, given the market generated by an increasing population. The process by which population and technology can lead to development will be explored later. In the next chapter we shall survey the technological innovations and inventions which revolutionized economic activity and production in modern Europe.

BIBLIOGRAPHY

Blackwell, William, *The Beginnings of Russian Industrialization 1800–1860,* Princeton: Princeton University Press, 1968, chap. 4.

Clough, S. B., *The Economic History of Modern Italy,* New York: Columbia University Press, 1964, chap. 5.

Deane, Phyllis, and W. A. Cole, *British Economic Growth 1688–1959.* Second edition, New York: Cambridge University Press, 1967, chap. 3 and statistical appendices.

Habakkuk, H. J., and M. M. Postan, Eds. *Cambridge Economic History of Europe,* VI, New York: Cambridge University Press, 1965, especially chaps. 1 and 2.

Hagen, E. E., "Population and Economic Growth," *American Economic Review,* XLIX, No. 3 (June 1959), pp. 310–327.

Heckscher, E. F., *Economic History of Sweden,* Cambridge, Mass.: Harvard University Press, 1954.

Lyaschenko, P. I., *History of the National Economy of Russia,* New York: Macmillan, 1949.

Maddison, Angus, *Economic Growth in the West,* New York: Twentieth Century Fund, 1964, chap. 1.

Malthus, Thomas, Julian Huxley, and Frederick Osborn, *On Population: Three Essays,* New York: New American Library, 1960.

Thomas, Brinley, *International Migration and Economic Development,* Population and Culture series, New York: UNESCO, 1961. See especially for more recent theories on migration.

Thomas, Brinley, *Migration and Economic Growth,* New York: Cambridge University Press, 1954, chaps. 1–4, 7, 10.

Vicens Vives, Jaime, *An Economic History of Spain,* Princeton: Princeton University Press, 1969, chaps. 33–44.
Woodruff, William, *The Impact of Western Man,* New York: St. Martin's Press, Inc., Macmillan & Co. Ltd., 1967, chap. 3.

17

THE
ADVANCE
OF
TECHNOLOGY

The study of technology involves four considerations: the scientific basis, the engineering feasibility, economic efficiency, and dissemination of technical knowledge. The economist frequently concentrates on the third of these considerations. His question tends to be the following: At each level of technology, which techniques are economically efficient and which are not, and at what rate should they be utilized in production? The economic historian needs to study the other considerations as well in order to understand the pattern of economic change. He considers the trend of technological inventions and the industries, countries, and periods in which they occur. He evaluates the impact of these inventions on society and the economy. He also tries to trace the spread of technology from one location or industry to another.

SCIENCE AND TECHNOLOGY

The relation between science and technology is one between theory and application. Science has been described as "the theory of nature" and technology as the "cultivation of nature for practical purposes. . . ."[1] Science deals with the objective aspects of tech-

[1] A. G. Van Melsen, *Science and Technology,* p. 307.

nology. It explores the logical foundations of technological processes and the natural characteristics of matter. It tries to discover the laws according to which certain phenomena occur. Science explains why actions and reactions take place the way they do, regardless of the uses of the results. Its relevance is unlimited by time or space; it is bound only by its own laws. When a scientist searches for a scientific law, he is rarely aware of the uses to which it may be put; he is rarely discouraged if he fails to see its immediate usefulness; he cares only to discover the new knowledge which might help man to understand his environment and uncover the secrets of the unknown. If science deals with specific processes, it tells *why* these processes proceed the way they do; it tells *why* a motor starts when a spark is put to the fuel, or *why* a certain fertilizer affects plants in one way and not in another.

In contrast, technology shows *how* things happen. Technology is more specific than science. Each technological invention has within it a certain set of applications which determine its usefulness. Unless a technological invention is considered useful, it may never be applied. Technological inventions may be closely related to need, whereas science is objective.

However, it has become difficult to distinguish between science and technology. A scientist frequently finds himself exploring

new areas because of their potential technological benefits. These may be badly needed,
as is the case with scientific research associated with the techniques of war, with the
control of disease, or with improvement of
the soil. On the other hand, with the expansion of formal education it has become
highly probable that the technician will
know some of the theoretical bases for his
technical operations, just as the theoretician
may know about technology. Indeed, the best
results in both science and technology may
occur when the two reinforce each other. In
such a case the technologist can take shortcuts, basing his inventions on scientific
grounds rather than on repeated and costly
experiments. Such coordination can also
serve the scientist by providing him with
empirical tests to help remove the defects in
his theories.

While science and technology can overlap
and reinforce each other, it is still possible
for each to proceed separately. The scientist
will not stop his investigations because his
theories cannot be tested due to technological
limitations, nor will the technologist or engineer wait for science to provide a theoretical
background for his inventions.

Most of the early technological inventions
of the industrial revolution were introduced
by nonscientists and were in many ways
ahead of existing theory. France was more
advanced in science than Britain during
most of the eighteenth and nineteenth centuries, while the latter was far ahead in
technology. Businessmen developed highly
sophisticated enterprises long before economic theory developed as a science. It
should be noted, however, that the scope of
technological advance remains limited until
science provides the theoretical foundations
for further development.

The utilitarian nature of technology
widened the division between it and science
in the early years of the modern period.
Until recently science was sponsored mainly
by universities and educational institutions,
while technology and engineering found

their home in industry and business. Coordination was not easy and was much less
evident than it is today, when theory and
practice can be found jointly in industry and
educational institutions. This was another
reason that the early technological inventions were frequently devoid of a scientific
base.

DISSEMINATION OF
TECHNICAL KNOWLEDGE

One of the main ways of disseminating
knowledge has been artisan movement across
national borders. This was limited first by
the guilds and later, in the mercantilist
period, by national governments. Another
common method of dissemination has been
to send technical missions to other countries
to observe production processes and techniques. The usefulness of this method, however, is limited by the fact that a mission can
see only what its host shows. A third method
is to obtain products from other countries,
analyze their characteristics, and try to infer
the techniques by which they were produced.
This method is useful only under two conditions: it must be possible to infer the technique from the product, and scientific and
engineering activities must be coordinated in
order to translate the observations into technological application. A much more effective
approach is to get hold of the process, the
machine, or the tool itself, and analyze its
functioning. Studying a loom is much more
useful than studying the fabric. This method,
however, assumes that it is possible to obtain
machines from other countries, either legally
or by smuggling. Currently the most important means of transmitting knowledge are
literature and the meetings of professional
and technical experts. The extent to which
these methods are useful depends on freedom
of publication, patent rights, and the degree
of communication among professionals. As
will be seen later, such freedom was not
complete at the beginning of the modern

period. However, it became gradually more possible, especially after the establishment of professional societies and journals.

Frequently development in a given country is closely associated with the technological inventions original to that country. The assumption is that countries with more advanced technologies have an advantage and can develop earlier than others, as if original technical knowledge remained the property of the inventing country. Looked at from another standpoint, this assumption implies that emulation is either not possible or not as effective as original invention. An illustration of this argument is the attempt to contrast early and late comers, as was suggested by Gerschenkron in the theory summarized in Chapter 3. In this regard, we should observe the distribution of inventions among the European countries, the ease or difficulty of acquiring technical knowledge, and the relationship between the dissemination of such knowledge and the rates of development and industrialization. It would also be helpful to observe whether or not the rate of development was related to changes in the freedom of dissemination of technical knowledge among the countries of Europe. Furthermore, it should be interesting to find out what happened after a given technique was transmitted to a country, or to what extent the accessibility of a technique was a determining factor in development. It may be that no technique can be regarded as indispensable to development.

ECONOMIC APPLICATION OF TECHNICAL INVENTIONS

From an economic standpoint, the most important determinant of technological innovation is the impact on profit. If a product is already in existence, the producer may use a new technique to reduce costs, to increase revenue, or both. However, an innovation may also be used to produce a new product for which no traditional measure of costs or revenue is available. In this case the producer introduces the new product only if its profit expectations promise a rate of return at least equal to what he can obtain from traditional investment.

Innovation can reduce costs by substituting capital for labor, especially when a labor shortage has caused wages to rise enough to reduce profit expectations. Or it may cut down transportation costs or other capital inputs such as fuel and maintenance, or reduce accidents. Innovation can also increase revenue by creating new demand for the product, by increasing its variety or improving its quality, or simply by a demonstration effect. The advantages derived by one producer from the innovation may be disadvantageous to others in the economy. Nevertheless, to the innovating producer the change is economically justified.

Thus the introduction of new techniques hinges upon two conditions: Assuming that the technique is known, it will be adopted only if sufficient entrepreneurship exists and if competition in the market is permissible. In the absence of entrepreneurship, economic considerations become irrelevant. And unless competition is permissible there is no incentive to innovate. The individual producer will innovate only if he can use the new technique to gain an advantage in the market, or to prevent others from gaining such an advantage over him. For this reason it has often been charged that monopolies refrain from innovating on the assumption that they already have an advantage and are not in danger of losing it.

These economic considerations apply to the individual firm. However, innovation may be desired as a national objective, which may be economic, political, or military. Profitability in such cases becomes irrelevant, since national objectives outweigh material gain as represented by profits and financial returns. The individual producer may be assured a certain rate of profit through subsidy or tax exemption in order to reduce national dependence on other countries, to achieve a political goal, or to help establish new industries. The last of these goals is particularly important for late comers, since dependence on the international market might be too hazardous for new producers. The national government may also decide to restrict competition in order to permit innovations which otherwise might not be profitable or competitive enough to introduce.

When the market mechanism did not seem convenient, these various other approaches were used, not always successfully. When and to what extent they were successful will be explored in the following chapters. Here we shall survey the appearance of new inventions and explore briefly their potential uses in production and industrialization.

ADVANCES IN TECHNOLOGY

Improvement in technology is cumulative in two ways: Each advance is built on techniques known before, and each is built on theoretical advances in science. Since scientific and technological knowledge is never confined to any one country or region, it may be inappropriate to describe a technique as purely British, German, or American. Most techniques are the result of scientific and technological achievements from various countries which have accumulated over the years. However, since our interest lies in the impact of these advances on economic development and change, it may be helpful to note the place of origin of those inventions which contributed to change.

Technological advances varied in their importance and applicability to economic change. Probably those with the widest applicability occurred in the generation of power, the supply of fuel, and the processing of metals. These three areas are interrelated. Fuel is necessary to power generation and metallurgy is essential in the building of machinery to use the fuel to generate the

power. We shall survey the inventions relating to these three fields before considering those related to other, more specialized areas. A summary of technological improvements since 1700 is appended to this chapter.

Science and technology in energy, power, and metallurgy

Until the beginning of the eighteenth century the main sources of power had been man, beast, wind, and water. Man had also increased his power with such devices as the lever, the spring, the crane, and beam press. Nevertheless, the amount of energy he could apply was still relatively limited. Wind and water mills could generate little more than a 5- or 10-horsepower capacity. The breakthrough came with the steam engine.

The steam engine. The steam engine was based on the theoretical knowledge of gravity and the atmosphere and the application of this knowledge to water pumping. Although water pumps had been used, water could be drawn up to a height of only 30 feet. The explanation of this phenomenon was provided in 1644 by Evangelista Torricelli, a student of Galileo, who affirmed that atmospheric pressure was equal to 30 inches of mercury in height, the equivalent of 30 feet of water. The problem of pumping was to create a vacuum so that water could be raised. Denis Papin built the first atmospheric steam engine in France around 1690. Although he introduced the idea of a cylinder and a piston, he depended on the pressure of the atmosphere; hence the name *atmospheric engine*. The engine itself was a simple one but it provided the basis for later developments. Around the end of the seventeenth century Thomas Savery built his "fire" engine. This was used to pump water but only at atmospheric pressure, although Savery tried unsuccessfully to apply it at higher pressure. The next advancement came in 1712 when Thomas Newcomen, possibly independently of Savery, built a steam engine making use of atmospheric pressure. Newcomen made use also of Papin's idea of the cylinder and piston, but he added new features which made his machine usable:

Newcomen's boiler produced steam at atmospheric pressure. When this was introduced to the bottom of the cylinder, it was mainly the weight of the pump-rod, hanging from the other end of the beam, that caused the piston to rise. When the cylinder was full of steam and closed by a valve at the bottom, a jet of cold water to condense the steam was introduced into the cylinder through an injection-cock . . . with the result that the piston was forced down again by atmospheric pressure. As the piston-rod drew down one end of the beam, the other end rose, carrying with it the pump-rod, which sucked up water. To maintain the cycle of operations, the steam-valve and the injection-cock were opened and closed automatically by the movement of the rod of the injection-pump, which was attached to the beam.[2]

Newcomen's engine lifted 10 gallons of water to about 153 feet. This represents about 5.5 horsepower compared with the 1 horsepower of the "fire" engine. By 1729 this machine was being used in Hungary, France, Belgium, Germany, Austria, and Sweden; about a quarter of a century later it reached America.

The efficiency of Newcomen's machine was still limited partly because the cylinder was relatively small, and partly because much heat was wasted in reheating the water after condensing the steam to create a vacuum. The first problem was treated more scientifically by John Smeaton, who calculated the relationship between the height of water pumping and the amount of fuel to be used. By 1774 he had succeeded in doubling efficiency, mainly by building larger cylin-

[2] T. K. Derry and Trevor I. Williams, *A Short History of Technology*, p. 307.

ders. The problem of reheating was attacked by James Watt, who decided that if the cylinder could be kept hot, fuel consumption would be cut down considerably. In 1765 he came up with the idea of a separate condenser. By 1776 his new engine was in action. But Watt did not stop there. Between 1781 and 1786 he introduced the "rotative motion" or parallel motion, which made it possible for low-pressure engines to drive machinery directly. This mechanism admitted steam to each side of the piston alternately, thus making the engine do almost double duty. It was also the necessary step toward generalizing the use of the steam engine to other areas of industry and manufacturing.

The problem of efficiency remained a focus of attention. The next major advance came with the "compound steam engine," which worked under much higher pressure than that of the atmosphere and made repeated use of the steam before reheating. Compounding increased efficiency almost tenfold by 1803. Humphrey Edwards patented a compound steam engine in France in 1815. Various other people had a hand in building high-pressure engines and in compounding, among whom were Jonathan Carter Hornblower and Richard Trevithick of the United Kingdom, and Jacob Perkins and Oliver Evans in the United Kingdom and the United States. John McNaught in 1845 and John Elder in the 1850s improved further on the compound engine. By using more cylinders to use the steam repeatedly and by applying high pressure, they cut down fuel consumption greatly. Small engines became capable of big jobs because of the manifold increase in horsepower.

While application of the steam engine to various processes was spreading, improvements in it were continuing. Most important among them was the steam turbine. The idea of the turbine is to activate an engine by directly applying pressure to a rotary shaft or its equivalent which connects with the engine. Serious attempts to apply steam and wind pressure directly had been made as early as the seventeenth century. Hydraulic turbines were put to use in 1827 in France by Benoit Fourneyron and in the 1840s and 1850s by various others in western Europe and the United States. The steam turbines that were developed early in the nineteenth century were not very efficient. Trevithick built the "whirling engine," which made use of steam at a speed of 250 r.p.m., only a fifth of the potential power of the steam pressure applied. The breakthrough in steam turbines came in the 1880s, when Charles Parsons of the United Kingdom and Gustav de Laval of Sweden succeeded independently in building a prime mover at high speed. The first turbogenerator ran at a speed of 18,000 r.p.m.

Improvements in electric power. As early as 1660 Otto von Guericke invented a machine to generate a continuous supply of electricity. In 1729 Stephen Gray distinguished conductor from nonconductor metals. The distinction between positive and negative charges was made shortly after by Charles Du Fay in France. In 1752 Benjamin Franklin discovered the lightning conductor, which made it possible to protect buildings against electrical storms. The quantitative measurement of electricity became possible in 1754 when John Canton of Britain measured the current by recording the "repulsion of like-charged balls of pith suspended by threads." His method was later improved upon and standardized by Alessandro Volta of Italy. It finally resulted in 1787 in Benet's gold-leaf electroscope. In the meantime, the Leyden jar to store and discharge electricity was invented by Pieter Van Musschenbroek; it was the earliest condenser. In 1800 Volta reported to the Royal Society on his voltaic pile, which consisted of

. . . alternate plates of silver or copper and zinc . . . separated by flannel or paper soaked in brine . . . [and] pro-

vided a simple and convenient source of continuous current [by] . . . converting the energy released in chemical reaction, which would normally appear largely as heat, into electrical energy.[3]

From then on it was possible to build batteries.

In 1802 Humphrey Davy established the principle of the arc-lamp; namely, when "a spark is continuously struck between two pieces of carbon a brilliant light is emitted." In 1847 W .E. Straite demonstrated an incandescent filament lamp in Britain. The problem of the lamp was to create a sufficient vacuum in the light bulb and add a carbon filament. The vacuum could be created after the mercury pump was invented in 1865. Joseph Swan succeeded in developing a carbon filament by carbonizing a mercerized cotton thread. Thomas Edison achieved the same results in 1881 by carbonizing slivers of bamboo. By the end of the century a metallic filament had been developed; the incandescent lamp had become a reality.

The electric light depended on all the other work which had been done in the field of electricity. In 1820 the Danish physicist H. C. Oersted described the magnetic field that surrounds a conductor carrying an electric charge. His work was later supplemented by that of A. M. Ampère of France, who established the precise relationship between the strength of the magnetic field and that of the electric current that produces it. Michael Faraday put this knowledge to practical use as early as 1831 to produce a mechanical motion, which eventually resulted in the invention of the magnetic electric generator. Though many attempts to build generators had been made, the first successful dynamo was Z. T. Gramme's ring-armature dynamo introduced in 1870. It was driven by a steam engine and could supply a continuous current without heating. It was later replaced by

[3] *Ibid.*, p. 610.

the drum-armature dynamo of 1876, built in Germany by the Siemens and Halske Company. By the 1880s generators, dynamos, and batteries to store electricity were fully developed and widely used in Europe and the United States. In 1883 the first hydro-electric power station in Europe was inaugurated in Milan.

Internal combustion. Although internal combustion may be regarded as an improvement on the steam engine, rather than as a separate invention, it provided such efficiency and flexibility that it became a good substitute. Gas engines were built experimentally in 1794 in the United Kingdom and in 1843 in the United States. The first successful internal combustion engine was a one-cylinder coal–gas engine built in 1859 by Etienne Lenoir of France. In 1862 another Frenchman, Alphonse Beau de Rochas, built an internal combustion engine which was the forerunner of the four-stroke cycle engine. In 1876 N. A. Otto of Germany succeeded in building a four-stroke coal–gas engine which could substitute for the steam engine. A high-speed internal combustion engine using gasoline was achieved through the work of Gottlieb Daimler of Germany; it made the automobile possible. The oil engine introduced in 1890 by H. Ackroyd Stuart of the United Kingdom and the diesel engine built in 1892 by Rudolf Diesel of Germany were highly important in reducing the cost of fuel consumption.

By that time the power and energy sources responsible for industrialization were well known. The major developments of the twentieth century have been the jet engine built in 1937 and the use of atomic energy. The amount of energy that can now be harnessed has no precedent. However, the cumulative nature of technology renders the earlier achievements at least as important as those of the mid-twentieth century.

The generation and harnessing of power required two basic conditions: knowledge, both theoretical and applied, and the mate-

rial to build high-pressure machinery. The former came about gradually, as has been noted. Implementation was made possible by improvements in metallurgy and precision tools. The shift from wood to iron and steel was indispensable for building high-power machines, but these machines also required precisely designed and constructed parts.

Metallurgy. Man made use of iron as far back as the iron age. However, as late as the middle of the eighteenth century only pig iron was produced, cast in large pieces of irregular shape and of great impurity. This metal was brittle and inappropriate for high-power machinery. Impurities remained even after introduction of the blast furnace and the shift from charcoal to coke, both of which provided much higher temperatures for the smelting of iron. In 1776 John Wilkinson used steam power to blow air into the blast furnace. The coke blast furnace spread to France in 1785, to Belgium in 1823, to Austria in 1828, and to the Ruhr after 1850.

An important development was the production of malleable wrought iron. Experiments were made by Abraham Darby around 1709. The Cranage brothers of England succeeded in 1766 in making bar iron. However, both its quantity and its quality remained limited until the puddling process was invented by a Welshman, Peter Onions, in 1784. The credit for this process has usually been given to Henry Cort.

> The essential feature of the puddling process . . . was the "raking, separating, stirring, and spreading about in the . . . furnace," which gave the air full and fairly rapid access to the melted pig iron, so that it was decarbonized to the point at which it became malleable.[4]

This was the first step towards steel-making, since steel is iron with up to 1 percent carbon content. The problem of economy of production was still critical. Blowing cold

[4] *Ibid.*, p. 477.

air into the furnace reduced efficiency. A major step was taken when James Neilson introduced the hot blast furnace in 1829. By blowing hot air into the furnace, he reduced the waste of reheating cold air. This also kept the temperature of the furnace high enough to permit the use of coal instead of coke as fuel. The use of anthracite in iron-smelting was applied in America in 1833 and in Wales in 1837. Until that time Britain had been far ahead of all other countries in the technology of iron and steel. British methods were introduced on the continent gradually during the second quarter of the century.

The age of steel came in the second half of the nineteenth century. The major problem was regulation of the carbon content of the metal. Sweden had long been producing high-quality steel by "covering the bar iron with fragments of charcoal and subjecting it to intense and prolonged heat from a charcoal fire."[5] Further improvements were possible only at much higher costs than the market would allow. A major advance was made almost concurrently between 1856 and 1860 by William Kelly in America, Henry Bessemer and Robert Mushet of Britain, and C. F. Geransson of Sweden. Known as the Bessemer process, the new converter process permitted mass production and control of the carbon content. Hot air was blown on the molten iron to remove all the carbon, after which the required amount of carbon was added. Thus it became possible to make all grades of steel. An alternative process was the "open-hearth" process introduced by Wilhelm and Friedrich Siemens of the United Kingdom and Pierre Martin of France in 1863. The Siemens–Martin process allowed gradual and more controlled burning of the carbon. It also allowed utilization the scrap iron, which helped to remove impurities and reduce waste.

Both these processes had one major limitation. They required phosphorus-free ore.

<hr>

[5] *Ibid.*, p. 480.

Much of the known ore deposits, especially the rich mines of Alsace-Lorraine, contained phosphorus. The Thomas–Gilchrist "basic" process developed in 1877 solved the problem. Sidney Thomas of Britain and Percy Gilchrist of the United States discovered that if the Bessemer converter were lined with limestone, it would absorb and neutralize the phosphorus. Furthermore, the slag resulting from the lining was found useful as fertilizer.

Later improvements in steel manufacture were concerned with economy, fuel substitution, and sophistication, rather than with fundamentals. Between 1880 and 1900 the regenerative electric steel furnace was introduced in England and France, in that order. The use of electricity cut costs and made it easier to maintain a steady temperature in the furnace, making possible the production of uniform-quality steel. Alloy steel, which was superior in strength, elongation, and hardness, was developed between 1870 and 1916 in the United Kingdom, Germany, and the United States. Faraday had produced alloy as early as 1819, but only for experimental purposes.

The aluminum industry was given a new foundation with the development in 1886–1887 of the electrolytic method of aluminum production by P. L. T. Hérault of France and Charles Martin Hall of the United States. Finally, stainless steel was developed between 1903 and 1912 in the United Kingdom, the United States, and Germany.

Machine tools. The building of high-power machinery also required appropriate tools. The problem of precision was compounded by the difficulty of constructing large equipment. These obstacles directed attention to the machine-tool industry. The drill and the lathe had been in use for many centuries, but they lacked precision and strength. By 1700 some precision had been achieved, as illustrated by the clock-makers' lathe. In 1750 Antoine Thiout of France equipped the lathe with a tool-holding carriage which was moved longitudinally by a screw drive and thus made accurate measurement possible. Between 1768 and 1780 a similar carriage held by a threaded screw was attached to both the lathe and the drill by Jacques de Vancauson of France.

The screw was important in all new operations, and precision in screw-cutting was essential. Jesse Ramsden of Britain built a screw-cutting lathe in 1770 which became the basis for numerous improvements in the next three decades. Equally important was the cylinder for the steam engine. John Wilkinson built a boring drill in 1774 with which he bored a cylinder for Watt's steam engine with no more error than "the thickness of an old shilling." Although this was a significant error, the drill remained a standard tool until the middle of the nineteenth century.

Joseph Bramah of the United Kingdom was another major contributor to machine-tool technology. He is said to have had 18 patents, among which were patents for an improved water-closet, a hydraulic press, a wood-planing machine, the suction beer-engine, a device to print the serial numbers on banknotes, and a spring-winding machine. Henry Maudslay, Bramah's foreman, set up his own firm and in 1800 built a screw-cutting lathe equipped with a screw micrometer accurate to one-millionth of an inch.

This increased accuracy was complemented by the ability to produce large parts. James Nasmyth, who worked for Maudslay, invented a milling machine and a planing machine or shaper which could shape any surface with rectilinear dimensions. His most famous invention was the steam hammer, introduced in 1839, which delivered great force with full control. While "iron beams and plates could now be forged of larger sizes than ever before, the great hammer could, nevertheless, descend . . . 'with power only sufficient to beat an egg shell.' "[6]

[6] *Ibid.*, p. 353.

The first inventor to produce machine tools commercially was Joseph Whitworth, who in 1856 built a measuring machine with accuracy of one-millionth of an inch.

These technological inventions were concentrated in Europe and particularly in Britain. However, on the other side of the Atlantic what has become known as the "American system" was developing. The essence of this system was the production of fully interchangeable parts. The system became dominant in the second half of the nineteenth century. Although small arms played a major role in its development, the idea of interchangeable parts spread throughout the modern economy. By the middle of the nineteenth century standardized parts were manufactured for reapers, clocks, pumps, and many other machines.

Science and technology in agriculture

Technological and scientific improvements in agriculture are of two kinds: those originating in and peculiar to agriculture, and those that are adaptations of discoveries in the power and machine-tool industries or the biological and physical sciences. We shall treat both types together, emphasizing those relating directly to agricultural science. Actual utilization of these discoveries will be discussed later in conjunction with other economic and social changes in agriculture.

Early technological improvements in agriculture were concerned with tools and farming equipment and with the composition and quality of the soil. The seed drill introduced by Jethro Tull in Britain in 1701 was mainly designed to speed the operation of sowing, to sow at greater depth, and to seed with uniform and controlled spacing. However, it attracted attention only slowly. The selective animal breeding by Robert Bakewell, Charles and Robert Collings, and Lord Coke, all of them from Britain, was mainly an experiment in genetics. Late in the eighteenth century France also began to experiment in agricultural methods. As early as the 1770s A. L. Lavoisier set up an experimental farm. In 1782 James Cooke of Britain introduced a new seed drill which became the basis for the modern drilling machine.

The period of mechanization had already started. In 1786 Andrew Meikle of Britain built one of the first threshing machines, while Eli Whitney in the United States was working on his cotton gin, which he introduced in 1794. Also from the United States came the first cast-iron plow in 1797, the work of Charles Newbold and Robert and Joseph Smith. The next step towards a better iron plow was the development of a three-piece, cast-iron plow in the United States by Jethrow Wood in 1819–1822. The new plow had interchangeable parts consistent with the American system.

Labor-saving devices and other scientific improvements were also being introduced. In 1800 Robert Salmon of Britain introduced his hay tedder, which was a forerunner of modern hay-making. At almost the same time several people in Britain began to use bone-dust fertilizer, probably the first artificial fertilizer used in Europe.

The early years of the nineteenth century were a turning point in agriculture, since at this time scientific methods became widespread. Jean-Baptiste Bousingault of France focused attention on the use of chemicals in agriculture, while Humphrey Davy of Britain was working on the theoretical bases for soil chemistry. Davy's *Elements of Agricultural Chemistry* appeared in 1813 and was supplemented by Justus von Liebig's *Organic Chemistry in Its Application to Agriculture and Physiology*, published in Germany in 1840. It is interesting to note that there were few restrictions on the diffusion and communication of knowledge in science and technology. Von Liebig was aware of and drew on Bousingault's experiments. In the 1840s several people in Britain began to use guano and nitrate as fertilizers and expanded the application of artificial fertilizer. Experiments were also conducted at Rothamsted, in England, by Georges Ville

of France, and by several Russian scientists who were interested mainly in the morphology of the soil. As a result of these experiments, there was increasing interest in the manufacture of superphosphate, and in plant nutrition and pathology. However, no major improvements in scientific agriculture were forthcoming before 1900.

Although Johann Gregor Mendel of Austria developed the principle of heredity and introduced a "quantum conception into biology," his theory was not widely accepted before 1900, although scientific plant selection based on Mendel's work was practiced in Germany, Austria, and the Netherlands. However, with artificial fertilization and scientific selection fully established, attention was turned to protection. Interest in insecticide culminated in the development of DDT in 1939 in Switzerland. DDT until now has been the most powerful known insecticide; its lasting effects have recently spurred federal and state governments in the United States to reconsider the wisdom of applying it. The most recent scientific developments in agriculture have been artificial insemination and regulation of animal and plant growth hormones, both of which occurred in the 1960s and cannot be attributed to any one man or one country.

Power machinery. Meanwhile more sophisticated, labor-saving, heavy-duty machinery was coming into existence in agriculture. In 1826 Patrick Bell of Britain developed a new reaper with commercial potential. Five years later Cyrus McCormick and Obed Hussey of the United States developed a reaper with a cutting bar, which was a great advance as a labor-saving device. In 1831 William Manning of the United States built a mowing machine. In 1843 a stripper was developed in Australia, making it possible to strip the grain from the straw. A thresher and a portable thresher–winnower were developed between 1840 and 1860 in both the United States and Britain. An automatic twine-binder was introduced in the United States in 1877; it was the first relatively efficient self-binder. In the same decade a combination harvester was developed in the United States which cut, threshed, cleansed, and sacked grain in one operation. The latest major improvement came in 1936 with the development of the completely automatic combination harvester.

Between 1830 and 1850 several improvements on the plow were made in the United States. Wood and cast-iron plows were superseded by chilled-iron and chilled-steel walking plows which were tougher, lighter, and more efficient. Other improvements, such as the wheel and the disc plows, both introduced in the 1860s, made it possible to use the plow in the hard sod of the American prairies. In 1876 the stump-jump plow from Australia made it possible to clear and cultivate scrub land. Few other basic improvements in the plow occurred until the tractor created a revolution in agriculture. Developed on the principles of internal combustion, the tractor was introduced in the United States in 1901, although it did not come into general use until 15 years later.

Other improvements included drainage facilities, mechanization, and standardization of production. Cylindrical clay pipes for drainage were constructed in Britain by John Reed and Thomas Scragg in 1843. In 1879 de Lavel of Sweden developed a steam cream separator. In 1890 S. M. Babcock of the United States developed the Babcock centrifuge, which rated milk for its butterfat content, thus helping to control quality and marketing. In 1905–1919 Australia introduced the milking machine. Finally, cotton-picking was mechanized in 1929 in the United States. The mechanization of tomato, fruit, and vegetable harvesting is now underway.

Science and technology
in textiles and chemicals

Technology in textiles was also partly unique to the industry and partly an application of power machinery and of advances in chemistry. Minor improvements in spinning and weaving were introduced early in the

eighteenth century. However, the major advances came after the middle of the century.

Spinning. The first important advance in spinning was roller spinning, introduced in Britain by John Wyatt and Lewis Paul in 1733. Roller spinning made stronger cotton yarn which could be used as warp in weaving. The speed of spinning was increased about 30 years later (1764–1767), when James Hargreaves introduced the spinning jenny in Britain, making it possible to multiply the spindles operated by one person. The jenny was a light machine which produced yarn for weft rather than the strong warp yarn used especially in hosiery. Stronger yarn was made possible by invention of the power-driven water frame, introduced in Britain by Richard Arkwright in 1769. Ten years later the best features of the jenny and the water frame were combined in the mule, built by Samuel Crompton in Britain. The mule was hand operated, and combined the speed of the jenny with the strength and firmness of the yarn produced by the water frame. Improvements on the water frame were made after 1815 in what was known as the *throstle*, which produced strong yarn fit for power looms. While this machine was being developed in Britain, an American version came into use known as Danforth's frame. However, the major improvement in the mule came in 1825 when the self-acting mule was introduced by Richard Roberts in Britain. Finally in 1828 ring spinning was introduced in America by John Thorpe and Charles Danforth; it became standard equipment late in the century. By this time it had been improved greatly, mostly through American workmanship.[7]

Weaving. Power was used in weaving relatively early. Until the middle of the eighteenth century, the main advance was the invention of the flying shuttle by John Kay of Britain in 1733. Use of the flying

[7] Some attribute ring spinning to the United Kingdom.

shuttle with the hand loom permitted the weaver to remain seated, passing the shuttle back and forth across a wider piece of cloth than had been possible previously. It represented a big improvement in both quality and quantity. Kay's flying shuttle remained the standard loom, even after Edmund Cartwright of Britain introduced his power loom in 1785. The power loom was not perfected before 1800 and was little used before 1830, when many people in both Europe and the United States had made further improvements on it. A more successful hand loom was the Jacquard loom, introduced in France in 1802 by Joseph Jacquard for silk weaving. By 1840 it had been adapted for the mass production of figured fabrics and for lace making. The latter had already been mechanized in 1809, when John Heathcote of Britain introduced the bobbin-net machine. In 1813 John Leavers of Britain developed a machine which made intricately patterned lace. The next major breakthrough came when William Crompton of the United States introduced a power loom which could weave patterned woolen fabrics. Francis Knowles and George Crompton had succeeded in automating this loom by 1857. Another loom originating in the United States was the Brussels power loom, introduced in the 1840s by E. B. Bigelow for mechanical weaving of Brussels carpets. A completely automatic loom came in the 1890s from the United States through the efforts of J. H. Northrop. Although modifications were continually made, the only other major invention was the Sulzer loom, introduced in Switzerland by Rudolf Rossman in the 1930s. The Sulzer loom permitted simultaneous use of several shuttles, thus increasing the speed of weaving.

While these improvements were being made, other processes relating to textiles were undergoing change. In 1826 John Goulding of the United States introduced the Goulding condenser which improved carding so that the number of spindles on the mule could be increased. In the 1850s, M. Town-send and L. Batton of Britain introduced the circular-rib frame machine and the rotary movement to hosiery manufacture. Their inventions helped produce seamless stockings. Between 1846 and 1851 Elias Howe and I. M. Singer of the United States introduced the first household sewing machine. The knitting frame of 1866, introduced both in Britain and the United States, was followed by a knitting machine in 1867, also in both countries. This completed the mechanization of the textile industry. In the 1840s John Mercer of Britain introduced the mercerizing process which added luster and strength to cotton fabrics and yarn and reduced shrinking by applying caustic soda while the goods were under tension. His process stimulated chemical technology.

Chemical advances. Chemical dyes were successfully manufactured in 1856 by W. H. Perkins and others. Perkins discovered the mauve color dye and produced it relatively cheaply. In 1859 Verguin discovered magenta, from which many other colors could be produced. Next came blue and rosaniline blue, in both Britain and France. Scientists were also working on the synthesis of natural dyes. Karl Graebe and Karl Lieberman of Germany succeeded in synthesizing alizarin in 1869. Synthetic indigo was produced in 1897 but was not commercially manufactured until many years later.

These advances were related to basic developments in chemistry. For example, sulphuric acid was needed for dyes, bleach, explosives, and oil refinement. Until it could be produced in quantity and at reasonable cost, these other advances were limited. A new process of producing sulphuric acid using large glass jars was introduced in 1736 by Joshua Ward of Britain. In 1746 John Roebuck and Samuel Garbett of Britain improved this process by introducing the lead chamber, in which they could burn sulphur and saltpeter. This invention has been regarded as the beginning of the sulphuric-acid industry. Chlorine and soda were needed in bleaching and in the pulp and paper industries. Soda was also demanded by glass-makers and soap-makers and in textile manufacturing. Chlorine was produced in Sweden by C. W. Scheele in 1774. It was used as bleach in France by C. L. Bertholet in 1785. Soda was produced from potash in small quantities and at relatively high cost until the Leblanc soda–ash process was introduced by Nicholas Leblanc in France in 1787.

Improvements in the production of sulphuric acid were introduced in 1827 in France and in 1831 in Britain. The contact process introduced in 1831 in Britain by Peregrine Phillips used a catalyst and was superior to the lead-chamber process. An improvement over the Leblanc process came in 1866 with introduction of the ammonia–soda process in Belgium by Ernest and Alfred Solvay. The use of chemicals as explosives was revolutionized by the invention of dynamite in Sweden by Alfred Nobel in 1866 through the use of nitroglycerine. In 1869–1870 Walter Weldon of Britain produced chlorine from a byproduct of soda production, hydrochloric acid. A major advance in the production of caustic soda and chlorine came in both Britain and Germany in 1892 through electrolytic production. After that there were only minor modifications and improvements until the recent development of synthetic products such as plastics.

Science and technology
in mining and mineralogy

Mining is one of the oldest economic activities of man. Recent improvements relate to methods of extraction, safety, lighting, ventilation, haulage, and to the use to which minerals can be put. Most of these innovations were applications of techniques developed in other, more basic areas.

Until about 1800 the only inventions in mining were those relating to drainage which permitted deeper and safer mining. The steam engine used for pumping water

had its earliest applications in the coal mines. The early years of the nineteenth century saw the beginning of crystallography, primarily in France. In 1809 a reflecting goniometer to measure the crystalline forms of minerals was introduced in Britain by W. H. Wollaston. In 1819–1821 E. Mitscherlich of Germany worked on clarification of mineral species, especially by applying the principles of isomorphism and dimorphism. Also in the 1820s E .L. Malus of France discovered the polarization of light, which helped in optical examination of natural crystals.

While these scientific advances were occurring, practical inventions were being put to use. The first air-pump ventilator was introduced in Britain by John Buddle and John Nixon in 1807, making deeper and longer periods of mining possible. In 1813 Richard Trevithick introduced a rock-boring machine. Probably the most important invention of these early years was Davy's safety lamp, introduced in Britain in 1816, which improved lighting and reduced the frequency of fires in the mines. In the 1830s J. Guibal of France introduced the steam-driven fan to improve ventilation. John Buddle of Britain introduced the system of endless-rope haulage in 1844, thus reducing the cost of carrying. Both France and Britain introduced rotary, hydraulic, water-flush drilling, a system which eventually replaced the old system of percussion drilling. Industrial diamond drill bits were introduced in the 1850s in Europe and the United States. Also in the 1850s W. Bartlett of Britain introduced steam drilling, while N. Bickford introduced the safety fuse, reducing the hazards of blasting. In 1863 T. Harrison of Britain introduced a rotary coal cutter which could also be operated by steam power.

The 1860s also saw advancements in geology. Microscopic examination of minerals was introduced in France while scientific oil prospecting was inaugurated in the United States, Canada, and Austria. In the same decade ventilation was indirectly improved by the use of compressed air as a power source in mining. However, both productivity and safety were greatly improved when electric power was first utilized in the 1880s. Although there were other minor improvements, the major addition to mineralogy was the application of seismology in prospecting and mining in 1919.

Essentially the new era of prospecting was a search for new products from the earth, which had important technological implications. The discovery of coal-gas, for example, was important in various industries, including lighting. The use of coal-gas for lighting was investigated for almost a century before it was successfully applied in Newcastle about 1760. Its use for lighting did not spread until near the end of the eighteenth century; even then, it was only experimental. By 1804, through the work of William Murdock in Britain, commercial production of coal-gas became possible. French experiments were equally advanced by this time and coal-gas lighting in Paris began in 1819. A major improvement came in 1810 when Samual Clegg succeeded in purifying the gas by "liming the water through which it passed." He also invented the hydraulic main which held enough coal-gas to service many burners and to render gas lighting and heating of houses and factories possible. In 1819, Clegg's son-in-law, John Malam, perfected a meter to measure gas output, but this was not installed and the effects of uncontrolled gas-burning remained a problem:

> The yellow gas flare which heated the air, blackened the ceilings, and gave only a moderate degree of illumination for a great expenditure of gas at last gave way to the far more efficient incandescent gas-mantle, impregnated with oxide of thorium, together with a little oxide of cerium, invented by the Austrian, C. A. von Welsbach [around 1885].[8]

[8] T. K. Derry and Trevor I. Williams, *op. cit.*, p. 513.

Petroleum was in use long before coal-gas. Shale oil had been extracted for limited uses during the seventeenth century. However, the modern petroleum industry was a late comer. In the 1850s paraffin oil, extracted from shale, was used for lighting in Europe, while coal-oil extracted from an asphalt-like mineral was used in America. Kerosene (or paraffin, as it is known in Europe) was also being produced in America by Abraham Gesner from asphalt rock. However, the breakthrough came when the first American oil well was drilled in 1859. Improvements in drilling methods have been noted above. Until 1900 the main demand was for kerosene. The demand for gasoline was a function of the development of internal combustion and the automobile.

Science and technology in transport and communication

Telegraphy. Interest in long-distance communication was evident in ancient and medieval times, especially in periods of war and insecurity. The early methods were mainly visual, however. The modern system of telegraphy began during the French Revolution and the Napoleonic Wars, starting in France and spreading to England. In 1790 Claude Chappe of France introduced the idea, and three years later he applied it. His method was to establish a series of stations with semaphore arms and telescopes, about ten miles from each other. The semaphore arms communicated the message according to a code, and the signals were visually picked up with the help of the telescope. This method was applied in England a decade later, but instead of semaphore arms the stations were equipped with movable shutters.

A major advance came with electricity. Although discussions and experiments were conducted as early as the middle of the eighteenth century, success came only after the invention of the electric battery. In 1795, Francisco Salvà of Spain established a multiple-wire system, with a wire for each letter of the alphabet, which spelled out each word of the message by transmitting a shock to the operator. Using the same system, S. T. Soemmering of Germany, in cooperation with Baron Schilling, employed a magnetic needle and operated a single-wire system in 1836. From then on, the expansion of electric telegraphy was possible. Soon after, a universal code was invented by Samuel Morse in America. In 1845 messages were first printed out rather than written by hand; this was also an American invention known as House's printing telegraph; however the invention was patented by Sir Charles Wheatstone of Britain in 1860.

So far no sound could be communicated. Experiments were made in Germany on an electric telephone, but success was not achieved until Alexander Graham Bell of the United States discovered his magnetic amplifier in 1876. A third major improvement in communication was the wireless telegraph. Following Faraday's discoveries in electromagnetics, Clarke Maxwell showed that electric waves were similar to light waves. This idea was verified by H. Hertz, who stated that "a flow of current in one electrical circuit could result in a corresponding flow in a similarly 'tuned' circuit not directly connected with the first." Therefore, waves radiated at one place could be detected at another "by the appearance of a spark at a small gap in the receiving circuit."[9] Wireless telegraphy became a reality in 1885. In 1901 Guglielmo Marconi succeeded in communicating signals by wireless across the Atlantic.

Transportation. Economic development and industrialization are so closely related to the size of the market and to factor and product mobility that it is hardly possible to exaggerate the significance of transportation facilities. The importance of technological improvements in this field vary according to

their impact on load capacity, the speed of delivery, the distance that can be covered, and continuity of service regardless of weather and climate.

The best road system in Europe before the eighteenth century was in France. It was also in France that the first modern improvement in roads came. In 1764 P. M. J. Trèsaguet introduced a three-layer system of road-making, using stone as foundation and a layer of hard small stone for the surface. A similar method was developed in Britain by Thomas Telford in 1824. The next improvement was introduced by John L. McAdam, a Scot, in the 1820s. He based his system on three principles: Native soil, rather than stone, is the best road foundation; drainage is essential to keep the road dry; and the thickness of the road is immaterial. The surface had to be as compact as possible, and this could be accomplished by applying an "indestructible" and "impervious" cover, for which asphalt came to be used soon after. McAdam's method became the standard for road-building, although improvements were made in construction methods. For example, a horse-drawn, iron road-rolling machine was put to use in the eighteenth century. In 1859 it was replaced by the steamroller invented in France, which was improved in 1862. British steamrollers were introduced in 1866, while in America a stone crusher was built in 1859. Later improvements in transportation related more to the vehicle than to the road, whose basic principles remained the same.

Improvement in water transportation was mainly in the construction and powering of boats. Canal-building had been fully developed by the middle of the eighteenth century, with watertight beds and locks. Tunnels were built as shortcuts. River waterways were widened and improved, but few required any special technology other than the application of the power machinery already in use. However, the modern period saw the shift from sail to steam, from wood to iron and steel, and from small to relatively large

9 *Ibid.*, p. 624.

vessels. As early as 1746 a Frenchman, Pierre Bouguer, had explained the theoretical basis for floating iron ships and for making much larger ships than the wooden ones then in use. His theories were developed further by others, but their implementation waited for invention of the rolling mill, which could produce iron plates that were long enough to allow the traverse frame to be built with single bars. In 1787 John Wilkinson launched the *Severn*, a barge with cast-iron plates. In 1822 the first iron steamship, built by Aaron Manby, crossed the Channel. Iron steamships large enough to cross the Atlantic were first built in the 1840s.

Speed and capacity were increased by substituting the screw propeller for the paddle, as demonstrated by the *Archimedes*, built in 1838. They were further enhanced by the application of compound steam engines to ships, which reduced the capacity allocated for carrying fuel and increased the driving power of the ship. The first compound-engine ship, the S. S. *Brandon*, was launched in 1854. The other major technological development of the century in this area was the shift from iron to steel, which began in America during the Civil War. However, it was about 20 years before full utilization of steel was possible. By that time the problems of transportation had been solved for water transport.

Horse-drawn rail carriages were used in the late eighteenth century, especially for carrying coal and for haulage in drainage operations. In 1738 iron rails replaced wooden ones in England and by 1767 cast-iron rails were in production. A century later steel rails replaced iron in both Europe and the United States. Advances in iron and steel production had direct effects on the railway industry. The first locomotive was built in 1803 by Trevithick; his 25-ton machine traveled at 4 miles per hour. In 1813 William Hedley solved the problem of traveling up and down hills by showing that there is no conflict in having a smooth wheel run on a smooth rail. The major improve-

ment in rail transportation came in 1825 when George Stephenson increased the efficiency of his locomotive by increasing the draught into the fire-box and thus ushered in the railway age. The subway was introduced in London in 1863 and the tube followed in the same city in 1890. The first electric train was exhibited in Berlin in 1879, although electricity remained for a long time limited to local trams. Subsequent improvements in urban transportation concerned capacity, efficiency, and comfort, and did not involve major technological innovations.

Land transportation was revolutionized by the internal combustion engine, which used liquid fuel. The automobile revolutionized the transport industry. The idea of a power-driven carriage goes back to 1769 when N. J. Cugnot of France built his steam road carriage. Trevithick built another in 1801 and the three-wheeled steam carriage was perfected in 1831 by Sir Goldsworthy Gurney. However, this carriage was hard on roads, since rubber was not yet in use. A steam tricycle was built in 1887 in France by Leon Serpollet, who in 1894 equipped it with an instantaneous generator. Solid rubber tires, in use by 1871, and the steam traction engine developed earlier were major steps towards a successful automobile.

The history of the automobile began when Siegfried Markus of Austria mounted an engine on a handcart in 1864. The major step was taken by Karl Benz of Mannheim in 1885 when he built a single-cylindered light vehicle. Four years later he built a four-wheeled car which became widespread in Germany, but its speed was quite limited and it had only a 3.5 horsepower capacity. Gottlieb Daimler of Germany built the first high-speed car in 1886; another was built in Denmark in 1886; and a British pioneer car was tested in 1888. Experiments and production continued relatively slowly until 1903 when Henry Ford began mass production, which culminated in 1908 with the Model T, the first mass-produced car.

The twentieth century saw the development of the airplane, although designs of flying machines go back to Leonardo da Vinci. Balloons were used in France shortly after the middle of the eighteenth century, and have been ever since in various countries, for military and meteorological purposes. The first actual experiment with flying was made in 1852 by a French engineer, Henry Giffard, who used a 3-horsepower steam engine and a 3-blade propeller. In 1884 a balloon fitted with a 9 horsepower electric motor made a circular flight of about 5 miles. Germans attempted to build a rigid airship, not a pressurized one, with gas bags enclosed in the hull. Despite failures in 1897, later attempts eventually succeeded in building the airships that were used in the First World War. A major problem of these airships was how to take off safely.

Modern airplanes owe more to a different approach. Sir George Cayley, almost a century earlier, had concluded that fixed wings and a gliding potential or capability to maintain stability in the air were essential for flying. He began experimenting as early as 1804. Gliding experiments were continued and many gliders were built in the 1890s. Other experiments of various types were carried out in Australia, France, Britain, and the United States. The breakthrough came in 1903 when Orville Wright of the United States flew his tailless biplane for 12 seconds to a distance of 40 yards. By 1908 this invention was accepted in Europe and America. In the meantime a Brazilian had made the first flight in Europe. Success was also apparent in France and England about the same time, especially in the development of monoplanes. Thus began the age of flying. Space flight is a product of a different technology and is at present history in the making.

GENERAL REMARKS

This survey of technological developments has been designed to point out the landmarks in engineering technology that were applicable to industry, manufacturing, and agriculture. Where, when, and at what rate these applications were made will be discussed in the following chapters. However, a few observations may be made at this point. (1) It seems realistic to distinguish between science and technology, since development in one area was not a prerequisite for nor result of success in the other. (2) It is difficult to attribute an invention to a single person or a single country. The technological revolution would not admit of political boundaries or nationalism, at least not for any length of time. (3) Technological development was cumulative and inventions in different fields overlapped in both their foundations and applicability. (4) Regardless of their applications, these inventions were so numerous and radical that it is appropriate to regard this period as a technological revolution. Once these inventions had been achieved, it became difficult for economic and social changes *not* to follow. Hence, the revolution in technology was at the root of the economic and social revolutions of the last two centuries. (5) Finally, the evolution of technology shows clearly the relevance of history in understanding the present and the future. Technology may be considered a necessary but not a sufficient determinant of economic development: Without complementary changes in other areas—economic, social, and political—technology may remain feasible but unrealized, with little or no impact on the economy.

BIBLIOGRAPHY

Derry, T. K., and Trevor I. Williams, *A Short History of Technology*, New York: The Clarendon Press, 1960, Part II, material used by permission of the Clarendon Press, Oxford.
Habakkuk, H. J., and M. M. Postan, eds. *Cambridge Economic*

History of Europe, VI, New York: Cambridge University Press, 1965, chap. 5.

Ruttan, Vernon W., "Usher and Schumpeter on Invention, Innovation, and Technological Change," *Quarterly Journal of Economics,* LXXIII (Nov. 1959), pp. 596–606.

Van Melsen, A. G., *Science and Technology,* Duquesne Studies, Philosophical series 13, Pittsburgh, Pa.: Duquesne University Press, 1961.

Woodruff, William, *The Impact of Western Man,* New York: St. Martin's Press, Inc., Macmillan and Co., Ltd., 1967, chap. 5.

INVENTIONS
AND
INVENTORS,
1700
TO THE
PRESENT

All the tables in this appendix are adapted with modifications from William Woodruff, The Impact of Western Man, pp. 200–222, and T. K. Derry and Trevor I. Williams, A Short History of Technology, pp. 732–749.

Table 17.1. Inventions in power

YEAR	INVENTION	ATTRIBUTED TO
1700s	Atmospheric steam engine	Thomas Newcomen, UK
1740	Leyden jar	Pieter van Musschen-broek, G
1752	Lightning conductor and experiments with electricity	Benjamin Franklin, US
1765–1769	Improved steam pumping with separate condenser and later use of cutoff	James Watt, UK
1774	Accurately bored cast-iron cylinders for steam engines	John Wilkinson, UK
1774	Large cylinders developed	John Smeaton, UK
1781	Compound steam engine	Jonathan Hornblower, UK
1781–1786	Rotative motion	James Watt, UK
1800	Voltaic pile	Alessandro Volta, I
1800	Compound steam engine	Richard Trevithick, UK
1804	Compound steam engine	Oliver Evans, US
1815	Compound steam engine patented	Humphrey Edwards, F
1820s–1880s	Electric generator and motor	M. Faraday, UK; Werner von Siemens, G; Z. T. Gramme, F; Thomas Edison and Nikota Tesla, US
1820	Magnetic field discovered	A. M. Ampère, F; H. C. Oersted, D
1827	High-pressure steam boilers	Jacob Perkins, UK; Oliver Evans, US
1827	Hydraulic (creation) turbine water wheel	Benoit Fourneyron, F
1831	Electromagnetic induction	Michael Faraday, UK

(Continued)

Table 17.1 *(Continued)*

YEAR	INVENTION	ATTRIBUTED TO
1840s–1850s	Advances in hydraulic turbines	Numerous sources
1859	One-cylinder coal–gas engine	Etienne Lenoir, F
1862	Internal combustion engine	Alphonse Beau de Rochas, F
1870	Ring-armature dynamo	Z. T. Gramme, F
1876	Four-stroke coal–gas engine	N. A. Otto, G
1880s	Steam turbine	Charles Parsons, U.K.; Gustav de Laval, Sd
1885–1886	High-speed gasoline engine	Gottlieb Daimler, G
1890s–1960s	Atomic energy	Numerous sources
1890	Oil engine	H. Ackroyd Stuart, UK
1892	Diesel engine	Rudolf Diesel, G
1960s	Solar engines based on photocells	Numerous sources
1960s	Great developments in rocket propulsion	Numerous sources
1960s	Optical maser	Numerous sources
1960s	Magnetohydrodynamics, the process of generating electricity by shooting ionized gas through a magnetic field	Numerous sources
1960s	Solar energy, Tidal energy, Wind energy, Geothermic energy, and thermal energy of the seas	Numerous sources

KEY: *Countries of origin are abbreviated as follows:* D *Denmark,* F *France,* G *Germany,* I *Italy.* Sd *Sweden,* UK *United Kingdom,* US *United States.*

Table 17.2.   Inventions in metallurgy and machine tools

YEAR	INVENTION	ATTRIBUTED TO
1709	Coke-smelting	Abraham Darby, UK
1720	Cementation process of making steel	René Antoine de Reaumur, F
1740	Crucible or cast steel	Benjamin Huntsman, UK
1740	Cast-iron rolling process	Christopher Polhem, Sd
1750	Carbon content of iron ore discovered	T. O. Bergman, Sd
1750	Screw drive on lathe	Antoine Thiout, F
1761	Air cylinders	John Smeaton, UK
1770	Screw-cutting lathe	Jesse Ramsden, UK
1774	Satisfactory cast-iron cylinders for steam engine	John Wilkinson, UK
1776–1780s	Application of steam power to forging; first forge hammer	John Wilkinson, UK
1783–1784	Improvements in puddling and rolling	Peter Onions and Henry Cort, UK
1829	Hot blast furnace	James Neilson, UK
1831	Hot blast furnace	Friedrich von Faber du Four, G
1833	Iron-smelting with anthracite	W. Gessenheimer, US
1833	A process for silver extraction	H. L. Pattinson, US
1838, 1841	Steam drop-hammer	James Nasmyth, UK
1850s–1860s	Development of the steel converter	William Kelly, US; Henry Bessemer, and Robert Mushet, UK; C. F. Geransson, Sd
1850s–1860s	Siemens–Martin open-hearth sled	William and Fredrich Siemens, UK; Pierre Martin, F
1855	Aluminum	Henri E. Deville, F
1855	Tungsten steel	Franz Köller, Sd
1870–1916	Alloy steel	Robert Hatsfield, UK; F. W. Taylor, US;
1879	"Basic" process: neutralizing the phosphoric content of certain ores by using lime	Sidney Thomas, UK; Percy Gilchrist, US
1880s–1910	Regenerative electric steel furnace	P. L. T. Hérault, F; William Siemens and others, UK
1886–1887	Electrolytic method of producing aluminum	P. L. T. Hérault, F; Charles Martin Hall, US; Karl J. Bayer, G
1887	Cyanide process for extracting gold and silver	J. S. McArthur, R. W. and W. Forrest, and others, UK
1890s	Flotation techniques	Numerous sources
1900s	Oxyacetylene and electric welding	Numerous sources
1900s	Continuous casting and rolling mills	Numerous sources, UK, US, G
1900s	Direct reduction of iron	Various sources
1900s	Oxygen converter	Various sources, Au
1903–1912	Stainless steel	Harry Brearly, UK; F. M. Becket, US; B. Strauss and E. Maurer, G

KEY: *Countries of origin are abbreviated as follows:* Au *Austria,* F *France,* G *Germany,* Sd *Sweden,* UK *United Kingdom,* US *United States.*

Table 17.3. Inventions in agriculture

YEAR	INVENTION	ATTRIBUTED TO
1701	Seed drill	Jethro Tull, UK
1750–1800	Selective animal breeding	Robert Bakewell, Charles and Robert Collins, and Lord Coke, UK; A. L. Lavoisier, F
1782	Seed drill	James Cooke, UK
1784 or 1786	Threshing machine	Andrew Meikle, UK
1793–1794	Cotton gin	Eli Whitney, US
1797	First cast-iron plow	Charles Newbold, Robert and Joseph Smith, Robert Salmon, UK
1800	Hay tedder	
1800s	Bone-dust fertilizer	Numerous sources, UK
1819–1822	Development of a cast-iron, three-piece plow with standardized interchangeable parts	Jethrow Wood, US
1826	Reaper	Patrick Bell, UK
1830s–1850s	Introduction and improvement of chilled-iron and chilled-steel walking plows	Joel Morse, John Lane, John Deere, William Partin, and James Oliver, US
1831	Mowing machine	William Manning, US
1831–1833	Reaper with first successful cutting bar	Cyrus McCormick, and Obed Hussey, US
1832	Flax-heckling machine	Phillipe de Girard, F
1840	Roller milling of grain	[Anonymous], H
1840s	Guano and nitrate fertilizers	Numerous sources, UK
1840s	Superphosphate experiments and manufacture, plant nutrition and plant pathology	James Murry, J. B. Lawes, and J. H. Gilbert, UK
1840s–1860s	Further improvements in the plow	J. C. Pfeil, J. S. Godfrey, and J. M. Cravath, US
1840s–1860s	Thresher, portable thresher–winnower	Numerous sources, UK, US

Table 17.3   (*Continued*)

YEAR	INVENTION	ATTRIBUTED TO
1843	Cylindrical clay pipe	John Reed and Thomas Scragg, UK
1843	Stripper	John Ridley and John Wrathall Bull, Al
1865	Principle of heredity	Johann Mendel, Au
1868	Refrigerated meat-packing	P. D. Armour, US
1870s	Combination harvester	Numerous sources, US
1874–1875	Barbed wire	Joseph Glidden, US
1876	Stump-jump plow	R. B. Smith, J. W. Scott, and Charles Branson, Al
1877	Automatic twine-binder	J. F. Appleby, Jacob Behel, and others, US
1877–1879	Cream separator	de Lavel, Sd
1890	Babcock centrifuge	S. M. Babcock, US
1900	Scientific plant selection	K. E. Correns, G; E. Tschermark von Seysenegg, Au; H. de Vries, and others, N
1901	Internal combustion tractor	Numerous sources, US
1905	Gasoline engine tractor	C. W. Hart and C. H. Parr, US
1905–1919	Milking machine	Numerous sources, Al
1929	Mechanical cotton picker	John Rust, US
1936	Completely automatic combination harvester	Numerous sources, US
1939	Development of insecticide properties of DDT	Paul Müller, Sl
1960s	Widespread application of artificial insemination of livestock	Numerous sources
1960s	Plant and animal hormones and growth regulators	Numerous sources

KEY: *Countries of origin are abbreviated as follows:* Al *Australia,* Au *Austria,* F *France,* G *Germany,* H *Hungary,* N *Netherlands,* Sl *Switzerland,* UK *United Kingdom,* US *United States.*

Table 17.4.   Inventions in textiles

YEAR	INVENTION	ATTRIBUTED TO
1733	Flying shuttle	John Kay, UK
1733	Roller spinning	John Wyatt and Lewis Paul, UK
1764	Spinning jenny	James Hargreaves, UK
1769	Water frame (power-driven spinning)	Richard Arkwright, UK
1779	Spinning mule	Samuel Crompton, UK
1785–1787	Power loom	Edmund Cartwright, UK
1801–1802	Jacquard loom	Joseph Jacquard, F
1809	Bobbin-net machine	John Heathcote, UK
1813	Machine-made patterned lace	John Leavers, UK
1822	Roberts' power loom	Richard Roberts, UK
1825–1830	Self-acting mule	Richard Roberts, UK
1826	The Goulding condenser	John Goulding, US
1828–1829	Ring spindle	Charles Danforth and John Thorpe, UK
1836	Crompton's "fancy loom"	William Crompton, US
1840s	Mercerizing	John Mercer, UK
1845	Brussels power loom	E. B. Bigelow, US
1846–1851	First practical household sewing machine	Elias Howe and I. M. Singer, US
1850s	Circular-rib frame machine and rotary movement in hosiery	M. Townsend and L. Batton, UK
1856–1857	Automation of Crompton's fancy loom	Frances Knowles and George Crompton, US
1866	Knitting frame	Isaac W. Lamb, US
1867	Knitting machine	William Cotton, UK
1880s	Development of knitting machine	Benjamin Shaw and Charles Fletcher, US
1890s	Completely automatic loom	J. H. Northrop, US
1930s	Sulzer loom	Rudolf Rossman, Sl
1960s	Introduction of synthetic fibers	Numerous sources

KEY: *Countries of origin are abbreviated as follows:* F *France,* Sl *Switzerland,* UK *United Kingdom,* US *United States.*

Table 17.5.   Inventions in industrial chemicals

YEAR	INVENTION	ATTRIBUTED TO
1736	New process of sulfuric-acid manufacture	Joshua Ward, UK
1746	Lead-chamber process for production of sulfuric acid	John Roebuck and Samuel Garbett, UK
1774	Discovery of chlorine	C. W. Scheele, Sd
1785	Discovery of chlorine bleaching properties	C. L. Bertholet, F
1787	Leblanc soda-ash process	Nicolas Leblanc, F
1827	Absorption towers	Joseph-Louis Gay Lussac, F
1831	Contact process	Peregrine Phillips, UK
1856	Discovery of aniline dyes	William H. Perkin and others, UK
1861–1866	Ammonia–soda process	Ernest and Alfred Solvay, B
1866	Nitroglycerine used in dynamite	Alfred Nobel, Sd
1869	Alizarin synthesized	Karl Graebe and Karl Lieberman, G
1892–1894	Electrolytic production of caustic soda and chlorine	Hamilton Young Castner, US; Carl Kellner, Au
1900	Improvement of contact process	Rudolf Messel, G; Clemens Winkler, UK

KEY: *Countries of origin are abbreviated as follows:* Au *Austria,* B *Belgium,* F *France,* G *Germany,* Sd *Sweden,* UK *United Kingdom,* US *United States.*

Table 17.6.   Inventions in mining

YEAR	INVENTION	ATTRIBUTED TO
Early 1700s	Development of drainage in mines	Thomas Savery and Thomas Newcomen, UK
1800	High-pressure noncondensing steam engine	Richard Trevithick, UK
Early 1800s	Crystallography	J. B. L. Romè de L'Isle and R. J. Haüy, F
Early 1800s	Chemistry in relation to mineralogy	C. W. Scheele and J. J. Berzelius, Sd
1807	First air-pump ventilator	John Buddle and John Nixon, UK
1809	Reflecting goniometer	W. H. Wollaston, UK
1813	Rock-boring machine	Richard Trevithick, UK
1815 or 1816	Safety lamp	Humphrey Davy, G. Stephenson and W. R. Clanny, UK
1819–1821	Clarification of mineral species	E. Mitscherlich, G
1820s	Polarization of light	E. L. Malus, F
1830s	Ventilation	J. Guibal, B
1840s	Introduction of rotary, hydraulic, water-flush system of drilling	Beart, UK and Fauville, F
1844	Endless-rope haulage	John Buddle, UK
1850s	Improvements in rotary drilling	Numerous sources
1850s	Steam drilling	W. Bartlett, UK
1850s	Safety fuse	W. Bickford, UK
1860s	Microscopic examination of minerals	A. des Cloiseaux and others, F
1860s	Power transmission by compressed air	Numerous sources
1860s	Geological foundations of modern oil prospecting	T. Sherry Hunt, C; E. B. Andrews and Alexander Winchell, US; Hans Höder von Heimholt, Au
1861	Microscopic examination of metals	H. C. Sorby, UK
1863	Coal cutter	T. Harrison, UK
1880s	Field investigation for petroleum deposits	I. C. White, US
1880s	Power transmission by electricity	Numerous sources
1890s	Torsion balance	Roland von Eötvös, H
1902	Coal-face conveyor	W. C. Blackett, UK
1905–1915	Diamond drill as exploratory tool	W. A. J. M. van Waterschoot van der Gracht, N; M. M. Travis, US
1919	Seismography	L. Mintrop, G
1928	Electrical coring of drills	Charles Schlumberger, F

KEY: *Countries of origin are abbreviated as follows:* Au *Austria,* B *Belgium,* C *Canada,* F *France,* G *Germany,* H *Hungary,* N *Netherlands,* Sd *Sweden,* UK *United Kingdom,* US *United States.*

Table 17.7.   Inventions in transportation and communication

YEAR	INVENTION	ATTRIBUTED TO
1738	Iron rails substituted for wood	[Anonymous or general] UK
1764	Three-layer system of road-making introduced	P. M. J. Trèsaguet, F
1769	Cugnot's steam road carriage	N. J. Cugnot, F
1787	The *Severn*, barge with cast-iron plates	John Wilkinson, UK
1790	Semaphore arms used for communications	Claude Chappe, F
1795	Multiple wire system for communication	Francisco Salvà, Sp
1801	Trevithick's steam road carriage	Richard Trevithick, UK
1803	Trevithick's steam locomotive	Richard Trevithick, UK
1807	Steamship *Clermont* on the Hudson	Robert Fulton, US
1820s	McAdam develops his principles of road-making	John L. McAdam, UK
1825	Stephenson's locomotive initiates rail age	George Stephenson, UK
1831	Gurney's steam carriage	Goldsworthy Gurney, UK
1836	Single-wire system of communication	S. T. Soemmering, Baron Schilling, G
1838	*S.S. Great Western* initiates regular Atlantic crossings	Isambard Kingdom Brunel, UK
1838	Screw propeller	John Ericsson, Sd; John Stevens, US; Francis A. Smith and others, UK
1852	First experiment with flying	Henry Giffard, F
1859–1866	Improvements in road construction machinery	Numerous sources
1876	Bell's telephone	Alexander Bell, US
1879	Electric railway exhibited	Siemens & Halske Co., G
1885	Benz's first automobile	Karl Benz, G
1886	First high-speed car	Gottlieb Daimler, G
1887	Steam tricycle	Leon Serpollet, F
1901	Marconi begins transatlantic wireless telegraphy	Guglielmo Marconi, I
1903	First flight in airplane	Orville and Wilbur Wright, US
1903–1908	Mass production of cars developed	Henry Ford, US

KEY: *Countries of origin are abbreviated as follows:* F *France,* G *Germany,* I *Italy,* Sp *Spain,* Sd *Sweden,* UK *United Kingdom,* US *United States.*

18

DEVELOPMENTS
IN
AGRICULTURE

The place of agriculture in the economy was discussed in Chapters 4 and 12. However, under the conditions of the modern period, new aspects deserve emphasis. In a period of industrialization and economic growth, agriculture is expected to provide food for the urban workers; to buy the finished and intermediate products of the urban sector, such as machinery and chemicals; and to produce industrial raw material such as fibers and oil seed. Furthermore, agriculture is often expected to provide the labor force to man rapidly growing businesses. If agriculture fails to do these things, it is said to hinder development.

This framework has been the source of a policy-oriented theory according to which an agricultural revolution must precede an industrial revolution if the latter is to be successful. This idea has received wide circulation and acceptance, as shown in recent attempts to guide developing countries. However, its validity depends on the economic system under consideration. In a market economy, some agricultural development may be a prerequisite for industrialization. In a planned economy, some of the conditions necessary for growth may be satisfied by the plan, regardless of agriculture's behavior. In either case, however, unless an outside catalyst and outside capital are available, agriculture tends to carry a large part of the burden of industrialization by absorbing surplus population, providing capital, and responding to the demands of industrialization. Agriculture may also need to complement industry throughout the process of development.

European development was limited until agriculture was transformed in its institutional arrangements and its technical and productive capabilities. These changes were closely interrelated. The most prevalent of the traditional tenure systems which prevailed in Europe up to the beginning of the eighteenth century were the copyhold system (or *censier* in France) in northern and western Europe, and the serf system in Russia, Prussia, eastern, and southern Europe. Neither system provided sufficient incentive to innovate, invest, or improve the land to raise productivity. These institutional handicaps were reinforced by the fact that the market was not free and prices of agricultural products were usually regulated. The copyhold system broke down first, almost a century before the serf system. The apparent reasons for this change were usually political and social. Nevertheless, economic objectives, whether private or national, were always in the background, particularly where population pressure on the land was great.

INSTITUTIONAL CHANGES

The main institutional problems of the copyhold and serf tenures were related to the arrangements governing the disposal of land. The defects of both the copyhold and the serf tenures may be summarized as follows: As traditionally held, land was fragmented into strips and the operational unit was relatively small. The tenant and serf had little incentive to invest and improve it; furthermore, they lacked the means to do so. The landlord in the copyhold system was frequently an absentee owner or *rentier*. He had no interest in land operation as long as the fixed rent was paid. The serf-owner had little incentive to change, since he had virtually free labor at his disposal, and did not want to jeopardize his economic or sociopolitical position.

These tenure systems also had organizational defects which hindered improvement. Since the common land was collectively utilized, few improvements could be introduced. The open-field layout was another obstacle, since it required that the rights of way and grazing rights of others be safeguarded. Finally, both systems lacked room for flexibility and expansion. Since the land was the main source of livelihood, population pressure usually led to fragmentation into even smaller operational units.

Both systems had an important sociopolitical defect. The landlords in the copyhold system wanted to be free of traditional restrictions. The tenants or copyholders wanted to be free of their obligations to the landlords, especially of those that survived from the days of serfdom. The peasants under the serf system were dissatisfied because they had virtually no rights other than subsistence and even this was threatened by population pressure. Although the peasants wanted change in both systems, their main demand was freedom. The landlords, however, wished change mainly for economic reasons, either to improve agriculture or to forestall losses.

Change in these systems came about largely in three ways: by supportive legislation and the market mechanism, by a gradual change in national policy, and by revolt or uprising. In some cases governmental attempts to reform the tenure system were made in order to forestall uprisings.

Britain

The British was the first land-tenure system to undergo radical change. The enclosure movement of the eighteenth and nineteenth centuries was almost unique in its approach and effects.[1] British enclosures were economically motivated. Landlords and big farmers, who wanted to improve the land but were unable to do so under the traditional system, sought to enclose, or fence, their holdings after consolidating them into a single estate. This they accomplished either by buying the strips intermingled with their own, or by arranging an exchange with their holders. The landlords also wanted to abolish the common-land system and put the grazing land under cultivation.

The most common method of accomplishing these aims was to obtain a private Act of Parliament for enclosure in each separate village or manor. According to the law, enclosure could be enforced if the owners of two-thirds of the land agreed. In many cases one landlord owned two-thirds of the land or had enough influence over it to obtain a private Act. The peasants were, according to the law, to be compensated for their rights if they could produce documents verifying them. Alternative methods included buying out all other landholders, frightening them into agreement, or securing a special license to enclose from the king. These methods were quite effective. Between 1700 and 1844, 2700 private Acts were granted to enclose common fields and some wasteland. Another 1385 Acts were granted to enclose wasteland in the same period. After that period 164 and 508 Acts, respectively, were granted to enclose the two kinds of land.

In total, 4,464,189 acres of common land with some waste and 2,100,617 acres of wasteland were enclosed. Of the common field, 2,428,721 acres were enclosed between

[1] This movement may be contrasted with the sixteenth-century enclosures discussed above.

1761 and 1801 and another 1,610,302 acres between 1802 and 1844. This constituted more than 90 percent of all the common-field enclosures. Although a higher percentage of wasteland than of common field was enclosed after 1845, the period 1801–1844 still saw a larger share of wasteland enclosures than any other corresponding period, approximately 44 percent of the total enclosed.

The impact on land tenure and distribution of ownership was immediate. The landlords were able to consolidate their property, evict those who had no documented rights, and buy out the remaining relatively small holders. By 1883, 1.43 percent of all private landowners in England and Wales owned 73.94 percent of all the privately owned land, and cumulatively 3.98 percent owned 87.07 percent of the land. These larger holdings increased the incentive to use improved techniques. Traditional peasantry as a class was virtually annihilated, and large numbers of rural people found their way to nonagricultural occupations, especially to those opening up in the urban sector.[2]

Scandinavia

While the enclosure movement was taking place in Britain, a gradual and probably more egalitarian change was in progress in Scandinavia. The problems of fragmentation and the common land were known and discussions of reform had started as early as 1746 when Jacob Faggot, a Swedish surveyor, published his essay, "Obstructions to Sweden's Agriculture and Its Remedy." Faggot's main proposals were (1) to abolish the village compulsion and strip systems, and (2) to divide the common land among the individual owners. The Field Consolidation Act of 1749 was designed to educate and

persuade the Swedes to consolidate their fragmented holdings. However, little success was achieved even after the 1783 Surveying Act which gave individual holders the right to demand consolidation. Change began with the Act of 1807 which made consolidation compulsory. The Redistribution Act of 1827 completed the process of transferring land to individual farmers in consolidated tracts. All common land was divided among individual owners strictly according to their legal rights.

The process was similar in Denmark where it began in 1784, although Danish reform was slowed down by economic difficulties between 1816 and 1830. Both Sweden and Denmark achieved their results peacefully, always compensating or redeeming dues where dues were legal. A relatively large proportion of the farmers became independent family farmers with unified farms.

The Scandinavian enclosure movement contrasts strongly with the British movement in two respects. Since enclosure in Scandinavia was carried out by salaried civil servants, it was less costly and less subject to abuse or infringement on the rights of the peasants. Furthermore, the Scandinavian enclosures did not create large-scale farms, even though they enlarged the size of the operational unit. In fact, the farmer frequently accepted less acreage as the price for consolidation of his holdings.

France

The movement for change in western Europe was triggered by the French Revolution, although changes were not effectively consummated in many countries until after the middle of the nineteenth century. French agriculture of 1789 had changed little since the breakdown of serfdom. The *censiers*, like the copyholders, had hereditary tenure, paid fixed rents, and owed obligations which were hated remnants of the seigneurial serf system. Fragmented strip landholding was the rule. The Church was a large landowner.

---

[2] Whether the enclosures caused depopulation has been a subject of debate; the logic of the situation, however, suggests that internal migration could not have been avoided. The economic effects are hard to estimate since other influences were at work at the same time. More will be said on this in the context of social conditions.

Most landlords were absentee owners and paid little attention to farming. The peasants, whether *censiers* or *metayers,* suffered from taxes and tithes which were especially heavy because the nobility and the clergy were exempted from them. Population pressure on the land added to the peasants' difficulties. According to some estimates, in Limousin 58 percent of the peasants held less than 2 hectares each on the eve of the Revolution; in Leonais 76 percent held similar lots; and in Nord 75 percent of the peasants had less than 1 hectare each.

On August 4, 1789, the National Assembly, acting on behalf of the Revolution, abolished all traces of the feudal system: all the hunting privileges of the landlords, all exclusive rights to pigeon-houses, all feudal jurisdictions, and all tithes and dues. Rents, whether in money or in kind, were to be redeemable. However, reinterpretation of the law delayed its effective implementation until 1792. After that date the law was implemented *de facto,* since the peasants refused to accept any interpretation other than their own, holding onto their holdings and refusing to pay any dues or rents. The property of the landlords who left the country as political exiles and the land of the clergy, together with the common land, were put up for auction. The terms and rates of payment were changed again and again, sometimes in favor of small buyers, but usually in favor of the wealthier bourgeoisie. As a result, it has been claimed that a new class of landowners emerged, a bourgeoisie created by Napoleon from among his supporters.

The effects of redistribution were radical in some respects and quite limited in other The peasants became free of all hereditary obligations; they became full-fledged owners, but the amount of land they owned changed little; in general they kept what they had. No enclosure was implemented and the strip system remained unchanged. The common land was either sold or appropriated by the local authorities. The most important effect of the reform was its catalytic

influence in France and Europe as a whole. Even after the defeat of Napoleon and restoration of the monarchy, the effects of the Revolution could not be erased.

Germany

German agriculture in the sixteenth–seventeenth centuries contained both the copyhold and the serf systems, in the West and the East respectively. Some attempts to bring about change were made in the eighteenth century. As an expression of his interest in agriculture, Frederick the Great perpetuated the status of the serfs by making their tenure hereditary and by putting an end to the landlords' attempts to remove them from the land. He also managed to settle 4500 families on newly reclaimed land between 1750 and 1776 on tenure arrangements similar to those of other peasants. Reform came slowly in both East and West Germany. In the West, which was occupied by the French during the Napoleonic War, the peasants were freed and the remnants of serfdom abolished. However, perpetual rents, which had a legal basis, were retained until the 1848 Revolution made it necessary to remove them by compensatory redemption. But nothing specific was done to consolidate the common fields.

In the East, serious attempts to reform the tenure system were begun by Baron vom Heinrich F. C. Stein in 1807. The Edict of that year gave freedom of person to the peasant, so that he could choose his occupation and place of residence, but it said nothing about the land. In 1811 another Edict was passed providing that peasants with hereditary tenure could own their land by paying the equivalent of 25 years' rent or ceding one third of their land to the landlord as compensation. Those who did not have hereditary rights could acquire rights to the land by ceding one half of it to the landlord. In 1816 this Edict was amended to include only those who owed plow service, leaving out those who owed labor services. Since the landlords were interested in utilizing new methods, the Law of 1821 provided for "separation" between land of the squire and that of the peasant. As a result, enclosure became legally possible. However, the potential effects seemed so drastic that separation was not generally implemented.

Thus, in both East and West the peasants continued to hold fragmented farms; they lost part of the land they had held previously; and often they had to sell and move out or become wage workers because they could not make a living on their small farms. Especially in the East, the landlords were able to enlarge their holdings and continue their large-scale farming. The tradition of the Junkers was retained. Consolidation on a large scale did not come until the twentieth century.

Italy

A similar situation prevailed in Italy, which until 1861 was divided into separate states, as was Germany. There were differences, however, between the North and South of Italy. In the South and the Papal States, serfdom was still widespread, while in the North copyholds were more common. The Napoleonic occupation abolished serfdom, but after Napoleon's defeat the forces of reaction were successful in delaying complete abolition until unification came in 1861. Political unification was accompanied by the confiscation and sale of Church property to answer the financial needs of the state. These changes, however, did not affect the distribution of ownership or land fragmentation. Although public land was sold on the market and the number of owners increased between 1871 and 1946, tenancy also increased and the number of small holdings remained quite high. The increase in the number of owners was probably a result of the addition of 2 million hectares of arable land beginning in the 1920s. As late as 1958 83 percent of landholders in Italy had 2 hectares or less and owned only 18 percent of the total farmland. Remnants of the seigneurial system remained until recently,

when attempts to deal with the problem began.

Spain

The situation in Spain was even more complicated than in Italy. While the Napoleonic occupation abolished serfdom, the reform laws, which were many, were frequently repealed by the forces of reaction. Resistance to change in Spain came from the nobility, the clergy, and the municipalities, which represented the large landowners. Between 1810 and 1860 at least 18 laws were enacted for reform or counterreform. The problem was in part that of inheritance or entailment. The reform laws managed to suppress entailment to facilitate land transactions. They also stipulated that one-fifth of the sale price be paid to the treasury. Some of the laws also provided for enclosure, but these were repealed by the opposition. Between 1833 and 1876 large amounts of property changed hands as a result of disentailment. However, transfer through the market favored those who had the means to purchase land, not the peasants. By the end of the nineteenth century, 96 percent of the owners owned an average of 0.6 hectares and a total of 29.57 percent of all the land. In contrast, 0.1 percent of the owners, with an average of 598 hectares each, owned 33.28 percent of the land. In other words, the result was a system of *latifundia* and *minifundia* in which fragmentation was common and increasing because of subdivision through the equal inheritance laws. There is little evidence that much change has taken place.

Russia

Change was probably slowest in Russia and the other areas of eastern Europe. Russian agriculture was, at the beginning of this period, primarily a serf system. Serfdom had become well entrenched during the eighteenth century and no attempts at change were made until the middle of the nineteenth century, when peasant unrest and violence had become frequent. To avoid a repetition of the French *Jacquerie* and to safeguard the status quo with only minor modification, Tsar Alexander II began serious attempts at reform in the 1850s.

These attempts culminated in the Emancipation Act of January 14, 1861. The Act abolished serfdom and awarded the emancipated serf hereditary tenure of his house and garden, but the field land was transferred into hereditary tenure of the village as a whole. The *mir*, or village commune, was to allocate this field land among the villagers according to specified conditions. All rights and claims on the land were either transferred to the community, to whom the individual was made responsible, or were abolished, with redemption to be paid directly to the landlord. Although the serf was freed, in effect he had to ransom his personal freedom by surrendering some of the land to the former landlord. His complete emancipation was made conditional upon completion of all redemption payments, and until then he was under a "temporary obligation" to render the services requested by the former landlord. Temporary obligation was abolished in 1881. Freedom by redemption was facilitated by the government, which paid the landlord about 75 percent of the redemption value and took over the responsibility for collecting payments from the village communities.

The Act of 1861 applied only to serfs on private estates. In 1863 an Act was passed to emancipate the serfs on imperial land, which amounted to 2.9 percent of all private land in 1877. Imperial serfs received the maximum amount of land fixed by law against redemption payments extended over 49 years. The state serfs, who occupied about 40 percent of all the farmland in Russia at the time of Emancipation, were freed in 1866 by a statute which gave them all the land they had held, except forests, in perpetuity against money rents. In other words, they became free tenants. The rent was estimated in proportion to the individual peasant's income regardless of its source, but this arrangement was replaced in 1886 by a 49-year redemption arrangement. However, both the imperial and the state serfs became subject to the same village or communal tenure as the serfs on private estates.

At this time Russia also employed serfs outside agriculture, in mines, factories, and households. These were freed like the others. Those in mines and factories were awarded small land allotments, but household serfs received no land. Finally, emancipation reached the Cossacks in 1869. The Cossacks received two thirds of the land they had held, to be held in common subject to repartition. The remaining third was ceded to the army. The Cossacks were not required to pay redemption; instead, they had to serve in the army for 20 years and provide their own horses and arms.

The effects of emancipation at first seemed to be far-reaching, but soon it became apparent that the peasants had been freed from one master, only to be subjected to another. The amount of land they received was less than they had before, their losses ranging from 0 to 45 percent, according to the province. Furthermore, they lost the best land, since the landlord had the right to choose his retained holdings. As has been noted, not all the peasants received land allotments. In addition, the redemption assessments were often higher than the market value of the land and the peasants had no option but to accept the obligation. In fact the redemption payments often exceeded the peasant's total income from the land, even though the fixed payments declined in value because of inflation.

The landlords also suffered. Inflation reduced the value of the bonds they had received from the government. Their incomes from the land were also reduced. Many of them had to resort to selling land to maintain their living standards. Between 1862 and 1906, the gentry in 45 European provinces lost 43 percent of the land they held previously. Most of the purchases were made by the rising bourgeoisie and by some of the nobility and peasantry. The peasants were able to acquire some land with the help of the Peasants' Land Bank, an institution set up to buy land on the market and resell it to them on favorable terms. However, a new influence on land transaction was the rise of merchant speculation. Except for bringing land onto the market, emancipation had little economic impact. Fragmentation was not reduced, incentives increased little, and the scale of operation hardly changed. The landlords were unhappy and the peasants were unhappier. The political stability hoped for was not achieved.

The Revolt of 1905 precipitated a new attempt, known as the Stolypin Reform. This reform was intended to remove peasant grievances and to create a class of independent, well-to-do farmers. By an Edict of November 3, 1905 all redemption payments were abolished. On March 4, 1906 the joint responsibility of the commune for public obligations was canceled, and communal assemblies were deprived of the authority to impose forced labor on any member or to control his passport. The individual became free to choose his place of residence. However, the main provisions of the reform remained for Peter Stolypin to introduce. On November 9, 1906 he issued an Edict which made each land allotment the private property of the individual, gave him the right to separate from the commune without losing land, and arranged for the allotment, upon separation, to be consolidated in one piece as much as possible. However, separation and consolidation of holdings still required approval by a two-thirds majority of the commune members. Finally, the Edict entitled the individual to claim his share of common holdings such as meadows and pastures. This Edict was reaffirmed by the legislature in 1910.

Stolypin completed his reform with the law of May 29, 1911, which tried to consolidate holdings by making enclosure an individual right under certain conditions, with special attention given to technical improvements. However, the effects of this measure could not be fully realized. The tide was changing and the old regime was nearing its end. The Soviets lost no time in radically altering the tenure arrangements.

The Soviet reforms came on the heels of restlessness, war, revolution, and the abortive attempts of Kerensky's provisional government to forestall the revolt. The Soviets came in with a doctrine, even though they had no real plan. They instituted the change with the Land Decree of November 8, 1917, which was reaffirmed by the Decree of February 19, 1918. These provisions were mainly to abolish private ownership, tie landholding to actual farming operation, increase productivity, and promote collective farming. The Decree also made trade in agricultural machinery, seed, and products a monopoly of the state. These provisions were clear and explicit. However, the lack of a plan rendered implementation rather difficult. The Soviets experimented with War Communism,[3] which proved to be disastrous to production. In 1921 they shifted to the New Economic Policy (NEP), which permitted private trade in agricultural products after set quotas had been delivered at fixed prices. While the results of this policy were highly favorable to production, it compromised with the doctrine and therefore was regarded as transitory. In 1929 it was decided to embark on collectivization, a process completed by 1936 at relatively high costs to production and to animal and human life. However, the tenure arrangements decreed in 1918 were finally realized. In 1939, collective farms occupied 85.6 percent of all the sown area; state and cooperative farms occupied 9.1 percent, of which 0.6 percent was held by individual peasants; and 3.9 percent was held by individual peasants as gardens on collective farms. Henceforth,

[3] This experiment took place between 1918 and 1921. During the period emergency measures were used to secure food and overcome opposition.

fragmentation was no longer possible and the scale of operation was enlarged. The impact of collectivization on incentives has been the subject of many debates, most of which have been emotional or political. The reader will be left to make his own judgment.

Eastern Europe

The situation in eastern Europe has been less explored than that in the other European regions. Most eastern European countries were under the Ottoman rule, but their institutions were a mixture of Turkish and other European origins.

While Hungary escaped long-term domination by Turkey, she was under the influence of both Turkey and Austria during the nineteenth century. In 1867 Hungary freed itself from Austrian influence. Serbia, as part of Yugoslavia, rebelled against Turkish rule between 1805 and 1813, but its independence was not achieved until 1878. Rumania gained independence in the same year. Bulgaria also became free but only nominally; independence was achieved only in 1908. The other eastern European provinces remained under Turkish rule until 1918.

Thus the landlords and the institutions governing ownership in each of these countries were foreign to them. Serfdom with forced labor was the most common system of agriculture. Many observers have associated these institutions with the backwardness of agriculture and the economy in this area. Although the nineteenth century was a century of reform, the change came so gradually that economic conditions and production methods changed little. The struggle was for personal freedom from serfdom and for ownership of the land the peasants cultivated.

The year 1848 was a turning point in Hungary's agrarian history. The Decree of 1853 abolished the *robot*, or forced labor, and the payment of dues in money and in kind; the landlords were compensated by the state. The Decree abolished the payment of

tithes to the Roman Catholic Church. It also abrogated the institution of *aviticitas*, or hereditary entailment of estates which, among other things, prohibited ownership of property by peasants, burghers, and Jews. It permitted the landlords to sell their land. While the Decree did nothing for the landless serfs, it did encourage consolidation or separation of the individual's strips by a process called *commasatio*. At the request of the landlord or a majority of the peasants a commission would be set up to evaluate the property and *commass* or consolidate the holdings.

The Rumanian reform came in 1864. It was similar to the reforms of Hungary and Russia, with significant differences. While it freed the serfs, it distributed the land according to the number of cows or oxen a peasant had, with variation according to the district. The peasant also paid compensation installments according to the number of his cows or oxen, the rates varying also according to district. In the meantime the landlords were paid in full with government bonds. Under no circumstances were the landlords to lose more than two-thirds of their estates. The peasants who might be left without land because of this restriction and the newly married couples who had no holdings of their own were allowed to settle on state land. For 30 years no land received by the peasants could be alienated, even though compensation had to be paid in full within 15 years, during which time the landlords were to receive interest on the bonds at the rate of 10 percent annually. Finally, by allowing the cottagers and landless to settle on state domain, the government solved a problem which continued in other countries.

In Bulgaria certain improvements ending forced labor services by the peasants were introduced in the 1850s by the Turkish government. Though the institution of *angariya* or forced labor was formally abolished, labor services were still imposed and extracted by the landlords. The real change came only after political liberation from

Turkey in 1878, In 1880, the Law for Improving the Lot of the Farm Population entitled each peasant—including those who had full rights, the sharecroppers, and even the landless workers—to own the property he worked, as long as he had worked it for 10 years without interruption. The landlords were to be compensated for the land transferred. However, the problem was not solved, especially because the Turks, who were a majority among the landlords, were too embittered to cooperate. The problem arose again in the 1920s.

Yugoslavia experienced agrarian reform at different times in different provinces. Serbia, which gained autonomy from Turkey in 1830, was able to abolish the feudal tenure, *spahi*, in that year. It abolished the fief system, all the land reverting to the state. Every peasant was entitled to the land he occupied. The relative abundance of land made implementation easy. In Croatia-Slavonia, the serfs were liberated in 1848. All those with hereditary tenure were awarded the land they occupied, with compensation of the landlords guaranteed by the state. Furthermore, the occupational monopolies from which the peasants were excluded were abolished and freedom of occupation was established. An apparently major problem remaining was the *zadruga* or joint-family tenure. The reformers debated whether or not it should be abolished by law. It was not, because it was assumed that the institution would disintegrate once capitalism had advanced.

These eastern European reforms have been discussed in some detail for three reasons. First, they contrast with developments in the advanced countries of western and northern Europe. Second, the experiences of these countries are highly relevant to present-day developing countries, much more so than the experiences of England, France, or Germany. Third, the reforms did not solve the problems of agriculture in those countries.

At least four major problems survived

which were bound to revive agrarian unrest. The first was the question of the landless serfs who were freed, but had no security of employment and no landlord to employ them. They did not benefit from reform, nor were alternative opportunities created for them. Second, the reforms set no minimum size for the individual farm and therefore the inefficiency of the small-scale holding was not prevented. Associated with this was the problem of fragmentation, which was bound to follow from the inheritance laws that permitted division among the heirs. Finally, because of the small size of the farms, the sale of land and tenancy were bound to grow in importance and a class of middlemen was bound to evolve.

Early in the twentieth century unrest became evident. In 1895, 0.84 percent of the owners in Hungary owned 45.31 percent of all the land, while 52.3 percent of the owners had only 6.15 percent of the land. In Rumania around the end of the nineteenth century, 0.46 percent of the owners owned 49 percent of the land. In Bulgaria the peasants received land but were burdened with heavy debts at high rates of interest. Fragmentation was common in most areas. Incomes were low and dissatisfaction was violently expressed, as in the 1907 revolt in Rumania.

Following the First World War and the Soviet Revolution, the governments in eastern Europe were anxious to avert local revolutions. New reforms were introduced in 1918, 1919, and 1920 in different countries, most of which gave land to the peasants. In Poland, Czechoslovakia, and Rumania laws were passed with the objective of setting up independent peasant farms which would permit intensive cultivation. Land was to be expropriated from landlords owning more than a fixed amount and subdivided among the peasants. First to be subdivided was the state land, then Peasants' Bank Land, the lands of religious establishments, and private farms, beginning with those badly farmed. The ceiling set on private holdings varied from 150 to 500 hectares, depending on the quality of the land and the land/labor ratio. The excess land was to be expropriated against compensation and divided into lots of from one to five hectares. Implementation was fairly rapid in Rumania, but by this time the peasants were organized in political parties and were no longer satisfied with partial measures. The revolts of 1926, commonly known as the Green Rising, were expressions of the new peasant movement. The impact of these reforms is hard to evaluate. As with the Stolypin Reform, time was too short before another war and a takeover by a Communist regime changed the environment and made the Soviet system a model for agricultural change.

Ireland

One more case deserves special attention, namely that of Ireland. Although tenure arrangements were always closely related to political institutions, in Ireland two other complications arose. Even after Irish independence from Britain in 1783 and reunion with Britain in 1801, the country was internally divided between Protestants and Catholics. Due to a series of colonial movements, the Protestant minority controlled the government, owned the land, and manned the professions. The Catholic majority were the tenants, the beggars, and the workers, and were prohibited from government and professional positions. Therefore, a deep-seated schism prevailed and resulted in restlessness among the peasants. Their difficulties were further aggravated when a return to grazing after the Napoleonic War reduced the land available for cultivation. This problem was augmented by the squeeze of population pressure, the frequent failure of the potato crop, and a new wave of tenant evictions. In 1837 an Irish Poor Law was passed which required the landlords to pay the entire poor rate on holdings which had an annual valuation of £4 or less. To avoid this tax the landlords resorted to evicting the tenants on holdings in this category. These difficulties were relieved somewhat when population

pressure declined due to the death of about half a million people from the potato famine of 1846, and the emigration of a quarter of a million between 1831 and 1841 and another 1.14 million between 1851 and 1861. This 20 percent decline in the Irish population meant a rise of the land/labor ratio by a corresponding amount. However, neither the problem of unhappy tenancy nor that of small-scale holdings was resolved.

Reform attempts were made around the middle of the nineteenth century. The first bill provided for the extension of improvement loans to the landlords. By 1859, 180,000 acres had been improved, giving work to 25,000 people. Another Act was the Incumbered Estates Act of 1849, which released estates from entailment and made sale on the market possible. The Landlord and Tenant Act of 1860 and the Deasy Act made the relationship between the two parties contractual and provided for compensation of the tenant for his improvements on the land. The Landlord and Tenant Act of 1870 further legalized compensation for improvement, but was meant also to convert tenants into owners. Its effects, however, were minor. Only 877 tenancies were converted. Another experiment was the Fair Rent Act of 1881, which was passed to quiet agrarian unrest. Its results were equally modest, with only 731 conversions made. The first effective measure was the Purchase of Land Act of 1885, which provided for loans to the full purchase value of the land and for annuity payments lower than the rent value. As a result of this Act, 942,625 acres were transferred to 25,367 new owners, with an average size of 37 acres per holding. Another Act in 1891 made it possible for 46,834 tenants to own their land. However, most important was the Irish Land Act of 1903, or the Wyndham Act. This Act awarded the landlords a 12 percent bonus over the purchase price, paid them in cash, and allowed them to sell their remaining land to the government at given prices, and to repurchase these properties at the same easy terms offered to the tenants. Hence, resistance of the land-lords was reduced to a minimum. By March 1921, 219,423 tenancies had been converted into ownerships.

In 1922 Ireland was divided into North-ern Ireland and the Irish Free State. After some debate, the Land Purchase (Northern Ireland) Order of 1925 was passed making automatic the acquisition of land needed to convert all tenants into owners. The transfer of holdings was completed in 1935. In the Irish Free State purchase continued so that between 1923 and 1933, 110,000 additional units were appropriated, although not with-out difficulty and the passage of several pieces of legislation. An Act of 1933 can-celled all arrears on payments, cut all future annuities in half, and cut those of war vet-erans by 55 percent. By 1933, 93.8 percent of the agricultural land was owned by the peasants, and most of the tenants had be-come owners.

PRODUCTIVITY AND OUTPUT

Agricultural production and productivity in Europe underwent radical changes in the nineteenth century, although in most cases not before the second half of that century. In part the delay was due to the persistence of tradition, the difficulty of institutional re-form, and the failure to apply the new tech-niques of husbandry. In surveying the pat-tern of change, certain benchmarks should be kept in view, two of which have already been discovered: developments in technology and institutional tenure reform. In addition, attention should be directed to the impact of the Napoleonic War, the advent of the rail-road, expansion into new cultivable terri-tories, the trend toward free trade and the ensuing era of protectionism, the increased international division of labor in agriculture, and the expansion of socialism. Each of these events had an impact on a certain aspect of agriculture. The emphasis in the following discussion will be on the changes in agricultural techniques and organization and their impact on production and produc-tivity.

Pattern of agricultural development

The agricultural development of modern Europe occurred, roughly speaking, in three stages. The first was concerned mostly with institutional arrangements, property rights, and the security of the producer. The second stage was efficiency-oriented and involved mainly the adoption of new crops, changes in farm layout, and the use of fertilizer and tools which were not mechanically powered. The third stage was a combination of the above two with the application of mechani-cal power. These stages of course overlapped greatly. The early developers, the Nether-lands and Britain, were already in the second stage by the end of the eighteenth century; the majority, however, did not reach that stage until the third quarter of the nineteenth. The third stage started around the middle of the nineteenth century in Britain and the Low Countries, but for the majority it did not begin before the end of the century. In contrast, the United States started at the second stage and advanced smoothly into the third as power machinery became available.

The distinction among these stages, how-ever, is not chronological, but is related directly to output, yield, and the commercial-ization of agriculture. The changes in the first stage were mostly distributive. Although they had a small impact on productivity, they redistributed income and reduced the rigidity of the tenure arrangements. Yield and crop rotation, fertilizer, and selective breeding in the second stage raised produc-tivity perceptibly. However, the major im-provement came with mechanization, which cut the cost of production enormously and thus reduced the input/output ratio. This is the stage to which most countries aspired, but many have had difficulty attaining it, especially because it required more land and less labor than was available in Europe.

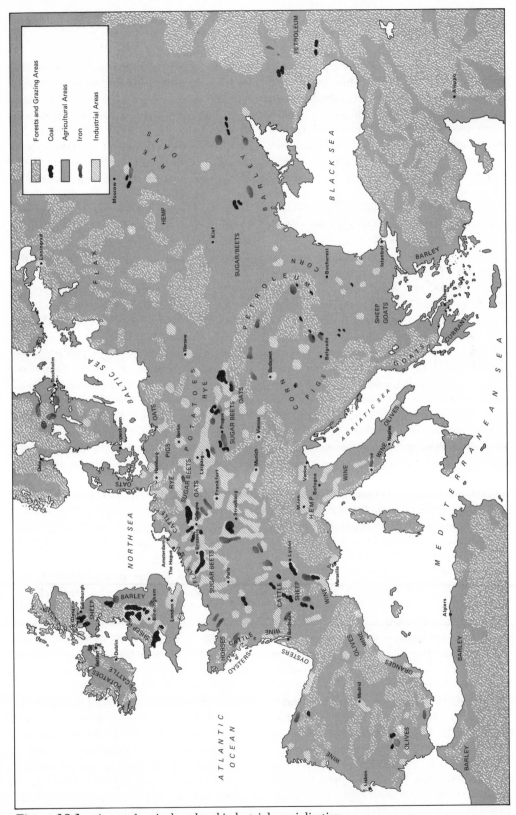

Figure 18.1 Areas of agricultural and industrial specialization.

Figure 18.1 shows agricultural areas of specialization in 1950. This pattern of specialization was fairly well established by the middle of the nineteenth century. Subsequent modifications were minor except for the recent encroachments of urbanization and industrialism on the arable land. This pattern was a result of the achievement of the third stage in many countries and of the exogenous influences—such as war, famine, and severe competition—which were experienced in the meantime.

During the eighteenth century and the early part of the nineteenth, only the Netherlands, Britain, and small parts of Germany and France had advanced conspicuously into the second stage of agricultural development. The Netherlands was ahead of all other countries, especially in the provinces of Flanders and Brabant. Most of the other countries were still preoccupied with tenure problems or were oblivious to the possibilities of advanced agriculture. The most important changes in agriculture in this period were the following: invasion of the sea, the wasteland, and the forests to enlarge the arable areas; more sensitivity to price and market conditions, a break with tradition, and introduction of more intensive farming; and reorganization of production and adoption of new crops to improve the yield or to avoid disaster. These developments will be treated below.

Reclamation

Reclamation of the land had been common in Europe for many years, particularly in the Low Countries. The growing density of population and the rising demand for industrial crops increased demand in general and had a positive impact on prices. The Dutch and British farmers were among the first to respond. The Dutch attacked the sea while the British invaded the marshes, swamps, and wasteland. By means of polders the Dutch were able to reclaim 927 hectares between 1690 and 1739; 1721 hectares between 1740 and 1789; 1318 hectares between 1790 and 1839, and 1568 hectares between 1840 and 1864. In East Friesland there was an invasion of peat marshes which reclaimed 7994 hectares between 1736 and 1794. These areas may seem small, but given the density of population, they were quite important. The British reclaimed about 750,000 acres in the nineteenth century.

Expansion of the arable, however, had at least three other sources: invasion of the forest land, conversion of the commons and grazing land, and settlement of previously unpopulated areas. Invasion of the forests was undertaken only partly to increase the arable land. In Sweden the primary purpose was to stimulate the timber industry, although a side effect was the addition of new agricultural land. Expansion of settlement into the forest land was also a means of solving the peasant problem and reducing population pressure on the available resources, as in eastern Europe. Conversion of the common and grazing areas into arable was a direct response to favorable market conditions and a result of the tenure reforms which converted communal or group tenures into individual rights in all the countries of Europe. The amount of land affected is not known. It may be inferred, however, from the fact that the land still fed increasing populations even though yield and labor productivity had not yet begun to rise. It may be noted that in Spain the conversion was due to a decline in the power of the Mesta in the eighteenth century, and also to a relative decline in the demand for wool due to the competition from cotton. Expansion of the arable in various parts of Spain between 1818 and 1861 was largely a response to population pressure; 4 million hectares were brought under the plow in this period. However, as Spain was unified and the effects of the second stage were felt there was a decrease in the arable. In the third quarter of the nineteenth century there was a tendency to give up the submarginal land on which farming was uneconomical.

The most important source of new land was expansion into previously uncultivated areas. This was particularly true of Russia and eastern Europe, where population was relatively scarce and land abundant. New lands were opened up to accommodate the landless, as in Rumania after 1864. The impact of this procedure was felt deeply after expansion of the railway made the eastern and southern parts of Russia accessible. The new grain country had an impact throughout Europe, as will be seen below.

The market and cultivation

Beginning in the eighteenth century farming methods changed in an attempt to use the land more intensively. This change was due not only to population pressure, but also to the desire to reap more output from the same amount of input. Its aim was a commercial one. Again the Netherlands led the way and Britain followed. Although most agricultural literature in the early years of the period came from Britain—where Arthur Young, Jethro Tull, and Lord Townshend were advocating improved and intensive agriculture—the Dutch were ahead in practice.

Crop rotation. Intensive farming was closely associated with the system of rotation, the composition of inputs and outputs, and climate and soil conditions. In the eighteenth century, various systems of rotation prevailed side by side, as the following summary shows:

1. Temporary cultivation (*Feldgraswirthschaft*), still used in Scotland, Ireland, Sweden, and elsewhere;

2. The infield–outfield system, in Scotland, Namur, etc.;

3. Continuous rye cultivation, in the eastern Netherlands, etc.;

4. Two-course rotation with a two-year fallow, in Andalusia, etc.;

5. Three-course rotation with a one-year fallow, general;

6. Free three-course rotation with a one-year fallow, general;

7. Regulated three-course rotation with a one-year fallow, general;

8. A rotation of four, five, six or more courses, usually in combination with extensive cultivation of pulses, in England, Friesland, Alsace, etc.;

9. Convertible husbandry, in Flanders, Groningen, England, Alsace, Schleswig-Holstein, etc.;

10. Rotation of crops with fodder-crops as catch-crops, in the Meijerij van den Holstein, etc.;

11. A rotation of crops with fodder-crops in the fallow year, in Flanders, Norfolk, etc.[4]

These systems of rotation are arranged in an ascending order of intensiveness which required progressively more capital and more labor per unit of land. However, two other conditions are also implied: To adopt a more intensive system, the farmer had to be a decision-maker responsive to the market. Second, the more intensive systems were closely associated with the growth of livestock farming, which used up the fodder and produced manure in return, as well as its direct output. Interest in livestock and in manure provided another impetus for intensive agriculture. The above conditions prevailed in the Netherlands and in Britain. Crop rotation of the last two types were facilitated by introduction of leguminous crops such as turnips and clover, which fed the cattle and restored fertility to the soil. The new rotation reduced the need for resting the land as fallow, and increased the total potential yield from the land, even though the yield per unit of input might not have increased. Since the cultivable area was increased, total output also increased, although without any significant effect on productivity, as Table 18.1 suggests.

The small change in productivity may be explained by the fact that agriculture was already relatively advanced and rotation had no great influence on yield per unit of input. On the other hand, the change from one rotation system to another had various

4 B. H. Slicher Van Bath, *The Agrarian History of Western Europe*, p. 224.

Table 18.1.   Estimates of yield in eighteenth and nineteenth centuries

CROP	KLONDERT (NETHERLANDS), 1740–1780 HECTOLITERS PER HECTARE	NETHERLANDS, 1851–1860 HECTOLITERS IN HECTARES AVERAGE IN SEA-CLAY REGION
Winter wheat	16–20	19.3
Winter barley	30–35	32.6
Oats	30	32.4
Field beans	18	18.5
Cole[a]	19	18.5

[a] Cole *refers to plants in the mustard family, including cabbage.*
SOURCE: *B. H. Slicher Van Bath*, The Agrarian History of Western Europe, *p. 282.*

effects, depending on which systems were involved and the general attitude associated with each. For example as late as 1879 in Rumania, where an intensive rotation system had not been adopted, the yield per hectare was only 7 hectoliters of grain, in contrast to Britain's 40.8 hectoliters. Taking the 1740–1780 average yield in the Netherlands as a standard, it may be suggested that the change from 7 to between 16 and 20 hectoliters per hectare was due to changes in the rotation system and other organizational changes. However, the addition of fertilizers and new machinery caused the doubling of the yield, from between 16 and 20 to 40.8 hectoliters per hectare. Similar, though less dramatic, changes due to rotation may be inferred in other countries, but the lack of adequate data precludes going beyond suggesting these observations.

Fertilizers and mechanization. The differences in yield cannot, however, be divorced from the development of new techniques and new tools. Until the middle of the nineteenth century, most of the countries of Europe were using primitive plows, sowing seeds which they themselves had always grown with little selectivity or improvement, depending on manure or natural fertilizer which was in short supply, and interested primarily in subsistence agriculture. Where agriculture had advanced, it had done so only on a few large estates, as in Prussia, or on experimental farms, as in France.

There is little evidence that artificial fer-

tilizers came into general use before the 1850s, and in many countries they were not common before the reforms which followed political independence or unification. Manure was used, but its availability was limited and far beyond the reach of most farmers since they had few animals and could not afford to buy it. The use of chemical fertilizer advanced greatly in the last quarter of the nineteenth century in most countries of western Europe, in Scandinavia, and to a lesser extent in the eastern and southern parts of Europe. While the available data suggest that chemical fertilizers were widely known, their application increased slowly and varied greatly from country to country. However, the pattern of utilization was uniform. The Low Countries led in the consumption of chemical nutrients and have continued to do so in the present century. Germany, Britain, and the Scandinavian countries followed; while Spain, Portugal, and eastern Europe used the least amounts. In all countries, however, there was a striking increase in the use of chemical fertilizers between the 1920s and the 1950s. This large increase was closely related to the use of the tractor.[5]

The same variations characterized the use of mechanical implements and inventions. Although the tractor was a relatively late innovation, there were implements in the nineteenth century which could have been

[5] For more detail, see *Cambridge Economic History of Europe*, VI, p. 656.

used to expand cultivation, to plow deeper, and to cut the cost of production by mechanization. These inventions were widely known, but there is little evidence that they were generally used before the late nineteenth century. Even the early horse-drawn machinery spread only gradually.

Several partial explanations may be offered for the slow adoption of these techniques. First, because land was relatively limited and the population was increasing rapidly, there was pressure to put as many people on the land as possible. Second, mechanization required capital which most farmers could not obtain. Third, most of the farms were so small that the use of machinery was hardly feasible. Fourth, mechanization and the use of fertilizer required complementary conditions—such as irrigation, training, and specialization—which did not exist under subsistence agriculture. Finally, there were few alternative opportunities available to reduce the fear that underemployment might result from adopting labor-saving techniques. It is not surprising, therefore, that mechanical harvesters were scarcely used even in Britain before the second half of the nineteenth century. Hay harvesters and reaping machines were by this time widely used. The jump in the use of machinery came around the end of the nineteenth century.

The scale of farming and the advance in technology in Britain during the nineteenth century lend credence to the assumption that Britain led the way in farm mechanization. The degree of mechanization may be inferred from the rapid decline in the amount of manpower engaged in agriculture, in spite of the increase of acreage under cultivation. It has been estimated that Britain had 40,000 reapers as early as 1870. This was almost equal to the total number of reapers in Germany and France combined. Germany, France, and Belgium were next in line in using threshers, reapers, and sowing machines. Between 1880 and 1930 the number of machines used in each category was

multiplied several-fold; the same was true in Norway.[6]

Machinery was a late comer in eastern Europe, in Spain, Portugal, Italy, and in Russia. The available data suggest that as late as 1935 less than 10 percent of the farms in eastern Europe used sowing machines, and less than 1 percent used threshers and reapers. In Spain as late as 1932 less than 2 percent of the farms had harvesters, less than .5 percent had sowing machines, and less than .25 percent had threshers. Even fewer had them in Portugal. In 1930 less than 5 percent of Italy's farms were mechanized. In this respect, Italy was about 30 years behind Germany and France. The steam plow met with even more reluctance, making headway only in Britain and Germany. In Britain it was adopted rapidly and was displaced only after tractors came into use, although the electric plow became common in the 1920s in Austria, Switzerland, Czechoslovakia, and Norway.

The available data on Russia are mostly in value terms. Clearly the expansion of cultivation into Siberia and the South of Russia, which flooded the grain market, affected the use of machinery. It is estimated that in 1862 52 Russian factories were producing farm implements; the number was 340 in 1879. It is not clear, however, what kind of implements were produced. The total consumption of farm machinery was about 4 million rubles in 1867, 8 million in 1890, and 15 million in 1894. After 1900 a relatively steep rise in the use of machinery occurred. The consumption in rubles was about 28 million in 1900, 61 million in 1908, and 109 million in 1913. It may be noted that as of 1890 Russia was producing more farm machinery than it was importing. In 1910 there were 811,000 threshers in use and 27,000 steam threshers. However, none of the modern machinery used in the United States or Germany was in use. In spite of the

[6] For statistical detail, see *Cambridge Economic History of Europe*, VI, p. 644.

relative increase in the use of machinery, Russian agriculture still depended mainly on draft animals and manual power. Mechanization came only after 1928 when the Soviets decided to collectivize and reduce rural manpower. Mechanization was also necessary as a substitute for the draft animals destroyed during collectivization as a form of resistance. The rate of mechanization, excluding the replacement of animals, rose from an index of 100 in 1928 to 450 in 1956. During this period the rural population active in agriculture was reduced by more than one-third.

Changes in productivity. Although total output was increasing, productivity per unit of land and of labor was relatively stagnant until the middle of the nineteenth century in the advanced countries, and until the end of the century in the others. Agricultural output in Britain increased from an index of 100 in 1700 to 111 in 1750 and to 143 in 1800. From 1800 to 1855 total output grew at an annual compound rate of 1.45 percent, and at an annual rate of about 0.7 percent from 1855 to 1900. Since the absolute number of people engaged in agriculture had not yet declined, the increase of labor can easily be exaggerated. Available data show that labor productivity in Britain was increasing at an annual compound rate of a little more than 1 percent throughout the nineteenth century, but that the rate was higher during the second half of the century than in the first. This is not surprising, given the more rapid adoption of labor-saving techniques in the second half of the century.

Agricultural labor productivity in Sweden, including forestry, increased from an index of 100 in 1861–1865 to 166 in 1896–1900 and to 247 in 1926–1930. During the same period labor productivity in Britain was far smaller, increasing from an index of 100 in 1867–1869 to 115 in 1894–1903 and to 140 in 1930–1934. This difference, however, may be due to the fact that British agricultural productivity had already ad-

vanced to a high level while Swedish agriculture was just beginning to move. Furthermore, the fact that the Swedish data include the timber industry tends to distort the comparison. However, it is clear that in northern and western Europe both production and productivity had advanced greatly by the end of the century.

At the lower end of the scale were Spain and Italy. Italian agriculture was almost stagnant up to the end of the nineteenth century. After 1900 it developed at a favorable rate until the Second World War, after which output increased radically. It may be noted that in the twentieth century fertilizers came into wide use in Italy. In Spain the output of all agricultural products, including farm animals, increased perceptibly during the nineteenth century; in some cases by 100 percent. However, the yield or productivity increased only for olives and grapes, apparently in response to market conditions and because these products were consistent with traditional agriculture and had a comparative advantage. The yield of olives increased by 50 percent between 1800 and 1900, while other agricultural products ahowed no apparent rise in yield.

These statistics should be interpreted very carefully. At best, they indicate trends. For example, no horsepower was given for machinery; no distribution of the use of fertilizer among farms was shown. Such use may have been concentrated in certain regions or farms. Northern and southern Italy certainly had different experiences. Furthermore, the results would look different had the comparison been made in terms of yield per hectare.

Nevertheless, trends can be observed. The Low Countries continued to lead in modernization, productivity, and intensity of farming. Scandinavia, Germany, and England came next with very little variation among them in rates of growth. An idea of the land yield can be arrived at from the estimates of Table 18.2. These figures show the Netherlands as the continuing leader, with France

Table 18.2.   Comparative yield in Europe and the U.S.A., 1938 (100 kilograms per hectare)

	WHEAT	RYE	BARLEY	OATS	POTATOES	SUGAR BEETS
Denmark	30.4	17.8	29.8	26.8	171.3	344.2
Netherlands	30.3	22.8	29.5	24.8	187.0	381.0
Eire	23.7	18.8	24.7	24.4	191.6	245.3
Britain	23.1	16.0	20.9	20.4	169.1	220.3
Germany	22.8	17.3	21.6	20.2	168.7	305.4
France	15.4	11.6	14.5	14.0	111.8	275.9
U.S.A.	8.8	7.3	11.3	9.7	77.7	250.6

SOURCE: Denmark, *p. 252.*

the lowest among the six European countries. The United States yield per hectare is still far below that of France. The obvious conclusion is that intensity of cultivation is positively associated with density of population. As long as land is relatively abundant, emphasis is put on economizing on other factors, in this case labor and capital. The United States surpassed all these countries in productivity of labor because of mechanization, fertilization, and more land-extensive farming.

Thus productivity was closely associated with institutional and attitude change and even more with the use of fertilizers and scientific principles. Mechanization was important in reducing costs, especially where wages were relatively high and labor-saving was economically advisable. In the majority of the European countries, the improvement came in the twentieth century. Only western Europe and to an extent Scandinavia experienced a major agricultural improvement earlier, and except in Britain this did not come until after the middle of the nineteenth century.

Reorganization of production

European agriculture faced several shocks during the eighteenth and nineteenth centuries to which it responded with specialization and reorganization. These shocks, which contributed to market and price fluctuations, included the awakening of the peasantry, discussed above; the Napoleonic War and the Continental Blockade; the advent of the

railroad; the mood of laissez-faire and the return to protectionism; and expansion into new cultivable land. Another great influence which acted as a catalyst to agriculture was the rise of the demand for capital generated by the new inventions applicable to agriculture. These various factors were reflected in the price levels of agricultural products, which in turn brought about adjustments in agriculture.

The rise in population stimulated the demand for food products and raised prices despite the expansion in arable land and food production. Moreover, the increasing demand for industrial crops resulted in recomposition of the product. The pressure was relieved only when new food supplies became accessible, at which time new adjustments became necessary. The demand for flax, hemp, sugar beet, and oil seed caused a shift from grains to these products.

The war and the blockade.   The first major shocks to agriculture were the Napoleonic War and the continental blockade. To put economic pressure on Britain, Napoleon tried to keep British products out of Europe and to prevent exports from reaching Britain. The policy had repercussions on agriculture throughout Europe. English farmers had to feed their country. Soaring prices resulted in an expansion of the arable. The same was true in Ireland. But when the war was over, the farmers found it difficult to face the competition of foreign grains. British farmers succeeded in passing new corn laws, which protected them against foreign competition as long as the price of corn was below a certain level. However, the effectiveness of the Corn Laws in restricting imports has been questioned. But the decline of prices after the war had a more severe effect in Ireland. A decline in arable and a return to grazing resulted, which was further stimulated by the increasing demand for beef in industrializing Britain.

The French farmers became used to the extensive market created during the First Empire. After the war they lost much of their advantage and had to adjust to the protective British policy. They responded with a similar policy without modifying the structure of their agriculture. The blockade also affected other countries, especially those that supplied France during the war. Some countries, like Belgium and Holland, responded by industrialization, expanding their cotton and sugar industries. Denmark expanded its wool industry to offset the loss caused by the blockade. When the war was over, these industries were unable to compete in the market. Some of these industrial areas turned to grazing and cattle breeding. However, one lasting effect of the war was the increase in the arable and hence in the agricultural capacity of Europe.

Specialization. The trend established in response to the Continental System received a blow when the railways began to expand and a new freedom of trade took shape. In 1846 the Corn Laws were repealed. Fear of famine began to decline and the emphasis on self-sufficiency no longer seemed justified. Even the potato failure in Ireland was not strong enough to shake the new attitude. Self-sufficiency became even less defensible when the railroads connected the Atlantic coast with the prairies of America and brought new lands under cultivation in Russia. The railroads and the improved trans-Atlantic vessels could now bring supplies of grain to the consumers of western Europe from Poland, South Russia, the American

prairies, and even India. The increased supplies brought down prices and forced farmers all over Europe to specialize and reorganize.

European farmers had either to compete on the market or to resort to protectionism. They managed to do both. The period known as the Great Depression of 1873 saw the return to protectionism in France, Germany, and other countries. Britain resisted protectionism at first and reorganized farming, concentrating on the production of fodder, some grains, and cattle. Wheat acreage was cut by more than 50 percent between 1873 and 1895. The Low Countries began to specialize in dairy production. Scandinavia, especially Denmark, decided to import fodder and produce poultry and dairy products for export. Denmark specialized in pork and its byproducts. The decision by Scandinavia and the Low Countries to specialize was reinforced by technical innovations. Refrigeration on ships allowed delivery of fresh products and removed the danger of spoilage. At the same time the cream separator and the milking machine were invented; both were adopted quickly, thus enhancing specialization. France continued the extensive production of grain, even though it required protection. Besides wine production, French agriculture has continued to stress small-scale farming. Flax, sugar beet, oil seed, and potatoes became staple products in various countries in response to the rising demand and the declining need to produce for subsistence, given the new safeguards against famine and starvation. The regions specializing in these products are shown in Figure 18.1 (p. 249).

The rise of cooperatives. Two other developments in European agriculture should be noted. The new improvements required financing, and the new implements required more land than the average farmer had in most countries. Both problems were handled by cooperation.

The problem of financing was resolved at

least in part by cooperative credit. Agricultural credit was not new. Germany established the first *Landschaft,* or Land Mortgage Association, in 1770 with the support of Frederick the Great. However, cooperative credit banks really began with the Reiffeisin Cooperative Bank in Germany in 1862. The new institution, unlike the *Landschaft,* was mainly for small farmers. It was quickly copied throughout Europe. In Germany there were 13,000 such banks in 1905 and 17,000 in 1910. Switzerland had 49 credit cooperatives in 1905; Ireland had 200; in 1906 there were 431 cooperatives in Belgium, and 1,461 in Italy. In 1907 France had 1,767 cooperatives of various kinds. Cooperative credit was least popular in Britain, in part because of the availability of substitute commercial banks. Moreover, British agriculture was controlled by relatively large farmers who had easier access to funds than the smaller farmers elsewhere. Only 11 cooperative banks existed in Britain in 1906.

The second problem, that of mechanization and scale of operation, was also solved by cooperation. Cooperation was consistent with the attitude towards welfare which the Scandinavian countries had held for almost a century. It was also consistent with the emerging socialist philosophy which cast doubts on the viability of competitive capitalism. Producer cooperatives seemed to be the answer, and Denmark set the pace in the rate of adoption. Producer cooperatives made it possible to use machinery by sharing or by collective securement and ownership. These cooperatives were also involved in marketing and purchasing, thus relieving the member of having to handle relatively small quantities himself and enabling him to enjoy more favorable wholesale terms. By 1909 about 3,000 producer cooperatives existed in Denmark. Even half a century later the Danish or Scandinavian example of producer cooperation had not achieved such acceptance or success in other countries. Only the socialist countries have gone

farther by collectivization, but this was a policy measure rather than a farmer response to market conditions. Other European countries have followed suit to a limited extent.

Both purchasing and production cooperatives were first initiated in Germany in 1860 and 1881, respectively. Eventually both types spread to Ireland, Britain, Switzerland, France, Belgium, and Italy, as well as to the Scandinavian countries. A sharp rise in the number of cooperatives took place in the last decade of the nineteenth century; Germany had 3,264 dairy cooperatives by 1906. In the same period, Ireland had established 270 cooperatives, Italy 600, and France 3,553, while Belgium had a mixture of 496 societies in 1905. Again only in Britain was the movement quite slow, reaching 142 societies in 1907. The reasons for this were probably the same as those that inhibited the growth of cooperative credit. Obviously the number of societies is deceptive since it does not indicate the size of the membership or the capital endowment of these associations. Nevertheless, it is clear that the movement was well established by the turn of the century as a solution to the problems of scale of operation and mechanization.

The role of agriculture. As these changes were taking place, other sectors of the national economies were also changing. Agriculture was becoming a less important contributor to the national income or the domestic product in each country. We have seen that the rural community became smaller and the agricultural labor force declined. The contribution of agriculture to the national income decreased almost as much.

The decline was most apparent in those countries that industrialized most rapidly. In these countries the relative contribution of agriculture declined, although absolute output increased. The decline was largest and fastest in Britain. Agriculture contributed 32.5 percent of national income in 1801, 20.3 percent in 1805, 6.1 percent in 1901, and only 4.7 percent in 1955. Germany experienced almost an equal decline but at a much slower rate, reaching down to 7 percent in 1958. Swedish agriculture declined from 49.1 percent of the national income in 1861–1865 to 32.8 percent in 1901–1905, to 18.2 percent in 1926–1930 and to 7 percent in 1950.

Another group of countries experienced a smaller relative decline. In these countries—including Norway, Denmark, the Netherlands, and to an extent France—agriculture continued to occupy a significant place in the economy in spite of mechanization and industrialization. These countries still derived between 10 and 15 percent of their national incomes from agriculture as late as 1950, although there has been further decline since then.

A third group of countries includes those in which agriculture continued to contribute more than 20 percent of the national income. Italy, Spain, Portugal, eastern Europe, and until recently Russia fall in this group. Agriculture in these countries remained underdeveloped, and industry was less advanced than in the first two groups. Italian agriculture, for example, contributed 56.7 percent of the national domestic product in 1861–1865, 49.2 percent in 1901–1905, and 27.3 percent in 1951–1955. As late as 1960 the contribution was still above 20 percent.

These differences are important only when analyzed in conjunction with the per capita income in each of these countries. Where the ratio declined greatly and the per capita income rose, as in Britain and Germany, the advance in industry must have been extensive. Where the ratio declined less while the per capita income increased, agriculture must have developed at the same time as did industry, as in the Netherlands, Norway, and to an extent France. Finally, where the ratio of agriculture's contribution declined least and the per capita income did not rise as much as in the other countries, both agriculture and industry must have remained relatively underdeveloped. This was the case in the last group of countries mentioned, and is also true of most of the present-day developing countries.

SUMMARY AND CONCLUSIONS

European agriculture has experienced radical changes during the last two centuries. The rate of change and its magnitude varied from one country to another. These changes came first in institutional and tenure arrangements. Adoption of new implements and methods of farming came next, and was followed by mechanization and the use of power machinery. The results of these changes cannot be isolated and explained in cause-and-effect terms because of the multiplicity of intervening variables. For simplicity, the effects may be summarized in two groups: direct and indirect.

The direct effects relate to agricultural production, organization, and tenure. The changes experienced in the last two centuries have caused radical increases in production and productivity. The countries of Europe have been able to keep up with population increases and raise the standard of living of their rural populations. The interest in commercial farming has brought agriculture into the sphere of the market economy, or exchange, whether capitalistic or socialistic. Consequently, the tenure arrangements have become secure either as private or as collective property. The farmer as operator on the land has gained full security of his holding and of any improvements he might make on it.

At the same time, the farmer has become responsive to events in other sectors of the economy as well as to the conditions in other countries. Isolationism, which was closely related to subsistence farming, has faded into history. By the same token, however, the farmer has become more vulnerable to fluctuations in demand and supply outside agriculture, especially in view of his growing specialization.

Finally, a major effect of the changes in agriculture has been the liberation of the rural population from tradition, subjugation, and fatalism. The new individual has become freer, more mobile, and much more productive than his forefathers. He has also become more dynamic; he no longer accepts any situation as given, but tries to find solutions to his problems. The farmer has demonstrated his ability to adjust in the development of cooperatives to handle the problems of supply and production. Such a population represents the potential on which the new economies have been built.

The indirect effects of the changes in agriculture relate to other sectors of the economy. European agriculture made impor-

tant contributions to industrial development. Agriculture provided the food to sustain the urban workers. It also released the labor necessary to man the other sectors as well as overseas economies. By using machinery and fertilizers, agriculture created a market for industrial products. Probably its most important contribution was its response to industrial demand and the expansion of industrial crop production. This challenge and response formed the cornerstone of development. Although the agricultural revolution might have been a prerequisite for the industrial revolution, its greater significance lies in its step-by-step acceptance of the challenge and its timely response.

BIBLIOGRAPHY

Bandini, Mario, *et al.*, *Agriculture and Economic Growth*, Paris: Organization for Economic Cooperation and Development, 1965.

Chambers, J. D., and G. E. Mingay, *The Agricultural Revolution 1750–1880*, New York: Schocken Books, 1966.

Clough, S. B., *The Economic History of Italy*, New York: Columbia University Press, 1964, chap. 4.

Deane, Phyllis, and W. A. Cole, *British Economic Growth 1688–1959*, New York: Cambridge University Press, 1967.

Denmark, Geographical Handbook series, Washington: Naval Intelligence Division, 1944, chap. 11.

Eddie, Scott M., "The Changing Pattern of Land Ownership in Hungary, 1867–1914," *Economic History Review*, 2nd series, XX, No. 2 (Aug. 1967), pp. 293–310. Contains comparative data on other European countries.

Fairlie, Susan, "The Corn Laws and British Wheat Production," *Economic History Review*, 2nd series, XXII, No. 1 (April 1969), pp. 88–116.

Fay, C. R., *Cooperation at Home and Abroad*, London: P. S. King and Sons, 1908, pp. 79–179.

Habakkuk, H. J., and M. M. Postan (eds.), *Cambridge Economic History of Europe*, VI, New York: Cambridge University Press, 1965.

Heckscher, E. F., *An Economic History of Sweden*, Cambridge, Mass.: Harvard University Press, 1954, chap. 6.

Henderson, W. O., *Studies in the Economic Policies of Frederick the Great*, London: Frank Cass and Co., 1963.

Hobsbawm, E. J., *The Age of Revolution, 1789–1848,* New York: New American Library (Mentor Books), 1964, chap. 8.

Hooker, Elizabeth R., *Readjustments of Agricultural Tenure in Ireland,* Chapel Hill, N.C.: University of North Carolina Press, 1938, chaps. 1–6.

Lenin, V. I., *Development of Capitalism in Russia,* Moscow: Foreign Language Publishing House, 1956, chaps. 3 and 4.

Lyaschenko, P. I., *History of the National Economy of Russia,* New York: Macmillan, 1949, chaps. 17, 23, 36.

Mitrany, David, *Marx Against the Peasant,* Chapel Hill, N.C.: University of North Carolina Press, 1951, chaps. 8–10.

"New Agrarian Legislation in Central Europe. A Comparative Study," *International Labor Review,* VI. No. 3 (Sept. 1922), pp. 327–363.

Ojala, E. M., *Agriculture and Economic Program,* New York: Oxford University Press, 1952.

Statistical Abstracts of the United States, Washington: U.S. Government Printing Office, 1962.

Thompson, F. M. L., "The Second Agricultural Revolution, 1815–1880," *Economic History Review,* XXI, No. 1 (April 1968), pp. 62–77.

Tracy, Michael, *Agriculture in Western Europe* [Since 1880], New York: Frederick A. Praeger, 1964.

Tuma, E. H., *Twenty-Six Centuries of Agrarian Reform,* Berkeley: University of California Press, 1965, chaps. 5–7.

Van Bath, B. H. Slicher, *The Agrarian History of Western Europe,* London: Edward Arnold, 1963.

Vicens Vives, Jaime, *An Economic History of Spain,* Princeton: Princeton University Press, 1969.

Warriner, Doreen (ed.), *Contrasts in Emerging Societies,* Bloomington: Indiana University Press, 1965.

The relative decline of agriculture at a time when total output and per capita income were increasing was largely the result of the relative advance of the nonagricultural sectors. While the services or tertiary sectors also increased in relative importance, they did so primarily because new agricultural and industrial products were becoming available and required services for their distribution and exchange.

Industry and manufacturing absorbed large segments of the labor force, created demand for agricultural and service products, increased both the total output and the per capita income, and stimulated a more rational organization of economic enterprises. For example, a much larger part of the British labor force became engaged in manufacturing, industry, and mining in the nineteenth century. While 29.7 percent were engaged in these occupations in 1801, there were 42.9 percent in them in 1851 and 46.3 percent in 1901. Subsequent percentage increases have been minor. A similar change took place in the contribution of these sectors to the national income. The contribution in 1801 was 23.4 percent; it was 34.3 percent in 1851 and 40.2 percent in 1901. Eight more percentage points were gained in the first half of the twentieth century. This pattern of change was true of other countries, although it was later and less dramatic than in Britain. As late as 1861–1865 Italian industry employed only 18.1 percent of the labor force and contributed only 20.3 percent of the total output; in 1901–1905 the estimates were 24.3 percent and 21.3 percent respectively; in 1926–1930 they were 24.7 and 31.7 percent. However, a more rapid change came in the last two decades so that by 1951–1955 32.2 percent of the labor force worked in industry and contributed 45.8 percent of the total output. In eastern Europe, Spain, Portugal, and certainly Russia, the change was quite late, occurring mostly in the last half-century.

Industry and manufacturing stimulated the introduction and expansion of new products which had little traditional demand, and which required new elements of entrepreneurship and sources of finance. Since risks were higher than in agriculture, a relatively more aggressive attitude was necessary. A break with tradition had to be effected and new demands created. Unless these conditions could be satisfied, development did not proceed in response to the market. In some cases government policy and planning were substituted for the market to consciously foster change. The two approaches were sometimes combined in a policy of aiding the market by programs favorable to development.

Interest in development, whether private or public, was helpful, but by itself it was hardly sufficient. Success depended on available resources and technology, the nature of the product, the scope of the market, the complementary sectors, and the degree of competition from other countries. Certain products were easier to develop than others and industrialization was easier in certain periods than in others. However, some observations are generally applicable.

OBSERVATIONS ON INDUSTRIALIZATION

1. Economic science became more relevant in this period, particularly in industry. There was a growing tendency for nations to respond to the market and to specialize in those areas in which they had a comparative advantage. Where such principles were applied, there was a tendency toward freedom of trade and international competition. This tendency favored early industrializers, especially Britain. However, as international competition became stiffer, and as political, nationalistic, or doctrinal objectives were injected into the situation, the market mechanism became frustrated or even irrelevant.

Late comers to industrialization tended to depend on protection, government intervention, or total planning. They were less willing to accept the gradualism of the market or its cruelties. They were anxious to foster rapid industrialization along lines known in advance so as to preclude what they considered unacceptable results. France and Germany, which developed later than Britain, combined the market mechanism with government intervention and protection. Soviet Russia abandoned the market in its desire for rapid planned industrialization. Any evaluation of these various approaches is usually value-loaded. However, the reader will find it profitable to make his own evaluation from the sociopolitical standpoint, as well as from the point of view of economic theory and analysis or efficiency of allocation and production.

2. Textiles have traditionally been front-runners in development. This is a result of the relatively high demand for textile products, their place in domestic industry, and the technical feasibility of their manufacture. Textiles can be manufactured under many different conditions, with a wide variety of techniques, both primitive and sophisticated. Textiles are also highly divisible so that manufacturing can be carried out on various scales, including those requiring little initial capital investment.

However, even textiles are not uniformly susceptible to industrialization or development. Wool was traditionally the main raw material of textile manufacturing until cotton took over. Cotton had many features to recommend it. It had no tradition to break away from. It was less subject to climate and weather fluctuations. Its supply was more elastic than that of other textile raw material. And it could be produced relatively cheaply. Therefore, as soon as technical facilities became available, cotton proved to be the textile to develop.

3. Like technology, industrialization was cumulative in its progress and effects. Knowledge and skill were cumulative, as were the material resources. For example, once one raw material was obtained from an area, any other raw materials that existed there became accessible. Moreover, raw material was often purchased in exchange for a finished product.

Industrialization was cumulative in another way. As the demand for capital increased, financing became a limiting factor. Industrialization thus helped create the financial institutions which fostered further industrialization. And as industrialization proceeded, self-financing gained in importance and profits were plowed back into the business.

The cumulative effects of industrialization were in part multiplier effects and in part demonstration effects. As incomes rose demand also rose, and as new products came onto the market the expectations for more and varied consumption also rose. Industry had no option but to respond. Hence industrialization bred industrialization.

4. Industrialization is dynamic in the sense that modification becomes necessary as new techniques become available. Unless an industry adopts the latest techniques, it may lose its place in the market. On one hand, this dynamism may require radical reorganization which may lead to concentration of capital; on the other, it may require rapid capital depreciation to take care of technical obsolescence. To a certain extent these two aspects explain some of the features of industrialization in the late-comer countries noted by Gerschenkron in Chapter 3. To adopt the latest techniques and to face the stiff competition of the early comers required much larger-scale enterprises. Large-scale businesses required large amounts of capital and hence large banks and financial institutions; they also had to produce for relatively large markets, which often led to monopolistic practices or controlled markets. In contrast, early comers had to either modernize or face the threat of displacement by their emulators, who started their businesses with the latest technique.

This process was evident both within and among countries, and in it lay the seeds of internal concentration and international conflicts, as the history of the last century clearly suggests. In the rest of this chapter we shall survey industrialization in the various countries of Europe, the major industries developed, and the pattern of specialization. Some emphasis will be put on the rate at which the new technologies were adopted.

INDUSTRIAL INNOVATION AND GROWTH

The trends

The industrial revolution in Britain has been variously dated by different people, but all seem to agree that it began in the second half of the eighteenth century. France was, until 1815, producing more industrial products in terms of total value than England did. However, in terms of per capita output, productivity, or rates of growth, France was far behind. Indeed, most observers regard the fourth decade of the nineteenth century as the beginning of industrialization in France. Germany's development was more rapid than that of France, but it did not take place until after the middle of the century. Scandinavia was farther behind, industrializing in the third or fourth quarter of the nineteenth century. Eastern Europe had hardly industrialized before the first quarter of the twentieth century. Russia's industrialization has been a subject of debate. Some observers have considered 1890–1914 as the period of takeoff. However, in terms of percentage of labor force employed in industry and industrial contribution to the national income, Russia's industrial revolution belongs to the Soviet period, especially after 1928.

This brief survey suggests that a chronological examination of industrialization would be inappropriate. It is probably more enlightening to observe the period of rapid advance for each of these countries, taking the preindustrialization period as a point of departure. However, since the available data are not fully comparable, caution is necessary in interpreting the estimates.

The growth of industry in Britain shows a big jump after 1750. The domestic or household industries of the eighteenth century continued to grow, their real output rising from an index of 100 in 1700 to 152 in 1800. In contrast, total industry and commerce, which grew at relatively equal rates, increased from an index of 100 in 1700 to only 148 in 1750, although the rise was more dramatic after that. The index rose to 179 in 1760, to 199 in 1770, declined to 147 in 1780, but rose again to 285 in 1790 and 387 in 1800.

The rapid growth experienced in the last two decades of the eighteenth century may have been associated with war mobilization,

Table 19.1. World net income from manufacturing (Million international units)[a]

	AUS-TRIA	BEL-GIUM	BUL-GARIA	CZECHO-SLO-VAKIA	DEN-MARK	FIN-LAND	FRANCE	GER-MANY	HUN-GARY	IRE-LAND	ITALY
1860	—	—	—	—	—	—	615	689	—	—	—
1870–1874	—	—	—	—	—	—	750	966	—	—	146
1875–1879	—	—	—	—	—	—	—	1062	—	—	—
1880–1884	—	239	—	—	—	—	968	1250	—	—	209
1885–1889	—	265	—	—	—	15	995	1568	—	—	290
1890–1894	—	290	—	—	—	19	1171	1900	—	—	345
1895–1899	—	362	—	—	—	30	1480	2610	—	—	442
1900–1904	—	397	—	—	—	36	1490	3236	—	—	530
1905–1909	—	487	—	—	—	43	1798	3845	—	—	735
1910–1913	231	616	—	447	159	58	2245	3647	175	—	829
1920–1924	168	523	—	436	193	66	2365	3170	118	—	935
1925–1929	254	807	—	673	212	115	3310	4864	170	—	1395
1930–1934	198	665	115	550	245	117	3105	3945	—	—	1169
1935	268	751	—	434	311	176	3010	6372	186	—	1503
1948	269	826	—	—	343	250	2890	2330[b]	—	132	1510
1949	365	826	—	—	373	259	3180	—	—	149	1692
1950	432	843	—	—	416	294	3180	—	—	164	1948

but it continued through the first three decades of the nineteenth century. After that period a high annual compound rate of over 3 percent was maintained throughout the century except for the early 1850s and the 1870s. The first decline was related to the famines of the 1840s in Ireland, and to the beginning of the period of free trade and the advent of the late comers into the market. The second decline reflected the intensification of competition, the depression of the 1870s and the beginning of the period of protectionism. It should be noted, however, that these rates are averages which tend to hide short-run fluctuations.

German industrialization belongs to the nineteenth century. Certain attempts to improve the textile industries, mining, and porcelain were made during the days of Frederick the Great. However, actual development began after 1815 and more conspicuously after 1834 when a customs union, the *Zollverein*, was established to unify the market. The actual takeoff period is considered to have been between 1850 and 1870. During the last quarter of the nineteenth century Germany's industrialization was probably the fastest in Europe. In part this

was due to the nation's position as a late comer and emulator, and to the significant role played by political forces, especially after Bismark unified the country in 1871.

The industrialization of France was gradual, compared to both Britain and Germany, although French per capita income was comparable to incomes in both these countries. After the Napoleonic Wars many attempts were made to industrialize. New techniques were utilized and new enterprises set up. Nevertheless, the period of major growth was after the middle of the century. This delay was due in part to internal obstacles and rigidities in the socioeconomic structure, but it was also due to the relatively high dependence on agriculture and the lack of pressure for rapid industrialization.

A much slower growth rate characterized Italian industry, although a beginning may be observed around the end of the nineteenth century. A significant rise in Italian industrialization occurred only in the second decade of the twentieth century, and it was much more dramatic after the Second World War. In Spain three periods of industrialization have been noted. The first was prior to 1832, during which time there was only

	NETHER-LANDS	NOR-WAY	PO-LAND	PORTU-GAL	RUMA-NIA	RUS-SIA	SPAIN	SWE-DEN	SWIT-ZER-LAND	U.K.	YUGO-SLA-VIA
1860	—	—	—	—	—	73	—	—	—	1025	—
1870–1874	—	—	—	—	—	—	—	45	—	1478	—
1875–1879	—	—	—	—	—	—	—	59	—	1512	—
1880–1884	—	—	—	—	—	156	—	72	—	1759	—
1885–1889	—	—	—	—	—	208	—	93	—	1832	—
1890–1894	—	—	—	—	—	280	—	134	—	1982	—
1895–1899	—	—	—	—	—	411	—	236	—	2236	—
1900–1904	—	—	—	—	—	545	—	298	—	2347	—
1905–1909	—	—	—	—	—	622	257	356	—	2545	—
1910–1913	314	95	200	—	110	837	282	411	286	2806	—
1920–1924	368	104	260	—	77	181	310	409	244	3060	—
1925–1929	508	128	339	—	128	862	424	570	296	4020	—
1930–1934	584	134	293	—	150	1401	432	675	242	3920	—
1935	755	175	413	—	191	2740	—	948	222	5205	580
1948	947	274	—	—	—	—	555	1525	—	6201	—
1949	1070	287	—	—	—	—	536	1585	—	6632	—
1950	1175	303	—	55	—	—	584	1645	—	7186	—

a International unit (I.U.) is a standardized measure used for comparative purposes. "One I.U. of real income was taken as the quantity of goods exchangeable for $1 in the U.S.A. over the average of the decade 1925–34" (p. 18).   *b West Germany only.*
SOURCE: *Colin Clark,* The Conditions of Economic Progress, *Table VII (opp. p. 335).*

scattered industry. The second period was between 1833 and 1869. During these years development was faster and mechanized techniques were adopted. However, rapid development came only in the third period, between 1869 and 1898. Since then manufacturing has continued at a relatively constant but slow pace.

Swedish industrialization became evident around the turn of the nineteenth century. However, if an industrial revolution existed, it certainly belongs more to this century. The Low Countries were quite advanced early in the twentieth century, but industrialization in the Netherlands and Belgium was gradual rather than revolutionary. Progress was steady and per capita output of industrial products compared favorably with any other European country throughout the nineteenth and twentieth centuries. In eastern Europe industrialization came only in the twentieth century, and has been especially rapid in the last two decades.

Observers of Russian economic history have noted rapid development in the last quarter of the nineteenth century, especially between 1890 and 1900. This may be called the period of takeoff in comparison with Russia's earlier history, if one gives weight to specific strategic industries. However, in terms of total industrial output, or of the potentialities of such a giant country, these developments were minor. Industrialization was scattered, uncoordinated, and not easily sustainable until it was taken over by the Soviet government, especially after 1928.

These observations of the pattern of industrialization are illustrated by the estimates in Table 19.1, although the recent past will be surveyed more fully in Chapter 24. These figures must be interpreted with great care. First, the estimates include a variety of manufactures, including food processing, buildings, textiles, and heavy industry. How much of the estimated values may be classified as industrialization is not clear. Second, they represent total manufacturing output regardless of the size of the population. A higher figure does not necessarily represent more industrialization than a lower figure.

Their significance lies rather in the light they shed on the rate of change in each country and the periods in which the rate seems to have increased radically. These estimates should be studied in conjunction with the population estimates of Table 16.1 (p. 202).

Given these precautions, the estimates of industrial output show that as late as 1860 the United Kingdom, with a smaller population than either France or Germany, produced almost 1.5 times as much as either of them. They also show that France never caught up with either Germany or Britain, a fact which suggests the continuing significance of agriculture in the French economy. In contrast Germany, which was far behind Britain, increased its industrialization so radically that it took the lead by 1890–1894. From that time until 1948, when East and West Germany were divided, Germany was producing more industrial output than Britain in most years.

The Low Countries appear to be relatively highly industrialized in these estimates. Belgium and the Netherlands combined had less than half of the population of Spain, and less than one-fourth of that of Italy. Yet each produced more industrial products than Spain, and their combined production exceeded that of Italy until 1950. On the other hand Sweden with a population slightly smaller than that of Belgium and about the same as that of the Netherlands was behind both of them until 1925–1929. Since then, however, Sweden has industrialized rapidly enough to surpass both. The Swedish experience is interesting because of the recent rapid change. From 45 million I.U.'s (International Units) in 1870–1874, the output increased to 356 million I.U.'s in 1905–1909, and to 1645 million in 1950, a rate almost comparable with that of Germany, although achieved half a century later.

Russia showed underindustrialization throughout the nineteenth century. As late as 1905–1909, Russia produced only 622 million I.U.'s, which was a little more than France's output in 1860 and less than that of Germany in the same year. The period of industrialization began in 1925–1929, and output increased from 862 million I.U.'s to 2740 million in 10 years. The value added in industry, in 1928 prices, increased from 6.5 billion rubles in 1928 to 54 billion rubles in 1940 and to 75.7 billion rubles in 1950, or about 12 times in 22 years and twice that much in the following 8 years.

These observations show that industrialization came at different times to different countries, even though science and technology had already made it possible. Furthermore, the rate of industrialization was not uniform; there were fluctuations for various reasons in the different countries. Only some of the late comers were able to develop more rapidly than the early industrializers.

However, these sketchy observations do not tell which industries developed and the rates at which they did. All the European countries experienced extensive changes in some industries, even though their total output might have remained limited.

The growing industries

In surveying the industrial developments in Europe, we will first examine some countries that hardly developed at all before the twentieth century—the eastern European nations and Russia—and others that developed late but slowly—namely, Spain and Italy. In the remainder of the section we shall discuss those countries which have industrialized quite extensively, whether early or late, namely, Sweden, France, Belgium, Germany, and the United Kingdom. We shall deal with each country separately, giving some comparative illustrations. The reader may find it profitable to undertake a systematic comparison.

Eastern Europe. The least industrialized region before 1900 was probably eastern Europe. The relative abundance of land and the rigidities of the political and social institutions seem to have kept agriculture the main source of income. Nevertheless, some manufacturing was carried out, mostly in domestic or putting-out industries. Available data are not sufficient to estimate the amounts produced before the end of the nineteenth century, however.

Hungary manufactured soap and tobacco in large quantities, but mostly for home consumption. Leather and hides were also processed. Wool, cotton, and linen textiles were produced mostly in the homes and for home use. Wax and wine were items of industry and trade. There were some sugar refineries. In heavy industry only very small quantities of iron and steel were produced. Earthenware products were made for local use and for trade. Hungary's economy remained, throughout the century, dependent on the production of raw minerals such as gold, silver, and salt; on cattle; and on the vineyards. Nevertheless, by the middle of the century some change was taking place. Steam mills had come into use by the middle of the century. It is estimated that by 1846 there were 40 industrial establishments in Budapest, 7 of which produced agricultural machinery. It is said that by the end of the century Budapest was an industrial center. In 1890 it had 371 factories and employed about 30 percent of its population in industrial production. By this time steamboats had come into use and some gas works and chemical industries had been established. Even ship-building had been expanded. Nevertheless, Hungary's industrial output was still one of the lowest in Europe even though the country had as large a population as Belgium and a larger one than the Netherlands throughout the period.

Rumania was similar to Hungary in the first half of the nineteenth century. Most of its manufacturing was carried out in Bucharest in domestic workshops. Textiles headed the list, especially cotton. Silk and fur were also produced, as were leather and glass. Other manufacturing was related to agricultural products. By the end of the century there was a decline in most of these industries, but in the meantime a new source of

industrial output was gaining significance. By the middle of the century petroleum was being produced by foreign capital and native joint-stock companies. The oil industries eventually became a monopoly of the Rumanian joint-stock company, *Steana Română*, which also distributed about 90 percent of all the oil produced. Production of oil increased from 30,000 double quintals in 1862 to 139,000 in 1873, 74,000 in 1886, 286,000 in 1896, and 1,341,000 in 1897–1898. It was up by another 25 percent in 1899. By the end of the century there were 73 refineries. However, only 10 of these were modern; the rest produced a petroleum of poor quality. The third quarter of the century saw the rise of two other industries: the timber industry, stimulated by the demand for railways; and ship-building, stimulated by oil and salt exports. While the development of petroleum was important to the economy, its impact on industrialization was limited, since few linkages were developed as a result. Rumania's industrial output remained among the lowest in Europe even during the first four decades of the twentieth century.[1]

Bulgaria and Yugoslavia were equally underindustrialized. Their main products were textiles, wines, baskets, mats, and other household items. Until around the end of the century most production was in domestic workshops. As late as 1930 Bulgaria, with a population twice that of agrarian Denmark, was producing less than half of the latter's output in manufacturing. Yugoslavia, with a population a little less than twice that of Belgium, was producing about two-thirds of the latter's manufacturing output as late as 1935–1938.

Russia. Pre-Soviet Russia had much in common with the eastern European countries. Attempts were made by the state and by private entrepreneurs to create new in-

---

[1] Some present-day oil-producing countries, such as Saudi Arabia and Iraq, also illustrate the limited impact of oil drilling on industrialization.

Table 19.2. Russian industry, 1804–1865

TYPE OF INDUSTRY	NUMBER OF PLANTS			NUMBER OF WORKERS		
	1804	1830	1860	1804	1830	1860
Textiles	1,006	1,351	2,416	69,742	184,333	303,832
Sugar	10	57	467	108	1,607	64,763
Iron	28	198	693	4,121	19,889	54,832
All others	1,646	3,706	5,986	20,117	46,425	81,191
Total	2,680	5,306	9,562	90,379	202,253	505,408

SOURCE: *William L. Blackwell*, The Beginnings of Russian Industrialization, *p. 423.*

dustries in the eighteenth century. Catherine II expanded industry conspicuously, especially textile factories and iron works. After a relapse, similar attempts were made in the first half of the nineteenth century. However, the breakthrough in industrialization, if there was one in the pre-Soviet era, came around 1890.

As early as 1710 there were 41 private and state plants in Russia producing iron. The number increased to 109 by the end of the eighteenth century. In 1725 there were 11 plants producing woolens and 7 producing linen; by 1812 there were 261 and 214 such plants, respectively. The expansion in the nineteenth century prior to Emancipation may be shown by the number of plants and workers in Russian industry given in Table 19.2.

The textile factories had as many workers in cotton as in wool in 1860. The number of people in the linen industry was a small fraction of the total. The machine industry expanded in this period from 19 plants in 1851 to 99 in 1860 and to 126 in 1865, with the number of workers increasing from 1,349 in 1851 to 17,284 in 1865. This general expansion was accompanied by some mechanization. Steam power was in use in 1805 and the first mechanical loom was used in 1808. By 1850 there were 2,000 mechanical looms; there were 18,000 in 1861. However, most of the weaving was done in the homes, which employed 80,000 hand looms in 1861. Finally, the mining industry, which employed 82,000 in 1804, was employing 245,000 in 1861. Given the population and

potential of Russia, this industrialization was still minor, however. Russian manufacturing output in 1860 was about 7 percent of that of the United Kingdom and about 11 percent of that of Germany or France.

The release of rural labor, expansion of the railways, the formation of joint-stock companies, the government's interest in development, and the European fever for industrialization in the mid-nineteenth century had a great impact on Russia. Traditional industries were expanded and new ones created. Russia's pattern of industrial development up to 1913 is shown in Table 19.3. As can be seen, the advances continued throughout the period except in 1908, which was a period of crisis because of an apparent overinvestment in the previous year and possibly the political unrest in 1905–1906. This advance in production was also accompanied by mechanization and the use of power. For example, there were 11,000 power weaving looms in 1861 and 87,000 in 1890. Most of the production, however, was still based on manual power.

This expansion can easily be exaggerated. With a population equal to the combined populations of the United Kingdom, France, and Germany, Russia's output was about 30 percent of that of the United Kingdom in 1910–1913, about 37 percent of that of France, and about 23 percent of that of Germany. As has been mentioned above, Russia's rapid and general industrialization came in the Soviet period. The Soviets had three main objectives in this respect: nationalization, industrialization, and the

Table 19.3.   Russian industrial production, 1870–1913   (Million poods)[a]

	1870	1887	1890	1900	1908	1913
Pig iron	21.3	36.1	54.8	176.8	171.1	283.0
Coal	60.0	276.2	366.5	986.4	1,608.5	2,215.0
Iron and steel	—	35.5	48.3	163.0	147.5	256.5
Oil	1.6	155.0	226.0	631.1	528.6	561.3
Cotton (requirements)	—	11.5	8.3	16.0	21.2	25.9
Sugar	—	25.9	24.6	48.5	76.7	75.4

[a] *Pood or pud: a dry measure equal to 16.38 kilograms or 36.116 pounds.*
SOURCE: Cambridge Economic History of Europe, *VI*, pp. 837–844.

spreading of industry to all parts of the country. They achieved all three objectives by planning, as will be seen later.

Spain.   Spain, which had been a leading commercial country, was left behind in the age of industrialization. Spain had crafts which had competed on the international market for centuries. However, a decline was experienced between 1650 and 1750. This has been attributed to competition from Britain and the Low Countries, the restrictive policies of the guilds, the deviation of Spanish prices from European prices, and political interventions. To correct some of these obstacles, the government in the second half of the eighteenth century tried to foster the building of large-scale factories. The fact that these factories were creations of the government has been considered a factor in Spain's economic decline in the early nineteenth century. As soon as government subsidy was removed, these factories declined, leaving Spain with only scattered industry, mostly in a putting-out framework.

Expansion and mechanization of textiles came between 1832 and 1869 when the mechanical loom and the steam engine were introduced. The self-acting mule was introduced in 1844, about two decades after its invention. Steam power was also used in the textile industry. The thrust of change in the cotton industry came after 1868. Data are not complete, but they do give some indications. In Catalonia alone there were 97,786 workers in cotton in 1842; in 1860 there were 125,000. The number of looms in the

same period increased from 27,204 to 37,640. The number of spindles declined due to mechanization. The horsepower applied in textiles increased from 2,095 in 1842 to 7,800 in 1860. In the third period the advance is indicated by the consumption of raw cotton, represented in Figure 19.1, which also shows the fluctuations in the cotton industry. In contrast to cotton, the silk industry declined in this period. While Valencia alone produced 800,000 kilograms of cocoons in 1852, Spain as a whole did not produce that much in 1900. There were no real attempts to modernize the industry. Woolens were expanded, although not as much as cotton.

Spain's industrial production also depended on mining. Spain has rich mines of copper, lead, iron, and mercury. The mining industry suffered a decline early in the nineteenth century, but was revived between 1839 and 1869, during which time 56 new companies were established in Catalonia alone. In 1868 the government leased the mines in perpetuity against a given royalty. From then on expansion became conspicuous, especially in the mining of iron ore and soft coal. The iron-manufacturing industry was also positively affected by the new developments. Soft-coal mines produced 450,000 metric tons in 1865, 946,000 in 1885, and 2,647,000 metric tons in 1900. The production of iron of all kinds was about 54,000 metric tons in 1865, about 135,000 in 1880, and 594,000 metric tons in 1900. The production of steel was minor until 1880, 445 metric tons, but reached 166,000 in 1900. It

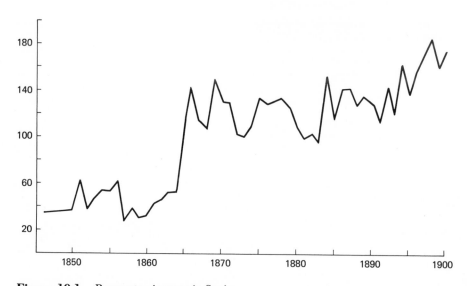

Figure 19.1   Raw cotton imports in Spain.
SOURCE: Jaime Vicens Vives, *An Economic History of Spain*, p. 671.

may be noted that processed iron contributed only 10 percent of the ore mined in
Spain. Exports took the rest.

The chemical and electrical equipment
industries were expanded late in the nineteenth century but their contribution to
Spanish industrialization was limited. Probably the most important industry was cork-
making. The cork industry had both positive
and negative effects. As the number of corks
exported increased from 500 million in 1860
to about 3 billion annually between 1890 and
1900, deforestation proceeded at a similar
rate with little attention paid to conservation. Spain has suffered the results ever
since.

These data show clearly that some industrialization took place in Spain, especially in
the second half of the nineteenth century.
Much of it, however, related to agriculture
and mining. The degree of mechanization
expanded gradually through this period, as
did the shift to steam power. The steam
engine capacity of Spain increased from
20,000 horsepower in 1860 to 220,000 in
1880 and to 510,000 horsepower in 1900.
Yet, in comparison with the other European
countries, Spain was still underindustrial-

ized. Spain was thus a late comer to industrialization whose growth rate was nevertheless not rapid.

Italy.   Italy's industrialization came probably as late as that of Russia and, except
for the Iberian peninsula, Italy was the
slowest nation in western Europe to industrialize. Some beginnings were made early in
the nineteenth century, but the pace was
slow. The country was divided and foreign
competition was very stiff. Therefore the
results were modest until unification, despite
the fact that some mechanization had already taken place. The textile industry was
expanding in Lombardy and Piedmont.
Some machine-building, arms manufacture,
and production of mechanical looms and
printing presses existed by 1860, employing
about 9000 workers in that year. Nevertheless, as late as 1870–1874 Italy's manufacturing output was less than one-fifth of that
of France, less than one-sixth of that of
Germany, and about one-tenth of that of the
United Kingdom. Indeed, most observers
date Italy's industrialization from 1880 or a
little later, when growth became continuous
until the 1930s and, after a slight depression,

Table 19.4.   Industrial change in Italy, 1881–1913

	MINING 1900 = 100	METAL WORKING[a] 1900 = 100	TEXTILES, SILK AND COTTON 1900 = 100	IRON AND STEEL CONSUMPTION 1900 = 100	BEER AND SUGAR OUTPUT 1900 = 100	CHEMICALS OUTPUT 1900 = 100
1881	71	22	54	62	1.7	8.7
1891	76	72	73	62	3.8	27.9
1901	103	103	105	100	122.0	102.4
1911	89	377	128	287	309.0	259.7
1913	98	381	134	272	465.0	280.9

[a] *Including oil.*
SOURCE: *Alexander Gerschenkron,* Economic Backwardness in Historical Perspective, *extracted from Appendix I, pp. 367–421.*

continued at a slow but steady pace. However, as late as 1948 Italy's output of manufactures was half that of France, about fourth that of the United Kingdom, and slightly more than that of Sweden, which had one-sixth of Italy's population in 1950.

Italy's problem was one of duality between a highly industrialized North and a highly underindustrialized South. The aggregate figures hide this fact, as well as the industries that developed. Table 19.4 shows the distribution of industrial growth among the various sections. In evaluating his own findings, Gerschenkron concludes that mining developed slowly although steadily throughout the period. A relapse was apparent at the beginning of the twentieth century. Metal-making developed at a high rate, especially between 1896 and 1908. Textiles developed at a moderate rate, although the very slow pace between 1901 and 1913 resulting from difficulties in the silk industry was a serious setback. It may be noted further that beer, sugar, and chemicals developed at a very high rate. In addition, Italy continued to produce woolen textiles, which expanded at almost the same rate as cotton in this period. Another industry in which Italy had a tradition, ship-building, was revived, although on a relatively small scale. The production of electricity was an important factor in Italy's industrialization; from 3 million kilowatt hours produced annually between 1881 and 1891, the annual production between 1911

and 1920 reached 3192 million kilowatt hours. The trend was continued in later years. These observations suggest that the big jump in industrialization in Italy came between 1891 and 1901 and became very dramatic in the first decade of the century. Indeed, if one may speak of an industrial revolution in Italy, it should be placed between 1891 and 1911.

Sweden.   Transformation of the Swedish economy began early in the nineteenth century. The mining industry grew at an annual rate of 3 percent between 1830 and 1860. The textile industry expanded more than 20 fold in that period. The value of industrial production grew about 10 percent a year. Nevertheless, while Sweden's population was more than 80 percent of that of Belgium in 1880, its manufacturing output was less than one-third of the latter's.

The 1870s may be regarded as the beginning of sustained industrialization. From 1870 to 1914, Sweden's industrial output grew at an average annual rate of 4.4 percent, compared with a 2.8 percent growth rate of the national income. The value of industrial output in the same period multiplied seven-fold and investment in machinery was multiplied nine times.

Sweden's industrial development was closely associated with timber, iron and steel, chemicals, and engineering. Timber was important for its own sake and as the

Table 19.5. Annual percentage rates of growth in Swedish industry

INDUSTRY	1867–1869 TO 1892–1895	1896 TO 1912
Paper, pulp, and graphic	6.1	11.0
Gravel, stone, caly, etc.	6.0	5.0
Food and tobacco	5.1	4.0
Chemicals	4.5	7.3
Metal and engineering	3.7	7.0
Timber	3.7	2.0
Iron and steel	3.2	2.2
Textiles	2.6	5.6
Leather, hair, rubber	1.7	10.0
Capital goods	5.2	6.2
Consumer goods	3.3	6.1

SOURCE: *Lennert Jörberg, "Structural Change and Economic Growth: Sweden in the 19th Century,"* Economy and History, *VIII (1965), p. 33.*

source of paper and pulp. Sweden was the first country to adopt a chemical pulp factory which produced high-quality paper. Her steel remained of the highest quality and all the latest techniques were adopted immediately upon their invention. Mechanization and use of power were rapid once they had become technically feasible. From a steam-engine capacity of 20,000 horsepower in 1860, Sweden grew to a capacity of 510,000 horsepower in 1896.

The pattern of growth of the various industries is shown in Table 19.5. The order in which these industries have been presented is not indicative of their relative significance. Even the changes in their growth rates may be deceptive. For example, the traditional industries such as timber, iron and steel, and even textiles could not be expected to grow at the same rates as the new industries which started at a very low level. The significance of these industries will be seen in the next section. However, within this period of less than half a century, Sweden was transformed from an underindustrialized agrarian economy to a highly industrialized country. The output of manufactures was higher than that of the Netherlands and slightly less than that of Belgium; it soon surpassed both of them.

France. French industrialization was probably the most gradual in Europe. In fact, it may be said to have extended over the last two centuries. Therefore, its effects have not always been dramatic, particularly because industrial and economic developments experienced recurrent relapses. Since such relapses were often interpreted as symptoms of weakness among the established industries, a new start seems to have been expected after each one. From 1750 to 1850, French industries owed so much to government intervention, war, and protection that when they were left on their own they were unable to sustain themselves. Another problem, related to the above, was the country's political instability and the interdependence between the pattern of economic change and the political regimes in power. This interdependence is probably why French industrialization has often been divided into periods coinciding with the life of the respective governments: the Napoleonic era, 1815–1830, 1830–1848, 1848–1870, and 1870–1914.

Whether this periodization has any significance is not clear, except that until 1848 France was preparing for more rapid advance. Communications had been improved, finances had become accessible, and awareness of the need to develop had become more intense. The Napoleonic Code, which had reaffirmed and strengthened the institution of private property, and the Patent Law passed by the Assembly were important sources of security and incentives. A more direct stimulation to industry had come from Napoleon's continental system, which excluded British goods from the continent and thus secured a safe market for industries under French rule. As a result various industries had been expanded. Sugar beet began to replace sugar cane; Le Blanc soda replaced Spanish soda, which was no longer accessible; indigo from native wood was developed to substitute for the lost foreign products. The effects, however, were not always felt within the boundaries of France.

Cotton expanded in Ghent, woolens in Cologne and Aachen, and mechanical engineering in Belgium. Some of the advances were felt also in France itself, where machine-building and chemicals were expanded. However, as soon as the continental system broke down, some of these industries suffered serious relapses. Furthermore, the system caused dislocations in the port cities and industries which had depended on trade with Britain. It is therefore not clear whether the continental system was advantageous to development.

The reconstruction after the Napoleonic Wars and the following three decades witnessed additional expansion in various industries. Most of the emphasis was on building a framework of roads, canals, and railways. By European standards, France was quite advanced in industrial production, being exceeded only by the United Kingdom until the middle of the nineteenth century. New techniques were adopted as soon as they became available, although they spread quite slowly. The first coke furnace was established in 1785 and the first hot blast furnace was introduced in 1830, but many years passed before either technique came into general use. The Bessemer process was adopted as soon as it was perfected, although the puddling process spread very slowly. Yet France had 230 blast furnaces in 1819 and produced 112,500 tons of pig iron; steel production in that year amounted to 7,420 tons. In 1812 the consumption of raw cotton was 18 million kilograms, but it rose to 32 million in 1830. There were 70,000 spindles in 1818 and 500,000 in 1828. The expansion of woolens was even faster. Silk also continued to enjoy prosperity. Only linen remained relatively limited to domestic industries.

The pattern of gradual industrialization may be observed in some of the available estimates on various industries. Measured in thousands of metric tons, French consumption of raw cotton increased from 28.2 in 1831, to 55.7 in 1841, to 59.3 in 1850, to 93.7 in 1869. It went down to 55.4 in the great depression of 1873, but recovered soon after, reaching approximately 30 percent over the 1869 capacity within a decade. The consumption of raw cotton, however, fluctuated from year to year. For example, between 1870 and 1879 the yearly consumption ranged between 158 million and 87 million kilograms. Between 1900 and 1909, it was between a low of 193 million and 319 million kilograms. In the next decade it hit a high of 346 million kilograms. Textiles were the fastest growing industry next to metallurgy. Unlike cotton, wool continued to expand, although with much less mechanization. However, silk declined because of disease and foreign competition. In the 1840s an estimated 25 million kilograms of cocoons were made; this declined to 7 million in the decade 1856–1866. In 1870 production went up to 10 million and with minor fluctuations this level became normal. Although France did not have much natural coal, its output increased eight-fold between 1852 and 1931; this was still about 16 percent of Britain's output and about 18 percent of that of Germany. Pig-iron production increased from 406,000 metric tons in 1850 to 1,381,000 in 1869. In the 1890s pig-iron production settled at a little more than 2 million metric tons annually. The production of steel had a relapse between 1819 and 1847, but recovered after the new techniques were adopted. From 40,600 metric tons of the Bessemer and Siemens–Martin steel in 1865, the production increased to 110,000 in 1869, 151,000 in 1873, and to 333,000 metric tons in 1879. However, the production of wrought iron and steel exceeded 1 million tons in 1869, a figure which was surpassed only by Britain in that year. By 1886–1890 the combined output of wrought iron and steel was 1.3 million tons; it was 2 million in 1899, 2.4 million in 1908, and 5 million in 1913. In thousands of horsepower, France has a steam-engine capacity of 90 in 1840, 270 in 1850, 1,120 in 1860, 3,070 in 1880 and 5,920 in 1896. Between 1860 and 1879 the production of sugar beet was doubled, and in 1883, 406,000 tons of refined sugar were produced. In 1900 the output was 1.002 million tons; it was 15.762 million in 1912–1913. Finally, an important sector of the French economy was the mining of iron ore. Even after Alsace-Lorraine was lost to Germany, the mines of France were still rich. In 1904 France mined 7 million tons of iron ore, but in 1913 the output had risen to 22 million tons, making France the largest exporter of iron ore in the world.

While these developments were rapid and in some cases dramatic, France's industrial development was not revolutionary. If a revolution did take place, it came quite late.[2] In 1913, France was still far behind the two other relatively large countries of Europe in industrial output. France also still had a larger segment of its industry in the homes and depended on manual power, as will be seen below.

Belgium. Belgium, a country with one sixth of the population, produced as many manufactured products in the 1880s as Italy. For most of the nineteenth century, Belgium was probably the most industrialized country on the continent. In part this was due to the traditional interest of the Low Countries in manufacture. It was also due to the rich coal mines and to the advantages derived from Napoleon's Continental System. The Belgians were quick to adopt new techniques, to mechanize, and to emulate. The first Newcomen engine was built in Belgium in 1720–1721. Around 1800 the Belgians were using the frame and the mule. In the 1820s they introduced the coke blast furnace and were the first to shift to mineral fuel. In the 1840s Belgium was the largest coal-producing country on the continent and was the only serious competitor to Britain in the iron and machine-making industries. Textiles were developed early in Belgium and by

2 J. H. Clapham considered post-1895 to be the appropriate period.

1846 there were 360,000 cotton spindles. The mechanical loom was introduced in 1825, and by 1830 there were 700; there were 2,900 in 1839 and 3,500 in 1845–1846. By this time hand cotton weaving in Ghent had vanished. The wool industry was also undergoing mechanization. The mule was in use for woolens in 1818 and the self-actor in the 1860s. By 1846 Belgium had a steam-engine capacity of 38,000 horsepower, about equal to that of France.

Despite these developments, or because of them, the dramatic development in Belgian industry came in the second half of the nineteenth century. Coal production increased from 3.5 million tons in 1850 to 7.8 million in 1869 and to 10.2 million in 1873. By 1913 it reached 26 million tons. Raw cotton consumption in 1850 was 10 million metric tons; it was 16.3 in 1869 and 18.0 in 1873. A more dramatic expansion was experienced in the production of pig iron. From 145,000 tons in 1850, it rose to 607,000 tons in 1873. In 1850, the steam-engine capacity was 70,000 horsepower; it was 350,000 in 1869 and 1,038,000 in 1907, or almost half that of France.

While Belgium was a fairly early and rapid industrializer, there were problems reflected in the total manufacturing output. The small population limited the home market, and protective laws and customs unions limited the external one. This limitation may in part explain why total manufacturing output changed relatively little after 1913 compared with that of the United Kingdom, Sweden, and Germany. Nevertheless, relative to its population, Belgium was among the most industrialized European countries by the turn of the century.

Germany. Slow to begin, within less than half a century Germany became one of the two most industrialized countries in Europe and probably one of the three in the world, counting the United States. The unification of Germany, completed in 1871, was economically effective. The market area was vastly enlarged, resources were pooled, and the central government was able to apply uniform measures to encourage industrialization. Furthermore, although Germany did produce traditional products such as textiles and coal, much of its development was due to the establishment of and specialization in new products such as beet sugar, chemicals, electrical equipment, and steel.

As we have seen, Frederick the Great attempted to improve manufacturing in the eighteenth century. However, even after the Napoleonic Wars, Germany was still fragmented politically as well as economically. Economic unification began with the establishment of the *Zollverein* or customs union in 1834. Twenty years later most of the states had joined the union and in 1871 full economic and political unification was achieved, as shown in Figure 15.1 (p. 195). It may, therefore, be suggested that development began with establishment of the *Zollverein*. The pace of industrialization was slow, although efforts were undertaken on a wide front—communications, chemicals, textiles, and metallurgy, among others.

Most of the industrial development of the eighteenth century related to textiles and mining. Wool was the major textile item. In 1750 Berlin had 3,537 looms, of which 2,880 were in the woolen industry. However, from then on silk began to make headway. In 1761, out of 5,078 looms, 3,082 were in woolens. In 1780 both silk and cotton were expanding while woolen textiles were sliding in importance. Out of 5,752 looms in that year, 2,220 were in silk and 1,018 in cotton; only 2,286 were in wool and the rest in linen.

However, the number of looms is not very indicative, since many different kinds may be in use. The consumption of raw cotton and raw wool is more significant. In 1821–1830 only 7,000 tons of raw cotton were used annually, compared with 330,000 tons of raw wool. In 1841–1850, the annual consumption was 41,000 and 490,000 tons, respectively. However, wool was not able to keep up with cotton. Mechanization of wool

began about 1850, but by the end of the century one-sixth of the wool workers still depended on hand looms. The number of workers in woolens increased from 182,000 in 1882 to 238,000 in 1907.

The consumption of raw cotton increased to 116,000 tons in 1871–1875. By the end of the century the cotton industry was employing more than 300,000 people. The number of cotton spindles increased from 2.23 million in 1861 to 10.92 million in 1913. After the middle of the century power machinery in cotton expanded steadily. Nevertheless, even by the end of the century about one-sixth of cotton weaving was still done in domestic industry. In contrast silk, which had been a major industry in the seventeenth and eighteenth centuries, was dying out until it was revived by the advent of machinery. By 1913 Germany's silk industry was next only to that of France among the European countries. The revival was in part due to concentration on mass production in contrast to the previous emphasis on luxury silks.

Use of power machinery made rapid advances after 1860. The German steam-engine capacity in that year was .85 million horsepower; in 1870 it was 2.48 million, or 3 times what it was a decade earlier; in 1880 it was 5.12 million, and by 1896 it had reached 8.08 million, compared with Britain's 13.7 and France's 5.92 million in that year. Power machinery was applied in the mines, in metallurgy, and in other industries. The production of coal was between 5 and 6 million tons in 1850; in 1873 it was 36.39 million tons. By 1900, Germany was producing 109.3 million tons of coal and 40.5 million tons of lignite, and in 1913 the output was 191.5 and 87.5 million, respectively, which was about 6 times the coal output of France and only a little behind that of Britain.

Germany's most favorable position was probably in iron and steel. The rich mines of the lower Rhine and annexation of Alsace-Lorraine gave Germany a decided advantage. The production of pig iron in 1810 was 46,000 tons; by 1850 it had risen to 529,000 tons. In 1880 the output was 2.8 million; it was 8.5 million in 1900 and 14.8 million in 1910, at which time Germany was the largest pig-iron producer in Europe. Germany's superiority in steel production came a decade earlier. In 1880 Germany produced 1.5 million tons of steel, which equaled the output of France and was a third of that of Britain. In 1900 the output of steel was 7.4 million tons, the largest in Europe, and by 1913 it had risen to 13.1 million, or almost twice that of Britain, and was surpassed only by the United States. Germany's advantage in steel production and use of steam power had other effects. Engineering advanced greatly, but ship-building was almost nonexistent in 1870; between 1880 and 1910 the steamship capacity was doubled.

Two other industries were important in Germany, both of which related to education and scientific excellence: the chemical and electrical industries. Scientific chemistry made a breakthrough in the 1840s in Germany. Experimentation continued and Germany was able to bring science and technology together to exploit its rich chemical resources. Potassium salt, sodium chloride, and sulphur could be extracted from iron pyrites, coal, and coal tar, of which Germany had plenty. Rock-salt beds were abundant in Stassfurt, and after 1871 Germany exploited the mines thoroughly with the help of new machinery. In 1882 Germany produced 112,000 tons of sulfuric acid, or about one-tenth of the world's production. In 1907 the output was 1.4 million. Between 1897 and 1907 the production of ammonia increased from 84,000 tons to 287,000 tons. The mining of crude potassium salt from Stassfurt was about 2,000 tons in 1861; in 1881 it was 906,000 tons, and in 1911 it was 9.6 million tons. Germany processed the chemicals in highly organized, large-scale industries.

Similar achievements, though on a relatively smaller scale, were made in electrical equipment. These had to wait for invention of the telephone and the dynamo, and for the application of electricity to transportation. Progress came around the turn of the century. The number of workers in electrical industries remained relatively small, but between 1880 and 1900 it multiplied several times. The industry's success made Germany the leader in Europe and next only to the United States in producing electrical equipment. Thus within the course of a few decades, Germany's total manufacturing output became higher than those of France and Britain. In terms of per capita output, Germany had already achieved second place.

Britain. Finally, we come to the United Kingdom, home of the industrial revolution and for some time the "workshop of the world." The experience of the United Kingdom has usually been used as a standard of comparison to explain why a certain country developed or failed to develop and at what rate. The reasons for such comparisons are obvious. When other countries began to industrialize, Britain's industrial revolution was almost complete. While the United Kingdom had resources for development, so did other countries. Her unified market was not larger in terms of population than states or provinces on the continent. Although the rationality of the Reformation might have influenced Britain's development, Protestants lived in other countries as well. Mercantilism, colonialism, and the Empire might also have contributed, but Britain was not the only country to have such advantages. The reasons for Britain's early and sustained leadership are too complex to isolate or identify. But once the combination of factors had made the early start possible, development, being cumulative, continued at a fairly steady pace.

Britain's development began in the eighteenth century, when agriculture was undergoing a revolutionary change. Industrialization was closely related to the readiness of British businessmen to adopt new techniques. Engineers and entrepreneurs were eager to adopt and spread them across the Channel, even when such action was legally restricted. In fact, some techniques that originated in continental Europe found a more ready acceptance in England than in their homeland. As long as there was a market and profits could be expected, British businessmen were ready to invest and supply it, whether it was at home or overseas. Moreover, when tradition stood in the way, it was broken.

Wool, which was traditionally protected, had to give way to cotton, although it continued to expand throughout the nineteenth century. The consumption of raw wool was about 100 million lbs. at the beginning of the nineteenth century. It was 250 million lbs. in 1850 and 744.2 million in 1907. In 1850 there were 2.47 million spindles; in 1904 the number was 5.8 million. In 1850 there were 42,050 power looms. The number went up to 140,000 around 1880, but there was a decline to 104,000 by 1904. In contrast the expansion of cotton was much steadier and more radical. Hand looms in cotton ceased to exist around 1860, while power looms increased from 55,000 in 1830 to about 540,-000 in 1880 and to 805,000 in 1914. Silk and linen expanded gradually until around 1880 and then began to decline. By 1900 British silk production was barely double what it was in 1770, and the linen output was little more than double what it was in that year. In the textile industry as a whole the output grew from an index of 76 in 1770 to 199 in 1820 and to 1,050 in 1857. After a slump the index rose to 1,481 in 1872. As the above figures suggest, growth continued during the next half-century.

Britain has been a leader in the mining and consumption of coal. Improvements in technology were quickly utilized in coal mining and their effects were reflected in the output. From 11 million tons in 1800, production rose to 49.4 million in 1850, to 110.4 in 1870, and to 287.4 million tons in 1913. The rise in the production of pig iron

was equally dramatic. From a quarter of a million tons in 1800, the output increased to 2.8 million in 1850, 6.4 million in 1870, and almost 10 million in 1907. Britain's readiness to adopt new techniques may be illustrated by the production of steel by the Bessemer and Siemens–Martin processes. In 1865 225,000 tons of steel were produced, which was twice the amount produced by France, Germany, and Belgium together. By 1873 the output was 588,000 tons, and 6 years later it was more than 1 million tons. Another illustration of Britain's industrialization is its steam-power capacity. In 1840 Britain had 620,000 of the 860,000 horsepower utilized in Europe. In 1860 Britain's capacity was 2.45 million horsepower; it was 7.6 million in 1880 and 13.7 million in 1896, almost equal to the combined capacities of France and Germany in that year. These developments explain how Britain was able to maintain her leadership of Europe in per capita manufacturing output throughout the nineteenth century.

Productivity. The industrialization of Europe was important quantitatively and qualitatively. The amount of goods was increased enormously. Variety also was expanded. Mass production put more commodities at the disposal of many more people than had been previously possible. This expansion was the result of higher labor productivity, which was probably the most important feature of this development. The increase in productivity meant that goods could be produced at a lower cost and that therefore more could be produced with the same amount of input. The rate of increase in productivity in the second half of the nineteenth century was not exceeded until the recent jump which began in 1950, as Table 19.6 shows.

These rates are only indicative of trends. They do not show the fluctuations in productivity growth. They also hide the fact that productivity was growing more in industry than in agriculture, almost one-third more

Table 19.6. Comparative annual average growth of output per manhour

	1870–1913	1913–1950[a]	1950–1960[a]
Belgium	2.0	1.4	2.5
Denmark	2.6	1.5	2.9
France	1.8	1.6	3.9
Germany	2.1	0.9	6.0
Italy	1.2	1.9	4.1
Netherlands	1.1	1.1	3.7
Norway	1.8	2.4	3.9
Sweden	2.7	2.0	3.5
Switzerland	1.6	1.9	4.2
United Kingdom	1.5	1.7	2.0
Canada[a]	2.1	2.1	2.5
United States[a]	2.4	2.4	2.4

[a] *Included for comparison.*
SOURCE: *Angus Maddison*, Economic Growth in the West, *p. 37.*

between 1860 and 1930. This was true even in countries in which agriculture was quite advanced, such as Sweden and Britain. Finally, productivity increases were not general to all sectors of industry. The variations determined the pattern of specialization, at least to the extent to which production responded to the market. However, productivity increased in those industries and countries that were willing and able to adopt new technology. In a sense, the industrial revolution and the steady increase in labor productivity reflected the triumph of technology. Since that time technology has continued to advance as the productivity data of the 1950s demonstrate.[3]

THE EFFECTS: SPECIALIZATION AND READJUSTMENTS

Specialization is a feature of commercial or exchange economies, in which production has ceased to be mainly for subsistence.

---

[3] The triumph of both science and technology reached a new high in the landing of Americans on the moon, an effort which coordinated all the technologies and scientific achievements of the past.

According to the principles of economics, a country or a region specializes in producing commodities in which it enjoys a comparative advantage. Thus a country concentrates on those goods that it can produce at a lower comparative cost and buys from others those that can be produced more cheaply elsewhere. If all countries produce the goods in which they enjoy a comparative advantage and trade with each other to satisfy their demand for goods, they will be better off than if each tries to satisfy its demand by local production. These principles apply equally to specialization among regions within a country. However, they require certain conditions: Production and trade must be governed by market conditions; economic objectives must predominate; and input and output mobility must be free and feasible.

These conditions did not prevail for any length of time during the nineteenth century. While specialization might have been in part determined by the available resources, by transportation costs, and by skill and efficiency of production, the European pattern was dominated by government intervention, protectionism, and national economic objectives. Therefore, it should not be surprising that specialization was frequently in conflict with the principles of comparative advantage. The justification often used for such deviation, and rightly so, was that the early comers had an advantage and it was difficult to compete with them without protection. This position explains the readjustments that took place in the last quarter of the nineteenth century, especially after the 1873 depression and after France and Germany had acquired the capacity to compete in industrial output.

Specialization may be approached in terms of regions or on a national level. In the nineteenth century regional specialization was determined primarily by the available resources, the means of transportation, and skills. For example, where coal or iron were relatively abundant, mining and metallurgy tended to develop, at least until the age of the railway, when transportation of voluminous loads became possible. Again, until the days of the steam engine, water power was an important determinant of industrial development. However, often specialization was determined by political motivations, as was the case in the growth of Moscow at the expense of St. Petersburg. The pattern of internal regional specialization was established around the end of the nineteenth century, and has continued, as shown in Figure 18.1 (p. 249).

Specialization of one country relative to others is best reflected by the pattern of trade. Specialization by a country tends to increase total exports and imports and change the composition of trade. By observing the changes in the list and magnitude of a country's exports and imports, we should be able to form an idea of its pattern of specialization. In the preindustrial era most exports and imports were primary agricultural products, with the exception of textiles and some luxury items.

This pattern continued for those European countries that were slow to develop until late in the nineteenth century. Russia, for example, continued to export grain, flax, hemp, and later oil. Its imports consisted of manufactured goods, including machinery. Although its import of machinery was declining by the end of the century and domestic production was increasing, it can hardly be said that pre-Soviet Russia specialized in machine production. On the other hand, Soviet Russia had, for doctrinal and political reasons, to be self-sufficient, and it therefore expanded all kinds of industrial production, including heavy industry. A major feature of Soviet policy was to expand industry to all those districts that had the resources for it, rather than concentrating it in the area around Moscow.

Spain continued to specialize in raw wool, ore, cork, and other primary products, but showed little industrial specialization. Spain remained dependent on other countries for manufactured and finished products, as did

eastern Europe, where industry was a late comer and specialization was limited to agriculture and primary mineral products, such as oil in Rumania.

The pattern was different in the countries which succeeded in industrialization. The United Kingdom, the first to industrialize, became increasingly dependent on imports of primary products and more specialized in certain industrial products. The major item of import until 1850 was raw cotton, followed by foodstuffs such as grain and tropical items. Hemp, flax, hides, and wool were the only other major imports for industrial purposes. The only other item added to this list before 1913 was timber, of which the United Kingdom had very little. Oil and oil seed became significant imports after that date. In contrast, until 1935 Britain's major export item was cotton yarn and textile, which ranged from 12 to 26 percent of all exports. The United Kingdom imported the raw material, processed and finished it, adding about 60 percent of the gross value of the finished product, and exported it. Woolen yarns occupied second place until 1875, but declined to third place in 1900, to fourth place in 1913, and to fifth place by 1935, even though woolens continued to range between 6 and 9 percent of all exports. Coal, which occupied sixth place in 1850, was fourth in 1875 and second in 1900; however, it declined to third place in 1913, and back to fourth in 1935. From 11 percent of total exports in 1900, coal dropped to only 6 percent in 1935. Iron and steel were becoming important, occupying third place from 1850 to 1900, second place in 1913, third place again in 1935. Between 1875 and 1935 iron and steel contributed 8 to 9 percent of all exports. Machinery, though a specialty of the United Kingdom, constituted only 3 percent of its exports as late as 1875 and 5 to 6 percent as late as 1913. However, in 1935 machinery and vehicles contributed 14 percent of all exports. Machinery alone was exceeded only by cotton yarn and textiles, although all textile exports were still ahead of any combination of related products. Thus the United Kingdom maintained its specialization in textiles, machinery, coal, and iron and steel. Chemicals and dyes, which were major exports, did not exceed 4 percent of total exports.

France, which was next to industrialize, imported raw material for its textile industry, especially cotton. Local production of wool was still relatively high until around 1850. Oil, sugar, and machinery were major imports until 1935. However, from 1875 to 1913 the largest import was raw wool, which ranged from 8 to 10 percent of the total. Cotton imports declined in importance after 1900. Between 1900 and 1935 coal and coke rose from third to first place, ranging from 7 to 9 percent of total imports. It may be noted that machinery, a major import item until 1913, was no longer as important in 1935. France exported textiles, especially silk cloth, which occupied first place between 1830 and 1913. However, its significance declined from 25 percent in 1830 to 6 percent in 1913, mainly because other products grew in importance. Except for wines and luxury items, only textiles were important exports before 1900. However, by 1913 France was exporting machinery, especially motor vehicles, and chemicals. And in 1935 iron and steel joined the list and occupied first place, constituting 6 percent of all exports. In that year textiles of all kinds including artificial silk were only 12 percent of all exports.

Germany's development came in the second half of the nineteenth century. Until then Germany had exported textiles, engineering skills, and metals. That pattern continued until 1880. Germany imported more cotton and wool than any other item until 1935. In 1880 raw cotton and wool and textile yarn contributed 26 percent of all imports. This percentage, however, declined by 1900, while imports of foodstuffs including grain were increasing. During the early years of the twentieth century, Germany imported copper, hides, iron ore, petroleum, and oil seeds in addition to raw textiles and

foodstuffs. Germany's exports changed radically after 1880. In that year the major export item was textiles, which amounted to 24 percent of the total. Chemicals came next, amounting to 8 percent, grain to 5 percent, and metalwork to 4 percent. By 1900 this pattern had changed. Iron and steel occupied first place and retained that position until 1935, amounting to between 8 and 17 percent of all exports. Though chemicals were a German specialty, their significance in percentage- terms was minor. Textiles were still important, amounting to 15 percent of all exports. However, machinery, coal, and sugar were major new exports, each contributing 5 percent of the total in 1900; 7, 5, and 3 percent respectively in 1913; and 9 percent for machinery and 6 percent for coal in 1935, when sugar lost its relative significance. Machinery, including electrical machinery, constituted 14 percent in that year. Chemicals recovered their importance and amounted to 8 percent in 1935. New export items in the twentieth century included paper and paper products, paints and varnishes, and glass and glassware. The engineering and scientific ability of Germany is clearly reflected in this pattern of trade.

The Netherlands, which had lost some of its earlier primacy, continued its pattern of trade participation, although on a smaller scale. It imported raw materials and finished them for export, or exchanged them for similar goods of a different quality. For example, the Netherlands imported a little more cereal than it exported, and both imported and exported raw and manufactured textiles. The same was true of iron and steel and of copper. The country seems to have been constantly short of coal and wood while its exports included paper and sugar in addition to the dairy products which had become a major specialty.

A similar pattern characterized Belgium. Belgium's imports were mainly primary products such as raw textile material, cereals, timber, coal, crude minerals, and chemicals. Later in the twentieth century, Belgium imported machinery as well. Belgium's industrial development, however, was clear. In 1900 Belgium exported finished textiles, railway carriages, glass, and cereals. By 1913 iron and steel, zinc, and rawhides were added to the list of major exports. After 1913 iron and steel became major export items.

Machinery, clocks, and textiles were exported by Switzerland. The Swiss economy is interesting because local resources were very scarce and all exports depended on imported raw material. It may be said that Switzerland actually exported skills and services in the form of value added to the raw imports.

Sweden's specialization is probably the most conspicuous of all the countries discussed. Lacking fuel, Sweden imported more coal than any other item of trade as late as 1913. Metals and machinery came next, ranging from 11 to 15 percent of total imports. Raw and manufactured textile imports ranged from 9 to 18 percent of total exports until 1913. Cereals were another important item of trade, ranging between 8 and 10 percent of total imports. Chemicals became important imports after 1913. In contrast, Sweden's exports were much more specialized. In 1900 timber constituted 50 percent of all exports, while paper and paper products added another 3 percent. Metals, mostly steel, constituted 12 percent, and metal goods amd machinery added another 6 percent. Minerals, especially copper, were 6 percent of total exports. While timber exports declined after 1900, paper and wood pulp increased. Together timber, wood pulp, and paper constituted 42 percent of all exports in 1913. As timber exports declined further, wood and coke manufacturing became more important. Metals, minerals, and later machinery were the only other major exports. One of the later developments in Swedish exports was electrical machinery. In addition, Sweden has always managed to export live animals and animal food.

This pattern of specialization in Europe has been somewhat modified in recent years, at least in the order of significance of the items of trade. The modification has been a result largely of the wars, of nationalism, and of the catching up of the previously underdeveloped areas, especially Russia and eastern Europe. Nevertheless, the basic structure of specialization, which was fairly well established around the First World War, still holds for most countries of Europe.

CONCLUSIONS

The industrial revolution is a measure of relative change. Within its own frame of reference, each industrializing country experienced an industrial revolution. This observation follows from the fact that industrialization requires certain preconditions and that it is cumulative. Once the prerequisites have been satisfied industrialization begins, and once it has started its progress tends to become more rapid, at least until a certain level has been achieved. The countries of Europe have industrialized to some extent, although their degree of success has varied. The results of industrialization have encouraged specialization and international division of labor. Although all countries have tried to produce certain common products, there seems to have been no inclination toward autarchy, at least not before 1913, except perhaps in a giant country like Russia which had the capacity to produce its own inputs and consume its outputs.[4]

Industrialization raised total output and productivity per manhour. It also increased responsibilities and the vulnerability of the trading nations to world market conditions. In part, these complications were due to the social and political factors that invariably intervene and distort the economic process.

Europe's industrialization depended heav-

[4] An exception could also be made of the United States for a long time, and can almost be made of present-day China.

ily on the utilization of new technologies and new sources of power. Moreover, the industrialization of the late comers seems to have been stimulated by the creation of new products and the concentration on mass production at the expense of luxury items.

We have surveyed the trends and magnitude of change. The differences between one country and another must be explained in terms of the obstacles and facilities available, such as transportation, financing, the role of government, and the organization of industry and labor. These will be studied in the following chapters.

BIBLIOGRAPHY

Aggardi, Mario Ferrari, "One Hundred Years of Italian Economy," *Review of Economic Conditions in Italy*, Vol. 15, no. 4, (1961), pp. 287–309.

Bergson, Abram, and Simon Kuznets (eds.), *Economic Trends in the Soviet Union*, Cambridge, Mass.: Harvard University Press, 1963, chap. 4.

Blackwell, W. L., *The Beginnings of Russian Industrialization*, I (1800–1860), Princeton: Princeton University Press, 1968, Part V and appended tables.

Habakkuk, H. J., and M. M. Postan (eds.), *Cambridge Economic History of Europe*, VI, New York: Cambridge University Press, 1965, chaps. 5 and 9.

Clapham, J. H., *Economic Development in France and Germany, 1815–1914*, New York: Cambridge University Press, 1928, chaps. 10 and 11.

Clark, Colin, *The Conditions of Economic Progress*, Third edition, London: Macmillan, 1960, chap. 6.

Clough, S. B., *The Economic History of Italy*, New York: Columbia University Press, 1964, chap. 3.

Deane, Phyllis, and W. A. Cole, *British Economic Growth 1688–1959*, New York: Cambridge University Press, 1967, chaps. 5 and 6.

Ellison, H. J., "Economic Modernization in Imperial Russia: Purposes and Achievements," *Journal of Economic History*, XXV, No. 4 (Dec. 1965), pp. 523–540.

Gerschenkron, A., *Economic Backwardness in Historical Perspective*, New York: Frederick A. Praeger, 1965, chap. 4 and Appendix I.

Goldsmith, R. W., "The Economic Growth of Tsarist Russia 1860–1913," *Economic Development and Cultural Change*, IX (April 1961), pp. 441–475.

Goris, Jan Albert, *Belgium*, United Nations series, Berkeley: University of California Press, 1945, chap. 12.

Heckscher, E. F., *An Economic History of Sweden*, Cambridge, Mass.: Harvard University Press, 1954, chap. 6.

Henderson, W. O., *The Industrial Revolution in Europe*, Chicago: Quadrangle Books, 1961.

Henderson, W. O., *Studies in the Economic Policy of Frederic the Great,* London: Frank Cass and Co., 1963, chap. 5.

Jörberg, Lennert, "Structural Change and Economic Growth: Sweden in the 19th Century," *Economy and History,* VIII (1965), pp. 3–46.

La Force, J. C., "Royal Textile Factories in Spain, 1700–1800," *Journal of Economic History,* XXIV, No. 3 (Sept. 1964), pp. 337–363.

Lyaschenko, P. I., *History of the National Economy of Russia,* New York: Macmillan, 1949, chaps. 25–26, 33.

Maddison, Angus, *Economic Growth in the West,* New York: Twentieth Century Fund, 1964, chap. 1.

Vicens Vives, Jaime, *An Economic History of Spain,* Princeton: Princeton University Press, 1969, chaps. 35, 44.

Warriner, Doreen (ed.), *Contrasts in Emerging Societies,* Bloomington: Indiana University Press, 1965, pp. 61–101, 162–199, 237–241, 267–272, 344–361.

Woodruff, William, *The Impact of Western Man,* New York: St. Martin's Press, 1967, chap. 7.

The enormous developments in the production of agricultural and nonagricultural goods could be realized only if inputs could be secured and conveyed to the production centers, and if the finished products could be distributed to buyers at home and abroad. As the tempo of production increased, the capacity to transport material had to increase as well. And as the product composition varied and faraway input and output markets were tapped, more enduring means of transportation had to be secured.

This interdependence between transportation and production has led some observers to explain development at least in part as a function of an expanding market. Means of transportation enlarge the market by unifying its various segments into a whole, thus increasing the elasticities of supply and demand for the accessible commodities. Thus the larger the market, the higher the probability that shortages will be relieved and gluts avoided. The means of transportation determine in part the size and efficiency of the market.

EFFECTS OF THE
TRANSPORT REVOLUTION

The nineteenth-century developments in transportation were revolutionary in enlarging and unifying markets within and across national boundaries. These developments were made possible by the demand for and the profit expectations inherent in the new transport industries, and by technological advances. The effects of the transport revolution were both quantitative and qualitative. On the quantitative side, more goods and people could be transported for longer distances and at much lower costs. With the application of new technology, especially steam power and iron and steel, larger volumes and heavier articles could easily be transported at lower costs than had been previously possible. On land and on water, there were no more volume or weight restrictions on transporting goods.

The qualitative effects were equally important. Speed is probably the first change that comes to mind. Speed is a matter of stabilization of the market and of convenience. Greater speed simply means that more goods can be transported per unit of time. Whether goods are transported slowly or rapidly, it is the unit cost that matters. However, the knowledge that goods can be received on short notice tends to reduce speculation and price fluctuations. A more significant effect of the new means of transportation was what has been described as its "ubiquity." Steam, rails, and iron and steel made mobility a continuous process, independent of seasons, of climate, of terrain, or of load. While wind and tide had previously determined the arrival or departure of ships, now steamships could plan their timetables regardless of these factors. While land transportation had depended on the terrain and the seasons, the railway went through tunnels, over bridges, in summer or in winter. Man's mobility became assured and his demand for goods could now be satisfied as long as it was backed by purchasing power. The market was both unified and perpetuated by man's ability to apply the new technology to transportation.

Two other qualitative effects followed from these changes. The harnessing of power to move more men and material increased comfort and conserved human energy. With comfort, however, came the discipline of the mechanical environment. Man had to adjust to predetermined time schedules. A new business psychology was evolving and the transport revolution was an important factor in its development. Man could now plan in precise terms his goings and comings and his business transactions. The coordination of timetables in different localities and countries helped to strengthen the trend towards enlarging and unifying the market.

Indirect effects

The impact of a new means of transport usually begins to be felt long before the service itself can be made available. The transportation industry affects the economy and society by forward and backward linkages and by its influence on social and political relations. As the producer of a service, transportation creates demand for machinery, fuel, and skill. The miners who produce the raw material; the industry that produces the iron, steel, and wood; and other industries which produce accessories for the means of transportation are directly affected by its growth. Since transportation services must be supplemented by catering services at the terminals, the latter also grow in response. Of course, the same is true of all other industries. However, because transportation had to be a large-scale operation and

reaching all regions within a country, the dynamic impact of its growth tended to be more widely felt than of other, less far-reaching industries.

Put differently, the new means of transportation tended to be great absorbers of real capital, which had to be produced before it could be utilized. By generating incomes, they stimulated increased expenditure and money circulation. Thus their construction was a catalyst for economic change. It also required large amounts of funds. Institutional arrangements to facilitate the financing of the new methods were often developed, as the history of investment banking clearly shows.

It is true that means of transportation were not always constructed in response to a market demand for service, nor were they always an effective catalyst to the economy. Failures, however, were due to the absence of other prerequisites for development. For example, when new railroads were built for military or political reasons, the catalytic impact on the economy could not be sustained unless other favorable conditions prevailed, such as entrepreneurial readiness, resources, or some kind of comparative advantage. Moreover, the forward and backward linkages of new transport construction are predicated on the assumption that the machinery and other raw and intermediate materials are produced domestically. If these are imported, many of the backward linkages accrue in the country of origin. If capital is also imported, the profits and the changes that result from them accrue to the exporting countries. Therefore, the forward linkages are also diminished at home. When these complications are compounded by a lack of resources to be exploited by the extended means of transportation, the economic effects of expansion may indeed be modest. Examples of such problems will be discussed below.

The impact of the transport revolution on social and political relations can hardly be exaggerated. Means of transportation bring people into closer contact with each other. Where contact prevails, communication grows. With communication comes organization. Is it possible to think of a national political party or trade union in the absence of modern transportation? Indeed, national political organizations became significant only after the transport revolution had become a reality. Until then such parties were elite in the sense that the communication of political views was restricted to their leaders. Social movements were also local in character and any apparent solidarity between two different localities was based more on empathy than on organization. If only because it provided for rapid dispersal of newspapers, the new means of transportation were an important factor in creating national social and political movements.

Where means of transport were expanded, major changes in the economy and society developed, and where they failed the economic, social, and political changes were limited. Developments in transport and communication and changes in the economy and society complemented and reinforced each other. The ability of each to respond to the challenges created by the other was and still is basic to the socioeconomic development of a country.

APPLICATIONS OF TECHNOLOGY

Modern means of transportation are creations of the last two centuries. Their history was closely associated with the development of the steam engine. However, the demand for more and better transportation facilities was apparently high long before the steam engine could be put to use. Previous efforts had been directed primarily towards the improvement and extension of road networks and of canals and waterways. The major road improvements were the building of safe, all-season roads, usually on existing roadbeds. The principles of drainage, surfacing, and compacting represented in the McAdam process were major improvements, and that process has continued to be the standard method of road-building.

These improvements, however, had only modest effects on the speed, weight and volume problems. The wheeled, horse-drawn wagon remained the main vehicle on these roads. The challenge of rising demand for greater inland mobility of inputs and outputs had to be met in other ways. Waterways seemed to be the answer and Europe began to feel the canal-building fever. Between the middle of the eighteenth and the middle of the nineteenth centuries, thousands of miles of new canals were built and old waterways and rivers improved. New construction methods were utilized to guarantee dependable waterways. In the absence of mechanical power, waterways were useful only in good weather and good climates and under favorable riverbed inclinations. They were more usable downstream than upstream. They also had to be supplemented by land transportation, which meant frequent loading and unloading. Nevertheless, canals and waterways filled a major gap, especially in transporting voluminous items such as timber, ore, and raw material. No doubt the improvement and extension of canals were effective means of cutting the cost of transportation. The application of steam power to shipping was also a major improvement. In fact, some observers have claimed that canals remained highly competitive with the railroads for many years.

The revolution in transport came with the application of steam. The railways on land and the steam lines on the sea enabled Europe to control nature, unify the market, and enjoy an all-year, all-terrain service. The age of the railways began in the 1820s in Britain. Within half a century, railway networks had been constructed in most western European countries, and attention was transferred to transcontinental lines. Wherever the railway went, a new economic environment was created. New resources were tapped and new markets exploited. The railway fever was so high that when the main lines in the home country had been constructed, investors searched for ventures elsewhere. Railway-building was profitable, whether construction was in response to the market or by contract with the government. In some cases special industries were established to supply the railways. Production of rails and locomotives became full-scale industries in Britain, Belgium, Germany, France, and Russia.

While the railways were being expanded, work was continuing on steamships. Although steamboats came into use about the same time as the railways, they were limited to short distances, mainly because of the difficulty of carrying sufficient fuel for long voyages. Ocean steamships became more common around the 1860s when the compound steam engine was perfected. This shift coincided with the age of steel, which made it possible to construct large, durable, dependable, ocean-going steamships. With the railway and the steamship, distance was conquered, the market was expanded, and mobility democratized. The reduction of transportation costs made it possible for more people to move around and put more goods within their reach.

The automobile and the airplane completed the revolution by adding speed and independence of movement. The car, with internal combustion, reduced distance by traveling at higher speed, but its main effect was to make individual transportation facilities available. The small passenger car reduced the individual's dependence on large-scale transportation, and undoubtedly created a social revolution. The airplane reduced distance even more, although air travel has thus far remained restricted to certain economic groups and certain commodities of relatively light weight and high value—except for war materiel, the movement of which rarely follows economic principles.

THE EXPANSION

The expansion of transportation differed in quantity and quality from one country to another. The more industrialized countries expanded their networks more extensively, but in virtually all countries the expansion of transportation preceded the general economic development known as the industrial revolution. Even in Britain, where the industrial revolution presumably predated the railways and the steamship, the expansion of the roads and canals gives credence to this observation.

Roads

Roads have always existed in various degrees of utility and extensiveness. Some countries had more roads than others because of more economic activity, more governmental attention, special military requirements, or some other unique consideration. One of the most interesting situations was the widespread highway construction for the Mesta in Spain. The sheep walks from one end of the country to the other were governed by strict rules as to width, quality, and maintenance. Moreover, fair towns all over Europe had to guarantee access if their fairs were to prosper. Such factors, as well as the military requirements of Napoleon's campaigns, created many miles of roads. Rarely, however, were they constructed according to a plan, to connect the main parts of a country with each other. When such a heritage existed it was mainly the economic factor that led to its construction.

By 1800 Britain and France had fairly complete road networks. France had a tradition of public interest in roads and canals and had seen technological innovations in road-building. Trésaguet's method had been introduced in 1764 and in 1769 a road steam carriage was invented, as noted in the appendix to Chapter 17. Napoleon continued the tradition, expanding the networks in France as well as in other countries which his armied occupied. He classified roads as imperial or departmental; the state cared for the former and the local authorities for the latter. During his reign Napoleon is said to have built or repaired over 13,000 leagues (39,000 miles) of roads. However, many of them were neglected for some years after his defeat. When their repair was resumed around 1820, many had to be shifted to more appropriate locations.

Until the late eighteenth century, British roads were less extensive and not as well built as those of France. However, the demand was growing and the technology changing. Telford's and McAdam's methods of road-building were reinforced by the turnpike system of financing and maintenance. By 1820 Britain contained 21,000 miles of turnpike under the supervision of local turnpike trusts which charged tolls for managing and maintaining them. The major roads, such as the road to Ireland, were subsidized by the government and built by private entrepreneurs. The impact of road-building in both France and Britain was to reduce the time spent on the road and thus the cost of transportation. When stagecoaches were regularized as means of transportation, it is estimated that between 1800 and 1830 travel time in Britain was cut by two-thirds and the cost was cut in half.

The best example of Napoleon's road construction may be seen in Germany. Around 1815 roads east of the Elbe were few and in disrepair and were financed by tax levy. West of the Rhine there were many good roads. Prussia alone had 419.8 miles of them. Expansion and improvement, however, were modest. As late as 1841 the total mileage had increased to only 1,280.1 miles and these had been built with government direction and financing. The Netherlands was probably the only country on the continent that had a road system comparable to that of France. In eastern Europe and in Scandinavia little road construction took place up to early 19th century. In the South, Italy had inherited a system of Roman roads. Although Napoleon's impact was also felt here, little improvement was evident until many years later. Spain expanded its road system through public control, but the quality remained low. Road-building in Spain came in stages and depended on the regime in power. Between 1800 and 1808 about 3,000 kilometers were constructed. After a long lull, construction was resumed on a modest scale between 1843 and 1856. Rapid expansion came after 1856, 7,822 kilometers being constructed in 12 years. By 1884 there were 23,215 kilometers of roads; there were 41,465 in 1908. However, in 1908 only about one-sixth of the roads were good enough for heavy loads and heavy traffic.

Waterways

By the early nineteenth century the cost per ton-mile of canal and river transportation was less than half that of land transportation. This explains the extensive use of canals in the more developed countries. Spain, however, had no canal-building movement, partly because there were no waterways to be utilized. Canals were important in France, Britain, the Low Countries, and Scandinavia. In Germany river transportation was more important. France had a tradition of canal-building and the post-Napoleonic era was rich in that respect. The French connected the Atlantic with the Mediterranean by the Languedoc Canal as early as 1650. The St. Quentin Canal was opened in 1810, and in 1869 the French built the Suez Canal which connected the Mediterranean with the Red Sea and the Indian Ocean. Between 1820 and 1850 canals connecting most of the major rivers were built, extending over several thousand miles. Unlike France, Britain built its extensive network of canals by private initiative through the turnpike system. These canals were mainly for the haulage of coal. Canals were built in Belgium, where the Ghent Ship Canal was opened in 1827; the Ghotha Canal in Sweden was opened in 1832 and the Tunnel-Kiln Canal in Denmark in 1839.

Major canals and bridges were built on the continent throughout the nineteenth century, such as the Kiel Canal in 1894 and the Dortmund-Ems Canal of 1899.

The use of canals and waterways received its greatest impetus after the introduction of the steamboat. River steamers soon became common in Germany, Scandinavia, France, and Britain. They used the paddle wheel and carried only enough fuel for short distances. Steam vessels large enough to go on the high seas were still not feasible. However, as steam was being put to use early in the nineteenth century, iron was gaining acceptance in ship-building. The first iron steamship to cross the Channel was built in 1822. The successful combination of steam and iron led to ambitious projects such as the building, beginning in 1835, of the *Great Western* and the *Great Eastern* by Isambard Kingdom Brunel of the United Kingdom. These ships were to be ocean-going, but the *Great Eastern*, which was completed in 1859, experienced great difficulties. The following excerpt gives an idea of the ship and the problems that remained to be solved.

As an advertisement of the structural possibilities of iron, the *Great Eastern* was a great success: as a demonstration of the economic use of coal she was a dismal failure.

The ship had a double skin of plates to the waterline with the frames between, supporting the machinery and huge coal bunkers; above this there were bulkheads placed lengthwise, designed like two Britannia Bridge tubes. . . . A feature of the design was the standardization of the sizes of plates, angle-irons, rivets, etc. Accommodation for 4,000 passengers was arranged on a total of five decks; even her coil-fibre rope, 47 inches in circumference, was record size. The fact that her tonnage of 18,918 tons was not equalled until the nineteenth century had closed may well argue that the basic conception was unsound, as events proved,

but the hull, with an approximate weight of 6,250 tons, made up of 30,000 plates held together by some 3 million rivets, proved to be in excellent condition when the ship was broken up in 1888—thirty years after the difficulties of her launching, which involved an unforeseen expense of £120,000, had driven the original company to virtual bankruptcy. The *Great Eastern* was never employed on the long passenger runs for which she had been designed, and *faute de mieux* did her best service as a cable-layer. The fatal defect lay in an underestimation of the quantity of coal which her combined paddle- and screw-engines—developing 6,600 h.p.—required to drive this huge ship at the designed speed of 14 knots. The steaming time required for the round voyage to Australia was about seventy-five days; the bunkers held 12,000 tons of coal, but the difference between the coal consumption that had been provided for and what was in practice required was of the order of 75 percent.[1]

The major problems of ocean steamshipping were solved with the invention of the screw propeller, first used in ocean steamers in the *Great Britain* in 1848, and of the compound steam engine in 1865. The shift to steam on long voyages thus became feasible, although until then steam had had little advantage over sail. In fact, all steamers going on long voyages had been forced to depend on sail for a part of the way. The transition was further stimulated when steel replaced iron.

The shift to steam was rapid in Europe as a whole; 93.4 percent of the merchant fleet had been transformed by 1913. Until 1900 the United Kingdom had the highest percentage of steamships in its fleet, followed closely by the Netherlands. However, by 1913 the Netherlands had taken the lead and several other countries had made rapid shifts

[1] T. K. Derry and Trevor I. Williams, *A Short History of Technology*, pp. 372–373.

to steam. The least transformed nation was Norway, only 76.1 percent of whose fleet consisted of steamships. It may be presumed that other countries were even less dependent on steam. For example, only 50 percent of the Spanish fleet depended on steam, the rest being sail. The shift to motor-ships (those with electric or internal combustion engines), which came after the First World War, was most extensive in Sweden, followed by Norway, and far behind by Germany. For some reason, the United States showed a distinct lack of interest in motorships, compared with Europe.[2]

The impact of the steamship can hardly be exaggerated. Nature was neutralized and carrying capacity was increased. More tonnage could be transported at lower cost. More comfort could be enjoyed and more regularity of travel could be expected. Low-value goods could now be transported at relatively low costs. More people could travel long distances at the lower rates. As late as 1900, Europe carried 71 percent of the net tonnage of the world. The percentage was slightly higher in 1913, but has fallen since then.

The shift to large steam and motor-ships must be viewed within the framework of expanding economies and the larger quantities of goods to be shipped and distributed all over the world. Data since 1850 show that the United Kingdom had the highest percentage of world shipping up to 1938, after which the leadership went to the United States. Until 1913 the United Kingdom carried more than one-third of world shipping. The share of the Netherlands continued to increase until 1913, after which it declined, although the absolute tonnage continued to grow perceptibly. The same was true of Germany and Russia. Italy's share started to decline around 1880, but stabilized after 1900. In all cases, however, the absolute tonnage increased. The reason for these declines

is that non-European countries increased their tonnage at a faster rate. Nevertheless, the growth of European tonnage was quite conspicuous. From 4.879 million tons in 1850, it grew to 13,988 million in 1880, and to 18.691 million in 1900. Between 1913 and 1960 the gross tonnage doubled. Although we have no data on the number of ships used or the average carrying capacity in each of these years, no doubt the carrying capacity of the average ship increased enormously.[3]

Railroads

While roads and canals are regarded as the trigger of the transport revolution, the most far-reaching effects came with the railways. They penetrated areas that had not been exploited, overcame the problems of volume and limited animal power, and were an all-season, durable means of mobility. As soon as the locomotive was perfected, private companies and governments were anxious to expand the lines. The railroad fever caught on quickly, and construction concessions were awarded in certain countries like Spain even before they were ready to build.

Railroad construction required government cooperation, even where it was in private hands. The authorities had to award concessions, regulate the lines, and sometimes encourage and subsidize construction. The late comers to industrialization learned from the earlier mistakes of Britain. The British railways began with little planning. Local lines were often constructed with no main line to connect to. Sometimes so many lines were built in a given locality that some went bankrupt. The government eventually tried to establish a network, but most of the construction remained in private hands. The continental countries were able to avoid some of these problems by laying down plans. In general, governments concerned themselves with the main lines and left the branch lines to private contractors. Eventu-

---

[2] W. Woodruff, *The Impact of Western Man,* p. 256.

[3] More details may be found in W. Woodruff, *op. cit.,* pp. 255–256.

ally, most railways became state-owned or were controlled as public utilities.

As noted, the United Kingdom led the way in railway construction. It may be recalled that road steamers existed in Britain before 1800. Rails were also used for haulage with horsecarts. The problem was to develop the locomotive and to construct rails sturdy enough to carry it. Sturdy rails were made successfully in 1816 and the locomotive in the 1820s. Soon after railway construction was begun by Acts of Parliament. However, there was little coordination between lines until the middle of the 1840s. In 1846 an Act was passed requiring all future lines to use a standard gauge. Coordination also resulted in the fusion of lines, so that traffic could be shared instead of regulated by cutthroat competition. Coordination was facilitated by extending the telegraph in conjunction with the railways. In 1869 all telegraph lines were bought by the government as a public utility; this made regulation of the railways easier.

On the continent, Belgium was the first country to construct a network of railways. As early as 1833 railway construction became a goverment responsibility. The government kept control of the main trunk lines, although beginning in 1842 concessions were given to private companies for the construction of connecting branch lines. Most of these concessions were awarded to British companies. However, the Belgian government soon started to buy the private lines as the opportunity arose. By 1880 about three-quarters of all the lines were in government hands, and most of the rest were by 1910. The service was well organized, the rates codified, and the lines well maintained at no loss. A unique feature of Belgium's policy was the construction of a local-service network of light railways reaching all population centers, under public authority. Between 1880 and 1910, a complete system was constructed, although the estimates of its mileage vary from one source to another.

Germany began its system of railways through private initiative. As early as 1833 a plan for a complete network was laid out by Friedrich List, who made Berlin the center from which six main lines radiated in various directions. Gradually the government of Prussia began to extend assistance to the railway companies and with it came control. By 1862 the Prussian government controlled 55 percent of all the lines. The southern German states copied the Belgian example from the start, taking full responsibility for the networks.

The public-utility aspect of railways was recognized in France from the beginning. Much debate took place before serious construction began. A general plan was laid out to connect all parts of the country. After 1842 the government took the responsibility for such overhead construction costs as roadbeds, bridges, and tunnels. The rest was left to private companies as concessions. However, reorganization in 1851 brought about the fusion of the various lines into six networks. To make the construction and maintenance of the railways profitable, the government guaranteed the railroad companies a certain income with the proviso that if their actual income exceeded the guaranteed level, the state would receive a share. In return the companies agreed to build subsidiary lines. The lines were virtually completed by 1860.

The Netherlands was more dependent than other countries on water transport, and therefore was slow in developing its railroads. Only short lines were built before 1850. However, in the second half of the century, a complete network was constructed. The start was slow also in Scandinavia, where the effort was undertaken jointly by government and private companies. The main lines in Denmark were always in the hands of the state. They were completed in 1880, but much remained to be done with respect to the connecting subsidiaries. Even by 1894 only 42 percent of the network was

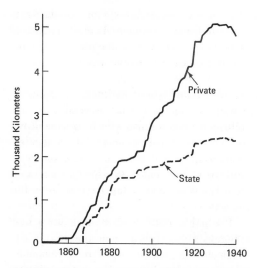

Figure 20.1 Private and state railways in Denmark. The sharp rises in state railways occurred as lines were taken over in Jylland and Eyn (1867), Sjaelland (1879), and Slesvig (1919).
SOURCE: Naval Intelligence Division, *Denmark*, p. 455.

completed. The rapid expansion that occurred after that date was mostly through private initiative under government supervision. The pattern of private–public ownership of railroads is shown in Figure 20.1. While the state owned about 80 percent of the lines in 1890, its share was reduced to about 50 percent by 1917, in contrast to the pattern in most other European countries.

Sweden's experience is interesting in a different way. In that country lines were usually built to isolated towns and villages to stimulate business and settlement. While a certain degree of mobility and initiative was stimulated, many of the lines proved to be uneconomical. When the private companies were in financial difficulties, the government advanced loans to help them. Gradually government control increased so that most of the lines were under public control by 1910. As a result of this process a complete network was built in the second half of the nineteenth century.

Spanish railroads were slow in starting, although many attempts were made in the

1840s. The major effort began after 1855, when a law was passed giving wide concessions to construction companies, most of which were foreign. The concessions included subsidies, long-term leases, and suspension of duties on imported construction material. Construction was interrupted between 1865 and 1875 because of political, military, and financial crises, but was resumed soon after. By 1900 a fairly complete network had been built.

Italian railways began mainly as private ventures, but most of the companies hit financial trouble and the state had to take over or rescue them. By 1880, the state already owned two-thirds of the lines. An attempt to keep the lines in private hands that was similar to the French plan was made in 1884. All the lines were grouped in four networks. The state owned the stations and the roadbeds, while the companies were responsible for the vehicles and their operation, with a guaranteed return of 7.5 percent of the paid-up capital. The excess return was to be shared by the state. This arrangement was not satisfactory to either the companies or the state authorities. Therefore, at the first renewal date in 1905, the contract was dissolved and the state took over almost all the lines. It may be noted that Italian railways had to overcome many difficulties of terrain. Bridges and tunnels had to be built. The St. Gotthard Tunnel, 14.9 kilometers in length, was opened in 1882 to connect with Germany and Switzerland. The longest tunnel in Europe, the Simplon, covering a distance of 19.5 kilometers, was opened in 1906, and so the network was complete.

In Russia and eastern Europe, railways were also slow and late in coming. Rumania, probably the most industrialized among the eastern European countries until 1913, began railway construction in the 1860s. The first line was opened in 1869. However, in 1883 there were only about 1000 miles of railways and there were less than 3000 in 1900. In 1879 the government began nationalization of the railways and the process was completed in 1888. Russia, which eventually built some of the most important lines in the world, began construction in 1859, at the initiative of the state and several joint-stock companies. It is estimated that between 1851 and 1860 about 108 joint-stock companies were established and that half of their capital was sunk in the railways. Private companies, however, soon lost their attraction and the state began to take more direct control or build its own lines. The period of major construction began about 1880, and about a third of the total mileage existing in 1903 was constructed after 1893, mostly by the government. The lines were designed to connect various parts of the continent, from the Caspian and Black Seas to the Baltic and the Pacific. By 1912 a large network had been constructed, most of it under direct government control.

This survey suggests that the rates of construction and distribution of railways differed greatly from country to country. Detailed data indicate that Britain was the first country to build a railway and that it continued to lead in the number of miles and percentage of total European mileage until 1860. Germany and later France caught up and surpassed Britain in mileage. However, in terms of density of railways, Belgium was the leader and Russia was behind most of the western countries. Britain's thrust came before 1860, while those of Germany and France came between 1860 and 1880. That interval was the initial construction period for most other European countries. Other countries increased their mileage four-fold in that period and almost doubled the new total in the next 20 years. For example, Italy had only 248.5 miles in 1850; Spain had 17 miles; Holland had 176; and Switzerland 15.5 miles. By 1870, Italy had 3728 miles; Spain had 3417 miles; Holland and Switzerland had 870 miles each. In another 20 years all these countries almost doubled their railway mileage. The two decades between 1860 and 1880 were also critical for Russia, which increased its mileage more than two-fold in

that period. Nevertheless, the Russian railway mileage remained modest compared with other countries in the West with comparable areas and populations.[4]

Effects of the railroad expansion. Transport development, especially of the railroads, had radical effects on the European countries. Not only did it increase mobility, but it was an important economic endeavor. The business aspects were most significant to those countries that were able to export capital and skill and to invest abroad, thus reaping secure and often high rates of profit. Britain was especially active in exporting capital, and British companies played a major role in the construction of networks all over the world. After 1850 the French became equally active, particularly after the establishment of the *Credit Mobilier* and other investment banks. Entrepreneurship in railroad construction reached such a level that some observers have tried to explain the great depression of 1873 as a result of overinvestment in railways.

While all countries rushed to build railways for internal transportation, the efforts went beyond national boundaries. Lines were built in India and Africa. Two lines originating in Europe deserve special attention. The first was the Berlin–Baghdad Railway, which was designed for political as well as economic reasons to connect Berlin with the Persian Gulf. Concessions for the line from Berlin to Ankara were awarded in 1888 and from Ankara to Konia in 1896. The rest of the line to Basra in Iraq was awarded in 1899. However, the construction was interrupted by the First World War and had to wait for another generation. The second important line was the Trans-Siberian line from Chelyabinsk in the Urals to the Pacific port of Vladivostok. The line, connecting the Baltic with the Pacific and covering 4607 miles, was the longest con-

[4] Comparative detailed data are given in W. Woodruff, *op. cit.*, p. 253.

tinuous railway in the world and was completed in 1905. Other lines to Siberia have been constructed since, but none has surpassed it in strategic or economic importance.

In retrospect, some writers have questioned the significance and "indispensability" of the railroads for economic growth. Although such questions have been raised largely in relation to American railroads, they are equally relevant to Europe.

Almost invariably the railroads were able to displace the canals and internal waterways. They reduced the cost of transportation so much that water transport could not compete. Most European countries were ready to subsidize their waterways to keep them in competition. Canals and waterways had a sentimental value for many groups in Europe. They also offered specialized services at favorable costs in some cases, such as in the mining areas, in the timber industry, and where the climate was especially favorable. The waterways were also often used as a whip to force the railway companies to improve their services or keep down rates. Nevertheless, the railways offered advantages not available from waterways at any cost. Not until the development of the automobile and especially the trucking industry was there to be a viable competitor for the railway.

The saving due to the reduction of transportation costs brought about by the railroads in America has been estimated at various rates ranging up to 7 percent of the national income. The railroads' contribution to U.S. gross national product has been appraised for certain years at 16 percent. It may be assumed that the railway's contribution in Europe was as much.

In one respect the railroad seems clearly to have been indispensable. As cities increased in size, their transportation required reorganization. The subway or underground railroad came to the rescue. London had an underground railway by 1863; New York built its subway in 1878; Berlin had one in

operation in 1885; Paris finally followed suit in 1900 and began the construction of its "subterranean town," which was indispensable for the survival of the city.

Motor vehicles

The automobile was important in several ways, other than as a technological improvement. The automobile industry had forward and backward linkages. It stimulated the iron and steel industry, the precision of the machine-tool industry, oil drilling and refining, and the rubber industry. In addition, it revived interest in road and highway construction. The car, whether for passengers or for shipping goods, proved to be more versatile than the railway and more divisible. Investment for car services was much easier to secure than investment for railroads, if only because of the divisibility of the service. Therefore, there was less need for government aid and control. The car also proved more flexible than the railroad, since it could run on all kinds of roads. The invention of rubber tubes and tires, replacing the solid rubber used on bicycles, added comfort and speed, making the car highly competitive with railways.

The rates at which the automobile came into use are not readily available for the early years of the twentieth century, partly because cars and trucks were not registered. Nevertheless, the available data show a rapid increase in the number of vehicles in operation. For example, Britain had 8,000 private cars in 1904 and 53,000 in 1910. The number of buses, coaches, and taxis was 5,000 in 1904 and 24,000 in 1910. Freight vehicles increased from 4,000 to 30,000 in the same period.

Estimates for other countries are available only for later years. Although they are useful primarily as approximations, they show certain clear tendencies. For instance, countries that had industrialized extensively had more vehicles than those with less industrialization. Countries with more railroads acquired more motor vehicles. Both observations are clearly illustrated by estimates for Belgium, the Netherlands, France, Germany, and Sweden. The converse was true in countries like Portugal, Hungary, Poland, and Czechoslovakia. The data on Germany present problems because of boundary adjustments and the effects of the war.[5]

These observations might suggest that motor vehicles were more complementary than competitive with railroads. This is only partly true. Motor vehicles were complementary to the extent that they connected outlying areas with railway terminals. However, highways were also constructed to carry men and material between points already served by the railroads. In this sense they were a competitor. Many railway lines were saved only by government subsidy and protection. Even Britain, which resisted taking over the railroads, eventually nationalized them, at least in part.

Motor vehicles completed the transport revolution. Air travel was more of a qualitative than a quantitative change. Furthermore, air travel has not spread widely until recent years and still remains relatively limited in most of the countries of Europe.

CONCLUSIONS

In conclusion, the following observations may be made:

1. Changes in transportation were closely related to industrialization and development.

[5] Data on motor vehicles may be obtained from the United Nations, *Statistical Yearbook*, various editions.

As countries developed they had to construct comprehensive transportation networks.

2. The pattern of change began with roads. Canals and waterways had a relatively short period of expansion, enhanced by the application of steam to water transport. The major thrust came with ocean steamshipping and with railroads. These two means rendered distance almost insignificant. The invention of motor vehicles was both complementary to and competitive with railroads. Expansion of motor vehicles followed the same distribution pattern among the different countries as did the railroads.

3. The development of new means of transport had direct and indirect effects. In economic terms there were forward and backward linkages. However, these linkages were more important in the countries that produced vehicles and fuel than in those which imported vehicles in order to secure the services. Probably the most important impact of transport development was the radical stimulation it gave to the mobility of both factors and products, and to social mobility and business organization. These aspects will be explored in later chapters.

4. Finally, the developments in transport were both consequences of and stimuli to improvements in technology. The industrial revolution included the changes in transport as integral parts of the total development in demand and supply, both of which changed as technology changed. Present-day experiences with development may be evaluated fruitfully in the light of these interdependencies.

BIBLIOGRAPHY

Clapham, J. H., *Economic Development of France and Germany, 1688–1959*, New York: Cambridge University Press, 1928, pp. 104–112 and chaps. 7 and 12.

Clough, S. B., *The Economic History of Italy*, New York: Columbia University Press, 1964, pp. 66–81.

Denmark, Geographical Handbook series, Washington: 1944, chaps. 13 and 19.

Derry, T. K., and Trevor I. Williams, *A Short History of Technology*, New York: Oxford University Press, 1960, chap. 13, material used by permission of the Clarendon Press, Oxford.

Fishlow, A., *American Railroads and the Transformation of the Ante-Bellum Economy*, Cambridge, Mass.: Harvard University Press, 1965.

Fogel, R. W., *Railroads and American Economic Growth: Essays in Econometric History*, Baltimore: John Hopkins University Press, 1964.

Habakkuk, H. J. and M. M. Postan (eds.), *Cambridge Economic History of Europe*, VI, New York: Cambridge University Press, 1965, chap. 4.

Heckscher, E. F., *An Economic History of Sweden*, Cambridge, Mass.: Harvard University Press, 1954, pp. 240–246.

Henderson, W. O., *The Industrial Revolution in Europe*, Chicago: Quadrangle Books, 1961, pp. 221–226.

Vicens Vives, Jaime, *An Economic History of Spain*, Princeton: Princeton University Press, 1969, chap. 45.

Warriner, Doreen (ed.), *Contrasts in Emerging Societies*, Bloomington: Indiana University Press, 1965, *passim*.

Woodruff, William, *The Impact of Western Man*, New York: St. Martin's Press, 1967, chap. 6.

Changes in technology, volume of production, and productivity in both agriculture and industry were possible only after major changes took place in the organization of business and methods of financing. At the same time, these changes in agriculture and industry made it necessary for new patterns of organization and finance to evolve. By organization is meant the management of the day-to-day bsuiness, the long-term decisions regarding volume and composition of the product, and in some cases supervision of marketing and price fluctuations. The problems of financing include securing initial and expansion capital. In examining the changes that occurred in the modern period, we need to ask several questions: Who made these decisions? Who supervised production and marketing? Where did the finances come from? And what changes occurred during industrialization and development? Although organization and finance are closely related, we shall treat them separately for convenience and clarity.

DEVELOPMENT OF
BUSINESS ORGANIZATION

At the beginning of the modern period, and in many European countries until the middle of the nineteenth century, traditional patterns of organization still prevailed. The production unit was relatively small. The putting-out system was common. The master artisan had a few journeymen to help him. He responded to the orders of the merchant who put out the work, or he made the decisions himself, if he produced directly for the market. The risk was borne by the merchant capitalist, or by the master artisan if he played the role of capitalist. However, risk was minimized by the protective guilds which regulated the market and by the government's mercantilist policies.

In the modern era several conditions changed and therefore required new methods of organization. The guilds were undermined. The market became more anonymous. The influence of the master artisan was reduced by the introduction of machinery. The productive unit became larger. The pressure to keep the process of production going increased because of the greater amount of capital sunk in machinery. The putting-out system became inadequate for the new market. Therefore, production moved to the factory. Protection was replaced by competition and security by risk. New kinds of decisions had to be made. Furthermore, the small amount of capital that had been sufficient was no longer adequate to initiate and sustain a modern business.

The modern production unit varied in scale and complexity from one business to another. The workers were gathered in under one roof and one supervision. The unit was indivisible in the sense that a certain minimum scale had to be achieved in order to utilize the new machinery and justify the overhead costs. The production process was ordered according to the pace set by the machine. The product was more standardized, and the volume larger. These were some of the basic features of what has been called the *factory system*. Production in the factory tended to be based more on economic rationality than had previous systems, which had tended to be rather informal and subsistence-oriented.

Effects of the factory system

The larger number of people employed and the increased overhead investment and volume of output had several important effects. (1) A new attitude toward production had to be developed. The factory required a discipline which had hardly existed previously. To keep up with the machine, work had to begin and end at given times. As long as the machine was in motion, work had to go on. The worker could no longer set his own rules. The machine or its owner established rules for all workers. (2) When machinery and standardization were introduced, the place of the master artisan was undermined. His craftsmanship was competed out of the market by less skilled but equally useful people. (3) As discipline became necessary, constant supervision was needed, at least until new habits were formed. This often led to the delegation of authority to a foreman, and as the size of the operation grew, more delegation of authority became necessary. This was the origin of the separation between the ownership of the business and its management. (4) As the master artisan was reduced to the level of a worker and as less skill was needed to operate the machine, labor security was affected. On one hand the worker could find a job in more than one factory. However, his security was also reduced; no worker was indispensable. (5) The alienation of the artisans,

which had started under the putting-out system, was completed. The artisans were no longer owners of the means of production or of their tools. The source of their incentives was now changed. Previously they had worked for profits; now as workers they had to work for wages which were specified in advance. (6) The factory system or gathering-in of the workers had social and political effects: It created new ways of communication and new bases of identification and organization. (7) The factory and the machine encouraged an increase in specialization and division of labor. The factory was a conglomeration of interdependent operations leading to the final product. Division of labor was closely related to mechanization and efficiency of production. Hence, the factory required a more rational, scientific management than had earlier systems of production.

Influences on business decisions

The method by which these problems were handled cannot be understood in a vacuum. At least three important influences have to be considered: the general attitude toward economic and business behavior; the dynamic nature of production; and national and international objectives. The attitude toward business went through a series of changes in the modern period. Mercantilism, which had prevailed almost from the beginning of the sixteenth century, had declined by the end of the 18th century and a new laissez-faire psychology was evolving. The new concept of individualism and free enterprise left all decisions to the market. It was thought that if each producer catered to his own self-interest, competition would result in optimum production. The more efficient producer would survive, the less efficient would be eliminated, and total production would be increased at the lowest possible costs. The ideal of free competition prevailed for a short period around the middle of the nineteenth century. In the last quarter of that century there was a rapid return to protectionism and controlled competition which influenced decision-making within the production unit, as will be seen below.

Management and organization are also functions of the scale of operation. Since the production process is dynamic, the scale of operation tends to change unless restricted by a conscious policy. As competition becomes more severe, the production unit can stay in business only by increasing efficiency, updating its machinery, and enlarging its size to reap economies of scale. Otherwise the producer may be competed out of the market. However, as the scale is increased the managerial responsibilities increase, the risks become bigger, and the need for more formal and objective decision-making becomes acute. These processes may be unavoidable in a competitive economy, for two reasons. On one hand, as efficiency increases profits increase. Reinvestment of profits means enlarging the scale of production. On the other hand, the more efficient firm tends to absorb the less efficient, either by buying it out or by catering to the market it previously served. In either case, the result tends to be a larger business enterprise with bigger responsibilities and probably greater risks, until competition has been effectively reduced and a certain degree of monopoly has been created.

Finally, national and international objectives often enter into decisions on economic issues. The management and organization of business must be seen in the light of the objectives reflected in government policy and social legislation. This factor is best illustrated in relation to international trade and the formation of contracts and combines, which tended to restrict or regulate competition after 1883.

CHANGES IN ORGANIZATION

Ownership and management

Business and industry under the putting-out system were mainly privately owned and managed. If the government played a role in management and organization, it was an indirect one. In some cases, as in the Russian state factories, management was an extension of the serf system except for foreign experts and engineers. The most common form of business organization was the small family firm. Although companies were established, these were mainly of limited membership based on blood or friendship. Company members bore risk and responsibility according to whether they were active or silent partners: The active made the day-to-day decisions; the silent partners provided most or all of the capital. The owners of individual businesses and industries came from various backgrounds. They might be landlords, yeomen, merchants, engineers, or self-made men. They carried the brunt of all decision-making and management. By the beginning of the nineteenth century, first in Britain and the Low Countries and then in other areas, a change was becoming apparent because of the need for more capital, more personnel, and a larger managerial nucleus. The minimum investment and scale of operation were larger than previously. There was therefore a tendency toward accumulation and concentration, and new forms of organization became necessary. The private company or partnership continued to prevail, but most of the larger enterprises sought to incorporate, even though the corporate structure had to submit to certain restrictions, such as disclosure, public statement of accounts, and limited membership.

Corporations. At the beginning of the nineteenth century in Britain companies could be formed only by Act of Parliament. Due to pressure for relaxation, a law was passed in 1832 stating that only a letters patent from the government was required to form a company. However, since the new organization was still based on unlimited liability, each member was responsible for losses to the extent of all his assets. The question of limited liability was approached in stages. In 1837 the issue was brought to the courts. In 1844 the company was declared a legal person that could sue and be sued as one unit. In a series of Acts between 1855 and 1862 limited liability was established, and incorporation with limited liability became possible for any seven people upon handing in a memorandum. Thus the joint-stock company became a legal entity and each investor became liable only to the extent of his investment. The division between ownership and management became unavoilable. A later modification, which came in 1892 in Germany and in 1907 in Britain, made it possible to form a private corporation of up to 50 members. Such a corporation was exempted from disclosure and publication of a statement of account, but could not offer shares on the market. This form became more popular than the "public corporation."

In France a company law was passed in 1807. Two forms of companies were possible. A joint-stock company, *société anonyme,* required authorization from the government whether it had limited or unlimited liability. The *société en commandite par actions* had unlimited liability for the active partners and limited liability for the sleeping partners, and was less carefully supervised by the government. The policy towards these forms varied until in 1867 limited liability was granted to all corporations and the need for individual authorization was removed.

Germany, being still divided into many states, had no uniform law. Generally any form of corporation could be established by special authorization. The change came after unification. A uniform code was introduced between 1870 and 1872, removing the requirement for individual authorization and making limited liability a general rule. Thus the public corporation, *Actiengesellschaft,* was established. The private company, *Gesellschaft mit beschränkter Haftung,* was legalized in 1892. These forms of company organization were eventually adopted by all other European countries.

Managerial problems. Management in the factory faced new problems of discipline, competition, and technological challenge.

Discipline was a matter of efficiency, since orderly continuation of production was essential to efficient use of machinery and to fulfill contracts. However, there was no uniform method of introducing discipline, since an ethos of mechanized production had not yet evolved. The problem was most severely felt in Britain, although other countries did not escape. British managers and factory owners differed in their approaches, but all of them tried one or more of three methods: the stick, the carrot, and the creation of a new ethos.

The workers were entering into an environment which contrasted greatly with their traditional work life. The hours were long and the work monotonous. Whole families were sometimes employed, including children who were paid less than the adults but performed some relatively important duties. To keep this kind of labor force alert and active was not easy.[1] The first method tried was a feudal approach, namely corporal punishment. Beating the worker to keep him on the job was common in most factories. It has been suggested that parents beat their children to spare them more severe punishment by the foreman. Corporal punishment was applied especially to apprentices, who were committed for a number of years and could not be dismissed summarily. Dismissal was more commonly among adults, who were the breadwinners of their families. Another punishment was to levy fines on the worker for any obstruction of work or damage to the establishment. If more than one individual were involved in such obstruction, legal prosecution was applied.

A more positive approach to the problem was to create incentives by giving rewards for good work. The most common method was to pay according to a piece rate determined by the employer. Sometimes a subcontract would be awarded so that a person could recruit his own help, including his

---

[1] The worker's conditions will be dealt with in the next chapter.

wife and children. Sometimes bonuses and prizes were granted to those who performed well. In addition public praise and possibly a promotion could be expected. Some of the most successful producers,—such as Robert Owen, Wedgewood, and Boulton—were model employers, but these were the exceptions.

These measures were short-term stopgaps. They helped production but did not reduce the need for constant supervision, prodding, and punishment. A more lasting approach was needed. The managers and employers tried to indoctrinate their workers regarding the efficacy of self-discipline, hard work, and high productivity. These approaches were general in Europe, although they were more extensively applied in Britain, where industrialization came early and rapidly, long before the labor force could be prepared for it. By schooling, preaching, bribing, and recognition, the employers eventually succeeded, but their success came after the workers themselves became conscious of their position. Since development of the capitalist ethos cannot be divorced from the labor and trade-union movements, it will be treated in that context.

The employer and manager had also to make decisions concerning production and marketing, expansion, competition, and investment. Managerial problems had become too big and too risky to undertake on an informal, intuitive basis. It was necessary to consider the facts of economic life and the relations between costs and revenues. It may be recalled that double-entry bookkeeping had been a common practice since the end of the sixteenth century. In the nineteenth century the efforts to improve management emphasized mechanization and new techniques. However, by the end of the century attempts were being made to reorganize the production process and increase productivity without changing the production techniques. These attempts primarily involved increasing the division of labor which was a common feature of the new economy. Scientific management, which developed near the end

of the century, was a product of the United States. It aimed at making sure that all inputs were utilized in the most efficient way. Its application and development in Europe belong more to the present century, although some innovations were made in France in the last decade of the nineteenth.[2]

Accumulation, concentration, and cartels

In his first volume of *Capital* Marx advanced his theory of capital accumulation under competitive capitalism. According to Marx, the profit incentive, which is the driving force in capitalism, makes it imperative for the capitalist to reinvest in his business for both simple and compound reproduction: He invests not only to replace the depreciated capital but also for expansion. Reinvestment is necessitated by competition and the advantages accruing from capital accumulation. The accumulation of capital reduces costs and gives certain firms an advantage over others, forcing some firms out of the market. Their place is filled by well-established firms, since they have an advantage that creates barriers against new entries into their market. As a result the number of firms declines and their average capacity rises. Thus the scale of operation is increased and this increase gives further advantages by promoting economies of scale. The expansion from within is termed *accumulation*. Expansion by absorption of other firms is *concentration*. Marx foresaw an increasing degree of the two overlapping processes under capitalism.[3]

This thesis has been widely discussed, but its evaluation has been clouded by at least three factors. First, its political and social implications are objectionable to adherents of the capitalist system, while they are applauded by its opponents. Second, it is difficult to measure concentration and accumula-

[2] It may be noted that the marginalist economic theory evolved in the last third of the nineteenth century and may have had something to do with the development of scientific management.

[3] See the section on Marx in chap. 3.

tion. What share of the market must be controlled by one firm before concentration is considered accomplished is not totally clear. Nor is it definite what the minimum or optimum scale of operation should be. Therefore, it is not always clear whether a firm leaves the market because of internal weakness or because of the aggressiveness of its competitors. Third, Marx did not set a time limit or a rate for the development of concentration. Whether a certain percentage increase in the scale of operation, given the size of the market, would constitute concentration cannot therefore be easily determined. Because of these complications, the Marxist interpretation of the history of industrial development and its critiques have remained unclear.

Accumulation and concentration. Nevertheless, the last quarter of the nineteenth century did witness some increase in scale, accumulation, and concentration. The railway networks had already been fused together, reducing their number and enlarging the size of the unit of operation. In both production and finance there was a tendency for more efficient or successful firms to grow. This was particularly true after the legalization of joint-stock organization and limited liability. Old establishments were reorganizing themselves into joint-stock corporations in order to gain access to public funds, and new ventures were almost invariably incorporated from the start.

The tendency towards larger-scale operations was most apparent in heavy industries and in the newer industries such as chemicals, but it was evident even in textiles.[4] It is estimated that the number of textile firms in Lancashire remained relatively constant between 1884 and 1911, but that the number of spindles doubled. In Germany only one firm produced as much as 19,500 tons of pig iron in 1853. At least a dozen firms produced that much each in 1870. In France the firm of

---

[4] The banks will be treated separately below.

François de Wendel increased its production from 22,370 tons of pig iron in 1850 to 6 times that amount in 1870. The firm of Schneider, Hannay and Company of Britain had 2 blast furnaces in 1859; it had 12 in 1871. The trend was the same in other countries as evidenced by Nobel in Sweden, Krupp in Germany, and Codurill in Belgium. In Germany in 1875, 64.3 percent of all workers were in establishments with 5 workers or less; 19 percent were in firms with 50 or more. This distribution was also characteristic of France in 1850 and of Belgium in 1846. By 1895, 68.3 percent of all German workers were in large establishments. The number of establishments in France increased from 6,500 in 1852 to 63,000 in 1912. Nevertheless, the average capacity of horsepower per establishment increased from 11.7 to 51.3 in the same period. By comparison with Germany, the concentration in France was modest, a vast majority of the establishments still employing 10 workers or fewer by the end of the century. The number of factories in Russia increased by about 30 percent between 1887 and 1908 while the number of workers doubled and the value of output increased threefold in the same period. Expansion was evident in metals, coal, and oil distillation, and in the horsepower utilized in the various industries. While the significance of this accumulation and concentration may be subject to interpretation, the tendency was evident to some degree in virtually all the industrializing countries of Europe.

Combinations. Profits are a function of both volume and price, or market conditions. To reduce competition and secure a viable segment of the market, entrepreneurs developed a new form of organization in the last quarter of the nineteenth century. This has been variously described as the combination, cartel, syndicate, association, or trust. Combinations tried to reduce competition by regulating price; by allocating market quotas, either by volume or by region; and by applying uniform policies towards labor. Gradually they extended their jurisdiction beyond national boundaries and took the form of international trade agreements in which governments became involved. In essence these combinations became virtual monopolies; their significance has increased during the twentieth century.

The trend was general in Europe in the last third of the nineteenth century and in later years the United States and Japan also became participants. Some cartels had existed early in the nineteenth century. J. and P. Coats holding company existed in Britain in 1826 with combinations in the United States, Canada, Japan, Germany, Russia, Spain, France, and Belgium. The Salt Union of Germany was established in 1828. However, when it was revived the cartel movement was strongest in Germany, where the first cartels were established around 1870. By 1906 there were 400 cartels in Germany covering most of the important items of trade. Metallurgy, coal and chemicals led the way on a national basis. In 1883 an international rail cartel was formed, and tobacco followed. Eventually glass-making, textiles, oil, and foodstuffs were also covered by such agreements. Germany took an important step in 1898 by legalizing combinations. The legality was reaffirmed a decade later. However, with legalization came regulation. A special cartel court was created to rule on differences. Britain was a little slower, but in 1883 the British industrialists joined the International Rail Syndicate. By 1908 cartels were common in Britain as well as in other countries. In 1914 there were over 100 international cartels. Scandinavia, the Netherlands, Belgium, Switzerland, France, and Russia were active participants or advocates of these agreements. Confidence in unrestricted competition had virtually disappeared. The movement was even stronger after the First World War. The structure of the steel cartel, shown in Figure 21.1 will give an idea of the scope of a cartel.

The cartel movement had political as well as economic effects and implications. On one hand it expressed a fear of competition and unlimited supply. Fear of glut in the market seems to have been a main factor in its development. On the other hand it implied an increase in the power of the industrial group, since government became directly involved in their agreements. These tendencies were reflected in national tariff policies and in what has been called the "New Imperialism" which characterized the last quarter of the nineteenth century. These developments may be regarded as ways of searching for markets and will be treated accordingly.

In search of markets

It is probably a truism to say that an exchange economy needs a market to survive. If the internal market is relatively small, external or international markets must be found. The search for markets varies directly with the insufficiency of domestic demand to use up the supply created by the productive capacity existing at any given time. To avoid glut, bankruptcy, unemployment, and economic decline due to insufficient demand, efforts will be expended to secure a market. This may be accomplished through protection of the home market, free access to international competition, division of the market among the producers by national or international agreement, or the creation and securement of new markets. The last of these is the colonial or imperialist solution.

During the period of European industrialization all these approaches were used, sometimes concurrently. In the early stages, when few countries had built a large industrial capacity, the tendency was to remove restrictions within and among nations. The philosophy of free trade became popular and late industrializers joined the early ones in allowing specialization and comparative advantage to regulate the market. However, the rapid increase in productive capacity and the apparent dominance of the early industrializers created doubts regarding the via-

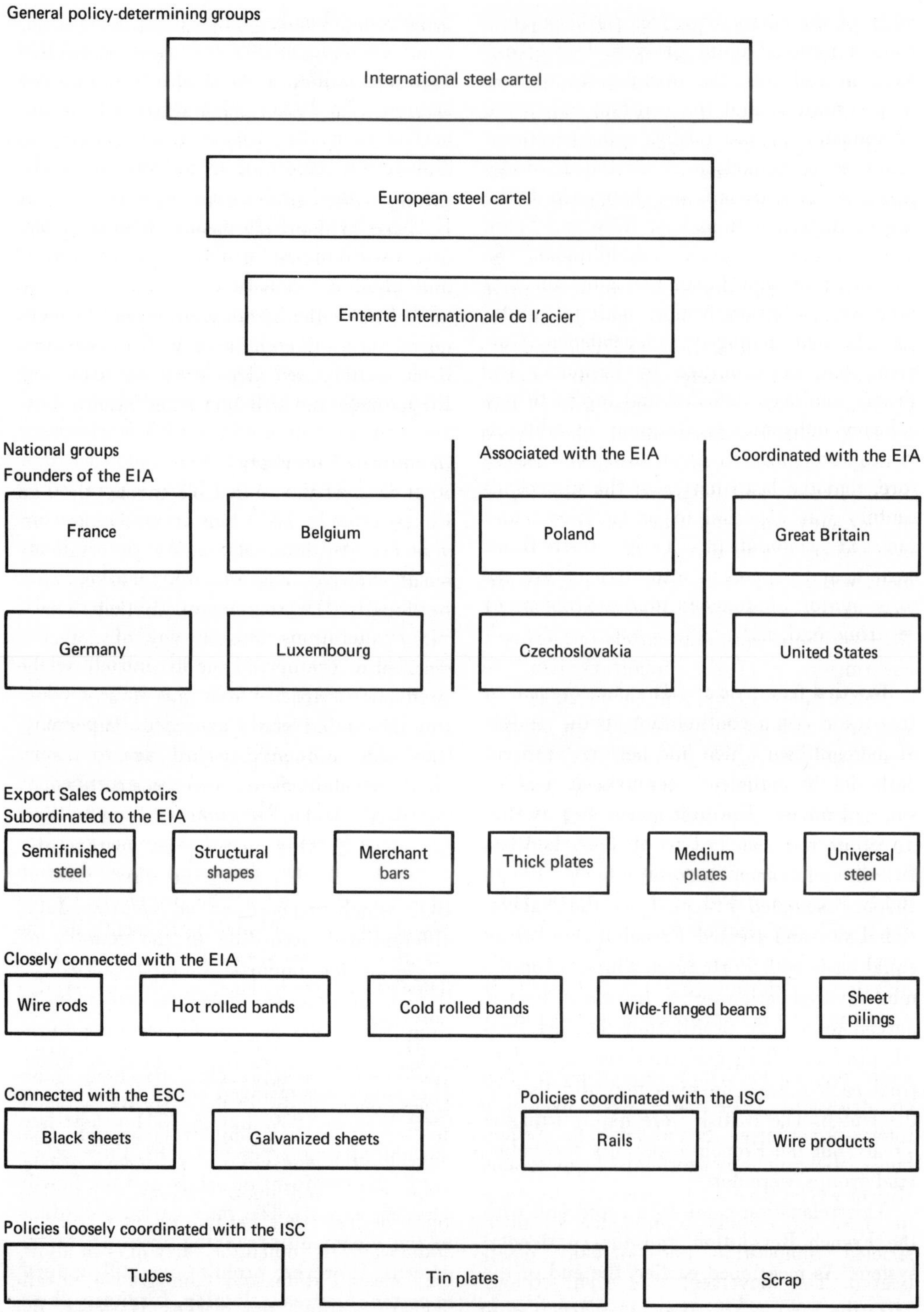

General policy-determining groups

```
┌─────────────────────────────────────────────────────────────┐
│                    International steel cartel                 │
└─────────────────────────────────────────────────────────────┘

      ┌─────────────────────────────────────────────────┐
      │               European steel cartel             │
      └─────────────────────────────────────────────────┘

         ┌──────────────────────────────────────────┐
         │        Entente Internationale de l'acier  │
         └──────────────────────────────────────────┘
```

National groups   Associated with the EIA   Coordinated with the EIA
Founders of the EIA

```
┌──────────────┐   ┌──────────────┐     ┌──────────────┐          ┌──────────────┐
│    France    │   │   Belgium    │     │    Poland    │          │ Great Britain│
└──────────────┘   └──────────────┘     └──────────────┘          └──────────────┘

┌──────────────┐   ┌──────────────┐     ┌──────────────┐          ┌──────────────┐
│   Germany    │   │  Luxembourg  │     │Czechoslovakia│          │ United States│
└──────────────┘   └──────────────┘     └──────────────┘          └──────────────┘
```

Export Sales Comptoirs
Subordinated to the EIA

```
┌──────────┐ ┌──────────┐ ┌──────────┐ ┌──────────┐ ┌──────────┐ ┌──────────┐
│Semifinished│ Structural │ Merchant  │Thick plates│ Medium   │ Universal │
│  steel   │ │  shapes  │ │   bars   │ │          │ │  plates  │ │  steel   │
└──────────┘ └──────────┘ └──────────┘ └──────────┘ └──────────┘ └──────────┘
```

Closely connected with the EIA

```
┌─────────┐ ┌──────────────┐ ┌──────────────┐ ┌──────────────┐ ┌─────────┐
│Wire rods│ │Hot rolled bands│ Cold rolled bands│Wide-flanged beams│ Sheet  │
│         │ │              │ │              │ │              │ │ pilings │
└─────────┘ └──────────────┘ └──────────────┘ └──────────────┘ └─────────┘
```

Connected with the ESC   Policies coordinated with the ISC

```
┌──────────────┐  ┌──────────────────┐      ┌──────────────┐  ┌──────────────┐
│ Black sheets │  │ Galvanized sheets│      │    Rails     │  │Wire products │
└──────────────┘  └──────────────────┘      └──────────────┘  └──────────────┘
```

Policies loosely coordinated with the ISC

```
┌────────────────────┐  ┌────────────────────┐  ┌────────────────────┐
│       Tubes        │  │     Tin plates     │  │       Scrap        │
└────────────────────┘  └────────────────────┘  └────────────────────┘
```

Figure 21.1 Basic structure of the international steel cartel.
SOURCE: Ervin Hexner, *International Cartels*, p. 397.

bility of the competitive free-market system from a national point of view. Overinvestment in railways, the opening up of new supply sources, and the constant expansion of industry in previously unindustrialized countries combined to cause the 1873 depression. This period also happened to be one of revived nationalism. Italy and Spain had just been politically rehabilitated. The United States and Japan had gone through processes of strengthening national unity. Canada had acquired independence. Germany had been unified by Bismark, and France had been defeated and forced to pay a heavy indemnity to Germany in addition to losing territory. It is not surprising, therefore, that the last quarter of the nineteenth century was a period of protectionism and renewed colonialism. Tariff restrictions, cartels, and expansion into Africa were the three major approaches to the problem of securing markets.[5]

Toward free trade.   The development of free trade was a continuation of the decline of mercantilism which had become apparent early in the eighteenth century, at least in some countries. The first major step in that direction was the Treaty of 1786 between Britain and France. According to this Treaty Britain exempted France from the Navigation Laws and treated French wines on an equal basis with Portuguese wines, or on the most-favored-nation terms. In return, France agreed to remove prohibitions against British products. Both countries also agreed to treat each other's linen as they did that of the Dutch. The British were happy with the Treaty but the French, especially the industrial groups, were not.

This relaxation came to a rapid end with the French Revolution and the continental system. As mentioned earlier, the end of the

Napoleonic War brought with it demobilization, unemployment, and new protective measures. Britain introduced new Corn Laws beginning in 1815, which restricted the import of corn. As early as 1810 Russia prohibited the import of manufactured goods, although this prohibition was relaxed in 1822 by levying high duties on some items. Austria also applied prohibitions and restrictions about the same time.

In France the manufacturers and farmers joined forces in seeking protective measures. High tariffs were introduced in 1814 and 1816 together with some prohibitions. Cotton yarn and cotton and woolen fabrics were prohibited. Iron imports were saddled with a 50 percent duty, and in 1822 it was raised to 120 percent. In 1826 these restrictions were tightened further, and most duties were raised between 100 and 400 percent. This system of restrictions remained in effect with minor alterations until the middle of the nineteenth century. Prussia introduced a tariff law in 1818, but it was quite moderate; the duties barely exceeded 10 percent. Only salt and playing-card imports were prohibited, both being government monopolies. Spain had more protective tariffs than Germany in this period. Its mercantilist policy was reaffirmed in the Tariff Law of 1825 which imposed an *ad valorem* duty, differentiated according to the country of origin of the imports. Imports carried in foreign ships were subject to excess duties from 50 to 300 percent higher than those levied on goods coming in Spanish ships. This policy was changed after the end of the Civil War in 1839, but in 1841 a new law introduced four types of tariffs, three relating to the continent of origin and the fourth covering exports. The rates varied according to the commodity, ranging from 15 to 50 percent. However, prohibitions still applied to cotton, footwear, clothing, furniture, ships of less than 400 tons, firearms, wrought iron, tin plate, and some agricultural products. Some reorganization and reduction of

[5] Colonialism can only in part be explained by this approach. However, the economic factor was probably the most important determinant of expansion.

duties were contained in the Law of 1849, but it still banned 14 items and levied duties on 1410 others.

In spite of these restrictions and prohibitions, there was an inclination toward freer trade. The *Zollverein* of 1834 united several German states in a customs union, thus removing all duties on the exchange of goods between them. However, between 1834 and 1838 heavier duties were imposed on import of manufactured goods from other countries. This period also witnessed the beginning of Friedrich List's arguments for protection of infant industries. His policies were not adopted before his death in 1846, although he had many adherents. Relaxation of restrictions took major strides in the 1840s. In Britain, the Navigation Laws were modified in the 1830s to allow for reciprocal agreements. Between 1849 and 1854 they were repealed altogether. The Corn Laws, which had been relaxed by replacing prohibition with duty, were repealed in 1846, effective in 1849. Only nominal duties on the import of grain were retained and these were finally removed in 1869.

Between 1850 and 1870 trade relations tended more and more toward free and unrestricted trade. The German states continued to join the *Zollverein* until 1871, enlarging the home market with few additional restrictions on the external market. In 1865 all duties on grain were removed, and in 1873 duties on iron and ship-building materials were abolished. The French, under Louis Napoleon, began by reducing the duties on coal, iron, steel, raw materials, and foodstuffs. The major step, however, was taken in 1860 when the Cobden–Chevalier treaty was concluded with Britain. The treaty, made for ten years, removed all prohibitions between France and Britain and reduced duties on all items which they had traded. The treaty contained a "most-favored-nation" clause. Most countries concluded similar treaties in the following decade. In 1866 the French modified their Navigation Laws to replace the prohibition

against ship imports by a 25 percent duty. The surtax on goods imported under flags other than that of the producing country was also removed. However, the surtax on goods imported through foreign markets, such as cotton from Liverpool or coffee from Hamburg, was retained. Also the monopoly on the coasting trade was retained.

Similar changes were made in Spain. In 1865 a law was passed authorizing the government to remove the differential flag duty on articles coming from Europe, but it was not effected until 1868, after Queen Isabella was dethroned. The Law of 1869 removed all restrictions and prohibitions on exports and imports. Duties were retained, but were reduced and graduated according to the item of trade. This law remained the basic framework of commercial policy until 1891, although modifications were introduced which tended to check its effectiveness. Russia removed prohibitions and gradually adopted a liberal trade policy. The Tariff Law of 1868 completed this trend, but it was not long lasting. The same trend could be observed in Scandinavia, the Low Countries, and Italy.

Return to protection. Free trade in an ideal form was not achieved in this period and the tendency toward liberalism soon came to an end. Freedom of trade was correctly conceived as favoring some countries over others, as inhibiting the advance of the late comers, and as inconsistent with revived nationalism. In other words, the policy of free trade seemed inappropriate in a world segmented into many national markets. Therefore, as soon as the pinch of the depression of 1873 was felt, a tendency toward protectionism emerged. The theories of Friedrich List and his disciples in the German historical school were brought back to life and embodied in protective laws in Germany. Other countries could hardly remain passive. Just as the tendency toward free trade was contagious, so was the return to protectionism.

Beginning in 1871, one country after another introduced protective tariffs. The French National Assembly reimposed higher duties in 1871 on coffee, sugar, tea, cocoa, and wine, and in 1872 restored the surtax on imports through third markets. The movement picked up momentum after 1879. A tariff law was passed in 1881 that levied *ad valorem* duties ranging from 10 to 30 percent on all manufactures. However, raw material remained free of duty. The rates were changed periodically until 1892 when higher duties were introduced by what has been known as the Méline Tariff, named after the secretary of the commission responsible for it. The major innovation of this tariff was to introduce a maximum and a minimum rate, the double-rate system, thus encouraging "most-favored-nations" agreements. It also increased the rates about 80 percent and assimilated the French colonies within the national tariff area. The rates were changed again in 1897, at which time bounties and subsidies to sugar manufacturers and silkworm producers were introduced. Attempts to abolish the double-rate system were made as late as 1910, but it was formally retained. Bilateral agreements were concluded with 62 countries, all of which paid the minimum rates.

Between 1878 and 1880 Germany introduced protective tariffs on iron, textiles, agricultural products, and various industrial products. The new duties were not prohibitive, but they were a beginning. Attempts to reduce them in the 1890s, after Bismarck's departure, were abortive. In 1902 the duties were raised again, but a more radical rise came after the First World War. The 1902 law was important in providing for reciprocal agreements, thus opening the way for bargaining. It may be noted that German tariffs were no more exorbitant than those of other countries at the time, with the exception of Britain, which resisted reimposition of tariffs virtually until the First World War.

Russia returned to protectionism in 1877 when duties were reimposed on locomotives, railroad rolling stock, and other heavy-in-dustry items. By 1890 high tariffs had been imposed on pig iron, textiles, coal, and finished metal goods. While revenue was the objective of these tariffs at the beginning, protectionist objectives were more characteristic of the Law of 1891, which raised duties 3–400 percent over their level in 1868. Russia, however, was also ready to conclude trade agreements: The tariff war with Germany between 1892 and 1894 ended with an agreement according to which lower-than-maximum rates were applied to trade between the two countries.

Spain resisted the return of protectionism and planned further liberalization and rate reductions. However, a country at Spain's stage of development has a hard time in resisting the general trend. New tariff laws were passed in 1891 and 1892. All trade exemptions introduced since 1882 were abolished and new protectionist rates were levied. The protectionist policy was completed by the law of 1906, which has been considered the basis of Spanish policy until the present.

This survey could be expanded to cover other European countries, but the trend has been clearly demonstrated. Only Britain was able to resist an early return to protectionism. In all cases, revenue was a minor objective of tariff law. The major objective was protectionism. These measures, like the cartel movement, were designed to guarantee a share in the existing markets to new and old industries. However, the expanding economies of Europe were also anxious to increase the size of that market. Therefore, a third approach was applied.

Territorial expansion. Colonialism was not limited to the last quarter of the nineteenth century, as the above discussion might imply. Britain acquired the Cape Colony in 1814 and expanded to Orange River in 1836. France established its power over Algeria in 1830. However, the major acquisitions were made after 1870. Germany had no territories outside Europe before that

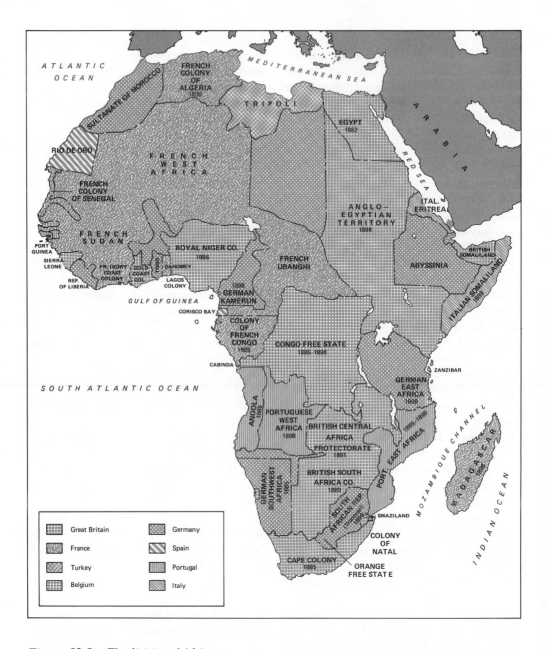

Figure 21.2 The division of Africa.

date, but between 1884 and 1895 its African colonies were acquired. The extent of the "New Imperialism" is illustrated dramatically by the map of Africa around 1900 (Figure 21.2). The figure shows how the continent was subdivided among the countries of Europe, including those that had no colonies before the last quarter of the nineteenth century. For example, the British colonies in 1860 covered 2.5 million square miles and contained 145.1 million people. In 1880, these estimates rose to 7.7 and 267.9 million, respectively; and in 1899 the area was 9.3 million square miles containing 309.0 million people. The colonies of France in 1860 covered 0.2 million square miles and held 3.4 million people. In 1880 the estimates were 0.7 and 7.5 million, respectively.

By 1899 the area dominated was 3.7 million square miles with 56.4 million people. Germany, which had no colonies before 1880, had 1.0 million square miles and 14.7 million people under its rule in 1899. Similar acquisitions were made in this period by Italy, Spain, Portugal, and Belgium.

What explains this new wave of imperialistic expansion? We have suggested that the pressure to create and secure markets was a major cause. Skepticism regarding this and other economic explanations of imperialism has derived from observations that imperialism was costly to the mother country, that the purchasing power of the markets it provided was limited, and that diplomatic and political objectives were at least equally important. Such skepticism results largely from a confusion between national or aggregate objectives and benefits and the objectives and benefits of special interest groups. The search for markets is directly related to special interest groups— those groups which need certain raw materials and produce goods that require markets. These were the groups which benefited economically from imperialism, whether they were ship-builders, producers of finished products, railway-builders and inventors, or civil servants and military officers of the Empire. Indeed, the mother country's unwillingness to withdraw from its colonies until forced to suggest that the benefits were positive and that these interest groups were powerful enough to influence the imperial policy of their country. It is not a mere coincidence that the formation of cartels, the return to protectionism, and the "New Imperialism" came at the same time, and only when industrial expansion and concentration had become widespread.

INNOVATIONS IN FINANCE

It should be clear by now that the organization of the enterprise was related to the methods of financing production and commerce. The new and expanded industries required much larger amounts of capital than had been needed earlier. It was necessary to develop new mechanisms and institutions by which resources could be pooled and funds could be raised. Such mechanisms include inducements to the income earner not to consume and incentives to invest. They also include the institutions by which savings can be channeled into investment at the right time and place and at costs that are consistent with the expected returns. Since economic expansion did take place, it follows that adequate financing was provided.

The problem of financing has been approached from various angles. Some have asked to what extent capital was a limiting factor in development. Others have taken the need for capital as a point of departure and concerned themselves with the sources and terms of financing. The implications of the first question are that the capital needed in the early stages of development was relatively small and that therefore traditional methods of financing were adequate. The second position implies that whether the amount needed was large or small, the problem of capital provision still had to be solved.

Investment capital can come from either domestic or foreign sources. It may be private or governmental, and it may come from present or past savings (hoardings). Foreign capital may be acquired by borrowing, by inviting investors, or by gifts, piracy, exploitation, or other adventurous means. Primitive accumulation during the mercantilist period and capital from profit inflation have been discussed above. These sources were no longer relevant after 1800, since the initial capital had already been accumulated, at least in the aggregate. Therefore, we shall concentrate on the domestic and foreign sources which were based on savings, past or present, and on the mechanisms by which capital was brought into industry.

Private saving and investment have always been practiced to some degree, even when the level of income was close to subsistence. Private sources continued to be important in industry as long as the demand could be satisfied with a relatively small supply of capital. Master artisans saved out of their income until they had enough capital to start a business of their own. Sometimes they received help from family and friends or sold property to secure the necessary funds. Partnership was another way of pooling resources for investment, as has been shown. People with accumulated capital often participated in business as silent partners, or were willing to loan the funds at given rates of interest. Sometimes deferment of payment was the way out. A landlord, for example, might agree to defer all rent payments until a business had reached a certain level of development. Once the initial capital had been acquired and profits had begun to accrue, expansion could be undertaken through self-financing out of profits.

These sources were too limited to finance large-scale ventures such as the railways or heavy industry, or to allow rapid expansion. Financing, whether domestic or foreign, was facilitated by the development of banks and joint-stock organizations and by the growth of stock exchanges which facilitated public lending and investment. The governments of various countries also played a major role in financing development.

The banks

Banking and credit have become common and accepted institutions long before the industrial revolution began. The modern period, however, witnessed a mushrooming of banks and an increase in the variety of organization. It has been noted that banks grew and were able to render services in the takeoff period in several European countries, although their effectiveness seems to have varied directly with their freedom from government intervention and restriction.

Britain. Britain, the first to industrialize, was also the first country in Europe to develop a widespread system of banks. Besides the Bank of England, which had been in existence since 1696, Britain enjoyed the services of a large number of local country banks after 1750. These country banks had agents in the city to carry out business on their behalf. Among other functions, they issued banknotes, accepted deposits, loaned money, and served as financial intermediaries. While the majority were private, after 1825 some of them were joint-stock banks. While the average country bank was relatively small, their large numbers provided a bank for every 17,000 inhabitants in England and Wales. The density, however, varied from one district to another. Country banks were a unique feature of the British system and their life span was short.

Around the middle of the nineteenth century the transition to joint-stock banking was underway. Joint-stock banks were authorized in 1826. By 1841 there were 115 joint-stock banks and 321 private banks. In 1875, the number of joint-stock banks had declined to 120 and private banks to 252; the respective figures in 1886 were 117 and 251. The right to issue was also becoming limited to a smaller number of banks, in part because of concentration. Many banks had branches. In 1864 there were 744 joint-stock and 272 private bank branches. The three largest joint-stock banks were the London and County with 165 branches, the National Provincial with 158, and the Capital and Counties with 99 branches. Six other banks had more than 50 branches each. In Scotland the concentration was much more rapid; by 1864 there were only 13 banks, all of them joint-stock banks of issue with branches all over the country. The next 20 years brought extensive concentration and amalgamation of banks in England. By 1910 there were 20 joint-stock banks with more than 100 branches each, and 3 of them had more than 500 branches each. In addition, there were probably 15 or 20 small joint-stock banks and a dozen private banks. The concentration in banking was more complete and more lasting than in industry, except in railways.

Savings banks had also evolved to help

the small income earners improve their lot. These were based on philanthropic objectives, the trustees and managers being unpaid officers. In 1817 there were about 80 savings banks in England and Wales and almost twice that number in Scotland; there were more than 500 banks in the United Kingdom by the 1840s. There were also bill brokers and discounting houses, but these did not issue credit or provide investment capital.

Banking was especially important for saving and investment because of its effects on limited liability and the stock exchanges. Until this time, the stock exchange had been limited to those investors who were able and adventurous enough to invest with unlimited liability. The new arrangements reduced the risk and created independence, since the investor remained liquid to the extent of the market value of his shares. The base for investment funds was thus enlarged and joint-stock companies could float their issues on the market. In place of private or family capital, capital from the public at large was tapped; hence the new concept of the public corporation.

France. Modern banking in France began shortly after the Revolution at the initiative of Napoleon. Before 1800 there were only a few small banks in Paris, all of which issued their own banknotes. Napoleon arranged with the director of one of these banks, the *Caisse des Comptes Courants*, for the establishment of the Bank of France. In two years a capital of 30 million francs was paid up. The bank opened its doors for business in 1800 and in 1803 its capital was raised by 50 percent and it was given a monopoly of banknote issue. Although the bank opened branches in other towns, these were closed soon after the fall of Napoleon and new banks of issue were chartered in various places. Their notes, however, had limited negotiability and their activities were mostly local. By 1848 a few more banks were chartered, but most of the activity was concentrated in the Bank of France, which had opened branches in 13 provincial centers by the middle of the century. Many small private banks also came into being in various parts of the country. These carried the brunt of money circulation and lubrication of the economy. Some of these private bankers were foreigners from Switzerland and Germany or former contractors to the French military. Insurance companies were also active financially, facilitating the recruitment of credit and money circulation. In addition some private credit companies were established which did not need government authorization.

France's major contribution to banking and financial operations came with the rise of joint-stock companies and the establishment of investment banks in the second half of the nineteenth century. The government took an active part in the new movement. After 1848 the provisional government created *comptoirs d'escompte* in all major cities. Their function was to discount bills, serve as intermediaries between the private sector and the Bank of France, and grant credit for various terms. The government of Napoleon III went further, establishing several other joint-stock banks, among which were the *Crédit Foncier de France* to handle mortgage credit, the *Crédit Agricole*, and the *Comptoir de l'Agriculture*. The most important new institution, which grew rapidly and died as rapidly, was the *Crédit Mobilier*, established in 1852. The *Crédit Mobilier* was the creation of Napoleon III and the Pereire brothers, who carried the services of the bank into Spain, Italy, Britain, Germany, Mexico, Russia, and many other places. Their innovation was the bank's investment function. It was not a passive institution. It promoted development both in France and abroad and provided the credit for it. It recruited domestic and foreign capital at a level never attained before. After many major achievements and a few embarrassments, the *Crédit Mobilier* was liquidated in 1867, but it left a great heritage and its example was later copied in various countries of Europe. The funds for this and other institutions were recruited by government prodding and contributions, by joint-stock flotation, and by reinvestment of profits. The stock exchange grew rapidly and Paris became a major international financial center. The few other banks that were established during the rest of the century were concentrated joint-stock investment banks much like the *Crédit Mobilier.*

Germany. Germany had, as noted previously, innovated in land mortgages and cooperative credit. Both of these facilities related mainly to agriculture. Credit facilities for trade and for government projects were also available, as they had been for a long time. The modern banking system began around 1830 at the initiative of the various state governments. The first bank of issue was authorized in Bavaria in 1835 as the *Bayerische Hypotheken und Wechselbank.* The second was established in Leipzig in 1838. The Prussian Bank was created in 1846 as a joint-stock bank of issue. Before 1860 several other banks of issue were established. Most of these, however, were absorbed by the Prussian Bank after it became the *Reichsbank* of the German Empire in 1875. Although these central banks were important in German finance, the private banks were more important for industry and development. The banks were closely associated with industry, first as sources of credit and subsequently as shareholders or controllers. Many of these banks were run by old financial institutions such as the Rothschilds, the Schicklers, and the Bethmanns, who had catered to government needs and accumulated fortunes. Joint-stock credit institutions fashioned after the *Crédit Mobilier* were established after the middle of the century. Various state governments were willing to grant charters, and joint-stock investment banks were fully established by the mid-1880s.

German banks were alway small in number but greatly concentrated, just as were the businesses in which they played a part. They had a relatively small number of local branches. The big banks were anxious to concentrate on big business and to absorb or control other big banks, leaving small business to the local banks. They were also anxious to establish foreign branches in the Near East, the Far East, and Latin America. The German banks extended their influence by acquiring interest in major banks in other countries including Italy, Britain, Austria, and the United States. Like the *Crédit Mobilier,* they also were directly responsible for creating joint-stock companies in industry, mining, and transportation both within and outside the country.

Belgium. Belgium was the first country to establish a joint-stock investment bank, the *Société Générale de Belgique,* with the personal help of the king. It had little success between 1822 and 1835, and was reorganized as the *Banque de Belgique* with the aid of the Rothschilds and French capital. Other banks were soon established; 47 existed by 1875. Branches and private banks took care of local business. The Belgian banks, like their counterparts in France and Germany, played an active role in industry. It is uncertain whether they did so on their own initiative, without government influence. Nevertheless, they were effective in promoting Belgium's early industrialization.

Italy. The Italian states had their own banks which had issued notes and carried on banking services for a long time. In fact, banking activities had been almost perfected in Italy before the modern period. However, the banking system which had something to do with the industrialization and development of Italy was a more recent creation, consisting of several relatively large banks. The Sardinian National Bank of Turin had resulted from the merger of the Bank of Genoa and the Bank of Turin in 1849–1850. There were other large banks, the Tuscan

Bank, the Tuscan Credit Bank, the Bank of Naples, and the *Banca Romana*, among others. Through absorption and liquidation, the Sardinian National Bank became the Bank of Italy, the only remaining bank of issue. Other banks also came into existence as joint-stock banks and participated heavily in investment banking and long-term credit. Apparently some of the Italian banks could not stand the effects of tying funds for long periods. Some were threatened with bankruptcy and had to seek help from the National Bank and from German banks. Others were almost totally crippled or went bankrupt, as did the *Banca Romana* in 1893. In fact, it has been observed that Italian banking, though it followed trends similar to those in other countries, was a failure as a joint-stock venture. Reorganization came near the end of the century with further amalgamation and concentration. It should be noted that financing of Italian industry depended heavily on foreign capital.

Spain.   Foreign investment, both direct investment and credit, was also very important in Spain. Although Spain had received large sums of precious metals which might have served her well in development, most of that capital was dissipated on nonproductive expenditures and found its way out of the country. When the time for development came, domestic capital was lacking. Spanish financial institutions were little help during most of the nineteenth century. At the beginning of the century, the banks had relatively small capital assets. Reorganization of the central banks was fairly successful, but private banks hardly existed at all in the first half of the century, and where they did, they pursued limited, traditional functions.

The second half of the century saw the establishment of the *Banco de España* in 1856. This was an amalgamation of two other banks, which had the obligation to create branches. The bank prospered, as did private banks in this period. There were also German and French banks in Spain. The

Spanish bankers' guild of Madrid was known as the "merchant capitalists," although it carried out no investment operations. However, the Bank of Barcelona and the Bank of Bilboa did invest in railways, mining, and commercial activities. The end of the century witnessed both expansion and concentration, but the investment function remained limited. The Spanish banks apparently remained passive instruments, even though there was a need for investment banking and a stock exchange had existed since 1831.

Sweden.   Sweden's capital was in the hands of merchant creditors throughout the first half of the nineteenth century. During this period, however, a tendency toward a modern capital market emerged. New banks were established and a system of borrowing and investing in bonds and stocks was created. Limited liability was not legally established until 1895, after which a corporate structure developed. Sweden's principal source of capital seems to have been inflated profits. Foreign capital contributed directly through investment in railways and indirectly through financing mortgage banks. The large merchant houses continued to be a source of capital. The banks also began to have some influence around the middle of the century. It should be noted that since foreign borrowing was carried out mainly by the government, exorbitant interest charges and control of local industry by foreigners were impossible. Even privately acquired foreign capital was largely in the form of loans. Thus control remained in domestic hands.

Though major banks were late in appearing, they did participate in development. A private bank, the *Stockholms Enskilda Bank*, played a major role in developing the timber industry. The joint-stock companies which began in 1863 eventually became the most important banks in the country. The central bank, the *Riksbank*, was not established until 1897, by which time, it has been suggested, the two strongest groups in the Swedish economy were the industrialists and the large banks. Between them these groups controlled all branches of the economy. It may be recalled that by this time cooperative credit had become fully established in Sweden.

Russia. Russia's experience was similar to that of the western countries in several ways. The state played an important role in establishing financial institutions. Stock companies began in the 1830s but were slow to develop before the Emancipation. A State Commercial Bank was established in 1817 to support commercial business. Various cities also created their own banks especially for discount services. However, the main effort to help industry came from private banks such as the House of Stieglitz and others owned by former Germans, Greeks or Italians. The limited investment effort of these financial institutions seems ironic in view of the legalization of limited liability as early as 1805 and joint-stock companies in 1807. Ten joint-stock companies were established by 1836 but these were mostly on a small scale. However, insurance companies expanded rapidly during the first half of the century.

After 1860 a virtually new banking system, in which the central and local governments played major roles, was created in Russia. The State Bank was created in 1860 and in 1875 it had 49 offices; there were 114 in 1900, and 137 in 1914. Under its auspices the State Bank created savings banks which proliferated from 72 in 1875 to 4781 in 1900 and twice that many in 1914. The cities, municipalities, and provinces were active in creating their own banks, mainly of the joint-stock form. The number of these increased from about 90 in 1875 to almost 10 times that number in 1914. In addition to the small credit and cooperative societies, there were commercial joint-stock banks, of which there were 39 in 1875 and 50 in 1914; their branches increased from 49 to 778 in the same period. Until about 1890 the banking institutions were passive instruments, limiting their functions to discounting, extension of credit, mortgages, and other such services. Since the state and local authorities were major depositors and borrowers, much of the capital accumulation came from forced savings. After 1890, however, the joint-stock banks became more directly involved in industrial expansion.

Until about 1908, foreign bankers were willing to undertake direct investment in Russia. However, after many failures, the French bankers especially were anxious to shift to indirect investment by acquiring shares in Russian banks. By 1916 foreign acquisitions in the 10 largest Russian banks amounted to 45.1 percent of the total ownership; 50.5 percent of these were acquired by French, 37.1 percent by German, 9 percent by British, and the rest by other bankers. Foreign banks also began to form syndicates with Russian banks and through them acquired interests in Russian industry. The Soviets changed all that, nationalized both the financial and the industrial establishments, and made accumulation and development a responsibility of the state. During the Soviet period financing was primarily from domestic resources, and mostly by forced saving, confiscation, and reinvestment of returns.

These various examples illustrate the structures of European financial institutions during industrialization. Two main points remain to be clarified: (1) To what extent was financing of development made easier? This question will be explored by examining the cost of borrowing. (2) To what extent was foreign capital important in the development of the various countries?

Interest and the cost of money

The cost of money or the rate of interest should, in a market economy, reflect the ease or difficulty of obtaining capital. Investment capital is reflected in long-term rates, while commercial and working capital is represented by the short-term rates.[6]

Although the available estimates of interest rates are neither complete nor reliable, certain trends can be easily observed.[7] The long-term rates in Britain during the eighteenth century were relatively stable from the third until the seventh decade. There was a perceptible rise after the ninth decade and the high rates continued until the second decade of the nineteenth century or until the end of the Napoleonic War. The nineteenth century was a period of almost continuous decline until the First World War, after which the rate fluctuated, with a low rate prevailing in the fifth decade of the twentieth century. The rate declined in the nineteenth century from 4.80 percent in the first decade to 2.47 percent at the end of the century.

The trend was similar in other European countries, with three differentiating features. In other countries, especially in France, there was more fluctuation in the middle decades of the nineteenth century. Second, in the twentieth century there was an upward trend in the rates in most European countries, except Sweden and Switzerland. The United States experienced only a minor reversal of the downward trend during the second to fourth decades of the twentieth century, and a new low followed. Third, the levels of the rates in the various countries were different. There was a significant rate differential between Britain and other countries throughout the eighteenth and the nineteenth centuries, which suggests that capitalists in Britain had easier access to capital than those in other countries. Britain invariably had the lowest long-term rates

between 1800 and 1919, when it was replaced by the United States. Switzerland had the lowest rate between 1950 and 1960, sharing that position with the United States. Belgium also seems to have had relatively low rates, compared with France, Germany, and Sweden. The differential between these rates would even be higher if the few available rates in countries like Spain, Russia, and eastern Europe had been taken into consideration.

The relation between industrialization and long-term interest rates may be gleaned from these comparative estimates. It should be emphasized, however, that this is not a one-way relationship. While easy access to credit may help development, development implies accumulation, relative abundance, and hence lower rates. This observation may explain the trend, especially near the end of the nineteenth century.

The short-term rates provide a somewhat different picture. While a general rate decline was evident in most countries, there was much more fluctuation in the trend and less consistency in the differentials between country rates. Furthermore, the fluctuations were much more dramatic, particularly during the late nineteenth and early twentieth centuries. No single country was able to enjoy the lowest rates consistently. The Netherlands had the lowest rate in the eighteenth century. Early in the nineteenth century this position was temporarily occupied by Britain. Soon after it was regained by the Netherlands and retained until 1859. After that date France and Britain seem to have competed for that position, the latter having an edge over France until around the end of the century.

It should be possible to discover a relationship between the growth of financial institutions and the decline of long- and short-term rates. It is tempting to conclude that the rates declined during the nineteenth century as a result of the development of banks, joint-stock, and other financial institutions, but observations from other periods do not

---

[6] The conception of long- and short-term rates is somewhat vague. However, in this context these rates are the best indicators of the relative ease of obtaining capital.

[7] The following observations are based on data from Sidney Homer, *A History of Interest Rates*, pp. 492–493 and 508.

Table 21.1. Foreign investment by selected European countries (Nearest $100 million)[a]

COUNTRY	1825	1840	1855	1870	1885	1900	1915	1930
United Kingdom	500	700	2,300	4,900	7,800	12,100	19,500	18,200
France	100	(300)	1,000	2,500	3,300	5,200	8,600	3,500
Germany	—	—	—	—	1,900	4,800	6,700	1,100
Netherlands	300	200	300	500	1,000	1,100	1,200	2,300
Sweden	—	—	—	—	—	—	100	500

[a] *Foreign investment in the table "is the total of outstanding investments in other countries, public and private, made on a long-term basis, converted into U.S. dollars at the current rates of exchange."*
SOURCE: *William Woodruff*, The Impact of Western Man, *p. 150.*

support such a conclusion. The relationship seems to depend on the structure of the financial institutions, government policy, access to foreign capital, and the relative amount of capital that has been accumulated.

The Role of Foreign Capital

The role of foreign capital in the early stage of industrialization and development can hardly be exaggerated. In the absence of domestic resources, a country must seek foreign capital. However, its significance is only partly a function of quantity. The quality of the investment is more important. Loans to monarchs or to finance imports of consumption and luxury items have little impact on development, compared with those financing railways, new industry, or the import of strategic capital goods. Furthermore, foreign capital is more significant when accompanied by skill and new technology.

The development of most European countries, Britain and the Low Countries being the only exceptions, depended heavily on foreign investment. Britain was a major exporter of capital until about 1870, after which France and Germany assumed that position. By that time, those countries had accumulated enough capital to require new markets for their capital and skill. The pattern of foreign investment can be seen in Table 21.1. These figures show clearly the early and significant part in foreign investment played by the United Kingdom. They also show the later advent of other countries into the field. However, these investments

were not all made in Europe. Britain's participation in European investment had declined enormously by 1900. In contrast, as late as 1915 half of France's investment and most of Germany's were in Europe. British capital reached almost all countries of Europe, through either loans to governments or direct or indirect loans to industry. The recipients included France and Germany, Spain, Portugal, eastern Europe, and eventually Russia. The railroads were major recipients in most cases. As late as 1913, British capital still operated in at least 10 European countries, including Russia, Germany, and France, and in 16 types of industrial endeavors.

British capital had accumulated because of heavy industrialization and therefore was in relative surplus. French industry was much less developed even by the end of the nineteenth century. Nevertheless, there was a relative surplus of capital because the French were less inclined to mechanize and use up the accumulating capital domestically. Between 1816 and 1851 96 percent of French foreign investment was in Europe. More than a third of the total was in Spain, a little more than a fifth in the Italian states, and 18 percent in Belgium. Between 1852 and 1881, Europe's share declined to about 70 percent of the total. Eastern Europe acquired a slightly larger share than previously, although the Mediterranean area still received more than a third of the total. As Britain was reducing its investments in eastern Europe, France's were increasing. Between

1882 and 1914, 38 percent of the new French investments were made in Russia and the Balkan states; this was about 60 percent of all French investment in Europe. Probably over half of the exported French capital was loaned to foreign governments. Although it is hard to determine how capital was used, French capital was instrumental in the railroads of eastern Europe, in the mines of Spain and Italy, and in metallurgy and textiles in Russia. By 1900 Paris was an international financial capital, rivaling London as a center for foreign borrowing.

German investment was mostly in Europe, although the Near East, the Far East, and Latin America later received a share. By 1914, a little less than 60 percent of German investment was in Europe. German investment came late, but it increased rapidly in the last quarter of the nineteenth century, although it remained modest compared with British foreign capital. Much of the German European investment before 1914 was concentrated in Austria-Hungary and Rumania. It was also concentrated in foreign governments' interest-bearing securities and thus did not involve direct participation or control of industry by German investors. Nevertheless, the German bankers, who were the major investors, did participate directly and bear the risk in various enterprises. Again the railways were major recipients. Public utilities in the Balkans and electrical plants in Austria, Hungary, Russia, Italy, and Spain were also favorite investment opportunities.

The experiences of less important capital-exporting countries were similar as far as the method and distribution of financing were concerned. In most cases, foreign investments created political complications, since the creditor country usually tried to protect the interests of its nationals in the debtor country. The consequences were not always harmonious or favorable. From the standpoint of development, one may wonder whether foreign investment was indispensable. Observers of Spanish development suggest that without foreign capital even the limited Spanish development might have been impossible. Investment in Italy was sometimes a life-saver, especially when the national financial institutions were in difficulty. Swedish development also owed much to foreign capital, as admitted by Swedish observers. The only possible, though tentative, conclusion is that foreign capital was indispensable to the extent that it provided strategic investment, was large enough to leave an impact, and was accompanied by basic skill and knowledge. How much of this capital was misallocated or designed for exploitation is not easy to determine, and whether such a price was justified can only be decided by the people in the capital-importing country.

GENERAL OBSERVATIONS

The industrial development of Europe was accompanied by several important changes in the organization and financing of economic activity. These changes were interdependent with development in a process of challenge and response, although sometimes the process was rendered ineffective by intervening obstacles. The changes may be summarized as follows:

1. Domestic industry was gradually replaced by a factory system which promoted standardization of output, regularization of work, and a larger-scale operation. The factory system was closely related to advances in technology and mechanization. Although it could have existed without mechanization it would have lost most of the rationale for its existence.

2. As technology advanced and the scale of production increased, there was a tendency toward specialization and division of labor, and with this a separation between ownership and management. This separation, in turn, gradually led to more rational decision-making.

3. Development was accompanied by concentration and combination, which were mechanisms to secure part of the existing

market, to regulate competition, and to reduce the advantages enjoyed by the early comers to industrialization. However, as development became more widespread, the existing market was no longer sufficient. Therefore, there was a tendency to restrict free trade, return to protectionism, and to search for outside markets both for consumer goods and for investment. This search was reflected in the "New Imperialism" which divided Africa and the remaining parts of Asia among the countries of Europe.

4. The new type of economic enterprise required larger-scale financing than could be secured by traditional methods. While individual savings and partnerships continued to be important, new institutions were also introduced or legalized. The joint-stock company became common and limited liability reinforced it. The stock exchange completed the framework for floating issues to recruit funds from the public. The "public corporation" came into being. This development was accompanied by the reorganization and expansion of banks and other financial institutions. These institutions also followed the trend toward concentration and amalgamation.

5. The development of financial institutions and the accumulation of capital were reflected throughout Europe in the declining rates of interest, especially on long-term loans. Accumulation was also reflected in the expansion of capital exports by the more developed countries, which also represented the search for new markets. The less developed countries of Europe were the main targets for the export of capital. They were anxious to import capital which promised to advance their development and make industrialization possible.

BIBLIOGRAPHY

Ashworth, William, *A Short History of the International Economy Since 1850*, Second edition, Toronto: Longmans, 1962, chap. 3.

Blackwell, William, *The Beginnings of Russian Industrialization 1800–1860*, Princeton: Princeton University Press, 1968, pp. 88–95.

Cairncross, A. K., "The Place of Capital in Economic Progress," in *Economic Progress*, L. H. Dupriez (ed.), Louvain: International Economic Association, 1955, pp. 235–248.

Cameron, Rondo, *et. al.*, *Banking in the Early Stages of Industrialization*, New York: Oxford University Press, 1967.

Cameron, Rondo, *France and the Economic Development of Europe, 1800–1914*, Second edition, Chicago: Rand McNally, 1965.

Clapham, J. H., *Economic Development of France and Germany, 1688–1959*, New York: Cambridge University Press, 1928, pp. 301–314 and chap. 13.

Clapham, J. H., *An Economic History of Modern Britain*, New York: Cambridge University Press, II (1932), chap. 9; III (1938), chap. 4.

Clough, S. B., *The Economic History of Italy*, New York: Columbia University Press, 1964, pp. 39–47, 124–132.

Clough, S. B., *France: A History of National Economics 1789–1939*, New York: Octagon Books, 1964, pp. 180–190, 212–234, 253–257.

Feis, Herbert, *Europe, the World's Banker 1870–1914*, New Haven: Yale University Press, 1930.

Habakkuk, H. J., and M. M. Postan (eds.), *Cambridge Economic History of Europe*, VI, Part I, New York: Cambridge University Press, 1965, pp. 450–454, 472–476.

Heckscher, E. F., *An Economic History of Sweden*, Cambridge, Mass.: Harvard University Press, 1954, pp. 246–251.

Hexner, Ervin, *International Cartels*, Chapel Hill: University of North Carolina Press, 1946, especially chaps. 1–2.

Homer, Sidney, *A History of Interest Rates*, New Brunswick: Rutgers University Press, 1963, especially Parts III–V.

Jenks, L. H., *The Migration of British Capital to 1875*, Camden, N.J.: Thomas Nelson & Sons, 1963.

Landes, David, *Bankers and Pashas: International Finance and Imperialism in Egypt*, London: Heineman, 1958, chaps. 1 and 2.

Liefmann, Robert, *International Cartels, Combines and Trusts*, London: Europa Publishing Co., n.d.

Lyaschenko, P. I., *History of the National Economy of Russia*, New York: Macmillan, 1949, pp. 557–559 and chaps. 33–34.

Manboux, Paul, *The Industrial Revolution in the 18th Century*, New York: Harper & Row (Harper Torchbooks), 1961, Part II, chap. 2; and Part III, chap. 3.

Marx, Karl, *Capital*, I, Frederick Engels (ed.), Samuel Moore and Edward Aveling (trans.), New York: International Publishers, 1947.

Mayall, Kenneth, *International Cartels*, Rutland, Vt.: Charles E. Tuttle, 1951, chap. 2.

Payne, P. L., "The Emergence of the Large-Scale Company in Great Britain, 1870–1914," *Economic History Review*, second series, XX, No. 3 (Dec. 1967), pp. 519–542.

Pollard, Sidney, "Factory Discipline in the Industrial Revolution," *Economic History Review*, second series, XVI, SS, No. 2 (Dec. 1963), pp. 254–271.

Rostow, W. W., *The British Economy in the 19th Century*, New York: Oxford University Press, 1949, chap. 3.

Stolper, Gustav, *et al.*, *The German Economy, 1870 to the Present*, New York: Harcourt, Brace & World, 1967, chap. 2.

Vicens Vives, Jaime, *The Economic History of Spain*, Princeton: Princeton University Press, 1969, pp. 46–47.

Woodruff, William, *The Impact of Western Man*, New York: St. Martin's Press, Inc., Macmillan & Co., Ltd., 1967.

Wright, Harrison M. (ed.), *The "New Imperialism,"* Boston: D. C. Heath, 1961.

22

LABOR ORGANIZATION AND SOCIAL MOVEMENTS

CONCEPTUAL FRAMEWORK

In the preindustrial as in the industrial society, labor has been one of the three main factors of production. The major difference between the two environments is that in industrial society labor increasingly has become wage labor, dependent on employment provided by the capitalist. The worker, regardless of his skill or specialty, owns no tools or machinery, carries no risk for the product, and makes no decisions concerning production. He owns his energy and skill and earns his living by selling his labor power to whomever will pay for it.

The labor market

An increase in the supply of labor power on the market, relative to the demand, tends to depress the price or the wage for which the worker can bargain. Thus any factors influencing the demand for or the supply of labor power will affect the level of wages. The prospective employer tries to pay the lowest possible price for labor, while the worker tries to obtain the highest one possible. In a free market, the two parties recognize the interdependence of their interests and try to find a wage acceptable to both.

The demand for labor is a derived demand. It depends on the demand for the product of labor, on the state of technology, and on the expected profitability of production. Given these determinants, it is to the employer's advantage to keep the labor supply relatively abundant in order to improve his bargaining position. Since he cannot control the supply, however, he may try to control the demand. This he can do by restricting production temporarily, by controlling a larger share of the market in order to shift the demand from one sector to another, and by changing the state of technology. By mechanization and automation, the employer may substitute capital for labor, thus reducing the demand for labor and rendering the supply relatively abundant, at least in the short run.

Employers tried all these methods during the nineteenth century and have done so ever since. In fact, failure to do so probably would have forced them to go out of business. Concentration, combination, and mechanization were in part designed to improve the employers' bargaining position in the labor market.

The worker was not passive, but for a long time he was weak, disorganized, uninformed, and incapable of bargaining because he required subsistence. To be able to bargain, the worker needs some degree of material security, information about market conditions, and the ability to move from one employer to another as he sees fit. In other words, he must feel on an equal footing with the employer. However, the individual worker is hardly ever in that position, especially if he must face a powerful employer on one side and compete with many other workers for his job on the other.

The worker's position also depends to a large extent on the political and social environment in which he functions. It is stronger or weaker depending on the social legislation governing industrial and labor relations. The more sympathetic the society, the more protected he feels and the more freely he can bargain with his employer. If the sociopolitical environment is unsympathetic, his position is weakened regardless of the genuineness of his claims. He has no recourse, since it is a part of the rationale of private enterprise that the employer should try to pay the lowest possible wage. Any deviation from this principle must be explained in terms of unknown or changing conditions so that the wage paid remains the lowest possible under the circumstances. The sociopolitical environment has a particular impact on nonwage bargaining items. An employment contract may include not only the wage, but the terms of payment— whether it should be in money or in kind, and whether it is per day, per hour, or per piece of output. It may include fringe benefits such as safety and comfort in the shop, vacation time, sick leave, pensions, and education. The likelihood of receiving these benefits is usually a function of the general social and political attitude towards labor and the distribution of power. Unless the worker has the support of the community at large, his position can be improved only if market conditions are strongly in his favor.

The workers cannot influence the demand for labor in the aggregate, but they can affect the demand for a given product and thus for the labor that produces it. They can also keep the demand relatively high by obstructing mechanization and substitution of capital for labor, although this tactic can be used only sporadically and temporarily.

The major influence on demand for labor is the supply of labor power, which is a function of the natural increase of population, internal migration, the life expectancy and age structure of the population, the level of skill, the system of education, and the social attitude toward work. The supply of labor will be higher if population is increasing rapidly, if migration from rural to urban areas is increasing, if life expectancy is long and women and children are expected to work, if the general level of skill is relatively high so that many people may compete for the same job, and if the number of years of schooling is relatively small. The converse of these conditions tends to restrict the supply of labor. The supply in specific regions or industries is also influenced by the ease of mobility. For example, a tight family structure or high transportation costs could easily restrict the supply of labor in a given region.

Although the natural population increase and international migration have some effect on the labor supply, internal migration has been the major source of industrial labor. Internal migration is a function of a supply push and a demand pull. Deterioration of local conditions can induce migration. However migration will materialize only if the prospects elsewhere are favorable. The push by negative forces at home must be reinforced by positive forces elsewhere. However, highly positive forces in another locality may be sufficient to create a demand pull by rendering local conditions relatively inferior. The push and the pull tend to induce migration until the expected benefits in the two areas have been equalized. As will be seen below, both forces were acting in nineteenth-century Europe to increase the supply of industrial labor throughout the period.

The workers may be able to influence the supply by changing forces of demand and supply in their favor, at least temporarily. For example, they may organize themselves into a union and bargain as a body against a few employers. But the more widespread the strike or the boycott is, the more difficult it is to sustain. The workers may be able to prevent internal migrants from entering the market, but this can be done only locally and only if other forces will cooperate. Internal migration cannot be totally restricted, especially if economic forces favor it.

The workers can secure long-term benefits only if they can recruit social and political support for their fight. Thus, the organization of labor can hardly be divorced from social and political movements. The system of government, the right to vote, and the attitude toward cooperation and socialism are all important factors. The formation of political parties is also influential. In the final analysis, however, two factors appear as the most important in determining the conditions of labor: the economic forces and rate of development prevalent at the time, and the internal organization and awareness of the workers themselves. The first determines the size of the cake in which the workers seek a share. The second determines their ability to recruit outside support and to restrict the supply of labor relative to the demand so that their share may be increased.

The problems of industrial labor are quite recent. Except in Britain, they arose generally after the middle of the nineteenth century, when internal migration from rural to urban sectors became widespread. At this time also industrialization was advancing and the demand for labor was rising. Most of the modern labor movements originated in the nineteenth century when changes in agriculture released large numbers of rural workers, industry became more concentrated, businesses formed combinations, and capital accumulation was greatly expanded.

THE IMPACT

Attempts to evaluate the impact of the industrial revolution on labor have resulted in a split between the pessimists and the optimists. The pessimists, including Karl Marx and Frederick Engels, Arnold Toynbee, Sidney and Beatrice Webb, John and Barbara Hammond, and E. J. Hobsbawm, have usu-

ally been concerned with the living conditions of the workers, the social aspects of the industrial society, and the qualitative advantages and disadvantages of the new environment. The optimists, like T. S. Ashton, J. H. Clapham, and J. D. Chambers, have concentrated on the economic and quantitative aspects. They have also raised basic questions regarding the methods of evaluation applied by the other school. They questioned the value of making short-run observations without looking at the long-run effects of the revolution on labor. More important, they asked why one should associate the conditions of life during the industrial revolution with the revolution itself. Why not compare these conditions with those that prevailed before the revolution or in places where no revolution took place? These questions could shake the foundations of the pessimists' arguments. However, not all their arguments depend on these issues. Long-run changes do not obliterate the short-run effects, many of which were direct results of industrialization. Moreover, the optimists have not as yet supported their argument by sufficient empirical data, although they have made a start.

We do not intend to resolve the controversy, nor even to discuss it in detail. Rather, we will survey the impact of industrialization as seen by labor and other sectors of society, and the reactions to it. The rationale of this approach is that a reaction can be interpreted only in the light of the reactor's conception of the situation. In other words, facts are important only as they are conceived by the people directly affected by them. Unfortunately, this approach is not a simple one. People do not always record their conceptions of the facts, and what has been recorded by writers, politicians, organizers, and others may tell only a part of the story. For this reason, the impact of an event can be evaluated only in the light of the reactions to it. This approach may thus be rephrased in the form of an hypothesis: The reactions reflect the apparent impact. If the impact were favorable, the reactions should have been harmonious. If the reactions were not harmonious, the impact must have been conceived as unfavorable.

Rapid industrialization took place at a time when the labor force was not prepared for machine technology and the towns and cities were not prepared for an influx of population. It came at a time when most governments were either uninterested or were inclined to keep their hands off business and therefore offered no protection to labor. And in most countries industrialization came before the remnants of serfdom and feudalism had disappeared. The workers suffered from these problems throughout the early stages of industrialization: their wages were low relative to their needs and expectations, the hours of work were long, employment security was lacking, and discipline was severe. In addition, they had to put up with poor conditions outside the shop. The influx of population put pressure on housing facilities and the limited utilities available. The workers had to live in very poor housing, with no sanitation facilities or utilities. In order to get a job or earn sufficient income, a man often had to bring along his wife and children, subjecting them to his poor working conditions. Furthermore, the workers lived under the constant threat of unemployment due to mechanization.

The influx of people into the cities came from three sources: the natural population increase, migration from one urban area to another where industry and manufacturing were being concentrated, and migration from the rural areas where land tenure changes had left many people landless or underemployed. Even though depopulation of the rural areas might not have occurred, contrary to the observations of the pessimists, the natural population increase in the rural areas found its way to the manufacturing and urban areas. The immediate effects tended to be a relative depression of wages, worsening of living conditions, and greater insecurity of employment. These conditions were common in Britain, France, Germany, Russia, and to an extent in Scandinavia.

Britain

A journeyman cotton spinner in Britain, speaking to a striking crowd in 1818, pictured the conditions in his industry eloquently. After describing the ostentatious living of the employers and the tyranny and ignorance of the master spinners, he described conditions of the workmen as follows:

The workmen in general are an inoffensive, unassuming, set of well- informed men, though how they acquire their information is almost a mystery to me. They are docile and tractable, if not goaded too much; but this is not to be wondered at, when we consider that they are trained to work from six years old, from five in a morning to eight and nine at night. Let one of the advocates for obedience to his master take his stand in an avenue leading to a factory a little before five o'clock in the morning, and observe the squalid appearance of the little infants and their parents taken from their beds at so early an hour in all kinds of weather; let him examine the miserable pittance of food, chiefly composed of water gruel and oatcake, broken into it, a little salt, and sometimes coloured with a little milk, together with a few potatoes, a bit of bacon or fat for dinner; would a London mechanic eat this? There they are (and if late a few minutes, a quarter of a day is stopped in wages), locked up until night in rooms heated above the hottest days we have had this summer, and allowed no time, except three-quarters of an hour at dinner in the whole day: whatever they eat at any other time must be as they are at work. The Negro slave in the West Indies, if he works under a scorching sun, has probably a little breeze of air sometimes to fan him: he has a space of ground, and time allowed to cultivate it. The English spinner slave has no enjoyment of the open atmosphere and breezes of heaven. Locked up in factories eight stories high, he has no relaxation till the ponderous engine stops, and then he goes home to get refreshed for the next day; no time for sweet association with his family; they are all alike fatigued and exhausted. This is no over-drawn picture: it is literally true. I ask again, would the mechanics in the South of England submit to this?[1]

While this speech was intended to incite the workers, it was a relatively mild description of the general conditions, even those of the mechanics. Available data suggest that the mechanics' wages were very close to those of the spinners until about 1825, although they surpassed them greatly afterwards.

More than two decades later, conditions were still very poor. Reports on textile factories made in the mid-1840s by inspectors and medical men testify to the depressing effects on the health of the children and women. Wages had not started to improve in real terms. Housing and sanitation were still miserable. Accidents in factories were frequent. Children were reported to be pale, thin, and small for their age, and girls reached maturity very early. The conditions had permanent effects on factory men which medical opinion attributed to occupational hazards. Similar observations were made of other industries. In mining, for example, children four or five years old were employed as long as they could be kept awake. The conditions obviously varied from one pit or factory to another, but the depressing working conditions were common in most of them. An important and prevalent complaint was against the truck system of payment, or the payment of wages in kind. The employers hedged against price fluctuations by shifting part of the risk, paying in goods

[1] Val R. Lorwin (ed.), *Labor and Working Conditions in Modern Europe*, pp. 43–44.

produced in the shop. The workers in Britain and elsewhere considered this system a major grievance.

It should be noted that the employers were not always or solely responsible for child labor. While they were anxious to recruit any labor, the parish administrations delivered the children either to make a profit out of their employment or to rid themselves of the burden of taking care of them. The weakness was in the social system as much as in the structure of the industrial labor market.

This depressed living standard for the workers in Britain was accompanied by low wages until about 1840. The average money wage in the United Kingdom, based on a survey of various districts, increased from an index of 75 to 124 between 1790 and 1810, or by about 75 percent. This was the period of the Napoleonic War and high inflation. The impact on real income is not clear. However, between 1810 and 1850 there was a decline from an index of 124 to 100, with a low of 98 in 1845. Prices declined steadily but gradually between 1815 and 1850 by almost 50 percent. Much of the price decline came in the decade of the 1840s, however. It is apparent that the real income of the wage earner improved little if any before the 1840s.

The decade of the 1840s brought improvements for the wage earners who were employed, but many were not and their conditions were further depressed by poor harvests. The major improvement came in the second half of the nineteenth century. Real wages in the United Kingdom rose from an index of 100 in 1850 to 132 in 1880, to 184 in 1900 and to 194 in 1906, almost doubling in a little more than half a century. As will be shown below, these improvements were not divorced from the reactions of labor.

France

The impact in France varied from town to town and from period to period. During the first half of the nineteenth century, industrialization was gradual and domestic industry was still widespread. Internal migration was not as rapid as it was in Britain. Nevertheless, some towns grew rapidly, suffering consequences similar to those in Britain. Mulhouse, which grew from a village into a large city in a relatively short period of time, faced serious housing problems. Slums in and around the city were created to supply labor for the expanding industry. The working conditions in the factories were bad: there was poor lighting and ventilation and few safety measures protected the workers. The wages were probably adequate for subsistence but there is little evidence of any improvement in real income before 1840. Temporary wage reductions in periods of industrial crisis were frequent. The hours of work were long. Hand workers stayed 18 or 19 hours on the job, while those in the mills worked 14 or 15 hours, although the hours decreased by the middle of the century. The employment of women and children was common at subsistence wages and under terrible conditions. Frequently the children worked the same number of hours as the adults in order to keep the machines going. An official report of 1821 from Alsace stated that:

> Several of the manufacturers—not content with having by the aid of these machines expanded their output beyond all measure—have given much greater scope to their cupidity by making children of either sex and of any age work day and night in their workshops to keep their machines going all the time and so double their profits. This policy has been made possible by the poverty of the inhabitants of this district. And so the poor children and young people, handed over to this new species of slave labour, lose their health and hardly retain a human appearance. This is a generation sacrificed to the cupidity of the manufacturers, a generation that shows no physical growth and

displays unexampled moral corruption. And the inevitable consequence will be that in a few years great difficulty will be experienced in finding men capable of bearing arms and of cultivating the land.[2]

Discontent with machinery and industrialization continued, since working conditions were not improved. Reports from Alsace and Nord in 1840 found that work hours still ranged between 13½ and 15 hours a day, with breaks totaling only 1½ hours. Slum conditions were still prevalent. In Normandy 60 percent of the workers did not earn enough money for their basic needs. Although not all of these grievances were results of industrialization, mechanization and the relatively abundant supply of labor tended to aggravate them in the industrial and urban districts. Although some improvements in real wages took place in the 1860s, the industrial workers were greatly dissatisfied. Wages rose, but so did prices, and periods of prosperity were followed by periods of crisis. In the process many people suffered, especially since there was little government sympathy for them. Throughout the century labor felt discriminated against and believed that industrialism was largely to blame.

Germany

The conditions in Germany in the early nineteenth century were even worse than in France. Many people had become landless, thus increasing the influx of labor into town. Industry was not expanding rapidly enough to absorb this labor force. Due to the competition of the factories, the domestic workers hardly earned enough to exist. The urban workers also complained of long hours, low wages, and poor housing. These conditions were aggravated in periods of crisis and poor harvests, such as the potato-crop failure of the 1840s. One of the workers described

[2] W. O. Henderson, *The Industrial Revolution in Europe, 1815–1914*, p. 107.

the situation in Cologne in 1848, in an address to the factory owners:

> The time for hypocrisy is over and done with. When you wanted to overcome the competition of foreign rivals you cut down our wages and you made no personal sacrifices. When you wanted to drive the goods of other German manufacturers from the home market it was the factory hands who had to work harder for longer hours. When you aimed at artificially raising the prices of manufactured goods you closed your works without turning a hair even although hundreds of workers were ruined. . . .[3]

The demands which were subsequently presented dealt with terms of dismissal, hours of work, overtime, sick pay, minimum wages, and procedures for arbitration and settlement of differences. One common grievance, in addition to the above, was child labor and the tendency of some parents to "sell their children into industrial slavery." These conditions prevailed during most of the century, and improvement came only when the pressure mounted and the whole system was threatened.

Russia

The conditions in Russia, although similar in some ways, differed in others. Industrial development in Russia was slower than in the three western countries. Rural labor was still tied to the land, even after Emancipation, because of the redemption system. Except in the St. Petersburg district, Russian industry was widely dispersed outside the cities. But although one would expect fewer of the hardships experienced in the West, this was not the case. Serfdom had left a deep impression on Russian society. Although it had been abolished in 1861 it continued to color the relationship between employers and employees. This was especially true in the case of factory serfs who continued to work in the factories after Emancipation. Prior to Emancipation the workers had been transferred with the job and treated as serfs. They had few rights other than subsistence. After Emancipation they were joined by former peasants who were new to the factory, to discipline, and to wage work. The workers faced the same problems of discipline, long hours, low wages, and poor housing that were common in the West. They expressed their resentment by hesitating to migrate to the factories, or by making their stay temporary if they did. They resented the heavy fines imposed on them for delinquency. They complained against living in barracks without windows, which leaked on rainy days. That there was hardly any difference between these conditions and those in their former villages did not seem relevant. The workers felt the misery and complained against it. Nicholas Nekrasov, in a poem, "The Railways," written in 1865, describes these conditions:

The road is straight; its banks are narrow;
Rails there are, and posts and bridges . . .
And Russian bones line that road.
Do you know how many of them there are, Vanya?
> We laboured in the heat and in the cold,
> Our backs were eternally bent,
> We lived in dug-outs, we starved and froze,
> We soaked in rain and died of scurvey . . .
The foreman robbed us, officials flogged us, Poverty crushed us.
We suffered all,
We, who are the warriors of God
And the peace-loving children of toil.[4]

A pamphlet of 1900 shows that the attitude of the workers had not changed:

[3] W. O. Henderson, *The Industrial Revolution in Europe, 1815–1914*, p. 38.

[4] S. P. Turin, *From Peter the Great to Lenin*, p. 28.

Our life is dark, and heavy; it is spent unendingly in tormenting, uninterrupted labor. Do we really live? Do we really experience the joyfulness of life in our close, dirty rooms, or within the noisy walls of the factory, where you cannot understand your own thoughts because of the rumbling of the machines? Do we really attain the happiness of life? We are born, marry, and die, and leave to our children the same eternal forced labor which we already inherited from our fathers and forefathers, besides the tormenting thoughts about our meager crust of bread. And beside us life runs its happy course, bright and light, the life of satiated and contented people—our bosses. We, sullen, sick, and exhausted, walk past them and see their contented life, we see that all the happiness of their lives is founded on our toil, sustained by the blood and tears of our forefathers, fathers, and children. . . . We hate the social order under which, at the price of the needs and of the unmeasured toil of millions, a small clique of parasites lives in happiness and luxury. We have a right to a share of the wealth which we create by our work. . . .[5]

These quotations, admittedly political, indicate the complexity of the impact of industrialization on the workers. This impact was due not only to objective conditions, but also to the workers' attitude toward other groups, by whom they felt deprived and mistreated. The above illustrations had parallels in other European countries, although in different degrees. In some cases the impact was much less because of slow development, the demonstration effect of what happened elsewhere, or insufficient education, awareness, or consciousness among the workers. Nevertheless, it is safe to suggest that as industrialization increased, the impact was more distinctly felt in all countries.

[5] Val R. Lorwin (ed.), *Labor and Working Conditions in Modern Europe*, p. 78.

THE REACTIONS

The impact of industrialization on the workers affected the rest of society. It was also determined by the actions and reactions of others in society, including businessmen, intellectuals and social philosophers, political groups, and the government. The businessmen, as noted previously, were concerned with production and profit. They used the stick, the carrot, and indoctrination. Sometimes they took the initiative, but in most cases they simply reacted to the pressures of the various forces in society, including labor. In general the business community was unwilling to concede any advantages to the workers unless it became apparent that further hesitation could lead to greater losses.

The intellectuals, social philosophers, and religious leaders generally reacted in two ways. They tried to educate the community in general and the workers in particular concerning the ills of society and the necessity of dealing with them. They also tried to mitigate the effects of these ills by sponsoring charitable societies and services. They played a major educational role, arousing awareness among the workers, supporting their cause, and encouraging them to demand and fight for improvements.

Political leaders and governments reacted in different ways. Generally they either restricted the activities of the workers or facilitated them by bringing about institutional and legal reforms. Since governments usually seek change only when the pressure for change mounts, the initiative invariably came from the workers and their leaders.

It should be noted that the labor leaders were not necessarily from the ranks of the workers. They simply identified with labor and espoused their cause, although they might also play various other overlapping roles. A social philosopher might be a political leader and government official. He might even, like Robert Owen, be a businessman as well, despite his sympathy for labor and welfare programs. In discussing the reactions of labor, we will therefore also explore the actions and reactions of the other groups.

The reactions of labor during the first half of the nineteenth century were colored by two major factors: an unsympathetic government and the beginnings of socialism. The workers' cause often became a lever for these two forces. Conservative governments restricted the labor movement to curtail socialism, and socialist groups supported labor to undermine the Conservatives. Gradually, the workers began to understand this mechanism and take advantage of it, especially in the last quarter of the century, by becoming political in their own right.

Labor's reaction took various forms, ranging from escapism and passivism to violence and rebellion and to political sophistication, which came with education, organization, and prosperity. The methods used and the successes achieved varied from one country to another, with Britain leading the way towards trade unionism and the politicization of labor.

The United Kingdom

Labor reactions. The history of the labor movement in Britain can be divided into four phases. The first was a period in which union organization was forbidden by law, and the workers had no political rights, although they were beginning to assume an identity. This period, which preceded the Reform Law of 1832, was characterized by spontaneous action by the workers, such as machine-breaking, disorganized strikes, and sporadic political agitation. After the Reform Law and until 1848 British labor assumed an identity and sought to obtain its objectives by legislation. The most characteristic movement of this period was the Chartist movement. The third phase extended through the mid-1880s, at which time the vote was extended to all male citizens. This period saw the establishment of organized labor, illustrated by the formation of the Amalgamated Society of Engineers. The last phase was one of union maturity and political activism, and acceptance by business and the rest of society. During this phase a transition took place, from a struggle for basic rights or benefits to the implementation of welfare programs.[6]

The labor movement's success in the early part of the nineteenth century was limited for various reasons. First, the workers were disorganized, not only because of their own limited awareness but because of legal restrictions. The Combination Laws of 1799 and 1800 had made it illegal to organize. Although these laws formally applied to both employers and employees, they were used only against the latter. Second, labor faced opposition or misunderstanding from many groups. The businessmen and the free traders opposed it on the assumption that it would interfere with trade. The Malthusians advocated letting improvement come through the forces of the supply of and demand for labor, while those who could not be supported would be removed by nature. Some monetarists advocated manipulating the money supply to remedy the grievances of the workers. Finally, the reformists thought that limited reform measures could mitigate the ills of society without causing radical changes.

While some workers escaped into pauperism and drunkenness, others revolted and attacked machinery, broke frames and spindles, and destroyed property. The Luddite movement, named after a fictitious King Ludd who was modeled on Robin Hood, reached a climax in 1818 with widespread strikes and machine-breaking. This movement came soon after the introduction of new Corn Laws in 1815 which protected the farmers and kept the price of grain high. The government responded to the violence

[6] Other systems of periodization have been proposed by E. Lipson and G. D. H. Cole. The differences between these approaches are minor and do not effect the substance of the discussion. See the bibliography.

with arrests, jail sentences, and executions. A government attack on a workers' meeting in 1819 became known as the Peterloo Massacre. Shelley described it in "The Masque of Anarchy" as follows:

I met Murder on the way—
He had a mask like Castlereagh—
Very smooth he looked, yet grim;
Seven bloodhounds followed him:

All were fat; and well they might
Be in admirable plight,
For one by one, and two by two,
He tossed them human hearts to chew,
Which from his wide cloak he drew.

Next came Fraud, and he had on,
Like Eldon, an ermine gown;
His big tears, for he wept well,
Turned to millstones as they fell;

And the little children, who
Round his feet played to and fro,
Thinking every tear a gem,
Had their brains knocked out by them.

Clothed with the bible as with light,
And the shadow of the night,
Like Sidmouth next, Hypocrisy,
On a crocodile came by.[7]

The Luddite movement was short-lived, but violent action recurred for several years. However, the general tendency was to promote reform, labor organization, and social legislation, rather than violence. The leadership, which was mainly nonlabor in origin, was divided. On one side were the promoters of reform programs to improve the conditions of the workers. Foremost among these were the Owenites. Robert Owen, himself a successful cotton spinner in New Lanark, conceived of creating a form of socialism by organizing with state aid "Villages of Cooperation" in which the poor would become productive and self-sufficient. The idea was

implemented by the creation of cooperative stores and some production associations, but its main impact was educational and almost Utopian. The movement collapsed in 1834.[8] In that same year Robert Owen became the head of the Grand National Consolidated Trades Union, which grew rapidly and died as rapidly.

In contrast to the peaceful gradualist Owenites was the forceful Chartist movement. Chartism was concerned mainly with economic objectives. Its demands were contained in a charter which called for their realization through parliamentary reform and legislation. The leaders of Chartism agreed on their objectives but not on method. Some were for gradual persuasion, while others thought that only radical and even violent action could achieve their goals. The movement soon acquired a political character and began to organize in various districts. Between 1830 and 1839 it had branches all over the industrial areas. Although the movement was intended to be peaceful, emotions were high and the government was impatient. The first clash with the police took place in London in 1839 and several were injured on both sides. A petition of the Chartists was debated in Parliament and rejected by a vast majority. In response the Chartists called for a general strike or a "National Holiday," which was never held. The leaders discovered their differences of opinion, their financial weakness, and the lack of adequate external support and therefore rescinded the decision to strike before the specified time. From then on actions of the Chartists were mostly minor skirmishes, although their educational and political impact can hardly be exaggerated. Before the middle of the century the movement virtually died, after its leader, Feargus O'Conner, was elected to Parliament. How-

---

[7] Roger Ingpen & Walter E. Peck (eds.), *The Complete Work of Percy Bysshe Shelley*, Vol. III, Poems. New York: Gordian Press, 1965, pp. 235–236.

[8] Robert Owen tried to implement his idea in America. However, his cooperative community in America, New Harmony, proved to be a failure, and in 1829 he returned to England to resume his efforts there.

ever, Chartism did crystallize the working class in the United Kingdom.

Government and business reaction. Government and political leaders in this period tried to enforce the law and at the same time to introduce legislation to improve conditions. In 1802 Sir Robert Peel introduced the first Factory Act, formally known as the Health and Morals of Apprentices Act, which regulated the employment and transfer of children. The Act, however, was badly received and had little effect except as propaganda. In 1813 and 1814 the Elizabethan Labour Statutes were repealed so that the state would no longer interfere in setting wages. Surviving apprenticeship laws were also repealed in order to remove all restrictions on the recruitment of labor. A more important piece of legislation was the Law of 1824 which repealed the Combination Acts and made the organization of labor possible. However, because of mounting pressure, an amendment was passed in 1825 making it possible to prosecute combinations for conspiracy. Also in 1824 the emigration of artisans became permissible.

The major breakthrough came with the 1832 Reform Bill, which extended the vote to businessmen and made it possible for them to be elected to public office. The Bill was important in various ways. First, it broke the monopoly of the old aristocracy in Parliament and acknowledged the advent of the new industrial society. Second, it gave a rationale to the workers' pressures for reform in the shop, since businessmen now had a voice in Parliament. Finally, the Reform Bill taught the workers a lesson. Feeling betrayed by the newly enfranchised group, they learned that they had no alternative but to depend on themselves. Therefore, movements like Chartism became meaningful.

A year after the first Reform Bill the first effective Factory Act was passed. The Act of 1833 prohibited the employment of children under 9 in textile factories other than those manufacturing silk, restricted the working

hours of children under 13 to 9 hours, prohibited the employment of young people at night, and established a system for inspecting factories. In 1834 the Poor Law was amended. Under the new law, Poor Law relief was put under the supervision of a national body of commissioners responsible to the central authority. Subsidy to wages was removed and outdoor relief to able-bodied people was restricted in order to force them into the labor market. Ten years later the provisions of the Factory Act were extended to women. In 1847 the Ten-Hour Day Act was passed, restricting the work of women and children to ten hours a day, but this was modified in 1850 and 1853 to ten and a half hours.

Union organization. The workers and unions reached maturity in the second half of the century, solidifying their internal organization and gaining legal acceptance. At least three major factors were now helping the workers. The economy had developed extensively and the employers could afford to pay higher wages and offer better conditions under the pressure of competition. The second factor was the shadow of the 1848 revolutions on the continent. Finally, the influence of socialism, reflected in the publication of Marx's *Communist Manifesto* in that same year, did not go unheeded. The most important factor, however, was the workers' growing awareness of their own role in the industrial society.

This awareness was reflected in the establishment of the first modern labor union, the Amalgamated Society of Engineers, in 1851. Earlier unions had been formed after the Combination Acts were repealed, but the Amalgamated Society was a "New Model." Although membership contributions were high, so were the benefits, which ranged from unemployment to sickness pensions. The Society had branches in various areas and was organized on a national level. It concerned itself immediately with working conditions. The employers became so disturbed that they organized the Central Association of Employers of Operative Engineers in the same year. The strike by the Society was answered by a lockout. Though the Society lost this first encounter, the gains in the long run were considerable, mainly because of the favorable impression it left on public opinion. Other associations were soon formed. When the Society was in trouble, the Christian Socialists came to its aid. Later the unions derived support from other segments of socialism, among them the Marxists and the Fabian socialists.

The progress made by the unions cannot be measured in numbers, since their influence went far beyond their own ranks. Nevertheless, the growth of the membership is indicative. As late as 1870 there were probably fewer than 150,000 union members in the United Kingdom, but this number was almost 6 times what it was in 1850. By 1900 the number had risen to about 2 million and to 5.29 million in 1917. However, progress was not continuous. In the 1870s and 1890s there were periods of decline, mostly in times of depression or crisis. Nevertheless, the unions were no longer in danger of being outlawed or suppressed. In fact in the 1890s a "New Unionism" evolved under which semiskilled and unskilled workers were recruited as members. The unions gained full economic acceptance as soon as bargaining became possible. The Molestation Act of 1859 made peaceful picketing legal and in 1869 the unions were empowered to prosecute defaulting officials. Their legal position was strengthened by the Act of 1875 which put the employers and the workmen on the same footing, thus giving the unions full legal security. They also gained political acceptance by the Acts of 1867 and 1884, which extended the franchise to the urban and the rural workers, respectively. Finally, formation of the Labor Party gave the workers the backing they needed. The Labour Representation Committee, formed in 1899, became known as the Labour Party in 1906.

The unions' success was not free of difficulties. They resorted to strikes frequently. There were 17 strikes in 1876, 24 in 1886,

and 111 in 1889. Between 1891 and 1899 there were no less than 700 work stoppages a year. The dock strike of 1892 is said to have been the turning point in which the unions proved their strength and ability to fight for their rights. In 1906 workmen's compensation was introduced; old-age pensions and the eight-hour day were instituted in 1908, and national insurance in 1911. The union struggle was no longer for survival or acceptance but for welfare programs and a larger share of the spoils of industrial society.

The recent history of unions has concerned consolidation or confederation and organization within the framework of national politics. The need for concerted action led the unions to concentrate their efforts and unite under the General Council of the Trade Union Congress (TUC). Prior to reorganization of the TUC, there were three main confederations, the Confederation of Shipbuilding and Engineering Union, the National Federation of Building Trade Operatives, and the Printing and Kindred Trade Federation. In addition there were six amalgamations which included many of the smaller local unions. There were also other independent general unions. While membership in a union has not been made a condition for employment, the silent pressure for joining has greatly strengthened the unions over the years. Reorganization of the TUC in 1921 made collective bargaining a standard procedure. The new constitution upheld the freedom of individual unions to negotiate on their own if they desired. The General Council, however, was empowered to deal with union disputes, supervise the conduct of member organizations, and negotiate with employers when requested to do so. These principles were still in effect at the end of World War II.

France

French industrial development was more gradual than that of Britain, but the awareness and reaction of French labor were no less intense or widespread. The 1789 Revolution abolished all guilds and declared all individuals free to pursue their own interests. But as combinations of union workers began to evolve, the Assembly reacted with restrictive measures. The Le Chapelier Law interpreted these combinations as guilds and thus prohibited them. The law covered both employers and employees, but enforcement was applied mainly to the workers. The Penal Code of Napoleon of 1810 included penalties against workers' combinations and against employers who tried to lower wages "unjustly or abusively." The workers were also required to carry workbooks to show whether the worker had deserted or had been honorably relieved of his job before he could be employed again. These restrictions remained in effect until the middle of the century. The workers resorted to the formation of bachelor workmen's clubs, mutual-aid groups, and resistance societies. Although these societies were illegal, they were tolerated without intervention unless there was violence.

Improvements through legislative action were slow. The first Factory Act, passed in 1841, prohibited employment of children under 8 and night work for those under 12. Those between 8 and 12 were granted an 8-hour workday, with a 12-hour day for those between 12 and 16 in establishments which had power-driven machinery or 20 workers or more. No further legislation was introduced until 1874, except for transitory regulations following the revolution of 1848.

The workers were not satisfied with their condition. They took leading roles in the revolutions of 1830 and 1848 and continued to form secret or mutual-aid associations. In response to the 1848 revolution the government set up "national workshops" mainly to dispense charity. These workshops proved a failure and starving workers demonstrated in June of the same year. The government responded violently in what has become known as the June Days, during which many were killed or injured. The workers' movement was crushed and little organization

took place until near the end of Napoleon III's Empire.

By 1864, however, the government's attitude seems to have changed and the workers were given the right to strike. In 1870 there were about 150,000 members organized in unions, half of them in Paris. However, some of the leaders were prosecuted for unauthorized association whenever it seemed convenient to the government. The government response reached its climax in the war between the Paris Commune and the provincial government. The Parisians refused to surrender the arms they had collected during the war with Germany. Instead, they attacked monuments and shot hostages. The government applied severe measures which resulted in the killing of 10–15,000 Communards, and many more thousands were imprisoned or deported. The Paris Commune, however, ended the Empire and started a new era for labor.

In 1871 began a period of relative peace and the organization of modern unions. Three of the workers' demands were soon granted. In 1877 a system of universal free secular education was introduced and amnesty to the Communards was granted. In 1884 the right of free association was introduced, although unions were required to register their constitutions and bylaws. Unions came out into the open and labor exchanges were established in 1886. They continued to be identified with political parties, although in the 1890s they became free of party domination. As in other countries, the tendency toward consolidation soon became apparent. In 1895 the General Confederation of Labor or *Confédération Gé nérale du Travail*, CGT, was established, and in 1902 it was fused with the Federation of *Bourses*, or labor exchanges. The theme of the CGT was revolutionary syndicalism, its focus of action being the local union. Until 1906 the CGT was mainly a craft union, but after that date it was affiliated with industrial unions.

The French labor movement of the 1890s

and 1900s was unique in its revolutionary syndicalism, which emphasized class struggle and direct action. It had little faith in parliamentarianism and advocated full dependence on the general strike. It also emphasized the interdependence of theory and action, with action forming the basis. Syndicalism grew from the lower ranks upward, and this fact appealed to those who were aware of the slow improvement in labor conditions achieved by other means. Although the CGT contained a large reformist group, decision-making was concentrated in the hands of the revolutionaries. Total membership remained relatively small. The number of union members in 1901 was 589,000; there were 836,000 in 1906 and 1,029,000 in 1911, one-third of the number in the United Kingdom.

This organizational structure lasted until 1920, after which splits were frequent. The Socialist Party split in 1920; the reformists in 1921. A Catholic union had already come into existence by 1919. Attempts to reorganize were abortive and labor unions became small minority organizations. At the initiative of the CGT and under the threat of Fascism, unity was restored in 1934, and collective bargaining became legal and acceptable. However, unity did not last long. In 1939 political differences regarding the pending war were brought to the fore and a split soon followed.

Thus French labor had limited organizational success, since it lacked the solidarity common in other countries. Benefits were still hard to obtain, and a class struggle seemed to characterize the labor movement throughout the period.

Germany

The organization of labor in Germany was late in developing, partly because industrialization came late and partly because of institutional obstacles. Freedom of entry into the trades was restricted up to the middle of the nineteenth century, and only small organizations were created. An effort was made by Stephen Born to unite these organizations into a consolidated group similar to Robert Owen's Grand National Consolidated Trades Union. Born created the Fraternity of Labor in Berlin in 1848, and this organization was loosely held together until 1854. In that short period the Fraternity of Labor succeeded in formulating and presenting labor demands to the Frankfurt Parliament concerning minimum wages and maximum hours, settlement of disputes with employers, regulation of apprenticeship, aid for the sick and needy, and the prevalent restrictions on labor and the right to organize. In response, the government took more restrictive measures which lasted for almost a decade and forestalled any serious attempts to organize. The leaders were exiled and the movement was suppressed.

Prohibitions on the right to organize were first relaxed in Saxony in 1861. The first organizations created following relaxation of the ban were mainly educational and nonpolitical. However, powerful forces were steering labor toward action. The provocative writings of Marx were well known. Ferdinand Lassalle insisted on the rights of labor to act politically and urged that political support be given only to those who supported the demands of labor. He also urged universal suffrage, the secret ballot, and the organization of a General German Worker's Association to realize those objectives by peaceful means.

The tide had turned; unions finally came into existence. The first interlocal union organization was the General Tobacco Workers' Union of 1865; the printers organized nationally in 1866; the tailors and woodworkers in 1868. However, attempts to create a national confederation were abortive. Unions were established on political lines: The Lassallians remained separate from the Marxists; and the less revolutionary, more reformist group had its own union, the German Trades Association, which was founded in 1868 and supported competition and mutual benefits, rather than a class struggle. There was also a white-collar union, *Gewerkschaft der Angelstelten.* The various liberal unions united in 1920 as the Federation of Unions of German Workers, Employees, and Civil Servants or *Gewerkschaftsring Deutscher Arbeiter-Angstelten und Beamtenverbände.* The socialist-oriented unions had united as early as 1871 on the premise that all workers alike are exploited under capitalism. In addition to these there was an interdenominational Christian union.

The reactions of the employers and the government were unfriendly, especially as the number of strikes rose in the 1870s. Bismark tried both suppression and reform to remove grievances. Antisocialist restrictions were accompanied by welfare programs to undermine the unions' struggle. Nevertheless, as soon as the antisocialist laws expired in the 1890s, organization was resumed by both the politically affiliated and the free unions. In 1891 there were 62 national unions with 277,659 members; in 1900 there were 58 unions with 680,427 members; by 1914 the number of unions had declined to 48, but the membership exceeded 2 million.

The unions offered their members travel aid, unemployment benefits, insurance against sickness and disability, and mortuary help. They also represented to the employers their demands for better wages and terms of employment. However, benefits were not quick to come, especially after the employers had formed their own associations, combinations, or cartels and were able to fight back. Therefore, the unions often resorted to the strike as the only means of achieving their demands. In 1890–1891 there were 226 strikes and lockouts. In 1900 there were 852 strikes and lockouts involving 115,761 workers. In 1913 there were 2,600 strikes and lockouts involving a quarter of a million workers. During this period wages rose and collective bargaining became accepted as a means of reaching agreement and compromise.

While the unions were fighting a losing battle, social legislation helped to improve the conditions of the workers. Insurance against work accidents was introduced as early as 1871. Between 1878 and 1886 laws were introduced to raise the level of technical skills and regulate the employment of apprentices. Sick-fund insurance was introduced in 1883 and invalidism insurance in 1888. By 1911 9 million workers, including agricultural, domestic, and even casual workers, were enjoying insurance benefits. Except for accident insurance, all programs were financed jointly by both workers and employers.

The First World War had a depressing effect on the unions, at least in part because of a split over support of the war, as in France. In 1917–1918 a revolutionary upsurge took place expressing opposition to the continuation of the war. The revolt of November 1918 resulted in a socialist-dominated government and a new era of cooperation between unions and government. The unions were given full freedom of association, in return for which they cooperated with and even saved the Weimar Republic in 1920. After the war the Nuremberg Trade Union Congress of 1919 decided to reorganize the free trade unions. Accordingly, the German Federation of Labor, *Allgemeine Deutsche Gewerkschaftsbund,* was established. To avoid conflict with the Social Democratic Party, the trade unions declared themselves politically neutral, thus making it possible for the leaders of the different unions to work together. By 1920 union membership had risen almost three-fold, with the majority concentrated in the free trade unions. The unions achieved great success during the 1920s in the areas of policy determination, collective bargaining, social benefits, and wage increases. These successes were checked only by the depression and by the Nazi government, which virtually brought the union movement to an end. The leaders were arrested; headquarters and offices were occupied, and all union property was confiscated. In place of the unions, the

Labor Front was established which was formally an arm of the government. It was 1945 before the unions revived.

Italy

Labor organization in Italy was also a late development, coming only after unification and some industrialization. A law of 1864 forbade the formation of trade unions and the strike was declared illegal unless the workers could show "reasonable cause" for such action, which was always subject to interpretation. Workers, therefore, resorted to the formation of mutual-aid societies and to politically oriented associations. Sometimes they formed unions, but these were quickly suppressed. These unions carried out strikes and demanded recognition. Official reports estimate that 634 strikes took place between 1860 and 1878 and 263 more by 1884. The formation of unions was made legal in 1889, and from then on labor organization into national federations proceeded rapidly. By 1902, 24 such federations had been formed with a Central Secretariat of Resistance representing about half a million workers. Collective bargaining became acceptable in the first decade of the twentieth century, at a time when strikes became more frequent and more violent in Italian industry.

Italian unions sought better wages and working conditions, but they were also strongly involved in politics. There were many influences encouraging this orientation. Marxist doctrines had become well known. Catholic groups were active in forming separate unions. The union movement was also closely associated with the Socialist Party. It is sometimes difficult, therefore, to distinguish the political activities of the unions from the economic. Political activity was somewhat frustrated by legal obstacles and internal divisions. It had some successes. In 1886 the employment of children under 9 was prohibited, those under 10 could not be employed in mines, and those under 12 were excluded from night work. This law was modified in 1902 so that work was prohibited for children under 12 and in mines for those under 14; and the labor day for young people under 15 was restricted to 11 hours. The workday of women was limited to 12 hours; and pregnant women were given a month's vacation with pay. Furthermore, a Superior Council of Labor representing employees, employers, and government was established to consider labor legislation. In 1893 a court of civic leaders was established to deal with industrial disputes. In 1895 insurance against injury on the job was introduced as well as old-age and invalidism pensions. In 1907 a maternity fund was established to help working women during childbearing. Factory inspection was extended in 1911. Nevertheless, the benefits to workers in general remained limited. The market alone could not deal with people's problems.

Until 1906 most labor unions in Italy were local organizations under a loose federation. In that year a new form of consolidation began with the establishment of the General Confederation of Labor (CGL or *Confederazione generale del lavoro*). This was a socialist organization and claimed the largest membership among the Italian unions. At its peak in 1920 it had more than 2 million members, but it declined to 10 percent of that number 4 years later. Another new organization was the USI, *Unione sindicale italiana* or the Italian Syndical Union, established in 1912. A year later it had 100,000 members. It was basically revolutionary in character. The CIL, *Confederazione italiana dei lavoratori* or Italian Confederation of Workers, Catholic-sponsored and opposed to both other confederations, was established in 1918. A fourth union, UIL, *Unione italiana del lavoro* or Italian Labor Union, was established also in 1918. The UIL was committed to national syndicalism, according to which the nation is more important than the class and internal class collaboration has precedence over international class collaboration.

This structure, however, was short-lived.

Fascism ushered in the corporate system, whose workings were as follows: Workers and employers were organized in unions and corresponding associations, respectively, except for professionals and artists for whose union there was no corresponding employer's association. In all, there were nine confederations, one each for management and labor in industry, agriculture, commerce, and banking and insurance, with a separate union for the professionals and artists. The unions were expected to negotiate collective agreements. In case of disagreement, conciliation was attempted and if this failed a special court ruled on the matter. Strikes and lockouts were prohibited. Each union had secondary organizations representing industrial and provincial interests. These associations dealt with the terms of work and remuneration, while corporations or guilds were set up to plan production and other economic matters. Twenty-one such corporations were established to deal with the industrial process, each representing labor and management equally.

The corporate system was actually more restrictive than suggested by the above outline. Rules were set up to govern all facets of work life: hours, holidays, vacations, grounds for hiring and firing, and remuneration. This system lasted through the Second World War. Following the defeat of Italy a free labor movement was established.

Scandinavia

Unlike the other countries, Scandinavia seems to have maintained a direct relationship between the earlier guilds and the unions. The guilds, which were strongest in Denmark, had left a legacy of organization which was helpful in union development. As industrialization and labor mobility advanced the guilds became anachronistic and a new approach seemed essential. Denmark had 270 guilds when they were abolished in 1862. Sweden abolished the guilds in stages. In 1846 Swedish guilds were replaced by "trade associations" to protect the master

artisans, but these were abolished in 1864. Norway, where guilds were least developed, prohibited the formation of new guilds in 1839, and in 1869 abolished all guilds except the Bergen bakers' guild, which lasted until 1894.

Even while the guilds were in existence another form of organization was developing. The journeymen, who had little hope of becoming masters, developed their own associations within the guild system to protect themselves and to perform mutual-aid functions. When the guilds were dissolved, these associations were permitted to continue. Eventually some of them evolved into modern unions.

Denmark was the first of the three countries to industrialize and to develop trade unions. The first attempt was made by the socialists, who in 1871 formed the International Labor Union of Denmark, which was dissolved a year later by the authorities. In the following years some local craft unions got together and in 1874 formed the Free Trade Union Central Committee, which lasted only three years. The movement began to gain momentum in the 1880s when economic conditions started to improve. In the last two decades of the century union organization was very rapid; 684 new local unions came into existence between 1895 and 1899. This growth was facilitated by four major forces: acceptance of unions by the employers, government sympathy, the growing political power of labor, and economic prosperity. And as soon as local unions became a reality, the Copenhagen unions took the initiative in forming national unions.

Swedish labor was about ten years behind the Danes, and therefore was greatly influenced by developments in Denmark. The Danes provided the example, but they also exerted pressure for organization by discriminating against unorganized Swedish labor. An important force in Swedish labor organization was the journeymen associations, some of which transformed themselves into unions. Another influential force was the rapid growth of industry. Unlike the situation in Denmark, industrial labor became more influential than craft unions. Centralization was rapid. Swedish labor developed central city unions as early as 1883, and by 1890 there were centrals in all the major cities. National unions also developed relatively early, the first being established by the printers in 1886. With national unions came an enormous increase in membership. In fact union membership multiplied four-fold in the first five years of the century.

Norway's labor began to organize about the same time as Sweden's. A carpenters' local union was established in 1872 by members of a former guild. Permanent unions first came into being in the 1880s, and by 1900 there were 250 locals with centrals in all the major cities. Federation came about before the end of the century.

The Danish Federation of Labor, *De Samvirkende Fagforbund,* and the Swedish Federation of Labor, *Landsorganisasjonen i Sverige,* were established in 1898. A year later the Norwegian Federation of Labor, *Arbeidernes Faglige Landsorganisasjon,* was created. This almost simultaneous federation was a result of an intercountry congress held in Stockholm in 1897, which resolved on the achievement of unity in national federations. However, in Denmark and Sweden there remained a high degree of decentralization, in contrast to the almost full centralization evident in Norway. In order to achieve unity and centralization, the Scandinavian unions agreed to maintain only a loose relationship with the socialist parties.

The federations of both Denmark and Norway included most of the unions in the country. However, in Sweden important unions remained outside the federation, among them the Syndicalist Union Center, established in 1910, and the union of white-collar employees in private industry and government. Nevertheless, federation membership in all three countries has increased

almost continuously since 1900. Labor organization has reached a vast majority of the workers. Mutual benefits, collective bargaining, and the protection and education of the members are still basic functions. The strike has continued to be the standard tool.

An interesting feature of labor relations in Scandinavia was the development of employers' associations on almost the same lines as labor unions. The employers' associations came into existence soon after the labor federations were formed, in 1898 in Denmark, in 1900 in Norway, and in 1902 in Sweden. They usually included most of the large enterprises. They abided by uniform policies to the extent that no employer would enter into collective bargaining without advance approval by the association, and resolutions taken in annual congresses became policies for all members.

While negotiation with employers' associations may be more difficult for the unions than negotiating with individual employers, these associations represented the employers' recognition of unions and their adherence to collective bargaining with them on an equal footing. Nevertheless, disputes arose frequently and many days of work were lost in strike or lockout. However, the government always managed, by compulsory arbitration whenever collective bargaining failed, to bring about an agreement. To avoid work stoppage, labor courts were set up in all three countries to deal with disputes arising from interpretations of existing agreements. A labor court was established in Denmark in 1910, in Norway in 1915, and in 1928 in Sweden. The courts were constituted from labor, management, and the public, which was usually represented by members of the judiciary. This arrangement lasted through 1945.

The apparent harmony that prevailed in Scandinavia was facilitated by long-standing welfare policies. Social legislation helped to improve conditions in general and to reduce the grounds for conflict between labor and management. In all three countries living standards were raised by government policies concerning housing, medical insurance, education, and unemployment. Furthermore, real wages have risen perceptively since 1900. Average real hourly wages in Denmark rose from an index of 81 in 1900 to 147 in 1925 and to 192 in 1949. In Norway, the rise was from an index of 69 in 1900 to 148 in 1925 and to 215 in 1949. In Sweden, the rise was from 82 to 151 to 219 in these years. Scandinavia thus provides an example of cooperation between the various forces in society, recognition of pending problems, and a conscious effort to deal with these problems to the mutual advantage of all concerned. The experience of Scandinavia also shows how much can be done if institutional changes are taken seriously and not simply made on the books.

Russia

The labor movement in Russia provides almost a direct contrast with that of Scandinavia. The movement there was more restricted and political than in the western countries. Serfdom, which had kept the peasants tied to the land, also supplied labor for the factories, and labor conditions were a continuation of that system. The state and the employers joined hands in sustaining it as long as possible. Oppressive legislation, the police, and even the military were used to prevent the formation of unions or the organization of labor.

Probably the earliest form of labor organization was the *starosta*, or monitor system, according to which monitors were elected by the workers in the shop to supervise wage payments and labor conditions. As leaders, these monitors often suffered more severe punishment than the other workers during strikes. The workers were far from passive. They formed secret organizations, made demands on their employers, and when such demands were not granted resorted to work stoppage. Evidence of strikes goes back at least to the 1824 iron foundry strike. Between that time and the Emancipation there were many strikes, but neither successful organization nor effective reform legislation resulted.

Labor legislation was introduced in the eighteenth century. In 1741 regulations were enacted dealing with hours of work, wages, medical aid, and other work conditions. In 1785 a law established a ten-hour day and a six-day workweek. These laws, however, were not enforced. Serfdom in various forms continued to be the rule rather than the exception. The "Rules of Employment of Persons Freely Hired" of 1857 reaffirmed this long-standing system. The Emancipation did little for factory workers other than to give them the freedom to desert, which they were already doing in large numbers. The work of minors was regulated in 1882 by reducing their day to 8 hours and prohibiting night work for children. In 1885 night work in factories for boys and girls under 17 was prohibited. The first effective legislation to stop the government from intervening between labor and capital was passed in 1886. It required employers to maintain a good bookkeeping system to protect the workers' wages. It also regulated the imposition of fines. In 1897 an Act reduced the workday to $11\frac{1}{2}$ hours, or to 10 if the work was done in 2 shifts.

Throughout this period the workers felt exploited and reacted with violence, strikes, and organization. The 1890s were a period of both prosperity and militancy. Socialists, among them V. I. Lenin, were active despite police oppression and arrests. The number of strikes multiplied for both economic and political reasons. An attempt to improve the situation was made in 1903, when an ordinance gave the workers the right to be represented in the shop by elected officials, although only with the consent of the employer. The ordinance also made the employer responsible for all accidents. Previously he had been responsible only for those accidents for which he was directly to blame. An interesting attempt to contain the labor movement was the decision of the Ministry of Interior to create labor organizations "under the guidance and supervision of the Secret Police," the first of which was the "Society of Workers in the Moscow Mechanical Trades" created in 1901. These attempts had little success. The General Strike of 1905 in St. Petersburg, demanding better conditions, resulted in a revolution, a massacre, and widespread strikes throughout the country. The unions won, and organization became legal in 1906.

The basic principles of Russian unionization included no party affiliations, internal democracy, and unification in trade councils. Union membership increased only modestly in 1907, especially after government reaction removed some of the liberties won by the workers and created strong employers' associations. Total membership in that year was less than a quarter of a million members. There were attempts to consolidate the unions by region, by faith, or by trade, but their impact was minor. On the eve of the First World War, labor unions still had limited membership and faced strong opposition, but they were even more intensely militant. Even attempts by the government to ameliorate the situation through reform legislation had a very limited impact. The war virtually put an end to union activity. A new phase began in the Soviet period.

Under Communist rule private property no longer existed. The conflict between capital and labor was theoretically removed. Therefore, it was presumed that trade unions should have no cause for conflict with the employers who represented them. However, this view was recognized as unrealistic for political and economic reasons. After lengthy debates, Lenin decided that the unions should have an important role to play both in helping management and in protecting the workers. The unions should be encouraged but they should be politically and religiously nonpartisan. They would protect the workers against bureaucratic and managerial inefficiencies. In this light cooperation between the unions and other agencies

seemed possible. While certain liberties of the members were restricted, such as mobility and the "right" to strike, the functions of the unions were similar to those in the West; namely to improve the conditions of the members, resolve disputes, and promote conciliation.

This apparent harmony was shaken seriously when the First Five-Year Plan was adopted in 1928. Stalin, determined to implement his programs, felt that no conflict could be allowed to jeopardize the economic plan and that any opposition by the unions was a deviation from Marxism. From then on two policies were pursued by the government: keep the unions quiet and expand welfare programs. Both were realized under the direction of the Communist Party and the state. The social programs introduced in Soviet Russia touched on all aspects of life in the home, the school, and the factory. The improvements have reached the core of the grievances which usually cause labor and management conflicts.

SUMMARY AND CONCLUSIONS

The countries omitted from the above discussion either differed little from those mentioned or had limited labor organization. It should be noted that the fact that labor organization came late in a country does not necessarily mean that the country was underdeveloped. In Belgium, which was one of the early developers, full legalization of labor organization came only in 1921, several years after the establishment of a national labor confederation.

The various experiences outlined suggest that labor organization has followed a pattern. At first, workers joined in sporadic local movements to demand better conditions. These were often temporary movements and frequently depended on violence. When they brought little success the workers resorted to persuasion and to the organization of units for mutual aid and protection.

As identification with political parties developed and the size of the urban proletariat increased, organization proceeded rapidly. The final effort was to confederate in national unions, free them from political domination, and adopt collective bargaining and the strike as standard approaches.

In all countries there was a close interdependence between national politics, the system of government, and union organization. The more inclined a society was to democracy and constitutional government, the more opportunity it offered for organization. Britain, the most democratic country in the western tradition, had more advanced unions and more developed labor legislation. The more rigid or nationalistic the government, the less union organization could develop. The tsarist government in Russia, the dictatorship of Bismark, and Catholicism in Belgium all tried to obstruct the development of unions, both by restrictive measures and by social reform. In all these countries union organization was delayed.

Labor organization also seems to have advanced most in countries in which labor identified itself with a political party. This was true even when unions decided to remain formally neutral as far as party politics were concerned, as in Britain and Scandinavia.

Apparently labor organizations were fully convinced that their interests and the interests of the employers were in conflict and that no gains could be made without a fight. The sooner their right to strike was recognized and collective bargaining became accepted, the more harmonious the relationship with the employers became. This relationship became the basis for a system of cleavage and consent that contained class conflict. In general, this conflict was contained rather than eliminated. The exception to this tendency was experienced in Soviet Russia, where labor was integrated in society and class conflict became irrelevant to the trade unions.

Containment of the conflict coincided with a change in attitude among labor, government, and the employers. New social legislation often reduced conflict by removing some of labor's grievances. However, it should be noted that the efforts of labor were often obstructed by violent government reactions, and containment was sometimes a result of oppressive measures. As labor succeeded in achieving recognition and better conditions, its original ideals were modified. Labor became content to acquire benefits without seeking the transformation embodied in the early revolutionary socialist doctrines. Gradualism became more acceptable than revolutionary change.

Unions proved to be sensitive to ideology, faith, and occupational specialty. Organization sometimes followed religion or political ideology. The schism was most clearly apparent between the socialists and the Catholics. The craft and industrial workers also maintained their autonomy. However, as collective bargaining became acceptable and the strike emerged as the major weapon in the hands of labor, it became increasingly apparent that unity was necessary for success. This tendency was reinforced by the growing concentration in business and the establishment of employers' associations. To be able to finance strikes and bargain with these powerful associations, labor unions resorted to confederation on a national level. Confederation to create a "countervailing" power became normal throughout Europe.

While labor organizations characterized all the countries of Europe, their success varied from one country to another. Achievement of objectives depended on at least four factors: the degree of labor's awareness, the role of government, the economic conditions in the country, and the national heritage. The more aware labor was, the easier it was to organize and to achieve objectives. The Scandinavian unions were particularly successful for this reason. Awareness, however, should be distinguished from political activity. French labor was probably the most politically active, but in an anarchist tradition. Its lack of unity or strong organization tended to limit its success. Success was determined also by the genuineness of the sympathy shown by the government in each country. Legislation was not sufficient, since frequently the laws were ignored by the authorities, as they were in pre-Soviet Russia. The experience of Denmark illustrates the importance of a sympathic government. The Scandinavian experience also illustrates the significance of national heritage. The welfare policies in Scandinavia and the strong guild tradition tended to support labor organization. Similarly, the British heritage of conciliation and compromise reinforced labor's demands for full recognition. In contrast, the autocratic heritage of tsarist Russia, imperial Germany, and to an extent France made labor organization less readily acceptable. In these countries labor had a more difficult job organizing and instituting collective bargaining.

Probably the most important determinant of union success was economic progress. Labor tended to achieve more success in times of prosperity than in times of crisis or depression. This was partly because the market mechanism favors labor in periods of high demand and hampers it in periods of labor surplus and unemployment. In periods of prosperity the employers are in a better position to make concessions and are more anxious to avoid work stoppage. In periods of unemployment or depression, however, labor tends to be financially weak and somewhat disorganized. The problem is clearly illustrated by the hard times faced by labor in Britain before 1840 and in the depression of the 1870s. The 1870s and 1880s were hard on labor in all countries, in contrast to the great upsurge enjoyed in the 1890s and 1900s.

This general formula seems applicable to fluctuations in the various countries considered. An exception was the attitude toward labor in times of war and national emergency. Although the demand for labor was high in such times, labor activities were almost invariably restricted unless unions voluntarily chose to cooperate. This was the case during the Napoleonic War, during the Franco-Prussian war of 1871, and during the First World War. Nevertheless, labor always came back, and labor organization proved to be a part of industrial society.

BIBLIOGRAPHY

Ashworth, William, *The International Economy*, Toronto: Longmans, 1962, chap. 4.

Bull, Edward, *The Norwegian Trade Union Movement*, ICFTU Monographs on National Trade Union Movements, No. 4, Brussels International Confederation of Free Trade Unions, 1956.

Clapham, J. H., *The Economic Development of France and Germany, 1815–1914*, New York: Cambridge University Press, 1928, pp. 265–267, 322–338.

Clough, S. B., *The Economic History of Modern Italy*, New York: Columbia University Press, 1964, chap. 5.

Cole, G. D. H., *A Short History of the British Working-Class Movement, 1789–1947*, London: George Allen and Unwin, 1948.

Deane, Phyllis, and W. A. Cole, *British Economic Growth*

1688–1959, New York: Cambridge University Press, 1967, pp. 21–25 and price graph following page 350.

Denmark, Geographical Handbook series, Washington: Naval Intelligence Division, 1944, chaps. 8 and 9.

Dunham, A. L., *The Industrial Revolution in France, 1815–1848,* New York: Exposition Press, 1955, chap. 8.

Engels, Frederick, *The Conditions of the Working-Class in England in 1844,* London: Allen and Unwin, 1958.

Galenson, Walter (ed.), *Comparative Labor Movements,* Englewood Cliffs, N.J.: Prentice-Hall, 1952.

Gordon, Manya, *Workers Before and After Lenin,* New York: E. P. Dutton, 1941.

Goris, Jan-Albert (ed.), *Belgium,* Berkeley: University of California Press, 1946, chaps. 13 and 16.

Gualtieri, Humbert L., *The Labor Movement in Italy,* New York: S. F. Vanni, 1946.

Hammond, John L., and Barbara Hammond, *The Skilled Labourer, 1760–1832,* London: Longmans, Green, 1920.

Hammond, John L., and Barbara Hammond, *The Town Labourer, 1760–1832,* New York: A. M. Kelley, 1967.

Hammond, John L., and Barbara Hammond, *The Village Labourer, 1760–1832,* New York: A. M. Kelley, 1967.

Henderson, W. O., *The Industrial Revolution in Europe, 1815–1914,* Chicago: Quadrangle Books, 1961, pp. 38–44, 106–108, 120–126, 165–167, 184–189, 231–240.

Hobsbawm, E. J., "Economic Fluctuations and Some Social Movements Since 1800," *Economic History Review,* 2nd series, V, No. 1 (1952), pp. 1–25.

Lipson, E., *The Growth of English Society,* Third edition, London: Adam and Charles Black, 1954, chaps. 9 and 14.

Lorwin, Val R., *The French Labor Movement,* Cambridge, Mass.: Harvard University Press, 1954.

Lorwin, Val R. (ed.), *Labor and Working Conditions in Modern Europe,* New York: Macmillan, 1967.

Plummer, Alfred, "The General Strike During One Hundred Years," *Economic Journal,* Economic History series, No. 2, I (May 1927), pp. 184–204.

Rimlinger, G. V., "The Expansion of the Labor Market in Capitalist Russia: 1861–1917," *Journal of Economic History,* XXII (June 1961), pp. 208–215.

Rowe, D. J., "The Chartist Convention and the Regions," *The Economic History Review,* Second series, XXII, No. 1 (April 1969), pp. 58–74.

Samuelsson, Kurt, *From Great Power to Welfare State,* London: Allen and Unwin, 1968, chaps. 4 and 5.

Sturmthal, Adolf, *Unity and Diversity in European Labor,* Glencoe, Ill.: The Free Press, 1953.

Taylor, Philip A. M. (ed.), *The Industrial Revolution in Brit-*

ain, Triumph or Disaster?, Problems in European Civilization series, Boston: D. C. Heath, 1958.

Turin, S. P., *From Peter the Great to Lenin*, London: Frank Cass and Co., 1968.

Webb, Sidney, and Beatrice Webb, *The History of Trade Unionism*, Longmans, Green, 1920.

Windmuller, John P., *Labor Relations in the Netherlands*, New York: Cornell University Press, 1969, chaps. 1–3.

23

ECONOMIC CHANGE, FLUCTUATION, AND POLICY

As we have seen, change from the pre-industrial to the industrial economy was accompanied by new business and labor organizational arrangements. The change has also affected the role of government in economic policy. The role of government in modern times has been influenced by the nature of industrial society and the instabilities apparently inherent in it. Fluctuations in output, employment, and prices, which were common in the medieval and mercantilist periods, continued to be so in the capitalist era. In previous periods, fluctuation was caused mainly by war, harvest failure, famine and disease. The impact of these factors, with the exception of war, has been reduced greatly in the modern period. However, man's dependence on the market has kept the economy vulnerable. Any factors influencing the market can result in inflation or recession. The impact of such fluctuations has become more widely spread and more severely felt as the market has become larger and as workers and employers have become more dependent on it.

Business fluctuations have been classified according to the length of the cycle, the severity of the rise or decline, and its scope. The longest cycle, which describes secular trends which can vary up to 50 years from peak to peak, is known as the Kondratieff cycle, after the Russian economist who first discovered it. The medium cycle, the Juglar, varies between 8 and 10 years. The short cycle varies between 3 and 5 years. The number of years given suggests a relative duration rather than the precise length of a cycle, which varies too greatly to be specified. The fluctuation is classified as a recession or depression when there is a decline, and as an inflation or hyperinflation when there is a rise in the indicators. In either case, the situation usually incites action to restore stability and sustain development and growth in real terms. In the modern period people have apparently become resigned to the instability of the economy and the necessity to deal with its symptoms rather than its causes. Since the latter are inherent in the market economy, they cannot be eliminated without destroying the economic system altogether.

RECURRENT FLUCTUATIONS

The magnitude of fluctuation and its meaning vary according to the criteria used. Inflation may cause just as much hardship as deflation, even though its impact may fall on a different group. Both inflation and deflation are reflections of price movement. Yet prices do not always indicate the real changes in output and employment, especially over short periods and in economies in which credit is common and the market is

Table 23.1. Years of economic decline in selected countries

COUNTRY	APPROXIMATE DATES OF DECLINE[a]								
Britain[b]	1763,	1773,	1784,	1793,	1803,	1810,	1815,	1825,	1836,	1847,
	1857,	1866,	1873,	1883,	1893,	1907,	1920,	1929,	1937	
Italy[b]	1866,	1869,	1874,	1881,	1883,	1889,	1892,	1908,	1918,	1927
Spain[b]	1827,	1847,	1866,	1876,	1886,	1892				
Sweden[c]	1876,	1885,	1890,	1900,	1907					
France[d]	1787,	1792,	1797,	1811,	1826,	1846,	1857,	1873,	1882,	1908

[a] *The specific years vary a little according to the indicators and weights used by the different outhors.*
[b] *Indicated by a price decline following a period of expansion.*
[c] *Indicated by a decline in industrial production and industrial employment.*
[d] *Indicated by a combination of the above indicators.*

dominated by contractual agreements between business and labor. Furthermore, fluctuation in one sector may not occur in other sectors of the economy. Therefore, averaging prices or output to measure the magnitude and impact of a cycle may distort the real economic picture.

Most of the information available concerns the period following the French Revolution, although estimates of earlier British fluctuations have been made. Between 1789 and 1914 three secular movements have been observed, each of which included a period of decline and one of expansion. The periods of expansion have been roughly delineated as falling between 1789–1816, 1844–1875, and 1890–1919. The periods of decline fall roughly between 1817–1844 and 1875–1890. The period following World War I was one of reconstruction, recovery, and expansion; it was followed by the depression of the 1930s. The Second World War distorted the trend again and brought havoc to many economies. Since 1950 Europe has enjoyed a general expansionary trend. However, these long cycles have little significance except for analytical purposes. Policies are usually concerned with the short or medium cycles, which are often characterized by specific crisis high points.

The critical years of decline in selected countries are shown in Table 23.1. Similar patterns may be estimated for other countries. Crises recurred in all countries after industrialization had begun. The interval between critical years of decline varied from one country to another, ranging from two to more than ten years. The critical period came at different times in different countries, suggesting a lag in the transmission of a crisis from one place to another, although some crises remained restricted to the national level. Three international crises may be distinguished. The first was the 1873 crash. The second came as the aftermath of the First World War. It brought severe unemployment in Italy and Germany and a hyperinflation which may have contributed to the rise of the corporate state in Italy and the Nazi government in Germany. Finally, there was the depression of the 1930s, which was so severe as to shake confidence in the monetary and economic policy tools which had prevailed in all capitalist countries.

These crises, both national and international, had a great influence on the role of government in the economy, not only because of their recurrence but also because of their magnitude and impact. The crises in Sweden were less severe than those in some other countries, but even there the impact was far-reaching. Industrial production increased 37 percent between 1871 and 1874, but declined by 16 percent in the next 3 years, the equivalent of a decline of 53 percent in the growth rate. A rise of 27 percent between 1904 and 1907 was followed by a 7 percent decline in the following 3 years, or

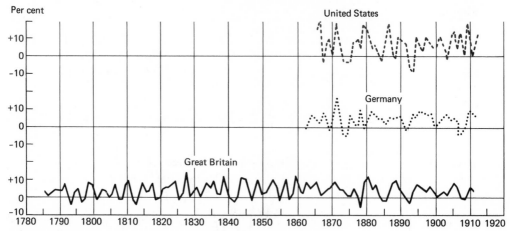

Figure 23.1   Rate of percentage change of industrial production.
SOURCE: Joseph A. Schumpeter, *Business Cycles*, II, p. 493.

the equivalent of a decline in the rate of growth of 34 percent.[1]

Industrial production also fluctuated cyclically in industrial Germany, the percentage rate of change being negative in 1862–1863, 1869–1870, 1874–1875, 1879, 1891–1892, 1901, and 1907. In several other years the rate of change, though positive, was close to zero, as shown in Figure 23.1, which compares Germany with Britain and the United States.

A different indicator of the magnitude of fluctuation is the trend of gross capital formation, shown in Figure 23.2 for Italy. The severity of the decline in the 1880s, in 1908, and after the First World War is clear. The fluctuations of the 1920s and 1930s were especially serious because of their rapid recurrence. As mentioned above, the crisis which followed the First World War was instrumental in the creation of the corporate state under Mussolini.

It may be noted that fluctuations in Spain were related mainly to commercial and agricultural developments until the latter part of the nineteenth century, after which monetary

and market conditions became more influential. However, the relation between production and prices is not clear-cut. Fluctuations in Spain are described in Figure 23.3. These graphs show the frequency and magnitude of fluctuation and the apparent interdependence between production and the value of issues on the market. After 1880, however, the commodity price index declined while industrial production continued to rise. This trend was due mainly to government policy and the fact that prices had risen more than they should have in the previous period. The deflation was part of the stabilization trend.

The effects of fluctuations in France have been noted briefly in discussing the recurrent political revolutions. Even in the absence of revolutions, however, crises often caused severe unemployment, bankruptcies, and starvation. Unemployment sometimes reached 50 percent in certain localities, as in 1811, 1846, and in the depression of the 1870s. Unemployment and slack in production were also common during crises in Britain and Germany, although the rates were usually modest compared with those in France.

Price rises can be as troublesome as declines. The most serious was the hyperinflation experienced in Germany after the First World War. The value of the currency de-

[1] For more detail, see Lennart Jörberg, "Structural Change and Economic Growth: Sweden in the 19th Century," *Economy and History*, VIII (1965), p. 45.

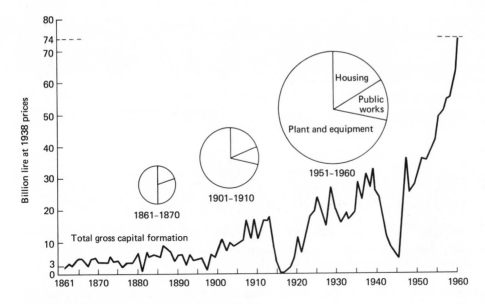

Figure 23.2   Investment fluctuation in Italy.
SOURCE: S. B. Clough, *The Economic History of Italy*, p. 374.

clined by more than 10,000 percent between 1913 and 1922, and by the end of 1923 the mark had virtually no value. Confidence in the economy was totally lost. The government faced a problem much more serious than those caused by price declines. The revival in the mid-1920s was brief and the severe unemployment which followed was an important factor in bringing Hitler to power.[2]

Causes of fluctuation

The causes of these fluctuations cannot be treated in detail, although a few of the more common ones may be noted. Demobilization after a war always created a crisis, partly because of the sudden increase in the labor supply and because much of the investment in the war period was not productive. Once the war was over, the productive capacity failed to satisfy demand, and the economy was unable to absorb the labor released by demobilization. This was the situation after the Napoleonic War, the Seven Years' War,

and the world wars. The relatively mild impact made by the end of the Second World War was due to conscious government policy. Another common cause of fluctuation was the tendency toward speculation and overexpansion in periods of prosperity. This was the case in the 1820s, in the early 1850s, in 1871–1873, and around 1900. The tendency toward overexpansion has been regarded as inherent in capitalistic production and the market economy, especially when accompanied by specific investment fevers such as the railway fever, expansion in construction, and speculation in wartime. For this reason, it has been constantly debated whether or not such crises can be prevented.

ECONOMIC POLICY

The government has always played an important role in the economy as buyer, protector, guardian of rights and property, source of finance and encouragement, employer, and producer. The details of government activity in the modern period have been surveyed in previous chapters. There-

[2] For details, see Gustav Stolper, *et al.*, *The German Economy, 1870 to the Present*, p. 84.

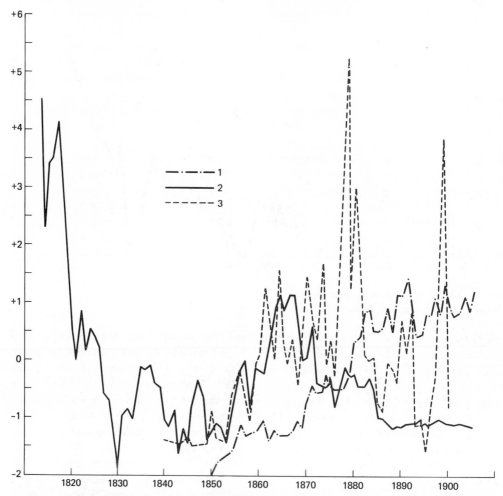

Figure 23.3   Nineteenth-century business cycles in Spain.
Line 1 is the average of the mean deviation in indexes of the chief
industrial products and the trade balance; line 2 is the same for
the general price index; line 3 is the same for value of issues.
SOURCE: Jaime Vicens Vives, *An Economic History of Spain*, p. 740.

fore, only a summary survey of the changing
trends will be presented here.[3]

The government has emerged as a
monopolist of the mint through its charter-
ing of the central banks. It has consistently
regulated international trade and the balance
of payments. Gradually it has also become
involved in welfare, planning, and even production. The degree of government partici-

[3] The student may independently gather these
details to illustrate the general tendencies noted
in this chapter.

pation is difficult to measure, since the
amount of change depends on one's reference point, in terms of both time and government structure. It is important to
distinguish between local and national
government. Local government has always
participated in the local economy. National
government and the national economies are
new creations. It is with them that we will be
concerned in this chapter. Finally, participation may be measured in terms of volume or
in terms of the strategic importance of gov-

ernment activity in the economy. Although 10 percent of total expenditure is relatively small, it may prove quite significant if it is controlled by a single management such as the government. It is important to know also whether such expenditure is made for consumption or for capital formation.

Government participation in the economy may be direct or indirect. Direct participation relates to government activity as buyer, seller, or producer. As a buyer the government controls part of the effective demand. As a producer it is a source of income and a supplier of commodities and services. Its influence on employment and prices in either capacity is great. Government participation may also be indirect, setting the stage for economic activity and change. Legislation can determine the direction and nature of economic activity, although not its intensity or the volume of production. The government may influence the relations between employer and employees, but it cannot guarantee harmony. Finally, the government can facilitate production and trade, but it can assure them only if it participates directly.

As a point of departure, we may recall the role of government in the mercantilist period, during which the polity and the economy were fused and the government regulated economic activity. Prices and wages were subject to control. Exports and imports were directly regulated. Relations between employees and employers were codified. Economic activity was determined by the degree of national unity achieved in each country. To a certain extent, mercantilist policies were never eliminated, although modifications have occurred in the modern period. However, the trend towards free trade has been predominant.

Laissez-faire policy

The decline of mercantilism, where and when it occurred, came at different times and rates. The economic role of government changed to permit freer trade and economic activity in the domestic and foreign markets.

The government carried out programs to remove restrictions: Tariffs were reduced; most prohibitions were abolished; guilds were suppressed; and labor and employer combinations were tolerated as long as they did not interfere with competition and economic freedom. The government remained active as guardian of social conditions and ethics. It also supervised the expansion of trade, both by removing obstacles and by concluding treaties. The bilateral treaties of the 1860s illustrate the active role the governments of most European countries played in international trade. Legislation to regulate business and labor organizations between 1840 and 1870 illustrate their domestic role. Factory legislation exemplifies their attempts to cope with the new conditions created by the industrial economy. In all these areas government participation was mainly indirect. The government was content to set the stage for economic change and let the market forces determine the results. This at least was the pattern in Britain, where the philosophy of free trade was most accepted.

However, the government did participate directly in production and industrialization even while free trade was being promoted, especially on the continent. It played an important role in the formation of banks and the building of railways by encouraging, subsidizing, and holding shares. Except in Britain, most of the major banks and railway lines were government creations. In many cases, as in Scandinavia, Spain, and Italy, the government borrowed foreign capital to finance development. Most of these forms of participation were traditionally in the government's domain, although their scope may have increased slightly because of the development of national markets and the strengthening of central government and because of the more frequent economic crises. When the era of free trade began to decline, however, the government assumed new roles.

The supervision of foreign exchange and the balance of payments, which began in this period, has continued. Growth of a national government usually encouraged unification and regulation of the currency by means of central banking and control of the mint. Until the Napoleonic War money included gold, silver, banknotes, and negotiable credit instruments. However, since the ratio between the metals and the price of gold and silver fluctuated, so did the international exchange rate. The nineteenth century saw a greater emphasis on a stable exchange rate and less on the accumulation of gold and silver.

A major step was taken in 1821 when the British government adopted the gold standard: Gold became the only metallic standard, and silver currency and banknotes had a fixed ratio to it. The Bank of England stood ready to convert these currencies into gold at the fixed ratio upon request. Henceforth, fluctuation in the exchange rate was theoretically possible only within a small range determined largely by the cost of transportation. To maintain price stability, the government also regulated the supply of money, whether in note issue or credit. Thus a loss of gold could be offset by expanding the circulating money, thus mitigating the effects on prices.

The gold standard was adopted by other countries half a century later. Germany adopted it in 1873. The Latin Monetary Union—composed of France, Belgium, Italy, and Switzerland, and formed in 1865 —switched to the gold standard in the 1870s. When Russia adopted the gold standard in 1897, it made it virtually universal. Bimetallism was no longer practiced in Europe. The gold standard remained in effect until the depression of the 1930s, although convertibility was suspended occasionally, especially during wartime.

The decline of laissez-faire

The last third of the nineteenth century witnessed the economic development of several European countries. It began with a depression and was characterized by the New Imperialism and a return to protectionism. In all these areas the government was an important influence on the economy. This period also witnessed the growth of revolutionary and evolutionary socialist groups. The government played an important role in socioeconomic relations, either by improving conditions to remove grievances or by suppressing radical and socialist forces. New functions, both direct and indirect, were assumed by the government. Expenditure on military and expansionist activities was greatly increased; legislation and new tariffs to regulate foreign trade were introduced; combinations and cartels were legalized; and new international agreements were concluded.

The government became more conscious of public utilities and a wave of nationalization began. The railways were the first target, but soon other means of communication were taken over, among them the telegraph and the telephone. The government was also active in extending the transcontinental cables. In Germany and Scandinavia the government was concerned with housing, and subsidies, especially by local governments, were common. Public education was fostered in France, Germany, and Scandinavia. Most governments also became involved in social insurance against accidents, disability, old age, and gradually against unemployment. They also set up courts to arbitrate between labor and capital, thus assuming the role of supreme judge in economic relations.

Nevertheless, when World War I came, Europe was still talking of free enterprise, minimum government intervention, and the ability of the market and monetary policy to cope with crises. The wars and the depression of the 1930s were to shatter that confidence and promote new approaches, as the next chapter will illustrate.

GENERAL REMARKS

The growth of the industrial economy brought with it a tendency toward fluctuation and crisis. Crises were often aggravated by the total dependence on the market, competition, and individualism. Their impact was usually reflected in unemployment, decline of output, and even political unrest. Therefore, the government found it necessary to institute policies to cope with these problems. However, to remain consistent with the philosophy of free enterprise, the government tended to emphasize indirect action. Manipulation of the money supply by various measures known as *monetary policy* remained the standard technique until the First World War, although some direct measures such as construction and housing were undertaken for their own sake or for humanitarian reasons.

In fact, however, free enterprise began to decline with the return to protectionism and the New Imperialism. The role of government increased on both the domestic and the international scenes. The trend was further crystallized during the first half of the twentieth century, to which we turn next.

BIBLIOGRAPHY

Ashworth, William, *A Short History of the International Economy Since 1850*, Second edition, Toronto: Longmans, 1962, chaps. 5, 7–9.

Cameron, Rondo, "Economic Growth and Stagnation in France, 1815–1914," *Journal of Modern History*, XXX (1958).

Clough, S. B., *The Economic History of Italy*, New York: Columbia University Press, 1964.

Clough, S. B., *France: A History of National Economics, 1789–1939*, New York: Octagon Books, 1964.

Dillard, Dudley, *Economic Development of the North Atlantic Community*, Englewood Cliffs, N.J.: Prentice-Hall, 1967, chap. 21.

Einzig, Paul, *The History of Foreign Exchange*, New York: St. Martin's Press, 1962, Parts IV and V.

Hobsbawm, E. J., "Economic Fluctuations and Some Social Movements Since 1800," *Economic History Review*, II, No. 5 (1952), pp. 1–25.

Kondratieff, Nikolai D., "The Long Waves in Economic Life," *Review of Economic Statistics*, 1935; reproduced in *Readings in Business Cycle Theory*, American Economic Association, New York: McGraw-Hill, 1951, pp. 20–42. Many other selections in this volume are also relevant.

Kuznets, Simon S., *Secular Movements in Production and Prices*, New York: Augustus M. Kelly, 1967.

Maddison, Angus, *Economic Growth in the West*, New York: Twentieth Century Fund, 1964, chap. 4.

Rostow, W. W., *British Economy of the Nineteenth Century*, New York: Oxford University Press, 1948, chaps. 1 and 2.

Schumpeter, J. A., *Business Cycles*, I and II, New York: McGraw-Hill, 1939.

Stolper, Gustav, *et al.*, *The German Economy, 1870 to the Present*, New York: Harcourt, Brace & World, 1967.

Triffin, Robert, *Our International Monetary System: Yesterday, Today, and Tomorrow*, New York: Random House, 1968, chaps. 1 and 2.

Vicens Vives, Jaime, *An Economic History of Spain*, Princeton: Princeton University Press, 1969, chap. 48.

24

THE RECENT PAST: AN OVERVIEW

It is hardly possible to study history without being tempted to draw analogies to the present. An attempt will be made to bring this study as close to the present as possible, even though such an attempt is bound to be either too detailed to fit in the available space or too brief to satisfy the reader. For Europe and the world, the last half-century has been rich in both failures and achievement. It seems appropriate, therefore, to at least outline the recent trends, with the hope that the curious reader will refer to at least some of the many works on this period.

We have noted the relationship between the recent and more distant past. The continuity in international trade, labor movements, and business organization before and after 1914 has also been briefly sketched. The present discussion is an attempt to give the reader a comprehensive outline showing the complexities, the interdependences, and some of the problems of this period, together with some solutions. Since 1914 there have been two world wars, a severe depression, and a recovery in Europe that is almost unprecedented. The changes and policies associated with these events have touched all aspects of European society. A new economic and political power structure has evolved. Reasons for security and insecurity have both been aggravated. How many of the past failures can be avoided and what

successes can be repeated? Is it possible to avoid a world war or a depression? Can we avoid a Malthusian solution to the population problem? Can the advantages of competition be enjoyed without suffering the consequences? And can industrialization and growth be achieved without polluting the environment and prematurely depleting the resource? These are difficult questions to answer. However, past experience shows man's ability to deal with his problems. If the past can be used as an indicator, it seems reasonable to expect that major problems can be reduced or even avoided. Even the cost of such policies can be reduced through application of intelligence, experience, and will.

THE NEW FRAMEWORK

The recent period has witnessed the evolution of a new framework in Europe. As a result of World War I Germany returned Alsace-Lorraine to France and lost parts of Schleswig to Denmark and large areas to Poland; small territories went to Lithuania and Belgium, and some areas were put under the jurisdiction of the League of Nations. The Turkish Empire ended and new independent states were created in its place in southeastern Europe. Its territories in the Middle East were surrendered and the vacuum was filled by Britain and France. These changes were of economic importance to the extent that they affected the size of the market, the distribution of natural resources, and the freedom of trade in a given region. Probably the most serious economic impact, however, was that of the Treaty of Versailles, which imposed burdensome reparation payments on Germany, as will be seen below.

The Soviet revolution changed the balance of power almost from the beginning. It made communism a reality and an apparent threat to the capitalistic countries. Although Soviet Russia was for the next two decades too weak to be a direct and immediate threat, the mere establishment of the new system was sufficient to change the European frame of reference. However, a counter force was becoming more involved in the affairs of Europe. President Wilson broke the isolationism which had dominated the foreign policy of the United States. The United States' involvement was closely associated with the economic trends of the next half-century, and has become progressively more so.

World War I was followed by a period of international distrust, vengefulness, and insecurity. The peace settlement antagonized Germany and taxed its resources seriously. Other European countries were too insecure to cooperate in making it easier for Germany to keep its side of the agreement, although later Britain and the United States became a little more cooperative. The interwar period saw a revival of nationalism and protectionism. Yet, except for Soviet Russia, the economies of Europe and to an extent of the United States were so interdependent that when the depression of the 1930s came it was difficult for any of them to escape it. Thus the interwar period was full of contradictions. While becoming more interdependent, the European economies were also going through a nationalist revival. The development of the corporate state in Italy and of national socialism in Germany are good illustrations of the trend. To a certain extent, the depression was a result of these contradictions, augmented by the failures of the economic and monetary policies of the period.

World War II brought a different atmosphere as its aftermath. Germany was divided between East and West. Two new camps developed, the socialist and the capitalist, with Soviet Russia and the United States, respectively, as their leaders. The political blocs eventually evolved into economic blocs. The impact was much more far-reaching than a simple division would suggest. Britain, which had dominated the international scene for two centuries, was losing ground. The Soviet Union was gaining, while the United States was becoming the unchallenged political and economic leader. The European countries were in a sense required to choose between East and West. Economic relations followed a similar pattern, whether by choice or by the dictation of circumstance. Another contrast with the post-World War I period was the greater cooperativeness of the countries involved, possibly as a result of the two-camp division. It is probably the first time in history that a defeated country has been aided by the victor in rehabilitating and reconstructing its economy, as was the case with Germany, Italy, and Japan after World War II. The results have had an impact on the economies of virtually all the countries of Europe.

A more dramatic change has been the reversal of the imperialistic policies of the preceding half-century. A few countries became independent after the First World War, especially those which were under Turkey's domination. However, after World War II a new attitude towards the rights of man developed and all people became anxious to gain independence. The European countries which had subdivided Asia and Africa lost their possessions one after the other. More than 50 new nations have come into being since the end of the war and joined the United Nations as independent states. This proliferation of independent nations has changed the structure of the market for the European countries and made new institutions for international trade and investment necessary. These relationships have been further complicated by the competition between East and West for the friendships or loyalties of the former colonies. The European countries have been forced to create a new atmosphere in order to maintain a flow of trade and capital between them and the new nations and to prevent a vacuum developing in their own economies.

The recent period has also witnessed a demographic change in Europe. Its population including Russia declined from 26.4 percent of world population in 1900 to 21.4 percent in 1960. Nevertheless, the European population increased from 423 million to 641 million in these years, net of emigration and of the casualties of the two world wars, although French population declined between 1911 and 1919. It may be noted that emigration in this period became restricted, since most of the receiving countries introduced regulations which reduced it perceptibly. About 8 million people emigrated from Europe between 1911 and 1920, about 7 million in the 1920s, and only 1.2 million in the 1930s. Even by the 1950s emigration was only about 5 million, while population had increased considerably.

The impact of this increase in population on the economy was mitigated by two factors. First, the size and composition of the labor force were modified by extending the period of schooling and by regulating the employment of women and children, at a time when the hours of work were being reduced. Second, the continued advances in technology tended to offset the pressure of population and raise productivity, thus helping to raise the standard of living and prevent a Malthusian trap.

At the same time, Europe's resources were being expanded. The use of oil as fuel increased the available energy, sometimes to the disadvantage of the coal industry. More

energy was harnessed by the expansion in the use of internal combustion. Both the automobile and the airplane belong essentially to this period. Electricity became more widely used. The electric motor was an important competitor to the steam plow. The tractor was also introduced early in this period. However, except for the jet engine, introduced in Germany in 1939, the major inventions in power production have been in the area of atomic energy, which came only after the end of World War II. The first nuclear reactor to produce electric power was introduced in 1951 in the United States and the first nuclear power station was built in Britain in 1956.

Resources have been increased also by the application of insecticides and artificial insemination. Synthetic fibers such as plastics and nylon have added to productive capacity. Synthetic rubber provided another resource. Chemicals and artificial growth regulators or plant hormones have helped agriculture and increased the capacity for food production. The details of these new technologies were discussed in Chapter 17. However, it is important to recall in this context that recent years have been rich not only in invention but even more in innovation, scientific management, and introduction of new products, all of which have changed the structure and quality of the economies of Europe. However, these achievements have been accompanied by a high cost to the environment as a whole. Ecologists are now drawing attention to the effects of water and air pollution and the insufficient attention paid by man to his environment. They are also pointing out the dangers of insecticides and herbicides as pollution sources and as killers of wildlife as well as hazards to human life. While these problems have only recently received serious attention, efforts have been expended to cope with them in various countries of Europe.

The rest of this chapter will outline the major trends in production and employment, the market structure and international trade, government policy and the welfare state, and the place of Europe relative to the rest of the world.

OUTPUT AND EMPLOYMENT

On the eve of World War I Europe contained all the elements necessary for continued growth and development. The market had been enlarged, the resources were available, and technology offered many opportunities which remained to be exploited. However, the war caused havoc in the European economies. Its effects can hardly be divorced from the instabilities of the 1920s and the depression of the 1930s, whose impact remained through the next world war.

Total output

The impact of the wars and the depression was differentially distributed according to the country's involvement in the war, its interdependence with other nations, and the vulnerability of its economy to monetary fluctuations. The changes may be indicated by the index of the total output of the various countries. Although this index does not take changes in the population and labor force into consideration, it does show how total output varied over the years. The year 1913 has been taken as the base year, whose output was set at an index of 100 for each country.

The output in Belgium, on which comparable data are not fully adequate, had been restored and increased to 127.8 in 1929, after which a decline set in. In 1938 the output index was 122. World War II took its toll, but 3 years after the end of the war the index had climbed to 135. Since then total output has continued to increase and by 1960 it had reached an index of 193.7. In contrast, Denmark overcame the effects of World War I by 1922 and increased its total output to 117.7 in 1923. Except for a decline of 3 index points in 1932, Denmark seems to

have escaped the fate of most other nations during both the depression and World War II. Output continued to increase; the index was 160.5 in 1938 and 189.7 in 1948. By 1960 it reached 298.7.

The wars' effects on France were much more severe, which is not surprising, given that country's involvement in the wars and in monetary markets. In 1920 France's output index was 77.6 and in 1923 it was still below the 1913 total, at 95.3. After that date output increased to an index of 130.6 by 1929. The depression hit France hard, the output index declining to a low of 107.1 in 1936. However, its impact might have seemed less severe because of France's low rate of population growth, compared with other European countries. Hardly had the effects of the depression been reversed, when war broke out. Another decline was experienced during and after World War II; total output stood at an index of 107.7 in 1948. Since then growth has been rapid and by 1960 the index had reached 208.8.

The impact of war and depression on total output was probably most severe in Germany. The hyperinflation of the early 1920s slowed down reconstruction, and by 1926 total output in Germany was only 92.9 on the index. Reconstruction of the economy succeeded in raising total output to 1929 levels, after which another decline reduced the index from 104.9 in 1930 to 94.9 in 1932. The policy of National Socialism reversed the depression, largely by mobilization, so that by 1938 output had reached an index of 149.9, a level which was not restored again until about 1950. Since then total output has increased so rapidly that the index in 1962 was 327.4, or more than 3 times its level a decade earlier.

Italy suffered less destruction than Germany and its economy came under government regulation earlier. The wars' effects on total output were much less noticeable. By 1920 total output had risen to 106.6 on the index scale and it continued to rise slowly until 1929. The depression caused a decline

Table 24.1.   Indexes of soviet industrial production

REFERENCE	1928	1937	1940	1950	1960
Official Soviet	100	446	646	1119	2065
Hodgwan	100	371	430	646	—
Jasny	100	287	330–350	411	—
Clark	100	311	340	—	—
National Bureau	100	257	279	421	688
Shimkin	100	274	296	434	715

SOURCE: *Robert W. Campbell*, Soviet Economic Power, *Boston: Houghton Mifflin, 1960, p. 48.*

from 132.9 to 125.7 index points in 1930, followed by minor changes until 1935 when the index stood at 144.1; it reached 153.8 in 1938. World War II was followed by a period of reconstruction and rapid expansion. The prewar level was restored in 1949–1950, and by 1960 the output index had reached 287.9, compared with 161.8 in 1950.

The rising output trend was least affected in the Netherlands, Norway, and the United Kingdom. Only minor relapses took place in these countries during the depression, and since postwar reconstruction was fairly rapid total output continued to rise. Consequently, change during the 1950s was less dramatic than it was in some of the other countries. In the Netherlands total output rose from an index of 194.0 in 1948 to 350.7 in 1960; in Norway it rose from 248.2 to 373.4, and in the United Kingdom from 177.3 to 244.3. The trend in Sweden was different after World War I; the 1913 level was not restored until 1923. Total output continued to rise until 1930, reaching an index of 127.0. A decline came with the depression, down to 110.0 in 1933, but recovery was rapid. By 1938 the index had risen to 154.6 and in 1948 it was 201.1. Even then growth continued to be rapid. The total output index reached 311.0 in 1960.

The United States' experience was similar to that of the Netherlands and Norway up to 1929. However, the depression was so severe that total output declined from an index of 163.4 in 1929 to 117.7 in 1933 and returned to the 1929 level only in 1938. The post-World War II period was one of continued

expansion. The index of output rose from 269.6 in 1948 to 403.1 in 1960, the highest of any country, relative to the 1913 index.[1]

The experience of Soviet Russia is not easily comparable to those of other European countries or the United States because of the radical changes in the structure of the Soviet economy and the difference in the quality of the data. Soviet development is usually measured in terms of 1928 as a base year, this being the highest output year before collectivization and somewhat equivalent to the level of 1914. Soviet development was concentrated on heavy industry until late in the 1950s, and therefore the available data may be somewhat misleading. The reader may glean some of the discrepancies from the different estimates shown in Table 24.1. Whichever of these indexes is used, it is clear that production increased enormously and that the depression had little impact on Russia. The economy was relatively closed, fully planned, and hence protected against international disturbances. The Second World War had a more severe impact, but Soviet Russia was able to restore the prewar level quickly and resume expansion. It may be noted, however, that expansion in agriculture was much less dramatic. Change in agriculture was mainly institutional, as has been noted above.

The eastern and southern European countries which became independent in 1918 and

[1] The above figures have been adopted from Angus Maddison, *Economic Growth in the West,* pp. 201–202.

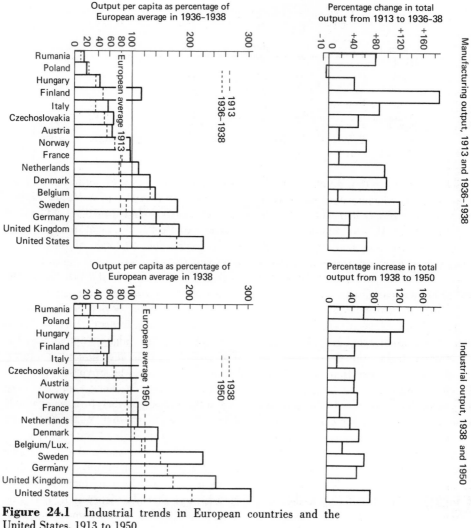

Figure 24.1   Industrial trends in European countries and the
United States, 1913 to 1950.
The 1938 data for Austria, Czechoslovakia and the United States
actually refer to 1937.
SOURCE: Ingvar Svennilson, *Growth and Stagnation in the Euro-
pean Economy*, p. 207.

Communist after World War II experienced
little industrialization in the interwar period.
Agriculture continued to be the main source
of income and tenure reforms were still a
subject of controversy. The depression had
the same effect on these countries as in the
rest of Europe, with a sharp decline between
1930 and 1933, followed by a slow revival.
The early revival has been explained as
partly due to the interdependence between

these countries and the German economic
policy which dominated them. Their genuine
development, however, came after World
War II.

These trends may be seen in Figure 24.1,
which may be used to compare eastern and
western European countries, and European
countries including Soviet Russia with the
United States up to 1950. It is clear that
manufacturing increased little between 1913

Table 24.2. Unemployment as a proportion of the labor force

	BELGIUM	DENMARK	FRANCE	GERMANY (WEST)	ITALY	NETHERLANDS	SWEDEN	SWITZERLAND	UNITED KINGDOM	UNITED STATES[a]
1913	3.1	2.0	1.0	1.9	1.7	1.5	1.1	1.0	1.2	4.3
1920		1.7		1.7		1.7	1.3		1.8	3.9
1921	6.1	5.1	2.5	1.2		2.6	6.4		9.6	11.4
1922	1.9	5.1		0.7		3.2	5.5		8.1	7.2
1923	0.6	3.3		4.5		3.3	2.9		6.6	3.0
1924	0.6	2.9		5.8		2.6	2.4		5.8	5.3
1925	0.9	3.9	1.1	3.0		2.4	2.6		6.4	3.8
1926	0.8	5.4		8.0		2.1	2.9		7.1	1.9
1927	1.1	5.9		3.9		2.2	2.9		5.5	3.9
1928	0.6	4.8		3.8	1.7	1.6	2.4		6.1	4.3
1929	0.8	4.1		5.9	2.5	1.7	2.4	0.4	5.9	3.1
1930	2.2	3.6		9.5	4.3	2.3	3.3	0.7	9.3	8.7
1931	6.8	4.8	2.1	13.9	5.8	4.3	4.8	1.2	12.6	15.8
1932	11.9	8.7		17.2	5.9	8.3	6.8	2.8	13.1	23.5
1933	10.6	8.3		14.8	5.6	9.7	7.3	3.5	11.7	24.7
1934	11.8	6.8		8.3		9.8	6.4	3.3	9.9	21.6
1935	11.1	6.2		6.5		11.2	6.2	4.2	9.2	20.0
1936	8.4	6.3	4.2	4.8		11.9	5.3	4.7	7.9	16.8
1937	7.2	7.5		2.7	5.0	10.5	5.1	3.6	6.7	14.2
1938	8.7	7.5	3.6	1.3	4.6	9.9	5.1	3.3	8.1	18.9
1950	6.3	4.1	1.4	7.2	8.7	2.0	1.7	0.5	2.5	5.2
1951	5.7	4.5	1.3	6.4	9.2	2.4	1.6	0.2	2.2	3.2
1952	6.8	5.9	1.3	6.1	9.8	3.5	1.7	0.3	2.9	2.9
1953	6.8	4.4	1.6	5.5	10.2	2.5	1.9	0.3	2.6	2.8
1954	6.2	3.8	1.6	5.2	8.7	1.8	1.8	0.2	2.3	5.3
1955	4.7	4.7	1.5	3.8	7.5	1.3	1.8	0.1	2.1	4.2
1956	4.0	5.3	1.2	3.1	9.3	1.0	1.6	0.2	2.2	4.0
1957	3.2	5.0	1.0	2.7	8.1	1.2	1.7	0.1	2.4	4.2
1958	5.0	4.7	1.1	2.7	6.4	2.3	2.0	0.2	3.0	6.6
1959	5.5	3.0	1.3	1.9	5.4	1.8	1.8	0.1	3.1	5.3
1960	4.1	2.1	1.3	0.9	4.0	1.1	1.6	0.1	2.5	5.4

[a] For comparison purposes.

SOURCE: *Angus Maddison, Economic Growth in the West, p. 220.*

and 1938 in Rumania, Poland, Hungary, and even Czechoslovakia, although total output increased by more than 40 percent in all of them except Poland. In contrast, all four countries experienced almost a doubling of industrial output between 1938 and 1950, their growth rates being among the fastest in Europe, as was the growth of their total output.

Unemployment

To put these output changes in perspective, changes in population and the labor force should be taken into consideration. Crisis in the economy was usually reflected in the level of unemployment, even when employment was increasing. The data on unemployment suggest that the effects of war and depression were different from those suggested by the output index. France, for example, which had suffered a decline of total output, was more fortunate than other countries in keeping unemployment figures relatively low. Even during the depression, unemployment in France did not exceed 5 percent.

In contrast, all other countries had serious unemployment in the postwar periods and during the depression. Table 24.2 shows these comparative data. Belgium had 6.1 percent unemployment in 1921, but for the following 8 years unemployment was virtually nonexistent. The depression years were hard and unemployment rose from 2.2 percent in 1930 to 11.8 percent in 1934 and remained around 8 percent until World War II. Unemployment after World War II ranged from 6.8 percent in 1951–1952 to a low of 3.2 percent in 1957. The early 1920s witnessed relatively high unemployment in Denmark, the Netherlands, Sweden, the United Kingdom, and even the United States, but the period of unemployment was relatively short in all these countries except the United Kingdom. After it started, unemployment seems to have persisted with some fluctuation until the big jump during the early 1930s, at which time severe unemploy-

ment was common to most countries, especially Belgium, Germany, the Netherlands, the United Kingdom, and the United States. The rates of unemployment in the latter were the highest. Except in Germany, unemployment also persisted throughout the 1930s, until the war and mobilization eliminated it.

In the postwar period France, the Netherlands, Sweden, Switzerland, and the United Kingdom had very low rates of unemployment. In the other countries unemployment was 5 percent or more in the early 1950s, after which it began to decline, although in Italy, the United States, and Belgium the rates remained relatively high. The differential rates of unemployment after World War II may be explained mainly in terms of government policy and planning. France, for example, has practiced planning more than any other western country and therefore can keep the average rate of unemployment low. Sweden has instituted a policy of full employment. Other countries have worked towards that goal, but only after redefining full employment to tolerate a higher rate of unemployment. In the United States, for example, 3.5 to 4 percent unemployment is regarded acceptable. In contrast, unemployment in Soviet Russia does not formally exist, since the plan is designed to employ all resources. However, there is no consideration of underemployment, which has been characteristic of various countries including those with a plan. Thus in the last two decades governments have become more sensitive to changes in unemployment rates and are no longer willing to let the market resolve the problem. Government policy has been tailored to deal with fluctuations in most European countries.

MARKETS, BLOCS, AND INTERNATIONAL TRADE

The pattern of economic change in the recent period has been closely associated with market conditions and liquidity. International trade and finance reflected the difficulties faced in the market. After World War I international trade was burdened by the effects of the war. Germany was subjected to extensive reparation payments to other countries, which were themselves burdened with war loans from the United States. The loss of productive capacity, the disorganization following the war, and the lack of confidence in the postwar institutions caused havoc in the levels of international demand and liquidity. Germany was unable to pay reparations regularly, while the other countries could not pay their debts unless they received reparations. The gold standard had broken down and convertibility was suspended by most countries. Even the successful attempts to overcome hyperinflation in Germany were not sufficient to restore confidence or increase liquidity enough to revive trade.

Attempts were made to ease the situation. Britain, in the Balfour note of August 1, 1922, declared that it would demand from debtors only what it owed to the United States. The United States came up with the Dawes Plan on September 1, 1924, according to which reparation payments were scheduled and tied to specific sources of revenue, and were initially financed by an international loan. While some improvement followed, the situation had already gone too far and the crisis continued. Britain and some other countries which had restored convertibility were soon forced to give up the gold standard. After the depression started each country was looking out for its own interests. Governments were afraid of long-term international debts and even short-term debts to finance imports. Tariffs and protectionism were revived or reinforced and cartels were strengthened. The monetary system had in effect broken down.

The depression years are hard to evaluate, since the period was too short to allow the results to be fully evident. Mobilization and war changed the economic framework, disposed of inventories, engaged the labor force, and regulated both wages and prices.

The war also created a new system of cooperation among nations. The Axis and the Allies each developed arrangements for transferring resources which made trade in the strict sense of the term irrelevant. Under the lend-lease method the Allies were able to secure the necessary equipment and war materials regardless of foreign exchange or liquidity problems.

The situation after World War II differed from that of the post-World War I years. There were no war debts. Lend-lease transfers were generally canceled. No reparations were imposed on the defeated countries, except those that Germany volunteered to make many years later. Because of the Fascist and Nazi experiences, World War II left the world anxious to avoid lasting bitterness. Rather, there were feelings of war-weariness, and a desire to build a better world and to avoid a return to the economic difficulties of the depression.

Among the problems which loomed large after the war were those of maintaining liquidity and preventing a depression. Reconstruction was necessary both to put the European economies back on their feet and to create liquidity through an efficient monetary and exchange system. International cooperation seemed to be the key to both problems. Cooperation was achieved by the development of the eastern and western blocs. The eastern bloc depended primarily on planning, regulation by the state, and limited convertibility within the bloc. Its operation has been described in various terms, ranging from full cooperation to exploitation of the satellites by the Soviet Union.

The western countries approached the problem of international payments in various ways. Since return to the gold standard was out of the question, a gold exchange system took its place. The dollar served as the main reserve currency in the West, although the pound sterling fulfilled the same function. Liquidity, therefore, meant adequate reserves of gold or dollars and to an extent of pounds sterling. Transfer payments as economic aid were begun as early as 1943 through the United Nations Relief and Rehabilitation Administration (UNRRA), coming mostly from the United States. The United States also approached the problem in another way. To encourage recovery and liquidity in Europe the Marshall Plan was introduced under the Economic Cooperation Act of April 1948. Aid was extended to those countries that needed it, amounting to more than $12 billion in about 4 years.

However, these were temporary unilateral measures. To provide a more permanent solution, the European Payments Union (EPU) was established in 1950 to clear payments among members of the Organization for European Economic Cooperation. In 8 years of existence the EPU settled about $46 billion of transactions with a working capital of only $350 million. The International Monetary Fund and the International Bank for Reconstruction and Development (World Bank) were established in 1944, although they became operative a little later. The Fund acted as a currency pool or revolving fund to help members deal with temporary deficits in the balance of payments. However, it could impose reforms before extending loans to the members. The World Bank was created mainly to help in financing productive long-term investments. Although the means at the disposal of the Bank were relatively small, it was important economically and encouraged cooperation. Both the Fund and the Bank played important roles in economic and monetary reforms in certain countries.

Agreements to remove trade restrictions were designed to expand trade. The first viable measure was the General Agreement on Tariffs and Trade (GATT), which aimed mainly at sponsoring bilateral agreements like those of the 1860s. A more directly involved institution, though narrower in scope, is the European Economic Community or the Common Market, which includes six European countries—France, Germany, Italy, Belgium, the Netherlands, and Luxem-

bourg—built on the foundations of the European Coal and Steel Community. The Common Market came into being in 1957 when the six countries signed the treaty of Rome. It aimed in part at creating a free-trade area and a common policy towards nonmembers. No doubt political and social objectives were in the background. The impact of the Common Market was felt immediately, as reflected in the move by the "Outer Seven" in 1959 to create a similar free-trade area, known as the European Free Trade Association. The Free Trade Association includes the United Kingdom, Norway, Denmark, Sweden, Switzerland, Austria, and Portugal. The pace of the Association, however, was much slower than that of the Common Market, and its impact has been much less felt. The eastern European bloc also formed a "free"-trade area. Europe was thus divided into three main trade areas with varying degrees of freedom.

However, restrictions on trade with the rest of the world have been modified only slightly. Tariffs are still imposed on both industrial and agricultural goods. Exchange controls have not been eliminated. Free trade is still a distant dream. The reason for this lies mostly in the changed economic structure, the commitment to full employment and the welfare state, and the expansion of economic planning. Domestic problems may also have rendered more freedom of trade impractical.

These measures have been adequate to deal with the problems of trade and liquidity, but they have not solved them. The recurrent crises and devaluations in various countries suggest that new approaches are still needed to smooth the flow of trade. Nevertheless, Europe has continued to dominate world trade, of which it held 58 percent in 1913, 52 percent in 1938, and 53 percent in 1960. The share of the individual countries has changed slightly. Britain, for example, controlled 17 percent of world trade in 1913, 14 percent in 1938, and only 8 percent in 1960; Germany held 13 percent, 9 percent, and 8 percent, respectively; while the share of France declined from 8 percent in 1913 and has remained relatively stable around 5 percent since 1938. Newly industrializing European countries, including those which have since World War II gone into the eastern bloc, have acquired a large share of the trade.

BUSINESS, LABOR, AND GOVERNMENT POLICY

The present structures of the various European economies were basically laid out in the interwar period. Concentration, confederation, scientific and technical management, government participation, planning, and social security were all continued and reinforced after World War II.

The eastern bloc

The Soviet Union and its eastern allies have relied on planning, public ownership, big business enterprises, and formally abolition of class conflicts. Emphasis on heavy industry has been common to all of these countries to some degree. The plan usually determined what should be produced and the managers were expected to comply. Wages and prices were fixed. Raw material and finished products were allocated. Trade, whether domestic or foreign, was directed by the plan. Labor, business, and the government were supposed to be partners since all of them owned and produced in the service of the same cause. Strict implementation of the plan continued to be the rule until the 1950s, when questions were raised regarding rational and efficient allocation, the absence of material incentives and rewards, the efficiency of price determination, and the prescribed composition of the product. Pressure mounted to reduce the inefficiencies which were considered inherent in what has been described as the "command economy." Reforms were introduced under which a certain degree of decentralization has taken place, incentives and rewards for more efficient performance have been encouraged, and

higher wages have been paid to workers in industry and agriculture. More consumer goods are being produced. However, all these reforms have been introduced within the framework of planning and public ownership of the means of production.

Variance from the Soviet socialist system was most pronounced in Yugoslavia, which split with Russia in 1948. In that country the workers play an important role in industry. In each enterprise they elect a workers' council and a managerial board. Together with the unions, the board determines wages, prices, and the composition of the product. The government controls investment and growth through the central bank and by regulating the allocation and prices of certain basic raw materials. In that sense industry is nationalized. The plan sets targets which the government tries to achieve by controlling investment. Public services, new enterprises, and basic industries are actually planned. Agriculture, on the other hand, has remained in the hands of farmers and farm cooperatives. The individual farmer was originally permitted to own up to 60 acres, but this was reduced to 25 in 1951. Farmers are encouraged to join collectives and cooperatives which are better equipped with machinery. This flexibility can hardly be divorced from the slow rate of development in Yugoslavia, compared with most other countries in both eastern and western Europe.

Germany and Italy

Germany and Italy underwent centralization and corporatism during the interwar period. Both processes encouraged more state control at the expense of business and labor. However, in both cases, private ownership was maintained and business became identified with the state. Businessmen directed industry on its behalf and reaped the profits for themselves. Labor was largely suppressed.

After World War II Germany was *de facto* divided. East Germany essentially followed the pattern of the Eastern Bloc. In

Italy and West Germany attempts were made to return to a more liberal economic system. By July 1948 most of the price controls in West Germany had been abolished; price determination was left to the market. Prices rose and production continued to expand. The government encouraged investment by a tax-exemption policy with good results. The Central Bank applied monetary measures as added encouragement. An important feature of the new economy was the fear of mass unemployment and the government's readiness to take direct action against it. In 1950 plans were made to undertake construction and other projects to prevent unemployment. Nevertheless, a market economy has been fully reinstated, with the understanding that the government should remain active in combatting crises and in guarding social and economic welfare. The new system has been based on the motto of the Social Democratic Party: "Competition as far as feasible, planning as far as necessary."

However, controls were still imposed on currency exchange and the prices of steel, flour, housing, and electricity. As late as 1966 there were controls on agriculture and housing. While free competition was considered basic to the new regime, cartels and large businesses were maintained and even encouraged. As early as 1923 a Cartel Decree had put restraints on actions that might abuse the cartels' power. In 1957 a new cartel authority was established to supervise their behavior. By 1962, 260 new cartel applications had been filed, in addition to at least 3000 cartels that existed in 1930. Concentration, whether in cartels or in other forms, has increased progressively in the last few years.

Germany has continued to regulate entry into the market by legislation. The Artisan Charter of September 17, 1953, reinstated the requirement for "proof of competence" as a prerequisite for admission to the crafts. In 1957 "proof of expertness and reliability" was made a requirement for entry into retail trade; a new business can be established, at least in some trades, only after it is shown that the market demand justifies it.

The German government has also played an active role in agriculture. To render agriculture competitive in world markets, the government disseminated information on conditions in the market and extended subsidies to influence the direction of production. Subsidies were given for the use of fertilizer; low-interest loans were extended as a counterpart to the Marshall Plan funds; and tax reductions were applied to agriculture. As a result an agricultural revolution has taken place, including extensive mechanization and modernization with government help and direction.

An interesting feature of the last decade in Germany has been the "reprivatization" of public property. While continuing to control major industries such as railroads, electricity, water, and gas, the government has begun to disperse shares in these public properties to less propertied citizens. In addition there has been an active government policy in housing, social insurance, and education.

Labor unions, which had virtually vanished in 1933, were reinstated in Germany, but in a different form. They were unified within the General Trade Union Federation (DGB or *Deutscher Gewerkschaftsbund*) in 1949, although the specific industrial unions retained their autonomy. Although half the labor force was unionized, conflict was infrequent, partly because the unions were willing to cooperate in the period of reconstruction and because of their hopes for the future. Prosperity helped confirm their expectations. Furthermore, management was seeking cooperation of the unions in the shop. A system of codetermination was established for iron and steel by the Law of 1951, according to which the supervisory board included equal representation of labor and shareholders, with a neutral member appointed jointly. A labor member was also to represent the union on the management board and the shop council. Since then unions have tried to introduce codetermination in other industries with some success.

Italy also tried to return to a more liberal economy. However, the difficulties were great. Currency reform and credit control took various forms before stability was achieved. The government took direct economic measures in the postwar period, notably in agrarian reform. Land distribution, credit expansion, and the creation of cooperatives were extensive. The results, however, have been variously evaluated.

The success was much more clear-cut in industry. As in agriculture, the government immediately assumed direct responsibility. A plan was established, showing priorities among reconstruction measures and the rates at which they should proceed. The plan aimed at reducing unemployment and the differences between northern and southern Italy, increasing exports, and maintaining a stable balance of payments. However, it was only a general guide to be followed rather than enforced. It was facilitated by full government ownership of some industries such as banking and transportation, and partial ownership of others. It is interesting that the government used instruments created by the Fascist regime to control the economy. In 1937 the Institute for the Reconstruction of Industry (IRI) was created to take over frozen banks and companies in crisis. After World War II the IRI was reactivated as a public corporation to function as a public holding company to help the members. It was backed by the Treasury and empowered to borrow money on the open market. Separate branches of the IRI held stock in different industries, the IRI's shares varying from 10 percent to full ownership. Another holding corporation was the *Ente Nationale Idrocarburi* (ENI), which played the same role in oil, gas, transportation, minerals, and chemicals. Other public corporations were also established, making the state a partner or owner in industry, and therefore a decision-maker. The government also set up

financial institutions, the most important of which was the *Instituto Mobiliare Italiano* (IMI), which dealt with the United States Export–Import Bank, and helped coal and steel, ship-building, development in the South, and other industries.

In addition the government devoted attention to welfare and education. In the early 1960s about 28 percent of the government budget was committed to education, housing, and welfare. While maintaining a market economy, the government has thus managed to influence the economy by direct participation. While some sectors were nationalized, others were influenced by joint decision-making or by subsidy and international agreements.

The revival of trade unions after the war soon showed that the differences of opinion and ideology which had prevailed in pre-Fascist Italy still existed. The largest union, *Confederazione Generale Italiana del Lavoro* (CGIL) represented the Communist ideology and was opposed to the reinstitution of the market economy, unlike the Christian (Catholic) union, the *Confederazione Italiana Sindacati Lavoratori* (CISL). The Social Democrats had a separate union, as did the neo-Fascists. As a result, the labor movement in Italy has been divided and has cooperated little in reconstruction. Labor objectives have remained confused with political objectives. Nevertheless, the unions have managed to carry out collective bargaining, and have frequently gone on strike for political or economic reasons. Although the minister of labor may arbitrate, his decisions are not binding. In general labor unions have been concerned with wages and living standards. As early as 1920 they also tried to participate in management by organizing factory committees. However, little success was achieved until 1944–1945, when Mussolini gave them virtual control through membership on labor–management councils. After the war these councils were generally devoid of real power. The only parties to support them were the Communists and socialists. Labor's only achievement until 1950 was recognition of "the right of workers to collaborate in the management of business enterprises in the ways and within the limits established by law."[2]

In both Germany and Italy employers' associations were revived after the war. However, their functions were restricted, since there were many other forces to fight their cause and since they preferred to stay out of organized politics. There were two main functions which they served: They provided an organization for collective bargaining, and they undertook social improvements to aid reconstruction and stability. The relations of management with labor were more harmonious in Germany than in Italy, in part because of the differences in the levels of unemployment and prosperity, and because of the greater militancy of Italian labor.

Scandinavia and Britain

The experiences of Scandinavia and Britain were quite different. Both countries experienced continuity and a strengthening of already established trends. After the war both saw the development of an affinity between the unions and the political party in power, even though in Britain there was a clear division between party and union.

British unions cooperated with the state as a partner, particularly when the Labour Party was in power. This partnership was reinforced by the government's decision to nationalize major industries such as coal, steel, transportation, electricity, and the Bank of England, in all amounting to about 20 percent of the total economy. The nationalized industries were set up as corporations and labor was represented in management. Relations with labor were greatly improved, especially because nationalization had long been one of labor's objectives.

Labor was also appeased by repeal in 1946 of the 1927 Trades Disputes and Trade Unions Act, which restricted strikes and lockouts.[3] Furthermore, the government introduced large-scale social security programs, spread industry into the country, and passed the Town and Country Planning Act in 1947, by which ultimate control of all types of land was vested in the national government. This Act was modified in 1953, however.

The government was interested in business efficiency as well as ideology. Nationalization was in part aimed at rescuing ailing industries, and those who were expropriated were fully compensated. Mechanisms were set up to help those industries which were not nationalized, through both finance and protection. Previous trends towards concentration and growth of the private sector continued. British business has recently been charged with relative stagnation, since little innovation has taken place. Machinery has not been brought up to date and scientific methods have not been adopted as widely as in Germany or the United States. The degree to which this charge is true is hard to measure, especially since the international market in which British industry competes has not been left completely free.

Most of the features of the mixed economy of postwar Britain were common also in the Scandinavian countries. However, nationalization was not undertaken in the latter, mainly because some industries had been public since their construction. The Scandinavian countries paid more attention to national planning and direct intervention in the market than did Britain. Planning in Britain was mostly piecemeal, relating only to the nationalized industries. In Scandinavia, the plan was a directive for the government and a guide for others. The government saw to it that the plan was followed, either by budgetary methods or by direct

---

[2] Walter Galenson, (ed.), *Comparative Labor Movements*, Englewood Cliffs, N.J.: Prentice-Hall, 1952, p. 466.

[3] At the moment there are threats of reimposing some restrictions.

participation and competition in the market. Cooperation of business and labor was usually obtained by consultation during the construction of the plan.

Welfare has been a major objective in all Scandinavian countries. Attempts have been made to guarantee full employment and to maintain a stable relationship between prices and wages. This policy has been based on a partnership among government, labor, and private employers. Both labor and the employers are highly organized and centralized. In many cases, a strike has been avoided simply by announcing its date; since the labor unions are so well organized, a mere announcement can close a shop. The relationship between unions and cooperatives has also remained very close. Labor is stronger because it can compete on the market through the cooperative associations. Consequently, the objectives of labor have been generally realized. However, the employers' interests have also been guaranteed. In essence mutual acceptance has guided the behavior of the various sectors, each of which is strong enough to deal with the others on equal terms. Collective bargaining has been the accepted method of wage determination. While compulsory arbitration is resented in Britain, government intervention is accepted in Scandinavia as consistent with the idea of partnership.

France

The pattern in France has some similarities with each of the German and Italian patterns as well as some of the Scandinavian tendencies, although it is unique in many ways. German occupation and the rise of the Vichy regime left an impact on labor, business, and the place of government in the economy. The year 1936 was a landmark in French labor history. The sit-in strike of that year was the first of its kind in France and its effects were long-lasting. The CGT obtained a virtual monopoly over labor affairs. The Employers' Association (CGPF) lost its power and was forced to reorganize. The government reestablished its authority over arbitration and the settlement of disputes. Collective bargaining became accepted, but it was for the government to designate the organizations "most representative" of labor and employers to be parties to the bargaining. The Vichy regime was a victory for business but not for the Employers' Association. Under it a version of the corporate system was established. By a Law of 1940 organization committees, manned by businessmen, were created for the different industries. Further concentration and cartelization of industry followed. Quotas were allocated, prices fixed, and entry restricted. Under this system labor unions were virtually dissolved.

Upon liberation both the unions and the employers reorganized. Some continuity was maintained, however. Labor, which had been active in the liberation movement, came back with dignity. Its role was enhanced by the fact that the provisional government under De Gaulle nationalized the coal mines, gas and electricity, the 34 largest insurance companies, and the 5 largest banks. These were in addition to the already nationalized railroads, potash mines, and aircraft plants. The workers played an active role in the management of these nationalized industries through representation on their boards of directors. They also shared in the administration of social security and served on the Monnet Planning Commission. The major labor organizations were the CGT and the CFTC, although other new organizations appeared, such as the *Confédération Générale des Cadres* (CGC). The employers' Association was also revived but more slowly.

Although decentralization of industry gave rise to local trade associations, a national association, the *Conseil National du Patronat Français* (CNPF) was created combining the various associations. The CNPF agreed to cooperate with the government, accept planning, and examine social questions. The General Assembly of the CNPF was made broad enough to represent both small and big business, although big business remained in control. However, the CNPF was mainly ceremonial in function, unlike the militant labor unions. Both labor and the employers' confederation maintained their autonomy. However, conflict was widespread in both groups, especially in labor, which continued to be politically active. The CGT, which represented Communist elements, was not homogeneous in commitment or orientation, as the failure of the 1947 strike showed.

Collective bargaining was resumed after the war. Once again the concept of "most representative" was used to designate the parties to negotiation. The government thus reaffirmed its control, especially since all agreements had to be approved by the Minister of Labor. The Minister of Labor could also decide whether the agreements reached by negotiation should be extended to other industries. Minimum wage rates were also determined by the government through a commission which used the family budget as a basis.

The role of government in France was extensive in two other areas. All relations within nationalized industries were regulated by statute rather than by contract. Accordingly, the government could establish precedents for modifying relations with labor. Moreover, to overcome the destruction and disorganization caused by the war and move the economy toward reconstruction, the government adopted planning as an official policy. Under the direction of M. Monnet, a plan was built which aimed at utilizing the profit motive, keeping a balanced budget, and promoting efficiency. The plan was also designed to maintain regular consultation with business. However, it was used mainly as a guide, and when private investment fell short of the target, the government filled in with public funds. Although business promised to cooperate, opposition soon developed from both business and labor. Nevertheless,

the system was sustained and strengthened in later years.

Fiscal policy

Recent decades have witnessed another major change in the role of government, especially with respect to stabilization of the domestic economy. Commitment to welfare and full employment and the bitter experiences of the depression have made it clear that monetary policy is inadequate to stabilize the economy or advance growth. The practical difficulties faced in the depression and in the postwar periods were reinforced by the theoretical arguments of John Maynard Keynes in England and Knut Wicksell in Sweden on the importance of aggregate economics and the role of effective demand. Keynes expounded the theory that equilibrium in the economy may be reached at less than full employment. To avoid such a situation investment expenditure can be manipulated to bring about full employment. However, the only agency that can handle economic matters on an aggregate level is the government. Hence, fiscal policy seemed the obvious answer. Monetary policy continued to be utilized but taxation and government expenditure were now also employed for stabilization purposes.

This change in part explains the increase in government expenditure in the last half-century, although expenditures might have increased as a result of the military situation. Table 24.3 shows the changes in government expenditure since 1870. Big jumps are evident between 1913 and 1938 and again between 1950 and 1960. The rate of change cannot be explained easily, since it occurred for different reasons in different countries. However, in most countries, including the United States, the percentage of GNP spent by the government almost doubled between 1913 and 1938, reaching more than 10 percent in all countries except Norway with 9.9 and Denmark with 9.3 percent. With a percentage of up to 17.7 percent, as in Sweden in 1960, the government

Table 24.3. Government current expenditure on goods and services as a proportion of GNP at current prices

	1870	1913	1938	1950	1960
Belgium	—	—	—	9.8	12.1
Denmark	—	—	9.3	10.3	12.6
France	—	—	13.0	12.9	13.3
Germany	—	—	23.1	14.4	13.6
Italy	9.7	9.8	16.3	11.1	14.5
Netherlands	—	11.0[a]	11.4	12.6	13.5
Norway	3.8	6.3	9.9	10.6	14.6
Sweden	4.7	5.6	10.4[b]	13.9	17.7
Switzerland	—	—	—	—	12.1[c]
United Kingdom	4.9	7.2	13.5	15.6	16.6
United States	3.7[d]	4.2	10.1	10.6	17.2

[a] *1921.*
[b] *1938–1939 average.*
[c] *1959.*
[d] *1869–1878 average.*
SOURCE: *Angus Maddison*, Economic Growth in the West, p. 103.

became capable of stabilizing the economy, maintaining full employment, and implementing its plan indirectly by putting pressure on other sectors. Thus, without fully abandoning the market, the government can guide development and change and handle crises.

While the experiences of the various countries have differed, certain common features can be observed. The role of government has been enlarged. Monetary policy has been supplemented by an active fiscal policy. Social legislation has aided the market or compensated for its failures in raising the living standards. Labor and employers have again become partners to collective bargaining in determining wages and conditions of production, while the strike has remained labor's major weapon. In all countries except Germany and to an extent Britain, a plan has been used as a guide with differing degrees of enforcement. Concentration and combination have survived and have even been encouraged in all countries, although attempts have been made to avoid abuses of power. In virtually all cases labor has become a partner in the management of business. Finally, full employment and price stability have been basic policy objectives, even though their attainment has been far from common or complete.

The environmental impact

Economic growth and industrialization have seriously polluted the European environment. Water pollution is caused by sewage, a perennial problem, and recently by chemical wastes and effluents of the industrial economy. Among the pollutants are synthetic detergents high in phosphate contents, cellulose pulp waste that forms a film on the water surface, nutrient salts, toxic effluents, and radioactive waste. Water is also polluted by oil discharged from ships after washing their oil tanks, by wastes from food manufacture, by herbicides and insecticides, and even by fertilizers. Air pollution is caused by some of these in addition to the exhaust and fumes of automobiles and factories and by military testing and war activities.

A forceful description of water pollution is given by a Soviet observer :"The Oka is also an interesting river. If you go to a restaurant on its bank not far from a perfume factory, you will be served a royal dish: carp with a rose aroma, perhaps, or a pike with magnolia scent. You can have still tastier dishes: perch cooked in Benzene, bream in Kerosene or turbot in first-class lubricating oil."[4] The poisoning of more than 400 million fish in the Rhine in June 1969 exemplifies the serious effects of water pollution in Europe. The dead fish, in addition to being an economic loss, littered the river over international territories and aroused several nations to argue for an agreement to protect international rivers and waters.

Air pollution in Europe has been equally serious. It has been estimated that modern technology in Great Britain produces annually 2 million tons of smoke, 1½ million tons of grit and ash, 5 million tons of sulphur gases, billions of gallons of hot water, and unknown quantities of toxic by-products.[5]

The environment has also suffered from the high concentration of people and industries in certain regions in the different countries. The effects of urbanization and industrialization have been maldistributed among the regions. France offers a good example: Paris has 15 percent of the French population, 25 percent of all government workers, 33 percent of all college and graduate students, 65 percent of all artists and writers, 54 percent of all newspapers and publishing houses, 50 percent of the country's business turnover, headquarters of 65 percent of all companies, 25 percent of all industrial workers, 50 percent of the electrical construction industry, 56 percent of the aeronautics plants, 64 percent of the automative industry, 76 percent of the pharmaceutical industry, and 80 percent of the motion picture industry.[6]

The fight against pollution in Europe has so far been limited to research, debate, and experimentation. Conferences have been held and proposals made, but action has been rather limited. For example, attempts to protect the beaches and international waters from oil pollution have been frustrated by the fact that ships discharging oil on the high seas are difficult to identify and the shipmasters have little incentive to carry the cost of treating waste oil in ports. The protection of river water, especially rivers that pass international boundaries, has been carried out mainly in terms of bilateral agreements. Forty such agreements have been concluded between European countries in the last two decades, but these are primarily voluntary arrangements since there is no way of enforcing them. The bilateral agreements have been very vague; actual implementation of any purification program would require funding, and private industry has not been willing to undertake it, nor have national governments come forth with subsidies.

The disposal of sewage into the rivers, the main source of pollution, is usually a domestic question. Without local pretreatment of sewage and sanitary disposal of chemical and industrial wastes, pollution is bound to remain. Sometimes the problem is the technical one of finding alternative treatment methods or substitute inputs that would cause less pollution. In other cases the technological problems have been solved, but the material incentives have not been high enough. For example, many industries in the Soviet Union have had funds allocated in their budgets for the construction of purification installations, but they managed to avoid spending these funds. Indeed, the major complaint has been that enforcement of the regulations against pollution is lenient, not that funds and technical knowledge are short.

An exceptionally successful project of water protection and management has been the Ruhr Valley program in West Germany. The project is a cooperative association, known as *Genossenschaften*, of several major industries in the region. The association provides facilities for purification and

---

[4] Marshall K. Goldman, ed., *Controlling Pollution* Englewood Cliffs, N.J.: Prentice-Hall, 1967, p. 54.

[5] *London Times*, July 3, 1969, p. 9.

[6] Ambassade de France, *France. Town and Country Environment Planning*, New York, 1965, p. 11.

reuse of the water for industrial purposes and thus for treatment of the waste in a nonpolluting manner. Each industrial outfit has the option to use the facilities of the association against a fee or treat its sewage at its own cost, but no industry is allowed to pollute the water. The program, which has been in existence for more than three decades, has received public support and subsidy, but so far it has not been imitated extensively.

A promising invention for the protection of water has come from Sweden. It is known as the vacuum sewage system. This system separates toilet waste from other domestic wastes and treats each separately and more economically. It also uses air instead of water to convey the toilet waste, and thus uses only about 10 percent of the water normally used in a toilet.

The Soviet Union has recently taken measures against water pollution. Legislation passed in April 1970 was comprehensive although enforcement has been sporadic. At present there is apparent success as shown by efforts to save Lake Baikal, the largest body of fresh water in the world, from industrial waste. A purification system, also the largest of its kind in the world, has been installed to treat sulphurous and saline material dumped in the lake; new industries that might pollute the lake are forbidden; and the wood pulp plant which has been causing pollution will be closed down unless its waste can be diverted away from the lake.[7]

Other attempts to prevent water pollution have concentrated on reducing the polluting contents of detergents such as phosphates and other nutrient substances. Swedish companies and housewives seem to have agreed on using detergents with less of these substances, even though the cleaning results may be less than otherwise possible. There

are indications that a reduction of these substances has been successful in Britain and in the Scandinavian countries, but the effects are not yet sufficient to reach a conclusion.

The campaign against air pollution has been fairly extensive, especially in the case of carbon dioxide caused by the burning of fossil fuel. Britain passed a Clean Air Act in 1956 that restricted the use of coal and high-sulphur-content petroleum in some cities; now requests are made to extend the restriction to the rest of the country since the results have been favorable, especially in London. Sweden has passed legislation requiring all cars to have exhaust cleaning equipment beginning with the 1971 models. Furthermore, attempts are being made in Sweden to reduce the sulphur content in furnace oil and the lead content in gasoline. In a more drastic step, Sweden has banned for two years, beginning January 1970, the sale of DDT and other chlorinated hydrocarbons used as insecticides; Denmark has made the ban more permanent. The Soviet Union has expedited the construction of gas-purification installations four fold between 1952 and 1962, at least in the Russian and Kazakh Republics. DDT production has recently been prohibited and measures have been taken to protect forests and wildlife.

In most European countries, however, a broader perspective has been applied to the problem of pollution. A certain degree of regional planning has been recommended or implemented. Land use has been controlled and new industries have been allowed only if they met conditions which would be in harmony with and harmless to the rest of the environment. France, for example, has adopted a town and country environment plan that would guide decentralization of people and industries and spread the benefits more widely in the country and reduce congestion in the urban areas. Sweden has adopted an environment-protection law that supervises the establishment of new industries. The Soviet Union has made it mandatory to have sanitary doctors and public

[7] "Soviet Pollution Fighters Sense Victory in the Battle of Lake Baikal," *The New York Times*, August 23, 1970, p. 2.

health officials in every industrial enterprise in the country. The objective in all these plans is the protection of the environment against further deterioration under the impact of technology and industrialization.

These efforts, however, have not resolved the apparent conflict between technological and industrial development and the protection of the environment against pollution. Advanced technology in agriculture and industry is indispensable for feeding an increasing population and raising its standard of living, yet these same processes are polluting the water and air and endangering the environment. Insecticides and herbicides protect the crops and increase agricultural yield, but they also pollute the water and air and endanger wildlife as well as human beings. Ironically, they may also protect man against diseases such as malaria. Preventing the harm may entail foregoing the benefits, unless technology finds a substitute that is equally useful but less damaging to the environment. The people of Europe have become aware of these conflicting objectives. They led the world in industrialization, and may lead in protecting man and his environment against the hazards of industrialization.

EUROPE BETWEEN CAPITALISM AND SOCIALISM

Such a characterization of Europe may be interpreted in two ways: One describes it as divided between the capitalist and the socialist blocs; the other suggests that it represents an economic system which falls between the two. Both interpretations are to a certain extent correct. Clearly Europe's position has changed considerably, and the pace in world politics and economics is being set by parties other than the European countries which controlled it until 1914. The two world wars, the depression, and the end of United States' isolation at the time when Soviet Russia had already started toward extensive political and economic develop-

ment, gave Europe a new position in world affairs. Having lost most of its colonies, having suffered in the wars so much that at least temporary reliance on the United States was necessary, and facing Soviet Russia, whose economic system and ideology are a radical departure from capitalism, Europe found the new situation inevitable. The adjustments are by no means complete.

Europe has been divided between East and West, with only a few countries remaining nominally neutral. The majority have willingly or unwillingly become tied either to Soviet Russia or to the United States in defense treaties such as the North Atlantic Treaty Organization (NATO) and the Warsaw Pact. Even those countries which have not formally joined these blocs have shown preference for one or the other. It is apparent that there is no room for neutrality, since the European countries are not strong enough to stand on their own in case of a conflict.

The European countries have tried to create a third force to balance the power of the United States and Soviet Russia. However, traditional enmity, the effects of the war, and the economic insecurity of the new environment have made such attempts useless. Economic agreements such as the Common Market have been tried as means of creating political unity, but have met with little apparent success.

European economies have advanced rapidly. The areas of underdevelopment have been reduced and new problems have arisen, including rivalry abroad and impatience at home. International economic rivalry has been contained by institutional arrangements, such as market allocation for various commodities, regulation of international prices, and the assurance of a certain degree of liquidity. Nevertheless, the balance-of-payments problems have not been eliminated and foreign aid has been indispensable. The western European countries have depended heavily on the United States, while the eastern European economies have been tied to the Soviet Union. Thus problems of international payments have become the responsibility of the two major powers, and Europe has become subject to a greater economic dependence than ever before. It is not surprising, therefore, to hear it said that "If America sneezes, Europe catches cold." In eastern Europe, a Russian sneeze might mean pneumonia.

The pressure at home has been equally troublesome. When a country is in the early stages of development, austerity and sacrifice may seem justified. However, once development had advanced, it seems unreasonable for poverty, relatively low wages, or poor social conditions to prevail. Dissatisfaction with such conditions may be especially aggravated in a country influenced by a socialist ideology which preaches equality, harmony, and welfare. Both the example of the Soviet Union and the pressure of domestic socialist and humanitarian elements have rendered such conditions unbearable. The depression and recurrent cyclical fluctuations have made it clear that the market cannot resolve these problems and might actually aggravate them.

Accordingly, the western and northern European countries have moved away from capitalism. However, they are not anxious to adopt socialism. They have therefore resorted to an economic system which combines some features of both systems. While basic industries and utilities have been nationalized, the private sector has remained in control of about 80 percent of these economies. While social security has been instituted as a right, private ownership has remained the basic institution. While planning has been adopted by many countries, imple-

mentation has been partial or half-hearted. While monopolies and cartels have been regulated, size and concentration have been encouraged. And while full employment and price stability have been proposed as national objectives, the measures designed to realize them have been far short of those used in the socialist countries and little more extensive than those used in the United States. The European countries outside the eastern bloc have adopted "mixed" economic systems, traveling "the middle way" between East and West. While that middle way deviates from classical capitalism, it does not lead to socialism. In many ways it is a modified capitalism in which the market is supplemented by policy measures, without compromising the basic institutions of ownership, inheritance, and competition. Whether or not this structure is stable is hard to say. To a large extent its stability depends on the government's willingness to use policy to prevent depressions, and the ability of the decision-makers to prevent the outbreak of another world war.

In spite of these problems, Europe and the countries in it still wield enormous economic power. Many of them rank next only to the United States in per capita income, next only to the Soviet Union in welfare expenditure, and are as up-to-date as any other country in technology and productivity. The change in relative position may be healthy, and some countries have accepted it as such. On the other hand, uncertainty and a middle-of-the-road policy may lead to more rather than less conflict, especially in the event of a decline in markets, overexpansion, or failure to regulate the economy sufficiently.

BIBLIOGRAPHY

Ashworth, William, *A Short History of the International Economy Since 1850*, Second edition, Toronto: Longmans, 1962, chaps. 8 and 9.

Basch, Antonin, *The Danube Basin and the German Economic Sphere*, New York: Columbia University Press, 1943.

Clough, S. B., *The Economic History of Italy*, New York: Columbia University Press, 1964, chaps. 7–10.

Dillard, D., *Economic Development of the North Atlantic Treaty Organization*, Englewood Cliffs, N.J.: Prentice-Hall, 1967, Part IV.

Friis, H. (ed.), *Scandinavia Between East and West*, Ithaca: Cornell University Press, 1950.

Goldman, Marshall I. (ed.), *Controlling Pollution*, Englewood Cliffs, N.J.: Prentice-Hall, 1965.

Hohenberg, Paul, *A Primer on the Economic History of Europe*, New York: Random House, 1968, Part III.

Jacobsson, Per, "Western European Growth Experience," in *Proceedings of a Symposium on Economic Growth*, New York: American Bankers' Association, February 25, 1963.

Landauer, Carl, *A History of European Socialism*, I and II, Berkeley: University of California Press, 1959.

Lewis, B. W., *British Planning and Nationalization*, New York: Twentieth Century Fund, 1952.

Loucks, W. N., and W. G. Whitney, *Comparative Economic Systems*, Eighth edition, New York: Harper & Row, 1969, chaps. 14–21.

Maddison, Angus, *Economic Growth in the West*, New York: Twentieth Century Fund, 1964.

New York Times, The, "Soviet Pollution Fighters Sense Victory in the Battle of Lake Baikal," August 23, 1970, p. 2.

Otto, Nathan, *The Nazi Economic System*, Durham, N.C.: Duke University Press, 1944.

Stolper, Gustav, *et al.*, *The German Economy, 1870 to the Present*, New York: Harcourt, Brace & World, 1967, Part VII.

Svennilson, Ingvar, *Growth and Stagnation in the European Economy*, Geneva: United Nations, 1954.

United Nations, Economic Commission for Europe, *Annual Reports 1966–8*, supplement No. 3 [Printed in France]. Contains references to bibliography.

Windmuller, J. P., *Labor Relations in the Netherlands*, Ithaca: Cornell University Press, 1969, chap. 3.

Woodruff, William, *The Impact of Western Man*, New York: St. Martin's Press, 1967, chap. 7.

INDEX

Designed by Michel Craig
Set in Bodoni and Spartan
Composed, printed and bound by American Book—Stratford Press, Inc.
HARPER & ROW, PUBLISHERS

71 72 73 74 7 6 5 4 3 2 1

DATE DUE

OCT 3 0			
NOV 2 6			
SE 11 '85			

DEMCO 38-297